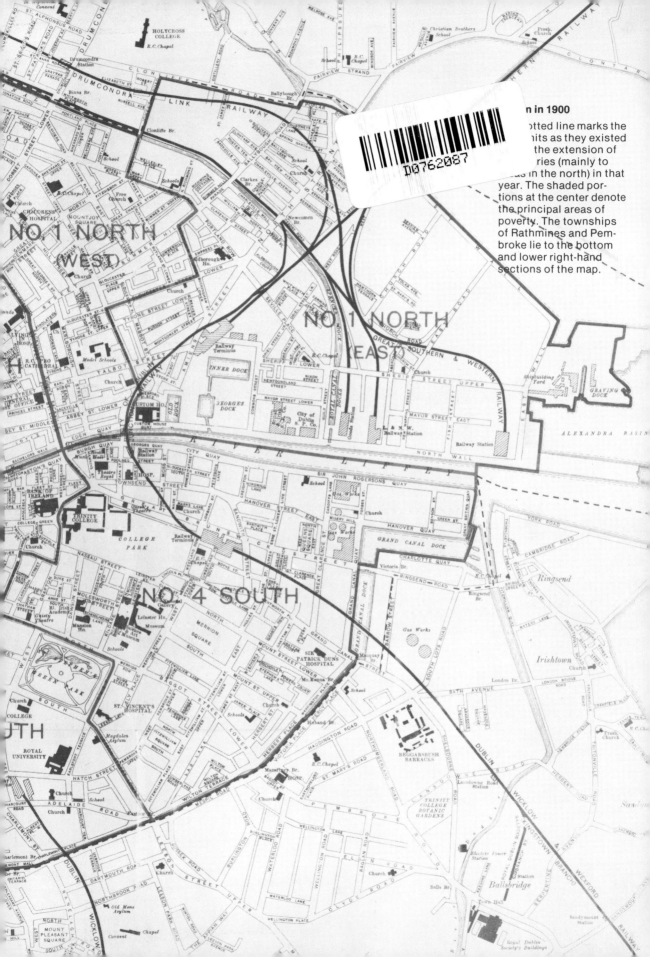

...n in 1900

...tted line marks the ...mits as they existed ...the extension of ...ries (mainly to ...as in the north) in that year. The shaded portions at the center denote the principal areas of poverty. The townships of Rathmines and Pembroke lie to the bottom and lower right-hand sections of the map.

"Dear,
Dirty
Dublin"

"Dear, Dirty Dublin"

A City in Distress, 1899-1916

JOSEPH V. O'BRIEN

University of California Press/Berkeley/Los Angeles/London

Lines from "To a Shade" are reprinted by permission
of Macmillan Publishing Co., Inc. from *Collected Poems* of William Butler Yeats.
Copyright 1916 by Macmillan Publishing Co., Inc.,
renewed 1944 by Bertha Georgie Yeats.

University of California Press
Berkeley and Los Angeles, California

University of California Press, Ltd.
London, England

© 1982 by The Regents of the University of California

Library of Congress Cataloging in Publication Data
O'Brien, Joseph V.
  "Dear, dirty Dublin."
  Bibliography: p.
  Includes index.
  1. Dublin (Dublin) — History. 2. Dublin (Dublin)
— Social conditions. I. Title.
DA995.D75027   941.8'3   79-64662
ISBN 0-520-03965-3   AACR2

Printed in the United States of America
Designer: Jim Mennick

1 2 3 4 5 6 7 8 9

Contents

Foreword   vii
Preface   xi

Part I   THE LEGACY OF THE NINETEENTH CENTURY
    1   Dear, Dirty Dublin   3

Part II   THE CITY
    2   The Faded Capital   39
    3   Politics and the Dublin Corporation   70
    4   Public Health   101
    5   Housing   126

Part III   THE PEOPLE
    6   Poverty   161
    7   Police and Crime   171
    8   Labor   199
    9   War and Rebellion   241

Epilogue   275
Appendices   281
Notes   309
Bibliography   325
Index   333

In memory of my mother and father.

Foreword

> Wallpurgies! And it's this's your deified city?
> —*Finnegans Wake*

A man's high deed, we learn from Vergil, is to found a city. Thus out of a vagueness of shores, coasts, buffetings, wars and driving fates, the long first sentence of the *Aeneid* clambers with its hero to a syntactic rock at the phrase *dum conderet urbem*: until he could lay, we may put it, the city's foundations: whereafter sprang up a race, therefrom forefathers; whence (for climax, with metrical trumpets) the proud *altae moeniae Romae*: lo, the high walls of Rome.

What you say of it after it is founded, Juvenal said: that the topless towers are rickety, the slums inescapable, the noise unbearable, the streets piled with filth. A whole tenement will topple, killing everyone inside it and whoever else may be passing at the luckless moment.

James Joyce tended to share with Vergil the city-founder's emotions. During the seven years, 1914-1921, in which he built his imperishable Dublin of the mind, it was light and movement and specifiability that caught him—"Grafton street gay with housed awnings lured his senses"; "Bare clean closestools, waiting, in the window of William Miller, plumber, turned back his thoughts"; and if Leopold Bloom looking down at the Liffey employs the word "sewage"—"Reuben J's son must have swallowed a good bellyful of that sewage"—still it is but one word with no special emphasis. It is not from Joyce but from Jonathan Swift, the city's Juvenal, that we must form our ideas of what city waters bear away:

Sweepings from Butchers' Stalls, Dung, Guts, and Blood, Drown'd Puppies, stinking Sprats,
all drench'd in Mud, Dead Cats and Turnip-Tops come tumbling down the Flood.

Do not object that Swift's poem contains London place-names, or that it dates from two
centuries before Joyce. When James Joyce left Dublin the Liffey's waters still bore away
all manner of offal, sluggishly, and the stench in summertime was notorious. It was not
until 1906 that the main drain system commenced to deposit city sewage out beyond the
harbor. That was long after such a procedure had been instituted in London, but turn-of-
the-century Dublin was a retarded city indeed.

Few cities exist as radiantly in the mind as that Dublin, site of the Literary Revival
that was the most publicized Irish event since the potato famine. Our notions of it, like
our notions of Shakespeare's London, are vivid, credible, and wholly literary. It contained
the Abbey Theatre, which we are not encouraged to remember could seat at most 562
people and was often three-fourths empty. It contained W.B. Yeats, when he was there,
which was not often, his address of record being 18 Woburn Buildings, London. It contained Lady Gregory, though only for brief visits once in a long while ("My imagination," she wrote, "is always the worse for every sight of Dublin"). And it contained James
A. Joyce only until the moment he could get abroad with the U.C.D. degree which in the
opinion of Italian authorities did not even qualify him to teach English.

Of these it is Joyce who has invented the city for us, "with meticulosity bordering on
the insane," and if there were parts of Dublin that Joyce did not know, notably the Ascendancy quarters Yeats frequented, there were also parts he knew but elected to omit. If
we hear of Stephen Dedalus's sister Dilly drinking weak cocoa with the oatmeal water for
milk while the cat eats a mess of eggshells and charred fish heads off the floor, not only
are we encouraged to blame this squalor on the improvidence of Dilly's father, we are
given no hint that it is genteel squalor indeed compared with what might have been
found a few blocks away.

"The room with two bedsteads occupied by a family of six, a bundle of straw on the
floor where the husband slept, the wife ill with typhus fever, the little girl being treated
for typhoid, the window overlooking a small yard covered in excrement with the foul
privy directly beneath"—so runs one of the milder delineations in *"Dear, Dirty Dublin":
A City in Distress*. It is the author's paraphrase of what an inspector witnessed in 1876,
touring the worst slums in Europe. The next words he quotes—"The homes of men have
become the living sepulchres of the people"—happen to gloss a witticism of Leopold
Bloom's: "The Irishman's house is his coffin." (The place that is the Englishman's castle
is his home, but "home" is not an Irish word. The Irishman has no home, merely a shelter
that he rents.) A third of the city's families lived in one-room tenements, and the death
rates, the highest in Europe, were comparable to Calcutta's.

As for the streets Bloom walks, it assists a reader's imagination to learn from Joseph
O'Brien that because the paving was not laid on anything firm, "the unprotected subsoil
inevitably seeped through to the surface under the wear and tear of traffic," and "rain and
inadequate scavenging did the rest, producing in the press recurrent diatribes against the
scandalous state of the streets especially during those periods when financial stringency
in the Cleansing Department resulted in the dismissal of the street-cleaning staff." When
such a staff was available it confronted, per mile per year, not the tonnage of filth a London or an Edinburgh sweeper would have coped with, but twice that tonnage. Whether
or not Dubliners were dirtier than Londoners, their city was probably the dirtiest in the

kingdom, one reason perhaps that Bloom fills mid-morning time by paying 1s. 6d. for a bath. A letter is extant in which Joyce wonders how many *Ulysses* readers would perceive something unusual in this bathing.

Not a clean city; a city, though, of readers? No; for though in 1884 the Lord Mayor, inaugurating the Capel Street library, had set an example by checking out a book called *Self Help*, by 1908 when shortage of funds closed the entire system down only 6,000 books were on loan to about that many cardholders. One obstacle was that to obtain a card you had to know a property-owner who would vouch for you (Bloom is fortunate in knowing a man named Kearney). As for the National Library, familiar to every reader of *Ulysses*, it housed a noncirculating collection only and maintained a staff of merely 15 to serve more patrons—mostly college students—than the Library of Congress with a staff of over 200.

But a music-mecca surely? No, it catered chiefly to musical nostalgia. Dublin was unique among European capitals in lacking a hall suitable for orchestral works. Touring companies had little better to offer than *Martha* or *The Bohemian Girl*, and what we are told of Bloom's tastes—"On the whole, though favouring preferably light opera of the *Don Giovanni* description, and *Martha*, a gem in its line, he had a *penchant*, though with only a surface knowledge, for the severe classical school such as Mendelssohn"—makes him sound reasonably representative. One notes the swank word "penchant" afloat on its italics in this archly graceless sentence.

Theatre? This exchange from an 1892 committee hearing is illuminating:

> Q. As a matter of fact, I suppose the Irish are not great theatre goers?
> A. They are.
> Q. But there are only two theatres in Dublin.
> A. Yes.

By Bloomsday (mid-1904) there were three, the Royal having reopened 17 years after it burned down in 1880. Its forte proved to be wrestlers and performing dogs. That of the Gaiety was pantomime and farce, and of the Queen's, endless minor plays on Irish historical themes, the equivalent there in those times of the Western in America in these.

Such is the Dublin Joseph O'Brien presents, a Dublin of statistically supported generalizations so different from the Periclean Dublin of literary repute as to make you wonder about the informative power of literature. Yet Mr. O'Brien does not misinform, and neither does literature. O'Brien's sources are newspapers, committee minutes, investigators' reports; his Dublin therefore is the problem Dublin, an inventory of the themes for contemporary complaint.

Complaint could appeal to norms, notably London, the capital, we sometimes forget, of the United Kingdom to which Ireland had belonged since the Act of Union of 1800. In the ensuing century, the century that mastered the technology of the city, inoculating the citizens, laying water mains and sewer lines, paving streets and rationalizing transport, Dublin's lapses from amenity were conspicuous, and what they highlighted was not, as the English tended to suppose, some Hibernian absence of sensibility but something atypical in nineteenth-century Europe, sheer accumulating corporate poverty.

Since 1800 the city had possessed no economic base. The money that attends a functioning government had commenced to slip away soon after the government left. It was the fine Georgian row houses, no longer inhabited by the wealth that had built them, that got reclaimed as tenements. Efforts to regulate these were subject to the legal definition of overcrowding: less than 400 cubic feet of space per adult, half that per child. Thus a room 16 x 16 x 10 passed muster if it was inhabited by no more than five adults and three children. The inhabitants of these were the wretches who put up with rats on the stairways and overflowing privies in the yards.

Yeats knew the well-to-do, and could complain of "the daily spite of this unmannerly town" but, staying as he did in hotels on his visits to the city, he was unlikely to have brought to his notice the stench of its latrines. As for Joyce, his people are not the very poor but the people who would have been moderately well-to-do as recently as a half-century earlier. With their second-hand trousers and their frayed white collars, they expect policemen and barkeeps to refer to them as "gentlemen," and if no one in *Ulysses* seems to have much to do that is very compelling, that fact in itself reflects the long stagnation of the city's economy. If a principal event of Bloomsday is a funeral, one in the day's long train of funerals ("Every mortal day a fresh batch: middleaged men, old women, children, women dead in childbirth, men with beards, baldheaded business men, consumptive girls with little sparrow's breasts"), that reflects not only human destiny but a disease-ridden city's statistics; so does the fact that we read so many sentences about doctors and hospitals, or the fact that the rate of childhood mortality in the Bloom family has been exactly 50 percent. Once when the Blooms were "on the rocks" Molly made pin money by selling the cuttings of her hair, and that such an expedient is not regarded as odd is itself indicative. Scraping by was a Dublin norm. As often, *Ulysses* is most eloquent in its selective omission of what no one present would have thought noteworthy: the smells, the desperation, the horsedung in the streets.

In *"Dear, Dirty Dublin"* Joseph O'Brien tells us precisely the things Joyce's Dubliners are so accustomed to they do not remark them. Only when rendered surreal by the phantasmagoria of "Circe" can certain not uncommon phenomena achieve literary visibility. Thus in a fantasy of omnipotence Bloom ordains the construction of a wholly renewed city.

> In the course of its extension . . . numerous houses are razed to the ground. The inhabitants are lodged in barrels and boxes, all marked in red with the letters: L.B. Several paupers fall from a ladder. A part of the walls of Dublin, crowded with loyal sightseers, collapses.
> THE SIGHTSEERS: (Dying) Morituri te salutant. (They die.)

Tenements, we learn from O'Brien, were occasionally torn down, and then what was to be done with their inhabitants no one could decide. And it was, every now and then, a tenement house that was apt to collapse, killing everyone inside. One that collapsed in 1902 belonged to Alderman O'Reilly of Trinity Ward, a member of the Health Committee whose charge included the condition of tenements. *"Morituri te salutant,"* indeed!

No, literature in the long run misses probably nothing, though we may need a parallactic view to tell us what is being recorded. Parallax registers a displacement of viewpoint, and the view from O'Brien's research, surprising though it often seems, is no more incompatible with the view from literature than the views from your two eyes are incompatible. For this accuracy we owe thanks to O'Brien's kind of meticulousness, so different from Joyce's, so resourcefully employed. In enabling us to open a second eye on a city and a time that hang vivid before the eye of the imagination, he enriches immeasurably imagination's harvest.

—HUGH KENNER

Preface

Only a few cities evoke those clear images that feed the mind and imagination of successive generations or represent for posterity the spirit of an age: Johnson's London, Louis Napoleon's Paris, Brecht's Berlin. And so also the Dublin of Yeats and Joyce. This "literary" Dublin has long fascinated specialist and student alike. And little wonder, for ever since the creative genius of her most famous son reincarnated the wandering Ulysses in the person of a Dublin Jew, the city on the Liffey has become a "world city"—a world city of the literary imagination. There is another Dublin, again a Dublin of Yeats and Joyce, but one that evokes harsher images and nurtures little of the interest reserved for the milieu of dramatist and poet. This, the nether world of tenement and slum, of the poor and unemployed, is in large part the subject of this study.

The city as a field of study in its own right has over the past decade or so attracted the concentrated attention of social historians. Much of their concern is with the darker side of the urban experience. In fact, urban historians have been accused by professional colleagues of being obsessed with the "pathology" of the city as evidenced by an apparent desire to quantify misery. When Constantia Maxwell introduced her portrait of Georgian Dublin almost half a century ago, she half-apologized to her Irish readers for including such disagreeable features of the pre-industrial city as a lack of sanitation and the frequent appearance of epidemic disease. But no constraints deter the contemporary urban historian from wading knee-deep into the detritus of the urban past to retrieve some sense of the physical and emotional hazards, frightful living conditions and penurious circumstances that daily laid siege to the well-being of the less fortunate in cities and towns. This is strong stuff and suggests that in addition to a clear head the writer (and reader, too) had better possess a strong stomach. Yet the historian is the victim of his sources, and when these relate to an assessment of the urban experience they can, to say the least, discourage optimism. The characterizations are now familiar—"infernal wen," "cruel habitations," "eternal slum." In the case of Dublin the historical portrait exhibits the same dark hues and invites no less grim a description.

Dublin is something of a *rara avis* for the urban historian. In an age when towns and cities underwent rapid transformation under the urbanizing pressures of industrialism, the Irish capital was a city pretty much in decline. And of all the great Victorian cities none endured such long-lasting death throes. The great social problems that enveloped the urban scene about the time of Queen Victoria's accession were by the end of the century well on the way to solution in most cities or at least confined to ever-decreasing sectors of the population. Not so in Dublin. There, retarded material progress, lack of population expansion, widespread and continuing unemployment, an abominable housing situation, pockets of the direst poverty, and some of the most daunting vital statistics to beset any metropolis set it apart from its sister cities of the United Kingdom. Add to this its status as a colonial outpost of an Imperial Britain, the effects of the racial and religious distinctions dividing ruler and ruled, a rebellious nationalist ethos that issued in bloody revolt, and the Irish capital becomes unique among the great cities of Western Europe for the early part of this century. Yet this period of Dublin's history, which partakes in full measure of tragedy and despair, glory and excitement, has attracted little attention from the urban historian. Issues and problems of the historical city that elsewhere invite full-length monographic treatment appear in the case of Dublin only as fleeting references in the more general historical or descriptive works.* An ancient and historic capital deserves more than this even if the image so created, as in this attempt, be made to reveal those scars and blemishes rarely highlighted by the gentler touch of the architectural and literary historian. Here then is Dublin, warts an' all.

The present study covers the years 1899 to 1916, a framework that sacrifices decadal neatness to the arbitrary prescription of the writer. But the earlier year does seem a fair starting point for a confined study of early twentieth-century Dublin. For one, the municipal franchise was broadened in 1899 with the coming into operation of the notable Local Government Act passed in the previous year. Thus, in local politics at least, the direction of the city and its services now lay open to the influence of far more than the few "fit and proper" persons hitherto entrusted with municipal affairs. Also about this time some notable currents in Irish history seemed to have their confluence in the Irish capital; for example, the nationalist revivalism generated by reactions to an Imperialist war against the Boers, as well as the cultural reawakening occassioned by the experimental drama of Yeats and his circle. For the terminal point of the study, the year 1916 seems natural enough, a date fixed by the Easter Rebellion for its setting in train those events

---

*See, for example, the handful of isolated references granted the Irish capital in H. J. Dyos and M. Wolff, *The Victorian City* (London, 1973), a remarkable compendium of nineteenth-century urban life and forms that devotes an entire chapter to Belfast. There is no published work on Dublin to compare with Anthony Wohl's investigation of the housing question in Victorian London, G. S. Jones's study of poverty in the same city, or E. P. Hennock's analysis of municipal politics in Birmingham and Leeds. In fact, the only full-length published study of modern Dublin of more than passing interest to the urban researcher is in a foreign language, viz. Reinhard Stewig's *Dublin: Funktionen und Entwicklung* (Kiel, 1959), which is essentially a work of historico-economic geography and dependent for the period before 1922 on secondary sources of only general interest. Unpublished work offers more substance, as indicated by the annual register of research in Irish universities in *Irish Historical Studies* with research underway on aspects of social life and politics in eighteenth- and nineteenth-century Dublin, as well as notices of similar enterprises in *Urban History Yearbook*. But given the exigencies of modern publishing, it is unlikely that much of this will find its way into print. One acclaimed and pioneering thesis (M.A., University College [Dublin], 1971, by Mary Crowley; not examined by the author) on the social and economic history of late nineteenth-century Dublin deserves a wider audience.

that presaged a new historical era for Ireland no less than for its capital city. Within this framework the author has felt obliged to go beyond the narrower concerns of the urban historian in an attempt to convey a broader picture of the life of the city than might have been required had Dublin alone—the city and its people—borne, for the brief span of years now under consideration, the scrutiny of the social historian. There is another reason for the more comprehensive approach, one related to the wide-ranging fascination the Irish capital holds for that international audience nurtured on the early artistic achievements of the Abbey Theatre and the immortal peregrinations of Leopold Bloom. One suspects that for many among this faithful band of admirers the historical portrait of Edwardian Dublin extends little beyond the circumstances of a theatre riot in 1907 or certain events of June 16, 1904. The historian, naturally, finds this disconcerting: after all, the artistic web spun by the Abbey Players captured the minds of only a few Dubliners, whereas any actualization of Mr. Bloom's fictional companions must have yielded a highly selective component of the citizenry. The encouragement of an interdisciplinary interest does not therefore seem out of place. Not that the picture here presented offers more than one slice of Dublin life in a period that witnessed events of more momentous impact on the lives of citizens than had been experienced at any time before. There are, of course, other Dublins—elite Dublin, educated Dublin, religious Dublin—that await more committed and competent hands. If this present version of events generates the desire to fill these gaps, then it will have served one further purpose.

Part One of this study is mostly confined to nineteenth-century Dublin. It is intended to provide the necessary background without which a full appreciation of the crushing problems of unemployment, housing, and public health that persisted in post-Victorian Dublin cannot be realized. All cities experienced them to varying degrees and found them difficult to solve; though by century's end sanitarians in Britain no longer wilted at the recital of municipal death rates, and few if any of their reforming compatriots were faced with the pervasive crisis of urban housing that challenged their counterparts in Dublin. In reading the record from decade to decade, one is continually struck by the virtually unchanging nature of the complaints that emanated from within and without the Irish capital—a city unchallenged as the least healthy in the United Kingdom; notorious for the poverty of its inhabitants; appalling in the state of its working-class dwellings; even the most unsightly for its ill-scavenged streets. Part Two takes up the story in 1899 and delineates the form and functions of the city and its administrative institutions. Chapter 2 opens this section with an impression of the city, inevitably sketchy, as it appeared to contemporaries who contrasted the elegance with squalor, flocked to theater and music hall, witnessed the contretemps over John Synge's play and Hugh Lane's art gallery, boasted of an excellent tramway system while doing their best to avoid muddy streets, bemoaned the passing of the horse-drawn "outside car," and nodded dubiously at the appearance of the motor car. In Chapter 3 the municipal politics of the period are resurrected to reveal the civic tensions and political opportunism that outraged observers and invited the vilification of the daily press. The picture darkens in Chapters 4 and 5, where the regressive effects of disease and slum life, the legacy of decades of neglect, are treated at some length. The final section of the book focuses on the people of Dublin, or at least that large majority who were prey to the vagaries of market and master, trade and depression. Included also are those smaller components of the population—the underworld of criminal and prostitute as well as the secret world of revolutionary nationalist.

The highlights here are the labor struggles of 1913 and the Easter Rising of 1916. These latter, of course, are oft-told stories, but no work of this nature on this period of Dublin could avoid their inclusion. However, the present reconstruction of events eschews the more familiar political considerations and biographical details and instead puts the city itself in the center of the stage by examining the impact of civil strife and rebellion on the life of Dublin and its citizens.

In forming his picture of Dublin, the author has more or less been faced with the task of starting from scratch. The paucity of the usual published sources is evident from the bibliography. Fundamental to the task was the close reading of the daily newspaper for each year under review, in this case the *Irish Times*, an organ noticeable as much for its then Unionist bias as its exemplary reportage and (an added boon to the researcher) excellent index of the day's coverage. Indispensable, also, at every stage of the work was the vast resource of materials in the British parliamentary papers. The items found useful, both of major and minor importance, have for the most part remained unused by historians since they were first published as official documents. Other official material consists of the published records of the Dublin Municipal Council. Of private correspondence there is nothing tht might have added anything more than diversion to the record. More might have been expected from a municipal archive, but for this period none apparently exists, the victim to the flames of civil war. Yet it would be foolish to conclude that the future leaves nothing to be retrieved—a treasure surely awaits the researcher where some errant leprechaun has left it for safekeeping.

The idea for this book originated from an invitation to participate as historian in an interdisciplinary course of studies on the urban past and present introduced by the Thematic Studies Program at John Jay College of Criminal Justice. A generous grant from the Research Foundation of the City University of New York facilitated two research stints in Dublin, during which periods the author, alas, had little time to observe what the passage of years had done to exorcise the spirit of Dublin past. It is all too commonplace now to derogate many features of the modern city, but the historical researcher should be the last one to add his voice to this clamor, especially when that city is New York and its features the superabundant archival, library, and interlibrary loan resources of Columbia University and the Research and Newspaper Divisions of the New York Public Library. In this regard, I am grateful to my alma mater on Morningside Heights for her encouragement of Irish scholarship through the voluntary forum sponsored by the University Seminars, and for the research facilities and intellectual fellowship I have enjoyed as a member of the Seminar on Irish Studies. I also wish to acknowledge the kind and helpful service that has always eased my labors at repositories in Ireland, most especially at the National Library and Public Record Office in Dublin. A special word of thanks to Thomas L. McFarland, late of the University of California Press, for much encouragement and support along the way. It only remains to add that no amount of help from whatever source would have availed to make this book possible without the untiring efforts and limitless forbearance of my wife.

—J. O'BRIEN

John Jay College of Criminal Justice
New York, N.Y.

October 1980

Part I

THE LEGACY OF THE NINETEENTH CENTURY

Is it well that while we range with Science, glorying in the Time,
  City children soak and blacken soul and sense in city slime?
There among the glooming alleys Progress halts on palsied feet,
  Crime and hunger cast our maidens by the thousand on the street.
There the Master scrimps his haggard sempstress of her daily bread;
  There a single sordid attic holds the living and the dead.
There the smouldering fire of fever creeps across the rotted floor,
  And the crowded couch of incest in the warrens of the poor.

TENNYSON, Locksley Hall Sixty Years After

1

Dear, Dirty Dublin

Dublin is a miniature of London: it is built like a metropolis, and has its squares and great streets. It is not like any of the great provincial towns which are places of trade . . . nor is it, like Bath, a great theatre of amusement. . . . It exhibits the same variety of ranks as London. It has its little court, its viceroy, with all the attendants upon his reflected royalty; it has its Lord Mayor, and all the pageantry of city grandeur; it has its manufacturing, its mercantile, and its monied interests; it is the Westminster of Ireland, and is accordingly the *locus in quo* of judges, barristers, attorneys, etc. Almost everything we find in London may be found also in Dublin . . . it was formerly a great capital, the seat of legislation; it is now a great place of passage . . . it contains a large mass of human beings in the most squalid and wretched conditions . . . in Dublin he must step warily who desires to avoid the view of wretchedness. It is not possible to walk in any direction half an hour without getting among the loathsome habitations of the poor.

S.M.T., "Dublin in 1822," in New Monthly Magazine and Literary
Journal, IV (1822), 503-11

DUBLIN. Second city in His Majesty's dominions. Esteemed the fifth for magnitude in Europe. Possessed of one of the finest public avenues of any city. Its new streets graced by magnificent houses, the result of the "amazing increase and improvement" the metropolis had experienced in the eighteenth century. Such was the description offered to readers of the third edition of *Encyclopedia Britannica* in 1797. It was one with which residents and travelers with an eye for the visual imagery of the urban landscape could agree, for during the preceding hundred years the city had grown beyond the confines of the narrow streets and crowded alleys connecting its two cathedral churches. It was the economic prosperity of the middle years of the eighteenth century that gave the necessary fillip to the remarkable spate of building activity that, in the grimmer years of the present century, recalled the faded glories of Georgian Dublin. This was the Dublin of Thomas Cooley, James Gandon, the Parke brothers, Francis Johnston and other designers whose monuments to civic greatness—among them the Custom House, Four Courts, King's Inns, Royal Exchange, additions to the Parliament House (now the Bank of Ireland) in College Green—still stand. It was also the Dublin that soon bore in Dame Street, Westmoreland Street, D'Olier Street, and Lower Sackville (now O'Connell) Street the majestic stamp of that aptly named, government-appointed body—the Commissioners for Opening Wide and Convenient Streets. Since 1774, legislation had provided for the paving and flagging of new streets. Soon after, improved lighting—globes with double burners set 36 feet apart—contributed to the convenience and safety of citizens. As trading centers Dame Street and Parliament Street were hardly inferior to the best of London's streets. To the north of the city ran new thoroughfares unknown in Dean Swift's day: Gloucester, North Great George's, Dominick, Gardiner's, Dorset, and Eccles Streets. And south of the dividing waterway, familiarly dubbed Anna Liffey, were added Molesworth, Kildare, Merrion, Clare, Mount, Holles, Baggot, Hume, Fitzwilliam, Leeson, Harcourt, and Camden Streets. The mansions and town houses of the great and wealthy, built in the "best modern style," enclosed Rutland and Mountjoy Squares, on the north side of the city, and Merrion Square, on the south, all of which struck contemporary observers as affording the finest prospects in Europe to their fortunate residents. Close to one hundred Irish peers had town houses in the city, almost half of them in Sackville Street alone. The gaiety and brilliance of Dublin society in this period was sustained by the regal pomp of the Viceroyalty and, during the last quarter of the century, by the resurgent Irish parliament of Flood and Grattan. It has been well described by two of Dublin's best historians, Constantia Maxwell and Maurice Craig.

This life of culture, leisure, opportunity, and success, with its aristocratic club houses, masquerade balls in the Rotunda gardens, fashionable promenades along the spacious gravel walks of St. Stephen's Green, and levees at Dublin Castle, was enjoyed by few of the 170,000 or so inhabitants recorded by the Rev. James Whitelaw and his assistants in their 1798 census of the city. Cut off by race and religion from the upper class of English and Anglo-Irish Protestant society, most citizens could only join this world as spectators at the great military parades in Phoenix Park on the King's birthday. Or at a lower level, they could enter more fully into the spirit of that other great event, the Donnybrook fair. The usual urban division of rich and poor was in Dublin intensified by a corresponding division into a privileged class descending from an alien conqueror and a despised, distrusted, and barely tolerated native Irish stock. The social chasm between these two groups was nowhere more clearly discerned than in the eighteenth-century Penal Code, first designed to chastise the rebellious Irish after the Williamite wars and then maintained to suppress their aspirations to the expression of religion, ownership of land, pursuit of office, and benefit of education. Thus the Dublin masses, like most of their rural compatriots, were despised because poor and ignorant, degraded because Catholics. The severity of the Code had been mitigated by mid-century and had largely disappeared by the 1780s, but its effects, large and small, were a lasting obstacle to the forging of a common identity for all citizens. When John Carr visited Dublin in 1805, it seemed to him that the traveler's view of Dublin was marred because so many churches were without steeples: any passer-by might have told him that they had been forbidden to Catholic churches under the Code. He might also have thought it strange, or at least novel, that a residential area less than two miles from the city should be called *Irish* Town; again, a relic of medieval penal legislation that forced the Irish to live outside the city proper. Indeed, Dublin in the eighteenth century remained what it had always been, even in its ninth-century Norse origins—a city lacking much in the way of a distinctive native character. Its two cathedrals served the minority faith (there was no Catholic cathedral). Its buildings were designed by Englishmen, its municipal government run by a closed Protestant elite, its professional and merchant classes dominated by an Anglo-Irish component, its Castle the administrative center of British rule over the whole island, its very streets and bridges named for English notables and officials. Moreover, its development in trade and industry had long been restrained by the jealousies of English manufacturers; and now, as the century was drawing to a close, its one great industrial base, woolen manufacture, was doomed by the growing ascendancy of an industrializing England hungry for markets at home and abroad. Little wonder then that the vast majority of perhaps 130,000 Catholic inhabitants should be numbered among the denizens of those sections of the city described by another visitor, the Rev. Thomas Campbell in 1777, as rivalling "the worst part of St. Giles."

The political problems posed for England by the new and challenging independence of the Irish parliament in the years between 1782 and 1800 do not concern us here. Suffice it to say that the victory won by Protestant politicians could hardly have failed to whet the political appetites of middle-class Catholics for further concessions to the King's Irish subjects. Parliamentary reform and Catholic emancipation were the twin pillars that united for a time the Presbyterian radical in Belfast with the Catholic artisan in Dublin— the Irish manifestation of that heady spirit of democratic revolution issuing from Paris. The admission of Catholics to the parliamentary and municipal franchise in 1793 evoked not only gratitude but also the resolve to press for the ultimate Catholic Relief—admission to membership in parliament. However, in the context of "the constitution of 1782," this last concession could well herald the demise of the Protestant Ascendancy. Against such fears neither the oratory of Protestant sympathizers nor the latent rebelliousness of the Catholic masses could prevail. A rebellion did indeed occur in 1798, but it was suppressed with crushing severity and repaid two years later with the formal abolition of the troublesome Irish parliament.

The legislation that came into effect on January 1, 1801, establishing the United Kingdom of Great Britain and Ireland, was to affect more than the political destiny of the metropolis. For now that the seat of political power and influence lay solely at Westminster, Dublin began to lose its attractions for those aristocrats and gentry who had lent brilliance and polish to Dublin society. In 1800 some 100 peers and 300 commoners of the Irish parliament, many of them with families, resided in the capital, their presence supporting a flourishing class of tradesmen and shopkeepers. Gradually this wealthiest segment of the population withdrew from Dublin, and the noble residences adorning the best streets and fashionable squares exchanged their occupants for the new pace-setters of society—the professional classes, especially the barristers and attorneys, who thrived on the favorable admixture of law and politics in a city that retained in Dublin Castle a top-heavy bureaucracy and a focus of smouldering Irish discontent. The damaging effects of the Union on the social and economic life of Dublin were acknowledged by contemporaries and remembered by those who remained to experience the reduced status and prosperity of the capital. One of the more fateful consequences of the Act of Union was noted by one observer: "This measure [the Union] has seriously changed the appearance of Dublin; with the removal of its parliament the nobility of Ireland withdrew to England and left their palaces in Dublin either to fall to decay, or be converted into public offices, hotels, or charitable institutions . . . [or] *divided into two or three smaller and more convenient houses* for the present inhabitants of the metropolis."[1] At any rate, within a generation only a few residential peers remained, and as the raconteur Sir Jonah Barrington was to bemoan, "neither men nor manners" were as they had been in the great days before the Union. Such a lament would not have been echoed by those nationalist Irishmen who had survived the rebellion of '98 or recalled the retributive justice dispensed thereafter by local magistrates.

Of course, grass did not begin to grow in the streets of the capital as some of the more desperate opponents of the Union had warned would happen. The Wide Streets Commissioners continued to make improvements on a somewhat less grandiose scale, and a new Paving Board was established in 1807 with an initial grant of £40,000 for making sewers and laying down granite pavements. The completion of Merrion Square and the building up of Fitzwilliam Square were both undertaken after 1800. And the 3,000 or so new houses put up in the city between 1800 and 1830 represented extensions to existing streets and the filling in of empty spaces between Mountjoy Square and the Royal Canal, between Henrietta Street and the Circular Road, and about Portobello and Charlemont Street. But as the following tabulation for 1828 shows, palatial residences were few and 75 percent of the city's 17,314 houses were under £50 valuation:[2]

Classification based on valuation		Number
1st class	(exceeding £300 A.V.)	45
2nd - 4th	(over £150 to £300)	339
5th & 6th	(over £100 to £150)	653
7th - 10th	(over £50 to £100)	3,313
11th - 16th	(over £20 to £50)	6,561
17th - 20th	(under £20)	6,403
	Total	17,314

Also, a great deal of Catholic money went to make Catholic devotion more respectable through the erection of some imposing churches in Gardiner Street, Aungier Street, Marlboro' Street, Francis Street, and elsewhere: before the Union the Roman faith could only boast of one major place of worship in the city, namely, the Clarendon Street chapel of the Carmelites. Yet for the city itself something of culture, grandeur, and civility had been lost, not least by the fact that the great phase of civic development that had begun half a century earlier had virtually come to a close. Moreover, a process of internal migration had also been set in motion that gathered force from decade to decade until great sections of the city descended in turn from upper-class elegance to middle-class respectability and ended in a desperate and unavailing struggle against the creeping paralysis of social and structural decay. A select committee appointed to enquire into matters of local taxation reflected on these trends in a report published in 1822:

> It is true, that its [Dublin's] advance as a place of commerce, and as the seats of the courts of law, has counteracted in some respects the decline of its wealth and resources [since the Union]; but the increasing poverty of its inhabitants is still most melancholy and most rapid. Your Committee cannot give a stronger proof of this fact than by referring to a return laid before them, by which it appears that the number of houses certified by the collectors of the Paving Tax as insolvent, have augmented since the year 1815 from 880 to 4,719, and that at the present moment [1822] out of 16,138 houses liable to assessment, above one fourth are unable to contribute towards the local taxation. . . .

> Many of the most valuable houses and streets of the city of Dublin, as it stood in the
> reign of George I, have fallen into decay, and are now inhabited either by the most abject
> poor, or at least by the humblest traders and the poorer description of merchants and arti-
> sans. . . .³

By mid-century, as some observers claimed, Dublin was no longer the metropolis for the
rich who had departed (there were few men of great wealth) but rather the metropolis for
the poor who, it was feared, were flocking to the city in increasing numbers.*

The urban poor could hardly be blamed for their indifference to the political machi-
nations that had robbed their city of its status. The city fathers had always been indifferent to them. None of the decisions made about the great building activity of Georgian
Dublin was informed by the social conscience of a later Victorian generation. Already in
Swift's day hundreds of houses in the older parts of the city were in decay and the familiar lower-class tenement of the nineteenth century was in the making. There is hardly one
among those who have left us accounts of their visits to Dublin who was not visibly impressed by the startling contrast between elegance and poverty, which appeared sharper
in the Irish capital than in other cities.** The sympathetic Philip Luckombe was appalled
at the wretched condition of the inhabitants of mud-dried huts whom he encountered on
the outskirts of the city in 1779—"shoes and stockings are seldom worn by these beings,
who seem to form a different race from the rest of mankind." In the city itself indigence
marked even the "middling class" of people. Perhaps no description of lower-class life in
Dublin was more often quoted by contemporaries than the circumstances encountered
by the Rev. James Whitelaw in the course of his house-to-house survey in 1798:

> In the ancient parts of this city (called the Liberties),*** the streets are, with a few excep-
> tions, generally narrow, the houses crowded together, and the reres, or back-yards, of very
> small extent. Of these streets, a few are the residence of the upper-class of shop-keepers and
> others engaged in trade; but a far greater proportion of them, with their numerous lanes and
> alleys are occupied by working manufacturers, by petty shop-keepers, the labouring poor, and
> beggars, crowded together, to a degree distressing to humanity. . . . I have frequently sur-
> prized from ten to sixteen persons, of all ages and sexes, in a room not fifteen feet square
> stretched on a wad of filthy straw, swarming with vermin, and without any covering save the
> wretched rags that constituted their wearing apparel. . . . An intelligent clergyman of the
> church of Rome assured me that no. 6, Braithwaite-street some years since contained one
> hundred and eight souls. . . . From a careful survey, since taken of Plunkett-street, it appeared,
> that thirty-two contiguous houses contained 917 souls, which gives an average of 28.7 to a
> house.

---

*In point of fact, the influx of population had begun to level off at mid-century when a total of 258,000 per-
sons were recorded. But a remarkable growth (at least judged by later standards) had taken place, particularly
over the preceding three decades, during which numbers had risen from 186,000 (1821) to 204,000 (1831) and
232,000 (1841). Much of this increase doubtless represented the influx of the landless poor, of artisans attracted by speculative building ventures, as well as, in the late 1840s, of those fleeing famine and desolation for
the organized philanthropy of the capital.
**The various descriptive works of these visitors may be identified in the bibliography by referring to the au-
thors' names. Observations of other eighteenth- and nineteenth-century travelers are the subject of the works
by Constantia Maxwell also cited.
***The area in the southwest roughly straddling the diagonal that ran from St. Patrick's Cathedral to St.
James's Gate at Watling Street near the Liffey.

... This crowded population, wherever it obtains, is almost universally accompanied by a very serious evil; a degree of filth and stench inconceivable, except by such as have visited those scenes of wretchedness. Into the backyard of each house ... is flung from the windows of each apartment the ordure and other filth of its numerous inhabitants; from whence it is so seldom removed that I have seen it nearly on a level with the windows of the first floor. .... When I attempted in the summer of 1798 to take the population of a ruinous house in Joseph's-lane, near Castle-market, I was interrupted in my progress by an inundation of putrid blood, alive with maggots, which had from an adjacent slaughter-yard burst the back-door and filled the hall to the depth of several inches. ... The sallow looks and filth of the wretches who crowded round me indicated their situation, though they seemed insensible to the stench, which I could scarce sustain for a few minutes. ...

Seven years later John Carr was to repeat Whitelaw's dismal account and regret that nothing had been done by the authorities to ameliorate the dreadful conditions in the warrens of the poor. The "disgusting huts" Thomas Cromwell saw surrounding St. Patrick's Cathedral in 1820 made obvious the fact that the great church lay in the most dilapidated part of the city. The "huts" may well have been the wretched hovels of Mitre Alley that over twenty years later would be described by others as "a nest of infamy and filth." Indeed, the approaches to the cathedral were so mean and narrow that, when George IV stopped to pay homage at Swift's memorial on his visit to Dublin in 1821, a temporary carriageway had to be cut through the Palace Yard and Dean's Garden for the king and his entourage. But travelers did not need to visit the Liberties to witness misery, for the city swarmed with beggars, or so it seemed to their "victims." The city, of course, has been down through the centuries the magnet attracting all classes, those with skills to sell as well as the unskilled, the vagrant and vagabond. De Latocnaye was so disgusted by the "insolent" importunities of those who accosted him during his rambles through the city in 1798 that he "never felt less inclination to be charitable than whilst in Dublin." Though the numbers of beggars had probably decreased by the time of Thomas Cromwell's visit, their wretchedness remained, making them the butt of the joke that no wonder need be expressed about what English beggars did with their cast-off rags—they were sent over to the Irish beggars. The mendicancy problem was particularly acute before the establishment of the poor-law unions in 1838, since it was generally accepted that the Dublin charities and the tax-supported House of Industry attracted to the capital large numbers from outside districts in search of relief. In fact, so great was the lure of the House of Industry that the managers were forced to alter the regulations for admission in 1817 by peremptorily discharging the able-bodied poor, accepting thenceforward only the aged, sick, and insane—"the first experiment in the United Kingdom to exonerate the public from the gratuitous support of this class." Yet those same managers were obliged to admit that "with respect to the policy of leaving the poor of Dublin to their own exertions exclusively, we believe there is no city where it is less practicable, or where, if the attentions usually bestowed on the poor by individuals and institutions, were withdrawn, there would be more misery and crime."[4] A generation later, the 1861 census classified over 3,000 "beggars" in the province of Leinster, and doubtless most of those (80 percent of them females) operated in the city of Dublin. The needy poor who shunned the House of Industry were almost always sure of a meal at the Mendicity Institution, which also provided a penny for lodgings. When subscriptions ran low, it was not uncommon for the Institution to parade the mendicants through the streets of the city to stir the conscience of the rich. The consequences of such poverty dismayed Henry Inglis and Leitch Ritchie, both of whom passed through Dublin between 1834 and 1837. Inglis attended a cattle show in Kildare Street, "where half-eaten turnips of the cattle became the perquisite of ragged children." Ritchie saw two street waifs naked and shivering near the door of Thomas Gresham's hotel in Sackville Street, "but the indifference with which it was glanced at by the passers-by proved their daily and hourly familiarity with scenes of misery and destitution." Such a state of affairs, he thought, would not have been permitted by the police of any other town in Europe north of the Alps. Perhaps the most searing indictment was that of James Johnson, who visited the city in 1844:

> Dublin—rent and split—worm-eaten, mouldering, patched and plastered—unsightly to the eye, unsavoury to the taste, and not very grateful to the olfactories—here there is but one step from magnificence to misery, from the splendid palace to the squalid hovel. . . .
>
> . . . [And on the Liberties] winds and rain have *liberty* to enter freely through the windows of half the houses—the pigs have *liberty* to ramble about—the landlord has *liberty* to take possession of most of his tenements—the silk-weaver has *liberty* to starve or beg.

Naturally, such stories could be found in any other large city. The horrors of the Five Points district and Little Ireland remind us of the extremes of physical degradation endured by the poor of New York and Manchester. But Dublin was different in one fatal respect from other nineteenth-century cities. It was a city undergoing industrial decline and demographic stagnation at a time when others were experiencing rapid industrial growth and population increase. In these latter cities, brawn, skill, or luck might activate that upward social mobility that every opportunity facilitated. In this regard, the story of Belfast in the Presbyterian north offers a vivid contrast to the problems that faced Dublin in the Catholic south. Expanding from a mere 37,000 inhabitants in 1821, Belfast's population doubled within twenty years and by 1880 was well on the way to overtaking Dublin's relatively stable population of about a quarter of a million throughout the Victorian period (see Appendix B). Meanwhile, the northern town had become a major industrial center based on the production of linens, the engineering trades, and above all, shipbuilding. Moreover, its civic and business institutions demonstrated a remarkable ability to provide new housing and jobs for the spiralling population. This interdependence of population and industrial growth is well illustrated also, of course, by Bristol, Sheffield, Leeds, Manchester, Glasgow, and Edinburgh. None of these could boast 50 percent of Dublin's population in 1800, yet all exceeded it, with Glasgow and Manchester doubling it, by 1890.

The reasons for the lack of industrial performance in the Catholic parts of the country are manifold, and most have their basis in the history of the Anglo-Irish nexus. Some have been hinted at already: alien rule, penal legislation, racial and religious conflict, over a century of trading restrictions on native Irish enterprise. In addition, a disastrous system of land tenure, the bitter fruit of the Conquest, had brought forth a poverty-stricken peasantry that rendered worthless the normal symbiosis of rural hinterland and capital city. A case in point is the Dublin woolen manufacture. In the seventeenth century this trade lent opulence and respectability to the Coombe, Pimlico, and Weavers' Square quarters of the Liberties. A mortal blow was struck the industry when English competitors prevailed on the Westminster parliament in 1699 to forbid the export of Irish woolens. In the years immediately following, thousands were obliged to leave Ireland for want of employment.

Though it revived during the closing decades of the eighteenth century, the industry was in no position to compete without protection against the dominant British manufacture, and it sank into decay after the Union. In his *Sketches*, John Gamble relates that when he was in the city in 1810 he attended an exhibition of paintings where the proceeds of admission were used to relieve the distress of the clothiers.

The silk trade offered a further example of the decay of an industry that had been introduced in the Dublin Liberties over a century before by Huguenot immigrants. Jonathan Sisson, the representative of the Dublin silk weavers in the city council, outlined its fate before a select committee investigating the state of the industry in 1832. In 1824, he stated, 1,200 broad looms and 996 ribbon engines gave employment to an estimated 6,000 persons in all branches of silk manufacture. In that same year, however, the reduction of the duty on Italian silks followed by the unrestricted import of British and French products all but annihilated the trade in Dublin. By 1832 fewer than 150 looms remained.[5] In these years so great was the distress among the weavers that some 20,000 of them, along with their dependents, were reduced to a state bordering on starvation, and large numbers of females sank into prostitution. The shattering human effect of this extended misery was enough to extinguish, in the words of an official report, "all that hope and buoyancy of spirit for which the poor people of this city were remarkable in their better days." Pauperism prevailed where once prosperity reigned. Likewise, the linen industry gave way before the superior advances of the Belfast producers, while the famous Dublin tabinets fell victim to changing fashion. Nor were Dublin manufacturers, especially the distillers, helped by being forced to pay more for coal than their English counterparts by reason of the coal duties imposed between 1781 and 1832 to support the activities of the Wide Streets Commissioners. Ireland, of course, experienced economic growth in the post-Union decades, and defenders of the Union were quick to counter the arguments of repealers with data on increased exports of corn and livestock, greater consumption of tea and coffee, wines and spirits, the remarkable increase from Dublin itself in the export of porter, as well as the prosperity evidenced by the large sums of money raised for various political purposes. But Ireland also entered the industrial era without a national parliament that might have fostered and promoted native manufactures, without the skills and capital to create industries strong enough to withstand British penetration of the Irish market. Moreover, hundreds of thousands of Catholic tenant farmers throughout the country were victims of a system of land tenure that reacted unfavorably on the capacity for capital accumulation in the agricultural sector to support economic growth in the industrial sphere. And, if contemporary opinion be correct, English capitalists saw no incentives to investment in the general level of social and political unrest that was never entirely absent in Ireland. Thus the promise of economic advance—the boon that was to sweeten the bitter pill of political integration—was never quite realized for the metropolis. Maurice O'Connell, MP, detailed some of the changes that had occurred in the city since 1800 during the repeal debate in the Commons in February 1834: untenanted office buildings in commercial Dame Street; drastic increases in unemployment; a huge decline in the numbers of master carpenters and master bricklayers; a halving of the number of shipbuilders, and the virtual disappearance of anchor and sail makers.

The paucity of Dublin's commerce in the decades after the Union had a visible impact on Gandon's great creation, the Custom House. By the 1840s its purpose had to be adapted to other public uses, only its name suggesting functions that in the opinion of one observer might just as easily have been transacted in a cottage. And as the industrial revolution gathered pace, Dublin was left ever farther behind. Complaints of the hegemony of imported English manufactures became more frequent—boots and shoes (a feature of the new "monster" drapery houses), paper, furniture, soap, glass, and more. And as others were to claim, Dublin lost out as the *entrepôt* for some regional centers when it became cheaper to send shipments (tea, paper, and such) from England to, for example, Mallow via Cork rather than by rail from Dublin. There was no one great industrial outlet in Dublin such as the textile factories of the Belfast region or the cotton centers of northern England. A return issued in 1871 of the number of factories subject to official supervision under the Factories and Workshops Acts disclosed the very unfavorable position that Dublin held vis-à-vis the manufacturing centers of Ulster.[6] In county Antrim alone over 14,000 persons were engaged in flax spinning (an Ulster industry), compared to fewer than 500 in the entire county of Dublin. Cotton and wool manufacturing in the latter hardly engaged another 500 hands. In an Irish context Dublin appeared strong in brewing, paper milling, and printing, but again the numbers involved were small, totalling about 4,000 workers in all. There was no comparison with the busy English manufacturing towns where, in the borough of Bradford, for example, at least 30,000 persons were employed in the worsted industry. Thus, with limited industry (small-scale iron and brass founding, coachmaking, and so on) and few skilled workers outside the traditional building trades, Dublin had an undue proportion of its workforce engaged in casual, low-paying occupations that inevitably bound a great number of laboring-class families to a grim existence in the decaying purlieus of the city. The census of 1851 had already indicated the regressive trend. Of a combined adult (15 years and older) workforce of almost 120,000 persons, one-third (40,453) were employed either as general laborers or domestic servants, about double the rate prevailing in Belfast.

By mid-century the city had acquired all those aspects that were to become its most distinguishing features in the next couple of generations: low employment, overcrowding, insanitary housing, widespread poverty, and all their concomitant evils. The *Parliamentary Gazeteer of Ireland* published in 1844 provided a social dissection of Dublin that in the case of the older parts recalled the descriptive prose of the Reverend Whitelaw, though with little of his sympathy and concern. It divided the city into four quarters separated east from west along the line of Capel Street, and north from south by the River Liffey:

> South-west . . . retains, with hardly an exception, the contractedness of street arrangement, the crookedness and capriciousness of thoroughfare, and the coarseness, ugliness, or craziness of architecture, which so generally and distressingly characterize the city or town retreats of the lower classes of the Irish; and it has so abundant an intermixture of putrid lanes, and dense niduses of diseased, ragged, starving poverty, or of bold shameless, stenchy vice, as to appear, in juxtaposition to the south-east quarter, almost like a field of rubbish and manuring composts adjacent to a handsome and odoriferous parterre. It possesses, indeed, some redeeming features, and even objects of intense pleasurable interest, in a few of its choicer localities, and especially in its more ancient public buildings; still, in its general character, it is the St. Giles of Dublin,—a region which any stranger of delicate organs of perception will feel chary to enter.
>
> North-west . . . may be generally characterized as the retreat of the middle classes, the home of the better sort of tradesman; and as possessing a medium character of architecture between the poor and the opulent, or between the shabby and the elegant . . . and some

[streets], on the outskirts, are so sumptuous as to give the whole quarter the appearance of soaring gradually into the magnificence of the newest portions of the city.

South-east and North-east . . . form the real boast of the city, and vie with each other in the numerous features of urban brilliance and attraction; the portions nearest the other quarters and the quays are the abode of the wealthiest classes of trades-people, and the theatre of as proud arrays of shops and fashionable warehouses as any in the world; and the other and far larger portions are the stated residence of about two thousand families in circumstances of opulence, the home of not a few families connected with the learned professions and the fine arts, and the occasional retreat of a small number of noble families, and of some 15 or 20 members of the House of Commons.

The four quarters of the city were almost entirely enclosed by the North and South Circular Roads, and these in turn were bordered for much of their nine-mile length by the Royal Canal (to the north) and the Grand Canal (to the south). The city in effect was contained within a "ringed fence," slightly over three miles long by two miles wide, comprising some 3,800 acres and outside of which lay the Phoenix Park, the northern townships of Glasnevin, Drumcondra, and Clontarf, as well as the more exclusive, independent southern districts of Rathmines and Rathgar, Ballsbridge, and Sandymount. But these barriers to urban expansion did not prevent individual citizens from participating in that common nineteenth-century urban phenomenon—the flight to the suburbs, though, as elsewhere, the lack of cheap workmen's fares on railway and omnibus as well as the insufficiency of low-rent housing accommodation kept the laboring classes from joining in the migration. The inevitable result was that the city lost a growing number of middle-class families—commercial and professional elements as anxious to enjoy the salubrity of a suburban villa as they were hopeful to avoid the social problems and tax burdens of a city with streets in disrepair, houses in decay, industry in decline and inhabitants in distress. As early as 1854 the Collector General of Rates remarked on the considerable increase in the city of the number of houses under £20 valuation and a corresponding decrease in those of higher valuation. The burden of municipal taxes, he claimed, was responsible not only for the multiplication of smaller houses but also for the departure of citizens to the suburbs.[7] In fact, only two years before the city had undergone a general revaluation of property, which took into account the deterioration in the value of houses in almost all the older parts of the city as well as improvements in others. The net result was a new valuation of £541,000, a reduction of £120,000 even though the city had many more miles of streets to clean than in former years.

The area of the city most affected by the migration to the suburbs was the northeast quarter. The street directories of the period confirm the social profile offered by the *Parliamentary Gazeteer*. Here at mid-century, barristers, attorneys, and physicians abound in private residence, occupying almost every house in Old (Lower) Dominick Street, Gloucester Street, Lower Gardiner Street, Upper Dorset Street, Grenville Street, Henrietta Street, Summerhill, and elsewhere. In another three decades Gloucester Street, Dorset Street, and Summerhill are virtually devoid of the former class of resident, and the others

are undergoing a similar transition that within a few years would entirely transform their former character. By century's end all these areas—"the real boast of the city"—had become the sites of tenements and lodging houses, buildings whose former residents had been crossing the Liffey over the years to take up residence in Rathmines and Pembroke townships and in other suburban areas. Only the residential squares manage to resist the ugly transformation, though here too unfavorable trends could be discerned. Rutland Square, in the 1830s home to aristocratic families and the professional classes, has to a great degree exchanged private residences for schools, clubs (including in uncomfortable juxtaposition the Orange Lodge with John Redmond's National Club), hotels, and the offices of doctors and lawyers. Mountjoy Square, also occupied earlier by the upper classes, retains its largely professional character, but the great number of vacant houses signifies the conversion of many residences to offices and flats.

Official statistics also reveal the trend. In 1854 the rateable valuations* of Henrietta and Grenville Streets were £2,280 and £840, respectively. By 1879 these had plummeted to £1,040 and £323. Data for other streets suggest the same general dilapidation or reduced circumstances over the years. During the same period, however, the total valuation of Rathmines township increased from £30,728 to £98,065, while that of Pembroke township grew from £42,000 to nearly £90,000.[8] Rathmines, a "poor and obscure" village in 1820, was described in 1844 as a "beautiful and rather large suburb." Incorporated as a township in 1847, it recorded a population growth according to official returns from 11,052 in 1851, to over 20,000 in 1871, and almost 28,000 in 1891. Similarly, Pembroke, constituted in 1863 with a population of 13,200 and adjoining the southeast corner of the city, had grown to over 24,000 by 1891. Other smaller adjoining townships incorporated in the interim were New Kilmainham (1868) in the southwest, Drumcondra (1878) to the north, and Clontarf (1869) at the northeastern extremity. Therefore, whereas the population of the city itself showed no increase during the second half of the century (258,000 in 1851; 245,000 in 1891), that of the metropolitan area, as in other cities, was increasing—although that growth, a moderate 75,000 persons by 1891, was attributable solely to the townships. As everyone knows, the real Irish contribution to urbanization was made not in Dublin or Cork but rather in the teeming industrial centers of England and the North-American Atlantic seaboard.

The independent townships formed a more impassable barrier to the city's expansion than the "ringed fence" of Circular Road or Canal. Normally, the Victorian city solved the revenue problem incident upon the movement of residents to the suburbs by simple annexation of these areas. In Great Britain it was accepted municipal practice that whenever new districts arose as suburbs that were obviously extensions of the municipality itself, those suburban areas would be annexed to the parent city. Mutual consent of the parties involved was usually the preliminary to the private bill legislation or Local Government Board orders that extended the boundaries of borough and town. Thus a private act in 1862 enabled Rathmines to annex the district of Rathgar. When resistance was encountered, annexation might be decreed by legislation, though many suburban townships were able to resist takeover. A formal attempt by the Dublin Corporation to add the ratepayers of all but the Clontarf township (separated from the city by the demesne of

---

*The rateable value of a house denoted that amount at which the premises might in its actual state be reasonably be expected to be let from year to year.

Lord Charlemont) to its tax rolls was made in 1879. Appearing before the Municipal Boundaries Commission, municipal spokesmen pleaded for annexation as vital for the future of the city. The boon for the city lay in the proposed addition of over £230,000 to its £651,000 valuation (in 1880), thereby increasing its borrowing powers. Besides, new territory would yield the sorely needed virgin building land.

Every argument was brought to bear to buttress the case of the Corporation: the wear and tear of city streets caused by suburban merchants, traders, and cattle drovers; the use of the city's public institutions by suburban lunatics, hospital patients, and youthful offenders; the utter dependence of suburban business on the city's labor pool; the reliance on the city's disinfecting facilities when disease became rampant; the availability of the fire brigade in times of emergency; the supplying of domestic water by contract. The city's case could hardly be denied, for the townships were indeed normal extensions of a metropolis that was practically devoid of available building sites for new housing. Moreover, the suburbs boasted no great industry while their middle-class residents pursued their vocations and amassed their wealth in the city. Yet they escaped the burden of taxation that fell disproportionately on those whom the municipal suppliants dubbed their fellow citizens.

Suburban opponents countered these arguments with the claim that money earned in the city by suburbanites or in the townships by city workers was in whole or part spent in the city. As for the wear and tear they were alleged to cause on city streets, they saw little distinction between it and the traffic of hordes of city dwellers making their way to the bathing facilities at Sandymount or the beautiful slopes of the Dublin mountains. More to the point, however, was the present luxury of lower suburban taxes. After all, there was probably some truth to the oft-repeated contention that the first drift to the suburbs began out of fear of the revenue-hungry reformed (i.e., Liberal) Corporation of 1841, although one cannot make too much of this—the nineteenth-century middle-class urbanite recognized as clearly as his modern counterpart the disadvantages of living in a city faced with apparently insurmountable social problems. And the financial advantages of suburban living were real. For example, Lower Leeson Street (within the city) extended across the canal bridge to Upper Leeson Street (in Rathmines). But the resident on the Dublin side paid in 1878 a total of 6s. 10d. combined municipal and poor-rate, whereas the liability of his neighbor in Rathmines amounted to only 3s. 8d. The combined rates of the other townships were higher than those in Rathmines, but none exceeded 78 percent of the Dublin rate.[9]

After examining over eighty witnesses, the Commissioners fully endorsed the Corporations's proposal, added Clontarf township to the city for good measure, and tartly rejected the claims of those "who enjoy all the advantages and escape many of the disadvantages of the citizens." But these recommendations could not obtain the force of law, and for the remainder of the century Dublin was to remain a "cribbed, cabined and confined" place.

The existence of these townships highlighted by comparison two of the most intractable social problems Dublin had to face throughout the nineteenth century and well into the twentieth: a high death rate and insanitary housing. These were in fact *one* problem, for it was widely maintained that the death rate of the city could never be reduced so long as great numbers of the inhabitants continued to dwell in abominable tenement houses. In historical terms excessive mortality had generally been associated with the lack of pure air and wholesome water. The earliest sanitary law on the English statute book, an Act of 1388, prohibited the dumping of refuse, dung, entrails, and so forth into ditches and rivers near cities and towns. A century later another decree prohibited butchers from slaying beasts within the walls of London and other walled towns. By the time of Henry VIII much work had been done in the matter of sewage disposal, culminating in the great Statute of Sewers in 1531. Sanitary advances in the eighteenth century brought greater cleanliness and convenience to growing towns in the form of legislation for the paving, lighting, and cleansing of streets. The year 1717 saw the first such act regulating the paving and repair of the streets of Dublin, directing that a city "scavenger" carry away twice weekly the dirt, soil, and filth out of every street and lane, and enjoining the inhabitants to sweep before their houses in preparation. Subsequent legislation suggested the ineffectiveness of these measures in a growing city. Not until 1774 was the first of several official Paving Boards created whose responsibility was soon extended also to public lighting (1784) and the erection of public fountains (1786). But again, not too much confidence could be placed in the efficacy of these measures. As late as 1809 the paving and cleansing of the city, both long neglected, were being severely hampered by lack of funds, and the new Paving Board began to encounter a public health problem that was to figure greatly thereafter—the slaughter houses and dairy yards, "which infect not only the Neighborhood but the whole Town with the most noxious filth and effluvia, sufficient to breed a plague."[10] The Wide Streets Commissioners, too, did something for public health in the course of their work by abolishing many of the narrow lanes and alleys that had occupied the sites of new and wider thoroughfares. But concerted efforts to improve public health did not take on much immediacy in the United Kingdom before the great proliferation of towns and cities under the impact of the Industrial Revolution in the opening decades of the nineteenth century. The dangers of concentrating large numbers of people in conditions of extreme poverty, intolerable congestion, and insanitary circumstances were brought home all too clearly when Asiatic cholera first struck the cities in 1831.

The establishment of the office of the Registrar General of Births, Deaths, and Marriages in 1837 was the first effective step in the development of modern sanitation. Now, for the first time, the increasingly excessive mortality in towns in England and Wales was made patent, inviting private and public concern. Next, the Report of the Select Committee of the House of Commons in 1840 recommended legislation embracing the whole array of sanitary reforms sorely needed in populous towns and cities: construction of sewers; purification of water supply; provision of public baths; supervision of lodginghouses; appointment of local Boards of Health and Inspectors. Not until 1848, however, was the attempt made to deal comprehensively, though permissively, with public health matters in the great Public Health Act of that year, which provided for the creation of local health boards to effect sanitary improvements. But, as in the case of registration, the legislation applied only to England and Wales. Ireland had to wait until 1864 for her own Registrar General and until 1878 to benefit from the comprehensive Public Health (Ireland) Act consolidating all previous enactments and adding considerably to the powers of sanitary authorities.

Of course, some progress was being made in Ireland throughout the century. Vaccination, discovered by Jenner in 1796, was introduced to Dublin four years later, and in 1804 the private Cowpock Institution was established in Sackville Street to provide for free inoculation of the children of the poor. In 1820, prompted by the recent fever epidemics that affected an estimated 1.5 million persons throughout the country, the Marquess of Wellesley, Lord Lieutenant of Ireland, set up a General Board of Health in the capital to collect information and recommend preventive sanitary measures. The Board's report, published two years later, outlined such distressing circumstances among the poor—want of employment, exorbitant rents, pressure of tithes, severity of distraining laws, and the prevalence of wretched, comfortless, unhealthy dwellings—that it must at least have evoked sympathy if not concern for the social travail of the Irish people.[11] Next, public provision for vaccination was made that resulted in a considerable decrease in smallpox deaths after 1840, a trend bettered after 1863, when vaccination became compulsory for infants before they reached six months (reduced to three months in 1879), though serious loss of life would still occur in epidemic years, as in 1872, when over 1,600 persons were struck down in Dublin. Also, at mid-century, one of the more enlightened incursions of the collectivist state had arranged for the establishment, under the Medical Charities Act, of local dispensaries throughout the country where medical officers treated gratis the sick poor and dispensed vital medicines and drugs annually to nearly three quarters of a million people.

In Dublin meanwhile, the "reformed" Corporation had become involved in sanitary work when it assumed from 1850 on the various duties (drainage, paving, cleansing, lighting, and so forth) extended or transferred to it after passage of the Dublin Improvement Bill of 1849. This was the legislation that also authorized the city council to borrow on mortgage or bond, provide public slaughter houses and urinals ("*châlets de nécessité*") as well as levy an improvement rate not exceeding 2s. in the £. Improvement became the order of the day as the principal streets in the heart of the city were soon resurfaced in granite setts. The appointment of an Inspector of Nuisances (aided by a handful of police), the regulation of lodging houses, the erection of public privies, the establishment in 1866 of a permanent public health committee to coordinate and enforce sanitary improvements, the opening of a disinfecting facility, the appointment of Medical Officers of Health, and the building of a morgue (until 1871 post-mortem examinations were conducted in a shed connected with a dairy yard), an abattoir, and a Baths and Wash House all followed in turn between 1851 and 1885.[12]

All this activity, however, was not translated into a sanitary boom, and lack of money was a principal reason. The downward general revaluation of the city already referred to resulted in an annual loss of £12,000 to city revenue, which was felt for a number of years after 1852. The strenuous resistance of ratepayers to expenditure for sanitary projects also had its retarding effect: the council members could not easily ignore the protestations of those citizens (only a few hundred per ward) who elected them. From 1867 to 1876 the average annual expenditure for sanitary purposes only slightly exceeded £2,000. Indeed, the municipal poundage rates declined by 24 percent between 1874 and 1879. Furthermore, the Local Government Board for Ireland, administrative monitor of municipal waywardness, held a tight rein on the Corporation's rating powers and often turned a deaf ear to requests for increased borrowing powers. Well might the Corporation claim in answering its attackers that its meager sanitary expenditure should be blamed on the fiscal straitjacket it was forced to wear. Under the Dublin Improvement Act of 1849, borrowing was limited to £100,000 for all purposes, a restraint not removed until the Public Health Act of 1878 raised the limit to £620,000 for sanitary purposes alone. The same act

don main drainage, to produce plans for intercepting sewers to purify the Liffey by discharging the waste from the north and south sides of the city into the estuary at the North Bull Wall. After adopting the plan at an estimated cost of £200,000, the Corporation successfully promoted the Dublin Main Drainage Act of 1871 and invited bids for completion of the work. But the planners had not reckoned on the rise in prices for material and labor: the lowest bid exceeded £750,000. Although this high figure was reduced to less than £500,000, the entire scheme was dropped in 1876, the Corporation being unable to persuade the government to advance the required loan and unwilling to risk the taxpayers' revolt that sharply increased rates would have provoked. The scheme was later revived when the Public Health Act of 1878 gave the Corporation increased borrowing powers; but by then other priorities had intervened, for the Corporation decided instead to concentrate on the more urgent work of domestic scavenging and improvement of tenement houses where the system of privies and ashpits coupled with bad repair were viewed as a far greater hazard to the public health than the two-mile-long "stinkpot" in the center of the city. The result was that the city sewers continued to discharge their noisome contents directly into the Liffey for the rest of the century. (See Chapter 4, below, for details of the work of main drainage undertaken after 1896.)

The question the state of the Liffey had brought to public notice—the high death rate in the city—continued however to vex and dismay. The battle against dirt and disease was, of course, a general problem of the early nineteenth century. The ravages of epidemic disease in Dublin in those years as recorded in the reports of the Cork Street Hospital and other institutions make for somber reading: raging fever in the summer of 1810, which "scarcely felt among the rich, seemed to have levelled all its fury against the poor whose crowded habitations gave facility to contagion"; typhus epidemics from 1817 to 1819, which saw over 42,000 admissions (1 in 5 of the population) to fever hospitals and 2,000 dead; the dreaded cholera in 1832, with its 5,632 deaths in the city alone. Smallpox and cholera, though great killers, merely exacerbated the already high numbers of deaths from the usual zymotic or "catching" diseases (fever, measles, scarlatina, diarrhoea, diphtheria, and so on), respiratory ailments, and pulmonary consumption. Even England, galvanized to action by the moral impetus of Dickens and Kingsley and the collectivist bent of a Chadwick, saw no lasting victory in the struggle before the Public Health Act of 1875. In Ireland prior to a registration of deaths, the urgency could be masked by the lack of reliable mortality rates. Dr. William Wilde, whose study of mortality in Ireland was included in the census report of 1841, determined that the average age of death (i.e., the mean point at which death took place) in Dublin was 20 years. Other estimates also suggested the notoriety that was eventually to be accorded to official figures. According to Dr. Thomas Antisell, a member of the Royal Dublin Society, the average age of death in third-class districts of the city was under 5 years, while even in first-class districts it did not exceed 30. An investigation of 3,000 poor families carried out in 1845 by Dr. Thomas Willis, a local medical officer, led him to conclude that 22 percent of children did not survive the first year of life, 52 percent died before their sixth year, and only one-third of the working class as a whole survived beyond 20 years. Indeed, Dublin's appalling mortality rates, paralleled in Liverpool and other English centers at this time, appeared good by comparison with "the most unhealthy towns in Ireland," namely,

Drogheda and Galway, where, as Dr. Wilde calculated, the avarage age of death was 6 to 7 years. What incredible child mortality rates these figures suggest![16]

However unreliable the figures, it was unlikely at mid-century that any such horror stories would provide the catalyst for massive and urgent attention to the causes of the premature deaths of the citizens. After the experience of the Famine, a horror that dwarfed in scale all the ravages of fever, cholera, and smallpox combined, anything might appear normal. In Dublin itself the mid-century migration already described enabled the prosperous classes in the comfort of their suburban homes to divest themselves of contact with, and concern for, those less privileged classes struggling in their tenements. In their view the visible mud and dirt of deteriorating macadamized streets could seem as great a social evil as the rarely seen heaps of ordure lining the lanes, alleys, and yards of the developing slums.

After 1864, Dublin was forced to share with other major cities in Britain a reluctant prominence in the annual returns of the Registrars General. In 1866, for example, the Dublin death-rate, 33.1 per 1,000 persons living, compared with Glasgow's 29.3, Manchester's 31.9, Leeds's 32.5, London's (East End) 34 and was considerably less than Liverpool's 41.8, though one might surmise that the high rate in that city betokened the demise of many an Irish immigrant. In those early years of hesitant municipal involvement and permissive legislation in the field of public health, no large city in the United Kingdom could boast the acceptable death rates (13 to 18 per 1,000) that became common for English cities toward the end of the century. Nevertheless, in 1880, more than a decade after the establishment of the Public Health Committee, the rate for Dublin stood at an appallingly high 37.8, while all the large English towns, now benefiting under the Public Health Act of 1875, had effected progressive reductions in mortality rates. Dublin was not to enjoy these dramatic improvements. The annual death rate in the city at no time before 1900 was lower than 26.6, the annual averages for two decades ending 1889 and 1899 being 30.6 and 29.6, respectively. Naturally, much higher rates prevailed in localized areas within the city. A congested ward in the old city west of the cathedrals or surrounding the Four Courts would show rates 25 percent, or more, higher than the average for the city as a whole. The breakdown for a smaller area a row of houses with defective drainage, for instance—could yield a horrendous rate of 100 per 1,000, as did one such section of the city for a two-and-a-half-year period in the 1870s.

Child mortality, especially in the vulnerable under-five population, was particularly shocking; about 30 percent of all deaths in Dublin were of children in that age bracket, while 60 percent of those were of infants under one year. Up to 1875, few cities could boast an infant mortality determined as a fair rate by actuarial tables—under 150 per 1,000 live births. Dublin was unable to avoid statistical notoriety in the returns of infant mortality. There the annual average rate in the last quarter of the century was 171 deaths in the first year of life for every 1,000 children born. Even as late as 1898 the rate ran as high as 196 per 1,000. But few other cities could throw stones at the Irish capital in this regard, for such annual slaughter of the innocents gave reminder, until well into the first decade of the present century, of some of the sadder circumstances of life throughout the Victorian era. The death rates for children under five years were equally striking—over 290 per 1,000 when most other large cities approached the more acceptable level of 250 per 1,000.

Dr. Grimshaw, the Registrar General for Ireland, offered the following breakdown by so-cial classes for this type of mortality (the numbers express the percentage of total deaths that those of children comprised):

Professional and independent classes	6.6
Middle classes	22.6
Artisan class	25.9
General service class (laborers, etc.)	44.9 [17]

The impact of all this mortality is reflected in the city's demographic profile. The population of Dublin, as has been noted, hardly changed for the last five decadal cen-suses of the nineteenth century. It could not have been otherwise when the number of births in the city barely kept ahead of deaths, as shown by the records of the Registrar General for the last quarter of the century. For this period alone the proportion of deaths to births in the city averaged just under 97 percent per annum; the corresponding ratio for major English cities (Leeds, Sheffield, Birmingham, Manchester, and so on) generally ranged between 60 and 70 percent. In fact, Dublin experienced more deaths than births in 8 of these 25 years, while in two of the eight registration districts (those, predictably, con-taining the workhouses) a natural increase in population was never recorded. In the last decade of the century a mere 5,427 persons were added to the city's population by natural increase! Thus, with little influx of people from the rest of the country in this period— perhaps only enough to make up for the loss to the suburbs—it is no cause for surprise that the city's population in 1891 should have been fewer by about 13,000 than the 258,000 residents counted in 1851. The number would surely have been fewer still had not emigration from Dublin been smaller in proportion than that of any other county in Ire-land. [18]

In every aspect of mortality, Dublin in the last quarter of the nineteenth century held the unenviable record of being first among major towns and cities of Britain and Ireland. Indeed, from Brussels to Berlin, from Rome to Stockholm, and from Philadelphia to Boston, the death rates in major cities rarely exceeded those in the Irish capital. Pro-longed excessive mortality of this kind represented a cruel waste of human life, almost 3,000 lives each year when judged by the lower mortality of the suburbs. The Corporation was never allowed to forget this sorry record. The most effective and persistent spokes-man for better housing, better streets, and better health for all citizens was a self-appoint-ed watchdog of sanitary progress: the Dublin Sanitary Association, formed in May 1872 in the wake of the smallpox epidemic of the previous winter. Among its members were Dr. Thomas Grimshaw, F. W. Pim, of the prominent mercantile family, and a host of oth-er luminaries representing the medical, academic, and legal professions in the city. Had the Association's genuine concern and noble aims been matched by Corporate or govern-mental munificence, no doubt Dublin would have become the healthiest city in the Unit-ed Kingdom. Instead, constant prodding of the city fathers, even to the extent of plying them with unsolicited weekly lists of public nuisances, resolved the relationship into a running battle between the reputed forces of "good" (the Association) and "evil" (the Corporation). Nevertheless, for the next thirty years the Dublin Sanitary Association strove to educate public opinion on sanitary matters, monitor the progress of sanitary laws, and maintain that *salus civium suprema lex.* It was the Sanitary Association that in 1878 called on the Lord Lieutenant to institute a "searching inquiry" into the causes of the excessively high death rate in the city. The result was the first extended official inquiry into the state of public health in Dublin—the Royal Commission on Sewerage and Drainage.

The Report of the Commissioners concluded that the prime source and cause of the excessively high death rate in Dublin was the tenement system—the "great sanitary sore of the city." Originally built for one family but now occupied by two or more, the tenement, because of gross sanitary deficiencies, was highly unsuitable as a dwelling place. One example of a first-class house let in tenements was cited before the Housing Commission in 1885. This was a nine-room house in Upper Gloucester Street occupied by nine families comprising 63 individuals (the average rooms per family ratio for all tenements was 1.5). Two of the rooms were each occupied by a family of 10 persons. Of the 24,000 or so inhabited houses in the city in 1881, over 40 percent (9,863 houses) were let in tenements. It would be misleading, however, to ascribe to all houses occupied by, say, two or three families the pejorative connotation usually associated with the word "tenement." A moderate adaptation of a well-preserved town house could easily accommodate that number of families to a reasonable degree of comfort and convenience. A more useful measure of severe overcrowding is offered by the class of accommodation accorded to such houses. According to an old formula devised by Sir Thomas Larcom, fourth-class accommodation was represented by a first-class house (i.e., having over seven rooms with windows) containing six or more families, a second-class house with four or more, a third-class house with two or more or, by definition, a single-room dwelling. But even that criterion, as Table 1 shows, places over 40 percent of families in the very worst accommodation. These were the true inhabitants of the slums (i.e., any property judged insanitary or overcrowded, or where strikingly unhealthy conditions prevailed). Spread all over the city rather than confined to particular poor areas, these tenements therefore contained a huge proportion of the city's population. Indeed, almost 30,000 persons were living in 2,300 of them that inspection had revealed to be unfit for human habitation. In this respect, the Report of the Royal Commission recalls the doleful observations of those travelers of a generation before:

> Public sanitary works and main sewers will be of little avail if these tenement houses are left in their present neglected condition, without a proper supply of water and utterly without any privy accommodation. . . . The evils are, however, so enormous when inquired into; and when the localities are inspected, the sufferings of the inhabitants are so palpable and the misery so evident, that wonder is excited to find that opposition, the most difficult to overcome, rises from the greatest sufferers. The poor inhabitants have been born into, and have been brought up in the midst of their filthy and unwholesome surroundings, so that uncleanness seems to have become a sort of second nature. . . . The room tenements and their surroundings in Dublin are now so utterly neglected that there is a very wide margin for cheap, available, and effective improvement.[19]

As we have seen, the tenement had been developing since the very beginning of the century. The steps in the decline of a house originally occupied by a prosperous family suffering loss of income, to take one example, are fairly predictable: the acceptance of paying guests, conversion to a family hotel, descent to lodging-house, collapse into a state of vacancy and disrepair, and expiration as a run-down tenement. Thus did large costly structures, some still recognizable a century later by their lofty entrances, majestic architraves, and exterior mouldings, become the homes of the most miserable section of the population. Those mansions in the better areas that resisted this trend became instead the site of public offices, hotels, charitable institutions, and schools. Little was accomplished to prevent this overcrowding through the erection of new houses. Indeed, compared to that of other cities, the increase in the number of houses in Dublin from 1840 onward fell abysmally short of what was required to provide decent homes for the mass of inhabitants.

TABLE 1.   No. of Houses, Families and Occupation of Fourth-class Accommodation in Dublin and Belfast, 1841–91 (according to each census).

DUBLIN	1841	1851	1861	1871	1881	1891
No. of inhabited houses	20,109	22,244	22,935	23,896	24,211	25,766
Total houses	21,670	24,284	24,585	25,042	27,587	29,370
No. let in tenements (i.e., 2 or more families per house)	9,280	10,408	10,782	10,963	9,863	8,485
Total families	49,511	57,318	58,426	58,327	54,725	51,851
No. of families per inhabited house (average)	2.5	2.6	2.5	2.5	2.3	2.0
No. of families in 4th-class accommodation	23,197	28,039	27,290	25,952	23,360	19,342
Percentage of families in 4th-class accommodation	47	49	47	45	43	37

BELFAST	1841	1851	1861	1871	1881	1891
No. of inhabited houses	10,906	13,802	18,595	27,961	34,982	46,376
Total houses	12,068	15,100	20,190	29,918	41,271	52,017
Total families	15,172	20,312	24,981	36,654	41,542	51,256
No. of families per inhabited house (average)	1.4	1.5	1.3	1.3	1.2	1.1
No. of families in 4th-class accommodation	1,061	2,003	1,351	1,419	657	579

Accommodation for the worst-off families hardly improved at all between 1841 and 1881, only a drop from 47 percent to 43 percent being achieved in the number of families in fourth-class accommodation. The figure for 1891, though an improvement, still represented an intolerable situation, with 37 percent of families in the very worst of living conditions. At that rate of decrease it could take the best part of a century to provide something better for the poorest of the working classes than the type of dwelling that was increasingly being considered unfit for human habitation. Corresponding data for Belfast, admittedly a "new" town compared to ancient Dublin, invite sobering reflection on the historical circumstances that at all levels of society always appeared to favor the Protestant North over the Catholic South.

Of course, the "housing question" was hardly a matter of public concern in the United Kingdom before the middle of the century. Even the poor of the most congested quarters of London had to await the philanthropic work of Octavia Hill and John Ruskin in the 1860s before much activity was directed to the improvement of their abodes. As usual, activity in Ireland, philanthropic or legislative, followed England's lead. The first legislative recognition of the housing question in general was the (English) Act of 1851, promoted by Lord Shaftesbury to give local authorities the power to build model lodging houses for the laboring classes, in particular for single persons. Shaftesbury's enthusiasm also infected concerned private citizens, and in Dublin, under the lead given by the Sanitary Association, the idea of a philanthropic building society was canvassed in 1853. Queen Victoria and Prince Albert, who had had a triumphal tour of Ireland some years before and did not count the abject condition of the poor among their more engaging memories of the trip, let it be known to the Association that they were prepared to head any subscription list with a donation of £300 if enough support were found for the project.[20] However, public apathy was to deny the denizens of the Liberties the model dwellings, schools, and reading rooms contemplated for a few of them. Not until the (Irish) Act of 1866 (The Labouring Classes Lodging Houses and Dwellings Act) was the municipality given the power to effect what private philanthropy had failed to do; but here too good intentions spoke louder than action, for that Act lacked a compulsory clause for the acquisition of sites and included the ominous provision that expenditures were to be defrayed out of the rates. In fact, before the powers acquired under Sir Richard Cross' Act (the Artisans' and Labourers' Dwellings Improvement Act, 1875) extended to Ireland at the instigation of the Dublin Sanitary Association, the Dublin Corporation could not even boast the tiny success achieved by the private Industrial Tenements Co. (founded by Quakers), which began to build a handful of dwellings for poor laboring-class families in Meath Street in 1867.

The Cross Act authorized the Commissioners of the Board of Works in Ireland to make loans to local authorities and private bodies for the erection of working-class houses (i.e., artisan dwellings or laborers' cottages) in urban sanitary districts with a population in excess of 25,000. The monies so advanced were to be repaid with interest within 40 years (in England, 50 years). Prior to this act, the Board, over 8 years of operations, had sanctioned only 15 loans for such purposes, amounting in all to some £35,000 for projects housing about 550 families *in the whole of* Ireland. And since the Board had virtually no control over the rents borrowers might charge, the few houses built in Dublin by private companies or individuals had been let at rents that only the better-off artisan or higher shop assistant could afford. For example, of the 38 houses built by a group headed by Sir John Arnott in the neighborhood of Dominick Street, 24 were let at 7s. 8d. per week (£20 p.a.) and two at 10s. 9d. per week (£28 p.a.), rents that must have forced some occupiers to take in lodgers. Of the remaining 12 houses, 11 were let at 5s. 9d. (near the *maximum* rent the Board considered within the means of the better-off artisan in the more expensive districts) and only one at 3s. 10d. The newly organized Dublin Artisans' Dwellings Company (another Dublin Sanitary Association idea) had also begun to build, but even at rents slightly in excess of 5s. per week it was certain that only a very few working-class families would take part in any migration from decaying areas to the tidy row-houses that were beginning to dot the landscape in the city's northern districts. Some of the cheaper new houses had other disadvantages, as suggested by the Board's criticism of a proposed private scheme off the North Strand Road: "The cottages contain very poor accommodation, only a living room 17' x 9' x 7½' (high), but they are of a class much wanted and which speculators are not building. The living rooms have no light but what comes in over the doors; no bedroom has a fireplace; they are too low and the facing of Tullamore bricks would not stand the weather."[21] The Board may perhaps have been too critical in many instances, for at this early stage of its work only about one-half of the loan applications survived the close scrutiny of the inspectors. Nevertheless, the

Cross Act and subsequent legislation did stimulate building activity in urban areas. In the last quarter of the century, as the annual reports of the Board of Works reveal, about 9,000 Irish families (of which perhaps one-third to one-half were in the city of Dublin) were accommodated through schemes executed with the Board's assistance.

As far as the Dublin Corporation was concerned, the Cross Act armed this body with compulsory powers to deal with slum clearance. Thus the Corporation could now purchase for demolition and eventual reconstruction whole areas of insanitary and structurally defective houses. Again, loans from the Board of Works were to finance purchasing and clearing of unhealthy areas, laying of new streets, and making improvements for sewerage, lighting, and water supply. The site would then be leased to a private builder (anything smacking of municipal "socialism" was frowned upon) for construction of new improved dwellings. Thus did the Corporation make its first attempt to come to grips with the housing question. Three areas were selected for demolition: parts of the Coombe, Plunkett Street in the heart of the Liberties, and the Boyne Street section east of Trinity College, all ancient and decayed areas containing houses that in official parlance were "unfit for human habitation." All three sites were purchased, and the first two, after clearing and improvement, were handed over for private development to the Dublin Artisans' Dwellings Company: lack of funds prevented improvement of the cleared site in the case of the smaller Boyne Street area.

But the Corporation was badly burned in the entire transaction. It took several years after issuance of the demolition order in 1877 for the Corporation to surmount the legal barriers to obtaining possession of houses in the Coombe, and when compensation was finally fixed by arbitrators appointed by the Local Government Board, the Corporation discovered it had to pay at least ten-years' purchase of rents to owners of decayed tenements and as much as twenty-six weeks' rent indiscriminately to tenants and roomkeepers. The Coombe scheme alone came to £24,000, far in excess of what had been estimated. This story was repeated for the Plunkett Street scheme as almost £30,000 was expended for clearance and improvements. In any event, both areas were built upon by the Dwellings Company: the Coombe completed in 1886—210 houses for as many families; Plunkett Street in 1888—99 houses for 111 families.[22] Even so, the Corporation could congratulate itself on having taken the first small steps in municipal housing, for an element of subsidy was introduced to this worthy venture by the ridiculously small site rents of £200 per annum payable by the builder for land that would have brought in considerable revenue at open market prices. However, this experience made the Corporation wary of making further clearances except in cases of pressing social need or where representations were made by local ratepayers. There can be little doubt that of the displaced families, numbering about 2,500 persons for both schemes, most were unable to return as tenants of the new dwellings because of the rent structure imposed by the profit-making Dwellings Company: rents between 3s. and 6s. for two- to four-room dwellings. The vast majority of working-class families in the Dublin slums could afford no more than 2s. or so per week in rent.

Five other projects exhausted the Corporation's involvement in housing for the working classes in the remaining years of the century. These comprised flats and cottages throughout the city for nearly 500 families, which project the Corporation itself undertook to build (at *economic* rents, and with only small loss to ratepayers) because private builders were unwilling to invest in slum clearance. One of these schemes, the Bride's Alley development, replacing a frightful slum near St. Patrick's Cathedral, also involved the Corporation in huge and unexpected expenditure. Even with the municipality as landlord, not all the displaced tenants became the occupiers of the new "council flats." A survey made later in one case revealed that all but two families out of scores that had been dislodged had to find elsewhere the cheap accommodation they could only afford.[23] This displacement was inevitable considering that a mere 84 of the 500 or so new Corporation tenements were let at rents of 2s. or less. The number of families housed in the city by private enterprise in the same period (under schemes conforming to the provisions of the various Housing of the Working Classes Acts) hardly exceeded 4,000, only about one quarter of whom might have escaped from the slums. Therefore, public and private building activity in metropolitan Dublin had succeeded in providing accommodation for between 4,000 and 5,000 families, most of whom had to pay "economic" rents, in the 25 years since the first substantial steps had been initiated by the (Housing) Act of 1875.[24] Meanwhile, reflecting the continued destruction of older housing stock, the census figures for 1891 revealed that the number of inhabited houses in the city had increased by only 1,870 over the total for the year 1871 (see Table 1), and this at a time when houses in Belfast were being built at an average of over 2,000 *each* year. Moreover, large tracts of the city were falling into decay, for the operation of public health regulations resulted in the "detenanting" of several thousand houses, many of which were pulled down and remained as derelict sites. The capital was fortunate indeed to have experienced a demographic downturn in the second half of the century. A net population increase, especially any resulting from an influx of rural unskilled, would only have exacerbated the already severe congestion in the poorer working-class areas.

Thus, the housing problem facing Dublin Corporation was virtually insuperable. The "cheap, available and effective" solution urged by the Royal Commissioners in 1879 must necessarily have involved vast urban clearances, massive rebuilding, as well as considerable rent subsidies supported by increased rates and large, long-term loans. Also, the size of the tenement population was alarming and the number of families in need of immediate rehousing too great for any quick solution. And where in an overcrowded city, enclosed on all sides by townships anxious to preserve their middle-class character, could the detenanted be housed while reconstruction was in progress? Those evicted would of course be forced into houses in adjoining localities. Worse still, there was every likelihood that the occupants of newly constructed dwellings would not be those same evicted but rather the better-off artisans who could afford the "economic" rents charged by either the Corporation or the private builder. But neither ratepayer nor government, given the sanctity of private enterprise, was willing to expend or advance huge sums of money to provide housing for the working classes at uneconomic rents. The scale of activity on the part of public and private enterprise in the last quarter of the century indicates the extent of the failure to ameliorate, let alone solve, the housing problem in the city of Dublin. The Irish capital was to remain singularly free of what Engels dubbed the "spirit of Haussmann." There was to be no forced scattering of the working classes through the demolition of their centrally located homes to make way for great shops, warehouses, boulevards, and public buildings.

The bare statistics of housing accommodation also beg the question—how did the poor live? Life in the nineteenth-century tenement suggested an intolerable emotional and physical strain, a constant battle against debilitating disease, a daily assault on the senses of sight, hearing, and above all, smell. It was an experience to be avoided by all but the most intrepid social investigator, the ministering priest or parson, and those who were paid for their brief acquaintance with it—the sanitary inspector and rent collector. The external aspects of slum life—desolate and decaying houses; drunken street brawls, filthy lanes, courts, and alleys; ill-clad children; young faces with the mark of premature death; old faces ravaged by a lifetime of poverty and despair—these were obvious to all who dared to see. The twentieth-century reader can only know of it through the accounts of middle-class observers (the poor themselves have left none), which accounts in many instances reflect the latent ideological presuppositions of that fortunate segment of society. Hence the apparent disdain for the lower classes, the attribution of poverty to their intemperate habits, the belief that their depravity rendered them insensible to the degradation in which they lived, and, ultimately, the lack of concern for their plight. Even that most sympathetic of observers, the Reverend Whitelaw, who could hardly endure for more than a few minutes the stench that met him in one house, thought that the inhabitants were quite insensible to it. "Filth and stench," he wrote, "seemed congenial to their nature." Perhaps it is to be expected that our less socially conscious forbears should have regarded as less human than themselves people who could survive day after day in conditions of squalor that were quite literally a "disgrace to modern civilization." Nor had official sensibility yet learned to conceal by a simple change of name the unsavory reputation of the back streets—Dirty Lane (off Thomas Street), Cut-Throat Lane (Cumberland Street), Murdering Lane (Bow Lane), Dunghill Lane (Watling Street).

When Whitelaw made his pioneering investigation in 1798, he did so to make known to "persons of elevated rank and station" evils that their influence might ameliorate. On that score he labored in vain. For the next several decades the crusading spirit that marked his work was absent in Dublin, though, fortunately, there was no diminution in the amount of charitable work that had always brought some solace and sustenance to those in direst need. Instead we have a succession of travelers' reports, most of which share a tone of condescension and disgust at the "wretchedness and filthiness of the inhabitants," or the expostulations of newspaper editors outraged by the atrocious condition of streets and pavements that earned for the city the dubiously affectionate appellation "dear, *dirty* Dublin."* The severe fever epidemic that appeared in Ireland in 1817 did lead, however, to the earliest official investigation into the condition of the laboring poor in Dublin as well as in the rest of the country. The fever soon passed, of course, and with it the concern it had raised, but the brief report on the Dublin outbreak is of some interest. It was observed that fever had been general among the poor for many years in all parts of the city, especially in the more crowded and filthy streets, lanes, and courts. It is evident that the tenement system had already become a way of life in the working-class parishes of St. Michan's and St. Paul's in the northwest of the city: Church Street with 71 of its 181 houses let in 393 single rooms to 1,997 persons; 52 of the 85 houses in Barrack Street occupied by 1,318 persons in 390 rooms; and Nicholson's Court boasting only two bedsteads and two blankets in the entire court of 28 small rooms containing 151 persons! Dr. J. Cheyne, the medical investigator, displayed rare insight into causes for the tribulations of the poor. Noting that there had been a great scarcity of food and fuel at the onset of the epidemic and that the poor were clad in rags, he con-

*The phrase is attributed to Lady Morgan.

cluded that "many of them were in a state of dejection of mind from these hardships and from a general failure of employment."[25] It was unlikely that a more cogent analysis of an urban social problem was ever presented to the authorities before the appearance of the labor agitators at the end of the century.

As has been noted, it was only toward the middle of the century that the "condition of the people" generated lasting official concern and legislative action. The Select Committee on the Health of Towns (1840) resulted from the heightened interest in sanitary matters following those first forbidding reports of mortality in English towns by the Registrar General. Dublin was selected as one of the towns for investigation, and the evidence given reveals a state of affairs in the poorer districts that was to be repeated in more or less lurid detail at subsequent official and private investigations: the narrow courts of overcrowded tenements with their cellar dwellings devoid of light except through the door; the privies ("never cleaned until impossible to use") in lobbies and under staircases; backyards ankle-deep in human filth; adjoining ruined sites serving as dung yards; nearby slaughterhouses and dairy yards with their "noxious effluvia"; refuse-loaded streets lacking any regular system of scavenging; the common lodging houses from which issued the recurrent epidemics that killed, disfigured, or sapped the strength of the community; and pervading all, the noisome smell that put to flight every "respectable" witness to such scenes.[26] Even the elements made their special contribution to the surroundings, turning the oozy soil of the streets into mud lakes and creating hazards redolent of Swift's purple phrases in *A City Shower*: ". . . sweeping from butchers' stalls dung, guts and blood; drown'd puppies, stinking sprats, all drench'd in mud, dead cats and turnip-tops come tumbling down the flood." For their water supply most tenement dwellers depended on the backyard tap, while those lacking even that convenience incurred the extra journey to the local public fountain, the scene of frequent quarrels. This latter circumstance led several commentators to assert that the very poor, for lack of utensils, were forced to collect clean water in the very same vessels in which they carried effete matter to the privies; perhaps the truth, or at best a justifiable exaggeration to arouse official action. Needless to say, thousands of families had no opportunity to bathe or wash clothes, at least not until 1885, when the first and only Public Baths and Wash House was erected in Tara Street to serve the entire city.

These revelations induced the same response among sanitary "hobbyists" in the Irish capital that, as Enid Gauldie has shown in her excellent study of working-class housing, developed in reforming circles in English towns and cities over the next generation—the transformation of the housing question into a public health problem to be solved by sanitary legislation instead of by direct action to rehouse the poor. It could hardly have been otherwise at a time when laissez faire represented the social and political philosophy of the middle class. Nevertheless, the attack on filth did ensure that not only sanitary reforms, however inadequately executed, would be made but that the "condition of the people" question would continue to demand attention. When, for example, the Dublin Corporation applied to Parliament in 1846 for an Improvement Act, the resulting enquiry laid bare once more the tattered social fabric of the city. Such legislation was sorely needed to effect a rational approach to municipal administration, for as the system then stood two government-appointed bodies, the Wide Streets Commissioners and the Paving Board, operated and were funded (by Parliamentary grants and revenue from municipal taxation) independently of the elected town council. Thus, functions that one would normally associate with a municipal body—civic improvements, paving, lighting, cleansing of streets, making of sewers—were instead vested in nonelective Commissioners over whom the Corporation had no control. This incongruity gave rise to the ludicrous situation whereby the Corporation (which supplied the water) needed the permission of the Paving Board to break the streets in order that the Pipe Water Committee might repair its pipes, giving rise to the Board's complaint that the Corporation did more harm to the streets than all the inhabitants of Dublin put together.

At any rate, since the enquiry was designed to test the Corporation's fitness to assume the above-mentioned functions, it was natural that the condition of the streets and sewers in the poorer districts should come under scrutiny. Dr. Thomas Willis, whose work has already been cited, took the investigating surveyors, Messrs. Hayward and Brassington, on a tour of the congested St. Michan's parish. This quarter of the city contained 22,793 inhabitants and had a density in persons per house greater than any other Dublin parish— "a striking specimen of a poor district." The investigators were appalled and astonished, being obliged by the "filth and corruption of the atmosphere" to discontinue after an hour the inspection of interiors. "The wonder to our minds," they wrote in their report, "was not that disease, with its attendant miseries was rarely absent, but that human beings could prolong life at all in such dwelling places and under such circumstances. . . . Their present condition is a disgrace to a civilized country, and should be amended at any sacrifice; if not for their sakes, for the sake of the public health. . . ." As might be expected, a startling contrast was found to exist between the state of paving, cleansing, and sewerage of poor neighborhoods as against the opulent quarters of the southeastern districts. The Corporation's ability to deliver a sufficient supply of water to the citizens also came under sharp attack when it was found that the Pipe Water Committee had shamelessly neglected working-class areas. When the same charge was made at later investigations, apologists for the Corporation were wont to excuse the inaction of that body by claiming that it was useless to install water pipes and plumbing fittings in the worst class of houses—they would only be ripped out and sold within 24 hours. The Paving Board as a consequence was unable to guarantee to the eighty public fountains (the Board also controlled these) what recent legislation demanded—water for three hours in the forenoon, three in the afternoon. Still common was the four hours per day, three days per week supply. The Corporation obtained its Improvement Act in 1849, but most people had to wait considerably longer for the amenities of industrial civilization.

Of course, the published proceedings of parliamentary commissions and select committees, with their interminable questions and answers and often boring details, went largely unread by the public. It was not uncommon, moreover, for their recommendations to be ignored by the government. Nevertheless, that a public opinion was being created in favor of the amelioration of the plight of the poor cannot be denied, as is evident in the formation of the Dublin Sanitary Association (precursor of the organization mentioned earlier). That the aims of this body were not solely encompassed by the desire for clean bodies and sanitary toilets is evident from its Report for 1849, which suggests the demoralizing effect of their living quarters on the poor of the city: the husband tempted "to exchange in his hours of relaxation a dirty home, the society of a wife whom circumstances have forced to be untidy, and filthy children for the comparative cleanliness and cheerfulness of the public house"; the greater burden on the housewife unable to surmount the obstacles, including lack of a ready water supply, to maintaining a decent abode. "All these details and many others of everyday life among the poor," states the Report, "are sufficient to eradicate every desire for appearances, every yearning after home comfort with which the young wife may have originally set out on the journey of life." This was the kind of genuine though ineffectual concern that led to the attempt, mentioned earlier, to set up model lodging houses for the poor. It was on this occasion that Queen Victoria suggested in a letter to the Association that a condition be attached to their occupation whereby the future inhabitants would "be made to feel some shame at raggedness [which was] not a necessary accompaniment to poverty."[28] Her Majesty was not being uncharitable. She was merely displaying a normal upper-class disdain for the poor coupled with a characteristic English inability to understand the real nature of Irish distress.

Interest in working-class living conditions appears to have waned during the '50s and '60s, a period during which middle-class families departed for the suburbs to the south of the city in appreciable numbers. This was also the era of mid-Victorian prosperity in which Ireland to some extent also shared. The advance in wages enjoyed by the city's artisans and laborers may have put more food and drink in their stomachs, but as can be seen from Table 1, it did little to afford them better accommodation. In the decade of the '70s the pace quickened and the urban condition came under more general observation when newspapers like the *Freeman's Journal* and *Irish Times* and trade and professional journals such as the *Irish Builder*, the *Sanitary Record*, and the *Dublin Journal of Medical Science* began to press the issue of sanitary reform and, after 1875, the housing needs of the working classes. The popular daily *Freeman's Journal* conducted its own social survey—"In the Fever King's Preserves"—and published the results in August and September 1871. Little appeared to have changed since 1840: yards ankle-deep in filth and garbage; the foul effluvium of cesspools, dairy yards, and slaughter houses; the goats, pigs, and hens swarming in the enclosures of courts whose cheerless rooms swarmed with inhabitants; the lime kiln in Long Lane serving as a "hotel" for the destitute. The Coombe and the area surrounding St. Michan's Church still presented scenes of utter desolation, their worst lanes and alleys being likened to prolonged ashpits and urinals, owing to the old Dublin custom of throwing out filth into the streets. In this latter respect even royal personages got scant consideration. Charles Cameron, the resourceful overseer of the city's public health, once accompanied the Prince of Wales and the Duke of Clarence on a visit to the slum district: "Just as we stopped at a large tenement house a woman discharged into the channel course a quantity of water in which cabbage had been boiled . . . the Duke stepped into this fluid, slipped and fell. He was much startled and his coat and one glove were soiled."[29] A medical witness at the Royal Sanitary Commission in 1879 stated that he often while on his evening rounds narrowly escaped being showered with the contents of vessels used by the female poor to relieve themselves in their homes: it was commonly held that no respectable female would use the backyard privy.

One can hardly blame the poor entirely for the state of their streets: over 1,700 houses lacked either internal or external space for the construction of privies, and water closets were a rarity in tenement houses. Before 1882 there was no regular system of domestic scavenging. There was also no house-to-house cleaning of yards and sanitary accommodation like that performed in many English cities where the privy system was in general use and where sanitary authorities collected night soil and refuse and defrayed the cost out of the rates. The few ashpits and privies cleaned by the Corporation were done at a fee to owners, a practice that virtually excluded tenement houses from such operations. As late as 1884 the situation was bad enough for a concerned Superintendent of Cleansing to make the following report to the municipal council:

> It will be at once admitted that there is no city in the United Kingdom, similar in extent, population or importance to Dublin, in which the public thoroughfares are so abused as they are in this city, where in many instances [over 350 affected streets and lanes were listed] they serve as receptacles for house, fish, vegetable and other shop refuse and every kind of filth—the result is most offensive to the senses, demoralizing to the citizen, deleterious to the public health, discreditable to the Corporation, and a disgrace to the city . . . some of the back lanes are not alone used as ashpits by the people residing in or near them; they also serve as depots in which, night after night, cartloads of rubbish or refuse are deposited by persons who take advantage of the darkness or the temporary absence of the police.[30]

The tenement dweller had to endure other daily discomforts not of his own making—the presence of private and municipal manure yards, way stations for street sweepings and the contents of ashpits and privies. The private yards of MacClean's Lane held festering heaps 60 feet long and 20 feet high. The Corporation's "malodorous acre" at Marrowbone Lane had manure ("deodorized" with pulverized macadam) piled to the second floor height of adjoining houses. Not even these ill winds blew the city some good, at least to the degree they did in many English cities where the expense of scavenging was partly recouped through the sale of manure to farmers. The small amount of tillage land in the rural environs of Dublin precluded such a windfall for the city, though that sober fact did not deter the Sanitary Association from reminding the city fathers in a bizarre euphuism that they (or rather the working class) were sitting on "a veritable mine of wealth, more valuable than the sands of Pactolus, more real than the imaginary treasures of El Dorado." The extent of the scavenging problem and, by inference, the threat to public health is revealed by the report of actions enforced by the Public Health Committee during the thirteen years up to 1879—the repair of 17,497 privies and water closets; the removal of 12,804 accumulations of manure, of 3,418 pigs and other animals from dwellings, and of 9,839 pigs from yards. The average fine levied for the 43,000 sanitary offenders brought before the courts was a mere 2s., hardly a deterrent to the slum landlord.[31]

Dublin had achieved sufficient notoriety by this time for the *Sanitary Record* (London) to send its own "special commissioner" to report on the sanitary condition of the city it had recently condemned as "reeking with filth." Doubtless St. Giles-in-the-Fields or Saffron Hill nearer home could have equally earned attention, but evil conditions that in great English cities prevailed largely in confined areas existed in Dublin on a widespread scale. Hence its attraction for crusading sanitarians. The Commissioner was Henry Burdett, a fellow of the Sanitary Institute of Great Britain, and he spent over two months going about the city in 1876 observing abuses of public health that he charged to Corporate inertia, supineness, and incompetence. There was probably some justice to his charge in the case of the dirty streets, filthy yards, defective sewers, inadequate water supply, and the general pollution of residential environments by slaughter houses and dairy yards. Burdett had the fortitude to enter some of the homes, where he met sights that must have been duplicated many times over throughout the city—the room with two bedsteads occupied by a family of six, a bundle of straw on the floor where the husband slept, the wife ill with typhus fever, the little girl being treated for typhoid, the window overlooking a small yard covered in excrement with the foul privy directly beneath. As the *Irish Builder* claimed, "the homes of men have become the living sepulchres of the people." One of Burdett's interviewees, an Irish poor-law medical officer, was no less chilling in his assessment of the situation: "The Irish child is born and reared on the dung-heaps, and if ever there was a country where the 'survival of the fittest' was alone aimed at, sure ours must be the one entirely."[32]

As noted earlier, official investigations after 1875, such as those having to do with local government, extensions of boundaries, sewerage and drainage (all dealing with Dublin), tended to show increasing concern with housing. It was found that rents even in the worst of tenements were often beyond the capacity of the residents, varying as they did between 10d. per week for a single room in a tenement unsuited for human habitation to 5s. for two good rooms. Rents were generally less than 5s. per week so as to allow owners to apply to magistrates for summary ejectment for nonpayment. Consequently, unlicensed lodging houses proliferated as hard-pressed tenement occupiers attempted to make ends meet by taking in one or more strangers and imparting to the urban argot that catch phrase of rural Ireland—"the pig that pays the rint." In this way areas of exceptional density were created in the city. The system was described to the Royal Commission in 1879 as it operated in Bride Street: a young man lying in fever in the one room with three other adults sleeping in the adjoining unventilated "closet," the numbers sometimes supplemented by tramps; another dwelling containing four generations (an old woman, daughter, married granddaughter, and infant children) and male lodgers and mendicants in addition. This mixing of the sexes, with the implied danger to public morals, agitated the Commissioners as much as did the more real danger to public health. The same "disgraceful indecency" perforce prevailed within families—it could hardly be otherwise in a city where over 32,000 families out of a total of 54,000 lived in 48,000 rooms.[33] Thus, investigators were shocked to find that a 35-year-old woman slept in the same bed with her 40-year-old brother or that a man, wife, five children (the oldest, a daughter, aged twenty), and grandmother shared two beds in a room 10 feet by 9 feet. These cases, like many others, must have escaped the moral policing of each parish conducted as a matter of course by the various charitable organizations. The St. Vincent de Paul Society, for instance, made the separation of the sexes at night a condition of relief even for the poorest families, a requirement that one expects was more honored in the breach than the observance.

Such revelations hardly ruffled the public conscience and doubtless seemed of small concern to a government confronted in the early '80s by the national agitation of the Land League and Parnell's Irish parliamentary party. Yet similar disclosures of much more delimited urban congestion in London a few years later, in particular the Reverend Mearns' *Bitter Cry of Outcast London*, precipitated a national outcry and were partly responsible for the setting up of the Royal Commission on the Housing of the Working Classes in 1884. Apparently the imputations of incest and gross immorality that seemed credible to English readers hardly mattered in Dublin, where as clerical witnesses were wont to proclaim, the morality of the people was proverbial. Relevant also was the relative freedom from crime of any serious nature: it was easier to ignore the social degradation of the slums when they failed to be breeding grounds of crime or, as Mayhew imputed to the London slums, training schools for professional criminals. By far the most threatening "criminals" in Dublin were the common drunks and disorderly prostitutes. Drunkenness had, of course, long been recognized as the great psychological release of the working classes in general and the Irish in particular. Many witnesses of the lower depths of urban life conceded that mass intemperance was hardly avoidable in the circumstances. Hence the persistence of the distinctive Irish "waking" of the dead, despite the priests' bitter denunciation of the drunken orgies often associated with such apparent necrolatry. The extremes of poverty must surely also have been responsible for the occasional elemental outbursts that doubtless entered into the folk memory such as the great whiskey fire of 1875. On that occasion a malt-house and bonded warehouse went up in flames in the Liberties and sent an intoxicating stream of burning malt and Irish whiskey down Ardee Street. Scores of people had to be dragged off the streets insensible, having lain in the gutter to lap up the life-giving liquid. More serious was another fire in Thomas Street two years earlier, when a mob of 20,000 or more looted shops as the fire spread, assaulted police, and stoned the military until routed by bayonet charges.[34] But orgies of revelry and looting were few and far between; death, disease, and poverty being infinitely more common along the mean streets of a distressed city.

The nineteenth century—that "great age of cities"—was unkind to Dublin. At its end the Irish metropolis was no longer the proud second city of the empire, nor did it rank at all with the great cities of Europe. As municipal councillors were to complain before the Select Committee on Industries in Ireland in 1885: "There is no other large city in Europe that has declined so rapidly of late as Dublin . . . things are getting worse every day."[35] When the Irish capital was now compared with other cities it was, alas, only to highlight conditions of poverty and mortality, which in them had been to a very great extent banished as mass social evils. The situation in Dublin, of course, was only one instance of the regressive nature of the colonial relationship that rendered major Irish social and political issues, ranging from the tenure of land in the countryside to the municipal franchise in towns and cities, subject to the legislative fiat of the British parliament. Only very late in the day did that body concede that Irish social problems were worthy of consideration on their own merits instead of being solely bones of contention with truculent Irish nationalist politicians. And given the overwhelming rural character of Ireland as well as the political goals of the Irish parliamentary party, it was inevitable that those concessions should be largely determined by rural needs or the more generalized nationalist aims, viz., the abolition of landlordism, a scheme of local government, a national university system of Catholic education, and ultimately, an Irish parliament. In the field of housing legislation, for example, the most effective measures by far were the various Labourers' Acts that provided modern standards of comfort for rural workers on very favorable financial terms made possible by subsidies from the Treasury.

As we have seen, after 1872 or thereabouts every attempt was made to focus attention on the social ills of the capital, in particular on the woeful lack of proper housing for over one-third of the city's population. The various official investigations from 1876 onward performed a valuable service in their delineation of the city's social and structural decay. Sanitary inspectors, medical officers, clerics, and reformers all bore witness to the fact that thousands of families existed all along on the borderland between habitual privation and absolute destitution. Considering the paltry action taken to reverse that situation, one is tempted to conclude that these various witnesses were enrolled as participants in a series of civic rites designed to evade the reality of improvement by the semblance of concern. Most contemporaries placed the entire blame for the city's ills on Dublin Corporation, but that judgment ignored the difficulties, both political and financial, under which that much-abused body had to labor. Before 1840 the Orange-dominated municipal council, the voice of Ascendancy and bigotry, operating under the principle of self-election and absolute control of admission to the franchise, certainly invited the contempt of most citizens for its exclusion of Catholics from the roll of freemen on political and religious grounds. Even as late as 1835, 42 years after the passing of the act granting corporate privileges to Roman Catholics, members continued to be exclusively Protestant in religion and almost wholly Orange in temper. At the same time barely half-a-dozen Catholics sat among the hundred or so grand jurors for the city—"a monstrous revolting feature" of civic life, exclaimed Daniel O'Connell. That this political ordering should endure to safeguard the Protestant ascendancy was defiantly asserted in the House of Lords 5 years later in a last-ditch attempt, supported by some Irish peers, to defeat the reforming provisions of the Municipal Corporations (Ireland) Act as it applied to Dublin. The Dublin Catholics won their reform only to find that the city fathers had been neither honest nor efficient. They had so plundered the resources of the city through huge loans and alienation of property that Daniel O'Connell, the first Lord Mayor following the reforming legislation of 1840, had to suffer the indignity of seeing the property of the Corporation, including the insignia of the mayoralty, placed under seizure by the Master of the Rolls as a result of a suit brought by the previous administration's creditors.[36]

The new and reformed Corporation hardly justified Protestant fears that the Council chamber would become a "normal school" for agitators. The qualification for town councillor and alderman presumed assets of £1,000 in property and occupation of a house within the borough to the value of £25. And the potential municipal voter by virtue of his status as a £10 householder was subject to a residential requirement of almost three years (in contrast to *one* in English boroughs) as well as liability to all rates, including the poor rate. Thus exclusivity as well as a narrow franchise was maintained: middle-class Protestants merely yielded power to aspiring middle-class Catholics. Witness, for example, the municipal burgess roll as late as 1898—fewer than 8,000 electors in a population of 245,000 compared with Belfast's 40,000 burgesses and a population of 256,000. Such a narrow franchise could be depended on to safeguard the interests of property holders, not compel owners to put drains and sanitary conveniences in their tenement properties. In mitigation of the Corporation's lackluster record in caring for the citizenry, one must note that after 1840 the Corporation was saddled for years with both debts and the expense of miles of streets in gross disrepair. And as indicated above, the downward general revaluation of the city in 1852 resulted in a loss of revenue that was sorely missed in the subsequent decades of sanitary concern. And since statutory limits on rating powers were imposed by Parliament, sympathizers would point to the fiscal strait jacket imposed on the Corporation in assigning blame for the city's ills. The Corporation did not even possess the right to collect its own rates, a task assigned (until 1890) to a government-appointed Collector General whose costs of collection were an unnecessary added expense to the city. Others saw the decline of the city consequent upon the withdrawal of the "leading merchants and citizens" from any involvement in municipal life—a phenomenon of the 1870s not unknown in British and American cities of the period. If these solid citizens, Conservatives (and usually Protestants) who had been shut out of Liberal (and usually Catholic) wards, could be induced once more to undertake their civic responsibilities, it was suggested that a reassured Parliament would lighten the restrictions that barred municipal prodigality. And there were some concerned citizens who offered the debatable view that the problems of the city were attributable to the exclusion of the artisan class from the municipal franchise.

The real solution, of course, could not be broached—massive social investment on the part of the state itself. For doing so would have involved a departure from the principles of laissez faire that must have repercussions in England itself, with its equally great social problems. A more modest approach would have looked to the ratepayers to provide the huge subsidies that were required to mount an all-out attack on the city's worst problem—housing. Even when the resurgent Irish constituency effected a political revolution in municipal life with the appearance of Parnell's National League in 1881, the "true" representatives of the people were no more successful than their Liberal predecessors in loosening the pockets of Catholic ratepayers or inducing in them a concern for the plight of their less fortunate coreligionists. The real concern of most Irishmen, of course, was now to become the issue of Home Rule and the restoration of the land to Irish tenant farmers. In an era when rural distress and agrarian agitation dominated the Irish scene and Irish nationalism dominated politics, little consideration could be expected for the urban problems of the Irish capital. The Victorian era came to a close for Dublin with no promise of a golden age of growth and prosperity. True, as one economic historian has pointed out, "Despite its large slumland, Dublin revealed all the characteristics of a relatively prosperous city."[37] One in which, however, an apparent economic vigor rested with only a few exceptions (brewing, milling, for instance) on the retail trade and petty shopkeeping. The households of the well-to-do in the suburbs may have increased the opportunities for female domestic servants, but middle-class capital more often than not found its way into foreign and colonial stocks. The failure of Dublin to duplicate the success of a Belfast or Birmingham has led another Irish historian to speculate that human rather than material factors may have operated to retard industrial growth as the Catholic middle classes aped their Protestant betters in the single-minded pursuit of professional status for themselves and their children, thus denying much-needed skills and capital to the riskier pathways of industry and commerce.[38] In another context this is perhaps what the President of the Queen's College at Cork had in mind when he complained to the Select Committee on Industries in 1885 about the lack of good technical education in the country and its consequences: "I am sorry to say that the majority of the young men would prefer to be clerks or anything in which they were not called upon to labour."[39] But then again, those who might have wished to "labour" would most likely have had to seek their opportunities in Belfast or Birmingham rather than in Dublin. At any rate, the paucity of manufactures, an insufficiency (or misdirection) of capital, and an inability to compete with the products of British industry stifled economic progress in the Irish capital. And in social terms, also, the want of employment, prevalence of poverty, and inadequacies in public health and housing ensured that for some more years the hopes for a future of progress would have to defer to a concern for the social failures of the present. Housing was the fundamental social problem, however, and would only be solved after the passing of too many decades of the twentieth century. This was, perhaps, the cruellest legacy of the nineteenth century.

 *Part*

THE CITY

"Whether our natural life is great or mean, whether our social virtues are mature or stunted, whether our sons are moral or vicious, whether religion is possible or impossible, depends on the city."

HENRY DRUMMOND

2

The Faded Capital

Dublin is less an aggregation of buildings than a collection of personages.

JAMES STEPHENS

My imagination is full of Ireland when I no longer see it, and it is always the worse for every sight of Dublin.

LADY GREGORY, Seventy Years

IN MANY respects Dublin at the end of the nineteenth century presented the face of an eighteenth-century metropolis. For during the preceding century, the lack of any substantial industrial development coupled with the absence of widespread general building activity allowed the continued existence of Georgian residences (alas, not always for the use originally intended) and the preservation of a rich architectural heritage of fine public buildings. Indeed, this constant visual reminder of earlier glories is credited with preventing the worst excesses of Victorian building seen elsewhere.[1] The harmonious results are still much in evidence in what has been described as the "Augustan delicacy" of Dublin's inner suburbs, most notably in the modest row houses of Sandymount, Phibsborough, and Drumcondra. Yet by century's end, nothing could disguise the fact that Dublin was, as the phrase went, a hundred years behind the times—a faded capital. All those problems, social and civic, that had loomed so large in the closing decades of the nineteenth century were carried over, in varying degrees of severity, into the next.

In 1901 the census recorded a population for the city of 290,000, an increase of 45,000 since the previous census. But the growth was less than appeared because 30,000 persons had been added by the incorporation in 1900 of the former townships of New Kilmainham, Glasnevin, Drumcondra and Clonliffe, and Clontarf. Thus, the population of the city grew by only 5 percent over the decade, about half the growth rate of the still independent suburban townships that lay to the south and east of the city. But the latter (Pembroke, Rathmines, Blackrock, Kingstown) added only 93,000 persons to the population of the entire metropolitan area. The citizens were predominantly Roman Catholic in religion, as many as 81.8 percent in 1901 and increasing to 83.1 percent in 1911, when a total of 304,802 persons were enumerated, testimony to the continued though slow decline of Anglo-Irish Protestant Episcopalian (Church of Ireland) elements (see Appendix A).

Though their numbers might be on the wane, Dublin Protestants (Episcopalians mostly) continued to wield a disproportionate share of the social power and influence that derived from their status in the occupational hierarchy. In the medical and legal professions, according to the 1901 census, the non-Catholic elements exceeded 50 percent of the total in each case, and that this imbalance was to be slightly redressed at the next census was almost certainly due to the decline of the Protestant population: there were fewer doctors in Ireland in 1911 than there had been in 1881. Likewise, Roman Catholics were decidedly in the minority in banking (42 percent), engineering (32 percent), pharmacy (44 percent), and only had a slight majority as accountants. These disproportions in relation to strength in the population were repeated in the county area outside the city, where Catholic doctors, for example, were less than one-third of the total. Even where social recognition did not especially depend on professional status, such as in official appointments as commissioners of the peace, the number of J.P.s who professed to be Roman Catholics was remarkably low. In 1911 the magistrates list for the country borough revealed that only 84 of 233 J.P.s (i.e., 36 percent) were of the majority faith, a proportion that though exceeding the county's (29 percent) was well under that for the country as a whole, viz., 46 percent. Perhaps most remarkable of all was that in "Protestant" Belfast the number of Catholic J.P.s at the same date corresponded exactly with their denominational ratio of about 25 percent in the city's population.[2]

The city of Dublin, or rather that part of it that lay within the canals, retained its quadripartite division, but three sectors had continued to suffer from the inexorable push to the southeast quarter. The old core centered at the Liberties remained a constant reproach to the civic authorities for its poverty and squalor. On the opposite side of the quays, in the section extending west of Capel Street to the Royal (now Arbour Hill) Barracks, lay pockets of blight rivalling in frightfulness the worst slums of the Liberties. Naturally, the city's two workhouses were located in these quarters. It was the third area of decline, the northeast, that had really suffered from the flight of the solid middle-class elements after mid-century. At an earlier period the homes of the resident gentry extended from Dorset to Gloucester Streets between Granby Row and Mountjoy Square. Now little more than the Square itself stood testimony to the former elegance of the entire district. Cavendish Row, Great Denmark Street, Gardiner's Row, and Gardiner's Place had lost their character as first-class private streets. Within a stone's throw and to the south the tenements of Summerhill were fast evolving. And hard by Gloucester Street, likewise in incipient decay, lay the notorious bastion of iniquity framed by Lower Tyrone (formerly Mecklenburgh), Mabbot, and Montgomery Streets—whither, in Gogarty's well-known limerick, Joyce went "down to the kips" in 1904. Fortunately, most of the rest of the northeast, much of it newly built over the previous half-century, betrayed the somewhat less genteel aura of respectability with which the stoical and hard-working elements of the artisan and lower-middle classes faced the world. Here, also, ran the noble length of O'Connell Street,* though better known for its breadth, which with more pride than conviction was accounted the widest thoroughfare in Europe. It had long since exchanged private elegance for the bustling hotel trade and rows of fancy shops: its

*During this period officially known as Sackville Street but the name used by nationalists is employed throughout the book. A formal resolution of Dublin Corporation to change the name to O'Connell Street was made as early as 1884 but a court injunction obtained by residents of the street prevented a change, and the original name remained the official one until 1925.

O'Connell Bridge and Sackville (familiarly, O'Connell) Street before the turn of the century. The rain is no deterrent to riders on the open tops of the Sandymount trams as they enter and leave the city. The Liberator's statue dominates the southern end of the city's main thoroughfare as does Nelson's massive column the center. The white façade of the Metropole Hotel is on the left and just beyond is the imposing colonnade of the General Post Office. The Smith O'Brien statue in the foreground was later removed to its present site near the monument to Dr. John Gray, seen here between O'Connell and Nelson.

modern façade broken by Johnston's Post Office; its center dominated by Admiral Nelson from his 134-foot-high perch atop a pillar whose pedestal reminded Dublin's citizens of great British victories.* At the southern end of the street, O'Connell (formerly Carlisle) Bridge, paved, incidentally, with stone setts from quarries owned by Charles Stewart Parnell, led the way to the grandest quarter of the city.

*The famous landmark is now no more: in the early hours of March 8, 1966, it was blown up by persons unknown, Nelson and over half the stone column crashing to the ground. Officialdom removed the stump some days later.

As in the other photographs of these central thoroughfares, the streets lack the bustling crowds that distinguish the modern metropolis on a typical working day. The tram (still horse-drawn in 1897) is ever present and animals outnumber bicycles. Note the "sandwich-man" about to pass by the gates of the Provost's House, Trinity College.

In the southeast there was no suggestion to the passer-by of the mean streets or desperate habitations encountered freely elsewhere. For that one had to search out the neglected courts, lanes, and stable dwellings in the rears of fashionable houses. These latter too were in stark contrast to their decayed counterparts north of the Liffey. Though no longer boasting aristocratic residents, their late-nineteenth-century inhabitants represented the highest classes of Dublin's social and mercantile groups that still chose to live or conduct business within the confines of the city. The classical architecture of the Georgian period here shone resplendent,[3] for interior discomforts were consoled by imposing exteriors (the familiar front doors and windows, tall and narrow; the varied tracery of fanlights; the wrought-iron railings and lamp standards) of houses able to prevent by the opulence of their environment the intrusions of the avaricious middle lessor and resist (until the 1970s, at least) the blandishments of the urban "developer." Here, also, lay the

The Bank of Ireland (formerly, the Parliament House) is on the left. Foley's statues of Burke and Goldsmith flank the entrance to the College while Grattan looks on in oratorical pose. William III's equestrian statue, which had survived a century of desecration, finally succumbed to a land mine in 1929. Note the "outside car," Dublin's unique mode of conveyance, at the bottom of the picture.

seat of learning (Trinity College), a center of finance (Bank of Ireland), the height of fashion (Grafton Street), together with the museums and other institutions of art and culture without which a city must lose its spirit. There was much in Dublin to attract the tourist—the historic associations of College Green (no longer a "green") and the old Parliament House; the architectural bravura of Gandon's Custom House; the enduring wonder of the Book of Kells at Trinity College; the triad of monuments to Grattan, Goldsmith, and Burke; the National Art Gallery; the Zoo (famed for its ability to breed lions in captivity); the Punchestown Races in April; Horse Show Week in August; even Nelson on his pillar in O'Connell Street or "Guinness and oysters" at the Red Bank restaurant. But contemporary observers rarely omit, also, to mention the air of decay and melancholy that appeared to have invested the city. Shops closed early and streets rapidly became de-

Along the Dublin quays: the view from Capel Street (Essex) bridge, ca. 1897. Lower Ormond Quay is on the left, running into Bachelor's Walk on the far side of Wellington (the Metal) bridge. McBirney's department store is on the right, near O'Connell bridge, and beyond, partly occluded by the "loop line" elevated railway crossing, is Gandon's Custom House. The Metal bridge is here seen fulfilling a function that gave much offense to the civic-minded—on this occasion broadcasting a message for epileptics.

serted. Places of entertainment were few, so few in fact that a select committee in 1892 was astounded to learn that Ireland contained only 7 or 8 theaters in all, 2 of them (the Gaiety and the Queen's) being in Dublin:

> Q. As a matter of fact, I suppose the Irish are not great theatre goers?
> A. They are.
> Q. But there are only two theatres in Dublin.
> A. Yes.[4]

London alone boasted about 40 theaters and as many large music halls.

Many would have conceded that Dublin at the turn of the century had already lost whatever cultural vitality or civic élan it once possessed. William Dawson, an acute observer, has left us his impressions of a city lacking a cultivated musical taste, having artistic pretensions, and being in great peril of sinking into provincialism.[3] The arbiters of public taste naturally bemoaned the sad decline that saw citizens flock to enjoy the lunacies of the English music hall when more legitimate institutions languished for want of public support. A common complaint was that no city in Europe was as destitute as Dublin of indoor or outdoor amusement for its people, an argument used by the City Coroner at the Public Health Inquiry of 1900 to explain the popularity of the public house, "the only meeting place for the poor." Dubliners liked to boast of the city's musical traditions, to recall endlessly that Handel first presented his *Messiah* to the world in Dublin and that the famous Mario and Grisi had created the great days of Italian opera at the old Theatre Royal. The opera companies still braved the rough Irish Sea crossing but sometimes to the despair of critics who shrank from the cult of the *Bohemian Girl* and longed for something other than the standard repetitive fare.

Dublin now possessed three theaters—the Gaiety, the Queen's, and the restored Theatre Royal—and two music halls. The Round Room of the Rotunda was the venue for the newfangled animated pictures and the latest "bioscopic revelations," while the Antient Concert Rooms in Great Brunswick Street catered to elevated musical taste in infrequent musical performances by local companies and just as infrequently provided an outlet for local amateur adventures into serious drama. The 1,800-seat Gaiety theater, in South King Street, was the capital's premier place of entertainment. It was here that Shaw was exposed to theatrical life in the years just prior to his departure for London. The Gaiety played a large part in the social life of the city and in rescuing the citizens "from the martyrdom of ennui." It was famous for its pantomime productions since producing Edwin Hamilton's *Turko the Terrible* in 1873. But the old tradition of the stock company was abandoned here, the management preferring to rely entirely on the visits of the various London companies, among which were included as regular annual visitors since the mid-1870s the Carl Rosa Opera company and the D'Oyly Carte. Minor drama, farces, and musical comedy were the regular fare of the Gaiety productions, though the theater was also the only venue for any recurring presentations of the works of Shaw and Ibsen, the latter producing critics' groans that there was little audience in Dublin for the realistic drama. Usually a week of Shakespeare or a visiting diva would relieve the monotony of the *Belle of New York* or the usual deadening dramatic fare. The aging Bernhardt made fleeting appearances on a handful of occasions, generally remaining for just one day, with the 1912 visit producing only a matinee performance on Friday, November 8. Melba sang on one Wednesday afternoon in 1908. Mme. Tetrazzini appeared in 1910, and there was a week of Pavlova in 1912. But these were few and far between and did nothing to recapture the glories of an earlier period. And with a paucity of first-rate theaters, no one could now in truth claim that a Dublin audience was a good test of the merits of a play or insist as of old that a play that survived the "exacting ordeal of a run in Dublin" was certain to succeed elsewhere.

The great days of the old Theatre Royal ended with its demise in 1880, burned to the ground as the curtain was about to be lifted on a benefit performance of the annual pantomime in aid of a local charity. It was reopened in 1897 with a 2,300-seat capacity on its old Hawkin's Street site and quickly became the home of Hippodrome and musical comedy. The unending feast of wrestlers, performing dogs, and mumming birds was relieved, fortunately, by the regular appearances of the English operatic and theatrical companies for their Dublin "season" of two or three weeks. Henry Irving and Ellen Terry visited until 1904, and the productions of Mrs. Patrick Campbell's company were staged on several occasions. The Royal also had its visiting divas, or diva rather, for only one of them graced its stage—Melba appearing twice in 1911 but only for midweek *afternoon* performances, one year too soon, alas, to attract the representative audience that the new and general weekly half-holiday might have provided. However, her working-class fans had already had the opportunity to hear her in an evening performance eleven years earlier at the Royal University hall. The Royal was also responsible for bringing Fritz Kreisler and the Imperial Russian ballet to the Dublin audience. Minor drama mainly distinguished the smaller Queen's Theatre in Great Brunswick Street, where the *Colleen Bawn* was always sure of an airing and full liberty was given to the dramatic talents of the manager, J. W. Whitbread, who produced an endless stream of plays on Irish historical themes to justify his theater's claim as the "Home of Irish drama."

The opera lover was well served in Dublin, though he could no longer expect to hear, as his grandfather had, the great Italian companies. The mainstay of opera in Dublin was now the visiting English companies, primarily the Carol Rosa and Moody Manners companies. The mainstays of operatic performances were the old favorites. No season was complete without *Bohemian Girl, Carmen, Faust, Lily of Killarney, Il Trovatore, Maritana,* and the *Daughter of the Regiment.* There was a different performance every night, a circumstance that must have put as much strain on the performers as on those critics who felt that the *Bohemian Girl* or the *Lily of Killarney* was entitled to a well-earned rest. The Moody Manners company had an annual season at the Theatre Royal for most of the period, while the Carl Rosa company produced its standard fare at the Gaiety. Yet attempts were always made to introduce Wagner to the Dublin audience. In fact, one of the companies' leading tenors was the Limerick-born Joseph O'Mara, who added the Wagner parts to his repertoire and later toured with his own company, appearing at the Gaiety in 1915 and 1916. Moody Manners rarely lost the opportunity to test Dublin audiences with *Lohengrin* or *Die Meistersinger,* though we have William Dawson's evidence that "Wagner did not pay" in Dublin. Yet some audience still remained, for the Quinlan Opera Company also persevered to present *Tristan, Valkyrie* and, for the first time in Dublin, the *Ring* during its 1911-13 seasons at the Royal.

The high point of every theatrical season was the Christmas pantomime, which often extended well into February. The Gaiety advertised itself as the "Home of Pantomime," not drama or opera. Yet the "pantos" were a very necessary part of the theatrical year, for they were highly profitable and enabled the managers to survive from season to season. Indeed, one might say they were vital in a city with such little employment for females, if only for the work given to hundreds of seamstresses each year in making up the elaborate costumes. When the Queen's began to produce pantomime after 1909, all three theaters in the city were given over to this craze once each year and, of course, all at the same time, giving the Dublin theatergoer the choice of *Cinderella, Sinbad the Sailor,* or *Puss in Boots.* In December 1916, when the three theaters as well as the Empire Palace Music Hall were each producing a panto, the *Irish Times* felt obliged to offer that unhappy conjunction as a "sad commentary on modern changes in social life." Popular, cheap entertainment was to be had at the city's two small music halls the Empire Palace and the

Tivoli. Condemned by the serious-minded, the music hall was the real mecca for the masses, providing an endless stream of vulgarity, ribald songs, Box and Cox situations, and the perennial jokes at the expense of drunks, lodgers, policemen, and mothers-in-law. The Empire was the successor to Dan Lowrey's Star Variety Theatre, on Dame Street, and was every bit as titillating or vulgar: the "beautiful bicycle princesses" and "funny nigger comics" of the 1880s now replaced by "pedestal clog dancers," "two real Hebrews" and, to stretch credulity even further, "nine real American negroes." Similar fare was available at the Tivoli (formerly Lyric) Theatre of Varieties, on Burgh Quay, once the site of Daniel O'Connell's Conciliation Hall. Since they were generally forbidden to produce plays or pantomime, the music halls presented short sketches of 30 minutes or less as well as the usual variety acts of boomerang throwers, acrobats, boxing kangaroos, performing pigs, and the like. The following is a typical English music-hall tableau of the period, and for all its lunacies the entertainment was well worth the price of admission to the cheapest seats, which was little more than the cost of a pint of porter or a packet of cigarets:

> *Tableau.* Interior of the enchanted castle (The temptation of Guido). 10—Guido is received in the enchanted castle by Hymen; but to test his love Hymen causes some pretty women from different countries to appear. 11—Dance Mauresque by three African ladies. 12—Circassian dance. 13—Nautch dance by five Indian ladies. 14—March; and entrance of the baron, his daughter, and the jester. They cannot recognise in their new neighbour the poor Guido, whom they had formerly treated with contempt. 15—Bohemian polka. 16—Scene; Guido resists all temptation. 17—Lielda appears veiled, and dances a gavotte. 18—Guido, who recognises her, expresses his love. Coralia cannot hide her jealousy, but Lielda disappears at the bidding of Hymen, and Guido in despair is about to kill himself, when the goddess stops his arm, and leads him to the abode of eternal felicity.[6]

Soon the popularity of the music halls was threatened by the appearance of the cinematograph, an indispensable feature of urban life by about 1910. In 1914, 27 cinemas were subject to Corporation bylaws. "Dublin a city of picture palaces" became the new cry of complaint, and those most concerned were the guardians of the people's faith. The wrath formerly reserved for the "shameless" beauty choruses and "immoral" plays was now visited on poor theater managers anxious to entice patrons with alluring posters on the hoardings. Alderman M'Walter was concerned about Sunday performances offending the clergy and inveighed against the "large number of aliens and Jews" who were alleged to have opened picture houses in the city (James Joyce was one of those "aliens"). Bishop O'Dwyer of Limerick once threatened a theater owner in his diocese with excommunication because of his "immoral" presentations.[7] Thus the Dublin Vigilance Committee added cinemas to its list of evils and was eventually instrumental in getting both Messrs. Allen and Company (the billposting contractor) and the theater managers to first submit objectionable advertisements for screening before being placed on the hoardings. Nevertheless, Theda Bara continued to enthrall her fans in *Infidelity* at the Bohemian Picture Theatre.

At a higher level of artistic endeavor, the struggle to establish a solid classical music tradition in Dublin was long and unavailing. In the latter part of the nineteenth century, the effort was marked by disappointment and neglect. The old Theatre Royal burned down in 1880, and Michael Gunn, the Dublin impresario, built a large concert hall, Leinster Hall, on the site a few years later. Great hopes were expressed for the future of musical life in the city on its opening in November 1886 with appearances by Adelina Patti and Mme. Albani. But variety shows and popular concerts soon became the staple fare of the hall until it was demolished to make way for the new Theatre Royal in 1897. Musical tastes in the meantime were served by the Royal Dublin Society, the Dublin Musical Society, and a very small number of amateur musical associations. But the R.D.S. only conducted a series of Monday afternoon chamber music recitals for a selective audience of members. The Musical Society, however, was aimed at a larger audience. It had been organized in 1876 to produce "choral and orchestral works of the highest class," to recapture perhaps the spirit that had nurtured musical Dublin when Handel gave *Messiah* to the world in a local music hall over a century before. Instead it was the losses incurred in mounting a performance of that same work in 1899 that induced the Society to threaten to suspend its operations. The following years brought renewed financial difficulties and poor attendance, with the result that performances ceased entirely after 1902. Fortunately, by that time a new musical venture—the Dublin Orchestral Society—had been launched by an expatriate Italian, Signor Michele Esposito, able successor to Sir Robert Stewart as the leading figure in musical life in Dublin in the early twentieth century. He was engaged as a piano teacher at the Royal Irish Academy of Music in 1882 and over the years had given an annual piano recital at the Antient Concert Rooms. In 1897 he won the Feis Ceoil prize for his cantata *Deirdre* and repeated the feat five years later with an Irish Symphony. With the establishment of the Dublin Orchestral Society in 1898, "a new era in the history of Irish music" was ushered in by Gluck, Mozart, Beethoven, and Wagner to "empty chairs in great numbers." A repeat concert produced the same dismal results. Within a year the *Irish Times* was both noting the gloomy and financial difficulties for the Society and berating the public for its lack of interest in the noble endeavor (one observer saw fit to attribute the musical crisis to the high fees demanded by the players' union—*plus ça change!*). The same paper pondered wryly in an editorial that the streets of the city might soon be thankful to retain even the services of the Italian organ grinders of Chancery Lane.

The Orchestral Society was made up of about 60 performers mostly recruited from local theater orchestras but with the amateur element predominating. Consequently, the five annual winter concerts usually had to be given on weekday afternoons when the players were available, except for an evening performance during Holy Week, when the main theaters were closed. In general, three of the five concerts were held on weekdays (Monday through Friday) at around 4 P.M., thus inevitably ensuring an audience composed mostly of middle-class ladies. Until 1910 the venue for these creditable performances of entirely classical music was the exhibition hall of the Royal University at Earlsfort Terrace and thereafter under the same pattern at the Gaiety Theatre. But the wonder is that the Society survived, for the financial difficulties and lack of adequate support from the public was unwavering. The notices continuously bemoaned the empty chairs even though the admission charge was as low as 6d. The Society was almost disbanded in 1903, when the Foundation Fund became exhausted, and again in 1908, when it was unable to cover a deficit of £200, eventualities that no one interested in the tarnished musical reputation of the city could contemplate. So thanks to the tenacity of Signor Esposito it managed to survive from year to year in a hand-to-mouth fashion, grateful for the niggardly £50 annual award from the Dublin Corporation (though even this was finally disallowed by the Local Government Board) and ignoring entirely the suggestions of those who thought that the only way to attract audiences was to include "light orchestral music" in the programs. In fact, Esposito was so little deterred by adversity that he undertook an additional musical venture in December 1905—a series of Sunday afternoon orchestral concerts "to interest the artisan classes in popular classical music at popular prices." These were usually held at the Antient Concert Rooms and appeared to be quite successful, again only classical works being offered. However, with only about 30 players it was impossible to mount any of the heavier orchestral items. Yet they represented a laudable attempt to improve public taste and were certainly more successful than the corresponding and equally worthy efforts of James Larkin to bring serious drama to the working classes in 1913.

None of the other musical efforts in the city was as ambitious as those of the Dublin Orchestral Society. A variety of small oratorio and chamber music societies were conducted by musical worthies such as Vincent O'Brien (Dublin Oratorio Society), Charles Marchant (Orpheus Choral Society), and John Larchet (Amateur Orchestral Society), but these too appeared infrequently and were entirely of an amateur nature. Each musical season, however, brought highlight performances from visiting artists and orchestras, though these tended to become fewer in number as the years went by. Up to 1907 the Hallé Orchestra appeared almost every year, though only for two engagements, usually at suitably raised prices. Not until 1913 did another orchestra of renown, the London Symphony Orchestra, perform, and then the venue was in the suburban reaches of County Wicklow at Bray. A few individual performers made their mark in the musical annals—Kubelik, Paderewski, Cortot, John McCormack, Caruso, and Mischa Elman. But at such inconvenient times! McCormack sang on a Tuesday and Thursday afternoon, Caruso on Friday at 3 P.M. And unless the voice of the great Italian tenor carried beyond the confines of the Theatre Royal, few of the ordinary citizens could have heard him at gallery prices of 5s. The appearance of the youthful Elman in 1905 created some embarrassment for Signor Esposito. Fearing the worst, he sent an open letter to the newspapers urging a good attendance. Alas, the matinee-only midweek performances at the Theatre Royal drew but limited audiences, "so far below what they might have been as to represent the reverse of encouragement to any enterprising musical director to place rare and important opportunities such as these at the mere caprice of the musical public."[8]

The pretensions of the city to musical taste continued to invite sarcasm. Even the redoubtable Professor Mahaffy of Trinity College lent the weight of his authority to the great debate—why had musical taste declined in Dublin?—at a meeting of the Royal Irish Academy of Music in 1906. The "social decadence of the city" was responsible, he affirmed. Had not all the people of taste and refinement departed for the suburbs? For what person of refined tastes, he asked, could stand the burden of rates, the clatter of trams, the mud of the streets, and the incessant cries of mendicants and hawkers.[9] But one might question whether in fact there was a real audience in city or suburb for the kind of music that was the standard fare of other cities of any cultural importance. Was it not that no real musical tradition had survived to nurture the enthusiast or sustain a school of musical talent? It was not only the writers of books who exiled themselves from Dublin or sought expression and reward elsewhere. They had been preceded by the writers of music—Field, Balfe, Stanford. In Dublin there was no orchestra of repute nor any that could bear comparison with Richter's Hallé in Manchester or Harty's London Symphony. Certainly, the lack of a good concert hall suitable to the production of important works did not help the situation. The Earlsfort Terrace Exhibition Buildings had served for occasional concerts, but it was taken over after 1908 by the new college of the National University, the latter incidentally lacking a chair of music. Thus had Dublin ceased to be a musical center and become the only capital city in Europe without a suitable concert hall for orchestral works, a situation that was to persist for decades. Patrick Pearse, as spokesman for the Gaelic League, rather intemperately proclaimed that the Dublin of his day produced "nothing but Guinness's porter—her contribution to the world's civilization."[10] He and other nationalists also inevitably blamed the decay of the city as an intellectual and artistic capital on the hegemony of imported (English) popular culture. A less politicized judgment would have seen very slim chances indeed for the development of public taste and cosmopolitan manners in a city virtually deprived of its bourgeois base and evincing a character of widespread general poverty and depressed living standards. And, as elsewhere, there resided in the city in those opening years of the twentieth century that distrust of the avant garde (sometimes tinged with an active sectarian philistinism) which produced those regrettable incidents associated with the Abbey Theatre and the Municipal Gallery of Art.

There was more hope for the fortunes of Irish traditional music, which also, by this time, had almost sunk into oblivion. Here the awakening nationalist and cultural identity of Irish Ireland came to the rescue with the founding of the Feis Ceoil Association. Established to preserve the Gaelic musical heritage and encourage the work of native composers, the Association held its annual Feiseanna in Dublin, awarded prizes (the young light tenor James Joyce won a medal in 1904), and generally benefited from the supportive activities of the Gaelic League. Thus the city was able to take the lead in reclaiming an interest in older musical forms that, if they did not exactly enthral, at least offered a welcome riposte to variety-show inanities.

The Abbey Theatre was living proof that those many reports of Dublin's artistic demise were somewhat premature. Indeed, looking back many years later, the literary-minded Augustine Birrell recalled the Dublin of his days as Chief Secretary for Ireland as indicating "a leap to the front rank of thought and feeling altogether novel. . . . Irish literature and drama, Messrs. Maunsell's list of new Irish publications, and the programme of the Abbey Theatre became to me of far more real significance than the monthly reports of the RIC [Royal Irish Constabulary]. The plays of John Synge and Lady Gregory, the poems of Mr. Yeats, A.E. [George Russell], and Dora Sigerson, the pictures of Orpen, Lavery and Henry . . . the bewitching pen of Mr. George Moore . . . were by themselves indications of a veritable renaissance."[11] It was a renaissance, however, that in many ways operated only within the elitist ambit of Russell's "evenings" in his Dublin apartments or Lady Gregory's weekends at Coole Park. Though he cast his net wider than most, Birrell may have been among the first in a long line to apotheosize the vitality of cultural forms in Dublin by reference to the Abbey Theatre alone. Surely a partial judgment, considering the nature and scope of that then modest but enduring enterprise. The Abbey Theatre had its immediate origins in the Irish Literary Theatre Society, which had been organized in 1899 by Lady Gregory, Yeats, and others to direct Irish artistic talent into new creative channels. Yeats's own play *The Countess Cathleen* had its first performance in May of that year. It offered a foretaste of the resentment this new creative force, when expressed in the English language by Anglo-Irish playwrights on native Irish themes, could stir up among those Gaelic Irish nationalists who were deeply suspicious of and almost congenitally insensitive to the nationalist pretensions, cultural or political, of the Ascendancy class in Ireland. Despite these ominous stirrings there was sufficient confidence and foreign intervention (the money of Miss Horniman of London) to transform the venture into the Irish National Theatre Society in December 1903.

The object of the new Society was that of the old—to create an Irish national theater for the production of plays in Irish or in English by Irish writers and on Irish subjects. In Dublin no theater could be established except by Letter of Patent, and at the subsequent patent hearing at Dublin Castle the Society's application was strongly opposed by the city's three major theaters—the Gaiety, Queen's, and Theatre Royal. All three were naturally covetous of their claims on the Dublin theatergoer. Their legal representatives sought to prevent the grant of the patent by suggesting that the previous productions of the Society had been run on lines of a "somewhat immoral, anti-religious or highly political character." Witnesses for the Society stressed the advantages that would accrue to the populace from an encouragement of artistic taste. Previous productions had helped make people *think*, thought W. F. Bailey, the Irish Estates Commissioner. Think about politics and excite animosity between England and Ireland, countered J. P. Moriarty, K.C. But the Solicitor General, finding that the Society's plays betrayed none of the dangerous tendencies imputed to them, duly authorized the grant, though restricting the company to Irish plays "or such dramatic works of foreign authors as would tend to interest the public in the higher works of dramatic art" (hence the occasional adaptation of French authors by Lady Gregory in later years). In December 1904 the Abbey began as a small, 562-seat theater at the junction of Marlborough and Lower Abbey Streets. Yeats, chastened by the earlier reception of his own work, had already expressed a dislike for "plays that express political views" and promised that that decision would guide the policy of the new theater.[12] Unfortunately, this cautious tactic did not save him from the wrath of the Dublin audience, for very shortly his prophecy that the battle for dramatic freedom in Ireland would rage around John Millington Synge was realized.

The rift that had been developing between Yeats and his broad conception of drama as an artform, untainted by considerations of nationalist expression, on the one hand, and self-appointed custodians of Gaelic culture such as journalists Arthur Griffith and D. P. Moran, on the other, came to a head in 1907 with the production of Synge's famous play, *The Playboy of the Western World*. The *Playboy*, billed as a comedy in three acts, opened at the Abbey Theatre on Saturday, January 26, 1907. The furore that had earlier greeted Yeats's depiction of the noble Countess Cathleen as one who would sell her soul to the devil to save the Irish peasantry from starvation was as nothing compared to the rampage occasioned by Synge's conversion of one of those same peasants into a parricide. Unprepared, the first night's audience created no scene, though finding offense at the casual invocation of the "holy name." Prepared, Monday's crowd nearly created a riot. No sooner had the play begun (the first offering, *Riders to the Sea*, had passed without incident) when, as if at a signal, raucous demonstrators prevented anyone from hearing the actors. Amidst the hissing and feet-stomping could be heard the redemptive strains of "The West's Awake" and "Nation Once Again." Not one to shrink from the assault on art, Yeats was quick to condemn his fellow citizens and hint at the sectarian bitterness and chauvinist demagogery he now felt distinguished the city:

> When I was a lad Irishmen obeyed a few leaders; but during the last ten years a change has taken place. For leaders we now have societies, clubs, and leagues. Organized opinion of sections and coteries has been put in place of these leaders, one or two of whom were men of genius. . . . There are some exceptions, as heretofore, but the mass only understand conversion by terror, threats and abuse.

The play continued its week's run with great difficulty and with police on hand to eject disturbers, who, presumably, were less vociferous than at the Monday performance since, as the *Irish Times* observed, "some of the most hotly-resented phrases [the word "shift," a female undergarment, for example] were . . . wisely omitted." The episode reflected little credit on a section of the middle class and nurtured an imputation of philistinism that was hard for the city to live down. Even that paragon of Dublin theatergoers, Joseph Holloway, branded Synge the "dramatist of the dungheap" and coupled him with Yeats and Lady Gregory as "degenerates of the worst type." The *Freeman's Journal* described the play as "calumny gone mad." The *Irish Times*, while admitting Synge's "error in taste," nevertheless sympathized with the plucky stand of the National Theatre Company, condemning both the Sinn Fein party and the "organised tyranny of clap-trap patriots." A more pointed criticism of the hecklers was that of a female letter writer in the *Irish Times*: "If he [Synge] should venture into the streets which surround the Abbey and describe in all its unlovely detail the typical life and language of Dublin slums, he would certainly produce a drama less calculated to satisfy the idealistic inspirations of the Abbey 'pit.'"[13] The affair had serious repercussions on the box office. By 1909, as Yeats noted in his memoirs, the Abbey was playing to an almost empty theater, and mounting debts were cleared years later only through the cooperation of the players in accepting reduced salaries. At any rate, the *Playboy* returned to the Abbey without incident, although, as the players' American tour confirmed, audiences could still be riled. In Ireland itself as late as 1912 the actor John Martin Harvey felt obliged to abandon a provincial tour with the play because of complaints from those arbiters of public taste whom Yeats had dubbed "an ignorant, undisciplined bourgeoisie." These latter had been given their watchword by D. P. Moran in his dismissal of the "Shabby" Theatre as "that metamorphosed morgue [a reference to the former use of the theater's dressing rooms] wherein the National Theatre Company hold intermittent inquests on the Irish peasant."[14]

By this time, however, criticism of Abbey productions was proceeding from more artistic sources. Disappointed by the tiresome repetition of peasant plays (no imitation of urban life here!) and a glut of box-office-oriented farces and melodramas, critics Edward Martyn and Ernest Boyd began to press for a repertory theater conceived on broader lines, one that would give to an Irish audience the master dramas of European genius. Certainly the Abbey had not gone to any great length to honor the license it had obtained to produce the "higher works of dramatic art" by foreign authors. To its credit, of course, the theater had displayed what Shaw called "inspiriting courage" in putting on in 1909, in defiance of Dublin Castle, the latter's *The Shewing-Up of Blanco Posnet*, a play rejected by the English censor. And there were also Lady Gregory's occasional eccentric adaptations of Molière and, in 1913, the production of two Strindberg plays. The so-called "literary freaks" of the New Drama also surfaced from time to time at other theaters in the city, but they hardly formed a durable component of the commercial theatrical scene—a *Doll's House* (one performance) at the Antient Concert Rooms in 1903, a few days of *Hedda Gabler* in 1904, more fleeting Ibsen productions at the Gaiety in later years and, apart from Shaw, not much else. From 1915 onward Martyn's Irish Theatre began to canvass audiences for Chekhov and other writers whose works had long been denied to Dubliners. But such productions, infrequently mounted and available only to tiny audiences, did little to allay the fears that the dramatic traditions of the Irish capital, such as they were, had decayed under the stultifying monopoly of the Gaiety and Theatre Royal, which, as commercial theaters do, gave the public what it desired—hippodrome, musical comedy, and the old-fashioned, sentimental repertoire—and rendered Dublin, as the *Irish Times* complained, a "parasite to the theatrical enterprise of London."

Another contretemps was the long-drawn-out affair of the Municipal Art Gallery. The city already had a small though excellent National Gallery of Art flanking the Library and Museum on the grounds of Leinster House, home of the Royal Dublin Society. Containing mostly Old Masters, the National Gallery had few examples of the work of modern artists. It was to remedy this and create, as he said, such "a standard of taste" that Hugh Lane, art dealer nephew of Lady Gregory, offered his fine collection of modern art to the city of Dublin in 1905. The only condition laid down by the benefactor was that a suitable building be erected by the city within a few years as a permanent repository for the collection. Lane's enthusiasm and canvassing soon attracted gifts and money to support the venture: two Corots from the future King George V and a contribution from President Roosevelt. Meanwhile, no. 17 Harcourt Street (a late eighteenth-century mansion—or rather half of it—originally built for the notorious Lord Clonmell) was acquired by the Corporation pending selection of a permanent site, and the new Municipal Art Gallery was opened free to the public on January 20, 1908. The occasion was a momentous one in the artistic history of the city, for the gallery boasted over 280 works of art in a unique collection of French impressionist and other continental painters as well as the work of artists who were Irish by birth or descent.[15] On Lane's insistence the gallery was to have evening hours (8 to 10 P.M.) to convenience working-class citizens. By contrast the National Gallery closed each day at 6 P.M. and charged admission on Fridays and Saturdays (a practice not abolished until 1912). Dublin now had a celebrated gallery of modern art that included paintings of British and Irish artists, being Lane's unconditional gift to the city, in addition to his conditional gift of 39 paintings by French artists, which would also become the permanent property of the city as soon as the Corporation provided a permanent site for the collection. But circumstances were inauspicious from the beginning, for the Corporation's Libraries Committee to which had been assigned the administration of the gallery had developed a financial crisis. Thus, the gallery was in great danger of being closed down within days of its opening in the temporary premises at Harcourt Street. The problem lay in the Corporation's inability to apply the proceeds of the rates to the maintenance of the building. It took another four years before Dublin and other county boroughs were empowered by Parliament to strike a half-penny rate for the support of galleries of art under the Public Libraries (Ireland) Act of 1911. Until then the citizens had to depend on loans and the munificence of (now) Sir Hugh Lane and others who kept the gallery open from year to year and brought welcome additions as gifts from artists and private collectors. Indeed, past performance had shown that very little in the way of a restoration, re-creation, or elevation of public taste—from the preservation of cathedrals to construction of playgrounds in the Coombe—had been effected without essential private effort and philanthropy. The National Gallery itself had been brought to completion in 1864 largely through the agency of private contributions, and as late as 1901 Tim Healy, MP, felt constrained to bring its "starving" condition before the House of Commons (at a time when thousands of pounds were being expended by His Majesty's Government on the National Gallery in London): "We have to maintain our Art Gallery by a system of bazaars to which we are asked to take tickets at five shillings each."[16]

Lane, ever anxious that Dublin should rival the artistic attractions of a Glasgow, Birmingham, or Manchester through possession of a permanent gallery of modern art, was determined to see the project through. He might have guessed that his one-man struggle to make Dublin an art center could prove as difficult as the corresponding efforts of those interested in conferring some musical eminence on the Irish capital. The exhibitions of paintings at the Royal Hibernian Academy had revealed the weakened state of art patronage and collecting in Dublin. At the 1901 exhibition, according to one source, only 13 of 379 pieces exhibited were sold.[17] By 1912, with no action forthcoming from the Corporation, Lane's patience was beginning to run out. In November of that year he threatened to remove from the gallery the highly prized continental pictures (39 valuable paintings by Corot, Courbet, Degas, Manet, Pisarro, Renoir, and other artists who were to form the nucleus of the permanent collection) at the end of 1913 if the Corporation by that time had not firmly decided to fulfill the terms upon which the original gift had been made. Lane had waited five years and could hardly be blamed for the threatening pose he now adopted. For, indeed, the Harcourt Street building, adjoined by premises on either side, presented a serious fire hazard. Moreover, space and lighting were inadequate in what had until recently been described as a "dingy dwelling." Worse still, a roof had fallen in in one of the rooms, though the five Rodin sculptures there escaped destruction. The threat precipitated both comment and action. An appeal for funds was launched by the private committee organized at a meeting in the Mansion House. This brought an anxious letter of support from one of Dublin's most famous sons, George Bernard Shaw, as he recalled the debt he owed to the city's other (the National) gallery for the taste and knowledge in fine art he acquired there as a boy; though he might have refrained on this occasion from adding the misleading jibe: "I was sometimes the only person in that gallery except the attendants."[18] Only £4,000 had already been received in subscriptions, and an estimated additional £17,000 or more was needed to be added to the £22,000 promised by the Corporation, which, as it turned out, proved to be a foolhardy pledge of the Dublin ratepayer's devotion to the cause of art.

The first blow was struck by William M. Murphy, a former Nationalist MP and one of Dublin's leading citizens. In an open letter to the press published on January 18, 1913, he expressed his grave doubts of the need for another art building in addition to the National Gallery, ignoring that the proposed institution would house the most representative collection of modern art in the British Isles. Let the Corporation do what it can by private subscription and keep out of the pockets of ratepayers, he pleaded, adding speciously: "I would rather see in the City of Dublin one block of sanitary houses at low rents replacing a reeking slum than all the pictures Corot and Degas ever painted." His opponents wondered whether he would therefore recommend the sale of such existing national treasures as the Ardagh Chalice and Tara Brooch for that purpose. Neither could they recall what he, as a very wealthy man, had ever done for the poor of the city. They might also have noted the contrast in the actions of one transportation magnate (Murphy was the mogul of the tramways system) to destroy an art gallery and those of the former

Dublin railway king, William Dargan, who in his day had been the prime mover in the establishment of the National Gallery of Art. The hopeless campaign dragged on for some more months while subscriptions continued to come in, over half of the £11,000 collected being sent from Canada and the United States. At first it was believed that Merrion Square Park would prove suitable as a site for the gallery, but the residents of the Square refused to give up the private recreational facilities their keys afforded them. "I cannot think except with horror of its quiet gentilities invaded by endless streams of gaping visitors," retorted George Moore. Lane himself also refused to consider that site, discouraged as he was by the poor attendance at the National Gallery in the vicinity. Then St. Stephen's Green was mooted, a suggestion that brought another mock cry of horror from Moore, who feared that before long someone would wish also to erect a nursing home there. But Lord Ardilaun was quick to remind everyone that such a union of nature with art did not accord with the terms of the gift he had given to the city. Matters got somewhat desperate when there was talk during the summer of a permanent bridge site on extensions over the Liffey at either the Grattan or Wellington (more popularly known as the Metal) Bridge. This was only to invite ridicule. If the paintings themselves should escape the sparks from steamboats passing beneath, visitors would hardly be unaffected by the exhalations from the river: one could imagine the emptying of the gallery with each receding tide. The idea, unfortunately, was supported by Lane himself, who had the English architect Sir Edwin Lutyens draw up a design for a gallery, in the best Florentine fashion, at the site of the Metal Bridge. Even the representatives of labor added their voices—the poorer classes would benefit first through jobs during construction and thereafter from the pleasure and education afforded by the paintings. The president of the Royal Hibernian Academy was so carried away by the grand prospect that he predicted the resolution of the slum problem, for "if [the poor] could be got to look at the beautiful side of life, they would rouse themselves and clear away the blots on their surroundings"![19]

Some members of the Corporation now felt that the city's honor would not survive the diversion of municipal funds to the pockets of a foreigner (Lutyens was only half-Irish!). Lane made matters worse when, displaying all the intellectual arrogance of the art patron, he attempted to bulldoze the Corporation into accepting his choice of both site and architect. Although the council had adopted the Bridge site on a vote in March, public criticism of the decision had precluded further action in that regard. So the controversy raged on. Those who thought the pictures should be put *in* the Liffey and not over it got powerful support from W.M. Murphy: "The mass of the people of Dublin don't care a thraneen whether Sir. H. Lane's 'conditional' pictures are left here or taken away." Nor should one have expected them to care, for surely the fate of artists and art in general has at all times depended on that elite of wealth to which Murphy belonged. Finally, on August 1 Lane gave the Corporation six more weeks to come to a decision and meanwhile removed his pictures from Harcourt Street to place them on exhibition at the Mansion House, an ominous move that caused the *Irish Times* to reflect that they had now travelled about half the distance to the North Wall, the terminal for English-bound steamers. The affair came to a head in mid-September, when councillor Sarah Harrison introduced a motion in the municipal chamber seeking approval of both site and architect, as Lane desired, under a guarantee from the Mansion House committee that both the donor and the committee would provide any funds needed in excess of the contribution promised by the Corporation. The resolution lost by two votes, though another motion by councillor Cosgrave seeking to reject any scheme that excluded Irish architects from competing for work also lost on a tie. Finally, on September 19, Miss Harrison reintroduced her resolution only to have it succumb (25 votes to 32) to Cosgrave's amendment rejecting the bridge site as "expensive, unpopular and highly impractical." The Nationalist members were divided in the final voting, with Labor voting against and both Sinn Fein and Unionist councillors voting for the amendment. Thus, with the Corporation's refusing to be bullied, Lane withdrew his "conditional" gift of 39 pictures (valued at £70,000) and presented them to the National Gallery in London, where they were ultimately to reside and become the subject of extended controversy between two governments over rightful ownership following Lane's ill-fated death aboard the *Lusitania*. Thus did the affair ignobly conclude, doing little, as John Lavery, the artist, observed, to corroborate the Celts' character as an art-loving people. Lane's grand scheme had foundered on what he perceived, perhaps rightly, as a "want of public spirit in the year 1913," a year in which, as events described in a later chapter may suggest, a public spirit was indeed in short supply. One good result, however, was the saving of the Metal Bridge, a structure condemned by contemporaries for its ugly hoardings and inconvenience (the ½d. toll was not removed until 1919) but now regarded as an indispensable element of that charming prospect from O'Connell Bridge.

Those who regretted this turn of events deemed it inevitable in a city where people with money were more likely to spend it, as one disappointed citizen reflected, "on horse racing and motor driving than in the purchase of pictures." In this respect, of course, the average citizen or substantial ratepayer of Dublin was hardly unique. Art had not exactly been a matter of civic pride anywhere in the United Kingdom for quite some time, a contrast it might be noted with the courtly traditions of continental countries such as France and Germany, where the "high culture" of opera, drama, ballet, and art had been institutionalized as national or regional treasures. Yeats, who like Lane had also experienced the distrust of his countrymen, was unreserved as he heaped poetic scorn on his native city— "the blind and ignorant town"—for what it had done to

> . . . A man
> Of your own passionate serving kind who had brought
> In his full hands what, had they only known,
> Had given their children's children loftier thought,
> Sweeter emotion, working in their veins
> Like gentle blood, has been driven from the place,
> And insult heaped upon him for his pains,
> And for his open-handedness, disgrace. . . . [20]

Though Ireland might produce musicians, painters, and writers of great talent and genius, Dublin, a victim of historical circumstances beyond her control, proved unable to develop the cultural ambience that one should expect in a capital city of ancient lineage. The ensuing decades did little to brighten the picture. Indeed, in some respects the situation worsened when, for example, the cultural complex of museum, library, and gallery encircling the Royal Dublin Society in Leinster House lost its expansive capacity, through the dislodgement of the Society, to make way for the two Houses of the Free State parliament. And only long decades of neglect, public apathy, and official parsimony could have produced the *cri de coeur* on the state of the arts in Ireland that was the Bodkin Report of 1951. Among the criticisms of Professor Bodkin were the "negligible and precarious" status of the fine arts in Irish universities, the neglect of the National Art Gallery, the "reprehensible amount of iconoclasm" that had been prevalent in Dublin during the recent past (he feared for the removal of Nelson's Pillar!) as well as the refusal to open the National Museum to the public during evening hours. Bodkin became something of an iconoclast himself when he also condemned the "1916" collection at the latter institution as unscholarly and tendentious: "likely to do more harm than good to the taste of our people and to excite the ridicule of intelligent foreigners."[21] But that was 1951. As for the Dublin of Leopold Bloom, whatever else it was, it was not, as the effusions of some captivated souls would have us infer, a reincarnation of Periclean Athens.

There was, of course, another avenue to the life of the mind available to the ordinary citizen, namely, the reading of books. In Dublin, as in any city of the period, this opportunity necessitated the provision of widespread and readily accessible public libraries. Dublin had its private and specialized libraries of distinction: Archbishop Marsh's antiquarian collection, Trinity College, the Royal Dublin Society, the Royal Irish Academy, and King's Inns. The National Library was a public institution availed of largely by scholars of the Royal (after 1908 the National) University. One suspects that it attracted few working-class readers, for not only was it a noncirculating research collection but one gained access only by introduction or on the recommendation of a property holder. It was, incidentally, woefully understaffed and the victim of governmental parsimony. In 1901 it had a staff of about 15 (including six "boys") and approximately 500 daily readers, the latter figure, it was noted, exceeding the attendance at the Library of Congress with its staff of over 200. There was also the small fee-paying (10s. per year) Mechanics Institute library and newsroom (one penny admission for nonmembers) in Lower Abbey Street, but few of its members were reputed to be artisans. Therefore, free general libraries were sorely needed for the working classes in the densely populated districts in the western parts of the city. The rating powers to establish such facilities had first been conceded in the Public Libraries (Ireland) Act as far back as 1855, but in the succeeding 30 years only the little towns of Dundalk (in 1858) and Sligo (in 1880) had availed of the Act. Dublin finally followed suit in 1884, choosing the occasion of the Library Association's annual conference and visit to the city to open its first public libraries. No one could complain that they were not convenient for working-class readers, being located in reconditioned premises at 106 Capel Street, adjacent to the Hall of the Trades' Council, and at 22 Thomas Street.

The opening of the libraries in October 1884 was a gala occasion; the Lord Mayor became the first borrower at Capel Street branch of a suitably exemplary volume—Smiles's *Self Help*. It was hoped that wealthy citizens would be found to contribute books as freely as that class had done in British towns. The initial response was encouraging, with almost 3,000 volumes pouring in from local benefactors along with contributions from such literary notables as Mathew Arnold and copies of his own works from the then Chief Secretary, G.O. Trevelyan. Some 2,500 borrowers (75 percent of them "working class") soon registered; the only test for admission—stringent enough in the circumstances—being the signature of a burgess and a "decent exterior and becoming conduct." An imposing Libraries Committee was appointed by the Corporation to monitor selections and ensure that no works of "polemical controversy" or of an "immoral or infidel character" were introduced. The committee included Sir Samuel Ferguson, who was to pronounce on works of art, Sir Robert Stewart for music, and, inevitably, clerics in the areas of history, biography, and natural history. The libraries were to remain small, however, not possessing much above 6,000 volumes in all and barely exceeding the number of books boasted by the little library at Dundalk at a time when the public library systems of Manchester, Liverpool, Birmingham, and Leeds each had over 135,000 volumes. But a greater measure of the effectiveness of the new Dublin libraries was the large attendance at the newspaper rooms: about 900 persons per day, many of them undoubtedly worn-out old men in search of warmth and shelter. It was hoped that each ward of the city would soon boast its own library, but these plans were never realized, for city revenue was eaten up by expensive main drainage construction, artisans' dwellings, and other urgent projects. There was no fear that the borrowers' list might be swamped, for when the burgess roll was assimilated to the larger parliamentary franchise in 1899 following the Local Government Act of the previous year, the conditions for borrowing (burgess or signature of burgess) were altered to limit membership only to the smaller number of ratepayers or those securing the signature of a ratepayer.[22]

The first public library established in its own premises was that at Charleville Mall, North Strand, in December 1900, and this was followed by a fourth branch library at Lower Kevin Street in 1905, a facility designed to serve the needs of the adjacent Technical School. Meanwhile, plans were also underway to establish a central library in Great Brunswick Street in fulfillment of a Carnegie grant. Not everyone regarded public libraries as the unalloyed blessing they were to laborers, artisans, and their families (the middle classes generally used the subscription libraries). There had always been some opposition to the growth of the public library movement either from rates-conscious citizens or those intolerant elements who could only see evil in the dissemination of fiction. Other threats stemmed from those who would have preferred censorship. In 1906, for example, Dr. M'Walter, then councillor of North City ward, presented a motion in the council that the Irish-language Bibles presented to the Public Libraries Committee by the 100-year-old (Protestant) Hibernian Bible Society be returned. The motion, though supported by notables of the stature of T. C. Harrington, MP, and councillor Lorcan Sherlock, was rejected, however. Some would have preferred denominational libraries for their Catholic countrymen. Catholic Truth Society conferences, for example, rarely missed the opportunity to descant along these lines. The opposite argument was the usefulness of the library in guarding against "the allurements of brightly-lit public houses," much as the old Repeal reading rooms in Irish villages in the 1840s were supposed to have diminished card playing and alcohol consumption. But a more effective barrier to the spread of public libraries was finance. As we have already seen in the affair of the Municipal Gallery, the library system in Dublin was in a poor financial condition, mainly because of the restriction on expenditures to a rate not exceeding 1d. The slow growth of the Dublin libraries is evident from the figures in Table 2. In fact, in 1890 Dublin could only have compared with Great Yarmouth (population 46,000) in holdings, readership, and expenditure. By 1912 the city could hold its own against Reading (population 75,000).

By 1908 library funds were only sufficient to pay employees, and on January 25 of that year the city suffered the indignity of seeing its public lending libraries closed on the order of the Town Clerk. The library rate was only bringing in about £3,500 per annum,

TABLE 2. Comparison of Growth of Libraries in Select U.K. Cities.

PLACE	LIBRARY SYSTEM OPENED	TOTAL NUMBER OF VOLUMES		VOLUMES ISSUED (IN 1000s)		EXPENDITURES (IN £s)	
		1890	1912	1890	1912	1890	1912
Dublin	1884	7,500	36,393	65	196	1,030	3,556
Belfast	1888	14,234	84,563	201	488	7,035	8,534
Bristol	1886	73,000	165,313	632	820	4,429	13,148
Manchester	1852	200,000	413,888	1,649	2,754	12,020	32,732
Liverpool	1852	147,000	315,863	1,135	2,000	13,661	34,000

SOURCE: *Parliamentary Papers,* 1890–1891 (LXI), no. 5; 1912–1913 (LXVIII), no. 266.

an amount insufficient to pay wages and maintain service without borrowing. Indeed, the Libraries Committee had already drawn on the borough fund both to pay expenses and purchase for £2,500 the valuable library of the late Sir John Gilbert, historian of the city of Dublin. This action had brought surcharges of over £1,700 on several members of the Corporation's Estates and Finance Committee by the auditor of the Local Government Board. Thus, the libraries could not have been reopened had not the City Treasurer guaranteed to make himself responsible for the payment of salaries until the end of the fiscal year in March. Naturally, there was little money for the purchase and repair of books, and no one came forward to offer libraries or make substantial gifts of books to the citizens in emulation of Hugh Lane's efforts in the field of art. Indeed, the greatest benefactor of the library system was a foreigner, Andrew Carnegie. Ironically, the Corporation was vainly begging the Local Government Board for permission to double the library rate to 2d. and so help resolve the crisis at the very time when the Chief Secretary was delivering noble sentiments in praise of libraries at the Lyceum Library in Liverpool in celebration of its 150th anniversary. In September the newsrooms were closed but rescued immediately through the generosity of a local citizen and the provision of free copies of the newspapers by their publishers. As further embarrassment, when the newly built central library in Great Brunswick Street was taken over in 1909 it could not be opened to the public through lack of funds for books, equipment, and upkeep (the Carnegie gifts, it should be noted, provided for buildings *not* books). It remained for two and one-half years "like a canal without water." Though the newsroom was formally opened in December 1911, it took another two years before the lending and reference departments were made available and then, happily, under the U.S.-pioneered provision of "open access." Judged by the number of public library borrowers, however, Dublin did not appear to be a very bookish town. When the system was forced to close in 1908, only 6,000 books were on loan, a number roughly equivalent to that of readers' tickets. Thus Dublin, with a population of over 300,000, had about as many borrowers of books from public libraries as did the little English borough of Gloucester (pop. 53,000). Expenditure for books, newspapers, periodicals, and binding in the fiscal year ending March 1916 totalled £650, certainly an improvement over earlier years, but this at a time when Belfast's system was spending over £700 on books alone. By 1920 the libraries again faced disaster, and expenditure for the aforementioned purposes had dwindled to less than £400, or a paltry £70 per branch and not one-tenth of what was to be spent annually in another four years. Such a continuing financial crisis rendered credible the claims in 1920 that not a single book had been purchased for several years.

Neither was Dublin a great center of publishing. Of the ten firms operating in the county, scarcely five would have qualified as book-trade publishers in the ordinary sense. They included Maunsel and Company, which though publishing "books by Irish authors and relating to Ireland" saw fit to break up the type of James Joyce's *Dubliners* rather than scandalize an uncaring public in 1912. Another, the Dun Emer (later Cuala) Press, managed by Miss Elizabeth Yeats, deserves an honored place among the list of those private presses dedicated to restoring the art of fine printing and book production. Mention might also be made of the creditable record of the Irish language revivalists in nurturing an interest in Gaelic through the publication by the Gaelic League of numerous works (from lesson and phrase books to the stories of the Rev. P. O'Leary) in that language, an endeavor supported by the weekly bilingual *Claideamh Soluis* and the annual Oireachtas (convention) held in Dublin every spring under the auspices of the League. Bookshops were in goodly profusion, however; although some doubt was expressed of the strength of their patronage when publishers and booksellers, according to the *Irish Times*, had come to regard Dubliners as "very indifferent customers." The city was rather well served by newspapers, with dailies representing the various political interests. The premier daily as measured by circulation figures was the Unionist *Irish Times* (circ. 45,000). The twin dailies *Freeman's Journal* (40,000) and *Evening Telegraph* (26,000) stood for support of the moderate goals of the Irish party. Competing with these in political opinions were the Conservative *Daily Express* (11,000) with its ally, *Evening Herald*, and the *Daily Independent* (20,000) and *Evening Mail*. The two last-named nationalist dailies were controlled by William Martin Murphy, who in 1905 brought out Ireland's first Sunday newspaper. In addition to the *Weekly Freeman* and *Weekly Irish Times*, there were various other weekly journals serving lay and clerical interests as well as attempting to foster more robust forms of nationalism. The more noteworthy of these were Arthur Griffith's *United Irishman* and its successor *Sinn Fein*; the *Irish Catholic*, an organ of extreme Catholic opinion; D.P. Moran's *Leader*, Irish Ireland to the core and a fierce crusader against what it dubbed "Bungery" (i.e., the liquor trade); and, after 1911, James Larkin's *Irish Worker*.

With the probable exception of public libraries, those aspects of a higher culture embodied in museums, art galleries, and the superior forms of entertainment impinged but little on the mass of ordinary working-class citizens. Their "club" was the local trades hall, public house, or illegal shebeen, their relaxation the inanities of the music hall. Besides, in the class-ridden society of the Victorian era their own social perceptions operated to make them regard as the preserve of their "betters" those citadels of wisdom and culture that were, or at least thought to be, alien to their way of life. They were not encouraged to think otherwise. Perhaps only their "children's children," as Yeats put it, would find that sweeter emotion working in their veins. Furthermore, experience at the British Museum and the Museum of South Kensington, where evening openings for the working classes had been tried, was used to demonstrate the futility of directing their minds to loftier thought. When similar privileges for the Dublin working classes were requested by an Irish MP, he was advised, on the authority of the director of the National Gallery in Dublin, that the pictures "could not be properly inspected" under artificial light![23] This was hardly the view of the representatives of labor or even of Hugh Lane, who had the Harcourt Street gallery open until 10 P.M. each weekday and on Sunday afternoons.

The kind of recreation attractive to most citizens, especially to the youth, was that provided by public parks and playgrounds. Dublin was noted for its attractive interior

The buildings along the western boundary include the Royal College of Surgeons (right of center) and the Unitarian Church (left of center). At the upper left is the temperance hotel of T. W. Russell, MP, and in the background rises the spire of St. Patrick's Cathedral. The equestrian statue in the Park is of George II.

spaces, enclosed for the most part by capacious Georgian houses. But there were only four of them in the city, and all were private grounds vested in Commissioners by acts of Parliament and set aside for the exclusive use of occupiers (each having a key) of the surrounding homes. In the north side of the city, the deterioration of the Mountjoy Square area bolstered the Corporation's desire to have the Square itself thrown open to the citizens—the congested city needed that additional "lung" in 1899. The number of professional families in residence had been reduced greatly with the appearance of offices and dwellings let in flats. But only an act of parliament could overturn the Commissioners' opposition to any conversion of the 4-acre Square to public use. Thus, like its three counterparts (Rutland, Fitzwilliam, Merrion Squares), Mountjoy Square was to remain in private hands and out of the reach of the citizens and the neighborhood's children for decades to come. The remaining "open space" within the city suitable for public casual enjoyment was the attractive 22-acre park of gardens and walks known as St. Stephen's

Green. This "lung" of the city had also for long been denied to the citizens, having only been opened in 1880. Nor did the circumstances of its opening do much credit to the Corporation. The idea of converting it from private to public use had first been broached in the 1860s, but in the parliamentary session of 1864-65 the Corporation had actually expended over £500 to *oppose* the bill providing for the opening: the municipality feared the loss of rents should the park, as expected, be handed over to a government department for administration. Eventually, by 1876, it was opened provisionally on Sundays only, but after four more years and a generous grant of £20,000 by Lord Ardilaun, the park was finally given over to the citizenry, vested in the Commissioner of Public Works, and maintained out of government funds.

Taking all five areas together, they amounted to less than 50 acres, a very small amount of interior space (even were it all available to the public) to satisfy the recreational needs of almost 300,000 persons. In this, as in many other aspects of urban amenities, Dublin lagged dismally behind her wealthier counterparts in England and America, where, especially in the latter country, huge sums of money were being spent on children's playgrounds to avoid its being spent in catching young criminals.[24] The Corporation had provided three small playgrounds in the poorer districts before 1900 (for example, the half-acre St. Michan's Park on the site of Newgate Prison, the medieval town jail). But not until much later were adequate facilities provided for the youth of Dublin, most notably in the Iveagh play center, near St. Patrick's Cathedral, which was established in 1915 through the accustomed generosity of Lord Iveagh.

None of these areas already mentioned had facilities for athletic recreation. For this the active citizen had to reach the magnificent Phoenix Park on the outskirts of the city. This huge area, over 1,700 acres in extent and almost all of it open to the public, made up in amenities what it lacked in convenience of access. The Park contained the world's second oldest zoo, the Dublin Zoological Gardens, of which observers remarked that it had begun to attract more working-class visitors after improved tramway service was instituted in 1899. Many families must have been deterred by the 1s. weekday admission (children, 6d.) to the Zoo, which amount was beyond the capacity of most workingmen to pay even when on two days (Wednesday and Saturday) these charges were halved. But, happily, Sundays and holidays brought greatly reduced prices (adults, 2d.; children, 1d.). The Park was also the venue where daily was waged the battle of two civilizations as the games of the Gael (hurling and football) vied with those of the Gall (soccer and cricket), while elsewhere the polo enthusiasts imparted a touch of Imperial splendor. Nor did the natives (or rather the nationalist component among them) have it all their own way. Of the 32 separate playing fields in the Park, in the section colloquially known as the Fifteen (actually two hundred) Acres, only three were allotted to Gaelic games, the rest to soccer. This was a matter of some concern to the Gaelic Athletic Association, whose protestations over this "injustice" reached the floor of the House of Commons on two occasions between 1904 and 1906. On one of these, Thomas O'Donnell, MP, was reminded by the Chief Secretary for Ireland that the Phoenix Park was a royal park and as the property of the Crown "did not belong to the citizens," that fields were allotted in proportion to players, and that the applications from soccer teams greatly exceeded those of the Gaelic clubs. This latter assertion was apparently confirmed by the available statistics of applications for the use of the playing areas (yearly figures refer to the year ending 31 March):

	1913	1914	1915[25]
Association football (soccer)	2,272	2,217	1,452
Gaelic football	52	23	28
Hurling	38	27	20

Organized spectator sports, on the other hand, left nothing to be desired, for teams and venues built up their partisan following and traditions: the Parnells and Hibernian Knights in contention at Croke Park (Gaelic football); soccer wizardry from Bohemians, St. James' Gate, and Shelbourne at Dalymount Park; legal mayhem in the rugby (the favorite spectator sport) skirmishes of Wanderers, Bective Rangers, and others at Lansdowne Road and Croydon Park.

Whatever the shortcomings of the city itself in regard to enjoyment and recreation, the environs of the city offered unmatched vistas of natural beauty in the Dublin hills and Wicklow mountains beyond. And one had only to pass through the adjacent village of Ringsend ("turn up your nose," warned one traveler) to reach those sandy shores that extended for another five miles to Ireland's "bay of Naples"—Killiney. And to the good fortune of citizens, these and other wonders were all within easy access by bicycle (at least by those who could afford an investment of eight guineas or more), tram, or railway; from 1899 onward, the tram provided Sunday afternoon trips "at phenomenally cheap" fares for those desiring to inhale the "ozone of the channel." For Dublin, thanks to private enterprise, had managed to keep pace with the needs of urban transportation and had, by the turn of the century, become a pioneer in the United Kingdom in the extent and efficiency of its electric tramway system.

Trams were a familiar feature of the city since their introduction in 1872. From the outset they provided service beyond the boundaries of the city—to Sandymount, Rathmines, Rathfarnham, Kingsbridge, and Dollymount—and became, even more so than the railway, "the true ship of the suburbs."* Thus they too played their part in the decline of the city by facilitating the migration of the middle classes to the outlying townships. All lines converged on Nelson's Pillar, then, as its former site is now, the mecca of all public conveyances. Every means of conveyance, of course, was horse drawn, from tram to cabriolet (four-wheeler) to the more than one thousand jarvey-driven "outside cars" beloved by tourists. Not until 1896 was general electrification of the tramway system undertaken—a blow to blacksmiths and harness makers, a boon to street sweepers. The moving force in the conversion within the city was the same W. M. Murphy already mentioned in another context. He had to overcome considerable prejudice in the Corporation and outside against granting the necessay wayleaves. By 1899 the great Ringsend power station for high-voltage distribution was placed in operation, and soon horse traction disappeared entirely. The transition was completed during 1901, but the conversion had not been an unmixed blessing to the citizens. For about four years immense disruption was created across the city as mile after mile of thoroughfare was ripped open to make way for the heavier and wider-gauge rails of the new system. There was objection to the unsightly criss-cross of poles and overhead wires strung out along all routes. The company spokesman had the correct reply: "When once they are put up, people become used to them and nobody seems to take any notice." A city that had occluded its finest building

*The phrase is John Harvey's.

(the Custom House) from public view by means of an ugly railway bridge was unlikely to halt the march of progress to consider alternative and probably more expensive solutions.

The new trams were a great success, becoming one of Dublin's minor glories as they traversed nearly 50 miles of the city and its environs. The minimum fare was 1d. (double the rate in Glasgow), and as late as 1912 the Corporation was being importuned to set up a rival motorbus service if the tramway company did not cut its minimum rate in half to benefit the poorer citizens. Though the trams were limited by law to proceed at no more than 8 miles per hour, this restriction was ignored in practice: even horse-drawn vehicles moved at 10 or 12 miles per hour. Every accident was reported and newspaper editorials recalled the "grand old days" of ten years previously, when one could go about the streets in comfort and safety and the most dangerous mode of locomotion was the "penny farthing." In fact, the citizen had more to fear from horse-drawn traffic, as is evident from statistics of street accidents compiled by the metropolitan police. The figures issued for the years 1909 through 1913 reveal that fatal and nonfatal accidents from horse-drawn traffice outnumbered those caused by the city's electric trams by well over 2 to 1 in each case. The total number of fatalities was small, however—about 15 per annum, a rate comparable with that of Edinburgh and Liverpool, though only half the annual rates of Glasgow and Manchester.[26]

The most startling transportation innovation was, of course, the motor car, which made its appearance in Ireland after 1896. Numbers were small, naturally, given the high initial cost (Humber, £275; Peugeot, £395) and maintenance. Thus, for a time, "automobilism" like horse riding was the exclusive privilege of the wealthy, popular with doctors on their daily rounds and with shooting enthusiasts who now found it more convenient to visit their rented country residences. Some satisfaction was doubtless felt in Dublin with the announcement in the daily newspapers that Guinness and Company were planning to use motor cars to deliver porter to quench the thirst of bibulous suburbanites. Yet Irish country roads must have deterred many a driver, for in these early days of the phaeton, voiturette, and charabanc the ride must have been more of an adventure than a luxury. The poor surfaces (there was no local steamrolling) were a threat to safety, and the severe winter weather almost rendered them impassable, especially in the southern half of the country. Up to April 1, 1904, only 58 motor cars had been registered in the city of Dublin since their first appearance. This compared with higher numbers in Belfast (74), Glasgow (135), Manchester (311), and London (2,758). But through the activities of the Irish Automobile Club (founded 1902), the interest created by the holding of the 1903 Gordon Bennett Trophy race in Ireland, and the reduction in prices, car sales increased appreciably thereafter, a total of 138 private and 9 commercial vehicles being registered on September 30, 1905. Horace Plunkett, ex-MP for Dublin South and founder of the cooperative movement in Irish agriculture, was greatly surprised to find two tenant farmers arriving at an agricultural show in their motor cars in 1904. By 1912 the £100 car was firmly on the market and no Dublin firm was considered "up to date" unless it had at least one commercial delivery van. By June 1915 the Corporation was registering over 140 motor cars each quarter to add to the 1,500 or so automobiles already being driven by residents of Dublin.

Inevitably, as with the appearance of the trams, complaints mounted from all sides. Charges of "negligent and furious driving" emanated from those who bemoaned that the public thoroughfare was becoming the arena for testing how fast man could travel. Yet here too accidents of all kinds were more likely to be encountered with horse-drawn traffic. The city's first motor ambulance came a cropper while on duty in February 1914, after only a few weeks of service, when it struck a lamppost to avoid a draycart, the patient suffering the inconvenience of completing his journey to the hospital on a stretcher. The fearless Captain Purcell, the city's fire chief, suffered a serious accident in 1916, when his horse (he was riding to the scene of a fire) bolted up Grafton Street and tossed him from the trap, an incident that recalled the near loss to Ireland of a favorite son, Michael Davitt, when he was thrown from a sidecar in 1899 on another of Dublin's treacherous streets. The speed limit was 20 m.p.h. but with the more lenient attitude adopted by the police in Ireland (as contrasted with that in England) this rate was generally exceeded. Despite this alleged leniency, however, the number of arrests for dangerous driving was remarkably high compared with any other city's in the United Kingdom. For the three years 1910 through 1912, for example, such arrests of automobile drivers totalled 263 for Dublin, compared with considerably lower figures for Glasgow (86), Belfast (39), Liverpool (107), and Manchester (139). Indeed, the Dublin driver in these early years of the automobile era acquired a reputation for reckless disregard of traffic safety. According to police records he drove faster and more dangerously and with more disrespect for the law (failing to stop after an accident, and so forth) than his counterpart in any other city in the kingdom, excepting London. Carmen were aggrieved that the "infernal machines" caused their horses to shy. And more astute observers perceived that the chaos of traffic and parking of cars boded ill for the future. With foresight about seventy years premature, the *Irish Times* warned that "no one who walks through Dublin can be ignorant of the indubitable fact that vehicular traffic is getting beyond the control of the authorities." Nor could those with an eye to the future fail to discern that, with the displacement of the horse by the motor car, one form of pollution (animal dejecta) was being replaced by the hidden dangers of another (the products of the internal combustion engine). This state of affairs was not helped by two of the city's most famous inanimate objects: the Pillar, which blocked cross-traffic at the center of O'Connell Street, and the Parnell Monument (unveiled in 1911), which had a similar effect at the northern end of the street (one marvels at the prescience of those who kept the O'Connell Monument at the southern end off the line of traffic between Eden Quay and Bachelor's Walk). The unfortunate siting of the Parnell statue could have been avoided had the Corporation insisted that the Committee headed by John Redmond, leader of the Irish parliamentary party, subordinate art to the "sordid considerations of convenience." As the *Irish Times* observed wittily: "The great leader was a brilliant obstructor when alive. It is not necessary to his fame that his monument should preserve the tradition." These inevitable growing pains of the twentieth-century city were compounded by the proliferation of the motor-driven taxi-cab. The increase after 1906 was remarkable. In London, for example, only 96 licenses to operate motor cabs were issued in 1906 as against over 10,000 for horse cabs of all kinds. By 1911, however, the number of motor-cab licenses exceeded 7,000, whereas those for horse-drawn cabs declined to fewer than 4,400. In Dublin the situation was quite different, owing to the tremendous opposition generated in the Corporation and elsewhere.

The decision to allow taxi cabs to operate in the city rested not with the Corporation but with the police, who were under the control of the British government through its officers in Dublin Castle. The Corporation did not have power to set speed limits since this too was the prerogative of the Local Government Board. Such absurdities were not unusual in Irish government (the National Gallery of Art was administered by the Department of Agriculture and Technical Instruction). Perhaps many felt gratified at the Corporation's subordinate role in this matter, for that body, given its way, would have limited the speed of motor cars to that of horse-drawn traffic (a resolution to this effect was passed in 1911) and resisted the "tide of progress" by preventing the taxi-cab service various English companies had applied for between 1908 and 1910. These latter could not be held off forever, despite the strenuous resistance of jarvies and carmen who set up an Anti-Taxicab Association to sustain their cause. The convenience of professional men and commercial travelers, racing spectators and theatergoers, shoppers and suburbanites had to prevail, of course. Approval to commence the service was duly granted by the Commissioner of Police, and the first motor taxi-cabs made their appearance in the city on November 1, 1911. The ride was quite expensive: 10d. per mile and a minimum charge of 2s. 6d. and, initially, an additional half-rate for the "wasted" journey from the garage. It could not have been the most convenient service since the cabs could be hired only at fixed stands, not hailed at will by the user. Of all European cities, it was alleged, Dublin shared this distinction only with Constantinople. Nevertheless, the motor car had triumphed over the horse—a serious loss, according to one rueful observer, "to the social life and pleasant traditions of the Irish capital."[27]

Few urban problems of the period evoked such sustained criticism as the condition of the streets. This, after all, is what appeared most obvious to the casual observer. It was a problem of very long standing and certainly could not have been as serious at the turn of the century as half a century earlier, when inadequate paving (or none at all), disrepair, and neglect had turned the streets of the city into oceans of mud or mountains of dust with alternating changes of weather. At least no one complained then as did one council member in 1847, when he likened the condition of Guild Street and the surrounding North Wall area to the backwoods of America: "the mud there would swallow up a man." The reformed Corporation began paving main thoroughfares in the 1850s, the superior asphalt being used in Grafton and Henry Streets. Not until the Public Health Act of 1878, however, did borrowing facilities become available for more extensive operations. But critics continued to berate the Corporation for the abominable state of the streets. After one or two days of rain (a not infrequent occurrence) even a main thoroughfare such as O'Connell Street became almost impassable to pedestrians owing to pools of liquid mud. The problem lay in the type of surface employed for paving.

McAdam's great invention had indeed turned sour after mid-century, when omnibuses and other heavy vehicles began to grind down the smoothed stones of macadamized roadways. Though well suited to country roads and village streets, this surface had become entirely unsuitable for city traffic. Yet 80 out of 110 miles of road surface in Dublin were of macadam as late as 1880, the remainder consisting largely of granite setts and employed mostly for heavily used streets. The choice of surfaces lay between asphalt, wood, granite, and macadam. Asphalting, though desirable, only added to paving costs and, moreover, under the weather conditions encountered in Dublin gave a poorer foothold to horses. Wood, though useful as a noise-deadener—and therefore often preferred outside churches, hospitals, and the like—absorbed too much manurial filth and besides fared ill under the hooves of horses. Hence the widespread use of stone paving (setts) and macadam, with the latter predominating owing to the advantage of lower initial cost, a major consideration for a penny-pinching Corporation. Neither of these two surfaces was ideal, because the lack of a firm concrete base beneath the roadway, usually the case in Dublin, meant that the unprotected subsoil inevitably seeped through to the surface under the wear and tear of traffic. Rain and inadequate scavenging did the rest, producing in the press recurrent diatribes against the Corporation for the scandalous state of the streets, especially during those periods when financial stringency in the Cleansing Department resulted in the dismissal of street-cleaning staff. The worst areas were the miles of neglected lanes, alleys, courts, and passages off the main thoroughfares. Though open to the public many such lanes and alleys were technically "not in charge of the Corporation" and hence were among the worst-scavenged parts of the city. There were 264 of them in 1899 and 894 (38 miles in total length) in 1911—vast accumulators of dirt, refuse, and nuisances and an enduring disgrace to the public health of the metropolis.

Dublin was hardly alone among cities of the period in inviting public odium over streets that more often than not left the pedestrian's feet immersed in mud and horse droppings or his nostrils assailed by swirling clouds of dust and pulverized particles of macadam. Sanitarians repeatedly warned of the pathogenic effects of roads thickly powdered with dried manure, attributing to the floating particles a host of ailments ranging from sore throat and nasal catarrh to conjunctivitis and pneumonia. But other cities were generally better paved, better scavenged, and better cleansed than Dublin. Not until 1903 did the capital adopt the common practice of watering streets before sweeping and then only in main thoroughfares, except again when long spells of dry weather or financial exigencies decreed economy. And critics did not fail to point to the unpalatable reports that revealed Dublin generated twice as many tons of street sweepings per mile per year as even larger cities such as Edinburgh and Leeds. Yet considerable improvements were effected over the years, though even those incurred resentment from the Stonecutters' Society as concrete began to be employed for some street pavements after 1907. Complaints of dirty streets hardly diminished, and citizens were not put off by the Cleansing Department's choice of scapegoat—the poorer citizen who allegedly indulged in the traditional Dublin habit of throwing refuse into the streets. Few appeared to disagree with the stricture of the *Medical Press* in labeling Dublin as "without doubt one of the most dirty cities in the kingdom."[28] Even as late as 1924, when Dublin Corporation was restructured by the Minister of Local Government of the Irish Free State, the condition of the streets remained a popular brickbat with which to usher the municipal council out of office.

Another aspect of the street scene, street lighting, received better attention and was solved more quickly. In any event, technology alone dictated progress in this area so that by the turn of the century conditions were a far cry from those fifty years earlier, when one witness at an official enquiry claimed he could not read his watch at the foot of a public gas lamp outside Gresham's hotel in Sackville Street. Electricity for lighting began to supplant gas toward the end of the century, when large power stations were set up in towns and cities, the technical problems having already been solved by Edison with his invention of the carbon filament incandescent lamp. The latter was especially vital for domestic lighting in homes and offices because of the unsuitability for this purpose of the older arc lamps that continued, however, to be used for street lighting. In 1881 the Mansion House, residence of the Lord Mayor, became the first building in the city to be lighted by electricity. Progress was slow, with public lighting initially confined to the vicinity of the City Hall, Grafton Street, and O'Connell Street—81 arc lamps in all in 1899.

By 1900 only a very small part of the city was lighted by electricity, a much larger area supplied with gas lamps but, as the *Irish Times* complained, "the great majority of the streets are plunged in almost Cimmerian darkness as soon as the shops are shut," bringing forth complaints from the police that they were unable to do their duty along the back streets because of the absence of lighting. The same newspaper three years later pointed up the lack of a 24-hour supply, but with the completion of the large-capacity generating station at the Pigeon House site in Dublin harbor, followed by the introduction of the more economical metallic-filament lamps in 1908, considerable improvement in service was effected. By 1909 public lighting in Dublin consisted of 4,444 gas lamps, 146 metallic-filament lamps, and 557 arc lamps. Few complaints were heard thereafter, and the electricity service was extended piecemeal throughout the city. The number of private consumers totalled 2,600 in 1910, almost a tenfold increase since 1903 and a figure that would be trebled within six years.[29]

"A city," as Robert Park once wrote, "is something more than a congeries of individual men and of social conveniences . . . more, also, than a mere constellation of institutions and administrative devices." Dublin had forgotten this. After a century of political subservience, social neglect, and physical deterioration, she had ceased to pay homage to the customs and traditions of her palmy days. Observing the city in 1914, Stephen Gwynn saw squalor hanging about her "like a draggled skirt on a beautiful woman." But the beauty too had faded, with blotches of decay at over a thousand ruinous sites and derelict spaces. Nor was dignity spared—the "inartistic and commercial spirit of the age" had erected a chaos of placard hoardings that spread like an unsightly rash across the face of the city and had occasioned mention in the Archbishop of Dublin's Lenten pastoral in 1901 for their "demoralising tendency." Could a city so disfigured be restored? If modern Athens, why not Dublin, where "lie the tradition and pride of an ancient culture second only to that of Hellas," or so thought the greatest city planner of his day, Patrick Geddes.

Dublin was not entirely immune to the pervasive atmosphere of "town planning" that was stimulating the civic consciousness in the decade or so before 1914. Geddes's own Cities and Town Planning Exhibition was brought over from England in 1911 under the sponsorship of the Viceroy, Lord Aberdeen. His lectures—calling for the conversion of derelict spaces to parks and gardens, the restoration of insanitary dwellings, and construction of cottages for skilled artisans on the outskirts of the city so the unskilled could inhabit the abodes they would have left—stimulated debate and were instrumental in the formation of the Housing and Town Planning Association of Ireland. That body hoped to create a public opinion that would transform civic life, in Dublin as elsewhere, in much the same spirit that Horace Plunkett's Irish Agricultural Organization Society was transforming the rural life of the country. Meanwhile, a certain urgency was imparted to civic problems after a tragic housing collapse in Church Street in 1913 and the subsequent Departmental investigation of the city's housing accommodation. So enormous was the housing problem that the majority opinion of the ensuing Report, appalled by its extent and gravity, called for massive and immediate rehousing of the poor on all available sites. The lone dissenter voiced a more reflective opinion: nothing less than a civic survey would be required to ensure that a reconstructed Dublin matched the beauty of its surroundings. Such a survey would have to embrace, in terms borrowed from Geddes, "all the factors hitherto left out of consideration—the topography, the means of communication, the industries (past, present, and future) and the movements, needs and occupations of the population."

Needless to say, the housing question remained mired in the mud of municipal impecuniosity. It was soon shunted aside by the greater dangers of war and eventually became victim to the birth pangs of the Irish Free State. But miraculously the idea of a civic survey took hold, helped along by the Town Planning Association and by the Civic Exhibition held during the summer of 1914. The latter was an interesting attempt to inform public opinion and attract attention to the vital needs of planning and civic betterment. Unwittingly or not, a proper tinge of seriousness was added by the choice of venue—the disused Linen Hall Barracks at Henrietta Street, with its lichen-covered walls and weed-grown squares, a physical reminder of the city's industrial decline. More to the point, the site lay on the northern fringe of the principal area of poverty, which extended for one-third of a mile south toward the Four Courts. It was quite an event, the first of its kind in Ireland, attracting 80,000 paying visitors over the course of six weeks to view exhibits on town and village planning, public health, and child welfare and be entertained by folk dancing, gymnastic displays, and the cinematograph. The inhabitants of the surrounding slums, who could hardly afford the 6d. admission charge, apparently benefited more materially, as was recalled by Sir Patrick Abercrombie many years later. The amusing episode took place on the final day of the exhibition, when Countess Aberdeen had to stand by helplessly (and given her charitable nature, doubtless willingly) as "an enormous flock of people . . . began one by one to remove the chairs and the tables and carry them off home" until not a stick of furniture remained.[30]

The more enduring results of the Exhibition were the international design competition for a town plan for the city, sponsored by Lord Aberdeen, and the civic survey eventually carried to completion by the Civics Institute and published a decade later. Neither eventuality ushered in the anticipated new epoch in Irish city life. They remained only to guide and exhort and, in the case of the Survey, to taunt. Some sobering reflections of that document are here quoted at length, for they provide some hints of the magnitude of some of the problems dealt with in the remainder of this book:

> Our civic problems, physical and administrative, cry out for immediate solution. In a progressive capital the want of modern educational facilities; the need of proper forms of juvenile recreation; indifference to historical associations, so valued elsewhere; the stagnation of industry and commerce; the inconvenience and costliness of transport, and the wretched habitations of the masses of the poor, cannot be allowed to remain as they are in Dublin. . . .
>
> As compared with the historic but modernised capitals of Europe, Dublin is 100 years behind the times in civic progress. It has become obvious that the ordinary measures are totally inadequate to deal with the situation. . . .
>
> Dublin of to-day presents to the visitor a lamentable picture! . . . The city's unkempt appearance is not confined to the poorer quarters. Citizens of all classes frequently endeavour to evade the byelaws framed under the Public Health Acts, and the building codes of the local authorities are obsolete. . . . Great tracts of Dublin are practically inaccessible hinterlands, hopeless and forbidding!
>
> Dublin of to-day needs a great awakening, a freedom from political and religious controversy, a subordination of the individual for the general good as well as a disregard of the sanctity of vested interests.[31]

CHAPTER

Politics and the Dublin Corporation

It is, unfortunately, the fact that the municipal administration of Dublin has been in the past in the hands of a comparatively small section of the community. The bulk of the population did not seem to understand or to care about civic affairs while the intrusion of politics into corporate elections disabled the professional and most highly efficient citizens from even seeking to represent Dublin in its Council. . . . The merchant princes of the city, the men of high culture, of wealth, and of experience in administrative affairs have been shut out from the Corporation by reason of their political opinions. Happily a change has come about. In recent years politics have been more and more avoided in municipal elections and in [Corporation meetings] . . .

Irish Times editorial, June 4, 1900

Taken as a whole the *personnel* of the Dublin Corporation is today thoroughly unsatisfactory. The most competent administrators in the city do not offer themselves for election because they dislike and despise the squalid atmosphere of jobbery and intrigue which envelops the City Hall.

Irish Times editorial, January 24, 1913

WHEN THE Irish parliament ceased to exist after the passing of the Act of Union in 1800, the focus of Irish politics shifted to Westminster, where some one hundred Irish representatives in the House of Commons carried the torch for legislative advances in Ireland. Naturally, the special nature of the social and religious cleavage in the country, divided between Ascendancy (Protestant) attitudes and a nationalist (Catholic) outlook, became reflected in the Irish parliamentary representation as soon as Catholics were elected in growing numbers after the achievement of Catholic Emancipation in 1829. This Irish parliamentary body, reflecting also party political development in England, was generally identified after mid-century as having Conservative and Liberal components. By 1886 certainly, in the wake of legislation extending the parliamentary franchise, that separation had hardened into clear-cut Unionist and Nationalist factions. The former, again for the most part Protestant Conservatives, represented the Irish opposition to any tinkering with the Act of Union and was strongest in northeast Ulster. The

Nationalists,* mostly Catholic and with a sprinkling of broad-minded Protestant feeling, were the moderate exponents of a constitutional reorganization of the British establishment in Ireland designed to place responsibility for purely Irish legislative measures in native Irish (Catholic *and* Protestant) hands.

These political differences were carried over into Dublin Corporation, that is, the municipal council of the city of Dublin and agency of such local powers as were devolved on it by the Municipal Corporations Act of 1840 and the Dublin Improvement Act of 1849. Municipal reform in 1840 ensured the subsequent domination of the council chamber by nationalist-minded Roman Catholics whose wealth and social status was inferior to that of the declining number of Conservative councillors and whose fitness for office was judged at election time by the degree of their support for repeal of the Union. But the progressive squeezing out of Conservative (Unionist) members was only the other side of the coin, a fitting retribution perhaps for the virtual exclusion of Catholics from municipal government in the four decades before passage of the Municipal Corporations Act, dubbed by its opponents as a "heavy blow" to the Protestant religion in Ireland. However, in an attempt to deflect the worst aspects of party strife in the interest of good municipal management, the practice was generally adhered to of dividing the mayoralty between Conservative and Liberal (i.e. Repeal) councillors, each faction agreeing to support the other's nominee in alternate years. This arrangement was finally dispensed with after 1882 with the marshalling of Irish political opinion by the aggressive grass-roots organization of the Irish parliamentary party, the Irish National League—standard bearer of the home rule and land agitation programs of a new breed of nationalist representatives at Westminster under the leadership of Charles Stewart Parnell. This trend also transformed the nationalist majority in the Dublin borough council from an independent-minded Liberal following into the well-dragooned Nationalist forces that were steered into office by the ward branches of the National League.

There was no chance that the more regressive aspects of party politics would ever be entirely removed from municipal government in the city of Dublin, the very seat of the British administration in Ireland. The fact of alien rule and its support by Conservative councillors imparted a political coloring to many of the actions and deliberations of the council. One of the first of the new breed of Nationalist Lord Mayors was Edmund Dwyer Gray, proprietor of the *Freeman's Journal* and, like Parnell, one of the few Protestant home rulers. His moderate nationalist views merited a rebuff from the Lord Lieutenant who declined to attend Gray's inaugural banquet in 1880, an insult that Gray returned by refusing to follow up his inauguration with the customary courtesy call at Dublin Castle. The cessation of the long-standing agreement on the rotation of the mayoralty soon followed: Nationalist retribution for the action of the then Conservative Lord Mayor, George Moyers, in blocking the conferring of the freedom of the city on Parnell in 1881. Thereafter, none but those with the necessary nationalist credentials attained the highest municipal office, and few councillors ever dared to run for election on any but a "politi-

*The term "Nationalist" (with a capital initial letter) is henceforth used in this book to designate the political followers of Charles Stewart Parnell and, after his death in 1891, those Irish politicians at Westminster and their supporters in the Dublin municipal council and elsewhere who looked to the attainment of Irish self-government along lines adumbrated in Gladstone's home rule bills. The Nationalists may thus be distinguished from their equally *n*ationalist compatriots in the Sinn Fein and Labour parties in local Irish politics.

cal" ticket. Nor was the council chamber free from political rancor even between Nationalist members when after 1890 the split in their ranks following upon Parnell's deposition as leader of the Irish parliamentary party divided them for a decade into Parnellites and anti-Parnellites, with the former always the dominant faction in the Corporation. This fighting between factions caused the most unusual turn of events of December 1896, which saw a number of Nationalist councillors support the Unionist candidate Sir Robert Sexton in his unsuccessful bid for the mayoralty against the incumbent Parnellite Lord Mayor. The conservative *Irish Times* was not alone in deploring the constant intrusion of political controversy into the meetings of the council. The nationalist *Freeman's Journal* also decried the trend, which had induced the electors to measure the fitness of a candidate for municipal honors "by his lung power in bellowing forth the catchcries and insults of a political faction."

Though the reformed Dublin Corporation was often referred to, in the absence of Irish self-government, as the premier representative body in Ireland, it could hardly be described before 1899 as a democratically controlled body. The burgess roll, which had numbered a little over 5,000 electors at mid-century, had increased only to about 8,000 by 1898, the year in which the Local Government (Ireland) Act democratized the franchise. Hitherto only rated occupiers (male persons of full age) in continuous residence within the borough during the preceding 2 years and 8 months qualified for inclusion in the list of burgesses. Thus, Dublin, with its huge number of lodgers and floating tenement population on monthly and weekly tenancies, compared poorly with Belfast (40,000 electors) and, moreover, with English cities where a residence of only one year was required. Yet despite this restricted franchise in a city of over 250,000 people, the character of those judged to be "fit and proper persons" to perform the civic duty of alderman or town councillor was the subject of much debate during the closing decades of the nineteenth century. Only those citizens in possession of real or personal estate or both to the amount of £1,000 over and above any debts or occupying a house in the borough of net annual value £25 or above and rated for the relief of the poor were qualified to sit as alderman or councillor. Up to 1880 or thereabouts some of the leading merchants and manufacturers in the city as well as individuals of acknowledged business acumen and social distinction formed an influential group within the municipal council. In the council for the year 1855, for example, there sat "merchant princes" of the stature of Sir Benjamin Lee Guinness, George Roe, and John Jameson, Jr., whereas almost one-quarter of the 60 members were either barristers or solicitors. In 1864 the proprietors of all three of the city's major newspapers (Capt. L. Knox, *Irish Times*; Sir John Gray, *Freeman's Journal*; A. M. Sullivan, *Nation*) held office as councillors. And throughout the 1860s and 1870s other leading citizens, both Protestant Conservatives and Catholic Liberals, continued to bear municipal honors—Sir John Arnott and Peter M'Swiney, the drapers, and wholesale merchants Sir James W. Mackey, John Campbell, Maurice Brooks, and Thomas Dockrell. But by 1870 prominent mercantile men were already being publicly chided for shirking their duty as citizens by refusing to present themselves at the annual contests for municipal office.[1] There was no such hesitation from the publicans and spirit grocers, who henceforth began to form the largest single interest group in the Corporation.

A distaste for the political partisanship introduced to municipal affairs after 1886, with the growing prospects for Irish home rule, doubtless induced some social luminaries to shrink from municipal contests: hitherto little excitement disturbed the annual elections and few seats were contested at all. This natural dislike among persons of social distinction for the rough-and-tumble of the electoral arena under these changed circumstances served to reinforce the lure of the adjoining townships where elected office still retained much of the exclusiveness (especially of the Unionist kind) of the pre-1840 era. However, social geography worked much more effectively in the long run to confine Conservative electoral fortunes (for most leading merchants and higher professional elements were loyal Unionists) to but three or four of the city's fifteen wards as increasing numbers of their Protestant constituents departed the city altogether for the advantages of suburban living. The minority interest in the city pleaded in vain for the redress of this imbalance in municipal affairs by calling for increased property qualifications for councillors as well as plural voting. But nothing could break the Nationalist hold on the Corporation from the early 1880s.* The municipal council retained a mercantile interest, of course, but it was no longer led by the "merchant princes." The council also boasted fewer members distinguished by titles of honor such as baronetcies and knighthoods, by official appointment as deputy lieutenants, or by the higher professional qualifications. Instead, in Dublin as in many other cities of the period, the council progressively fell into the hands of publicans, butchers, and other small traders who, it may be said, were as little representative of the mass of struggling citizens (except for their nationalist proclivities) as their own social superiors had been in an earlier period. But as the century now drew to a close, legislation was once again to offer the hope of some further transformation in the make-up of the municipal representation.

The revolutionary impact of the Local Government Act of 1898 was mainly felt in rural Ireland where a new system of local government by county and district councils replaced the unrepresentative, landlord-dominated and nominated bodies of grand jurymen and the like who had hitherto controlled local affairs. In Dublin, on the other hand, the powers of the Corporation were of long standing and had been extended by each successive act governing matters of public health and housing. Here the change was immediately felt in the enlargement of the burgess roll, which was now finally assimilated to the broader parliamentary franchise as exercised by male rated occupiers, leaseholders, freeholders, and lodgers of full age occupying rooms to the value of 4s. weekly (£10 per annum) and satisfying a one-year residency requirement. All special property qualifications for holding municipal office were abolished. And although women obtained for the first time the municipal franchise, the council of the newly styled "county borough" was to remain an exclusively male body until subsequent legislation rendered women eligible to seek municipal office after 1911, a privilege that understandably was continued to be denied to ministers of religion.[2] As expected, the 1898 act did not provide for municipal control of the police (even the home rule bills would have denied such control, if only for a time, to an Irish parliament), so the Lord Mayor remained as powerless to order the constable outside the Mansion House to clear traffic as he had always been. Nor did any authority extend to the courts system except for the Court of Conscience and Lord Mayor's Court, which handled small debts.

---

*This political dominance at the local level was also reflected in the city's four parliamentary constituency elections from 1885 onward. Before the general election of that year the (then) two city seats were usually shared between Liberal (i.e. 'repealer') and Conservative candidates and sometimes (as in the 1841, 1852 and 1859 elections) held by Conservatives alone. Starting in 1885, all four divisions elected Nationalist members with the exception only of the St. Stephen's Green division in 1892 and 1895.

Before considering the effect of these changes on local politics, it is appropriate to outline the powers, duties, and financial base of the Dublin Corporation. As an agency of local government, the council of the county borough derived its powers from Municipal Corporations Acts, various local Acts, and the Acts relating to public health and the housing of the working classes. It was also empowered to levy the poor rate to meet the expenses of the Boards of Guardians, which managed the workhouses of the North and South Dublin Unions. The council met in general session at frequent intervals but conducted the main business of administration through smaller standing committees responsible for finance and leases, improvements, public health, waterworks, paving, cleansing, lighting, and markets. These in turn supervised the work of the permanent staff of salaried employees distributed among the corresponding Corporation departments. The number of such staff was around one hundred at the turn of the century but rapidly increased thereafter to reflect the great expansion of engineering, electrical, and public health undertakings. By 1916 the number of nonmanual, full-time employees exceeded four hundred persons. Subsidiary committees, to which were appointed in some cases representatives of such groups as the Trades Council as well as private individuals, monitored the progress in the city of technical education, public libraries, and so forth. Also, members of the council were appointed to the boards of those public and private institutions receiving Corporation grants (city hospitals, Royal Irish Academy of Music) or levies (Port and Docks Board).

The Corporation obtained its income mainly from the poundage rates levied under the following headings: Improvement; Grand Jury Cess; District Sewer; Domestic Water; Measurement (a small rate assessed on the frontage of docks and public buildings); and, after 1907, Public Libraries. The Improvement Rate produced the most revenue and went to support the constant burden of expenditure for sanitary, paving, cleansing, and other works of improvement. The Grand Jury cess defrayed the costs of elections and registration of voters, maintenance of prisons and reform schools, but most of this assessment went to sustain the Richmond Lunatic Asylum and to honor the presentments of scores of industrial schools throughout the country for the maintenance of Dublin children sent there by the courts and chargeable to the Corporation in the absence of family support.

The Corporation also levied nonmunicipal rates to satisfy the presentments of the chief Commissioner of the Dublin Metropolitan Police (a statutory 8d.), the Port and Docks Board (the bridge rate, levied only occasionally), and the Poor Law Guardians. The poor rate was raised separately on the northern and southern parts of the city to cover the maintenance of the paupers in the two workhouses; hence the different poundage rates assessed on property valuation in the two halves of the city, the higher rate on the northern districts owing to the lower rateable valuation of that sector. The annual amount expended for the relief of the poor was generally in excess of £100,000, a considerable burden on taxpayers, considering that the corresponding assessment in Belfast was in most years little more than half the Dublin figure and occasionally, as in 1904, as low as one-third.

Of the additional sources of income available to the Corporation, the most important was the growing revenue from private and industrial electricity supply accounts. This rose from less than £10,000 to over £100,000 per annum between 1900 and 1916. Other major items included the rents from Corporation properties, proceeds from the sale of water for industrial purposes, and, since 1898, an annual sum of over £10,000 from the Tramways

TABLE 3. Dublin Corporation: Revenue from Local Taxation and Other Sources, Total Indebtedness, and Total Poundage Rates in Selected Years, 1900–1913 (year ending 31 March).

	1901	1904	1907	1910	1913
Improvement Rate	£136,043	£234,399	£279,218	£305,386	£295,049
Poor Rate	152,208	167,189	125,539	133,581	122,849
Other Rates	18,634	22,993	12,820	18,426	20,250
Grants from the Local Taxation Account	36,607	42,318	58,424	75,261	57,149
Receipts from other local taxing bodies	11,898	14,832	15,813	6,783	19,613
Receipts from markets, etc.	8,406	9,712	10,152	12,138	11,548
Receipts from dues, fees	13,387	6,793	7,888	11,452	2,528
Rents from land, houses, etc.	64,348	51,536	45,143	47,869	49,179
Receipts from Waterworks	(not shown separately—included in other receipts and balances)			39,636	34,448
Receipts from Electric Lighting		ditto		50,269	89,396
Money borrowed (loans or stock issue)	136,057	193,449	105,215	(not shown separately)	
Other receipts and balances	77,807	83,069	123,272	41,616	45,178
Total Revenue	655,395	826,290	783,484	742,417	747,187
Total Indebtedness (balance of loans and outstanding stock)	1,876,987	2,382,370	2,478,573	2,542,643	2,640,000
Total Rates (per £ of assessed valuation):					
North City	9s. 7½d.	11s. 1¼d.	10s. 4½d.	10s. 10d.	9s. 10d.
South City	8s. 10½d.	10s. 3¼d.	9s. 11d.	10s. 6d.	9s. 9¼d.

NOTE 1. Increase in revenue from Improvement Rate in 1904 reflects in part the assessment on the added areas after extension of boundaries.
SOURCE: *Parliamentary Papers*: Returns of Local Taxation in Ireland (Receipts). For 1901, see cd. 1382; 1904, cd. 2460; 1907, cd. 4018; 1910, cd. 5564; 1913, cd. 7289.

Company for wayleaves. At no time, however, was the Corporation's income sufficient to meet current expenses, which by 1916 were running close to £900,000 per year (including payments to the Boards of Guardians and others) and ranged from such large annual payments as £130,000 (electric lighting undertakings), £115,000 (paving and cleansing), £115,000 (interest on loans, dividends, and so on) to smaller annual amounts for the support of technical schools at Kevin Street, Bolton Street, Rutland Square, and Chatham Row (£30,000) and a sum rising to £2,500 in aid of scholarships for worthy applicants at University College (UCD). Annual revenue and expenditure were generally less in Dublin than in Belfast, especially after 1905, when Belfast Corporation began to undertake the management of that city's tramway service. By 1913 the receipts of Belfast Corporation were in excess of £1.2 million compared with Dublin's £.75 million, with over £500,000 deriving from the tramways and gasworks accounts.

Dublin, like most municipalities, resorted to borrowing to find the revenue she dared not extort from suspicious or resentful ratepayers. Projects large and small were only made possible through the issuance of stock or by recourse to the lending facilities of the

Commissioners of Public Works and private loans from assurance companies, friendly societies, banks, and others. The want of funds over the years had been responsible for the long delay in tackling the main drainage, a project undertaken finally through the sale of £700,000 of Corporation stock. Loans, stock issue, or both had facilitated every urban clearance and housing scheme, all new street construction, sanitary works, and electricity schemes as well as a multitude of smaller ventures ranging from the erection of children's playgrounds to the maintenance of an art gallery or the purchase of a private library. Borrowing was an even greater recourse in Belfast, which in contrast to Dublin operated municipal tramways and gasworks: the indebtedness of that Corporation amounted to more than £4 million in 1913 compared to slightly over £2.5 million in Dublin, but virtually all of this had been realized by the issuance of stock, yet another contrast to the less-favored southern capital, where outstanding stock issue represented only 63 percent of total borrowing. By 1916 the total indebtedness of Dublin Corporation stood at £2.75 million (over a two-fold increase since 1890) and included unpaid loans and outstanding stock in the following amounts: waterworks, £615,000; electric lighting, £600,000; main drainage, £570,000; housing schemes (under Parts I and III of the Housing of the Working Classes Act, 1890), £400,000.

There were practical and statutory limits also to the amount of debt the Corporation might incur. Every loan or stock issue added to expenditure, of course, by way of interest and dividend payments, monies that to some extent had to come out of revenue from the rates. The various municipal undertakings of Dublin Corporation, as with those of most other cities, usually produced a net loss after provision was made for payments credited to interest and sinking fund. Also, the Corporation's margin for borrowing under section 238(2) of the Public Health Act of 1878 was set at twice the city's rateable value. But the rateable valuation of the city of Dublin underwent only a moderate increase in the closing decades of the century and was the smallest of all the valuations of the large cities of the United Kingdom after 1900. Besides, the city's borrowing power was artificially limited until 1898 by the decision of the Local Government Board to include as chargeable debt in calculating the margin the huge sums borrowed during the 1860s in connection with the waterworks. Furthermore, the great extension of boundaries, which brought increased revenue and population to other cities, was denied Dublin: the extension won in 1900 was considerably less than that requested and brought in only 26,000 persons, about £90,000 additional valuation, and financial obligations in sewer construction and water supply that were deemed to exceed the value received. It had been felt all along that the city was undervalued by as much as £200,000, at the very least, inasmuch as there had been no general revaluation of property since the 1850s. When an attempt was made in 1906 to obtain such a general revaluation in the expectation that the greater revenue from an expected higher total valuation would enable a reduction of the poundage rates, the insistence of the Under Secretary at Dublin Castle that the Corporation pay half the cost of the work that would be involved shelved the project for a decade. Not until 1916 did the city benefit from a 15 percent increase in its rateable valuation, which increase for the first time brought the total sum for the 15 wards of the "old city" to over one million pounds.

As is evident from the foregoing, the municipal council was responsible for huge undertakings and a vast expenditure—upwards of £.75 million in revenue from rates, rents, and loans being spent each year by the Corporation and by those institutions, such as the

TABLE 4. Rateable Valuation of Dublin Municipal Borough, 1890–1915 (year ending 31 March) and Comparison with Other Cities (figures in thousands of pounds).

	1890	1895	1900	1905	1910	1915
Dublin: old city (15 wards)	683	700	727	779	826	869
added areas[a]	—	—	—	112	133	139
Total (20 wards)	683	700	727	891	959	1,008
Belfast	688	817	1,160	1,271	1,504	1,575
Birmingham	.	.	2,297	2,878	2,927	4,463
Bradford	.	.	1,368	1,538	1,557	1,590
Bristol	.	.	1,512	1,751	1,841	1,859
Edinburgh	.	.	2,363	2,723	2,905	2,970
Glasgow	.	.	4,780	5,580	5,916	7,308
Leeds	.	.	1,620	2,076	2,143	2,212
Liverpool	.	.	4,000	4,470	4,791	4,869
Manchester	.	.	3,109	4,071	4,497	4,703
Sheffield	.	.	1,400	1,694	1,827	2,005

[a]Townships added under the Boundaries Act, 1900, brought an initial increase of £94,000 to the valuation of the city and 5 new wards.
SOURCES: Annual Accounts of the Dublin Corporation; *Municipal Year Book*.

Poor Law Boards and Richmond Asylum, deriving income from the Corporation. In addition, its various committees administered the supply of water and electricity (gas and tramways being private monopolies), supervised cattle and food markets, baths and washhouses, and was landlord for a number of municipal ventures into public housing. Hence the great concern frequently voiced about the suitability of candidates for municipal office, a matter that took on some immediacy at the approach of the first municipal elections under the Local Government Act of 1898. After all, these were the years in which the municipal gospel was being elaborated in improving British cities, though the variant forms of it preached by the Fabian Society found few disciples in Dublin—here there would be little fear that infants would be brought up on municipal milk and in the fullness of time reduced to ashes in a municipal crematorium. The Act enjoined all 15 aldermen (1 per ward) and 45 councillors (3 per ward) of the city's 15 wards to resign so that all candidates for the new council could present themselves to an expanded electorate of almost 40,000 voters, including 6,600 females.[3]

Whatever trepidation was previously felt about taxpayers' money being spent at the behest of men whose business acumen derived from the management of grocery and butcher shops was now heightened at the prospect of there being added to the council men who, as contemporary concern expressed it, "will haggle over the price of a few shovels, because they do know something about shovels" but who might pass without criticism schemes involving considerable sums of money. There were many, therefore, who had distrusted the idea of extending the franchise to lodgers, a provision that had the greatest significance for Dublin, a city of lodgers. These included such a staunch representative of the Irish people as T. M. Healy, MP. "To continue the lodger vote in cities," he feared, "is to perpetuate a fraud," and he cited the usual objection of the widow with 7 "lodger" sons. He went so far as to introduce an amendment during the discussion stage of the Local Government Bill designed to remove the offending clause, but this was defeated.[4] He need not have worried, for both occupancy and residency requirements ensured that there would be no inundation of the burgess roll by lodgers. But on the surface his political fears might have been well founded. The voting workman was an unknown quantity who might come to realize that the domination of municipal government, in Dublin as elsewhere, by Nationalist councillors, while satisfying his patriotic instincts, had done little to improve his physical surroundings. Neither did the chances of elected artisans being nominated to sit on the Port and Docks Board appeal to those wealthy traders and shipowners who managed the Port of Dublin.

TABLE 5. Dublin Municipal Wards: Population, Valuation, and Number of Electors for Each Ward Under the Franchise Provisions Existing Before and After the Local Government Act, 1898.

	TOTAL POPULATION (1901 census)	POOR LAW VALUATION (1901)	NO. OF LOCAL GOVT. ELECTORS 1898 (pre-Act)	1899
North City: Arran Quay	31,109	£ 55,488	637	4,323
Inns Quay	24,940	44,301	621	3,628
Mountjoy	24,840	42,038	672	3,269
North City	8,784	52,500	368	1,785
North Dock	23,634	77,473	708	3,850
Rotunda	14,580	35,797	562	2,093
South City: Fitzwilliam	12,455	51,471	666	2,083
Mansion House	11,892	35,324	269	1,558
Merchants' Quay	25,434	37,603	622	2,757
Royal Exchange	7,648	52,512	380	1,283
South City	4,385	67,134	360	1,108
South Dock	14,766	56,328	654	2,088
Trinity	12,331	49,530	368	2,241
Usher's Quay	23,655	50,842	368	3,367
Wood Quay	20,654	34,081	709	3,286
	261,107	£742,422	7,964	38,719

SOURCE: *Freeman's Journal*, Jan. 16, 1899; *Parliamentary Papers*, 1901 (LXIV), no. 2 (Local Government Returns).

The now defunct assembly had contained 12 Unionist members and 48 Nationalists. In the January 1899 election nearly 120 candidates stood for the 60 vacancies. These included 18 Unionists, 10 Laborites, 88 Nationalists and 1 lone nominee of the fledgling Irish Socialist Republican Party. Organized labor, which had long been satisfied perforce with virtual representation by "labor" spokesmen from the Nationalist ranks, now ran its own candidates under the banner of the Labour Electoral Association. In contesting only 10 seats (not even 1 per ward), the Labour party had clearly demonstrated no resolve to precipitate a revolution in municipal affairs. Its election program purveyed the traditional trade union demands: local labor to be used as far as possible on Corporation contracts; fair conditions regarding wages and hours; only trade unionists to be employed on public contracts. The Nationalists entered the campaign divided on personalities, as before, but hardly differing in program—each side adopting a platform that looked to the extension of city boundaries, the improvement of the dwellings of the poor, the expansion of technical education, and the promotion of the "legitimate aspirations" of Labour. Naturally, they also agreed on the unifying symbols of national self-government and a Catholic University. Most Nationalists had swung round to the program of Nationalist unity championed by the newly formed United Irish League (UIL) with the result that the former majority Parnellite faction could field only a score of candidates.

There was as much curiosity as excitement at this first election under the broadened franchise, due mainly to the novelty of the labor ticket and, for the first time ever, the appearance of female voters at the polling booths. One condescending male observation had it that many ladies were present rather to assert a right than to support a cause and were alleged to have voted on the recommendations of their escorts. The results, as expected, perpetuated the previous domination of municipal affairs by Nationalist councillors with the United Irish League and Parnellite factions obtaining 27 and 18 seats, respectively. The remaining 15 were shared by Unionists (7) and Labour (8). More noteworthy was the fact that 30 incumbents (24 Nationalists, 6 Unionists), or exactly half the council, were reelected to the new chamber. The Unionist representation suffered badly, being reduced from 20 percent to under 12 percent, a loss of 5 seats of which 4 went to Nationalists. The Labour candidates headed the poll in three wards (thereby achieving aldermanic honors)* against the challenge of Nationalist stalwarts T. C. Harrington, Joseph Nannetti** and the late Lord Mayor, Daniel Tallon. This modest success of a handful of responsible and moderate trade unionists, who by no stretch of the imagination merited *The Times*'s characterization of them as a "transmigration of Fenianism," nevertheless induced mixed feelings in that organ of imperialism: ". . . the fact that the authority of [Irish parliamentary party MPs] Mr. Dillon, Mr. Healy and Mr. Redmond is challenged by a Fenian organization masquerading under the name of a 'labor party' may not be altogether disagreeable, but, if the movement should succeed, it can only be another blow struck at the interests of Ireland as a civilized and rational community." The *Freeman's Journal* crusading for the UIL felt relieved however: "from the workers has proceeded no sentence of doom against respected citizens and tried patriots."[5]

The 1899 election also reintroduced the old refrain about the want of substantial men of business in the council, of men who could supposedly be trusted to control the civic debt, reduce rates, and expose jobbery and nepotism. The absence of these individuals in municipal corporations was general throughout the United Kingdom and is variously explained. Certainly a lack of local patriotism and civic zeal embraced their motives in isolating themselves from direct involvement in civic affairs. A certain disdain for associating with men of inferior rank and education who were quite frequently predisposed to abusive or unparliamentary behavior must also have operated. Others perhaps saw pecuniary advantages in being able as private citizens to bid on public contracts that would have been denied them as corporators. And certainly many disliked the intrusion of "politics" into municipal affairs. One example of the latter was the action of the Unionist alderman, W. R. Maguire (of the brassfounding firm of Maguire and Gatchell, Ltd.), who resigned from the council in 1896, citing the constant political controversies and the disproportionate amount of committee time spent in relation to work actually accomplished for the good of the city. Thus in Dublin these men—the Guinness brothers, George Jacob, the biscuit maker, Marcus Goodbody, the tobacco manufacturer, W. J.

*The office of alderman conveyed no special authority, but the holder did enjoy a six-year term, a relic of the days when it was felt necessary to attract and secure through nomination the services of able men for as long as possible. The only other advantage was the privilege of wearing impressive scarlet robes on ceremonial occasions. Despite a general opinion that the office should be abolished in a more democratic age, both it and the longer tenure were retained.
**Nannetti, though a former President of the Trades Council, had allied himself with the Nationalists and was one of that party's spokesmen on labor questions. He was elected to parliament for the city's College Green division in 1900.

Goulding, the chemical magnate and chairman of the Great Southern and Western Railway, John Jameson, Sir John Arnott, Maurice Dockrell, and others—tended their immediate interests by securing safe positions on the Port and Docks Board and other bodies or quieted their civic consciences through philanthropy.

At any rate, except for the larger complement of artisans, the new assembly bore much the same occupational character as the old. Small groups of professionals, building contractors and small-scale manufacturers, and "commercial men" (company directors, insurance managers, secretaries, and so on) were overshadowed by the large merchant class of small traders (grocers, victuallers, merchant tailors, and the like), vintners (publicans and wine and spirit merchants), and licensed grocers. The professional interest was noticeably small for most of the period under review. Physicians never exceeded two in any year, whereas Belfast Corporation often boasted of eight or nine. And from the legal profession, not more than two barristers and five solicitors ever sat in the council. The liquor interest comprised the largest single specific occupational group, not unexpectedly in view of the local influence wielded by publicans and licensed grocers. More than any other group those in "the thrade" needed the protection that municipal office and political activism could afford, for they were constantly under attack by temperance crusaders and others bent on curbing the drink traffic through local ordinances or legislation. They had powerful allies, of course, in the great distillers and brewers—the merchant princes of Dublin's economic life—and in the Irish parliamentary party, which always depended on their contributions to the political war chest. Thus, among the Dublin wards there were few that did not send at least one representative of this interest to the council from year to year. Indeed, for a number of years three of the four incumbents of Merchants' Quay and Wood Quay wards belonged to the group. The number of councillors holding high social rank was negligible, but then it was hardly to be expected that aristocratic honors should fall profusely on such a "subversive" body as Dublin Corporation. The one baronetcy (Sir Thomas Pile in 1900) and two of the three knighthoods (Sir Joseph Downes in 1900, Sir Patrick Shortall in 1916) were conferred, however, on loyal Nationalist members.

After the 1899 election the municipal council resumed its normal election pattern of retiring one-third of the councillors in rotation each year and half of the number of alder-

TABLE 6. **Dublin City: Occupational Profile of the Municipal Council, 1899–1914.**

	1899		1902[a]		1905		1908		1911		1914[b]	
	no.	%	no.	%	no.	%	no.	%	no.	%	no.	%
Small merchant	19	31.7	24	30.0	28	35.0	33	41.2	32	40.0	24	30.4
Publican, wine merchant, licensed grocer	15	25.0	21	26.2	20	25.0	14	17.5	20	25.0	14	17.7
Builder/Contractor	3	5.0	6	7.5	4	5.0	3	3.7	3	3.7	7	8.9
Manufacturer	2	3.3	3	3.8	4	5.0	1	1.3	2	2.5	1	1.3
Commercial	8	13.3	8	10.0	7	8.8	11	13.8	7	8.8	9	11.4
Artisan	7	11.7	4	5.0	6	7.5	4	5.0	1	1.3	8	10.1
Professional	4	6.7	6	7.5	5	6.2	10	12.5	10	12.5	11	13.9
Member of Parliament	2	3.3	3	3.8	2	2.5	1	1.3	2	2.5	1	1.3
Gentleman[c]	—		5	6.2	4	5.0	3	3.7	3	3.7	4	5.0

[a] Membership of the council increased from 60 to 80 members after 1900
[b] 79-member council only; one seat vacant during 1914
[c] This category includes retired individuals and persons of unknown (but not artisan) status
SOURCES: *Thom's Directory* (annual); election nominations as reported in newspapers.

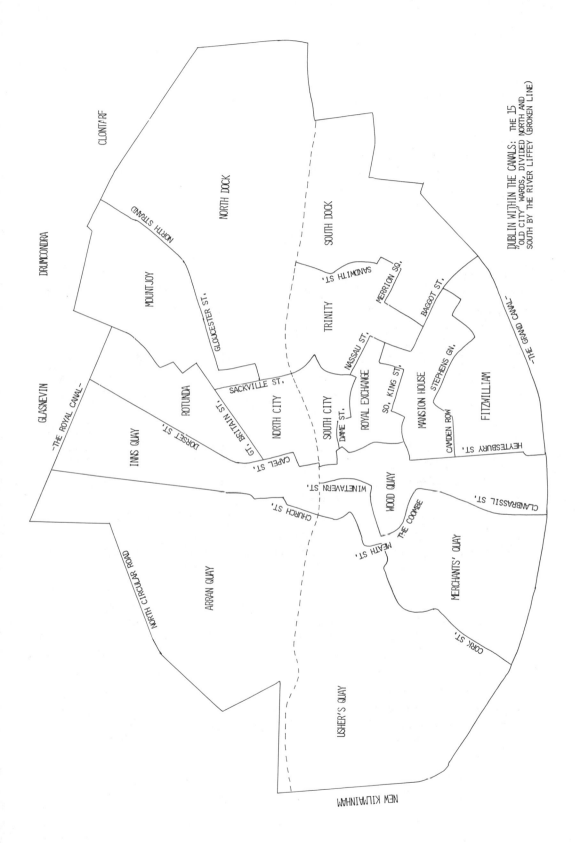

DRUMCONDRA

CLONTARF

GLASNEVIN

NORTH DOCK

NORTH STRAND

MOUNTJOY

GLOUCESTER ST.

–THE ROYAL CANAL–

ROTUNDA

GT. BRITAIN ST.

DORSET ST.

INNS QUAY

SACKVILLE ST.

NORTH CITY

CAPEL ST.

SOUTH DOCK

TRINITY

SANDWITH ST.

MERRION SQ.

NASSAU ST.

SOUTH CITY

DAME ST.

ROYAL EXCHANGE

SO. KING ST.

MANSION HOUSE

STEPHENS GN.

CAMDEN ROW

BAGGOT ST.

FITZWILLIAM

HEYTESBURY ST.

–THE GRAND CANAL–

WINETAVERN ST.

WOOD QUAY

CHURCH ST.

CLANBRASSIL ST.

THE COOMBE

MEATH ST.

MERCHANTS' QUAY

NORTH CIRCULAR ROAD

ARRAN QUAY

USHER'S QUAY

CORK ST.

NEW KILMAINHAM

DUBLIN WITHIN THE CANALS: THE 15 "OLD CITY" WARDS, DIVIDED NORTH AND SOUTH BY THE RIVER LIFFEY (BROKEN LINE) men every third year. The most important business to be taken up by the new members was the matter of extending the city boundaries by absorption of the surrounding townships, an action that required parliamentary approval. As indicated in an earlier chapter, the first attempt to incorporate these areas—especially Rathmines and Pembroke to the south, Drumcondra and Glasnevin in the north—came to nought in 1880. The arguments pro and con had changed but little in the meantime. In addition to land (for building) and people (80,000 and mainly middle class), the townships would also add £350,000 to the city's valuation, an increase of 50 percent. Belfast, for example, more than doubled its municipal area by an extension of boundaries in 1896, leaving Dublin the only major city in the British Isles that had not had its area extended during the previous half-century.

The most immediate purpose of annexation was to correct the inequity whereby the residents of the suburbs enjoyed all the facilities of the city (including hospitals, markets, abattoir, libraries, disinfecting stations, and fire brigade) without being liable to taxes collected through the rates. Over 45,000 suburbanites arrived in the city each day via foot, tram, or railway for work and business. Efficiency and economy demanded a centralization of municipal services and procedures in the greater Dublin area so that all might benefit from unified direction and combined effort in matters of sanitation and street improvements. With good reason the Corporation resented the townships' discharge of crude sewage into the Liffey (though this was a case of the pot calling the kettle black!) or onto the sloblands along its banks. Nor was it comforting to consider how many of the 45,000 daily visitors came from townships (Clontarf, New Kilmainham, Drumcondra) that had still not adopted the provisions of the Notification of Infectious Diseases Act. In the long term, however, it was the worsening housing problem that dictated the need for the revenue the suburbs could provide. In fact, the suburbs further complicated this issue by driving up the price of available land within the city since landlords took full advantage of the Corporation's pressing needs to provide municipal housing.

The annexation proposal was introduced at Westminster on February 14 as a private bill, a fairly expensive procedure that the Corporation could not avoid and could ill afford. Nationalist zeal for the measure was countered by Irish Unionist hostility, though the Conservative government itself maintained a strict neutrality during the progress of the bill. The Ulster Unionist MPs scored their usual debating points as they charged the Corporation with gerrymandering the wards, demonstrating open disloyalty to the Queen, and betraying all the evils associated with Tammany. Colonel Saunderson created calculated merriment with his characterization of Dublin Corporation as a "Greenwich Hospital for Nationalist wrecks." The majority of township commissioners, also Unionists, opposed annexation, and local witnesses hostile to the measure appeared before the private bill committee. The desire to maintain an independent administration in these townships was not unconnected with a distaste for the erection of artisans' dwellings in or about middle-class neighborhoods. Obviously, the townships had come to value the vested interest that resided in their lower rates of taxation and feared the probability of being saddled with part of the cost of solving the city's immense housing problem. As one witness declared, it was not the proper task of a municipality to house the poor "who would always exist in cities. . . . What could be done for them must be by private benevolence and goodness."[6]

The bill passed the Commons handily in June, though not without the embarrassment of its being opposed by Edward Carson and W. E. H. Lecky, the members for Trinity College, that Protestant stronghold located in the heart of the city. It was mangled in the Lords by an amendment providing for the cession of only the poorest of the suburbs, that is, New Kilmainham, an area largely inhabited by workers of the Great Southern Railway at Inchicore. The impasse could not be resolved so the bill was ordered anew for the following session. Its introduction for a second time in February 1900 afforded a rehashing of all the old arguments along with the novel but implausible one by a Pembroke parson who accused the Corporation of insincerity in its solicitude for the working classes because almost one-third of that body was in the retail drink trade, a conclusion that could hardly have appealed to the foremost supplier of that trade, namely, the city's leading Unionist and philanthropist, Lord Iveagh. Parliament received petitions against the bill from the surrounding townships and, strangely enough, from Trinity College, which through past favorable legislation contributed nothing to the revenue of the city beyond a 3½d. sewer rate. This time, however, a compromise was reached that added New Kilmainham, Drumcondra and Clonliffe, Glasnevin, and some county land comprising Donnycarney, Grangegorman, and other small areas (of combined total valuation, £90,000) to the city but denied it the more populous southern urban districts of Pembroke (comprising the townlands of Ringsend, Irishtown, Sandymount, Merrion, Donnybrook, Clonskeagh) and Rathmines (Rathgar, Ranelagh, Harold's Cross, Milltown), with their combined total valuation of about £260,000. This latter disappointment was softened somewhat by the Equalization of Rates Act, 1901, which gave effect to a recommendation that Pembroke and Rathmines make small annual payments to the city for a fixed number of years as their share of the costs of those city services that benefited suburbanites—public lighting, street maintenance, city markets, asylums, and such. Later attempts to induce these two districts to merge with the city likewise failed, and it was not until 1930 that the then fifty-year dream of annexation was finally realized. In the case of the added areas, the whole was divided into five new city wards—Clontarf East and West, Drumcondra, Glasnevin, New Kilmainham—each returning the usual alderman and three councillors. Consequently, the Unionist representation was given a boost at the subsequent municipal election. Of the twenty new members elected for these wards in January 1901 (thus bringing the council up to eighty members) nine were Unionists, raising their representation to sixteen, or the same 20 percent ratio they had enjoyed before 1899.[7] Indeed, had the original plan gone through of also incorporating Pembroke and Rathmines urban districts, the proposed ward changes would probably have yielded a sizable Unionist minority of about one-third in an eighty-eight-member council.

These changes augured no material threat to Nationalist political ascendancy. As Table 7 indicates, the Unionist party soon declined in strength, owing primarily to Nationalist incursions into the group's previously "safe" Royal Exchange and South City wards and similar penetration in the new Unionist stronghold of Clontarf. The party never really recovered from the debacle of the 1905 election, when not a single one of the eleven candidates fielded was successful. By the following year all the "old city" wards had been "purified," with the Unionists being confined to the added areas, a situation hardly relieved when Ernest Bewley, the cafe proprietor, intruded as a lone Unionist voice (one among sixty) from these fifteen wards from 1907 on. Thus, a handful of Unionist councillors (down to three by 1915), ably supported by the *Irish Times*, could only flail ineffectively at the increasing civic debt, its high municipal taxation, and a voter apathy that, to their prejudiced viewpoint, allowed the perpetuation of a corporate body lacking in intelligence, business capacity, and public spirit.

The laborite group also fared badly, proving unable to exceed the representation won in 1899 or rouse a majority of working-class burgesses to emulate their more politically conscious fellow citizens on polling day. The first two labor councillors to retire during 1900-1901 under the rotational system lost badly to Nationalist opponents. And the enlargement of the council in 1901 only confirmed the decline: none of the twenty new members represented Labour. In subsequent elections several labor candidates were dealt severe drubbings by their opponents; none more serious than the crushing defeat in 1904, by a Nationalist vintner, of W. Leahy, incumbent of Mountjoy ward and an artisan who had held his seat continuously since 1893. Nevertheless, the laborites, though few in number, could always expect to garner some support for their program from their Nationalist colleagues, particularly since the council chamber was the usual forum in which resolutions of the Dublin Trades Council on such matters as the enforcement of standard rates of wages and the like were brought to the attention of public and private employers. Such pressure in the old council had secured clauses in Corporation contracts enjoining subcontractors to hire local labor, pay not less than the minimum standard rate, and use regular tradesmen to perform tradesmen's work.

But the basic political weakness of the Labour group was not lost on their colleagues. One of the earliest resolutions presented by labor councillors to prevent nonunion labor from being hired by Corporation works departments was unsuccessful: it secured the votes of only six Nationalist members. Another resolution called for evening sittings of the council to accommodate members who were wage-earning tradesmen in carrying out their municipal duties. The idea was countered by councillor Harrington's smug suggestion that "those who spoke about the rights of the working men should think of some of the rights of others."[8] T.C. Harrington, the former Parnellite and then leading member of the Irish parliamentary party, was much distrusted by Labour. When he was nominated to serve as Lord Mayor in 1902, for the second year in a row, a forlorn objection issued from the Trades Council warning that the resulting avoidance of the usual inauguration procession for a new Lord Mayor would redound to the injury of the coachmaking trade. When he ran for an unprecedented third year in 1903, the Labour party put up its own candidate (Alderman Dowd, a registered plumber) to contest the mayoralty. Harrington's success, won over the votes of a score of Nationalist supporters of Dowd's candidacy, elicited murmurings about the hegemony of the United Irish League, and the Trades Council passed resolutions calling on Labour representatives to be trade unionists first and politicians after.[9]

In Dublin, however, politics always took pride of place. At the very first meeting of the Corporation after the election in 1899, the first order of business was not a much-needed declaration of war against the slums but a pledge of devotion to the cause of self-government and a promise to use every legitimate means to secure its triumph. But this was a task that could only be tackled successfully at Westminster or on the battlefield, in neither of which areas the Corporation operated. On the other hand, since Irish Home Rule interested few British politicians in 1899 (the Conservatives in any case were in office) such rhetorical flourishes were needed to remind the Irish people that local government was not to be confused with self-government and that it was not possible to "kill home rule with kindness." The opportunity to set a bolder face against imperial rule soon presented itself when the deteriorating relations between the British government and the Boers of the Transvaal reached a crisis in October. Irish nationalists, to whom self-government was denied, felt a natural sympathy with those whose nationality was threatened by a naked imperialism. A massive pro-Boer demonstration embracing a wide spectrum of local nationalist opinion was held in the capital on October 1, only days before hostilities commenced. The leading spirits of that gathering were the republican activist John McBride, organizer of the pro-Boer Irish Brigade, and the socialist republican James Connolly. A resolution of sympathy with the Boers was adopted that was forthwith transmitted to the municipal council for official endorsement. Lord Mayor Daniel Tallon, who had been fervently nationalist enough in 1898 to depart from tradition by dispensing with the usual military contingent in his ceremonial progression from the Mansion House to City Hall, failed the test of nationality on this occasion. But a Lord Mayor who had lunched with the Lord Lieutenant in Dublin Castle and was anxiously awaiting parliamentary consideration of the Corporation's claim for an extension of city boundaries was hardly likely to add to his difficulties by an act of open disloyalty to the Crown. The Corporation was now attacked for its seeming lack of support for national causes (only seven councillors had been present at the October demonstration), most notably by Maud Gonne in the pages of Arthur Griffith's *United Irishman*. Dissension again appeared within the council chamber in December, when councillor John Clancy introduced another pro-Boer resolution, which failed of hearing because a quorum of twenty members could not be obtained, a face-saving stratagem imputed to the collusion of the Lord Mayor and forty-three other "so-called Nationalists."

The hostility of Major McBride's well-drilled hecklers was also aimed at the new Nationalist organization, the United Irish League. The League had only just sealed reunion in the ranks of the Nationalists in Dublin by winning the allegiance of dissenting Parnellites in the municipal council. It had also demonstrated the strength of that achievement by a powerful show of force at the municipal elections in January 1900: in fourteen contests only one non-Nationalist candidate had been returned (a Unionist in South City ward); eight of the Nationalist victors were incumbents; and the several labor candidates were defeated, including one in Mansion House ward who had the endorsement of the pro-Boer, Irish Transvaal Committee. Notwithstanding, incidents such as had disrupted the council chamber in 1899 were certainly an embarrassment and could render difficult the slow task of extending the League's influence in the various city wards. Nor would this activity be made any easier by the tactics of political extremists whose appeals to Irish nationality offered a certain attraction (though not, of course, opportunity) to patriotic citizens at a time of England's difficulty. Thus, apprehension turned to alarm early in March, when John Redmond, the new leader of the reunited Irish parliamentary party, hailed the forthcoming visit to Ireland of Queen Victoria and expressed gratification at her announcement that for the future a sprig of shamrock be worn by the men of her Irish regiments on March 17 (St. Patrick's Day) to commemorate the gallantry of Irish soldiers (against the Boers) in South Africa[10]—a far cry from an earlier era when, in the words of the old ballad, they were "hanging men and women for the wearing of the green." These royal announcements were widely condemned by Irish nationalists as another ploy in the British army's recruiting drive in Ireland. For why else send the aged Queen to visit her resentful Irish subjects after "40 years of cold neglect"?

Considering the marked "disloyalty" with which royal occasions had been greeted during the previous fifteen years, one must conclude that royal visitors demonstrated more of a sense of duty than desire in preparing to visit Ireland. The dutiful sentiments that produced the following avowal from the municipal council on the occasion of the Queen's escape from the assassination attempt in 1882 could hardly have been credible in 1900: "We beg to assure Your Majesty that in no portion of this mighty Empire does there exist more generous and sincere loyalty to Your Majesty's person and throne than in your ancient City of Dublin." Already by 1885 the toast to the Queen at the mayoral banquet was being received with hisses along with the cheers. And the government could not easily forget the mass expression of disapproval throughout nationalist Ireland for the visit of the Prince of Wales in the same year, with Dublin Corporation voting 41 to 17 against taking any part in the official welcome. Two years later the council failed to prevent a Jubilee Address while the Lord Mayor absented himself from the procession that greeted the arrival in Dublin of the royal princes who were to usher in the festivities. The corresponding celebration in 1897 provoked riot in the city. Such nationalist manifestations often provoked the anger of the only loyal element in the city daring enough to tackle a nationalist mob—the students from Trinity College. Few years went by without end-of-term raids on the Mansion House to make off with a green flag: on one occasion in 1899 the students tore the flag to pieces in the college quadrangle. In the same year they desecrated the proposed site of the Wolfe Tone memorial atop Grafton Street and marched off singing "God Save the Queen."

When, finally, the royal visit was announced for April 4, 1900, the Corporation was inevitably divided on what official attitude to adopt. The Nationalist members were naturally anxious to avoid charges of flunkeyism yet unwilling to embarrass the Irish parliamentary party in its dealings with English politicians or in appeals to the goodwill of the British electorate. After all, formal obeisance on such occasions was, as a matter of course, to be expected from municipalities so honored by the royal presence. Lord Mayor Pile, a Protestant home ruler, proposed that a brief address of welcome be adopted for the arrival of, as Tim Healy put it, "a venerable lady to whom no extremist could be discourteous." But when it was further proposed to acknowledge Ireland as Her Majesty's loyal dominion, this proved too much for over one-fourth of the council. Nevertheless, the resolution carried 30 to 22 and bore the names of over 20 Nationalists and 1 laborite. William Redmond, MP, demonstrating less loyalty than his brother John, resigned his council seat in protest. Unionist propaganda in Ireland and England was quick to exploit the address that the Lord Mayor read to the Queen on her arrival at the city boundary at Leeson Street bridge. It was, according to these loyalists, an acknowledgment by Dublin Corporation of the abandonment of Ireland's claim to self-government, a tactic that restored unanimity in the council and prompted quick passage of a resolution reminding England that no loyalty could be expected from Ireland until her national parliament (then defunct for exactly 100 years) was restored. The majority, however, appeared to have better gauged the popular mood, for by all accounts the Queen was accorded a tremendous welcome by the people of Dublin. She signified her appreciation of the loyalty of Dublin Corporation by elevating the Lord Mayor to a baronetcy and dubbing councillor Joseph Downes, owner of a local bakery, a knight; the latter being promptly "elevated" to Lord Barmbrack by the Dublin wits. The Queen's death some months later prompted no letup in these political diversions in that the usual difficulties attended even the passing of an expression of regret to the royal family. But Her Majesty had the last laugh: her bronze statue on Leinster Lawn (erected in 1908 through Unionist subscriptions, though described as "the tribute of her Irish people") remained to taunt those nationalists who worried about such things, including after 1922 the deputies of Dail Eireann as they passed by to enter Leinster House.

Nevertheless, the pressure on the Corporation was maintained both within and without the chamber during 1900. In November, councillor John Clancy introduced another controversial motion—to confer the freedom of the city on Paul Kruger, President of the Transvaal. The police were on hand to record a scene that, according to the Chief Commissioner, "baffles description . . . for downright blackguardism it has no parallel. Between 40 and 50 young men entered the council chamber. When the Lord Mayor [Sir Thomas Pile] entered about 40 of them waved Boer and Green flags and cheered defiantly for Kruger. They used scurrilous language toward the Lord Mayor . . . it was discreditable to see the friendly way the hecklers were recognized by some members of the Council."[11] Clancy's proposal was ruled out of order but the clarion cry "three cheers for Kruger" rang in the Dublin wards for the duration of the Boer war, a constant taunt against those who accepted the finality of the imperial connection or sent their sons out in uniform to fight the Empire's battles.

The municipal elections of January 1901 afforded the electors the opportunity to pronounce on all these actions of their municipal representatives. The issue at stake, as the *Freeman's Journal* explained, was simply "flunkeyism versus nationality" and the "reconquest of the mayoralty" by Dublin Castle (a reference to the baronetcy accepted by Sir Thomas Pile). John Dillon, MP, clarified the issue in a speech to the electors of Arran Quay ward: "Nationalists of the Ward would strike a blow for the old cause and teach the flunkeys who had disgraced Dublin and the Municipal Council that they had no business to look for the suffrage of Nationalists. . . . For the future, if British ministers or the heads of English governments desired a welcome in Dublin they must come here with the charter of Irish liberty in their hands." And Lord Mayor Harrington echoed these sentiments at a UIL branch meeting in the following October: "If any man imagined that he, in taking up the office of Lord Mayor, would for a moment lay aside his political convictions and opinions, that man . . . should not vote for him."[12] Thus the recently won Nationalist unity was broken locally when "loyal addressers" found themselves under attack from their offended colleagues. The municipal voters were more indulgent, however, for of the six offenders (including two Unionists) seeking reelection only one lost and he the Labour candidate in Inns' Quay ward—a victory for the "flunkeys." Pile himself won a crushing victory over his opponent even though he had lately been described as the "best abused man in Dublin," having endured mob attacks on his inaugural procession as Lord Mayor in the previous year. A lone candidate in North City ward who ran on the republican and nationalist principles of James Connolly also suffered defeat.

Events such as these were a natural diversion in the otherwise dull routine of municipal politics and, of course, their repercussions had the greatest force at election time. And there was no letup in opportunities to assert the claim to exclusiveness in either nationality or religion. Thus, the accession of a King whose coronation oath obliged him to make insulting references to Roman Catholicism provoked further diversions. When the Corporation inevitably took umbrage at this, a formal objection from that body won tribute from Cardinal Logue, Primate of Ireland, but failed to impress the more politically astute Dr. William Walsh, Catholic Archbishop of Dublin, who reminded the city fathers in a letter read in the council chamber that their time could be more profitably spent on such vital questions as the educational, economic, national, and religious grievances of the Irish people.[13] The new King also failed to secure municipal representation at his coronation ceremony. Furthermore, when it was announced that Edward VII and his Queen intended to visit the Irish capital more protests were heard. The King tactfully postponed the trip until the war against the Boers was over, but his arrival in July 1903 produced no loyal address of welcome from the Corporation. Indeed, the wildest scenes were enacted in the council chamber when the usual resolution to present such an address was proposed: nationalists were always on hand in the crowded gallery for these challenges to national fervor. The complication this time was that John Redmond, who had just won a momentous land purchase act from a Conservative ministry, had expressed a wish that the Irish nation welcome their royal highnesses. Lord Mayor Harrington, Redmond's colleague at Westminster and one who had opposed the Queen's visit three years earlier, was at a loss to avert dissension among Nationalist councillors on the second attempt in as many weeks to pass the controversial resolution, the first having ended in uproar: "My chief hope is now in the Pope," he wrote to Redmond of the ailing Leo XIII. "If he dies before Monday we will have another adjournment," consequently enabling more pious considerations to intrude and the avoidance of further embarrassment. Neither, presumably, did Harrington as Lord Mayor wish to incur the odium that had been heaped on Lord Mayor Pile for his loyal action in 1900 on the occasion of the old Queen's visit. His Holiness failed to oblige, however, and the King lost his welcome by three votes—37 to 40—in a decision that saw Nationalists arrayed on each side along with Unionist (pro) and Labour (con) supporters. Harrington felt constrained to cast a safe vote with the majority but not so another prominent member, ex-Lord Mayor Dan Tallon, who was ejected by the voters at the subsequent municipal elections for his expressed loyalty to the Crown on this occasion. When His Majesty returned in the following year to lay the foundation stone of the new College of Science and indulge in the sport of kings at Punchestown, Leopardstown, and Phoenix Park, he was again ignored by the Corporation.

The acrimony among the Nationalists attendant upon these events did nothing to weaken their common control of the Corporation or allow any but a supporter of the United Irish League to hold the office of Lord Mayor. They could always depend on the support of voters (or perhaps on their apathy, since less than half of those eligible voted in most wards) to give them comfortable majorities of two-thirds or more in the council. Nationalist candidates were also assured of the powerful influence of the Catholic clergy at election time, especially if it was to protect the wards from socialist infiltrators, as became necessary in North City (1901, 1902, 1903), North Dock (1903), Wood Quay (1902, 1903) and Royal Exchange (1905) wards. James Connolly, who reportedly denounced the voters of Wood Quay as "priest ridden," found it tough going there in his unsuccessful bids for ward councillor, having to brave not only clerical denunciation but the threats of Nationalist thugs specially imported for duty at the hustings. And woe betide the dissident Nationalist who canvassed Unionist support, as witness the "charges" against councillor R.J. Dodd—the "loyal addresser" of Wood Quay ward—when he ran for reelection in 1903. "He had sought the support of Jews and Loyalists," declared the Reverend M'Gough, "and that was quite enough to urge them [the voters] to see that he got as few votes as possible."[14] He ran a poor second to the UIL candidate, only 15 votes ahead of Connolly.

A considerably more serious threat to the hegemony of the United Irish League was the rise of the Sinn Fein party after 1905. Long before the movement known as Sinn Fein attained national prominence after 1916, small groups operating under the aegis of Cumann na nGaedheal were at work at the local level in Ireland to further the goals of economic self-sufficiency and national self-reliance promoted at the turn of the century by Arthur Griffith.* The chief distinguishing mark of Sinn Fein was its insistence on the necessity of Irish parliamentary representatives withdrawing from Westminster preparatory to establishing a de facto political independence for the country. Hence, the practical knowledge of self-government to be gained in county and county borough councils would not be lost on those who hoped to realize the larger aims of the movement. As the so-called premier representative institution of Irishmen, the Dublin Corporation was a natural sounding board for those more voluble Irish Irelanders of Cumann na nGaedheal, the precursor of the Sinn Fein League. Before 1906 those associated with the movement had been content merely to transmit resolutions of various kinds for consideration by the municipal council: a protest against the "disgraceful" conduct of English soldiers in their nightly parading of Dublin's main thoroughfares; a request for the greater use of the Irish language, and such. In January 1906, however, Sinn Fein contested its first municipal election in Dublin and returned four candidates to join with five erstwhile Nationalists who now also identified themselves with the new political party. Among these were included Alderman Thomas Kelly, thenceforth the movement's leading spokesman in the council chamber, and councillor John T. Kelly (Sean T. O Ceallaigh), a member of the secret Irish Republican Brotherhood and a future president of an Irish republic. It was Alderman Kelly who consigned the Union Jack to the River Liffey at the inauguration of the city's main drainage in September 1906 and withdrew from the ceremony along with several colleagues rather than remain to toast the King.

Though numbering only nine members, the Sinn Fein party was now the second largest in the council, ahead of the Unionist party and the small group of Labour members sponsored by the Dublin Trades Council. The expressed antipathy of the Sinn Feiners to slum landlords and political bossism as well as the spirited nationalist sentiments of men like Thomas Kelly won the support of nationalist-minded laborite councillors. In fact, over the next few years Sinn Fein openly commended the names of several Labour members to the local electorate, with the result that well-known individuals such as Richard O'Carroll, general secretary of the Brick and Stonelayers' Society, and P. T. Daly, organizer for Jim Larkin's Transport and General Workers' Union, ran for election under the Sinn Fein banner. All this may have been as confusing to the voters as the UIL tactic of describing some of their own nominees as expressing both Nationalist and Labour viewpoints that, after all, were no more (and perhaps even less) incompatible than the various

---

*The same idea of self-reliance, including the English form of the slogan Sinn Fein (i.e., "Ourselves Alone"), was given poetic expression at a much earlier date in one of those patriotic ballads that became the stock-in-trade of the *Nation*:

> The work that should to-day be wrought, defer not till to-morrow,
> The help that should within be sought scorn from without to borrow.
> Old maxims these, yet stout and true, they speak in trumpet tone
> To do at once what is to do, and trust Ourselves Alone.

Quoted in C. G. Duffy, *Young Ireland* (New York, 1881), p. 165.

opinions on social and economic questions of Sinn Fein. Arthur Griffith, as mentor of Sinn Fein, deeply distrusted Larkin's brand of "new unionism" and came in for much abuse from the *Irish Worker* in 1911 during the great railway strike. Nevertheless, the alliance of Labour and Sinn Fein held in the municipal council, mainly because of the proletarian instincts of Alderman Tom Kelly, who was himself secretary of the Workmen's Hall in York Street.

The social standing of the Sinn Fein members was decidedly petty bourgeois, including among their number at various times a fruit merchant, coal merchant, electrical contractor, harness maker, publican, cab and car proprietor, newspaper manager, accountant, retired teacher, and grocery manager (W. T. Cosgrave, the future prime minister of an Irish Free State). But what really divided these forces was support for the program of the Irish parliamentary party in furthering Irish nationalism. The majority UIL faction generally gave unwavering support to John Redmond and his colleagues in the Irish party, whereas Sinn Fein wholly distrusted that party. When Sinn Fein requested the use of the Mansion House for a public meeting in September 1907, Lord Mayor Joseph Nannetti refused the request on the grounds that such a gathering would attack the party of which he, as MP for Dublin's College Green Division, was a member. In the council itself in the same year a resolution was introduced requesting that the Corporation urge the support of the Irish people for the general principles of the Sinn Fein movement; it lost 31 votes to 14.[15] In this latter as in most divisions in the council, the Labour members voted with Sinn Fein. Alderman Kelly contested the mayoralty on four occasions, losing each time. On another occasion (in 1908) the Sinn Fein party went so far as to support the candidacy of the Unionist Alderman F. Vance rather than the nominee of the UIL, a symptom of nationalist disarray that had not been witnessed since the mayoral election of 1897, when anti-Parnellites voted with Unionists in a vain attempt to oust the incumbent Parnellite Lord Mayor. Occasionally this mutual hostility in the ranks of Irish nationalists resulted in open fighting, as witness the wild scene attending a Sinn Fein motion of no confidence in the Irish party at a council meeting of June 14, 1909, when the diminutive John T. Kelly led the assault on behalf of the Irish Irelanders.

Sinn Fein, however, was winning more notoriety than support. In the four municipal elections of 1907 to 1910, the party either ran or endorsed 11, 9, 7, and 9 candidates, respectively, in contests and won only 4, 3, 4, and 2 seats, among which were 2 nominal Labour representatives. The year 1910 was a depressing one for the party, since it marked the beginning of the decline that saw the number of Sinn Fein council members reduced from 12 to 4 over the next three years, after which the party ceased even to present new candidates for election.[16] In that year 7 nominees (including P. T. Daly) lost to Nationalists of the UIL. A special meeting of Sinn Fein was held in Dublin a few days after the January election to review this sorry performance. It was easily enough explained as a reaction in favor of the Irish parliamentary party and its supporters following the Prime Minister's promise of home rule in his Albert Hall speech in December 1909, just weeks before the general election. But Alderman Kelly was more pessimistic, ascribing the failure of his colleagues to the "prostitution" of the franchise (reportedly float loads of whiskey and porter were in profusion) and describing his eleven years in the council as a waste of time. He advised his colleagues to withdraw from the Corporation (an austere interpretation of the Sinn Fein principle!) in order to conduct a more useful national propaganda.[17] More level-headed opinions prevailed and the Sinn Fein contingent remained, though sorely reduced in numbers, to maintain the pin-pricking policy of "insulting" royalty on every occasion. They alone refused to add their names to an expression of sympathy voted to the royal family on the death of Edward VII in 1910. In the following year they were more in tune with both public and official opinion in refusing an address of welcome to the new King and Queen on their visit to Ireland in July. Although George V was the first monarch to remove the offensive clause in the coronation oath that damned the Catholic mass as superstitious and idolatrous, this action was not enough for those who deemed His Majesty's government lax on the question of home rule. The days preceding the visit saw continuing demonstrations by republican elements of a kind that had not been seen since the hectic early days of the Boer War eleven years before. Only Lord Mayor J.J. Farrell (alderman of Mountjoy ward and one who opposed Queen Victoria's visit in 1900) announced his intention of conveying to the King the thanks of the Catholics of Dublin, though, tactically, he did so in the security of the Coombe Hospital rather than as traditionally at Leeson Street Bridge. This action incurred so much hostility from the militants that Farrell had to attend the unveiling of the Parnell monument later in the year under police protection. It did not, however, prevent his reelection as alderman in 1914. But no one challenged the response of the Catholic hierarchy at Maynooth, where Cardinal Logue, Archbishop Walsh, and the assembled bishops (with the notable absence of O'Dwyer of Limerick) offered the King a royal welcome.

As the political fortunes of Sinn Fein sagged, those of Labour were in the process of being revitalized by James Larkin's special brand of syndicalism, first with the "capture" of the Dublin Trades Council then followed by the establishment of an independent Labour party to contest the local elections.[18] Between 1899 and 1905 the Labour representatives, as Arthur Griffith remarked, had allowed themselves to be "nobbled" by the Nationalists, with few candidates being offered for election and the support of the Labour Electoral Association sometimes tendered to sympathetic Nationalists. The great hopes (or fears, rather) of inroads by the working classes into the political process with the enlarged franchise of 1899 never materialized. After 1905 all but one (Alderman Doyle of Rotunda ward, the only surviving nominee of the L.E.A. in 1899) of the few Labour members became merely the tail of the Sinn Fein party in the council. Before the January 1912 election only two Labour members remained—O'Carroll of the Brick and Stonelayers' Society, a Larkin supporter, and Alderman Doyle, who as a laborite of the old school might just as well be classified as a Nationalist. To these were now added four Larkinites (including Larkin himself) and the maverick Labour councillor from New Kilmainham ward, John Saturnus Kelly of the Irish Railway Workers' Union. Though this advance only put Labour back where it had been in 1899 in terms of numbers, at least there was little chance that the five Larkinites would be "nobbled." Larkin's activities since he had arrived in Ireland as a trade union organizer in 1907 left the employers in no doubt that the Irish labor movement had acquired a militancy and direction it had never before possessed. Likewise, it became evident to Irish politicians, more especially those at the local level, that a new political threat to their supremacy had been born, one that was soon to materialize formally with the creation of an Irish Labour Party under the aegis of the Irish Trades Union Congress.

Thus in 1912, for the first time in several years, the Nationalists found themselves under attack in wards (Merchants' Quay, North Dock, South Dock, Wood Quay) where they virtually reigned supreme. The election was also notable for the appearance of the first woman candidate for municipal office, Miss Sarah Harrison (portrait painter, friend of the unemployed, and tireless promoter of the Municipal Art Gallery), whom the Nationalists wisely left alone to defeat her Unionist rival. Larkin himself achieved the distinction of inflicting a crushing defeat to the incumbent UIL councillor in North Dock ward while his colleague J. Bohan accomplished an even greater feat in chasing his UIL opponent (Joseph Hutchinson, a Nationalist councillor who had served uninterruptedly since 1891) from Merchants' Quay ward. But it would take more than these victories to endanger the supremacy of the UIL and have social reforms in housing the working classes or feeding necessitous schoolchildren proceed at a pace other than that set by the Nationalist majority. Larkin's strident voice in the council chamber was stilled after barely six months of his ordinary three-year tenure of office—pursued by enemies who used his earlier conviction on charges arising out of a labor dispute in Cork as grounds for his disqualification.[19] However, by-elections in 1912 and the municipal election of the following January brought added strength to the Labour contingent, though at nine members even its alliance with Sinn Fein could present no more than thirteen votes to the Nationalists' fifty-five. Besides, six Labour nominees were defeated, a larger number than had actually won. And, also, the terrible labor unrest of 1913 (see Chapter 8, below) was now rallying both the enemies of Labour and those erstwhile neutral observers for whom the travail of the unemployed seemed less serious to the prosperity of the city than the vast disruption of trade and industry. It was in this year as well that the right of free access to the council chamber during the ordinary sittings of the council (a right that had often been abused in the past, especially when loyal addresses were under consideration) was denied: henceforth visitors would require a pass from a member of the council to gain admission.

Neither did the admitted socialist proclivities of Larkin and Connolly render the clergy neutral in the municipal contests. Labor agitators canvassing the Mountjoy ward, for example, were fair game for the curates at the pro-Cathedral who supported Lord Mayor Sherlock in the 1914 election by damning his Larkinite opponent as a member of "the motley crew of dangerous lunatics . . . socialists, syndicalists, Orangemen, suffragettes, decadent poets and armchair philanthropists." Elsewhere, voters were advised to join ranks to "smash Larkinism" and keep out the "poisonous doctrines of Robert Blatchford and Karl Marx," references perhaps that may have presumed too much on the intelligence of the average voter. Nevertheless, such diatribes by lay and clerical supporters of Nationalist candidates, especially in the aftermath of the violence and turmoil of recent months, were not without effect. Of the fourteen Labour candidates (including the socialist Walter Carpenter) in 1914, only two were successful and one of these (H. Donnelly, of New Kilmainham ward) was disqualified some months later for nonattendance at council meetings: he had to leave Dublin to seek work in Glasgow. Though several laborites made a good showing against heavy odds—six lost by only 200 votes or less—the pattern of defeat had been set and was repeated in the municipal elections of the following year, the last before the exigencies of war abroad and rebellion at home froze electoral politics for the next five years.

The municipal council was throughout a rather stable institution. Between 1899 and 1915 inclusive, 38 (63 percent) of the 60 seats representing the "old city" wards (i.e., excluding the added areas) were each held by no more than three individuals. These included 11 seats each represented by two members and 8 by only one member. As already

TABLE 7. Dublin Corporation: Political Affiliation of Council Members, 1899–1914.

AFFILIATION	1899		1902		1905		1908		1911		1914	
	no.	%	no.	%	no.	%	no.	%	no.	%	no.	%
Nationalist	45	75.0	58	72.5	65	81.2	55	68.7	61	76.2	56	70.9
	(note 1)											
Unionist	7	11.7	16	20.0	8	10.0	9	11.3	10	12.5	5	6.3
Labour	8	13.3	5	6.2	7	8.8	5	6.3	2	2.5	9	11.4
Sinn Fein	—		—		—		11	13.7	5	6.3	4	5.1
Independent	—		1	1.3	—		—		2	2.5	5	6.3
(note 2)												
Total	60		80 (note 3)		80		80		80		79 (note 4)	

NOTE 1. Includes (1899 only) Parnellites elected on separate ticket from Nationalist candidates supported by the United Irish League.

NOTE 2. Independents were never numerically large and did not exceed in any year the number reached in 1914. Though politically neutral in local politics, they sometimes demonstrated their Nationalist proclivities on such issues as support for Home Rule.

NOTE 3. The council was increased to 80 members in 1901 to accommodate representatives from areas annexed to the city under the Boundaries Act, 1900.

NOTE 4. One council seat vacant during 1914.

indicated, half of the members elected to the new county borough council in 1899 had served in the old restrictive chamber, some of them (Sir Robert Sexton; Aldermen Flanagan, Lenehan, Meade; councillors Brown, Burke, Kennedy, Kernan, Little, Macnie, O'Meara) for ten years or more. The record for the longest tenure was held by Alderman Flanagan, Nationalist member for Usher's Quay ward, whose name first appeared in the list of members in 1884 and remained there until 1919. A few wards resisted all attempts at penetration by other than Nationalist candidates, viz., Arran Quay, Fitzwilliam (after 1904), Mountjoy (after 1905), and South Dock. The 4 seats in two other wards (Merchants' Quay and North City) were never manned by fewer than three Nationalist members; and North Dock, Usher's Quay, and Wood Quay wards retained their Nationalist majorities for all but two of the seventeen years. Only the Unionists could boast of this kind of ward hegemony—for a few years in South City (1899 to 1902) and for much of the period in the two Clontarf wards. Sinn Fein could show this kind of strength only in Mansion House ward, where the party held all 4 seats in 1906 and maintained a majority there with the aid of a pro-Sinn Fein Labour member for the next four years. Labour likewise proved to be no threat to Nationalist ascendancy: the party failed to make any showing in 7 wards (Arran Quay, Clontarf East and West, Drumcondra, Fitzwilliam, Glasnevin, South City) and never held more than 2 seats in any ward except for 3 in New Kilmainham, a predominantly working-class district, during 1913 and 1914.

Thus, the Nationalists were at all times the controlling element in municipal politics, reserving to themselves the Lord Mayoralty as well as dominating those various committees manned by council members who determined the nature and extent of the annual expenditure of city revenue. This is not to imply that the Nationalist majority always operated as a solid front against their political opponents. Most of the Corporation's business was happily free of party posturing; otherwise the interests of citizens in the promotion of good government and proper management would have been ill served. Even on those occasions when one might have expected a closing of the ranks—a royal visit, an Imperial "difficulty," a coronation—allegiance, as we have seen, could be

TABLE 8. Dublin Municipal Council: Number of Members and Years in Office, 1899–1915 (Note 1).

MEMBERS SERVING AS:	UP TO 1 YR.	OVER 1 AND UP TO 2 YRS.	OVER 2 AND UP TO 3 YRS.	OVER 3 AND UP TO 6 YRS.	OVER 6 AND UP TO 9 YRS.	OVER 9 AND UP TO 12 YRS.	OVER 12 AND UP TO 15 YRS.	OVER 15 YRS.
Councillors only	25	35	40	49	28	9	4	2
Aldermen only	1	4	5	10	3	1	2	3
Councillors and Aldermen	—	1	—	3	5	9	3	4
Total (246 members)	26	40	45	62	36	19	9	9

NOTE 1. Councillors (3) and alderman (1) elected for each of 15 "old city" wards, 1899–1915, and for 5 wards in added areas, 1901–1915.

NOTE 2. Councillors normally served for a three-year term, retiring one at a time in each ward in successive years. To facilitate this rotation (since the entire council of 60 members was elected anew in 1899), the councillor with the lowest number of votes in the 1899 election in each ward served for one year only and the councillor with the next greater number for two years only before retiring or presenting themselves for reelection in the ordinary manner.

NOTE 3. Aldermen normally served for six years, with those from the northern and southern wards retiring alternately every three years. To facilitate this rotation system, those aldermen elected for the northern wards in 1899 served for three years only before either retiring or presenting themselves for reelection. Aldermen elected for the first time in 1901 for the wards of the added areas served until the 1905 aldermanic elections.

swayed. True, a resolution in support of the home rule program of John Redmond was always sure of passing the council, but the Nationalist ranks could divide on such issues as Labour's concern for the workingman or Sinn Fein's regard for the use of the Irish language. The Nationalist councillors, as the majority, became the butt of most of the criticism directed against the Corporation both inside and outside the council chamber. The Unionist members blamed them for manifesting the "exclusive spirit" that shut themselves out from all offices of honor, including the mayoralty and shrievalty. The nominees of the Labour Electoral Association, as good patriots, were decidedly less critical of their Nationalist colleagues, but even after the infusion of Larkinism in 1912, the Labour members, few as they were, could do little beyond urging the general cause of trade unionism and seeking to keep before the council the urgent needs of the working classes for better and cheaper housing. Sinn Fein, as self-styled standard bearers of a true Irish nationalism, were less indulgent of their Nationalist competitors, but their voice too soon faded, too weak to reshape the nationalist character of the council to accord with their own notions of self-government or to prevent such formal obeisances to the British notion of Irish self-government as a vote of thanks to John Redmond for his "securing" a Home Rule Act. Not until 1920 did Sinn Fein destroy the hegemony of the United Irish League in local politics and then under those changed political circumstances that two years earlier had resulted in a similar rout of Nationalist candidates at the general election.

Outside the Corporation, criticism also came from all sides and was less restrained. The *Irish Times*, the acknowledged voice of Unionism in Dublin (and, incidentally, the best newspaper in Ireland), was the most persistent critic and detractor, continually inveighing against the Corporation as a political debating society and an arena of jobbery and intrigue. And not a little of its anger was directed against those Unionist businessmen and professionals who instead of lending their competence and expertise to the work of City Hall "made their homes in the suburbs and allowed themselves to be represented by the councillor who secured the vote of the resident porter who polished the name plates on their city doors," deterred (so the paper explained) by the stormy confrontations, often descending to fist fights, in the council and by the political basis of decisions. It was James Connolly who took occasion to refer publicly to the political "corruption" prevailing in the capital whereby "persons were exploiting the working classes and making money by shouting Home Rule."[20] At another extreme, Bishop O'Dea of Galway (a Roman Catholic) warned his flock in 1911 that much abuse of power and the use of religious and political considerations attended the work of municipal bodies in Ireland.[21] Whether or not he had Dublin in mind, it is fair however to state that Dublin Corporation could hardly have operated on a more sectarian basis than, say, the "Orange" Corporation of Belfast. Every instance of mismanagement was used in the larger political arena by opponents of home rule as evidence that Irishmen were unfit to rule themselves. Unionist MPs in particular delighted to regale the Commons with tales out of school concerning municipal affairs in Dublin, such as accusing the city fathers of filling vacancies with ticket-of-leave men or, as the egregious Colonel Saunderson once claimed, making one individual an inspector of weights and measures for firing at a policeman![22]

The Corporation was also beset by various pressure groups, both nonpolitical and political, whose claims could not always be met. The Gaelic League harried the city council on behalf of the Irish language, promoting street names and bilingual signposts (usually successfully) and Irish as a necessary qualification for public appointments (unsuccessfully). Temperance groups decried the number of councillors associated with the drink traffic. The Irish Women's Franchise League, when not mindful of their political interests, took the time to champion the cause of free school meals for necessitous children *and* thrifty expenditure of the rates. The most assiduous watchdog committee after 1908 was the Dublin Citizens Association, which was supported by the city's largest ratepayers and numbered representatives from the biggest business establishments (Clery's, Switzer's, Arnott's, Dockrell's, and the like). Fiscal irresponsibility and high rates were its chief targets, but it also campaigned for municipal reform through the election of "men of substance" to the council. Finding the latter a vain quest, however, it finally settled for offering its sponsorship to any candidate who would subscribe to its program, which was sufficiently civic-minded to offend few and thereby attract candidates from all the political factions. The Association principally used its powerful voice—an echo, some thought, of the doughty Dublin entrepreneur W. M. Murphy—to preach the one civic duty it considered essential for a municipal councillor: Keep Down the Rates!

High municipal taxation was the most consistent single criticism leveled against the Corporation. And, indeed, it was high, higher generally than the poundage rates levied in such cities as Belfast, Birmingham, Bristol, Liverpool, and others. Little wonder then that the city fathers should be extremely circumspect about undertaking improvements and assuming long-term liabilities of any kind. In the years 1901 to 1913, the total (North) city rate never varied by more than 10 percent and in the latter year, when it stood at 9s. 10d., was at the lowest level of the entire period. Since high rates were regarded as the result of extravagance and mismanagement, the salaries paid to officials and workmen of Dublin Corporation inevitably came under suspicion. Doubtless this was the reaction of despair and frustration from those whose consciences would not allow them to point instead to the annual charges incurred as a result of municipal housing ventures. But the Corporation itself was a fairly effective monitor of wages and salaries inasmuch as all increases and adjustments came before the council for discussion. The rare occasions that saw Unionist and Sinn Fein members voting together were attempts to deny salary increases to officials and workmen. Resolutions were presented almost annually (most often by Alderman M'Walter) asking for cutbacks or postponement of salary and wage increases. In 1908 one such resolution asking for postponement of increases until a rate of 9s. 6d. (not enjoyed since 1898 and not ever again) could provide for them passed the council by a large majority. Fortunately, the resolution never went into effect, but considering that it would have meant some hardship for such lowly paid employees as library assistants and nurses, it is surprising to find the names of laborite councillors among the majority.[23] The handful of higher officials (town clerk, city treasurer, borough surveyor, law agent, comptroller, city architect, executive sanitary officer) were certainly generously paid (ranging from £750 to £2,000 per annum), as they were in Belfast, but otherwise the salary lists show little evidence of the kind of extravagance imputed to the Corporation. A comparison of salaries issued by the Local Government Board in 1901 reveals that both Dublin and Belfast had about the same proportion of officers in the various salary ranges. And as the lists indicate, the great majority of clerks earned less than £200 per annum: in 1916 for example, 75 percent were in this range in Dublin, whereas only about 6 percent earned £500 or above. The total salary account in 1902 was £36,000 (equivalent to about

11d. in the £ on assessed valuation) for some 140 officials and clerical employees. Fourteen years later, under the stress of greatly expanded city services and in response to increases in the cost of living, the corresponding figure was only £65,000 (equivalent to 1s. 4d. in the £) for about 400 salaried workers. Even though the Corporation's total annual revenue had changed but slightly in the meantime, the foregoing hardly suggests a wanton disregard for the fiscal conservatism of the taxpayers. As for the Corporation workmen, it was not likely that their wages were anything above the low remuneration prevailing for skilled and unskilled labor.

There were some "abuses" of course. An investigation by the Local Government Board in 1902 revealed certain aspects of administration, benevolent though lax, that greatly angered the ratepayers. In one instance some Corporation departments, as the newspapers informed their readers, had "kept the blind and lame upon the books at full pay for years after they ceased to be efficient." Actually, what was being condemned as squandering of the rates was the humanitarian response of an employer (the Corporation) to the inadequacies of the social system. In the absence of a pension scheme for Corporation workmen (one was not instituted until 1899), keeping a few old men "on the books" at least ensured that a lifetime of service found some reward. Yet the Lord Mayor (for the ultimate responsibility was charged to the council itself) felt constrained to agree with critics that "the facts revealed . . . were little short of a scandal."[24]

The Local Government Board, overseer for the government of the operations of all locally elected bodies in Ireland, also had the responsibility of conducting periodic audits of Corporation receipts and expenditures, a mandate that not infrequently produced some bitterness between the parties involved. In 1906, for example, the Corporation defied the board's auditor and refused to produce its books for his perusal in retaliation against that same auditor's previous criticisms of the Corporation's allegedly wasteful ways. This action was subsequently upheld in the courts, though on a technicality. Not unnaturally, Irish nationalists regarded such activities by a department of Dublin Castle as forced subjection to the scrutiny of a controlling body that was unrepresentative of Irish public opinion. And the scrutiny could hardly have been closer, as witness the trivial sums disallowed by the auditor for expenditures that did not meet with his approval. In 1907 surcharges were made against those councillors who in the normal course of their work on committees had authorized small grants to such worthy causes as Feis Ceoil, the Dublin Orchestral Society, and vocal competitions in the city's primary schools, charges that, happily, were remitted on appeal. A councillor was once surcharged twenty shillings for money he had repaid to a citizen who had humanely arranged to have a dying man brought to a hospital. In 1909 over 30 members and ex-members of the council were proceeded against for the recovery of £26 15s. 6d.[25] Similar action was taken, of course, against any offending local body, such as against the Guardians of the city's workhouses when they purchased coal at excessive cost (the auditor recovering the excess over the market price) or in a flush of generosity supplied porter to the paupers!

A favorite theme of some critics was the jobbery and corruption alleged to prevail in the Corporation and its departments. There is little hard evidence of this, but it seems fair to suppose that the jobbery and nepotism endemic to municipal administration were no worse and, given the moderate resources of the Corporation, probably less common than in other large municipal governments in the United Kingdom. Alderman M'Walter, tireless crusader for a host of civic improvements ranging from public lavatories for women to municipal milk depots for babies, attempted in 1912 to call a halt to political patronage by proposing that "no son or daughter, brother or sister" of any member be eligible for appointment to any post in the service of the Corporation unless by open competition. He was ruled out of order by the Lord Mayor and heard his motion denounced as "an insult to the Corporation and a reflection on Dublin."[26] True, a perusal of the salary lists discloses a Cameron as water analyst, a Cotton as Inspector, a Nannetti as an attendant, and *inter alios*, a Sherlock as a chief clerk. Yet however unseemly this may appear under present-day standards of municipal probity, it was hardly unusual or unexpected then for men who were devoting their time to public service to promote the honest claims of family members or close relatives for municipal appointments when opportunities were few and the most naked competition distinguished the job market. Whether one may claim, on the other hand, that Dublin Corporation was, to use Colonel Saunderson's acidulous phrase, a "Greenwich Hospital for nationalist wrecks" is another matter and certainly a gross exaggeration. But now that such statements can no longer "give comfort to the enemy," it may be allowed, at the risk of a pun, that the occasional misfit and party hack sometimes wound up in one or another of the wards.

Of official misconduct there was comparatively little, though from time to time the usual "vague and unsubstantiated charges" were current. One of the earliest allegations of bribery in the new borough council was levelled against two labor members in 1899 and arose out of the attempts by the London businessman, Saxe, to purchase the Corporation's monopoly of the electric lighting supply, which the two councillors were alleged to be furthering. The affair soon blew over and produced no more than the usual heated discussions in the council chamber.[27] Far more embarrassing than petty corruption was the sensational revelation at the Housing Inquiry in 1913 (see Chapter 5, below) that no fewer than sixteen members of the council (only one of them a Unionist) owned between them eighty-nine tenement and second-class houses. Among these were some of the most respected members of the Corporation, viz., Aldermen Downes, O'Reilly (Lord Mayor in 1908), Corrigan, and others. Five were aldermen, two having served in the council for over 20 years; five had served for 12 years or more; eleven had been reelected to office at least once. Such disclosures naturally appeared to justify the pillorying the Corporation had endured in the daily press over the years. Alas, there was no wave of voter indignation tha' would have sent the entire group packing at subsequent elections (although with the suspension of elections after 1915 only eleven would have had to face the voters). No fewer than six members were returned at subsequent elections (in 1914 and 1915), three of them unopposed. One of them ran successfully for alderman in the Rotunda ward only 3 weeks after the above disclosures while yet another defeated his laborite opponent for the councillorship in the same ward by two to one. Five others did not put themselves in the running, three of them through resignation. On one earlier occasion, however, the voters were not so indulgent; in 1907 councillor Parkinson of Mountjoy ward used his position as chairman of the Paving and Lighting Committee to make orders favorable to his own stone contracting business. He lost his bid for alderman in 1908 and declined to stand for reelection as councillor in 1910.[28] Nevertheless, there was every chance in Dublin that an incumbent put his electoral survival in greater jeopardy by tipping his hat to royalty than in demonstrating disregard for the well-being of the citizens.

The chief duties of a municipal body are threefold—to maintain order, conduct honest and good government, and promote the welfare of the citizens. The first, as we know, did not lie within the jurisdiction of Dublin Corporation. The second has been briefly treated above. In the third area of activity, the Corporation may be said to have been found wanting. Here a choice could be made—whether to indulge the minority of middle-class ratepayers by municipal thrift or make a frontal assault on poverty and poor housing accommodation by recourse to loans, public works, and inevitably, increased rates. As far as public expenditure was concerned, three main considerations faced the Corporation: whether to apply the receipts of the improvement rate and the proceeds of loans to main drainage, electric lighting, or urban clearances. Obviously, if the city of Dublin were to advance as a modern municipality the Liffey could not remain an open sewer nor could the main streets remain poorly lighted. Moreover, expenditure on these works was far more acceptable to the class that was taxed than would have been attention to the housing needs of the class that was dismissed as "unproductive." The accounts of the Corporation and the annual reports of the Local Government Board disclose where the priorities lay: increased expenditure and loans for public lighting with, as the Corporation itself explained, "obvious advantages from the point of view of traffic, morality, and social security"; extension of the profitable electricity supply service, total expenditure on which was approaching £900,000 by 1916; completion of the expensive main drainage works; enlargement of the Roundwood reservoir capacity; extension and improvements in the Fire Brigade service; reclamation of the disgraceful sloblands at Clontarf; street paving and repair. Elsewhere, as a Corporation report of 1910 promised, the "most rigid economy" would be maintained.[29] The expensive urban clearances and building undertaken by the Corporation up to about 1904 to remove "plague spots" and dens of prostitution were to yield to caution and frugality. The electorate from the slums could be held at bay—at worst with floatloads of porter, at best with appeals to patriotism and the promise of a new era of prosperity under home rule. It was the "political" thing to do and, as the annual municipal elections demonstrated, it worked.

The catchphrase "Dublin has the worst municipal government in the world" was much heard during these years, a canard invented by the *Irish Times*, the most constant and vehement critic of Dublin Corporation. Dublin lacked a civic spirit, it was claimed, and the chief cause purportedly lay in the character of the municipal council—of publicans extending the influence of the drink traffic, slum landlords perpetuating the evils of society, and politicians forever shouting "Home Rule." Municipal reform, it was held, would bring to an end a long career of civic inefficiency and mismanagement by ridding the council of misfits and political hacks. But this was to ignore the realities of the historical background, economic development, and contemporary political life, themes explored in some detail throughout this study. Local government in Dublin, as elsewhere in John Bull's Other Island, was fated to acquire the political coloration that defied any efforts of nonpolitical reformist elements to gain influence, though what these might have done "in the face of difficulties little dreamed of in English municipalities"* could not have promised any early solution of the city's manifold civic and social problems. But even opponents might have admitted that the municipality had endeavored to keep pace

*A singular phrase that introduced the section on Dublin in the *Municipal Year Book of the United Kingdom* from 1904 onward.

with the rest of the world in providing the essential amenities of city life not only as regards pure water and sewers, fire fighting and electricity supply, but also in the provision, however modest, of technical schools, public baths and food markets, children's parks and public libraries, and a gallery of art. The last word may be left to Lord Mayor Gallagher (neither publican nor slum landlord), whose spirited defense of the Corporation's achievements led him to recall how few great civic benefactors Dublin could boast (only Lords Ardilaun and Iveagh and Sir Hugh Lane came to mind) and wonder whether the alleged lack of civic spirit in Dublin should rather be "laid to wealthy classes whose numerous chateaux and spreading lawns, isolated by lofty walls, stud our environs."[30]

CHAPTER

4

Public Health

I know of no town that is comparable with Dublin from the point of view of the difficulties of its sanitary work . . . or that any other city presents such a condition of things.

PROFESSOR W. R. SMITH, President of the Royal Institute of Public Health, at the Dublin Public Health Inquiry, 1900

THE ACHIEVEMENTS of civilization are never more gratifying than when measured by improved standards of public health in cities and towns. In that context the appointment of the Registrar General for England and Wales in 1837 is more worthy of note than the accession of Queen Victoria in the same year. In 1837 the ravages of cholera were of recent memory in the United Kingdom and yet another fearsome visitation was due in the next decade. Though smallpox had already bowed to science, its toll of the unvaccinated in epidemic years gave cause for alarm. And typhus, typhoid fever, and tuberculosis, along with other communicable diseases that annually decimated the child population, continued to be an insidious drain on the national well-being. By the time of Victoria's death, however, typhus and cholera had been practically wiped out, the incidence of typhoid fever diminished to a fraction of its former virulence, and smallpox no longer any real threat. Several factors contributed to these beneficial results: the progress, naturally, of medical science; the humanitarian concern no less than the fear of epidemics that predisposed the middle classes to an invasion of both their liberty and privacy; the general betterment of living conditions and standards of personal and community hygiene; and, above all, the establishment of local sanitary boards, each under the supervision of a medical officer of health. The vital and pervasive activity of the boards is apparent from the powers that successive public health acts obligated them to exercise in such matters as water supply and sewerage; street cleansing and scavenging; refuse removal and disposal; inspection and abatement of nuisances; regulation of dairies, slaughter houses, workshops, and such; inspection of food for public consumption; erection of houses for the working classes; inspection of common lodging houses, tenements, and cellar dwellings; provision of baths and washhouses; control of infectious diseases; even the preventing of wakes.

The public health of the city of Dublin was supervised on behalf of the Corporation by that body's Public Health Committee. The establishment of the Committee in 1866, in the midst of a cholera epidemic that took the lives of nearly 1,200 citizens, was the first substantive step taken to bring the city into line with the sanitary improvements then being effected in the cities and towns of Great Britain. By the end of the century some notable improvements such as have already been alluded to had been made—particularly in the provision of the Vartry water supply, the reduction in the number of tenement houses, the general introduction of water closets, the virtual elimination of cellar dwellings, the halving of the number of slaughter houses within the confines of the city, and the improvements in refuse disposal. During this period also the Public Health Department had established a disinfecting facility at Marrowbone Lane, a temporary Refuge in Nicholas Street for contacts of fever and smallpox, and an isolation facility for smallpox victims at the Pigeon House Fort. Of more general use and benefit to the citizens were the Tara Street Baths and adjoining Washhouse opened in 1885. These became immensely popular, providing reclining baths for males and females (6d. for a first-class warm bath), two swimming pools, and a laundry facility (1d. per hour). Curiously enough, the Baths acquired an even greater significance for the city's tiny Jewish community (2,048 persons in 1901), when in 1897 the Corporation added special Plunge Baths to accommodate the *mikvah* ritual of Jewish women. Thereafter, three or four score females of the orthodox sect fulfilled their monthly obligation at Tara Street and in so doing demonstrated a personal cleanliness that from the standpoint of public health was the envy of the Health Committee, which observed that the Baths "appear to have a beneficial effect upon the procreativeness of the Jewish female, and goes far to account for her healthy offspring and the low infant mortality existing among the Hebrew community."[1] It is worth noting that when the Baths were closed for six weeks at the height of a water shortage in 1914, the ritual baths were made available for the sole use of these Jewish ladies. The various facilities at Tara Street were not free, however, admission fees being charged to all users. Similarly, at the only other Baths in the city, the Mendicity Institution on Usher's Quay, admission was also payable, a circumstance detrimental to the cleanliness of the Great Unwashed.

Mortality rates, whether of children or adults, were the standard by which the general public judged the effectiveness of the public health administration of the municipality. Despite more than thirty years of activity by the Health Committee, the annual death rate in 1899 was higher than it had been in any year since 1880. At 33.6 per thousand living (only slightly below Calcutta's), it exceeded that of any large city in Europe or the United States and compared to mortality in London, Edinburgh, Leeds, or Glasgow represented an annual waste of some 3,500 lives. As in 1879, when even higher rates were suffered, the appalling figures brought unwelcome recrimination from the press and public and phrases such as "the Dublin holocaust" and "terrible slaughter" were bandied about freely, much to the discomfiture of the Health Committee. The severest criticism came from the medical profession. Following a tradition established a quarter of a century earlier by the *Sanitary Record*, the *Lancet* appointed a special sanitation commissioner to report on the conditions that were wreaking such mortal havoc on the poor of the city. These "special commissioners" invariably chose to highlight in their reports the very worst conditions in some of the poorest quarters, judging perhaps that the more horrible the tale told the more anger generated and, consequently, the quicker the remedy. The stories related in *Lancet* between November 1899 and January 1900 were, as ever, most depressing: the "barbaric uncleanliness" of the people; the ill-regulated private slaughter houses that contaminated the air and subsoil, such as one found near St. Andrew's National School in Townsend Street, where "hundreds of children breathe the effluvia wafted to them from the hideous quagmire of blood and offal"; the dead-end courts used for defecation or prostitution; the alleys where refuse of every description accumulated and decomposed; the dark recesses in the hallways of filthy tenements that reeked of urine and fecal matter; and all about—"sordid misery, dilapidation and dirt."[2] The report might just as well have been a paraphrase of the dolorous litany of abominations offered to the readers of the *Sanitary Record* in 1876.

Such scenes of seemingly ineradicable degradation inevitably gave full rein to the prejudices most English observers had come to direct against the "filthy habits" of the Irish. An agricultural people brought up in small villages and rural districts, it was claimed, fail to comprehend in the city the mechanism of a water closet. In any event, the Irish were held to be more dirty than the English and, lest there be any misdirected imputation, the Protestant cleaner than the Roman Catholic. Was not Elliott's Home for Children (a Protestant institution in Townsend Street) an "oasis in the midst of its dreadful surroundings"? The truth of the matter of course, then as now, is that the poor of Dublin, like the poor of London or Glasgow or elsewhere, were in general "dirty" not because of race or religion but rather because they were forced by circumstances to exist in abject poverty, untouched for the most part by that consciousness of refinement, manners, taste, and bodily hygiene that material success must bring. These and other disclosures, however, did produce the expected official response—a lengthy inquiry into the state of public health in Dublin and the cause of the high death rate.

The committee appointed by the Local Government Board held public meetings at City Hall during February and March 1900.[3] Among those giving evidence were the Registrar General, medical officers of health and other members of the medical profession, town councillors, Corporation officers, representatives of philanthropic and reform bodies, and the clergy. One owner of tenement property was heard from, but no one spoke with the voice of the slums. All were cognizant that only twenty years before a Royal Commission had sat in the same council chamber to conduct a similar investigation into the sanitary condition of the city. The social circumstances then were certainly more daunting than those that marked the Dublin of 1900: better domestic scavenging, a reduction in the number of tenements, and the issuance of sanitary bylaws had effected considerable improvements. There was, however, little cause for congratulation. The committee felt obliged to confirm the conclusion arrived at earlier by the Royal Commission that the tenement houses of Dublin—overcrowded, dilapidated, dirty and ill-ventilated—were still the prime cause of the excessively high death rate. Other factors cited in 1879 as offensive to public health also reappear in the later investigation: defective house drainage to main sewers, slaughter houses and refuse dumps in residential areas, the continued sewage pollution of the Liffey. All this, in the opinion of the committee, tended to the "production of a state of lowered vitality favourable to the contraction of disease, and to fatal result when contracted." And, moreover, since mortality rates were the incontestable standard by which the healthiness of cities was measured, Dublin accordingly was the least healthy city in the United Kingdom (see Table 9). In comparing Dublin with London (chosen because its mortality approached closely the average death rate in 33

TABLE 9. Annual Death Rates (per 1,000 living) in Dublin and Selected Major Cities of the United Kingdom, 1899–1913 (note 1).

	1899	1901	1905	1907	1911	1913
Dublin County Borough	33.6	26.8	23.1	25.6	24.1	23.1
Dublin Registration Area (notes 2, 3)	29.7	24.5	21.2	23.1	21.4	20.1
Belfast County Borough	22.7	22.4	20.4	21.0	17.0	18.4
Birmingham	20.8	20.5	16.2	16.2	16.7	14.8
Bradford	19.4	16.8	15.2	14.8	15.1	15.1
Bristol	18.5	16.0	14.6	13.2	15.2	12.8
Leeds	20.6	19.3	15.2	15.3	16.5	15.5
Liverpool	25.6	22.3	19.6	19.0	20.2	18.2
London (Administrative county)	19.8	17.6	15.6	14.6	15.2	14.3
Manchester	24.6	22.1	18.0	18.1	17.1	15.8
Sheffield	21.3	20.4	17.0	17.1	16.1	15.8
Edinburgh	19.2	19.4	16.1	16.2	16.0	15.6
Glasgow	21.3	21.2	17.8	18.5	17.8	17.3

NOTE 1. Figures represent crude death rates as reported by the Registrars General. The usual *corrected* rates (i.e., adjusted to allow for differences of age and sex distribution with the general population) offer a somewhat better comparison between cities. In general, this adjustment yields an increase over the crude rate of between one and two full points for most cities, including Dublin.

NOTE 2. The Registration Area includes, in addition to the county borough, the suburban districts of Rathmines, Pembroke, Palmerston, Crumlin, Stillorgan, Blackrock, Kingstown, Finglas, Glasnevin, Coolock, Drumcondra, Clontarf and Howth.

NOTE 3. A contributing factor to Dublin's high mortality was its large population of sick, aged and infirm paupers. For example, of the 10,681 deaths in the Registration Area (pop. 349,000 in 1891) in 1899, 1,677 took place in the workhouses. Compare this with the number of workhouse deaths in English registration districts: Birmingham (pop. 245,000), 761; Bradford (pop. 216,000), 320; Bristol (pop. 289,000), 429; Leeds (pop. 223,000), 365.

SOURCE: *Parliamentary Papers:* Annual Reports of the Registrars General for Ireland, England and Wales, and Scotland.

large towns of England and Wales), the committee revealed the higher mortality in Dublin at *every* age period; almost three times greater for persons between 5 and 20 years and over twice as great for those between 20 and 35. Twenty years earlier these statistics were much more favorable to Dublin, an indication of the city's difficulties in attempting to emulate the gains made elsewhere in safeguarding the lives of the urban masses.

The germs of infectious disease had always existed in an evil alliance with poverty, malnutrition, dirt, and overcrowding. Perhaps one should also include ignorance of the kind that could only be banished by advances in medical knowledge. The science of bacteriology is only as old as Pasteur's investigations of the mid-nineteenth century; and the great leaps occurred only with the maturing genius of Koch, Ehrlich, and others in the closing decades of that century: the discovery of the genococcus as the cause of gonorrhea, of the bacilli causing influenza and dysentery, of an antitoxin against diphtheria. And not until the present century were the bacilli of scarlet fever and whooping cough isolated and a germ identified as the agent of syphilis. And surely no medical advance could have been as dramatic or welcome as Dr. Ehrlich's discovery of a specific remedy for syphilis (Salvarsan) in 1910. But only in the past generation have the newly developed toxoids and vaccines provided that degree of relative security from the horrors of communicable disease unknown to our less fortunate ancestors.[4] At the turn of the century, however, infectious and communicable diseases accounted for over one-third of all deaths in Dublin. The trend had become evident in the late nineteenth century and only improved slightly up to 1916, the proportion of deaths due to those causes in the latter year being one-quarter. The diseases contributing most to the high death rate of the city fell into three main categories: the zymotic diseases; tuberculosis in all its forms; and local diseases of the respiratory and circulatory systems. The concern of public health officers centered on the first two groups for these were, in theory, preventable diseases.[5] Dublin, like most cities, had been scourged by them for as long as one could remember: typhus, smallpox, scarlet fever, and cholera in the 1860s; smallpox and measles in the '70s; typhus and scarlet fever in the '80s; measles in the '90s; and in every year the constant drain of typhoid fever and tuberculosis.

The most virulent of the so-called preventable diseases, measured by the number of deaths caused, are indicated in Table 10. As can be seen, the diseases of childhood were the most prevalent in the zymotic category. In Dublin in 1899 and succeeding years, the principal epidemic diseases were measles, whooping cough, and diarrhea, the victims being almost invariably children under 5 years of age. Less fatal in impact generally, though still great killers of children, were scarlet fever and diphtheria. One should not infer from the table any particular predisposition in the children of Dublin to contracting, say, measles or the diarrheal diseases. The year 1899, for example, was an epidemic year for measles in the city (the second in 3 years and the last of such magnitude), and all large cities were affected from year to year to a greater or lesser degree depending on when and where epidemic struck. The city, however, compared very unfavorably in the case of diseases that mainly attacked adults over 25, namely, typhoid (or enteric) fever and tuberculosis. Also, through her very high rate of mortality (the highest of all the large towns and cities) Dublin maintained the unenviable reputation of being the unhealthiest city in the United Kingdom. In fact, the table makes the city seem less unsafe from the public health standpoint than it actually was, owing to the inclusion by the Registrar of the healthier suburban districts in the registration area. Death rates for the county borough averaged 7 percent higher in this period than the rates for the entire metropolitan area.

It will be realized that recorded deaths represent, to borrow George Rosen's striking phrase, merely "the tip of a vast ice-berg of ill health." For every fever death, ten or more nonfatal cases languished under the prostrating symptoms of typhus or typhoid. Scarlatina deaths reflected an even smaller fraction of the total cases treated. Nor could the "conspiracy of silence" surrounding venereal disease fail to hide that hospital deaths from syphilis and gonorrhea were, on the average, a mere 2 percent of the cases treated annually, a figure that, given the nature of the disease, is probably an understatement of the total number affected. Likewise, the extremely high rate of tuberculosis deaths in Dublin stood grim testimony to the lingering fate in store for countless thousands. The struggle of public health authorities to combat these and other communicable diseases did not depend entirely on the development of therapeutic drugs and vaccines. Dublin had early adopted the Infectious Disease (Notification) Act of 1889, which required sanitary officers to take appropriate action (disinfection, isolation, and so on) upon notification by attending physicians of the occurrence of certain epidemic diseases. The townships of Pembroke and Rathmines followed suit, but neighboring districts such as Blackrock and Kingstown did not adopt the Act until 1902 and 1905, respectively, a circumstance that meanwhile, in the opinion of the public health authorities, constituted a serious menace to the city. However, the poverty, overcrowding, defective sanitation, intemperance, and ignorance of ordinary hygiene that prevailed in the homes of the Dublin

TABLE 10. Deaths from Selected Causes in Dublin and Selected Major British Cities in 1899 (rates per 100,000 living).

REGISTRATION AREA	MEASLES	SCARLET FEVER	WHOOPING COUGH	DIPHTHERIA	DIARRHEA, ETC.	ENTERIC (TYPHOID) FEVER	TB (PHTHISIS)	OTHER TB
Dublin (city and suburbs)	186	14	43	17	142	52	368	218
Birmingham	58	11	30	25	161	29	207	66
Bradford	36	50	31	13	111	21	153	66
Bristol	14	4.5	43	11	118	12	161	63
Leeds	61	16	28	55	85	22	189	95
London (Admin. co.)	47	7.9	38	43	92	18	182	67
Lambeth borough	63	13	44	55	107	22	184	80
Sheffield	81	22	18	143	205	75	156	106
Edinburgh	30	19	73	18	67	16	214	106
Glasgow	83	31	50	16	85	27	221	98

SOURCES: Annual Reports of the Registrars General for Births, Deaths and Marriages in *Parliamentary Papers*: 1900 (XV), cd. 295 (Ireland); 1900 (XV), cd. 323 (England and Wales); 1901 (XVI), cd. 777 (Scotland). Rates calculated by author.

poor were a far greater source of evil than the stray infection that could be blamed on suburbanites. Nonetheless, statistics show a marked improvement in the public health of the city from 1899 onward. By 1916 the number of notifiable cases of infectious disease had been cut in half, with the greatest gains being made in the febrile category. The death rate had also been reduced, but at over 23 per 1,000 it was still at a scandalous figure and about 25 percent higher than the rates even in such large industrial centers as Birmingham, Leeds, Manchester, and Sheffield. Only Liverpool with its huge Irish population approached the Dublin figures. Moreover, long-standing evils in the form of infant mortality and rampant tuberculosis were resisting the best efforts of public and private health agencies.

TABLE 11. Infant Mortality: Deaths of Children Under One Year per 1,000 Live Births in Dublin and Selected Major Cities in the United Kingdom, 1899–1913.

	1899	1901	1905	1907	1911[a]	1913
Dublin County Borough	187	171	145	160	165	160
Dublin Registration Area (city and suburbs)	185	168	143	156	156	153
Belfast County Borough	159	154	136	136	128	144
Birmingham	191	187	154	147	164	129
Bradford	181	168	144	124	138	128
Bristol	158	131	122	100	141	96
Leeds	171	188	151	130	158	135
Liverpool	198	188	153	144	154	133
London (Administrative county)	167	149	131	116	128	106
Manchester	206	199	157	146	154	129
Sheffield	194	201	167	145	140	128
Edinburgh	176	148	133	127	118	101
Glasgow	172	150	131	130	139	129

[a] Figures uncharacteristically high for most cities in 1911 owing to epidemic diarrhea during the summer of that year.
SOURCE: *Parliamentary Papers*: Annual Reports of the Registrars General for Ireland, England & Wales, and Scotland.

Child mortality in general and infant mortality in particular were by far the most pressing problems of public health authorities in this period. Their influence on actuarial general life tables was clearly evident. At the turn of the century, a mean life expectancy of just under 49 years was promised a male child at birth, but at age five his mean future life time extended to his 61st year: not until he was well into his fifties could he expect to reach the biblical three-score-and-ten. Today, when congested American cities can achieve infant mortality rates of 20 (per 1,000 live births) or below, it is sobering to reflect that populous British cities as late as 1916 were rather fortunate to have rates as low as 89 (London), 111 (Glasgow and Belfast), and 116 (Liverpool). Others were less so, especially the Dublin metropolitan region, with its high rate of 153 per 1,000. Moreover, statistics revealed that excessive infant mortality implied excessive child mortality and correspondingly excessive mortality throughout adult life. Little wonder, therefore, that investigators should warn of "national inferiority" to counter the complacent argument that infant deaths were but nature's way of weeding out the unfit. For it was popularly held that the children of the working classes were "fine healthy little creatures," hardy enough to endure the physical demands of life in the slums. Doctors and undertakers knew better. The pneumonia wards of Dublin hospitals held more than their share of newsboys and other street-trading children from working-class homes whose miserable physiques and ill-clad bodies predisposed them to early death or frail adulthood. And more visible signs of "degeneration" were seen in the constant procession of "worn-out mothers dragging to and from hospitals week after week, stunted children in rags and variously diseased; and, on each return journey, to some dark, damp basement or other unsanitary dwelling, hugging a large bottle of medicine, gratefully believing that the science and charity of the twentieth century have done all that is possible for them and their offspring."[6] On the average in each year, one in three deaths was that of a child under five years, but in particular months, this rate could almost double. Observers were naturally appalled by the long line of funeral corteges that, at the worst of times, daily plied the route from the city to Glasnevin cemetery.

In assessing the causes of infant mortality, public health authorities could only offer very general conclusions.[7] In fact, well over a third of these deaths were officially classed as "wasting" diseases—the "atrophy, debility, marasmus" that concealed fatal diseases of varied origin attributable to congenital defects, premature birth, syphilis, as well as lack of pre- and post-natal care. Less than 10 percent of infant deaths would normally be traced to the common infectious agents of disease. Diarrhea, bronchitis, and pneumonia were by far the most dangerous ailments during the first year of life. Thus, the official view tended to direct attention to influences affecting mortality in general—poverty and social conditions, domestic and municipal sanitation, conditions of housing, the magnitude of the birth rate—while also stressing factors of more direct relevance, such as the age of the wife at birth, the quality of natal care, or the extra-domestic employment of mothers. Predictably, it was found that infant mortality was higher in urban than rural areas, high among the poor and low among the well-to-do, highest in the most densely populated wards in any given town. Other factors alluded to included the abandonment of breast feeding and the unavailability of sterilized milk supplies. Popular belief added less reliable explanations that were usually founded on the evils of alcoholism and were widely held by temperance crusaders. It was believed, for example, that the number of infant deaths was materially increased by "sleeping over," that is, the accidental suffocation of infants by drunken parents during sleep. Another exaggerated notion that obsessed middle-class reformers was the alleged practice of parents "putting away" their offspring to collect infantile insurance, a recourse supposedly encouraged by the routine issuance of death certificates by doctors in the case of children. This purported evil drew the attention of a select committee of the House of Lords in 1890, and the Bishop of Peterborough championed a bill to abolish the "premium for murder" made possible by the Friendly Societies Act of 1875. Such Christian gentlemen were in fact lending credence to the bizarre notion that their brethren in the slums regularly neglected their infant children or worse for the sake of a few nights' debauch secured by the penny premium. And they needed no more confirmation of their fears than the high proportion of insured among the child abuse cases prosecuted in the courts. Yet these outlandish ideas were taken at face value by Lord Mayor Pile at the 1900 health inquiry when he damned infant life insurance as an incentive to neglect and a "crying evil" in Dublin.

Infant mortality in Ireland, a predominantly rural country, was always lower than in the rest of the United Kingdom. Throughout the second half of the nineteenth century, the Irish rate was generally only two-thirds of the combined average for England and

Wales. And though the latter countries showed immediate and marked improvement after 1900 (from 154 to 91 per 1,000 by 1916), Ireland managed to maintain its favored position. For the Irish capital city, however, the reverse was true, though in this case its misfortune was shared by several of the major British cities (see Table 11), at least until 1907. Thereafter Dublin did not enjoy the rapid improvement achieved in such cities as Birmingham, Liverpool, Manchester, and Sheffield. But then no other city in Britain was so afflicted with the evils of low wages, poverty, unemployment, and bad housing. Surveys had amply demonstrated that infant mortality in the families of the unskilled was double that for middle-class groups. Likewise, the rate for families occupying one-room dwellings greatly exceeded that among families in more favorable circumstances.[8] Dublin, according to the 1911 census, had over 21,000 families (one-third of the total) living in one-room tenements with 60 percent of them having three or more persons. The vicious circle was completed by the aggravating circumstances of ignorance, alcoholism, and the lack of personal cleanliness. It was for these reasons, which pertained as much in English and Scottish as in Irish towns, that the Notification of Births Act was passed in 1907. It was adopted by the Dublin Corporation in 1910 and provided that all births in the city be notified within 36 hours to the district medical officer. In this work of instructing mothers in the care and feeding of infants, the Health Committee's female sanitary staff received vital assistance from the volunteer "health visitors" of the Society for the Prevention of Infant Mortality as well as the very active Women's National Health Association. It was this last-named organization that also operated the city's only depot for the sale of pasteurized milk (though only about 20 gallons per day to the poor of Arbour Hill) in hermetically sealed bottles: Dublin, unlike some English cities, had no municipal milk depot even though Liverpool, which had operated one since 1900, had demonstrated that the death rate among depot-fed children reached only 78 per 1,000 births, almost half the average annual rate for the Irish capital. Yet for all the concern and effort, infantile mortality in 1916, as in 1900, would be described by the same adjective—"appalling."

In the matter of disease the immediate problem for the public health authority was the minimizing of infection. In this it was served by the Infectious Disease (Notification) Act, which the Corporation had adopted after it was introduced in 1889. Here the family or attending physician, under penalty of a fine, was required to notify the district health officer upon the appearance of typhoid, typhus, measles, scarlet fever, diphtheria, erysipelas, smallpox, or cholera. Tuberculosis was added in 1909 after adoption of the TB Prevention Act. The data on typhus is suggestive of the scope of the public health problem facing the Dublin health authority. An acutely infectious and highly contagious disease whose predisposing condition was overcrowding and poverty, typhus had always been found most frequently among the poor in large cities. The disease, characterized by great prostration of strength, severe nervous symptoms, and peculiar eruptions on the skin, was transmitted by the human body louse (a fact unknown until Nicolle's demonstration in 1909) through the sucking of blood from febrile patients. All the conditions of human misery in which the disease thrived existed in full measure in Dublin, and it is remarkable that at a time when typhus deaths had in the normal course of events become something of a rarity thirteen of them were recorded in Dublin for 1913, whereas no more than two such deaths were reported for the whole of England and Wales. Much more serious as a cause of death among adults was typhoid, an infection traceable to contaminated water supplies, impure milk, and so forth. Fortunately, deaths from this cause in Dublin were

halved after 1903, an improvement attributable mainly to the abolition of the old privy-
ashpit system (11,000 of them between 1879 and 1900), the closing of local oyster layings,
and the halting of shellfish gathering from the polluted foreshores of the Liffey at Clontarf and Dollymount. Here again, success in this struggle had to await the twentieth century for the role of the "carrier" to be established and the availability of antibiotics to
reduce the 10 to 25 percent chance of death encountered with this disease. For these and
other diseases contagion was everywhere: at the public fountain in Smith Alley or
Taaffe's Court, surrounded with fecal matter; around the manure heaps and waste products of slaughter houses in Moore St., Townsend St., Chatham St., and other residential
areas; from the common sanitary accommodation in tenement yards, where one facility—
a "wretched, horrid, stinking closet"—could be the resort of 12 families; in the one-room
dwellings of the poor where, as was too often the case, the tubercular son or daughter en-
dangered others; in the ill-managed and poorly supervised common lodging houses, the
homes of drifters and vagrants; in middle-class homes from a cook's cough on the salad;
in the overcrowded churches, theaters, and music halls; and, above all, in the schools,
those "centers of infection" where compulsory attendance had not been matched, in Ireland at any rate, by the medical examination of schoolchildren.

Even the old Irish custom of waking the dead (and wakes were frequent in Dublin)
was a danger, and not for the reasons they were condemned by the clergy: the alarming
outbreak of bubonic plague in Glasgow in 1900 had been traced to that cause. Indeed,
something of a panic was created among medical officers in Dublin on that occasion,
cognizant as these individuals were of the vulnerability of the capital to any epidemic.
Certain "plague spots" dominated the infectious diseases reports,[9] predictably the poorer
areas of Summerhill, Townsend Street, Bride Street, North King Street, Benburb Street,
Great Britain Street, and elsewhere, though no area produced as many cases of disease as
the city's two workhouses. Nor did the Notification of Diseases Act appear to be entirely
effective. According to some observers, Dublin doctors were lax about notification and,
in addition, there was the deep-rooted prejudice among the poor of Dublin against their
removal to fever hospitals, derived presumably from the traditional fear of the workhouse
and its association with ill health. Local Government Board figures reveal that between
1905 and 1915 only an average of 1,800 infectious cases, less than the total for healthier
Belfast, were notified in the city each year. Notwithstanding the great improvement after
the turn of the century, the number seems less than a true measure of the unhealthiness
that yielded as many as 9,000 notifications in both 1899 and 1903. Concealment is also
suggested by the figures for TB, which before 1909 were running at around 500 notifications per year but doubled thereafter with the opening of the new TB dispensaries.

Tuberculosis proved to have the most prolonged impact in all countries, well justify-
ing in Western countries the sinister descripton of "white peril." Its incidence reached a
peak around the turn of the century and declined, though slowly, in the developed areas,
where it has now long since ceased to play a morbid role in death statistics. It was often
called the "Irish disease" by English observers because of the apparent ineradicable hold
it had taken in the country. The *Encyclopedia Britannica* noted the "well known suscepti-
bility of the Irish" and offered in evidence that the TB rate among the Irish in the United
States was three times greater than among native Americans and considerably higher
among children than among corresponding groups of other immigrants. But TB is not
hereditary. It is a disease of poverty, and its eventual decline coincided with improved liv-

ing standards and conditions, cheaper food, and the establishment of sanatoria for curable cases. Ireland did not always have its unwelcome preeminence in this category of disease. In fact, TB death rates were lower than in either England or Scotland before 1879 and did not exceed the rates in those countries continuously until 1887. By 1900 the gap had widened considerably, yielding death rates of 290 and 190 per 100,000 of the population in Ireland and England, respectively. Given the higher incidence of TB in urban over rural communities, even that comparison is too favorable to Ireland, which, in contrast with England, was then predominantly rural. Worse still, the form of the disease that took hold in Ireland had its greatest toll among young adults. These grim facts regularly evoked a cry of anguish from the Registrar General. The following from his 1906 Report is typical:

> 15.8% of deaths in Ireland are sacrificed to a disease which is in a great degree preventable. It is a difficult matter for me to dissociate myself from responsibility in such appalling circumstances and I cannot feel that my duty terminates in merely collecting and classifying these most depressing statistics. Year after year these facts are published, and although the members of the medical profession are strenuous in trying to awaken the public mind to a state of affairs that can only be considered as destructive to the community, yet, comparatively speaking, our countrymen are not alive to the dangers which threaten them.

The true etiology of this disease was established by Koch's discovery of the tubercle bacillus in 1882. Although its infectious nature had been determined in 1865, it was widely believed to be a hereditary disease because of its enduring hold within families predisposed to infection. Constantly active, it did not depend on epidemic or seasonal occurrence to strike down its victims. Tuberculosis took many forms, attacking the meninges (tubercular meningitis), the intestines in children, the spine and bones, and even the skin (lupus). However, it was its partiality to the lungs, producing the wasting disease commonly known as pulmonary consumption (i.e., phthisis) that accounted for almost two-thirds of the TB death rate. Infection generally resulted from inhalation of dried airborne tubercle bacilli from the sputum of its victims. Thus the disease was easily spread among adults by coughing and spitting, especially the latter, which was decried by *Encyclopedia Britannica* as "a perfect curse" in Great Britain. The ingestion of milk or other dairy products from tubercular cattle was a ready source of infection among young children: hence the growing importance attached to pasteurization of milk and the sanitary control of dairies and cowsheds. Concern had long been felt over the high correlation between bad housing or population density and tuberculosis. Hence, tenement life and overcrowding in certain occupations (the clothing trades, for example) were effective agents in spreading the disease among the working classes. Predictably, statistics had shown that the death rate from TB was twice as great among artisans and general laborers than among professional and middle-class groups. Likewise, alarming rates were found to exist in workhouses and lunatic asylums. And statistics alone could not disclose the full ravages of TB because many deaths ascribed to influenza, simple continued fever, and the like would have been due to antecedent tuberculosis. In fact, while the average mortality from the zymotic diseases was decreasing in the closing years of the nineteenth century, that from tubercular causes was on the rise.

Public attention was drawn to the disease in Dublin perhaps for the first time by Dr. Joseph Kenny, MP, in his evidence before the Dublin Hospitals Commission in 1886, just about the time that Ireland was losing her favored position in this aspect of public health. Then the issue was the large number of phthisis cases in the workhouse hospitals, attributed by Kenny (Medical Officer for the North Dublin Union) to the notorious overcrowding in the Poor Law institutions. However, some doubts still existed whether TB was infectious, as Kenny believed, and the question lagged for over a decade. In 1899 the Royal Academy of Medicine held a conference in Dublin on the prevention of TB, pointing out that tubercular diseases were the most destructive of all fatal diseases in Great Britain and Ireland, causing a vast amount of poverty and misery, especially among the working class. It recommended that a branch of the newly founded National Society for the Prevention of Consumption be formed in Dublin. The matter had already been taken up by the ever-active Dublin Sanitary Association and a branch was established in the same year, just at the time when the alarmingly high death rate in the city was generating its own call for action. The result was the previously mentioned Committee of Inquiry held in 1900 to inquire into the public health of the capital. There, in contrast to the almost total absence of mention at the Royal Commission twenty years before, TB figured prominently in the Inquiry. Expert witnesses spoke of the terrible toll tuberculosis had taken in overcrowded and unsanitary districts of the city in the years 1894-97: 96 deaths in 181 houses in Church St.; 32 deaths in 24 houses in Upper Gloucester St.; 491 deaths in the North Dublin Union (population 2,200).[10] Sad stories were repeated of the results in the familiar one-room tenements: healthy families migrating from country to city to take up residence in undisinfected quarters having a continuous history of inhabitants dying from consumption—hardly a member of the family would be alive in five years; daughters nursing consumptive mothers and both dying within months of each other; young adults in the last stages of consumption sleeping in the same bed with healthy siblings; the poor and unemployed living largely on bread, porter, and tea and unable to withstand the ravages of the disease when contracted. Inevitably, statistics also obtruded to highlight the plight of Dublin, revealing that in the ten years 1891-1900 the death rate from phthisis alone was 34.5 per 10,000 of the population for the Registration District, a figure that would be increased by 15 to 20 percent for the city alone. The corresponding rate for London was 18.2, which was higher than the rates pertaining in Edinburgh and Glasgow. As might be expected, Irish cities approached the Dublin rate—in Belfast, 34.1; Cork, 33.6. Comparable figures for densely populated American centers were Boston, 24.9; Chicago, 16.6; New York City, 24.2; Philadelphia, 21.8; San Francisco, 28.4 (1900 figures). Dublin, however, was not the worst of cities, for higher rates generally prevailed in Paris.[11]

After these revelations, the chief of the Health Department, Sir Charles Cameron, attempted to get the Corporation's approval to make TB a notifiable disease under the 1889 Act. The motion was rejected in the council chamber. Many doubtless felt that such action would be futile in a city such as Dublin, whose circumstances would render it unable to cope with the numbers and many of whose inhabitants, though afflicted with TB, nevertheless were forced to continue working to support families. There were no local TB dispensaries and no sanatoria. A bacteriologist for the examination of sputum was not appointed to the city's Health Department until 1910. In all of Ireland there were but two hospitals specifically for consumptive cases, the fee-paying (minimum 7s. per week) Royal National Hospital for Consumption at Newcastle, County Wicklow, and a small facility at Breda, County Down—both of which were opened in 1896. At first the Newcastle

hospital could accommodate only 24 patients, but by 1914 its facilities had been expanded to number 127 beds. By the latter date only another three sanatoria had been provided
to give a total of 306 beds for the entire country. Convalescent cases were cared for in
city hospitals and those in advanced stages of the disease in hospitals for the incurable
and hospices for the dying. The afflicted would continue to bow their heads in submission to "the will of God," and mothers would hearken to the popular nostrums for sickly
children—"Her own dear little self again thanks entirely to Scott's Emulsion . . . good
after hemorrhaging from the lungs."

Concern, however, continued to mount, ironically at about the time the disease in Ireland had begun to peak in 1902 and was commencing its slow decline. TB became the
most important public hygiene question of the day, with over 1,300 persons per year in
the city dying from its attacks. Preventive measures assumed considerable importance.
When the census forms were collected on April 3, 1911, those from infected houses were
first directed to the specially provided disinfecting chamber at the census office. The old
habit common among Irishmen of placing a pocket handkerchief beneath the knees at
church was denounced as an abomination. The kissing of the Bible in administering
oaths was discontinued in favor of raising the hand. And the traditional superstitious
dread of the "night air" had to be banished and people taught that sunlight and fresh air
were deadly enemies of the tubercle bacillus. The idea of a sanatorium to be erected
through a levy on ratepayers was endorsed by Dublin Corporation in 1906. However, voluntary effort was more immediately effective and went some way to answering the strictures voiced at the Public Health Inquiry in 1900 that the educated classes in Dublin
displayed no sense of responsibility, sympathy, or public duty in regard to the poorer citizens. This effort was best represented in Ireland by the Women's National Health Association, founded in 1907 by the energetic Countess Aberdeen, wife of the Lord Lieutenant.
This Association was one of the most active of its kind—establishing branches throughout the country, often with the support of the Gaelic League; arousing rich and poor
alike to the grave problems of public health; organizing the Health Exhibition of 1911;
even securing the election of its members as advocates on District Councils and Boards
of Guardians. Its fully equipped caravans carried the fight against "bad air, bad food, bad
drink and dirt" throughout the west and northwest of Ireland. It campaigned everywhere
for good health by distributing literature and sponsoring lectures, disinfecting rooms and
reporting insanitary houses, providing school breakfasts, teaching people to grow their
own fruit and vegetables, and even selling hot milk (pasteurized, of course) during winter
to the football players in the Phoenix Park. In Dublin, also, it established the pasteurized
milk depot in 1908 through the generosity of the American philanthropist Nathan
Strauss. Other projects in the city were the formation of numerous "babies clubs" for the
education of mothers and a nursing service to care for TB sufferers in their own homes.
In addition to establishing a suburban Preventorium at Sutton for persons exposed to infection, the Association also leased part of the Corporation isolation facility on Pigeon
House Road in order to set up a small (24-bed) hospital for TB patients, naming it the Al-
lan A. Ryan Home in honor of another American benefactor. And it was instrumental in
securing a £25,000 government grant for the construction of the Peamount Sanatorium
near Lucan. In this project the W.N.H.A. encountered considerable opposition from local county residents who objected to the "importation of disease" into the district. In
July 1912 a mob partially wrecked the almost completed building.[12] Nevertheless, the new

hospital was opened one year later and, with accommodation for 217 patients, proved to be considerably larger than the 50-bed Corporation-sponsored Crooksling Sanatorium, which had recently begun operations on a 300-acre site in the Dublin mountains. The superior work of the W.N.H.A. was recognized at the 1908 International Congress on Tuberculosis held in Washington, D.C., when the Irish organization shared with a New York voluntary group the grand prize for effective work in the prevention and relief of tuberculosis.

This great anti-TB crusade also secured passage of the Tuberculosis Prevention (Ireland) Act in 1908. When adoption of the measure was being considered by Dublin Corporation, opposition was expressed on several grounds. Some felt that the operation of the Act would confer on Dublin the bad name that the TB statistics published by the Local Government Board had already given to Ireland. It was held that the notification and registration procedures for infective cases would be an interference with a man's liberty and livelihood since known sufferers would be dismissed from employment. Others pointed out that there was no adequate hospital accommodation for those requiring isolation. Fears were expressed by interested parties that exports of Irish lace would suffer, not to mention what all the unwelcome exposure would do to Irish tourism. However, with 10,000 or more cases in the city in various stages of the disease, opposition was beaten down and the Act duly adopted in October 1909.[13] Thenceforth, the local sanitary authority was armed with procedures for preventing the spread of tuberculosis by means of notification, disinfection, appointment of a bacteriologist, institutional treatment, local dispensary facilities, dissemination of literature, and distribution of drugs and "spit bottles." But most recognized, as they had all along, that the conquest of the disease in Dublin awaited the elimination of the terrible housing situation and the amelioration of a condition of widespread poverty. Yet the great battle against TB had begun that was to last for too many years in modern Ireland, a chastening fact illustrated by the eventual reduction of the death rate from the disease in Dublin to 16.6 (per 10,000) in the mid-1930s, a rate attained by cities such as London, Glasgow, and Edinburgh over 30 years earlier.[14]

The foregoing also suggests a further problem of public health in Dublin—hospital accommodation. True, the capital could be justly proud of the number of its hospitals; some nine general facilities accommodated in all some 1,000 patients in addition to ten specialized and workhouse hospitals and a few very small private institutions. No other cause so demonstrated the charitable instincts of the city's well-to-do than their support of the hospitals. Here, again, Viscount Iveagh's philanthropy was outstanding: in 1911 he donated another £50,000 for distribution to local hospitals to honor the visit to the city of King George V. About half of the hospitals received government grants and most benefited in a small way from the proceeds of the annual Hospital Sunday collection organized by the Protestant community. Several bore honored names in the annals of Irish philanthropy—Steevens' (opened in 1733), Mercer's (1734), St. Patrick's ("Swift's") and the Rotunda Lying-In (both in 1757), Sir Patrick Dun's (1798). One, the Adelaide Hospital in Peter Street, accepted only Protestants, a rule that sometimes excited public outcry when "papist" emergency cases were turned away. The Mater Misericordiae was the premier Roman Catholic institution, founded in 1861 by the Sisters of Mercy but ministering to all creeds. Though the largest and most modern of the general hospitals, it could then barely accommodate 250 patients, though by 1900 a further 100 beds had been added. The largest institution of its kind in Ireland was the 284-bed (in 1916) Cork Street Fever

Hospital. Excepting the Mater and Cork Street hospitals, the various facilities were quite small (under 200 beds), a circumstance some medical observers felt restricted both the instruction of students and the experience of practitioners. None of the Dublin hospitals, for example, could compare with the impressive Royal Infirmary of Edinburgh, the City of Glasgow Fever Hospital, or other large British institutions. Moreover, if the evidence given by Alderman M'Walter, M.D., to the Poor Law Reform Commission in 1903 is correct, it was the practice of some hospitals (the Mater was cited as example) to close for cleaning for one or two months of the year with the result that would-be patients were sometimes, and to their surprise and discomfiture, shunted off to the Union infirmaries. Yet although Dublin compared quite favorably with other cities in the number of hospital beds in proportion to population, this advantage was considerably lessened by the fact that the Irish capital required more extensive specialized facilities for infectious cases than did other urban centers, owing to the greater incidence of disease as well as the unhealthful living conditions of a large proportion of its citizens. Presumably the degree of medical care was as good as found elsewhere, despite the usual reservations in respect to overcrowding in the workhouse infirmaries or the disquieting report of the Board of Superintendence of the grant-aided hospitals, which revealed in 1900 that at the Meath Hospital (one of the few accepting TB cases) "soiled linen from the wards is sent down in the same hydraulic lift which is also used for food."[15]

The medical resources of the city, therefore, were strained to the utmost during epidemics; in 1899 when the fierce onslaught of measles caused nearly 650 deaths in the city alone, and during the smallpox scare in 1903 when 34 of over 250 cases resulted in death. Many middle-class individuals could recall the humiliation they had experienced as smallpox victims in 1894-1895, when the lack of proper facilities forced them to join hundreds of stricken paupers and other poor persons in the convalescent sheds set up in the grounds of the South Dublin Union workhouse. Other indignities beset those less well-off who were forced to undergo disinfection at the Public Health Department's Refuge in Nicholas Street. During the smallpox visitation of 1903, over 1,400 "contacts" underwent disinfection at this latter facility in circumstances that in some cases reflected little credit on its management. *Lancet*, in reporting the sworn statements at a magistrate's hearing, disclosed that on one occasion over 40 persons of eleven families, clothed only in blankets, lay huddled together in the rooms of the Refuge while the men walked about fully naked and drunk on the stout and whiskey with which they had been supplied. Happily, this attack of smallpox was the last of its kind in Ireland, and fortunately so, for thereafter the number of vaccinations to registered births began to decline, reaching the low figure of 61 percent in 1913, a situation rendered more menacing by the ill-judged activities of the English Anti-Vaccination League, a branch of which had been formed in Dublin late in 1911. The antivaccinationists provided the impulse behind the frightening decision of the Board of Guardians of the North Dublin Union to refuse to prosecute those who failed to obey the vaccination laws on the grounds that in their opinion vaccination was "uncleanly, revolting and a danger to public health"![16]

Even without epidemics, however, isolation hospitals would still be sorely needed if only to relieve the pressure on the general hospitals that, in contravention of good practice, had fever blocks attached to them in several cases. Recurring public health crises thus pushed the demand for isolation and convalescent hospitals for infectious diseases to be constructed outside the city. As the Board of Superintendence noted in its report for 1897, the demand for accommodation for patients in Dublin was almost always in excess of the capacity of the institution or its funds, enjoining medical staff to be careful in the selection of patients and give preference only to the most urgent cases. Moreover, private hospitals depended greatly for support on donations and subscriptions, and when these ran low institutions such as Jervis Street Hospital, which gave free services to the poor, were often obliged to curtail much charitable work. There were some farsighted individuals who saw the solution in hospital insurance and institutions maintained out of the rates, but these were voices crying in the wilderness (though one should not forget that great numbers of the Irish people were already receiving free medical treatment in local dispensaries throughout the country at the expense, ultimately, of the taxpayer). Dublin Corporation, however, was ill equipped to respond to demands of this nature. Though medical men might well regard infantile mortality to be a more important issue than home rule, the city fathers inevitably were more inclined to heed the ratepayers' insistence on fiscal responsibility than provide for the well-being of the sick poor. The Corporation could afford only its small annual grants to a few existing hospitals and, until it was aroused to construct the Crooksling sanatorium, maintain a small smallpox isolation facility on the Pigeon House Road, the annual budget for which hardly exceeded the cost of maintaining the Refuge. And, unfortunately, the much-needed isolation hospital for infectious diseases similar to the one that had been established in Belfast in 1901 never got beyond the discussion stage.

A public health problem peculiar to port and garrison towns was that imponderable "cosmopolitan canker"—venereal disease. It was complicated by the popular attitudes to VD, by the prudery that maintained a conspiracy of silence, and by religious sensibilities that deemed the malady a fitting scourge of vice. Explicit reference to VD in books or in the press was considered highly improper, and little heed was given to the dire warnings of physicians who treated its effects. Indeed, the Indecent Advertisements Act of 1889 (sec. 5) expressly forbade under penalty of arrest without warrant by any constable "any advertisement relating to syphilis, gonorrhea . . . ," a clause less injurious to the ubiquitous "quacks" than to public health. Not until the Royal Commission on Venereal Diseases met in 1913 to explore the incidence of VD in Great Britain and Ireland did the general public become aware of the prevalence and gravity of syphilis and gonorrhea. Naturally, there are no available statistics on the amount of syphilis in the population. Those with early syphilis are seldom acutely ill and the lesions of the primary and secondary stages may be insignificant and overlooked. The mortality from syphilis is not so much from those who acquire it as from those who inherit it. Of the recorded deaths from venereal disease (mainly syphilis) in Ireland between 1899 and 1916—a total of 1,984—over 69 percent were of children under five years.[17] In fact, some experts were wont to claim that if the deaths of children born alive with inherited syphilis were added to the total aggregate of premature and still births due to the same cause, syphilis would have ranked as a serious cause of infantile mortality. And, of course, tertiary syphilis was an underlying factor in locomotor ataxia and general paralysis of the insane, and possibly in a large proportion of the deaths from cardiovascular disease. Physicians were usually too kindly to certify deaths as due to syphilis when they could be ascribed to other contributory causes. Gonorrhea, on the other hand, was a common bacterial infection among adults and considerably more widespread than syphilis. Though usually self-limiting and less dangerous than other forms of VD, it was nevertheless a frequent cause of blindness among children until modern medicine eliminated that birth hazard from infected mothers. Moreover, upward of 90 percent of females with gonorrhea, according to Top and Wehrle, are completely without symptoms or have such slight symptoms that they are unaware of the infection. Yet the dreadful threat of VD was generally ignored by public health departments as much as by the general public—as if in silent endorsement of the opinion of moralists and clergymen who regarded VD as a divinely ordained penalty for illicit sexual indulgence.

What little information we have on the extent of VD in Dublin derives from the committees and commissions appointed to inquire into the operation of the Contagious Diseases Acts, reports of the Army Medical Department, and figures supplied by hospitals treating VD cases. The Acts were first passed in 1864 and provided for the examination of "known" prostitutes. As *Lancet* tartly observed: "If the butcher's shop may be occasionally visited and inspected for diseased meat, why should the brothel be exempted?"[18] In 1866, amid the fiercest opposition and misrepresentation, a second Act gave the police power to enforce periodic medical examination of any woman in a "protected" district who resided in a brothel, solicited in the streets, frequented houses of prostitution, or was informed against by servicemen. The protected districts were the military stations and seaports mentioned in the schedule. In Ireland the Acts applied within a certain radius of the military garrisons in Cork and the Curragh and at the Queenstown naval station. Dublin, the arena for the largest numbers of soldiers, prostitutes, brothels, and "clients" in the country, was not included. Presumably, as with London, the inclusion of highly populated cosmopolitan centers would present an impossible task to the police and bring the Acts themselves into disrepute. In fact, renewed agitation against the legislation began in 1870 following an attempt to extend it to the entire civilian population, and after several motions for repeal were averted in the Commons, compulsory examination was abolished on a snatch vote in 1883 followed by final repeal of the Acts in 1886, much to the dismay of most responsible medical opinion. However, the Contagious Diseases Acts, despite some demonstrated worth in military districts, were reputed to have had little effect upon the prevalence of VD in general: after all, "clandestine" prostitutes and unregulated infected males are always much more numerous than "public" women.

Evidence given before the various appointed bodies between 1869 and 1882 testifies to the virulence of the disease in Dublin, though decreased there as elsewhere since the days of the dreaded "black lion." In 1869 it was in "a very bad form indeed." Two years later it was claimed that there had never been "so much true syphilis at any time existing as there is now in Dublin." In 1880 over one-third of the 4,357 troops stationed in the city were admitted to hospital for VD; 940 had cases of syphilis. And, finally, in 1881 the select committee was given the alarming information that in one Dublin-based regiment the commanding officer had complained that over a ten-month period some 43 percent of his unmarried men had been incapacitated by VD. Indeed, one is tempted to suggest that the prostitutes of Dublin were doing far more than republican-minded nationalists to weaken the sinews of the Empire. These claims were corroborated by the annual reports of the army medical departments. Between 1860 and 1868 Dublin was among those military stations most noted for the proportion of soldiers admitted to hospital suffering from venereal disease. In 1865 it held the unenviable first rank among the 24 stations listed and was in the top 4 for five of those years. From 1869 to 1878 Dublin was always among the 5 garrisons in the United Kingdom that had the highest ratios of men constantly ill from VD, the city again holding first or second place in 1869, 1870, and 1872. Between 1870 and 1873, when the examination of soldiers was strictly enforced, Dublin was second only to London among 28 garrison towns in the number of admissions for primary venereal lesions. The city had gained such unwelcome notoriety at least as far as the army was concerned that in 1885, when it seemed likely that the Contagious Diseases Acts that had lapsed were about to be repealed, *Lancet* warned: "If the Acts are not soon restored to their former state of efficiency, we shall have all our military and naval stations in a state closely resembling that of Dublin."

The army did indeed acquire an embarrassing prominence among the world's military forces for the prevalence of VD in the ranks in the later years of the century. Whereas the Home and Indian armies had hospital admission rates of 204 and 438 per 1,000 troops, respectively, in the years 1890-92, for example, corresponding returns for other armies showed Germany with only 27.2, France 43.6, Russia 43, Austria 63.5, Italy 71.3, and the U.S. 77.4. In 1898 the commander in chief of the army felt obliged to issue a general order to all company officers on the need to rid the service of this reproach in the matter of a disease that was by far the greatest single cause of military inefficiency due to sickness. Little wonder that Arthur Griffith, no lover of the British army or its recruitment tactics in Ireland, should hold it up in the pages of *Sinn Fein* as the most immoral army in Europe. He might, however, also have noted that no mean contributor to that record were the garrisons stationed in Ireland. From 1899 to 1905 the 20,000 or more troops in the country in each year had the highest incidence of VD of the four countries with the exception only of 1903, when the Irish Command was second to Scotland. In the same period the Dublin station, one of 15 or so in the U.K. with garrison strengths in excess of 1,000 men, also had the highest prevalence of the disease in all years except 1902, when it held third place.[19]

Dublin was fortunate to be among the few towns that had a special hospital for venereal diseases. This was the Westmoreland Lock Hospital, founded in 1792 and soon treating well over 1,000 patients a year. It was the only hospital of its kind in Ireland until 1869, when similar institutions were established near the Curragh military camp and in Cork City. Initially, the Lock provided accommodation for about three hundred men and women but this practice was changed in 1821, when thenceforth only females were admitted. This reduced accommodation by about 50 percent, with consequent reductions in the total number treated. Also, the progressive reduction in government grants eventually restricted activities so that by 1850 only 100 beds or fewer could be afforded. Thus the Lock was unable to provide for all those applying for admission. Yet between 1821 and 1853, 26,500 cases were treated, yielding an average annual intake that was only slightly reduced for most of the remainder of the century. The Lock was situated in Townsend Street—"a monument of moral degradation" in a densely populated, poverty-stricken area. It really was more of a reformatory than a hospital, an utterly cheerless place where patients endured a dreary and monotonous stay of one or two months in gloomy wards with only a tiny yard for exercise. Patients were obliged to wear drab hospital garb to satisfy the moral reservations of the hospital governors: "If we allowed these swell ladies from Mecklenburgh Street . . . to flit about in pink wrappers and so on, it would be a distinct inducement to others less hardened to persevere in that life in the hope that probably they would arrive at similar distinction."[20] Catholics and Protestants were kept in separate wards, and more explicably, married women contaminated by husbands were separated from the common prostitutes. Iron bars and locked doors rein-forced the classifications . The hospital had no power to compel patients to remain until cured, so that a considerable number usually left before treatment terminated. Besides, there were always those who could not stomach the matron's and chaplain's reading, and even withholding of their mail, and would soon depart. Nor is it unlikely that the frugal normal diet drove some back on the streets: breakfast—1 oz. butter, 6 oz. bread, ¾ pint of tea; dinner—6 oz. bread or 1 lb. potatoes, ¾ pint of milk, mutton chop (excepting Fridays when gruel was served instead); supper—4 oz. bread, ¾ pint of tea. Even the inspectors of the Board of Superintendence of the Dublin Hospitals usually shrank from visiting the Lock: "a dreary place from which one comes away depressed . . . a visit to it and to the Hospital for Incurables on the same day gives food for thought" (1909 Report); "as usual, came away from inspection with the sense that while all other institutions are advancing, this is obsolete, is standing still and that question of how the class of patients for whom it exists can be best treated remains to be answered" (1912 Report).

The Lock was always short of funds for it was non-fee-paying and neither shared in the proceeds from Hospital Sundays nor received subventions from Dublin Corporation. Since venereal disease was always "too delicate" a subject to bring before the public, ap-peals to private charity were out of the question. The facility was maintained entirely out of government grants. Its only additional income between 1899 and 1916 was two be-quests amounting to £2,500, which allowed sanitary and other repairs that enabled the provision of porcelain instead of metal baths, an important advance considering the cir-cumstance that metal baths were frequently out of use for repainting. The War Office, understandably, added another £1,125 in the years 1899 to 1906 but, unaccountably, noth-ing further thereafter. The amount the Lock received in donations is testimony to the dis-regard of the citizens for its services to public health: £35 between 1901 and 1906 and a solitary £1 per year (from a reformed prostitute with a heart of gold, one assumes) from 1907 to 1913; nothing thereafter. The number of cases (mostly first admissions) treated per year between 1899 and 1916 averaged 462, a little more than half the number treated twenty years previously. But it would hardly be wise to surmise from this that the preva-lence of VD had decreased. True, syphilis tended to diminish in virulence and would be on the defensive after 1910, when salvarsan would come on the market. But gonorrhea, it was noted, was on the increase. The senior surgeon at the Lock Hospital told the Royal Commission on Venereal Diseases in 1914 that in his opinion there was just as much VD in Dublin then as in former years, though he explained that its character had changed, re-sulting in a milder form that allowed more women to avoid the stigma of a stint in the Lock. Even the character of prostitution itself had changed, the "professionals" who had availed of the Lock as a matter of course being replaced, since the suppression of the brothels after 1887, by a better class of female—servants and shop or factory girls for whom acquaintance with the Lock would spell disgrace.* The ages of the patients at the Lock also appear to have changed. The chief surgeon maintained in 1910 that few suffer-ers sought admission until compelled by age or poverty. During 1877-83 over 80 percent of adult patients were between 20 and 30 years, though even these were older than the 15-to 20-year-olds who had comprised the inmate population a generation earlier.[21]

Unlike female patients who could undergo treatment at the Lock or be rehabilitated

*For further comments on prostitution in Dublin see Chapter 7 below.

at the several Magdalen houses operated by nuns, male VD sufferers were restricted to those few hospitals that tolerated their admission. Alone of the general hospitals, Steevens' Hospital maintained a dozen beds for "the worst class of male syphilitic patients" ever since the Lock was closed to men after 1820. A number of extern patients were also treated elsewhere. The services they received may have been something less than professional, considering that no training in the treatment of venereal diseases was provided outside the Lock and the governors refused to allow clinical instruction of medical students there. In any event, a fair estimate of the total adults (first admissions) treated each year for VD at the Lock and elsewhere would amount to somewhere between 500 and 600 cases. If Dublin can be judged like other large cities, then that estimate represented at the very least only about *one* percent of the total amount of VD cases in the city at large. For this estimate we have only the authority of the Royal Commission on Venereal Diseases, which after hearing evidence from England and Ireland concluded that "the number of persons who have been infected with syphilis, acquired or congenital, cannot fall below 10 percent of the whole population in the large cities, and the percentage affected with gonorrhea must greatly exceed this proportion."[22] Whether the morale and faith of a Catholic people would suggest that such an estimate would have been an exaggeration in the case of Dublin is anybody's guess. It was true, however, that in the case of VD-related deaths Dublin managed once more to achieve notoriety: its rates of 1.5 and 1.53 per 10,000 of the population for deaths from VD and paresis, respectively, were almost double the corresponding figures for London.[23] The treatment of venereal disease eventually saw its own revolution in the introduction of penicillin in the early 1940s but, alas, there was no revolution in the modes of thought that continued to sacrifice innocent victims and impetuous youth on the altar of ignorance and, in Ireland, of doctrine.

Fortunately, not all public health problems were as intractable as those of disease. The Public Health Department was able to achieve its share of success in other areas, though not always as rapidly so as some hoped. The 30-year-old public mortuary, a godsend when first erected, had itself become a nuisance and was finally replaced in 1900 so that the post-mortem area no longer ventilated into the coroner's court room. On the other hand, the Corporation steadfastly refused to provide a public lavatory for the women of Dublin, despite the constant entreaties of Alderman M'Walter: it will be recalled that the famous "meeting of the waters" under Tommy Moore's "roguish finger" in College Street (long a subject for local merriment) was created entirely by the men of Dublin. Even as late as 1915 a decision finally to erect such a facility at Aston's Quay near O'Connell Bridge fell afoul of the local merchants, who condemned the proposal as "objectionable" and were successful in delaying its completion for several years. But one great success of the Health Department over the years was the gradual abolition of some 12,000 privies throughout the city. By about 1907, therefore, Dublin, except for some small sections of the townships annexed in 1900, could boast of the water carriage system as the sole agency for the removal of human excreta. In this at least the city was far ahead of such English centers as Sheffield, with its remaining 16,000 privies, or Nottingham, with its primitive pail system for 35,000 houses as late as 1911. Street cleaning posed its own special problems. Day after day and year after year, the 500 men and 160 horses of the scavenging department emptied over 20,000 dustbins (supplied to householders by the Corporation at cost) and conveyed the refuse from these and from the streets and ashpits to the Destructor at Stanley Street, to the sloblands at Clontarf, and to the reclamation area that was later to become Fairview Park. Until 1906 a portion of the unsalable house refuse (300 tons daily) was taken to one of Dublin's less pleasing attractions—the Eblana hopper barge moored in the river facing the Custom House at the Tara Street railway station. There the noxious heaps would gather daily pending removal out to sea. Considering that the dustbins (one for each tenement house) were also used as receptacles for all kinds of slops and filth and that loads of manure were frequently disposed of via the barge, the crosswinds must have put many an admirer of Gandon's Custom House to flight. One complainant compared the Eblana's presence to what would transpire if the refuse of the metropolitan district of London should be allowed to run into the Thames from the terrace of the House of Commons. However, with the increase in capacity of the Destructor the "pestilent and hateful" Eblana was able to make its last voyage in 1906. Thereafter the tramway system was employed to cart most of the disposable refuse to the foreshore (in the dead of night, naturally) where years later the Fairview recreation grounds would emerge. But the scavenging of the city could never be entirely successful, not only because of the habits of the slum dwellers but owing also to the existence of numerous streets, courts, lanes, and alleys that were not obliged to be cared for by the Cleansing Department. Almost 900 of these filthy areas bore the signpost "not in charge of the Dublin Corporation." It was to clean out these that the Corporation sent the teams of unemployed in lean years when the British Treasury doled out funds under the Unemployed Workmen Act. The Corporation's practice after 1901 of cleaning tenement yards only on payment of a guinea by the landlord advanced neither the cleanliness nor the public health of the city. And the hindrance of legal technicalities in the interpretation of the sanitary acts inevitably weakened the chances of forcing owners of tenement houses to abate nuisances and correct sanitary defects. As far as the slum landlord was concerned, the difficulties were due to "the extreme filth and dirt of the tenants and their mode of living." And when these habits were challenged, the reply made the superintendent of the cleansing department despair of ever keeping the city clean: "I was told it would give the Corporation men something to do," an attitude as destructive to public health as the reason for tolerating contiguity to manure heaps in the back streets of the city—"where there is muck there is luck."[24]

A novel approach to public health that caused considerable amusement in Dublin around 1911 was Sir Charles Cameron's campaign against the common housefly. The fly is no longer a menace in modern cities but in the early twentieth century, before privy vaults, dairies, and cowsheds were banned from urban centers and before the automobile had replaced the horse, it was a real concern to public health authorities for its role in transmitting typhoid fever and dysentery. The summer swarms of 1911 were apparently menacing enough for the Health Department to risk a deficit in its lean budget by offering a reward for their capture—"Best House Flies, 3d per bag" ran the newspaper captions. The poor response suggested halving the size of the paper bags issued at the Marrowbone Lane depot: 6,000 flies were perhaps too much for one child to catch. Nevertheless, Cameron was pleased to note in his official report for 1912 that the previous year's massacre was so successful that no one presented a bag at the depot! But the ridicule persisted. Some wondered how many of the brown bags were tested for their noise value. A more enterprising character suggested the time was opportune to import the pests for sale to the Corporation. Those with foreign experience offered their advice on the construction of mesh screens for windows. Even Jim Larkin took time off from his herculean labors to educate the public to their responsibilities in the matter, suggesting that "bags be opened and pinned to the middle of the clothes line . . . flies will then walk along the line from both ends and, as a result of the impact when they knock heads together, will fall senseless into the bags." Or, alternatively, they could put salt on their tails![25] Doubtless Sir Charles was not amused nor were the correspondents of the medical journals who noted an exceptional plague of flies in the autumn of 1913 feasting on the heaps of rubbish in back lanes and courts, on the decaying vegetables and fish offal that usually laid for days in the gutters of the streets, and on the exposed produce of the street markets, where the hazard was sometimes increased, according to one of these gentlemen, by dogs urinating on the bundles of rhubarb![26]

The control and inspection of dairy yards and slaughter houses was another continuing problem of public health. As late as 1916 there were still over 200 dairy yards, 25 percent less than in 1900. London with its huge population had fewer than 40. There were also over 50 private slaughter houses, a number that had not changed significantly in fifteen years. These were separate problems of long standing, though conditions had certainly improved since the 1870s, when there had been twice as many slaughter houses and Mercer's Hospital had to buy out the adjoining dairy yard in Digges Lane to get rid of the offence of cows, pigs, horses, and heaps of manure. The Corporation had no power to refuse registration to dairymen even in congested districts and once registered, renewal was not required. The fine for operating a nonregistered dairy was only nominal. The result was that from November to May in each year up to 6,000 cows alone were housed in the city and contributed 20,000 loads of manure to market gardeners, local farmers, and workmen at labor on the reclamation of the foreshore. The committee that sat in 1900 to consider the health of the city found no valid objection to the presence of dairy yards, *provided* they were not in congested districts and that the relevant sanitary regulations were strictly enforced. The latter was found not to be the case. And, of course, here lay the danger to the milk supply for a city that had no municipal depot for pasteurization. Dublin received its milk supply from two sources: the rich grass lands of counties Limerick and Tipperary and the city and suburban dairy yards where animals were fed on mashes, tubers, and swill, inducing in them a form of chronic alcoholism that resulted in non-nutrient milk. This, however, was the least of the dangers facing the consumer, as is evident from the many reports from local government board inspectors on the manner in which great supplies of milk were produced despite the known agency of polluted milk in the transmission of tuberculosis, diphtheria, and other infectious diseases. Reports of local medical officers of health frequently related stories in similar vein to that told by the officer for Howth district: " . . . two men who were milking had their hands covered with cow manure from the udders of the cows, which they neglected to wash before milking. In the process of milking, the filth from the men's hands was gradually mixed with the milk." An officer of the public health department of the Local Government Board gave evidence before the Irish Milk Commission in 1911 that milk came into Dublin from districts where cow-keepers were not even registered. It was milk from cows kept by a lockkeeper on the Royal Canal that was responsible for the deaths from typhoid of at least 15 persons (including several constables at Phoenix Park police headquarters) in one section of Dublin in 1899. Another, an Inspector of Dairies, deplored the primitive milk-storage facilities he had seen on a farm in a district that lacked a creamery—crocks under a bed! Even superstition extended these horrors: the belief that the washing of the cow's udders retarded the flow of milk or that the burying of a bovine fetus in the stable prevented future abortions. When the Corporation in 1908 promoted a bill calling for stricter sanitary regulations, the Dublin Cowkeepers' and Dairymens' Association were able to exert sufficient pressure to have removed "objectionable" clauses providing for the licensing of dairies and butcher shops. As late as 1917 it was concluded at another investigation that the milk obtained by nurses at infant welfare centers was so bad in bacteriological character that a water supply giving evidence of the same state of contamination would have been classed as a dangerous menace to public health.[27] Obviously, with infantile mortality and tuberculosis so rife in the city, the responsibilities both of the education-oriented Irish Agricultural Organization Society in the country at large and of the Inspecting Veterinary Surgeon in Dublin itself were grave indeed.

The public abattoir located in Blackhorse Lane near the Prussia Street cattle market became something of a public joke in the city, the licensed victuallers being wont to boast that they actively boycotted it, thus avoiding the rent they would have had to pay while stock awaited preparation and dressing. It had been the intention of the Corporation to abolish all private slaughter houses as soon as the abattoir was built. Unfortunately, the structure when completed in 1881 was placed a few yards beyond the then city boundary on county land, whereupon the city butchers contended that the temporary slaughter-house licenses granted since 1851 need not be surrendered. They were not forced to close their private facilities, testimony perhaps to the political influence of traders whose voices were second only to those of the publicans in the council chamber: their chief spokesman was William Field, parliamentary representative of the St. Patrick's Division (Dublin City) in every election between 1895 and 1918. Influence prevailed to enable the butchers to retain their licenses even after the land on which the abattoir stood was incorporated into the city in 1890: the slaughter houses could thenceforth be closed only through purchase by the Corporation, an obvious impediment to their speedy abolition. In 1916 over 120 victuallers used the services of 53 private slaughter houses while some 50 butchers continued to avail of the abattoir. By contrast, Belfast had only 5 private slaughter houses in 1900, all others having been closed on grounds of public health and the existence of a public abattoir. Of the 3,000 to 4,000 animals slaughtered each week in Dublin, only about 25 percent passed through the abattoir. Hence the usual spectacle of hundreds of cattle being driven from the pens at the market where they were bought, not across the street to the abattoir but in wayward procession through the city to the various private yards in the heart of residential areas—to Moore Street, Townsend Street, Chatham Street, Westland Row, Thomas, Francis, Dorset Streets, and elsewhere. The barking of dogs, lowing of cattle, and shouting of drovers may have added a certain picturesqueness to the local scene redolent of life in old Dublin, but these also created chaos for traffic and extra work for the scavenging department. Notwithstanding, mass excitement and general merriment were sometimes created by a crazed animal such as the occasion in 1908 when a bull escaped from a yard at Sir John Rogerson's Quay and rushed westward, in and out of shop windows, reaching Kingsbridge Station and following the railway tracks to Inchicore, stopping only when it charged head on into a train at Ballyfermot bridge, all the while being pursued by mounted constables and sundry citizens.

The situation remained a positive nuisance if not also a danger to public health. The Master of the Coombe Hospital told the committee of inquiry in 1900 that, when an unfavorable wind blew from O'Keeffe's knackers yard, the staff was prevented from eating their food owing to the frightful stench. Many of the yards were in wretched condition with ramshackle huts and shanties forever splashed with blood, offal, and entrails. Animal lovers must also have been appalled by the inhumane methods of killing in Dublin—pole-axing of cattle and throat-cutting of sheep. Sir Charles Cameron, never one to pass up a good story or conceal a local nuisance, recalled the case of a butcher inserting a good lung in the carcase of a diseased animal to fool the public health inspector. Issuing orders for the destruction of unsound meat (the latter a hazard among the poor since the days of the old Bull Alley market) became a regular activity of the Health Department, almost 400 a year being issued from 1906 onward. One might fairly wonder where the thousands of pounds of infected and diseased meat removed from the abattoir for destruction by private jobbers wound up.[28]

Happily, against this dolorous litany we may set one great twentieth-century achievement—the completion of the main drainage, a project rivaling in scale that other great work of the previous century—the Vartry water supply. It will be recalled that the famous "Liffey smell" arose because the river acted as a giant cesspool for the collection of the sewage of a city of over a quarter of a million persons: the excreta of humans and animals, the road sweepings and surface water, and the products of industrial waste. At the western end of the city, the river received also the sewage of Kilmainham (via the Camac river) as well as that of the village of Chapelizod on the opposite bank. The estuary itself along the shores of Clontarf and Irishtown was similarly fouled by the drainage from the townships of Rathmines and Pembroke, and the bathing as far out as Sandymount was often destroyed. The situation in the city became intolerable at low tide, especially during the weeks of summer heat, so much so that it often became necessary for the Cleansing Department to send its men armed with brooms onto the exposed sides of the river in the early hours of the morning to sweep the offensive deposits back into the river to minimize the daily assault on the olfactory nerves of the citizens. More serious was the locking of the main sewers for several hours each day as the high tide closed the tidal valves. The high death rate in the city had often been attributed to this retention of sewage in defective house drains. The worst effects of this situation had been alleviated by the gradual replacement of house drains and the installation of pumping stations to take the surplus sewage at these intervals and thus prevent the inundation of the lower parts of the city along the quays. At any rate, anything that would banish the stink from the Liffey could only have the wholehearted support of the citizens and please foreign visitors.

The massive project had, as will be recalled, first been mooted as far back as the 1860s but had faltered through difficulties of financing. Though the Corporation again took up the matter after the Public Health Act of 1878 resolved this difficulty, the scheme was further delayed until necessity itself decreed action in 1896. A payment of £65,000 to the War Office for the repossession of Pigeon House Fort secured the site of the outfall works and work began. For most of the next decade, disfigured thoroughfares, street trenches, and pedestrian gangways became a familiar sight and inconvenience along the Dublin quays. Intercepting conduits were built for the old sewers both north and south, commencing near Phoenix Park gate and Kingsbridge railway terminus and ending at Eden and Burgh quays before connecting together under Hawkins Street and continuing beneath the city through Ringsend to the treatment plant at the Pigeon House fort. There the clarified effluent would enter the estuary while the sludge would be conveyed six miles out to sea and discharged there. The foundation stone of the outfall works was laid on August 28, 1900, in a ceremony that was marred for some spectators when the Lord Mayor proposed a toast to Queen Victoria. The entire project was all but completed by 1906 and formally opened on September 24 of that year. Needless to say, even greater consternation was caused on that occasion when the King's health was drunk.

Designed for a future population of 325,000, by 1906 the system was providing for an area representing 215,000 of the population and through negotiation of further loans in 1910 it was hoped to connect another 88,000. The operation of the main drainage soon demonstrated in unexpected fashion what had been happening over the years in the old intermittent-flowing sewers. In 1909 the system had to be closed down for two weeks to allow the removal of the huge quantity of detritus that had been carried from the old tide-locked sections of the connections and had clogged the 8-foot diameter terminal conduit. The main drainage was to cost the taxpayers over £600,000, considerably more than the original estimate of £350,000 but small cost if the senses of present and future citizens were to be spared and if the Recorder of Dublin could once again exercise his ancient right of hooking two salmon in the pellucid stream into which the Liffey was expected to be transformed between Kingsbridge and the North Wall. But the complaints against the Liffey's stinking tide would continue to be heard. Even as late as 1975 a report in the *Irish Times* looked forward to the day when the Camac river could be redirected in its course so as to eliminate the major pollution problem in the Liffey and do away with the famous smell.

The part of Dublin's story here recounted offers grim evidence of the slow and painful attempts to combat some of the worst features of urban life and eliminate the greatest dangers to the lives of individual citizens. The guardians of public health needed strong shoulders to bear the unrelieved burden of a set of social statistics that placed the capital in the front rank of unhealthy cities. A host of circumstances—the habits of the people, the inadequacy of bylaws, the dirt of the streets, the nuisance of knackers' yards, even the common housefly—appeared to combine with the ever-present causes of disease in reducing the effect of the most salutary efforts of the authorities. True, the completion of the main drainage was a great step forward, but even this could not materially affect the city's death rate. The root of that problem lay elsewhere and would not be achieved so cheaply. Sir Francis McCabe, a member of the Royal Commission in 1879 and a witness at the Health Inquiry in 1900, gave the greater part of the answer to it in his own assessment of the public health of Dublin:

> I think the Committee will gather from what I have said that I look upon the tenement dwellings of Dublin as the prime source and cause of the high death rate, and that there is only one remedy for it. It is a very great task to face that remedy; but I think you will never reduce the death rate of Dublin to reasonable proportions and keep it permanently low, until you remove to the suburbs a very large proportion of the population of Dublin. . . .[29]

The immensity of that task and how the remedy was faced form the subject of the next chapter.

5

Housing

The truth is that the proverbial slum dwellers delight in their surroundings. The one-room tenement was the dwelling of their forebears, the box bed had sufficed for the home of their early days and they have no soul that longs after better, cleaner, and healthier conditions . . . the cry of the slum dweller is to be let alone, to be allowed to live and die amidst the squalor and dirt.

Sanitary Record, August 11, 1904

I cannot conceive the existence of the present condition of the houses of the working classes except upon the supposition of the long subordination of the interests of the poor and humble to vested interests in their disease, misery and vice.

The Recorder of Dublin, *Lancet*, April 4, 1908

FEW IF any books that set out to evoke the Dublin of Yeats and Joyce can refrain from ringing the changes on the oft-repeated allegations of contemporaries that the city was not only a hot-bed of vice and intemperance but a disgrace to civilization as well for its hideous tenements. Doubtless there was much exaggeration in these claims, especially regarding the immorality and drunkenness. However, well-founded statistics based on detailed investigations done for local and census purposes revealed a housing problem of such dimensions that little exaggeration was needed to excite the sort of remarks quoted above. Indeed, the housing of the working classes presented an almost insuperable challenge to those who directed the affairs of the city in the early years of this century.

The nature of this social question as it confronted nineteenth-century Dublin has been sketched in an earlier chapter. Essentially, inadequate housing and unsanitary accommodation had consigned over one-third of the population to conditions of intolerable overcrowding and, most often, ill health. In fact, health and housing were so allied in the public mind that concern for the proper housing of the working classes was the natural consequence of the high death rates and rampant disease that instilled fear in all classes. This was abundantly clear from the lengthy investigation of the Royal Commission on Sewerage and Drainage in 1879, which revealed that the city's working-class population, about 70 percent of the whole, occupied about 30 percent of all houses. Virtually all lived either in tenement houses or in the second- and third-class cottages that formed the hidden courts and alleys of the city. Over 2,000 of these structures were officially declared unfit for human habitation. There was good reason therefore for the sweeping away of the menacing "fever nests" and growing support for the construction of decent and healthy dwellings for working-class families. As we have seen, the tenement system had been developing all through the nineteenth century, though at an accelerated pace after 1830. Over 3,000 of the worst abodes were closed by the Public Health Department between 1879 and 1900; and while many of these were repaired and reoccupied, over 1,000 of them lay in ruins all over the city by the latter date. Certain sections of Dublin acquired a lasting reputation for the squalor of their surroundings and the misery of the inhabitants. One of the worst areas lay west of Moore Street as far as the Linenhall Barracks and North Brunswick Street and thence southward to the river. There the slums of Church and Beresford Streets, Mary's and Cole's Lanes, and the courts and alleys surrounding the Ormonde Market abounded, places so wretched and dangerous that even collectors of the rates were deterred from entering them without the protection of the police. A rival scene of desolation on the other side of the Liffey encompassed the Coombe and the Liberties extending northward to Christ Church Cathedral and framed by the ugly tributaries of Ashe Street, Bride's Alley, Meath and Plunkett Streets, and the byways of Francis Street. These were the central areas of poverty, but outside them ran further gashes in the fabric of the city at Summerhill, Townsend Street, Upper and Lower Mount Street, and the lanes to the rear of Merrion Square.

As has been stated in an earlier chapter, the first demolition order for the clearance of an unsanitary section of the Coombe was issued by the Corporation in 1877. This was followed three years later by a similar order for the houses in Plunkett Street. Both sites were demolished and replaced with asphalted pavements and small, neat red brick cottages with internal scullery, separate water closet, and external coal storage for the 320 mainly artisan families that could afford the relatively high rents charged by the developer, the Dublin Artisans' Dwellings Company. This company was the only substantial private builder undertaking construction of housing for the working classes. Its area of operations included, besides the city, Rathmines, Kingstown, and Bray. By 1900 the company had built about 2,500 separate dwellings (block flats, cottages, and houses) mainly in the city and in the Harold's Cross section of Rathmines township. However, by 1907 its operations ceased entirely, victim to the uncertainty of the money market. In 30 years of building it had managed to provide model dwellings for 3,300 families or, at most, 15,000 persons. Excepting the Coombe-Plunkett Street schemes, which it undertook because the purchase and clearing of each site was done by the Corporation and the land leased to it at attractively low rents, the Dwellings Company generally conducted its operations outside the so-called central areas of poverty and dilapidated housing. Only the well-paid tradesman and skilled worker could afford the three- and four-room cottages at rents of 5s. 3d. and 7s. per week that represented the bulk of the new housing in the city in such sections as Inchicore, Infirmary Road, Aughrim Street, Oxmantown Road, Arbour Hill, Kirwan Street, Dominick Street Upper, Clanbrassil Street Lower, Blackpitts, Cork Street, and Rialto. Purchasers of shares in the company were assured a commercial dividend of 5 percent, and among the largest investors were members of the Guinness family, ever ready to reciprocate the favor of the workers with contributions for their welfare. In addition to the activities of private speculators,* the only other nonphilanthropic housing construction of note was that undertaken by the Dublin and Suburban Workmen's Dwellings Company, which put up close to 300 cottages in Cork Street area. Some further private ventures of the railway, tramways, and brewing companies accommodated another few hundred families.

"Five percent philanthropy" (actually, 3 percent or less) was also at work in the city. The aptly named Housing of the Very Poor Association, brainchild of Sir Charles Cameron, purchased six houses in Derby Square-Werburgh Street in 1898 and refurbished them as single-room dwellings for 39 families (190 persons), each house with range, beds, water supply, lavatory, and let them at moderate rents. It also built eleven houses on the site of an old brewery in Summer Street off Marrowbone Lane, housing 620 persons in 118 separate rooms. The Association failed, however, to attract subscribers despite annual appeals for public support and was forced, as it stated in its 1913 report, "to rest on its oars," thus lending credence to the belief that while speakers dwelt forever on the horrors of the slums, few indeed were prepared to do very much about them. The socially and politically active women's alumnae organization, the Alexandra College Guild, did similar good work for 47 families in the six houses they managed in Summerhill and Grenville Street, adding for good measure a small library in which "there was a constant demand for Dickens"! Renovation of another seven houses in Grenville Street was sponsored by the Social Service Society of Trinity College, not to emulate the social consciousness of young intellectuals in English or Scottish towns but merely to ascertain as a confined experiment whether it was possible for an ordinary landlord carrying out the ordinary laws to make a decent profit (it wasn't). The philanthropy of these ventures was laudable but, alas, too small to make much difference to the overall problem. Moreover, it was always hedged in by the need that schemes be conducted, as Miss Octavia Hill insisted, "on thoroughly sound commercial principles, and not as a charitable undertaking."

The greatest philanthropic work in housing the working classes was undertaken in 1889 by Viscount Iveagh when he established the Guinness (later Iveagh) Trust with a gift of £50,000. Dublin and its citizens already owed much to the Guinness family: Sir Benjamin had restored St. Patrick's Cathedral; his son, Lord Ardilaun, had opened up St. Stephen's Green; and now another son, who had built and handed over complete to the Corporation the Iveagh Market in Francis Street, was to lend a hand in destroying the slums of Dublin. The building of 336 model tenements in Kevin Street in 1894 was followed six years later by the clearing of Bull Alley, once a thriving butchers' quarter between Patrick and Bride Streets just north of St. Patrick's Cathedral but which over the years had descended to so low a condition as to be described rather unkindly in a Dublin Sanitary Association report as comprising "filthy, foul-smelling, half ruinous dwellings inhabited by a low and degraded collection of people." Soon the Bull Alley scheme saw the creation of the Iveagh Buildings, providing accommodation for 250 families in one-to three-room flats (70 percent of which were two rooms) at an average rent of 2s. per room, which included rates, services of a chimney sweep, venetian blinds, and small quantities of coal at reduced prices. This project also included a public swimming pool as well as the well-known Iveagh Hostel, a 508-bed lodging house for "impecunious

*The Civil Service Building Society was also active in this period, but it built, as the Board of Works noted, only "for a superior class of persons."

commercial men" where for 7d. per night those fallen on hard times could obtain a sleeping cubicle, use the reading and smoking rooms, and enjoy that rarity—hot water—in the bathrooms (towel and soap 1d. extra). King Edward VII, who certainly would have been more comfortable at Punchestown Races, nevertheless felt obliged to inspect this latest answer to a vital question of the day when he visited Dublin in 1903. Indeed, Lord Iveagh himself was so touched by the occasion that he forthwith donated £50,000 to be distributed among the various Dublin hospitals, an act of charity that he repeated on the occasion of the visit to Dublin of Edward's successor in 1911. Others were less gracious, especially that baiter of the Ascendancy, D. P. Moran of the *Leader*, who suggested that the work of Lord Iveagh in the Dublin slums might better be observed on any Saturday night. . . .

Meanwhile, the Corporation had been forced into municipal housing when private builders shied away from the legal expenses and harsh economic realities of slum clearance. Between 1887 and 1901 the Corporation had built flats and cottages for over 400

Dublin old and new. The recently erected block flats of the Iveagh Trust look down on the old clothes market in Patrick Street.

families in former unsanitary parts of Benburb (formerly Barrack) Street, Blackhall Place (between Ellis Quay and North King Street), Bow Lane (near "Swift's" Hospital), and St. Joseph's Place (off Dorset Street). It had also begun the clearing and rebuilding of Bride's Alley in the shadow of Christ Church, a project that when finally completed in 1911 provided homes for a further 174 families in blocks of four-story flats.

The magnitude of the task before public and private building enterprise was conveyed by the census of 1901: 21,429 *families* living in fourth-class accommodation, 2,000 more than the corresponding figure in 1891. The census also revealed for the first time the number of one-room tenement dwellings in the city. A startled public was to discover that over 72,000 of their fellow citizens (one quarter of the population) lived in 21,747 single rooms of which 12,925 were occupied by three or more persons. If we consider only those housing operations in the central slum districts, the record suggests that by 1900 or thereabouts public and philanthropic building had provided houses or block-type dwellings for approximately 1,700 working-class families, or an estimated 8,000 persons (assuming an average based on the census of 4.5 persons per family). This was a mere drop in the ocean—"oases in a desert of squalor." Though, of course, another 2,500 families or so had been accommodated elsewhere in the city by the Artisans' Dwellings Company.[1] Yet a start had been made in an agonizingly long campaign to rid the city of its worst scars. For the moment, the lugubrious connotations of Plunkett Street were exchanged for the heroic in Thomas Davis and John Dillon Streets. White's Lane, a "hotbed of drunkenness and crime whose inhabitants were a terror to the neighborhood," was redeemed as St. Joseph's Place. Bride's Alley no longer appeared as Sir Charles Cameron once described it—"like a city after a bombardment." And Bull Alley became fit for a king to visit. However, each condemned, derelict, and rebuilt site had yielded displaced families in search of cheap shelter far greater in number than those that replaced them in the new dwellings. They found it in places like Gloucester and Gardiner Streets, which already by the 1880s were starting their heady descent from once-stately single-family houses into dingy single-room tenements.

The tenement, of course, was not unique to Dublin. It was a common feature of most old towns. The contrast was most extreme when Dublin was compared with relatively modern cities such as Belfast and Birmingham. Accommodations in Ulster's first city had been sufficient over the years to avoid any recourse by the Corporation to the borrowing privileges available under the Housing of the Working Classes Acts. Not until 1910 was the first local government building scheme completed there under the 1890 Act. In Belfast fewer than 700 houses were classed as tenements, and nearly 90 percent of the population (60,000 greater in 1901 than Dublin's) lived in houses of four rooms or more, though many of them were jerry-built structures whose deadly monotony of line offended the artistic sense of the new breed of town planner. The tenement was such an unusual feature of Belfast housing that when the Commissioners investigating the health of the city in 1907 found "a few streets" with houses built for one family occupied by *two*, they dubbed this "a serious blot" on the city: in Dublin they would hardly have found more than a few of that city's 1,000 streets without a house built for one family occupied by five and more. In Birmingham the number of persons inhabiting the slum areas of St. Mary's and Nechells wards was 2,500, hardly one-fortieth of the total number in need of decent housing in Dublin. In Manchester and Liverpool in 1911 less than 6 and 2 percent of all families, respectively, lived in one-room tenements; 85 percent and 74 percent, re-

TABLE 12. Housing in Dublin: Number of Families in Each Class of Accommodation, 1891/1901/1911 (note 1).

CLASS OF ACCOMMODATION	1891	FAMILIES 1901	1911
1st class (occupancy of 1st-class house by one family)	4,694	4,635	4,599
2nd class (note 2)	13,279		
3rd class (note 3)	14,536	33,199	37,202
4th class (note 4)	19,342	21,429	20,564
Total families	51,851	59,263	62,365
Total inhabited houses:			
old city (15 wards)	25,764	27,404	28,938
added areas	—	4,657	6,539
Totals	25,764	32,061	35,477

NOTE 1. Data for 1891 is for 15 wards, i.e., the extent of the city of Dublin before reconstitution as a county borough and the addition of 5 wards for the added areas in 1900.
NOTE 2. Denotes occupancy of 2nd-class house (5-9 rooms) by one family or 1st-class house by two or three families.
NOTE 3. Denotes occupancy of 3rd-class house (1-4 rooms) by one family; 2nd-class house by two or three families; 1st-class house by four or five families.
NOTE 4. Denotes occupancy of 4th-class house by one family; 3rd-class house by two or more families; 2nd-class house by four or more families; 1st-class house by six or more families. (Houses of the 4th class were a negligible factor, numbering only 11 and 4 in 1901 and 1911, respectively.)
SOURCE: Census of Ireland: City of Dublin; 1891, 1901, 1911 (Table VIII).

spectively, occupied four or more rooms per family. But in Dublin fully one-third of families, the majority of them consisting of three or more persons, lived in these same one-room abodes. Even Glasgow, for all the talk about its cursed back-to-back houses and two-room tenements, approached only 60 percent of Dublin's total for one-room tenements, and this gap was rapidly widening in its favor. One had to single out the most populated London metropolitan boroughs (Finsbury, Shoreditch, Stepney) to obtain degrees of congestion and unsuitable dwellings comparable to those in the Irish capital.[2]

Such evidence of Dublin's unfavorable housing situation vis-à-vis circumstances in other cities was much exploited by the daily press and by reformers, churchmen, and public health administrators. Loosely used as a criterion for overcrowding, the one-room tenement dwelling with more than two occupants became, like tuberculosis, a pervasive evil that had to be attacked. Just as the disease invaded all classes of society, the tenement cast its shadow in every section of the city, forming a major portion of the buildings in scores of streets. Over 5,000 separate tenement houses were on the registers of the public health department. A survey of *Thom's Directory* for any year suggests how pervasive the evil was. In 1899, for example, over 80 streets are listed whose tenement, vacant, or ruinous sites represent over 40 percent of the total number of houses in each street. Of the 37 houses in Bull Alley, shortly to be demolished, 36 were let in tenements, with the remaining one in ruins. Likewise Bride's Alley, Chancery Lane, Cumberland Street South, Grenville Street, Hoey's Court (birthplace of Jonathan Swift), Luke Street, Mercer Street Upper, Montgomery Street, Newfoundland Street, Newmarket, Power's Court, and Watling Street. In populous streets with houses in excess of 50 were the following percentages (in parentheses) of tenement and derelict structures: Abbey Street Upper (45), Bride Street (63), Bridgefoot Street (72), North Brunswick Street (50), Church Street (51), Clar-

Typical Dublin tenement houses, with inhabitants *en fête* for the photographer.

ence Street North (74), Cook Street (59), the Coombe (53), Cork Street (42), Francis Street (49), Gloucester Street (55), Meath Street (44), Patrick Street (68), Townsend Street (58), Tyrone Street Lower (79), Wellington Street (58).

Certainly, the one-room tenement was not of itself necessarily the lowest form of habitation. After all, the term "slum dweller" was most often indiscriminately employed by middle-class types only to signify their detestation of the rough habits of the working classes. These so-called slum dwellers were not distinguished then or later by any alacrity to leave their tenement abodes for the mean, barracks-like flats of the Corporation or the barren wastes of suburban sites. One observer who had long experience with these people through his activities on behalf of the National Society for the Prevention of Cruelty to Children reflected at the Dublin Housing Inquiry in 1913 that "the masses never conquered these [slum] conditions nor rose above them; and the one fact borne in upon me is that they are largely impervious to their surroundings, and when pinched or hurt their trust in God for a better tomorrow is supreme. Nowhere did I find a revolt against the housing conditions; on the contrary I found expressions of fear that anything was going to be done which would limit the tenements by the destruction of houses and that they would be rendered houseless."[3] This latter fear was well founded, as the previous experience of Corporation clearances in Dublin and elsewhere had demonstrated all too painfully. The familiarity of old surroundings, acquired friendships, the vital comforts of the local pub, the privilege of buying "on tick" at the corner grocer, the avoidance of tramway fares, and especially, an affordable rent—all these were usually enough to make up for the noise, smells, and inconvenience of a "two-pair back" in the heart of the city. Was a vanman, charwoman, or casual laborer living alone in one room in Church Street worse off for accommodation than a family of seven in two rooms rented from Lord Iveagh, with or without the venetian blinds?* Reformers and do-gooders thought so. Where three or more slept in one bed were there not certain advantages regarding warmth in unheated tenement rooms? Reformers and do-gooders could see only the moral risks involved. But we can hardly blame them for wishing to impose on the lower classes the standards of decency and comfort they had created as a mark of the modern civilization they had brought into being. And the slums were a disgrace to that civilization. Few could believe that the Earl of Dudley, representative in Ireland of a government many held responsible for the country's ills, was greatly exaggerating when he stated that he "had seen the misery of Irish peasants in the West, but nothing compared with what existed at their own doors in Dublin."[4]

According to the census, Dublin had 32,061 inhabited houses (excluding that 10 percent or so that at any time were normally closed or uninhabited) in 1901 and 23,501 of these were each occupied by one family (i.e., by a single occupier or head of household). This left 8,560 houses of all classes containing two or more families each. At least 5,197 of the latter were registered tenements under the bylaws, according to the figures of the Public Health Department, but to that total would have to be added another 1,500 or so second- and third-class houses or cottages in courts and alleys, each normally occupied by one family, to arrive at a more reliable estimate of the unsuitable housing in the city.

*Families of 5 to 7 persons were not uncommon in the Iveagh Buildings' two-room flats: in one case, for example, such an apartment was occupied by a father, two sons (aged 28, 20), three daughters (24, 31, 36), and one grandchild aged 15.

TABLE 13. Dublin: Total houses, registered tenement houses, and tenements of one room in each ward of county borough, 1901 and 1911.

	TOTAL HOUSES (note 1)		NUMBER OF REGISTERED TENEMENT HOUSES (note 2)		NUMBER OF ONE-ROOM TENEMENT DWELLINGS (note 1)	
	1901	1911	1901	1911	1901	1911
Arran Quay	3,424	4,541		452	1,680	1,477
Clontarf East	574	658		2	1	34
Clontarf West	758	1,099		—	32	58
Drumcondra	1,293	1,803		1	62	98
Fitzwilliam	1,679	1,711		195	704	781
Glasnevin	1,095	1,861		15	64	99
Inns Quay	2,623	2,586		444	1,977	1,789
Mansion House	1,058	918		318	1,428	1,206
Merchants' Quay	3,204	3,271	(figures for wards not available)	553	2,008	1,974
Mountjoy	2,850	2,932		474	2,439	2,650
New Kilmainham	1,365	1,600		64	184	161
North City	1,290	887		261	755	881
North Dock	3,096	3,354		323	1,916	1,808
Rotunda	1,524	1,425		347	1,402	1,884
Royal Exchange	940	649		272	737	680
South City	819	502		102	322	253
South Dock	1,824	1,763		342	1,200	1,145
Trinity	1,220	1,005		303	1,358	1,185
Usher's Quay	2,308	2,656		418	1,627	1,308
Wood Quay	2,516	2,376		436	1,851	1,662
Totals	35,460	37,597	5,197	5,322	21,747	21,133

Number of one-room tenements occupied by		1901	1911
	1 person	3,278	3,604
	2 persons	5,544	5,310
	3–5 persons	10,078	9,234
	6 or more persons	2,847	2,985

NOTE 1. Data from Census 1901/1911 (Tables III and X)
NOTE 2. Figures as supplied (1911 only) by Public Health Department of Dublin Corporation at the Dublin Housing Inquiry in 1913 [see *Parliamentary Papers,* 1914 (XIX), cd. 7317, pp. 311–12]

Section 29 of the Dublin Corporation Act (1890) defined a tenement for purposes of registration as "any house (not being a common lodging house) occupied by members of more than one family, and in which the average rent charged to the occupiers shall be less than 7s. a week, and the lowest rent charged to any occupier shall be not more than 5s. a week." Every tenement house was inspected about eight times a year for compliance with public health regulations. In this way the Public Health Department had been able to close, in most cases permanently, several thousand tenement houses and cellar dwellings classed as unfit for human habitation during the years 1899 to 1913.

A common violation of sanitary regulations in tenement houses was overcrowding. Overcrowding in Dublin was defined as less than 400 cubic feet for each adult (200, each child) in nonsleeping accommodation and 300 (150) cubic feet in sleeping accommodation. But it proved impossible to enforce this regulation, for obvious reasons. The attempt to do so in Glasgow by *night* visitations of the sanitary inspector resulted in some amusing sidelights at the Glasgow Municipal Commission in 1904, while, incidentally, shedding some light on the worst circumstances of working-class life of the period. Occupants attempted to avoid detection by hiding in presses, under beds, in cupboards, or on housetops! On several occasions two tiers of people had been found in one bed, one on the boards or on the mattress, the bedclothes then flung over and another living tier on top. In another case a son aged 22, a young woman aged 20, and a 16-year-old girl were found between the bed and the mattress; the father lying above the son and younger members of the family above the girls; the eldest girl "as naked as the hour she was born" and the mother lying on the floor!⁵ One obvious defect of the bylaws was that the only limit on the number of persons allowed to occupy one room was the rough-and-ready cubic feet regulation, so that a 16' x 16' x 10' room could legally contain up to eight persons (including three children under 10 years). Even a cow in his byre was entitled to 800 cubic feet under the laws regulating dairies and cowsheds.

The laxity of the Public Health Department in enforcing the laws in respect to overcrowding was dictated by the need to avoid the social problems that would ensue from any mass closings of tenement dwellings. Had this not been so, the police records of closing orders issued on civil proceedings to landlords would hardly have numbered a mere 82 for the 15 years 1899 to 1913. In the year 1914 alone, after the outcry generated by the Church Street disaster, in which several people were killed in the sudden collapse of a tenement house, no fewer than 320 such orders were delivered. Other health regulations were unenforceable on other grounds, some downright silly, such as the requirement that under penalty of fines every roomkeeper "shall cause the floor . . . to be thoroughly swept every day before 10 A.M." or that "every window of every room . . . used as a sleeping apartment, to be opened and to be kept fully open for one hour at least in the forenoon and for one hour at least in the afternoon of every day." Another impossible situation was introduced by the laws governing the provision of water closets—one to every 12 persons. The public health department also allowed this to become a dead letter, convinced by the experience that the more WCs in a tenement house, the more abuse of the facilities and consequently the greater dangers to public health. Sir Charles Cameron rarely let the opportunity slip in official reports or at public hearings to decry the careless and filthy habits of those in the lowest class of tenement houses, maintaining that even when transplanted to new Corporation flats they continued to make improper use of the WC, using it as an ashpit, a fowlhouse, a receptacle for boken jampots, and so forth. Like other witnesses, he was convinced that no self-respecting woman in a tenement house would ever use the backyard public WC, though tolerating her children's defilement of the yard or closet floor. Hence, sanitary conveniences had only to be provided for men and grown-up boys. In any event most yards were not large enough to accommodate the number of WCs that would be required by strict application of the sanitary laws. At least this was the argument used in 1914 at the Dublin Housing Inquiry to justify Cameron's instructions to his sanitary officers to be lax about enforcement of the laws regarding water closets. Although the bylaws provided for summonses and fines for abuse of WCs, they applied only where two or more *houses* had a common WC, thereby allowing the tenants of any house with its own WC, regardless of the number of families, to escape penalty. The Corporation felt no compunction therefore in making formal admission at the Inquiry that of the city's 5,322 tenement houses, 1,161 having 20 or more persons per house were each provided with but one WC! Among the worst of these at one time was 10 Francis Street—two WCs for 107 inhabitants.⁶

The defects of these tenements were many. Their condition was generally dilapidated

—cracked walls, leaky roofs, rickety stairs, broken windows, worm-eaten floors. Basements became receptacles for dirt or, worse, sufficed as cellar dwellings for the most destitute of the population. Many were situated in narrow courts and alleys and had neither sufficient airspace nor provision for backyards. There were no effective arrangements for regulating the cleaning of halls, lobbies and stairs; in any event, water was not laid on at each floor, being available only at the single common tap. This general lack of washing facilities lends credence to the story that it was common for neighborhood mothers to bathe their young children in the ornamental waters of St. Stephen's Green. The free access to unlit hallways at all hours rendered them the haunts of prostitutes, criminal elements, or derelicts looking for a place to sleep. The early riser might have to throw something down the stairs on his way to work to frighten the rats away. There were no proper cooking arrangements, and washhouses were such a rarity that clothes were strung on lines inside the rooms to dry or hung out the windows as "flags of distress." The Corporation had no power to compel owners to put decaying tenements into repair except where conditions contravened the sanitary laws or the structure was unsound. Therefore, representations made to owners might lead at best to repair of a fanlight or the painting of a door. Public apathy, tenants' habits, landlord resistance, and to some extent, a demoralized sanitary staff all combined to perpetuate a number of evils. Meetings of the Corporation often degenerated into unseemly altercation as one councillor, generally from the Labour contingent, traded accusations with the Chairman of the Health Committee regarding alleged pressure on the sanitary staff to postpone prosecutions of slum landlords.[7] For its part the Dublin Corporation averted criticism by pointing to the objections of organized ratepayers, many of them owners of tenement property, to any strengthening of the bylaws that imposed stricter obligations on owners or served to increase the rates. And ultimately, its most effective weapon in countering those who demanded action in regard to the housing of the working classes was that alternative housing at moderate rents was not available in Dublin for those who would be displaced by the mass closure of insanitary dwellings.

In the previous quarter century much had happened to mitigate the plight of the laboring classes. The general course of wages had been upward until 1900, hours of labor had been reduced slightly in many trades, improvements in the cost of living, the proliferation of modern creature comforts, and improved standards of health had all gone hand in hand. The one element that had remained unchanged from decade to decade was the living conditions of the class of unskilled labor, especially those who resided in the thousands of tenement and other houses that in fact if not in law were an affront to standards of decent living. The Dublin Tenement Houses became the standard topic of Corporation meetings, health congresses, statistical societies, philanthropic associations, and newspaper editors. What little we know of the domestic arrangements of their inhabitants comes down to us second-hand from the witnesses of their misfortune in reports that were doubtless often colored by moral outrage and human sympathy to stir the social conscience, yet still suggestive of grim realities. A room is rented by a woman to four permanent lodgers. She sleeps in a small bed at one end while along a wall are two beds placed end to end for the lodgers (two of each sex). In a corner is a ragged mattress and bed clothes that serve as the sleeping place of temporary lodgers (6d. a night)—husband, wife, and three children. Evidence at the police courts also reveal conditions: a husband and wife, brother, seven children, of which one is in the latter stages of consumption, in

The rear of an insanitary cottage dwelling in Faddle's Alley, off Clanbrassil Street.

one room. A murder in the Coombe discloses that three couples occupied one room, with separation by curtains. A landlord is charged for maintaining his 18 overcrowded, back-to-back tenements in Taaffe's Row in an unfit state: the unlighted 25"wide staircases have no hand rails; there is a sickening odor from the doorless common water closets. Investigation of a typhus outbreak in Church Street finds thirteen families occupying 14 rooms and 4 closets. One family in 2 rooms and a closet consists of a husband, wife, wife's mother, and seven children between 1 and 17 years. Eight had been attacked by the fever. NSPCC inspectors discover three families (ten persons) occupying a room that formed the only means of entrance to another room equally overcrowded. In another case, parents and seven children sleep on the floor on which there is "not enough straw for a cat" and no covering. Utensils consist of a zinc bucket, a can, a few mugs and jam pots for drinking. The only furniture is a broken bedstead and stool. The investigation of a claim for compensation in connection with the detenanting of Beresford Street in 1913

Taking water from the pump in one of the ruinous courts off Beresford Street.

reveals two rooms and a closet occupied by a family of fifteen, the eldest a 19-year-old boy. "And what are the rest," asked the court of an apparently distracted father. "I couldn't really say whether they are boys or girls," he answered, "but they are there now (loud laughter). There's a child a fortnight old, but you wouldn't count him (renewed laughter)." The labor troubles of 1913 also added to the legend of despair, for the phrase "O'Leary's Room"* came to encapsulate the hardship of life in the tenements. The court cases in connection with assaults on (and by) the police on the night of August 31 disclosed that William O'Leary, his wife and six children (aged one to thirteen years), a brother, and consumptive child inhabited a single room in a tenement.

The Housing Inquiry of the same year also offers a depressing record of life in these dwellings. One of the more eloquent witnesses at that hearing was Walter Carpenter, erstwhile socialist colleague of James Connolly, who claimed that there was not a house yet built in Dublin that was fit for a working-class family to live in. At the very least, he thought, every house should be supplied with a bathroom so that a man's shirt need not be taken out of a pot for his dinner to be put into it. Those interested in the welfare of

*Coined by an editorial in the *Irish Times*, September 19, 1913.

children surmised that their lives were probably extended by spending so much of their free time in the streets rather than at home. And in the case of adults, it was felt that the allegedly low standard of efficiency of Dublin labor, especially of the bricklayers whose work was quantifiable, could only be explained by the debilitating circumstances of life in the tenements.[8]

A more exact guide to instances of overcrowding is afforded by the individual reports of the census taker as preserved in the manuscript schedules. Some glaring examples in the case of individual families taken from the 1901 census are given in Table 14. Among the worst examples of multi-family occupancy of a tenement house was 1 Francis Street: 15 families consisting of 63 persons occupying 16 rooms. The same street of 118 houses had each of 264 of its 407 families living in one room. In fact census schedules confirmed what critics had been saying all along about overcrowding as measured by the ratio of "one-room" families to total families in various streets of the city (figures in percent): Ardee Street, 55; Ashe Street, 74; Back Lane, 63; Benburb Street, 42; Brabazon Street, 79; Bride Street, 79; Cook Street, 74; The Coombe, 60; Dominick Street Upper, 82; Francis Street, 65; Gloucester Place Lower, 64; Hackett's Court, 78; Hoey's Court, 86; Michael's Hill, 50; Michael's Lane, 39; Montgomery Street, 85; Nerney's Court, 70; Purdon Street, 82; Spitalfields, 95.[9]

Not all houses, naturally, had fifteen families, nor did the majority of families, as we know, live in one-room dwellings, although as much as one-third of them did. Fully half of the 8,000 or so multi-tenanted houses contained in each case either two or three families. And of the remainder only about 10 percent were occupied by eight or more families. These figures, however, did not conceal the fact of the extraordinary number of single-room occupancies that characterized residence in thousands of these houses. The tenement was generally a four-story structure of the kind that because of size (i.e., number of rooms and windows) was classified as a first-class house. Two-thirds of all families in fourth-class accommodation lived in them. Rents varied depending on the floor and the view. Such a house let in single rooms would have four rooms on the ground floor (front and back kitchens, front and back parlors), two large drawing rooms (front and back, often partitioned) on the second floor, the "two-pair" (one room, front and back) on the third floor, and the top front and back above those. Drawing rooms and parlors, the largest rooms, commanded the highest rents. A typical rental schedule for the better class of Dublin tenement would have had the following range of weekly rents:

back kitchen	1s. 9d.
front kitchen	2s. 6d.
back parlor or drawing room	3s. 0d.
front parlor or drawing room	3s. 6d.
two-pair back	2s. 6d.
two-pair front	3s. 0d.
top back	2s. 6d.
top front	3s. 0d.

In a less well-kept house the rent per room would perhaps be reduced by 6d., and, of course, a family with two or more rooms paid correspondingly higher rents. By contrast, the rents in the block flats let by the Artisans' Dwellings Company were 2s., 3s., and 4s. 3d. per week for one, two, and three rooms, respectively; but that type of dwelling represented only 13 percent of all its lettings; the three- and four-room cottages at 5s. 3d. and

TABLE 14. **Selected Data on Individual Families as Reported in the 1901 Census.**

LOCATION	NO. OF ROOMS OCCUPIED BY FAMILY	NO. AND MEMBERS OF FAMILY	OCCUPATION OF HEAD OF HOUSEHOLD	OTHER INFORMATION
10 Hoey's Ct.	one	9 (parents, 7 children aged 4–16)	Painter	Two daughters employed as servants
14 Hoey's Ct.	one	8 (parents, mother-in-law, 5 children aged 1–13)	Laborer	—
1 Nerney's Ct.	one	7 (parents, 2 sisters-in-law, 3 children)		Sisters-in-law employed as servants
	one	5 (widow, 2 adult children, 2 children aged 5 and 14)	Fish dealer	Son a laborer
3 Nerney's Ct.	one	3 (2 brothers aged 30, 40; sister aged 35)	Laborer	Brother and sister also employed
6 Nerney's Ct.	one	8 (parents, 6 children aged 1–10)	Porter	—
23 Nerney's Ct.	one	7 (mother, 6 children aged 1–10)	None	—
1 Montgomery St.	one	8 (parents, 4 daughters aged 1–12, 2 sons aged 8, 10)	Quay laborer	—
3 Montgomery St.	one	8 (widow, 3 daughters aged 16–24, sister-in-law aged 56, nephew aged 26, 2 nieces aged 16, 18)	General laborer	One daughter, nephew and one niece employed
32 Montgomery St.	three	11 (parents, 5 sons aged 6–19, 3 daughters aged 4–9, and 37-year-old male boarder)	General laborer	2 sons employed as laborers
57 Montgomery St.	one	3 (2 females aged 26, 42; 1 male aged 38)	—	Occupants unrelated (two are boarders)
60 Montgomery St.	two	7 (1 female aged 24, 5 female boarders aged 4–40 and 1 "visitor")	Servant	All adults employed as servants

TABLE 14 (con't.)

61 Montgomery St.	one	3 (2 females aged 23, 30; 1 male aged 29)	—	Two occupants are boarders
67A Montgomery St.	three	10 (parents, 4 children, 2 female boarders with children)	General laborer	—
4 Brabazon St.	one	8 (parents, 3 daughters aged 2-13, 3 sons aged 1-9)	—	—
45 Bride St.	one	9 (parents, 4 daughters aged 2-16, 2 sons aged 7, 14; 28-year-old brother-in-law)	—	—
4 Dominick St. Upper	one	9 (parents, 2 daughters aged 3, 6; 5 sons aged 1-19)	Shoemaker	2 sons employed
4 Gloucester Place, Lower	one	10 (parents, 5 daughters and 3 sons aged 9-22)	General laborer	—
16 Mabbot St.	one	10 (parents, 5 daughters and 3 sons)	Coal laborer	3 older daughters aged 12-16 employed as servants
57 Mabbot St.	one	11 (parents, 2 daughters and 7 sons)	Float driver	3 sons employed
1 Newfoundland St.	two	9 (mother, grandmother, 2 daughters aged 7-16, 5 sons aged 1-14)	—	2 children employed
36 Newfoundland St.	two	12 (parents, 6 daughters aged 1-19, 4 sons aged 9-15)	Laborer	3 children employed

SOURCE: Public Record Office (Dublin). Manuscript schedules of 1901 Census: 71/34, 43/37, 39/86–87, 74/6, 76/31, 45/41, 39/47, 39/82, 39/91.

7s. being the common tenancy. The Corporation's single-room flats, of which there were only 65 among the buildings constructed before 1900, were let at 1s. 6d. to 2s. for a 15' x 10' x 8½' room, which according to the bylaws could accommodate a family of four. The two-room flat (floor area: 13' x 13', 13' x 8') was the predominant Corporation dwelling at this period and rents for the 300 or so that were available ranged from 2s. to 4s. per week.

It was generally maintained that a casual laborer or other low-paid worker in Dublin could not pay more than about 2s. to 2s. 6d. per week in rent out of an average wage of 15s. When it is realized that at least one in four male workers was a general laborer, porter, carter, or unskilled railway employee, it becomes evident that rents were an important aspect of the housing question. A large proportion of artisans, despite their higher wages, were also forced by economic circumstances to accept the stigma of tenement living. A survey of tenement-house families prepared by the Public Health department showed that 70 percent paid weekly rents of 3s. 6d. and under, while 60 percent of that number paid 1s. 6d. or 2s. 6d. The same investigation listed the occupations of some 25,000 heads of families occupying rooms in registered tenement houses. About half were in the class of general laborer, charwoman, porter, pensioner, carter, and the like and their recorded average weekly earnings did not exceed 20s. Official records also showed that over 400 notices to quit were served in the city each week for nonpayment of rent. In fact, one of the chief difficulties of municipal housing in Dublin continued to be the impossibility of providing accommodation at rents that the majority of workers could afford while at the same time avoiding recourse to the rates to make up the financial loss that would accrue. The City Treasurer even admitted at the Housing Inquiry in 1913 that tenants of the municipal flats in Bride's Alley tended to leave in search of lower rents. Not only were rents in Dublin much higher than in the rest of Ireland, but a Board of Trade study of rents in the U.K. revealed that of eighty-eight towns studied, in only two (including London) did the rents of working-class houses generally exceed rents in Dublin. In Belfast, where land was cheap and rates low, the rent index number was 40 percent lower than the Dublin figure when measured both in 1905 and 1912. According to the *Irish Builder*, "house rent in Dublin is high beyond all reason," a fact it held partly responsible for the continuing degeneration of one-family houses into tenements and lodgings.[10]

These drastic circumstances were widely known and commented upon endlessly. In England, as Enid Gauldie informs us, a solution to the housing problem became an electoral campaign need that based itself on working-class demands and middle-class sympathies. Similar demands and sympathies were not absent in Dublin. Unfortunately, given the immensity of the task that faced the municipal authorities, not even a wholesale desertion by the ratepayers of their wonted parsimony could have provided a lasting solution. The democratization of the municipal franchise in 1899 at least provided a forum for discussion of the housing question. Only a few months after the first municipal elections under the Local Government Act (which added a laborite contingent of eight members to the municipal council), the first of many resolutions was introduced at a Corporation meeting suggesting that a scheme of slum clearance and rehousing be promoted. At the ensuing discussion there was ominous reference to recent experience in clearing slum areas when huge sums had to be paid to buy out the owners, creating annual deficits that were charged to the rates.[11] Thus, since the Corporation did not as yet possess the favorable borrowing powers ceded by the "Clancy Act" of 1908, no large-scale clearances were contemplated. However, the agitation did not subside, for the year 1899 also saw the concern for public health create the conditions for close scrutiny of the housing problem in the Public Health Inquiry of the following year. That hearing concluded that improvement schemes could not but react favorably on the health of the city:

> The question of the housing of the poor of Dublin is one of magnitude. The provision of an adequate number of healthy dwellings by way of relief for the present overcrowding of population under unhealthy conditions in congested districts of the city, must, of necessity, be on a

considerable scale, and would probably involve several schemes for this purpose. . . . In these schemes it should be borne in mind that healthy dwellings are especially needed in Dublin for the very poor. Houses, therefore, intended with this object should be of the plainest kind, in order that such schemes may not entail heavy loss upon the ratepayers.[12]

The first scheme the Corporation took up after this managed to acknowledge both the healthful and frugal components of that recommendation. The Montgomery Street area west of Amiens Street was one of the most unsavory districts in the city, full of brothels and unlicensed beerhouses and comprising some of the most disreputable and unsanitary streets in Dublin. It was now proposed to clear a 2¼-acre slum between Purdon and Montgomery Streets to rid the city of yet another "plague spot" and erect healthy dwellings for the class known as the "very poor." Hitherto the Corporation had largely endeavored to attract as tenants of municipal housing the artisans or regularly employed laboring classes. Here, however, the need to provide for the casual laborers, low-paid porters and messengers, rag pickers, hawkers, sandwich men, and others whose margin of survival was barely enough to keep them out of the workhouse was fully acknowledged. Part of the £70,000 cost of the proposed scheme (including site costs of £5,000 an acre) was to be regarded as "unproductive expenditure made in the interest of public health." A better selection in the matter of the site could hardly have been made: at least the financial reservations of the ratepayers could be balanced by higher moral considerations. And there could be no doubting the general poverty of the inhabitants. The 122 families in the 30 houses, almost all tenements, declared their occupations to the census-taker in 1901 as follows: general laborers (coal, quay, and so on), 59; servants, charwomen, porters, and the like, 25; tradesmen, 7; dealers, 7; unstated (widows, unemployed, and such), 15; other, 9.[13] Although 480 dwellings were erected in 1905 with accommodation for about 2,000 persons, or six times the number displaced, they consisted entirely of barracks-style flats of five storys with interconnecting balconies. All but 80 of them were single-room tenements, let at 2s. 6d. and below. With dimensions of 14' x 11' x 8½', the rooms (excluding the scullery and WC) could hardly be called commodious or comfortable for a family of four. They were certainly dwellings "of the plainest kind" in houses that observers considered so plain as to be almost repellent. In fact, the Corporation had created the type of congested habitations it had been the object of municipal housing to abolish. Nonetheless, a memorial of "the ratepayers of Montgomery Street" expressed satisfaction at what had been attempted and requested Dublin Corporation to rename the street to, as it were, exorcise the spirit of its former evil. It duly became Foley Street and for good measure adjacent Mabbot Street became Corporation Street while the nearby and more iniquitous Tyrone Street, which had already undergone one transformation from Mecklenburgh Street, endured another as it descended to Railway Street. Purdon Street, commemorating the name of a former Protestant Conservative Lord Mayor, disappeared entirely. The memory (or, perhaps, the vice) proved too strong, however, for the Corporation found it impossible to attract sufficient tenants even at the low rents. As a result the rents had to be cut in half, to as low as 1s. per week, and a less desirable type of tenant had to be accepted. Naturally, the "Foley Street dwellings" became another white elephant that fed the anger and cynicism of critics for years. Even as late as 1913, one-third of the flats were untenanted. Patrick Geddes, in evidence at the 1913 Housing Inquiry, dubbed the scheme a "dramatic example of deteriorating process in action": in effect, the Corporation was preparing slums for the future.[14]

It had taken five years from the date of approval to acquire the property in 1900 to bring the Montgomery-Purdon Street area scheme to completion. Agitation for further action continued meanwhile. Two of the city's Nationalist parliamentary representatives, William Field and Joseph Nannetti, carried the campaign to the House of Commons, where they chided their English colleagues with the notion that paupers, lunatics, and criminals were better housed in Ireland than the wealth producers of the nation. Alas, they were unable to persuade the government that special legislative treatment should be accorded to Dublin, where, it was suggested, the housing of the very poor was done in the workhouses. The interests of labor in the matter were acknowledged when the Dublin Trades Council was invited for the first time to join town councillors and MPs at a Mansion House conference on housing for the workers in September 1903. Among the recommendations that emerged were the provision of incentives (i.e., rates remission) to stimulate private building enterprise, the erection of cottages on the outskirts of the city where land was cheaper, and cheap means of transit for workers. To this latter demand for a half-penny fare, the Tramways Company always turned a deaf ear. Though meetings of the Irish Trades Union Congress and the annual conventions of the Irish parliamentary party never failed to include the set speech on the "housing of the working classes," solutions to the problem proved to be as elusive as ever as far as Dublin was concerned.[15]

The result of all this activity was an attempt by the Corporation to give effect to some of the recommendations heard over the years. In February 1908 it decided to promote a bill in parliament designed to extend the period for which money for housing might be borrowed from 60 to 80 years, acquire without payment of compensation land that had lain derelict for 5 years, place all tenements under the supervision of drastic by-laws, which included their licensing at the discretion of the Corporation, and, taking a cue from the 1903 Mansion House conference, offer 10 years' remission of rates to encourage private building in order to help reduce rents in the city. The housing bill was to be accompanied by a Various Powers (Omnibus) measure dealing with general matters of public health enforcement. The discussion in the municipal chamber gave a foretaste of what was to come. With the Corporation debt at £2.7 million, the rates-conscious, middle-class Sinn Fein contingent led the opposition against any further pilfering of the public purse. Rather than place themselves in naked alliance with such obvious anti-trade union elements as the Chamber of Commerce and property-owners associations, Alderman Thomas Kelly and his Irish Ireland stalwarts couched their opposition in political terms, viz., that no Irish Corporation should petition a British parliament to grant them powers to act—to do so would be tantamount to acknowledging its right to legislate for Ireland. Whether the Dublin laboring classes were prepared to accept this political logic is not clear, but we do know that the minority Sinn Fein party suffered drastically in the municipal elections over the next few years. In this instance, however, the opponents of the bills received very effective support from the public gallery. So much disorder was created in the chamber that the police had to be called to quell the disturbance, thus forcing the Corporation to submit the issue to a referendum of registered voters. Newspaper editors and cartoonists had a field day pillorying the proposals.

Substantial citizens such as W.M. Murphy and Sinn Fein crusader Arthur Griffith led the public opposition. Murphy condemned outright the promotion of any private bill "in restraint of individual rights and liberties"—those of slum landlords, presumably. Corporation housing was, he wrote, "a waste of public money." When he rose to the "defense" of slum dwellers against expenditures for an art gallery in 1913, his own critics may be forgiven for having detected insincerity in his views in the light of his confessed attitude to working-class housing in 1908. Griffith advised the voters to "destroy these dishonest bills" because the Corporation already possessed sufficient powers to act under existing legislation. But he was being less than honest himself in so dismissing measures that would have armed the public health department against recalcitrant and dishonest landlords and with any luck (and government funds) pushed forward the timid campaign against the slums. Five out of nine voters in a poll of twenty-five thousand voted against the two bills (one of which, incidentally, would have provided free milk to needy schoolchildren) and they were consequently withdrawn.[16] Local wags quipped that no small credit for the defeat was due to the horse-car owners and drivers who thought that the "omnibus" bill was promoting taxicabs!

Thus chastened, the Corporation declined to increase the rates by 6d. in the £ as planned and earned the gratitude of its most constant critic, the *Irish Times*, thereby. So challenged, the biggest ratepayers in the city formed the Dublin Citizens Association to preach the lesson now painfully familiar: that high municipal taxation frightens away private capital, retards business development, reduces employment and wages, raises the cost of living, and mutatis mutandis, increases pauperism. That these same elements as well as newspapers like the *Irish Times* had for years been in the forefront of criticism of the Corporation for tolerating the continued existence of the slums gives some indication of the extent to which hypocrisy had triumphed over humanity in Dublin.

Some of the ground lost by the Corporation was shortly to be recovered by the independent action at Westminister of the Nationalist member for Dublin county, J.J. Clancy, MP (not to be confused with councillor John Clancy of South Dock Ward), with whose name the Housing (Ireland) Act of 1908 is linked. Hitherto the housing of the working classes was guided by the provisions of the great Act of 1890. This was the authority by which the Corporation undertook improvement schemes for areas declared unfit for human habitation by the medical officer of health (Part I) or proceeded against individual unsanitary dwellings (Part II). In pleading his case, Clancy observed how very little had been done to house the working classes in Dublin since the very first housing act—fewer than 5,000 houses constructed in close to 40 years. "The magnitude of the blot on the capital city of Ireland," he said, "amounts in itself to a national scandal . . . thousands of dens breeding tuberculosis."[17] The measure passed into law in December 1908. As a consequence the ponderously slow procedures of the 1890 Act, such as the necessity to obtain the approval of parliament for each order covering the compulsory acquisition of land, were simplified and speeded up. In addition, the "Clancy Act" gave to municipal authorities the extended borrowing period (80 years) called for in the Corporation's bill and permitted a two-year delay in the initial repayment of capital to the Treasury. It was also the first housing act to put into effect the principle of a state subsidy to stimulate building through the creation of an Irish Housing fund, which would provide grants-in-aid to lessen any burden on the rates. This Fund, sustained by certain monies collected in Ireland (Crown and Quit rents, and such), was never very large and was divisible (in proportion to amounts borrowed each year) among all municipal bodies with housing schemes for the workers in progress. For example, some local authorities received as little as £9 (Galway in 1909) or as much as £600 (Kingstown in 1911). Dublin's allocation averaged about £400 per annum. Yet the idea of supplementary funds supporting municipal housing suggested to some concerned citizens that a corresponding Mansion House committee might be established to solicit private donations, a tactic often employed to relieve the victims of disaster, whether from earthquakes in Sicily or unemployment at home. Alas, there is no record on this occasion of any rush to rescue the poor from their sordid living quarters.

The Clancy Act, by encouraging both an increase and acceleration in the disbursement of loans, gave hope but could hardly be expected to provide any immediate solution to the housing crisis. The usual three- to four-year delay would have to ensue between the adoption and final completion of any scheme. There was the difficulty of procuring sites whose land and compensation costs would not prejudice the adoption of particular schemes. The Corporation had also decided not to grapple with the difficulties of building cottages on virgin soil outside the city so that any major rebuilding in the city would likely displace thousands of families with nowhere to go but to other low-rent congested areas. Moreover, the cost of ridding the city of its "national scandal" was variously estimated to be between £3 and £4 million, or ten times the amount borrowed for housing since the purchase of the Coombe site in 1877. And doubtless rising costs for labor and material would greatly increase that estimate in the years ahead.

Since the Foley Street scheme only 4 projects had been undertaken to provide a mere 70 flats or cottages in the inner city and ultimately over 300 cottages in the added areas, mainly in the newer New Kilmainham ward (see Appendix D). Another scheme for the Cook Street area between Christ Church and the Liffey was adopted in 1909 and completed by 1914. The Cook Street scheme illustrates the difficulties and delays under which the proponents of municipal housing labored in Dublin. Much of the area was already in ruins by 1904, when a deputation from the neighborhood requested action. The reply of the Corporation's Improvement Committee cited the lack of funds and its lack of power to deal with derelict spaces not owned by the Corporation. The next report on Cook Street is dated 1907 after Sir Charles Cameron had declared its eyesore tenements to be unfit for human habitation, thus allowing the Corporation to proceed. It was decided to clear the site bounded by Cook Street and the adjoining Schoolhouse Lane, Michael's Lane, and Borris Court. Initially, 162 one- and two-room self-contained flats in three-story blocks were planned in the usual frugal style. The room plan for the two-room tenement provided for a living room 11¼' x 10½' and bedroom 10½' x 9½'. By 1910 nothing had been done, and in July of that year a "special commissioner" was sent by the *Irish Times* to photograph and survey an area that had become a center of squalor and ruin in the midst of which visiting archaeologists, not inappropriately perhaps, viewed St. Audoen's Arch and the ancient wall of the city. "Cook Street, once famous for making coffins," wrote the investigator, "is now busy preparing their contents." The Citizens' Association next entered the fray, seeing another "Foley Street" in such a scheme of minor improvement for a depressed area. The Corporation backtracked and finally decided to house 45 families in self-contained, three-room, two-story red brick houses instead of the 162 originally contemplated. The rents, set at 4s. 6d. per week, were obviously designed both to be "economic" and to lure the better-paid artisans who had declined to avail themselves of the Foley Street flats. A £10,000 loan was sanctioned by the Local Government Board in December 1911 and the buildings completed in 1913, nine years after the matter had first been brought to the attention of the Corporation.[18]

Meanwhile, the public health department continued to inspect, condemn, and detenant groups of buildings throughout the city. By 1913 over 1,300 derelict houses and sites littered every quarter of the city, giving visual evidence of massive urban decay. The human results were conveyed by the census: in the 10 years since 1901 the number of tenements of one room had decreased by only *614* (see Table 13); the number of inhabited houses had increased by 3,416 (or by only 2,155 if the number of uninhabited houses at each census is included)—barely enough to keep pace with the number of new families; and, worst of all, one-third of all families lived in fourth-class accommodation, this latter representing a mere 3 percent change for the better in that ratio (see Table 12). Sir Charles Cameron's annual report on the public health of the city for the census year 1911 included these official figures and, accordingly, generated renewed interest in the immensity of the housing problem. The *Irish Times* was the first to call for a Vice-Regal Commission to inquire into the situation. Despite the fact that this newspaper of the conservative Unionist party had never ceased to harry the Corporation for allegedly playing fast and loose with taxpayers' money, it nevertheless also played the leading nonofficial role in educating the general public to the housing needs of the city. The idea of an official investigation was taken up in the municipal council by Alderman M'Walter, MD, but it died there. The recently elected councillor Alfred ("Alfie") Byrne, as yet untuned to the Fabian strategies of his Nationalist colleagues, reminded the members that "the question of the abolition of the slums . . . has become so pressing that it is imperative that some decisive steps should be taken to deal with it immediately."[19] Other councillors descanted on the problem at ward meetings of the United Irish League where such concern bought votes. The holding of the Congress of the Royal Institute of Public Health in Dublin in 1911 also exerted pressure on the Corporation to undertake clearance schemes under Part 1 of the Act of 1890.

The public health department had outlined as early as 1898 the several areas requiring to be cleared: Ormond Market, Moore Street Market, Nerney's Court and Leeson Place. To these would be added over the years the nether worlds of Church and Beresford Streets, Spitalfields-Ashe Street, Crabbe Lane, Boyne Street, and elsewhere. Among the worst of these was the Ormond Market area, a rookery of tenements and ruinous sites about Mary's Lane whose condemnation and closing had been contemplated as far back as 1886. In 1903 the *Irish Times* described the courts and alleys behind Upper Ormond Quay as a disgrace to the city that should be reformed out of existence: "To pass through it is to endure odours of the most repulsive and sickening character. . . . We hardly believe that a worse spot exists in Europe."[20] In the following year the Local Government Board received a Corporation request for sanction of a £24,000 loan to institute the Ormond Market rehabilitation scheme, but so strong were the objections of the Houseowners and Ratepayers Association to Corporation expenditure to sweep away one of the worst rookeries in the city that the scheme was then dropped and not taken up again until 1912. Five more years were to pass before the first brick was laid in a scheme that saw capital costs and rents increase considerably over earlier estimates owing to the effects of the war. Before that conflict put a virtual stop to all building plans, the planning stage had been reached for a number of schemes, and large tracts of land at Cabra, Marino, and Dolphin's Barn were being eyed as future sites for development.

The proposed schemes (including Ormond Market) called for the erection of 1,700 dwellings to rehabilitate some of the worst parts of the city and provide housing for those displaced. Chief among these was the Church Street-Beresford Street area, the site of the terrible smallpox epidemic of 1903. So little could be expected from sanitary improvements in the surrounding houses that nothing less than total obliteration of the area would suffice. The urgency of doing something was conveyed by inspectors from the Improvement Committee of the Corporation who "were so strongly impressed on the occasion of their visit by the almost appalling conditions under which the people were striving to live in this human burrow, that the members of the Committee who had intimate knowledge of the facts had to urge upon the Municipal Council the absolute and pressing necessity for obtaining an order for the clearance of the area, even though the details of the proposed housing scheme could not there and then be agreed to." The area housed 308 families (1,540 persons) in tenements whose rents were as high as 3s. for one room and 4s. 6d. for two rooms. The Corporation proposed initially to rehouse 246 families in three-room cottages at minimum rents of 4s. 6d. The usual delays ensued, though this time they were caused by the attempts of laborite councillors to reduce rents and increase the size of bedrooms; only room areas of 107 and 76 square feet were planned for those of the largest (class A) cottages. To accommodate these demands, a minimum 1,000 cubic feet capacity was then allowed for each bedroom, with rents not to exceed 1s. per room. The Corporation next had to counter the objections of the Citizens Housing League, which reasoned that potentially valuable property in central wards (Church Street was within a stone's throw of the Four Courts) should not be used to house dockers and carters, a suggestion that received councillor John Clancy's curt dismissal: "We don't want town planning: we want to house the people first."[21] The result of delays and objections, however, was a radical modification of the entire scheme so that ultimately the number of houses was reduced to 146 while rents for the two- to four-room dwellings ranged from 4s. 6d. to 7s., a far cry from the 1s. per room desired by the champions of the working classes. The first tenants did not take up residence there until 1917.

Other projects also competed for attention in the years immediately preceding the First World War. The Spitalfields scheme in the Liberties contemplated the clearance of the unsanitary streets, courts, and laneways bounded by Meath Street, Engine Alley, Ashe Street, Spitalfields, and the Coombe. The Trinity Ward scheme was to deal with the condemned houses of Moss Street between Townsend Street and the river. Coleraine, Linenhall, and Lurgan Streets were the focus of rehabilitation in the vicinity of the disused Linenhall Barracks. Among the larger schemes were those planned for the McCaffrey estate at Mount Brown beneath the walls of the South Dublin Union workhouse (234 houses); Fairbrothers' Fields, a largely agricultural tract of land stretching from Chamber Street to Greenville Avenue between Love Lane and Blackpitts that would provide for the depressed Weaver's Square area (694 houses); and, finally, the Glorney's Buildings scheme at Summerhill (232 flats). Of these six projects only the Linenhall scheme was completed by 1914. The Local Government Board refused to sanction a loan for the Glorney's Buildings project and the remaining four were eventually completed between 1917 and 1927, having provided in all for but 1,140 of the 1,700 dwellings originally planned.[22] Some of them might never have gone beyond the planning stage had not the deaths of seven persons in a housing collapse in 1913 catapulted the housing question once more into the full glare of public discussion.

The collapse of old tenement houses was a comparatively unusual occurence, testimony to the alertness of the general public, the public health department, and the inspectors of dangerous buildings. Between 1904 and 1912 over 12,000 inspections were made and a little over half of these resulted in notices being served requiring repair or demolition. This activity, however, did not prevent the occasional mishap. In 1902 the collapse of a tenement in Townsend Street killed one person and injured others. What was embarrassing about this case was that the building was owned by Alderman O'Reilly of Trinity Ward, a member of the Health Committee. At least this revelation gave the lie to allegations that all the slum property of Dublin belonged to police inspectors, pensioners, and Primrose Leaguers. Seven years later two fatalities were recorded in the collapse of 12 North Cumberland Street, the subsequent investigation revealing that 26 notices had been served since 1901 without action being taken. In April 1911 several houses that had been condemned by the health department collapsed in North King Street and Church Street. Fortunately, the tenants had already been evicted, but one of the workers engaged on the demolition work in one of the Church Street houses was killed. By 1913 about 100 notices of dangerous buildings were being served each month so that by September 2, when another collapse took place in Church Street, over 600 known dangerous structures existed. All over the city could be seen walls shored up with baulks of timber, a condition that could portend further disastrous consequences with an increasing rate of motor-lorry traffic. No. 67 Church Street was reported by the sanitary staff as an apparent dangerous structure as far back as July 1911. A second report was made in February 1912, but on each occasion the inspecting officer judged the building safe after minor repairs had been effected. On September 2, 1913, no. 66 Church Street fell and brought no. 67 down with it. The sudden collapse took place at 9 P.M., before most of the 46 members of 11 families had retired. Had it occurred later in the evening, a far greater number than the seven bodies of three adults, two boys, and two small children would have probably been taken from the ruins.[23]

What made the Church Street disaster a local cause célèbre were the circumstances in which it occurred. The criticism of the city's housing conditions had been mounting for several years and was reaching a crescendo. D.P. Moran's *Leader*, long-time critic of most aspects of Irish life under British rule, added "slumdom" to its list of abusive catchphrases. "The slums of Dublin are a disgrace to any civilised city," it claimed, ". . . a hideous eyesore, a focus of moral and physical disease, an intolerable nuisance which ought to be swept away."[24] When the collapse took place, the entire area had already been marked for clearance and rehabilitation as one of the worst areas of the city. But, more important, it occurred on the heels of the most serious manifestation of labor troubles in the history of Dublin—the riots of August 30-31. Observers did not fail to point out that most of the members of the rebellious Irish Transport and General Workers Union lived in tenements much like those in Church Street and were, thereby, a "prey to plausible agitators." "Decently housed men would never have fallen such a complete prey to mob oratory," explained the *Irish Builder*. The "degradation of slum life . . . is today an active cause of our industrial unrest," intoned the *Irish Times* while also reminding employers and trade unions alike to consider the social benefits that could be derived from investment in schemes for the better housing of the poor. Some employers had built houses in the past (e.g., Guinness and Company, Watkin's Brewery, the railway and tramway companies), but these were solely for employees. Unions, naturally, were too poor and vulnerable to engage in such ventures, and in any event, such altruism and co-operation could hardly be expected to surface in an atmosphere of bitter hostility between masters and men.

Nevertheless, these seven deaths, tiny in proportion to the thousands of needless deaths each year in Dublin from preventable disease, were instrumental in persuading a reluctant government at Dublin Castle to institute an official investigation into all important aspects of the housing question in the city. The public conscience had been aroused and local citizens' groups, including the Women's National Health Association, pressed for the appointment of an independent and imposing Vice-Regal Commission as the only agency that could fairly assess a problem that had become a menace to the social order. A Vice-Regal Commission, similar to that which had met a decade earlier to consider the reform of the poor law in Ireland, would have enabled the best brains in the United Kingdom to formulate those answers to the housing problem that must have preceded legislative action in the House of Commons. The Chief Secretary for Ireland, Augustine Birrell, insisted however on relegating the matter to a committee appointed by one of his own administrative departments, the Local Government Board for Ireland, ostensibly on the grounds that the more elaborate hearing would entail greater expense and cause unnecessary delay. Inasmuch as the Board had been fully aware of all the circumstances of housing in Dublin over the years, especially through the annual reports of the public health department of Dublin Corporation, but had remained largely inactive, little was expected from the committee. The Corporation was particularly displeased at the selection of committee members, four officials of the Board of whom only one reputedly had much familiarity with the housing problem in the city. Nevertheless, there was some hope that the victims of the Church Street disaster might yet become the posthumous pioneers of reform.

The Dublin Housing Inquiry[25] took place in the council chamber of City Hall during November and December 1913. The Departmental Committee was instructed to investigate the general circumstances of the working-class population as regards accommodation and rents, assess the scope of existing housing legislation, and offer solutions to the city's housing problem. These matters were explored in exhaustive detail by seventy-six witnesses: city officials, councilmen and town planners, ratepayers and trade union representatives, social workers and medical officers, and the clergy of both faiths. The ubiquitous one-room tenant was not invited to give evidence and this was the committee's loss in many ways, not least for the refreshing examples of sardonic humor and caustic wit the Dublin working classes would have offered, as they did some weeks later at the Dublin Disturbances Commission (see Chapter 8, below). Invitations were sent requesting the presence of representatives from all trade unions, but, surprisingly, only three appeared at a time when the city was wracked by civil strife arising out of labor troubles. Much of the evidence gathered has already been used in this and other chapters to shed light on the living conditions in tenement houses and the extent of housing construction in the city during the previous quarter-century. The members of the committee personally visited a large number of houses in all parts of the city and proved to their own satisfaction that the depressing stories recounted by witnesses were all too true:

We have no hesitation in saying that it is no uncommon thing to find halls and landings, yards and closets of the houses in a filthy condition, and in nearly every case human excreta is to be found scattered about the yards and on the floors of the closets and in some cases even in the passages of the house itself. At the same time it is gratifying to find in a number of instances that in spite of the many drawbacks, an effort is made by the occupants to keep their rooms tidy and the walls are often decorated with pictures. . . . Of the many closets we inspected, it was the rare exception to find one that could be described as even approaching a clean condition . . . indeed it would be hard to believe how any self-respecting male or female could be expected to use [WC] accommodation such as we have seen.[26]

The published record of the inquiry is one of the most important social documents in the history of modern Dublin, delineating in great detail the living conditions, housing, rents, and wages of the working classes of the city in the closing years of direct British rule of the country. Elaborate information is also provided on the extent of municipal involvement in housing the working classes, in addition to copious statistics on the tenement and other dwellings occupied by the submerged element of the population. The most important evidence was furnished by the superintendent of the sanitary department, Charles Travers. He provided from official records the salient facts relating to the number and condition of tenement houses upon which the committee based its conclusions. City officials in general felt that the inquiry placed the Corporation on trial and pointed out, rightly, the considerable all-round improvements in the health of the city over the past 30 years. Most looked to some form of state aid to solve the crisis and thus avoid further assaults on the ratepayers. Remarkably, the chairman of the newly formed Housing Committee of the Corporation rejected outright the idea that it was the duty of that body to house the people who were unable to pay for their own housing; building houses at uneconomic rents, he argued, would only give a bonus to employers at the expense of ratepayers. In this he had the support of the Town Clerk, who exclaimed: "If they [the Corporation] are going to build houses for the people, I don't see why they should not provide them with umbrellas and top hats."[27] Naturally, ratepayer and landlord representatives endorsed these attitudes and placed much of the blame for the bad condition of tenement houses not on the parsimony of landlords but on the "nasty habits" of the tenants. Those whose evidence was based on personal contact with the lower classes and their problems saw wages as the issue. And no one who had lived through the struggles of Irish laborers from 1907 onward could doubt that low wages and unemployment were responsible for the great social ills of the capital. Clerical witnesses offered some glimpses of the destitution in the homes of the poor while not omitting to cite the danger of immorality in overcrowded dwellings and the accompanying evil of intemperance bred by poverty and despair. Predictably, town planners wanted town planning of the kind that would not perpetuate such affronts to aestheticism as red brick artisans' dwellings abutting the Four Courts. At the very least a civic survey should be undertaken, a view endorsed by a member of the committee. Labor spokesmen wanted stricter enforcement of the sanitary laws and housing bylaws, lower rents, and cheap workmen's fares to facilitate migration to the outskirts of the city. The committee president followed up this latter suggestion of ½d. fares with the Dublin United Tramways Company, but the reply received was that it was not possible without serious financial loss.[28] One wonders whether cost was a major factor in a decision to aid those who some weeks before had been wrecking company trams in the streets of the city while engaged in the titanic struggle of labor and capital, the latter personified by the chairman of that company, William Martin Murphy. The proceedings were, on the insistence of the committee, free of political posturing, though for one brief moment Lord Mayor Sherlock managed to flog a moribund horse: "Personally, I want to see Home Rule, which in my opinion would mean the creation of a great capital city worth living in."[29]

One of the real revelations of the Inquiry was the involvement of council members in the ownership of slum property. Ordinarily, most people believed that the majority of tenement houses in Dublin were owned by members of the upper classes resident in Ireland, England, or abroad who let them on lease to middlemen who in turn subletted rooms to weekly tenants. This was probably true enough. Ordinary human prejudice normally also supposed publicans and retired policemen to be among the class of slum landlords. But the extent of ownership by members of the municipal council was unknown though long suspected. In 1902, as indicated above, the investigation of a collapse of a house in Townsend Street revealed an alderman to be the owner. Then and later resolutions were presented in the council attempting to ascertain the names of owners of dangerous or condemned structures, but they failed on each occasion. Now, what was long guessed at was revealed to all: members of the Corporation whose political influence was won in several wards by the so-called "slum vote" were slum landlords—five aldermen and eleven councillors. Among the wards represented were Arran Quay, Inns Quay, Merchants' Quay, Mountjoy, and Usher's Quay, all noted for the prevalence of tenement houses. One of these landlords was Councillor Laurence O'Neill, a friend of the labor faction, who owned two houses in Smithfield (he was elected Lord Mayor in 1917). Even the chairman of the Housing Committee was tainted, acting in a private capacity as solicitor for the owner of tenement property. The total number of houses involved was not large—63 tenement and 26 second-class hosues—and 64 of these were owned by only three members.[30] Yet there was something shabby about the whole episode, though, strangely enough, the political repercussions (as discussed in Chapter 3, above) were minor. Disappointing too was an episode in the council chamber only weeks after the Inquiry when a resolution introduced by Alderman M'Walter to forbid future ownership of tenement property by any official of the Corporation was ignored.

The real focus of the Inquiry, of course, was the extent of the housing problem and what to do about it. The recent census had already provided the essential details, which, as has already been noted, showed over 21,000 one-room occupancies representing the abodes of over one-third of all families in the city. This was about the same proportion of families occupying the worst type of accommodation, the generally overcrowded fourth-class kind (see Table 12). In contrast to conditions in 1901, there was a 15 percent increase in the number of families occupying single houses, but these new families roughly equalled the number of new houses, most of which made up the considerable development of private homes in the neighborhood of Drumcondra, the township annexed in 1900. Thus, there still remained as in 1901 over 8,000 dwellings occupied by two or more families of which the great majority comprised the tenement abodes that decreed so much concern. There was some confusion in determining the exact number of tenement houses in the city, but the various figures cited differ only slightly. In any event, any such total could only be approximate not only because the number fluctuated but also because the Corporation was notoriously lax about registration. Concern lay only with the registered tenements and the so-called cottages (one- and two-story second- and third-class houses of the type found in courts, lanes, and alleys and generally considered to be unsuitable or unfit for human habitation). The figure used by the committee as compiled by the sanitary staff in 1913 was 5,322 tenement houses. To this total would have to be added the 2,413 cottages (see Table 15) to yield a total of 7,735 houses requiring repair, remodeling, or demolition.

TABLE 15. Particulars of Registered Tenement Houses and Second- and Third-class Cottage-type Houses in Dublin, 1913.

	NUMBER	FAMILIES	PERSONS	ROOMS
a. Tenement houses				
of the 1st class (note 1)	1,516	8,295	27,052	11,077
of the 2nd class (note 2)	2,288	10,696	37,552	14,877
of the 3rd class (note 3)	1,518	6,831	22,701	9,273
Total	5,322	25,822	87,305	35,227
b. Houses				
of the 2nd class (note 4)	1,124	1,121	4,961	2,704
of the 3rd class (note 4)	1,289	1,136	4,851	2,530
Total	2,413	2,257	9,812	5,234
Total a. and b.	7,735	28,079	97,117	40,461

NOTE 1. Houses that appear to be structurally sound but not necessarily in good repair.
NOTE 2. Houses so decayed or badly constructed as are soon likely to be unfit for human habitation.
NOTE 3. Houses unfit for human habitation and incapable of being rendered fit without rebuilding.
NOTE 4. Difference between number of houses and families represents vacant houses.
SOURCE: Dublin Housing Inquiry in *Parliamentary Papers,* 1914 (XIX), cd. 7317, App. XIX.

Some witnesses looked to the total abolition of the tenement system but this aim was unrealistic. Only the return with redoubled fury of the famous "gale of 1839" could have effected the sort of demolition work that human agency feared to contemplate, for where were the people to go? Priorities therefore dictated that reform should initially provide for those in houses deemed unfit for human habitation (third class) and families of 3 or more persons occupying only one room. This would yield according to Corporation data roughly 18,500 families for whom decent housing was a pressing need. In other words houses would have to be provided for about 85,000 persons, or 28 percent of the population.

The committee accepted these findings and endorsed the demand that "every working-class family should be provided with a self-contained dwelling of sufficient size to prevent overcrowding, and which admits of the separation of the sexes." But a state of affairs that had been slowly developing to crisis proportions over the best part of a century could not be corrected overnight. Almost four decades of municipal and private involvement had only provided new homes for scarcely 7,000 working-class families. And the present facts were these: over 25,000 families in tenement abodes and another 1,000 in unfit cottage dwellings. The committee produced its own estimate of the number of new houses needed based on the assumption that the first- and second-class tenement houses could be remodeled to accommodate 13,000 families, or about 6,000 fewer than already resided in these, though this approach for tenements of the second class, as the committee conceded, might be too optimistic. Thus, houses would have to be found for the dispossessed 6,000 as well as those 8,000 families occupying the third-class tenements and cottages, or in all 14,000 new houses *at a minimum*. The plan really contemplated the perpetuation of the tenement system, though in houses remodeled to provide the type of letting that would raise the moral tone. But it was the considered opinion of several Corporation witnesses that the fine old mansions of Lower Gardiner Street, Upper Gloucester Street, and Lower Dominick Street could be saved through reconditioning only if occupied thereafter by the well-to-do, and, of course, experience has proven that view to have been correct. Had it been possible to have revitalized the inner city by retaining a proportion of the "quality," the lamentable trends in the social geography of modern Dublin might have been arrested, and in the process the capital might have become (as Patrick Geddes, a witness at the Housing Inquiry, hoped) what it had been in the eighteenth century—"one of the most important secondary cities in the world."[31]

The Corporation was now asked to produce a plan within two years that would look to the building of 14,000 new houses and, eventually, the complete abolition of the tenement system as it existed. That body must have been displeased to find no support from the committee for its claim to an extension of boundaries, a theme often introduced over the years to excuse the slow progress of municipal housing. The committee figured there were sufficient acres of grass and tillage land on the outskirts of the city itself coupled with derelict spaces within to furnish adequate sites. The financing of an initial scheme was estimated at £3.5 million or about ten times the amount borrowed by the Corporation from all sources since 1881 to cover all its housing undertakings. This, obviously, was a sum quite beyond the capacity of the municipality alone to raise without considerable state aid. Little reliance could be placed on private enterprise to do its part, for the private companies had virtually ceased to build artisan dwellings after 1907, the inevitable consequence of soaring prices in the building industry. Indeed, that the building trade was slow in general in this period is suggested by the reduction of about 1,000 in the number of tradesmen recorded in the census of 1911 over the number working in the city ten years earlier. The committee had no hesitation, therefore, in placing a share of the responsibility for the solution of the housing problem at the door of the Treasury. The time had come for the government to bestow on the urban worker the benevolence it had already showered on the Irish rural laborer under the Labourers' Acts—a one-third subsidy for the building by county councils of model cottages at cheap weekly rents.[32]

The committee had done its job well, although the facts revealed were hardly entirely strange to local ears. Among the more unpleasant of these were the charges leveled by three members of the committee against Sir Charles Cameron and his colleagues in the Health Department, who were taken to task for deficiencies in enforcing the sanitary by-laws. The registration of tenement houses was also found to be lax (suggesting that more existed than had been enumerated at the Inquiry) and the inspection of dangerous buildings inadequately conducted. But a far more serious charge was made against Sir Charles alone, viz., his allowance of unwarranted tax rebates under the Dublin Corporation Act of 1890 to owners of tenements in certain cases even though the conditions of sanitary repair laid down in the legislation had not been fulfilled. Cameron defended himself by claiming that only leniency of this nature could have induced owners to place their properties in any tolerable condition, but this assertion rang hollow in light of the fact that aldermen and councillors were among the beneficiaries of his dispensations. Needless to say there was no disciplinary action taken against him, and he continued as executive sanitary officer in one of the most highly remunerated positions in the Corporation.

These revelations presented further opportunities to the enemies of Irish self-government to ridicule a stricken city as "the proposed seat of the Nationalist Parliament" and indulge in the favorite pastime of showering abuse on the Corporation. In fact, the latter was blamed for not deterring the alleged influx of rural laborers and their families into the city and this despite the fact that the Corporation had inserted a clause in its contracts in 1906 making two years' residence in the city a condition of employment only to have it disallowed by the Local Government Board. It was widely believed that the overcrowding of tenement houses had been aggravated over the years by a rural inundation to take up the thousands of jobs that had become available in the city during the construction of the tramways, main drainage, and electricity works. And as jobs fell off, this stream of laborers and their families were believed to crowd the workhouses or survive in casual employment. But there had always been a very large number of "foreigners" in the city. Counting only those from the other 31 counties the census data showed that the proportion was highest (35 percent of the population) in 1851, with a decline setting in after 1881, a time when the population of Dublin was relatively stable. By 1911 that proportion was at its lowest at slightly under 23 percent, although the total population of the city (304,000) had never been higher.[33]

Despite all this the committee expressed its confidence in the Corporation's ability to discharge its duties, provided increased powers were accorded it to deal with recalcitrant landlords. Indeed, the Corporation regarded the statistics of housing operations made public by the committee as vindicating the role it had played in providing homes for artisans and laborers. Despite intense opposition and great difficulties in obtaining finance, the Corporation had built to date almost 1,400 separate dwellings and had plans for an equal number, far more in fact than the 400 or so houses built by Sheffield Corporation, described as "a pioneer among towns in enthusiasm for housing reform."[34] In general not much enthusiasm could be generated for recommendations that envisaged, even with state aid, an increase in the rates. Costs were incalcuable if building land was to be provided, against the wishes of town planners, in the city itself, where the decisions of arbitrators were conceding prices to owners anywhere between £4,000 and £10,000 an acre. On the other hand, the decisions of individual families could complicate any scheme to bring them to virgin sites beyond the city itself. The little direct evidence we have on this score suggests that workers desired above all to live near their place of work and thus avoid daily tram fare. This was especially the case for the city's numerous dock workers and quay laborers in casual employment. And what of the shopkeepers who would remain "to starve in the city" after a mass migration to the suburbs of dispossessed families? One senses the desperation in the idea of one official of the Corporation that perhaps the Phoenix Park could be used for housing![35]

Everything hinged on the response of the Chief Secretary. There was the predictable horror expressed in his House of Commons speech on April 16:

> It is a very painful report indeed . . . a grave and serious document, in no way exaggerated. . . . It has put the state of life of the poorer inhabitants of that city [Dublin] in a manner which I do not think anyone can read without feeling grieved and, to some extent, shamed . . . this report cannot be allowed to rest . . . in the pigeon holes of offices . . . the state of things which now exists is horrible and intolerable.

That feeling soon passed however as Birrell continued:

> A large class of people living in an uneconomic way on 15s. or 16s a week! And you will
> thereupon say that the public must supply the money to build nice, clean, charming residences
> where they and their wives and their children can lead useful lives and the rent may be pro-
> vided for out of the pockets of other people. That is a rotten state of things. It is one we can-
> not possibly accept as the merest substitute for the conditions which should exist.[36]

The Chief Secretary's comments were a straw in the wind: the slums apparently were to
remain. There would be no government grants to bridge the gap between what the worker could pay in rent and what was needed to make municipal housing either self-support-
ing or a tolerable burden to ratepayers. And the government had little to fear in this
attitude from the Irish parliamentary representatives, members of a party whose greatest
social impulses derived from the needs of peasants and agricultural laborers. Over the
years the Irish party had been in the forefront of a long and sometimes violent agitation
to win the land of Ireland for its tenant farmers, a campaign that had culminated with the
remarkable land act of 1903 passed by a Conservative government and including a sub-
vention of some £12 million to facilitate the transfer of land from landlord to tenant. The
same solicitude for the plight of the agricultural laborer had led to the various Labourers'
Acts, with their own Treasury grants. But the call for decent homes for the submissive urban poor could generate no crusade beyond J. J. Clancy's conventional repetition of the
grim facts of Dublin housing during the Commons debate of April 16, a discussion in
which his colleagues intervened only to defend their slum-owning compatriots in Dublin
Corporation or to stress the corresponding needs of the agricultural laborer. Also, Birrell's raising of the specter of socialism in that debate could not fail to mute criticism
from Dublin, where priest and politician were close allies in their dread of the socialist
proselytizing of James Larkin and his colleagues in the Irish Transport and General
Workers Union. Moreover, there was the appeal to the natural self-interest of ratepayers
in the Chief Secretary's blunt dismissal of the idea of solving the rent problem for one
group of citizens by taking money out of the pockets of others. And, indeed, after the
embarrassing disclosures of the Housing Inquiry any further demands on the Dublin ratepayer could easily have led to an outcry that would have made the furore over the Corporation's attempt to promote a housing bill in 1908 rather tame by comparison. The
government might well fear the "chartless ocean" of state-aided municipal housing—as
Birrell explained, "it would be very difficult to make grants to Dublin and refuse them to
other towns in Ireland."

The housing question was returned unanswered to the Corporation, now diverted, as
was most of Ireland, by the climactic proceedings attending the closing stages of the
third and final home rule bill. Tenuous hopes would again have to be placed in industrial
expansion, employment, and investment or, more immediately, in extended loan periods
and lower interest rates and the paltry "stimulus" of the Irish Housing Fund. And a public nurtured in the principles of laissez faire would understand that the poor themselves
must also play their part: "It is not only a matter of model dwellings," said T. W. Russell,
MP, "but of model people and we cannot make people moral by bricks and mortar."
Thus rebuffed, the Corporation gave short shrift to the claims of town planners (and the
future of Dublin). William Cosgrave, the Sinn Fein councillor (and future leader of the
Irish Free State), reminded the Corporation's Housing Committee of the "enormous eco-

nomic disadvantages attached to the high-falutin' recommendations" of the Housing and Town Planning Association, which body had lately complained that too much consideration was being given to the working classes, with little consideration reserved for those better off. "The minds of the council were fixed on one idea," Cosgrave reminded his colleagues in May 1914, "the enormous improvement that must be made in the housing of the working classes." What the council might accomplish was indicated by Alderman Kelly: "It is in my opinion hopeless to do more than slightly mitigate the results."[37] At any rate it roused itself to add a new committee—the Housing Committee—to its deliberations. It was staffed by a member from each ward and there was little doubt that its activities would only continue the piecemeal approach of rebuilding the worst areas of the inner city.

Such improvements as would be undertaken could only be effected by the usual government-sanctioned loans, a recourse that must add to the Corporation's indebtedness and further increase the rates because of the necessity to cover the usual losses on municipal housing. When a council meeting was called in March 1916, for example, to discuss an expenditure of £8,000 for 32 houses in the pending Spitalfields scheme, many, including the Lord Mayor, opposed the plan on those grounds. Such lack of concern provoked from Councillor Sherlock, one of Larkin's former antagonists, an outburst that became the battle cry of housing reformers during the next few years: "Are the survivors of the war to come back to the foetid atmosphere of the tenements or the slums?"[38] (Though the money was voted, the project was vetoed by the Local Government Board as unsuitable.) It was useless to expect much attention from the state to the social crisis in Dublin while the Empire was locked in a death struggle with Germany. Still less did it seem possible after April 1916, when that Empire had been challenged in the streets of Dublin. There were some who sought to portray the Easter Rising as emanating from the mass discontent of the ill-housed and poorly paid laborers of the capital. Alderman Alfie Byrne, lately elected to represent his city in parliament, lectured his colleagues at Westminster in that vein a few weeks after the Rebellion. A visiting American was at a loss to understand why men and women in Dublin would rise in revolution with the certainty of losing their lives "until I saw how these men and women lived in one-room tenements." Although these expressions were more properly applicable to an earlier outburst—the industrial struggle of 1913—they nevertheless suggested the shattering impact the housing conditions of Dublin made on all who, however remotely, experienced them. Little wonder that the new Chief Secretary, H. E. Duke, should exclaim that the problem of housing in Dublin was "one of as tremendous a magnitude as faced any statesman in modern times";[39] or that the novel situation should arise in which the Corporation in 1916 felt impelled to canvass a $2 million (£410,000) loan from Boston bankers to build the much-needed houses, a plan that eventually fell through when the Corporation was unwilling to meet a 6¼ percent interest rate.

Only small relief was afforded—loans to complete the handful of schemes begun in 1912—before the problems of Dublin were swallowed up in the wider political struggle that was to shake the relations between Britain and Ireland between 1919 and 1921. Thereafter, those problems would rest solely with Irish men and institutions, unhampered by the attitudes, ideas, and enactments that had for so long stood guard over the destinies of the capital. Alas, however, the removal of foreign domination did not presage for one-third of the city's population what Lord Mayor Sherlock had confidently prophesied eight years earlier—a great capital city worth living in. As late as 1925 the housing situation in Dublin was described not as "question" or "problem" but as "a tragedy"—a judgment that was hardly refuted by the 1926 census, which revealed, as had those in 1911 and 1901, that over one-third of all families lived in one-room tenements. And the number of tenement houses and subletting of rooms was increasing as the city began to experience the growing influx of those affected by the "metropolitan spirit." Also, as in the past, the municipal authorities, still beset by financial difficulties and the disinterest of the investing public, bore the brunt of criticism. They were criticized for continuing to build the barracks-like flats that had always invited the scorn of town planners, "red forts" according to one clerical observer, whose propertyless inhabitants were "ripe for the communist organiser." And there was equal criticism for not doing enough, for throughout the 1930s and 1940s (until 1956, in fact), *Thom's Directory* introduced its urban statistics with the following remarks on housing in Dublin: "A great deal, but not yet nearly enough, has been done to clear unsanitary areas, to increase the number of open spaces, and provide healthy and cheap housing accommodation for the poor. . . . It cannot be denied that the narrow squalid streets, lanes and alleys to be found in the older parts of Dublin, and the congestion which exists in most of its poorer districts, are a serious blot on the city's reputation." Even as late as 1935, the City Manager addressed that question in words that could have been uttered just as appropriately by Sir Charles Cameron 20, 30, and 50 years earlier. "I am shortly about to attack," he promised, "the kernel of the great nut that has to be split and that is how you are going to house the man who has no money at all."[40] Yet by 1939 the housing shortage had become grave enough for the Corporation to plead for an official inquiry into the crisis. Many years were to pass before the great "municipal shame" was abolished and the recollection of Bull Alley and its pestilential neighbors became so dim in the memory that it would become fashionable to exalt the Liberties for its nostalgic associations with Italian organ grinders and Huguenot weavers. Such enthusiasms should be tempered with a passing nod for the generations of citizens for whom Chamber Street, Meath Street, Francis Street, and Cook Street had only associations of poverty and degradation.

Part

THE PEOPLE

I should like to say a few words about the chief characteristics of Dublin people. You are, I think, taken as a whole, an eminently tolerant, good-humoured, charitable people, endowed, moreover, with the quality, rare and delightful at all times, but especially so in this age of "hustle," of not taking life too seriously.

WILLIAM DAWSON, "My Dublin Year," in *Studies* (December 1912)

6

Poverty

Dublin is relatively the poorest [city] in the kingdom. There is a large number of people living on the absolute verge of poverty, and, if it were not for the passive type of character so largely represented among our people, there would be a regular rising in the city, for there are large numbers of people living on such small sums of money that we who know them wonder how they keep body and soul together.

REV. GILBERT MAHAFFY in evidence before the street-trading children committee, Parliamentary Papers, 1902

A DEEP social cleavage separated the prosperous middle classes and struggling working classes in the Victorian city. A small class of privilege and influence stood opposed to a much larger class of wage earners whose mode of dress and manner of speech, occupation and income condemned them to social inferiority and a life of more or less constant struggle for existence. In most essentials these contrasts survived into the twentieth century. The Dublin worker usually drew wages that effectively denied him and his family the standards of food, clothing, education, and housing enjoyed by his social superiors. But wide differences also existed within the working-class world. The earnings of the sober, aspiring artisan could provide, however frugally, a standard of living for his family that was entirely beyond the capability of the equally sober though hardly aspiring underpaid, unskilled laborer. Likewise, the casually employed, aged poor, and beggars were necessarily reduced to the degraded life in the slums, though fortunate nevertheless if they managed to escape the workhouse regimen of the habitual drunkard and vagrant. The differences became all too clear when one studied the nature of housing accommodation and standards of public health, thus revealing a predictable and marked improvement in mortality rates for those ascending the social ladder from tenement room to self-contained artisan dwelling.

The misery and degradation of a large section of the population of Dublin was all too apparent. It was impossible to deny the visible evidence of miserable housing conditions or refute the painful record of death and disease. These matters have been sketched in earlier chapters, where it is shown, according to reliable statistics, that over one-quarter of the citizens in 1914 were in pressing need of the essentials of decent living. It will be recalled that Seebohm Rowntree's famous survey in 1899 of poverty in York (a town, incidentally, with a sizable Irish population) revealed that 28 percent of the population of that city was lacking the minimum necessities of life. Considering the generally unfavorable economic position of Dublin vis-à-vis English urban centers, contemporary observers hardly erred in concluding that poverty in Dublin at the turn of the century approached alarming dimensions. The public symbols of this poverty were the shiftless mass of unemployed, hangers-on at the fruit, fish, and old clothes markets lucky to earn a shilling or two each morning as porters, the army of "sandwich men" trooping the city in ragged attire, barefooted street urchins, youthful street traders, the "Molly Malones" who gathered cockles in Dublin Bay in the morning to sell at street corners for the night's lodgings, the street musicians, idlers and corner boys as well as the ubiquitous beggar noted for generations for his pertinacity. Dr. MacDowel Cosgrave, an observer who sought to defend his city from the usual imputations as dirty and decaying, admitted in his popular guide, *The Dictionary of Dublin*, that the "higher class of solicitors" was noticeably absent there, the pavement artist being almost unknown. Pauperism, of course, was the surest evidence of poverty. About 6,600 paupers were in receipt of indoor relief on an average day in Dublin's two workhouses. In addition, these institutions attracted large numbers of citizens (about 11,000 annually) every Tuesday and Thursday morning for their portion of the bread, tea, sugar (and sometimes meat) distributed as outdoor relief. A less obvious sign of poverty was the widespread recourse to the "poor man's banker"—the pawnbroker who often stood between tattered dignity and the drab workhouse garb. In 1906, for example, over 4.5 million pledges were taken in Dublin, almost double the rate for Belfast.

It was this aggregation of the victims of industrial society, in Dublin as in the other large cities, that gave opportunity to those who saw in the fecundity of slum dwellers the reason for the supposed degeneration of the racial stock, a favorite topic of the time. There was, naturally, much physical evidence of the lowered constitution of the male urban poor. And one had only to consider the army's statistics to gauge the apprehensions of those whose job it was to select able recruits from among the thousands of fit and physically unfit specimens seeking enlistment. About one-third of all those inspected were rejected on medical grounds, but the physical standards of those who remained— average height 5'5", average weight under 130 lbs.—did little to allay the exaggerated fears of those who claimed that the army was left to rely on street loafers and town casuals. No wonder that in Dublin the metropolitan police (minimum height 5'9") should appear as "giants" to the general public when fitted out in heavy boots, greatcoat, and spiked helmet.

While it seemed quite admissible that poverty, ignorance, and neglect contributed much to the inferior physical characteristics of a particular segment of the population, there was no evidence whatsoever to support the nonsensical claims that these same elements established an hereditary retrogressive effect. But, then, race is a subject peculiarly creative of nonsense. And muddle-headedness, too, could add its pernicious influence, as in the following contribution to the debate by an Irish spokesman: "A few of them [Jewish pedlars] go round and do very great harm . . . they sell tea of the vilest character. . . . It is nearly impossible to keep the people from dealing with them. That is one of the causes of physical deterioration, because they are getting the vilest stuff from the Jews."[1] Happily, the voices of sanity also spoke to urge improvement of the social condition of the poor, preferably through the beneficent intervention of the state as the best guarantee of national vigor.

Among the widely accepted reasons for the mass poverty of Dublin were lack of employment, low wages, and intemperance. Catholic employers would hardly have agreed with Cardinal Vaughan's analysis of the condition of the poor—"the natural result of an utilitarian philosophy and of an inordinate growth of selfish individualism."[2] It suited the moral proprieties of the middle classes to defer generally to the notion that the condition of the poor was due to a state of "voluntary" poverty induced by profligate habits and, most of all, drink. People are poor because they waste their money, intoned otherwise sympathetic-minded clerics. They are careless and thriftless owing to a temperament peculiar to the Irish—not caring about much except politics, explained the president of the Royal College of Surgeons. And, declared others, they drink Guinness as a food, with even nursing mothers exalting its ability to increase the flow of milk.

Possibly the memory of excessive drunkenness in an earlier period colored people's attitudes. Only a generation earlier the number of arrests for drunkenness in Dublin exceeded by over five times the annual rate recorded after 1904. Yet the depredations of the few "habitual drunkards" and "incorrigible rogues" agitated politicians and people far more than the obvious causes of "involuntary" poverty in a city where manufactures were few and employment opportunities hardly existed for young people. That a certain amount of poverty was directly related to drinking is undeniable: both the police courts and the reports of social workers offer distressing evidence of families reduced to utter misery owing to drinking parents. To Seebohm Rowntree, something of an expert in the matter, the type connoted that "happy-go-lucky person who spends his income as soon as he gets it, who cares nothing for his home, . . . who may make very good wages, but who drinks them and eats them. Probably if he gets his wages on Friday, on Monday he is pawning his clothes. I distinguish him from the man who is genuinely poor and does not get a good wage, but leads a steady life."[3] Under this prescription, the wife of such a "happy-go-lucky" sort might be expected to exhibit equally low habits, an ignorance of household management, and indifference to the needs of her children. But, surely, where tens of thousands of persons lived on the absolute verge of poverty, intemperance could hardly have ranked high among the primary causes. And there were those among the middle class who recognized this well enough. "No wonder [they drink] when they have to live in degraded conditions," stated the Rev. Savell Hicks of St. Stephen's Green Unitarian Church as he condemned those who assigned the cause of poverty to alcoholism and accused the rich of reverting to worse than savagery for their neglect of the "white man's burden" in their own city. His stern judgment did not appear to be misdirected, for foreign missions, whether Catholic or Protestant, and international catastrophes, whether a Sicilian earthquake or a *Titanic* disaster, always touched the hearts and pockets of the citizens while the handful of philanthropic ventures at home languished for want of interest. As the *Irish Times* chided, "men prefer to discuss the moral effects of billiards to fighting the sin and wretchedness of their fellow Christians." In fact the *Irish Catholic*, more noted for fighting proselytism than the "evils" of billiards, made its own distinctive approach to social problems by occasionally reminding its readers that the poor were as well off as the rich, who also had problems!

Poverty robbed the citizen of physical efficiency, and the constant underfeeding of his children resulted in stunted growth and proneness to disease. Rowntree's survey of

York, where he examined some 2,000 children of the poor, disclosed that at age 14 the boys showed a deficiency of about 3" in height compared to the average normal standard. Significantly, low wages, old age or illness, and the loss of a breadwinner through death contributed to over 72 percent of the poverty he found there, the rest being attributable to excessive family size or loss of employment. In Dublin this cycle would have been repeated in all essentials with, perhaps, unemployment playing a greater role. Only investigators like Rowntree observed the worst effects of social distress at first hand. "How do these people live?" queried one cleric, baffled that a whole family still managed to survive with only a few shillings of weekly income, the man probably so physically enfeebled as to be incapable of more than a few days' work when it was available. The home environment was such that one would have to agree with the despairing cry of the drunk arrested for breaking a plate glass window (a perennial Dublin "crime"): "I may as well be in jail as the way I am." One tenement dwelling was described by a witness at the Public Health Inquiry in 1900: "I have been in a room in Dublin where 39s. a week was pretty steadily coming in. There was no bed—a heap of sacks and rags in a corner, no furniture, a broken box by the fireside, one damaged chair. The people slept in their clothes. . . . They never washed them—never took them off. The only fireplace was a grate of the oldest fashion, too large, without hobs, the bars broken. . . . I was shown a fire which was made of 4d. worth of cinders picked out of the waste heaps."[4]

Presumably only the most improvident of working-class families lived in such abject conditions, in circumstances that would have been more familiar to the unskilled casual laborers and their families. But it is certain enough that the 130,000 or so inhabitants of tenement houses and unsanitary cottages endured in some degree the myriad inconveniences of that type of accommodation. Among the worst conditions were those of the more than 21,000 families occupying one-room tenements, 85 percent of which consisted of two or more persons. Many of these were among the so-called "very poor"—that submerged tenth whose position continued to remain one of hopelessness and despair. Such families of five or more persons huddled together in one room, often with only a straw covering on the floor for sleeping, no furniture, neither fuel nor heat, not much more than a few plates, bowls, pan and kettle with which to prepare and serve food, and a bucket secreted in a closet for the relief of normal bodily functions. In circumstances like these, landlords were not surprised to find floorboards and bannisters pulled up and used for firewood or lead and copper pipe fittings cut away to realize a few pence to pay the rent and buy food or, as the landlord would rather claim, to spend on drink.

As might be expected, the diet of the people left much to be desired. Bread, porter, and tea were staple items in the food of the poor. In some respects that diet had deteriorated over the years as changing tastes or the technology of food service replaced the wholesome porridge or stirabout with tea and brown bread with white. Cheap bacon, odd scraps of beef, and a herring supplemented the fare of the breadwinner, whose choice of vegetables was invariably confined to potatoes and cabbage. Among the very poor, pig's cheek was a staple item as was the potato. In general butter was not available to these families when employment for the breadwinner was irregular. For those who could afford it, bacon was a leading component of diet, boiled bacon and cabbage being a favorite dish. The 2-lb. white baker's loaf was the bread in universal demand. Those adults endeavoring to sustain life on a daily regimen such as that revealed in Table 16 must have listened to the annual Lenten regulations in Archbishop Walsh's pastoral with some wonderment at being advised that to mediate their fast meat was allowed at one meal on Monday, Tuesday, Thursday, and on some Saturdays in addition to a normal diet of cheese and eggs! And even had they wished to, they could hardly have flouted those other episcopal expostulations that requested they shun the immodest presentations of local theaters, avoid betting and gambling, and not destroy the purity of their Christian morals by reading infidel tracts or immoral poetry. Where could they scrape up the money to indulge their passions unless, as with a pint of porter, it cost only 2d. to do so? What few pleasures remained must have been reserved for the husband. The wife in these circumstances, unless she drank, was resigned to overcoming the brutal inconveniences of her tenement room, which she left, if at all, only to give birth. Poverty was indeed, as Durkheim stated, "the best school for teaching a man self-restraint."

TABLE 16. **Dublin, 1903: Daily Diet of the Poorest Classes.**

| OCCUPATION | WEEKLY WAGES | WEEKLY RENT | NO. IN FAMILY | FOOD USED | | |
				BREAKFAST	DINNER	SUPPER
Tobacco spinner	6s.	1s. 9d.	4	Cocoa & bread (butter sometimes)	Bread & dripping (Stew on Sundays)	Same as breakfast
Tailor	10s.	2s. 6d.	2	Tea & dry bread	Herrings, dry bread & tea	Porridge (sometimes)
Van driver	15s.	2s. 6d.	6	Bread, butter & tea	Bacon & cabbage (herrings occasionally)	Tea & bread
Laborer	15s.	2s. 3d.	10	Bread & tea (butter sometimes)	Bread only	Bread, butter & tea (bacon sometimes)
Laborer	16s.	1s. 4d.	6	Bread, butter & tea	Bread, butter & tea (meat or bacon occasionally)	Bread, butter & tea
Laborer	17s.	3s. 0d.	8	Bread, butter & tea	Bread, butter & tea (meat & vegetables on Sundays)	Bread, butter & tea
Laborer	18s.	2s. 0d.	7	Bread, butter & tea	Bacon, bread, butter & tea (pig's cheek sometimes)	Bread, butter & tea
Laborer	18s. (wife earns 1s. 6d.)	4s. 6d.	7	Tea & dry bread	Tea & dry bread	Tea & dry bread
Laborer	20s.	3s. 0d.	5	Bread, butter & tea	Meat & vegetables	Bread, butter & tea
Painter	30s.	3s. 6d.	6	Bread, butter & tea (meat occasionally)	Meat & vegetables	Bread, butter & tea (cocoa for children)

SOURCE: Dublin Corporation: Public Health Report, 1904, pp. 114–19.

In the final analysis an individual's standard of living depended on the amount and frequency of his weekly wages. By this measure also, Dublin presented an aspect of grim poverty. There were proportionately far greater numbers of workers in, for example, Belfast or London in receipt of 30s. per week, perhaps the minimum income for a family of five if more than the barest needs were to be served. Evidence was introduced at the Dublin Housing Inquiry in 1913 that indicated that of over 21,000 heads of families occupying rooms in registered tenement houses and certain second- and third-class houses (i.e., the homes of half the working class) no more than 12 percent had incomes in excess of 30s. per week! Rowntree characterized primary poverty as those circumstances in which the individual obtained the food that would be just sufficient to enable him to do moderate work (viz., maintain "merely physical efficiency") together with an appropriate allowance for rent and clothing. His conclusion was that a family of four or five required 21s. 8d. per week in income to maintain this minimum standard. It should be noted that no allowance was made in this estimate for tobacco, beer, or ordinary amusements. The standard was computed in 1899 and, needless to say, would be in need of upward adjustment within a few years to allow for the rise in the cost of living. According to government estimates in 1904, about two-thirds of the income of a family of five earning a total of 21s. per week went towards food, leaving 7s. weekly for other necessities, including rent, drink, and tobacco. These earnings were in the neighborhood of what were received in 1914 by a huge proportion of Dublin's working-class families. Between 1904 and 1914 the retail price index for London, a city never far ahead of Dublin in the combined prices of food and rent, rose from 102.4 to 116.8 (1900 = 100). Thus, by 1914 it would seem that 7s. was a small amount indeed to cover rent, clothing allowance, tram fare, fuel, higher food prices, and drink (2d. the pint of porter, drawn "from the wood") or tobacco (10 cigarets for 3d.). By the latter date, experts such as Chiozza Money were suggesting a more realistic poverty line (to include an allowance for drink, tobacco, and amusements) in the region of £2 per week, a limit that few working-class families in Dublin had attained in 1914.[5]

TABLE 17. Earnings of 21,200 Heads of Families Occupying Registered Tenement Houses and Second/Third-class Houses (other than tenements): Dublin, 1913.

NUMBER OF FAMILIES	EARNINGS PER WEEK
21,200 (total)	—
18,816 (88.8%)	30s. and below
17,189 (81.0%)	25s. and below
14,604 (68.9%)	20s. and below
5,604 (26.4%)	15s. and below

SOURCE: *Parliamentary Papers*, 1914 (XIX), cd. 7317 (Dublin Housing Inquiry), Appendix XXIII. Figures adapted to exclude old age pensioners, owners, and persons with unascertained incomes.

The social condition of about 5,000 persons in 1,254 families in Dublin was the subject of a notable survey made in the summer of 1904 by Dr. T. J. Stafford, medical commissioner of the Local Government Board, and C.D. La Touche. Intended as a typical picture of conditions in a working-class district, the survey revealed that barely 12 percent of these families occupied dwellings that were satisfactory with respect to sanitation, sanitary convenience, air space, and cleanliness. Indeed, 60 percent of them lived in single-room tenements and TB was found to be present in 150 cases (12 percent). The average family income amounted only to 22s. weekly, but over 50 percent of families earned less than 20s., whereas not more than 10 percent earned 40s. or more per week. A separate study of 21 of the families presented in extensive detail their daily diet and expenditure and need not be repeated here, for it hardly differs in essential details from the information already cited in Table 16. Rowntree's poverty line was employed to ascertain their social condition and it was determined, based upon that standard, that 12 of the 21 families lacked the essentials for merely physical efficiency; all but 1 of the 12 comprising the class of unskilled labor. It could not be expected that any more extensive survey would have revealed different circumstances for the mass of families of unskilled laborers in Dublin. The conclusions of Stafford and La Touche were drawn up in 1907, but they may well be considered relevant for the remainder of the pre-war period and in respect to income might even have been too optimistic:

> In point of earnings it appears to us that in Dublin £1 a week is the minimum income needed to provide a family [of 3.3 man equivalents] with the prime essentials of life. This leaves no margin; but, judging from the habits of the people as ascertained in the present inquiry, that sum will be sufficient only if the family does not exceed four persons—two adults and two children. This is a grave conclusion from the standpoint of national increase, as it means that any tendency in the labouring population to increase in numbers must be accompanied by privation of some of the necessaries of healthy existence.[6]

The study is also interesting for the casual detail it provided on the social habits of the typical working-class family. Rents were paid on Mondays each week and Saturday was the day for settling accounts with the local grocery where articles were obtained "on tick" or with the pawnbroker in redeeming the pledges made on the previous Monday or Tuesday. Five of the twenty-one families enumerated had recourse to the pawn office. All but four enjoyed a Sunday dinner of meat and vegetables, which was also eaten cold on the following day. Meat dinners dropped off on the two following days to be replaced by fish mainly, with meat returning on Thursday. Friday, as expected, was predominantly "fish day" and, strangely enough, Saturday saw the smallest main course, mostly a "fry," or piece of meat without the addition of the usual potatoes and vegetable. The evening meal or so-called "tea" was invariably sparse, mostly tea and bread and butter, even on Saturdays, and most families also went to bed without a late supper. Though on paper the main meals appeared to be substantial and varied, they were probably inadequate to provide the energy requirements needed; for, as the survey showed, twelve of the families were below the poverty line and two others were on the very margin of poverty. The plight of the very poor was illustrated by the enumerated budgets of cases no. 9 and no. 14. The former, a family of six with an income of 18s. per week (poverty line = 26s.) had a Sunday dinner of mutton soup and bread (repeated on Thursday) and milk and porridge or rice on two other days. Other meals offered the dull monotony of tea, bread and butter. The charwoman with two children (average weekly income 10s., from earnings, charity, and outdoor relief) enjoyed no meat at all during the week of observation, her dinner generally consisting of potatoes enlivened by pea soup or cabbage. The children only received whatever milk was imbibed with tea, which was not always accompanied by bread. For almost all families such items as marmalade and jam would have been luxuries. Food and other necessities were bought from day to day in small quantities, which made the purchase of coal, for example, much more costly. Coal was the main fuel, an open grate providing not only heat but in most cases also the only means of preparing

food. Domestic lighting was invariably provided by oil lamps. The breadwinners must
have been in these cases remarkably temperate, for the amount of money left after expenditures for food, rent, fuel, and clothing left little with which to slake the thirst. In only
three cases was sufficient money held back by the husband to satisfy any craving for the
"creamy pint." Nor would the amounts entered under "sundries" suggest that the families ever enjoyed the theatrical and music-hall productions of local palaces of entertainment: only one budget showed a specific outlay for "amusements." Just under half the
weekly budgets were in deficit, suggesting that loans and the pawn office were often necessary to survival. Tobacco was also a rare commodity as was the purchase of a daily
newspaper. Only one budget disclosed the latter expense, but for others this want could
be rectified, though at some inconvenience, by a visit to the reading room of the nearest
public library. The purchase of clothing was facilitated by enrollment in "clubs" to which
weekly contributions were made, a device used by over three-quarters of the families. For
others, one suspects, new clothes must have been something of a rarity inasmuch as
clothes-conscious females were reduced to having old coats dyed and dresses made up
by the neighbor who was "handy with the needle." The remaining extraneous items of
expenditure were Sunday church offerings (1d. or 2d. where possible) and contributions
to friendly and trade societies. In one case, that of a 33s. per week artisan, there was
enough surplus money (3s.) for "photographs."

These early years of the century were characterized by distress for many families for
whom material relief could come only by way of public or private charity. Throughout
the period the Lord Mayor of Dublin administered a Coal Fund via the various charitable
societies of the city through which free coal was distributed to families devastated by unemployment or illness. Annual subscriptions to this effort amounted to little over £500
but ensured at least that 8,000 or so bags of coal were available for delivery to the poor
during the Christmas season. The continuing unemployment of these years put great
strains on the Corporation, whose own stringent budget kept relief for the able-bodied
poor via public works to a minimum. The employment offered under that program
(cleaning out back lanes and alleys, removing mud from the Tolka river bed and the Liffey foreshore, and such) was only temporary, and because of the need to distribute relief
as widely as possible, few men were employed for longer than a week. November
through March were the worst months for unemployment, and it was not an unusual
sight in Dublin for hundreds of idle men to gather at City Hall to importune individual
councillors for relief as they entered the council chamber.[7] During the terrible winter crisis of 1904-1905, the *Irish Times* instituted a "shilling fund" for the distressed poor in imitation of similar campaigns in England. Visiting opera companies could hardly avoid the
expected benefit performance for the poor of the city. But the most singular effort on behalf of the poor was the bequest of a local matron, Ada Hannah Lewis-Hill, who left
£10,000 of her fortune to the Lord Mayor, the income from which (after 1909) was to be
applied to the relief of the poor "during the winter months."

Those in need of continuing charity were aided by the city's many philanthropic organizations. Some believed that the best way to realize the poverty of Dublin was to observe the motley collection of down-and-outs gathered for the annual Christmas Dinner
of the Mendicity Institution, that old reliable that had been serving the poor of the city
since 1818. Its reports showed that over 100 meals (breakfast and dinner) were given free
each day to men, women, and children desperate to avoid the stigma of the workhouse.

An even older institution was the nonsectarian Sick and Indigent Roomkeepers Society, established in 1790 for the temporary relief of the poor. About 500 families were relieved there each month, but the amounts distributed were a pittance, again owing to want of subscriptions. The *Leader* once described the Society's laudable efforts as akin to "throwing snowballs into hell to lower the temperature" because of the lack of citizen support for its aims. Complaints about the meager contributions to voluntary effort were an annual refrain in Dublin; and in that context the occasional royal visits to the capital took on added importance, for the monarch never departed without leaving £500 or so for distribution to the poor. The St. Vincent de Paul Society was the largest lay Catholic charitable agency. It had over 30 branches in the city engaged in the work of visiting the poor in their homes and distributing relief to some 5,000 families. The most active non-Catholic agency was the Salvation Army, which began its work in Dublin in 1888. Those drumbeating, concertina-playing "soldiers" of the Army braved many a hostile mob in the city in their efforts to aid the poor, for their presence on the streets of a Catholic city evoked no Christian response from sectarian bigots. Their good work in providing clothes for the poor, "rescuing" women, furnishing the means for "prodigal sons" to return home, and feeding the hungry was often rewarded with cowardly assaults or arrests for obstructing traffic (i.e., causing a hostile crowd to gather). Apparently the Army found it impossible to continue the work of its "slum sisters" because of the religious prejudices of the people, a hostility often vented also, to judge by the newspaper reports, against Protestant clergymen. Various other voluntary bodies of small dimensions engaged in disparate activities dispensing penny-dinners to the poor, distributing flowers (primroses and cowslips!) among the poor of the north side (North Dublin Flower Mission), rescuing for institutional laundry work the young Protestant wayward women (Dublin Prison Gate Mission), maintaining a Home for Catholic working boys not living with parents, and providing free education and support for children attending the various "ragged schools" conducted by the clergy of both faiths.

The proliferation of night shelters and common lodging houses also suggested distress. The Corporation had erected a nightly lodging house in Benburb Street in 1887 to accommodate about 70 persons each night at 4d. per bed. The Salvation Army ran a shelter in Peter Street that included a meal of meat hash for the same charge. The St. Vincent de Paul Home in Great Strand Street was free of charge. It was established in 1912 through funds provided by Archbishop Walsh and was the first free night shelter for Catholic homeless men. Nightly accommodation was provided for 50 persons in addition to a frugal meal. For its first year of operations, reports show that 34,736 men (about 100 each night) had to be refused admission, so great was the demand.[8] At 8 Bow Street the old Night Asylum for the homeless poor also had to turn away far more applicants than the 100 or so men and women it sheltered. Indeed, the Asylum provided little more than shelter from the elements, for there were no facilities, lodgers being obliged to sleep on the floor. It was the resort of only the very poorest citizens—charwomen or old brokendown men who were unable to gain admission to the casual wards at the workhouse. The Poolbeg Street Shelter for Men also attracted the very poor—coal porters and "sandwichmen" who for 2d. per night could sleep on a leather bed stuffed with hay (4d. for spring mattress and sheets). The best known of the male lodging houses was the hostel opened by Lord Iveagh in Bride Street in 1905 for the more sober and respectable of "impecunious commercial men." For women the preferred institution was the Night Refuge in

Brickfield Lane, off Cork Street, which was managed by the Sisters of Mercy and invited women and girls of good character. Those who desired more permanent accommodation and could not afford an established residence were forced into the privately owned common lodging houses. These had an evil reputation as centers of disease, congestion, and immorality. Keepers often divided the rooms into pens by erecting wooden partitions and allowing up to three persons in a bed. Not until the adoption of a bylaw by the Corporation in 1917 was the letting of a bed in a common lodging house to two or more males over ten years of age prohibited.

The last resort of the poor in any region was the Union workhouse. Dublin had two of them: the overcrowded North Dublin Union workhouse and infirmaries in North Brunswick Street, accommodating about 2,700 paupers, and the huge workhouse of the South Dublin Union in James's Street, with 3,800. On the average, about 33,000 persons, not all from Dublin city or county, were relieved annually—men, women, and children; epileptics, lunatics, and the disabled—all subject to the tender mercies of the Master, Matron, and Poor Law Guardians. The city of Dublin was always numbered among those Unions in Great Britain and Ireland that contained the highest proportion of paupers and persons on outdoor relief. Workhouse relief under the Poor Law Act of 1838 was first organized in the city in 1841 to be followed a few years later by the concession of outdoor relief for the disabled, widows with children, and others. The North Dublin Union workhouse occupied the site of the former House of Industry, to which the beggars picked off the streets by patrolling constables had been consigned at the discretion of magistrates. More sinister associations distinguished no. 1 James's Street, site of the former infamous Foundling Hospital, where between 1786 and 1826 over one-third of the 75,000 infants admitted—"offspring of sin, or of sorrow untold"—died in the nursery.[9] Large numbers of inmates of the workhouses were infirm persons who had retired there to spend their last years, for there was no hospital in Dublin except the workhouse infirmaries into which the sick poor had a right to go. These institutions left much to be desired, having neither day-rooms for the sick nor separate wards for convalescents. Nursing, both as regards standards and sufficiency, was by all accounts very unsatisfactory. In 1886 three-quarters of the "nurses" in the Whitworth (North Dublin Union) Hospital had been graduated from pauper wardmaids. Although this practice was officially discontinued after 1897, Boards of Guardians often circumvented this order of the Local Government Board.[10] Other improvements may have occurred with the introduction of nuns to workhouse service, though their presence was not appreciated by all: the *Church of Ireland Gazette*, for one, felt obliged to question their employment and in the issue of October 9, 1903, repeated the old canard—". . . we have not always found Roman Catholicism and cleanliness in close alliance."

The strict discipline of the original Poor Law Act was long maintained, which was not surprising considering the fundamental principle on which relief was to be granted, viz., that the condition of the pauper ought to be, on the whole, less eligible than that of the independent laborer. One of the most outrageous rules in force was that no one member of a family would be admitted to a workhouse unless all applied for admission. Inmates were forbidden to have spirituous or fermented liquors, articles of food not allowed by the dietary (except on Christmas Day), playing cards, dice, or matches. If an inmate were caught playing cards, using profane language, or pretending sickness to avoid work, he was judged "disorderly," punishment being a reduced diet for up to 48 hours. Repetition of the offence within a period of seven days invited "refractory" punishment, namely, confinement for up to 24 hours and, again, a reduced diet. An example of personal discipline was the case of the female inmate placed in a dark cell for 7½ hours for using abusive language to an official, punishment that one kindly Guardian claimed would not be found outside Russia.[11] There was also separation of families within the workhouse as a consequence of the classification system, which provided separate quarters for able-bodied men and youths over 15, able-bodied women and girls over 15, the infirm of each sex, children of various categories of age and sex. Discretion was allowed the Guardians to separate females of "dissolute and disorderly habits" from those of superior character or to permit common living and sleeping quarters for married couples over 60 years, concessions that could hardly be honored in the overcrowded Dublin workhouses. While lunatics in general were transferred to the Richmond Asylum, many feeble-minded persons and insane epileptics were retained in workhouses and allowed to associate with other inmates. Neither were nonhospital consumptive cases separated from healthy inmates. Reformers considered it nothing short of a national scandal that the respectable poor should be associated with the vagrants, degenerates, and incorrigibles who often availed themselves of a few days' stay in the "casual" wards. Elements of the old discipline in their regard were evident in the stone breaking (2 cwt.) required of male tramps and oakum picking or washing duties exacted from females before their departure. No inmate received compensation for his or her labor, a circumstance that certainly made their condition less eligible. The able-bodied of both sexes over 7 years rose each day at 5:45 A.M. (one hour later during winter) and breakfasted from 6:30 to 7. Work lasted from 7 A.M. to 6 P.M. except for a one-hour dinner break at noon. The day ended soon after supper, when all were obliged to retire at 8 P.M. In the case of boys and girls under 15, however, three of the "working" hours were set aside for instruction in the three Rs.

By far the darkest feature of the Poor Law system was the condemning of children to a monotonous, cheerless existence as pauper inmates (over 5,000 in the whole of Ireland) confined to their workhouse schools, branded by their pauper dress, and necessarily commingled with the aged, sick, feeble-minded, vagrant as well as the able-bodied adult inmates. In the old days, before the suppression of the brothels, it was sometimes found that prostitutes gained admittance to the Dublin workhouses for the purpose of procuring young girls of sixteen years or older (these were free to leave) for the kips. About 1,000 (14 percent) of the paupers in the two Dublin workhouses were unfortunate children, most of them infants or very young. The mortality of children in the nurseries of the North Dublin Union was extremely high and became the subject of considerable comment in 1904, when it was disclosed that 327 babies out of fewer than 1,000 children had died there during the three years ended June 30, 1904, a figure that would have to be raised to 402 to include those children who perished on transfer to extern hospitals.[12] As might be inferred, there were no nurses in the workhouses with special experience in the management and care of children. According to the census of 1901, only about 150 children were then attending the workhouse schools, though several hundred more were benefiting from the humane "boarding out" system, and even this practice had its critics, being condemned because of those instances in which it was discovered that the small farmers and cottiers who had become foster parents were using the children as virtual slaves. Table 18 showing the particulars of workhouse inmates on the night of March 11, 1905, is most instructive, for it reflects in large measure the conditions pertaining in these institutions throughout the period:

TABLE **18.** **North and South Dublin Unions: Number and Classification of Workhouse Inmates and Number of Children Maintained out of the Workhouses, March 11, 1905.**

Number sick	1,898
Number aged and infirm	2,316
Lunatics, imbeciles, etc.	402
Sane epileptics	96 (12 in lunatic wards)
Illegitimate and deserted children	261
Legitimate children	708
Women entering to have (or with) an illegitimate child	138
Casuals ("ins and outs")	12
Vagrants	5
Other able-bodied	1,396
	Total: 7,232
Children boarded out	325

SOURCE: *Parliamentary Papers,* 1906 (LI), cd. 3203 (Vice-Regal Commission on Poor Law Reform in Ireland), vol. 11, pp. 11–12.

Those who complained of the burden that paupers placed on the rates often subscribed to the notion that workhouse inmates were somehow better off than 90 percent of the Dublin poor because the former were reputed to be better fed, clothed, and housed.[13] The truth, surely, was otherwise, for the overcrowding in both of the Dublin workhouses was notorious and few Dubliners would willingly give up their freedom for the bacon and cream the paupers were alleged to enjoy. "Meagre and monotonous" was how the inspectors of the Local Government Board described the dietaries of many Unions, fare that was, incidentally, below the standard of the large English institutions. The following is the dietary suggested by the Board for the aged and infirm as well as for those over 15 years and not engaged in work:

Breakfast	(8 A.M.)	8 oz. white bread and 1 pt. tea
Lunch (10:30 A.M.)		none
Dinner	(1 P.M.)	8 oz. white bread and 1 pt. meat soup (3 days)
		1½ lb. potatoes and 1 pt. meat soup (3 days)
		8 oz. white bread and 1 pt. new milk (Friday)
Supper	(6 P.M.)	8 oz. white bread and 1 pt. tea

Little wonder that the inmates should resort to "corruption" to obtain the tobacco, cigarets, and drink that were often smuggled in to temper the deadening monotony of their daily fare.[14]

Before the introduction of the Old Age Pensions Act in 1909, the social condition of elderly persons among the laboring classes was precarious in the extreme. A government return in 1899 estimated that of the 14,000 or so persons over 65 years in the greater Dublin metropolitan area, almost 7,000 (including paupers) earned less than 10s. per week and only 200 derived pensions from former employers.[15] Often ill or unable to find employment, the aged poor depended for their survival on relatives or, in the last resort, on the Poor Law Guardians. In too many cases their poverty and loneliness consigned them to the workhouse. There, paupers dying without friends or relatives to claim their bodies suffered the ultimate indignity of burial in the "pit" at Glasnevin or, it was hinted, dissection by medical students at the College of Science and Anatomy. Only a general system of old age pensions could alleviate the worst effects of poverty among the elderly, and this had been urged as far back as 1891 by Joseph Chamberlain and his followers. However, the lead given by Germany and Denmark was not matched in the United Kingdom until the reforming Liberal ministry of Asquith. Legislation was introduced that became law in August 1908 and came into operation on January 1 of the following year—one of the happiest days of their lives for hundreds of thousands of persons aged 70 and above in Great Britain and Ireland. "God's bounty" of 5s. a week (7s. 6d. for a married couple) had arrived for about 4,500 of the elderly (mostly women) in the city of Dublin provided certain conditions as to income could be met. Many more found their claims rejected because they or their spouses had been in receipt of poor relief during the previous year, though this pauper disqualification was removed by amending legislation two years later. Others found themselves ineligible through inability to prove age, a circumstance not unusual in Ireland, where there had been no statutory registration of births before 1864 and baptismal certificates were not always at hand. It is not known whether the investigators agreed with the avowal of the Bishop of Ross that an Irishman, "being exceedingly fond of genealogical information and discussion," might always be relied upon to be accurate about his age. At any rate, most of the dubious cases were resolved through presentation of other evidence (marriage certificates, baptismal certificates of children born before 1860, and the like) or even by observation of an applicant's appearance when oftentimes the benefit of the doubt had to be given.

It is a further commentary on the extent of poverty in Dublin that both old age pensions and the subsequent social legislation of 1911 made no immediate and appreciable reduction in the number of paupers, a striking contrast with the English experience. By 1914 the average number relieved in the workhouses in each year since 1909 actually exceeded by about 5 percent the numbers relieved during each of the five years before passage of the act. But significant reductions did take place in the case of outdoor relief, especially after the abolition of the pauper disqualification clause. So the workhouse remained to induce terror in the minds of some unfortunates and defy the efforts of reformers to place the sick poor in hospitals, the aged and infirm in almshouses, epileptics in institutions, and poor orphans and other children with guardians.

One of the more visible signs of poverty in Dublin was the horde of ragged children trooping the streets in all weathers, barefooted and insufficiently clothed. Almost any street photograph of the period offers evidence of their neglected appearance. The Industrial Schools were filled with these unfortunates, rescued by the State when found begging, wandering without home or guardian, or frequenting the company of thieves and other undesirables. Orphans and the destitute children of imprisoned parents added to their numbers as did the few unruly children committed by the courts who might otherwise have been sent to prison. About one quarter of the 1,300 or so children committed to Industrial Schools throughout the country each year were from Dublin. They ranged in age up to 14 years, with about half of them under 10 years. There were seven such institutions in metropolitan Dublin, including the earliest, established in 1869 at Lakelands,

The children of the slums.

Sandymount (for Roman Catholic girls), and the most famous (and one of the largest in Europe)—the Artane School, in which some 800 boys were under the supervision of the Irish Christian Brothers. Depending on their age at committal, children would spend up to 10 years or more under restraint until released to service or returned to parents or guardians. Not until the humanitarian provisions of the Children Act of 1908 were put into effect did it become possible for Industrial School children under the age of 8 to be boarded out to foster parents.

Juvenile street trading was as much evidence of straitened family circumstances as youthful enterprise. The practice was often merely a cover for begging, and the importunate behavior of the children toward their quarry made of them almost as great a public nuisance as the city's beggars. But there were as many defenders as opponents of this old practice, for in a city as poor as Dublin the 3s. or 4s. per week earned by a child hawking bootlaces, matches, flowers, or newspapers could make a measurable impact on his or her family's standard of living. It was also recognized that without such added income a substantial number of families in Dublin would become yet another burden to rate-payers. Needless to say the trading waifs were also defended by the newspaper proprietors, who well knew that their enterprise in the newer residential areas of the city meant increased circulation. On the other side, opponents condemned a system that brought children into public houses, kept them up late and away from school, and exposed them, especially the girls, to the moral and physical dangers of the city's night life. Many children apparently were already witnesses to these latter hazards inasmuch as a goodly proportion of them were reputed to emanate from the slum-ridden and brothel-infested quarter of Tyrone and Montgomery Streets.

Because it involved school-age children, the street trading system as practiced in Dublin, Belfast, and Cork became the subject of an official investigation in 1902. It was then estimated from police records that 433 boys and 180 girls aged 16 and under (i.e., less than 2 percent of all children in the age group 9 to 16 years) were engaged in street trading in Dublin. No one believed, however, that this was an accurate count of the numbers involved, which certainly exceeded 1,000 children. The trade was unregulated and consequently gave rise to some harrowing tales of child neglect. One such case was reported by a representative of the National Society for the Prevention of Cruelty to Children.

> On the night of 22nd of February, 1901, my attention was drawn to a crowd of people standing near Harcourt-street Railway Station. On going to the place I saw that a child was sitting on the steps of a house crying and shivering with the cold. She had a number of boxes of matches in her hands. She was barefooted, and badly dressed, with an old cape about her shoulders. . . . I took her in a cab to the South Dublin Union. . . . The child stated to me that the mother gave her a penny in the evening, and told her to go and buy matches and sell them. She further said she was out selling matches on Mondays, Tuesdays, and Fridays, and on Saturday nights she was out selling boot laces. The child was nine years of age. . . . Only last month the same child was again seen selling matches in the street. We shall now endeavour to get the child into an Industrial School.[16]

The pressing family circumstances that produced street trading by children are described in a survey of over 500 homes conducted by the Dublin metropolitan police. The youthful traders generally ranged in age from 10 to 15 years and mostly came from the poorest of working-class homes. Parents were described as either poor, respectable and industrious, or bad characters and indolent. In many cases, at least one parent had died. The weekly income of the father rarely exceeded 20s. and was sometimes supplemented by the 5s. or 6s. earned by the wife's charring. The survey combines cryptic accounts of a stoical struggle against adversity as well as graphic details illustrating cases of family drunkenness, abuse, and neglect. The following extracts from the police report suggest the drastic consequences that would follow for those families were the system of trading by young persons abolished, as some reformers urged.[17]

> Newsvendor, 13 years old. Father dead. Mother is a charwoman and earns 6s. per week, and stops in common lodging-houses. The boy earns 6s. per week and gives his mother 2s. per

week; he pays 1s. 9d. per week for lodgings, and supports himself on the remainder of the money.

Newsvendors, 9 and 15 y.o. Parents alive. Father has deserted them and mother for past twelve months. He is an idle drunkard living about Church-street. Each boy earns 3s. weekly, which they give their mother. They are at present homeless. . . .

Newsvendor, 14 y.o. Mother dead. Father a dealer in rags, bottles, etc.; earns about 6s. per week; one other child to support. Thomas gives his father about 4s. a week. The father is addicted to drink, has been arrested several times, and has no home, but lives in common lodging-houses, which are the resort of disreputable characters.

Newsvendor, 14 y.o. Parents alive. Father a labourer; unemployed. Mother also unemployed. Christy earns 5s. weekly, which he gives his mother. No other child in family. Parents idle drunkards. Condition of home most miserable, being dirty and without furniture, except an old straw palliasse thrown on floor.

Some of the evils enumerated at the investigation were soon corrected by the Employment of Children Act of 1903. Under its terms authority was given to municipal bodies to curb street trading and prohibit it to any child under 11 years. The Corporation subsequently took action to license the trade, drawing up specific regulations in 1905 and issuing badges, at 6d. each, to be worn by each trader to avoid arrest for unlicensed activity. The municipality soon had over 800 children on its rolls and was dimly aware that perhaps as many again were operating without badges. It also had the evidence of the police courts regarding the infringement of the regulations prohibiting trading by children under 11 years. A committee investigating these matters in 1909 came to the conclusion that as far as Dublin was concerned the issuance of bylaws had left the street trading evil practically untouched. A "smart little fellow" of 5 years was among 50 boys and girls brought before the Lord Mayor's court at William Street in 1908 for breaches of the bylaws for which hundreds were tried each year.[18] An unfortunate consequence of this type of arrest was that, although most offenders were let off with a caution or loss of the badge, some few children were invariably shuttled off to Reform and Industrial schools for several years or, before the reforms instituted under the Children Act of 1908, might spend a few days in prison.

Further attempts to limit street trading by the young always came up against objections that stressed that the poverty of a considerable number of families in the city was so great that total abolition would do more harm than good. In fact, when the Earl of Shaftesbury introduced a bill in the House of Lords in 1911 to prohibit trading by young persons under 17 years, the Dublin Corporation fought off an attempt to include Ireland in its provisions, Lord MacDonnell, the former Under Secretary, being instrumental in having Ireland excluded. While the opponents of street trading complained with some justice that the practice was creating a generation of wastrels unfit for anything but gambling, vagrancy, or crime and was pushing young girls along the road toward a life of immorality, defenders claimed, also with some justice, that abolition would only drive the children to idleness and that in any event it was better to be active on the streets than exposed to the unhealthy environment of the slums in which they lived. The evil was eventually recognized, however, in that deputations prevailed on the Corporation in 1915 to abolish night trading altogether and raise the age limit to 14 years (still 2 years under the limit in England). But by that time the establishment of labor exchanges had greatly reduced the numbers of older street traders because they were generally unable to obtain renewal of their badges as long as they could register for employment at the Exchange.

The charitable agency most in contact with these children was the Police-Aided Children's Clothing Society, an organization founded by the Philanthropic Reform Association on the model of those operating in Liverpool and Glasgow. The police were to be the eyes of the Society, recommending to its charity any child in an obvious state of neglect—provided the father's weekly income did not exceed 18s. As usual, the investigation of a thousand or so children each year revealed the familiar accounts of poverty. Like many charities in Dublin, it was perennially short of funds through lack of support, only £170 (a third of the amount needed) being received in 1903, for example, when nearly two thousand children needed to be clothed. Its difficulties in 1910 provoked the indictment by the *Irish Times* that "half the trouble and cost expended in sending money to sustain missionaries to the heathen would suffice to give the Dublin children a chance. . . . The people of Dublin ought to be ashamed of themselves for their neglect of the poor, especially of the children." Yet when Protestant organizations attempted to help the waifs and strays of the city, they were often greeted with charges, true or not, of proselytism. Their social concerns gave occasion for the bizarre admonition of priests, from whom the merest hint of proselytism put reason and charity to flight that "fathers and mothers should allow their children to die before their faces rather than hand them over to those who will take away their faith"! When the *Irish Times* issued its own attack on such fearful theology, it too was assailed for "rank paganism" and for forgetting that "religion comes before food in the stomach."[19]

The schools also gave evidence of the destitution and hardship suffered by children. In his 1906 Report on the city's sanitary circumstances, Dr. D.E. Flinn, medical inspector of the Local Government Board, claimed that 104 of the 167 national schools in Dublin lacked lavatory accommodation. A problem was also created by the educational system itself in the setting of hours of attendance from 9.30 A.M. to 3 P.M. Whereas in England a one-hour break at noon allowed children to go home for a meal, in Ireland there was only a half-hour break to be spent within the precincts of the school. No provision whatever was made for food, so that the poorer children were obliged to bring in scraps of bread or in some cases arrived with no food at all. Teachers often stated that some boys were too weak from hunger even to play during recreation. In such circumstances compulsory education seemed compulsory starvation or, as the *Irish Times* reflected, "legislative murder." One obvious solution would have been the provision of free school meals by the state, but middle-class sentiment against the alleged demoralizing effects of such would-be charity was strong in Ireland as elsewhere. Even Dr. Kelly, Bishop of Ross and one of the most sympathetic clerical spokesmen on behalf of the needs of the Irish poor, overcame his humanitarian instincts in this regard when he admitted at the hearings of the parliamentary committee on physical deterioration in 1904 that he "would prefer physical hardship and cruelty on the one hand by leaving them [schoolchildren] hungry, rather than demoralising them on the other." Fortunately, several private groups were organized in Dublin to serve free meals to necessitous children: the English act allowing the striking of a rate to provide meals for poor children did not extend to Ireland. Maud Gonne was the foremost spokeswoman for this cause after 1910. Her Ladies' School Dinner committee provided free meals for over 400 children in two of the poorest school districts in the city. And that crusade also triumphed with the passage in 1914 of the Provision of Meals Act for Ireland, yet one more recognition of the fact that public obligation became necessary when public charity broke down. The Act was duly adopted for the National and convent schools of the city, though the ½d. in the £ rate was not expected to provide for all those in need. Nevertheless, some 4,000 of the city's 39,000 primary-school children received thereafter one meal per child per day, the cost of each not to exceed 1½d.[20] Not the least of the benefits of this measure was the marked improvement in attendance in a school system that traditionally drew only 70 to 75 percent of enrolled students each school day.

Dublin, alas, was not able to keep pace with other cities in the solution of its social problems, for the capital and its citizens were subjected to mighty shocks from 1913 onward. The industrial troubles of that terrible year were followed by the hardships introduced at the outbreak of war—increases in the price of fuel, enhanced prices of foodstuffs, and cessation of employment. Irishmen, embarrassed by the receipt of foreign contributions to relieve Irish distress, cried that Ireland was a prosperous country—*except* for Dublin. There the distressing symptoms of poverty and sickness still stood challenge to the public conscience.

7

Police and Crime

In Dublin there is practically no serious crime . . .

Report of the Committee of Inquiry into the Dublin Metropolitan Police,
Parliamentary Papers, 1902

LAW AND order in the city of Dublin was maintained by a police force unique to the metropolis, the Dublin Metropolitan Police. The DMP was quite distinct from the Royal Irish Constabulary operating in the rest of the country and unlike the latter was unarmed. The police district extended beyond the old city to include the townships of Rathmines, Pembroke, Blackrock, Kingstown, Dalkey, and parts of the county and comprised six divisions in all. A seventh elite division, the "G" or detective division, operated in plain clothes and could exercise a warrant in any part of Ireland. Authority within the DMP was exercised by a Chief Commissioner and his assistant, while each division was headed by a superintendent, with inspectors and sergeants of various grades in direct command over the constables who made up about 80 percent of the total force. Sir John Ross (of Bladensburg) was Chief from 1900 until his resignation following the dismissal of Assistant Commissioner W. V. Harrel in connection with the Howth gun-running affair in July 1914 (see Chapter 9, below). The force numbered on the average approximately 1,180 men (of whom five-sixths were Roman Catholics), ranging from a low of 1,137 in 1899 to a high of 1,202 in 1911. It operated from 17 stations, of which 11 (Chancery Lane, Newmarket, Kilmainham, College Street, Lad Lane, Summerhill, Store Street, Green Street, Bridewell Lane, Mountjoy, and Chapelizod) lay within the city proper. Constables were mostly recruited from among farmer's sons, and there was generally no shortage of applicants, the annual intake (an average of 65 recruits) representing only some 20 percent of those desiring entry. In the ten years to 1900, the average annual resignations numbered under a dozen men, less than 1 percent of the entire force. Though the initial salary of a constable was only 25s. per week, rising to 30s. after 15 years' service, there were prospects of promotion to detective or to the higher ranks, security of employment, retirement with three-fifths pension after 25 years' service (two-thirds after 30), and other benefits that rendered the occupation of policeman an attractive career for otherwise unskilled individuals.

The DMP was an imperial force and, like the London Metropolitan Police in this respect, was free from the control of the local authority. One of the standing complaints of Dublin Corporation was the police tax levied on the citizens under an act of parliament and collected via the rates to support a body under the direct control of the Chief Secretary. This contribution averaged about 18 percent of the total cost to maintain the force, the remainder being made up by a grant from the Treasury (67 percent), the county of Dublin (7 percent), and various receipts (8 percent) due the force from hackney license fees, court fines, and so forth. Between 1901 and 1916 the total maintenance cost increased but slightly from £160,000 to £177,000, lending some credence to the perennial claim of the men that they were underpaid. The Corporation refused in 1905 to hand over its share of the police appropriation on the grounds that the rate (8d. in the £ and more than the levy in either London or Manchester) established in 1837 was proving to be an excessive burden on the citizens, owing to the city's increased valuation since that time. This was just one more aspect of the hostility with which the nationalist councillors treated most imperial institutions in Ireland. The tactic proved ineffective when the government exercised its statutory power to recover the revenue by appropriate deductions from monies due the municipality under the local taxation account.

Dublin, Belfast, and other Irish cities were the most policed areas in the United Kingdom. In 1901 Birmingham, Manchester, Leeds, and Sheffield—all cities of greater population than Dublin—had police strengths of 800, 1006, 507, and 515 men, respectively, all below the 1,172-man Dublin Metropolitan Police. Liverpool had an absolutely greater force with 1,360 men, but these were responsible for a population that exceeded Dublin's by almost 300,000 persons. There was one policeman for every 330 persons in the Dublin metropolitan district in 1906, whereas in Liverpool, Glasgow, Manchester, and Birmingham the rates varied from 1 in 480 to 1 in 580, with even greater disparities in other large cities.[1] The same trend was evident in Ireland as a whole, where the proportion of police to total population greatly exceeded the ratios for either England, Scotland, or Wales. There were of course sound historical reasons for this, inasmuch as the latter three countries never experienced the revolutionary unrest and agrarian agitation that characterized Fenianism and the successive phases of the so-called land war in Ireland. As the visible presence of an alien administration, the police became, therefore, the object of a natural hostility on the part of all shades of nationalist opinion, the more so because there was no professional criminal class in Dublin that could justify a force of over 1,100 men. This hostility was a sufficient hazard of their occupation for the men to use it to justify their claims for more favorable pay scales than enjoyed by Scottish or English police forces. Official representations of the men pointed to the fact that, whereas a record of employment with the London police was a passport to good employment upon retirement, the reverse was true for the DMP. The latter, it was claimed, were isolated from society, their wives insulted in common grocery shops, their sons ostracized. While it is true that police in Dublin were often subject to harassment on the job and discrimination off it, their case was probably overstated. One could hardly imagine a city in the United Kingdom more difficult to police than, say, Liverpool. And for every landlord who gouged excessive rent from a policeman, there were surely more who would gladly allow 6d. off the rent to obtain the stabilizing influence of a police family. Likewise, the alleged refusal of work to retirees by Corporation departments could be balanced by offers from the railway companies and "loyalist" employers such as John Jameson, Guinness's, and others.

The average age of DMP recruits at entry was between 22 and 23 years. Minimum regulation height was 5'9", one inch greater than that for RIC recruits. Visitors rarely failed to be struck by the "giant-like" stature of the DMP. However, it seems unlikely that this quality was possessed by more than a very small percentage of the men. Figures supplied by Sir Francis Head in 1852 reveal that only 23 of the 12,000-strong RIC boasted a height of 6'3" and upward while 85 percent of the force were under 6', for an overall average height of slightly under 5'10".[2] Since no geological time span separated that year from the early twentieth century, there is no reason to suppose that the force had changed much in stature in the meantime. Thus, assuming that the available pool of "giants" was equally restricted for the DMP, the average height of the men on that force was perhaps no greater than 5'11", which nevertheless certainly distinguished them from the normally smaller-statured citizenry. The average wait for promotion was around 8 years for sergeants, 16 years for station sergeant or, in the case of sergeants qualifying by examination, 7 years for inspector. There were complaints from the men that promotion was unduly slow owing to the absence of compulsory retirement after the normal 29 years on the force, and dissatisfaction was also generally expressed at the relatively low salary scales, particularly in relation to those pertaining for the London Metropolitan Police. A standing demand of the DMP, as a metropolitan force, was for equality with the London police. Conditions had been much worse before 1873, when the wage disparity between the two bodies rendered the Dublin force decidedly unattractive to the better class of recruit, who soon found alternative, better-paid employment with police forces in London and elsewhere. This situation was corrected when new wage scales were established that raised the pay of sergeants and constables by 50 percent. Thereafter, voluntary resignations virtually ceased and the number of applicants greatly exceeded the available positions even during the early 1880s, when the nationalist agitation of Parnell and his followers was at its height. In fact, the constant availability of recruits was a factor in the decision to deny the men's wage claims at the Committee of Inquiry in 1901, when once more equality with the London police was at issue. But this situation was also reversed when the war brought real hardship to those with moderate incomes. By 1916 the DMP was finding it almost impossible to secure suitable candidates, a situation that in the crisis-laden atmosphere of Dublin from 1913 onward caused considerable disquiet in Dublin Castle.[3]

The DMP was also wont to buttress its claim for special treatment by reference to certain "hazards" unique to the experience of policemen in the Irish capital. There was, as already mentioned, the prevailing current of hostility toward any Irish policeman on the part of nationalists because of his role in upholding the rule of an alien government. In Dublin this animosity rendered it difficult if not impossible, as the police themselves claimed, to fraternize with their fellow citizens. The Dublin pedestrian and driver also apparently presented special problems, for they were held to lack the "moral control" that distinguished the citizen of the English metropolis: "In London . . . a policeman has only to put up his hand, and it is sufficient. It is not so in Dublin," complained one traffic constable. This "contrariness" as regards traffic extended even to Dublin's upper classes for, as our constable further explained, "If you speak to a gentlemen . . . many of them will tell you that you are a 'cad of a policeman' or use some other offensive expression." The unhealthy state of the Irish capital, with its high death rate and recurrent epidemic disease, was also cited as evidence of the greater risks run in Dublin by either a policeman on the beat or a detective searching for stolen goods in the pawnshops.[4] To these unpleasant features of the life of a Dublin policeman was added the egregious restriction preventing marriage before five years' service. The expression or manifestation of political or sectarian opinions was strictly forbidden, but this injunction did not extend to the Society of Freemasons, the blatantly sectarian Protestant organization. This anomaly provided the occasion for a rare expression of indiscipline in the force late in 1916, when 150 constables attended a meeting in a show of support for the Catholic counterpart to the Freemasons, the Ancient Order of Hibernians. As a result 5 constables were dismissed from the force, but the point of their action was conceded when the Society of Freemasons was thereafter included among the list of "forbidden" organizations.[5]

The dull monotony of the policeman's working hours was shaped by the beat—the daily patrol duty assigned to about three-fifths of the force's 950 constables. Some 700 men from the A through D Divisions patrolled the city streets while most of the remainder covered the suburban districts of Rathmines and Pembroke (E Division) and the rural and urban districts extending along the coastal strip to Killiney (F Division). The constable, patrolling at the regulated pace of 2½ miles an hour, was obliged to give his attention to the condition of footways and shopfronts, obstructions and nuisances, even to seize stray dogs. Summonses would be issued on the spot for infractions of the Highway Acts or Hackney and Carriage regulations and offenses against the sanitary laws. Arrests were in order for drunken and disorderly conduct, prostitution, and offenses against the Vagrancy Acts. Those few constables not on patrol were engaged as jailers, court attendants, and guardians of public buildings. Also among the duties of a constable were visits to tenement houses to detect sanitary defects, to slaughter houses and nightly lodging houses to ensure observance of public health regulations, and most of all, to the city's more than 800 public houses to enforce the Intoxicating Liquor Laws. The 40 or so officers and men of the G (Detective) Division investigated crime, recovered lost property, and regulated the hackney and carriage trade. That such a large force of police should be patrolling the streets of a city that was remarkably free of any serious crime always elicited considerable hostile comment from local nationalists. The least offensive and most amusing of these came from Tom Kettle, MP, who suggested that only the need to restrain and suppress the riot and disorder created by the students of Trinity College could explain the considerable presence of the men in blue. Their presence would not have been described with such levity after 1912, when mass industrial unrest, gun-running, and seditious activity introduced occupational hazards of a kind that had not been experienced since Fenian days.

As already indicated, serious crime in Dublin never reached great proportions. Though the two greatest crimes of modern Ireland both occurred in Dublin—the assassinations of the Chief Secretary and Under Secretary in the Phoenix Park in 1882 and the theft of the so-called Irish Crown Jewels from Dublin Castle in 1908—they were quite exceptional. In the eighteen years under review in this study, the number of indictable offenses committed in the entire metropolitan police district (i.e., city and suburbs) averaged slightly under 3,000 per year in a population of over 390,000 (see Appendix E).*

*Police returns distinguished between indictable and nonindictable offenses. Normally, the term *crime* was reserved for the former while the latter, being less serious, were described as *offenses*. Under the law, indictable cases were triable before a judge and jury at Quarter Sessions or Assizes, whereas nonindictable offenders could be proceeded against summarily by lay magistrates (i.e., justices of the peace) attending petty sessions.

About 80 percent of this number consisted of offenses against property without the use of violence (minor larcenies and the like). Consequently, the number of really serious offenses such as murder, manslaughter, rape, burglary, and robbery were quite small by comparison. It was an exceptional year if more than two or three homicides were reported, though, of course, some heinous crimes went statistically unrecorded such as the discovery in July 1909 of the bodies of three infants in the refuse heaps unloaded at the Cleansing Department's destructor in Stanley Street. Indeed, an average of only 100 of the worst crimes (i.e., offenses against the person) were committed in the district each year, and half of these covered cases of abandonment and neglect of children and such misdemeanors as assault. Though the general character of a moderate incidence of crime is clear from the record, it should be realized that reported statistics cannot accurately reflect the overall degree of criminality in society. This is especially true, of course, in the case of sexual offenses, of which the greatest number of reported cases comprised "indecent assault" and averaged only 7 cases per annum. The crime of incest, which so agitated those concerned with the overcrowded conditions in tenement houses, was not separately reported until 1914, and little credence could then be placed in data that suggested two such crimes per year.

The larger category of crime was the type of minor offense for which no indictment was needed and offenders, as already explained, were disposed of summarily. The number of these offenses exceeded the more serious forms of crime by over ten times, but they hardly presented a reliable standard by which to measure the degree of criminality in the city. A large number of them partook more of a civil than a criminal character. Over half consisted of ordinary infractions of the police regulations, sanitary laws, traffic and vagrancy acts, as well as offenses in relation to dogs. Nevertheless, they also included cases of drunkenness, disorderly conduct, common assault, cruelty, vandalism, and prostitution. Thus, while these nonindictable offenses may not have indicated a great deal of criminal activity taking place, they did reflect in some measure the general state of disorder and demoralization in the community. Over 33,000 persons per annum were being brought before magistrates in Dublin in the closing years of the nineteenth century, and fully one-third of them were cases of assault or drunkenness.

At the turn of the century, therefore, contemporaries were not unduly alarmed at the nature and incidence of crime in the city. Indeed, they might have noted a remarkable decrease in Ireland as a whole during the previous half-century. The number of convicts (i.e., those imprisoned under penal servitude for three years and upwards) in custody in Irish jails declined progressively from over 3,400 in 1855 to 292 in 1901. The number convicted in each year showed a corresponding decrease, from 518 in 1855 to only 59 at the end of the century.[6] Of course, much greater numbers were confined at all times to local prisons for lesser offenses, although the decrease in committals was also notable in that regard: from 48,000 in 1855 to 32,000 in 1900, of whom some 50 percent were drunkards. The latter when arrested usually spent only four or five days in jail, but magistrates were

---

In point of fact, however, fewer than half of the arrested criminals in Dublin appeared on indictment at the Dublin Commission Court or before the Recorder in the borough court of Quarter Sessions at Green Street; the majority, either by legal convention or by choice in certain cases, were dealt with summarily in the police courts at Inns Quay where paid magistrates having at least 6 years' practice as barristers presided. In Dublin, the J.P.s, in contrast to practice elsewhere in the country, had mainly nominal duties, namely, the taking of affidavits, and so forth.

often criticized for their leniency especially in the case of those more extreme cases that invited repeated imprisonment. One such example from the reports of the Prisons Board was the female drunkard with 264 previous convictions who wound up in Grangegorman prison on 52 occasions in one year. Treatment not severity was needed for these unfortunates, and this need was partly met in the Inebriates Act of 1898, which for the first time provided for the compulsory committal of criminal habitual drunkards (i.e., those with three convictions in one year) to Inebriate Reformatories (one was established at Ennis, County Clare) instead of to prison. As Table 20 shows, Dublin shared in the downward trend both for serious and minor offenses, with the improvement in the former category being brought about mainly by the great reduction in crimes of theft. In 1900, for example, the number of crimes committed in the district was less than half of the number reported thirty years earlier. Naturally, a considerable number of perpetrators of burglaries, robberies, and larcenies eluded the police, and of those made "amenable" for these indictable offenses over one-third had the charges against them dropped or were acquitted in court (see Appendix E). Conviction for an indictable offense almost always resulted in imprisonment for the accused. Some 700 men and women were disposed of in this manner in Dublin each year, in addition to a small number of youthful offenders and children committed to Reformatories and Industrial Schools. Of the 30,000 or so nonindictable offenders, fewer than 2,000 on the average suffered imprisonment. Most of the remainder (the conviction rate here being around 80 percent) were subject to fines only, excepting those few juveniles sent to join their more aggressive peers in the Reform and Industrial schools.

Mountjoy or Kilmainham jail was the repository of offenders sentenced to prison by the Dublin courts. Mountjoy, situated within a stone's throw of one of the city's elegant residential squares of the same name, was built at mid-century to replace Newgate as a convict prison, but with the welcome closing in 1887 of the old Richmond Bridewell the facility was enlarged to include also a local prison for males avoiding sentences of penal servitude. It was further extended to provide for female convicts and other prisoners when the Grangegorman Female Penitentiary was closed in 1897. The county jail at Kilmainham (discontinued as a local prison after 1910) held males only. Both institutions took in a total of about 10,000 prisoners each year from various Irish counties. In 1899, 3,300 of them had passed through the Dublin courts, but this figure was gradually reduced until by 1914 fewer than 2,000 were being processed annually. Most served brief sentences of from one day to five weeks. While "inside," they were occupied for the most part with the familiar prison ordeal of stonebreaking, oakum picking, wood-chopping, and mailbag making. On release those in need could avail thmselves of the charitable solicitude of the certified prisoners' aid societies, of which there were three in Dublin, organized as usual along sectarian lines.

The foregoing hardly presents a picture of the kind of mass social disorder that has become all too painfully familiar in contemporary urban society. Yet, relatively speaking, Dublin could be described as a foremost center of crime in the United Kingdom, not only during the late Victorian era but also for the early years of the present century—a description that would not have been challenged by those who equated wickedness with misery. Sir Frederick Falkiner, the Recorder of Dublin for almost thirty years before his retirement in 1905 and the judge who most came in contact with crime, frequently took the opportunity to preface his remarks to jurors with a disquisition on the relation between crime in the capital and the depressing circumstances in the slums. Between 1870 and 1894 about half of all the major crimes committed in Ireland fell within the jurisdiction of the Dublin Metropolitan Police, except during the Land League years (1879-82) of nationwide disorder, when the ratio fell to one-third. But even the latter figure was remarkable enough, considering that the population of the police district was only one-fifteenth of that of the entire country. In prosperous Belfast, whose population began to approach Dublin's toward the end of the century, the number of major crimes in this period was small by comparison, well under 10 percent of the total for the Dublin metropolitan area, though the northern city quickly lost its "crimeless" status from 1895 onward. Not until the very end of the century did the pattern improve for the capital with the halving of the number of crimes, an aspect of the general improvement alluded to above. By 1899 the crimes committed in Dublin represented slightly over one-quarter of the total for Ireland and rarely exceeded one-third of it thereafter. But the capital, nevertheless, easily maintained its leading position, as Table 19 discloses.

TABLE 19. **Incidence of Crime in Three Major Irish Cities and Ireland as a Whole for 1910.**

	DUBLIN (DMP) DISTRICT	BELFAST	CORK CITY	IRELAND
	(rates per 100,000 of the population)			
Indictable offenses	852	541	215	221
Nonindictable offenses	8,169	5,397	4,963	4,343
Total offenses	9,021	5,938	5,178	4,564

SOURCE: *Parliamentary Papers,* 1911 (CII), cd. 5866 (Judicial Statistics of Ireland), p. xv.

A comparison with the eight major English cities was equally striking and almost always unfavorable to Dublin. In the incidence of crime (indictable offenses) alone, only Manchester in the earlier period and Liverpool in the later merited comparison (see Table 20 and Appendix F). The parameters of crime were similar in both countries. As in Dublin the really serious offenses represented only a small proportion of the crime in English cities; simple and minor larcenies remained the great contributors to crime statistics. Not until 1903 did Dublin lose the total ascendancy it had held in criminal matters and then only to Liverpool, a quite exceptional case by English standards. With this exception, the crimes committed in Dublin between 1900 and 1913 were greater even in absolute numbers than in English cities (Birmingham, Leeds, Manchester, Sheffield) with much larger populations. Indeed, more persons were arrested for simple larcenies in Dublin in each year than were apprehended for *all* indictable offenses in such populous centers as Bradford, Bristol, Leeds, and in most years, Sheffield. And the greater policing of the Irish capital may not be pleaded to mitigate its notoriety in this regard, for indictable offenses were crimes *reported to* the police not, as in the case of most nonindictable offenses, ones made known by the police themselves in their capacity as public prosecutors of minor offenses.

No city earned the notoriety Dublin held in the case of those offenses dealt with under summary jurisdiction. Even if allowance be made for the large number of civil orders issued to weekly tenants for repossession by the landlord owing to nonpayment of rent*

---

*These proceedings were included as "minor offenses" in the statistics of crime in Ireland *before* 1895. Thereafter they were reported separately as quasi-criminal matters thus avoiding the inflation in the number of apparent crimes that characterizes figures reported in the nonindictable category for 1894 and prior years.

TABLE 20. Number of Crimes (indictable offenses) and Persons Proceeded Against for Nonindictable Offenses (including rates per 100,000 of the population at each census) in the Police Districts of Dublin, Belfast, and the Greater Boroughs of England, 1871–1911.

	1871 NO.	1871 RATE	1881 NO.	1881 RATE	1891 NO.	1891 RATE	1901 NO.	1901 RATE	1911 NO.	1911 RATE
CRIMES:										
Dublin	4,401	1,304	3,771	1,079	2,610	741	2,696	691	3,429	824
Belfast	92	53	201	96	138	54	2,031	582	1,826	474
Birmingham	841	245	1,343	335	950	221	1,874	359	1,581	301
Bradford	360	247	192	105	152	70	885	316	1,413	490
Bristol	259	142	426	206	177	80	780	237	861	241
Leeds	718	277	937	303	364	99	1,053	246	996	224
Liverpool	3,680	746	4,298	778	3,320	641	4,087	597	12,803	1,715
London	12,982	341	16,203	344	11,343	203	19,496	297	18,298	253
Manchester	4,597	1,293	4,095	1,199	1,884	373	1,946	358	2,578	361
Sheffield	448	187	569	200	280	86	1,458	356	1,688	371
NONINDICTABLE OFFENSES:										
Dublin	37,483	11,103	45,580	13,036	56,808	16,126	29,736	7,621	27,050	6,504
Belfast	12,508	7,172	14,614	7,011	15,366	6,004	12,978	3,717	20,384	5,288
Birmingham	11,722	3,411	13,007	3,246	14,043	3,272	17,235	3,300	17,318	3,293
Bradford	3,232	2,216	4,531	2,476	4,721	2,182	3,435	1,228	3,904	1,353
Bristol	6,026	3,301	6,831	3,308	5,695	2,569	7,539	2,289	4,493	1,258
Leeds	6,043	2,331	7,962	2,576	10,934	2,975	8,477	1,976	9,485	2,129
Liverpool	43,926	8,904	45,507	8,238	46,795	9,035	34,591	5,050	32,007	4,288
London	97,800	2,568	115,761	2,456	144,354	2,580	165,952	2,532	156,091	2,158
Manchester	24,299	6,832	23,232	6,803	24,207	4,790	23,902	4,395	22,459	3,144
Sheffield	4,935	2,057	5,238	1,842	8,989	2,772	8,269	2,021	7,651	1,683

SOURCES: Judicial Statistics of Ireland; Statistics of the Dublin Metropolitan Police (begins 1894); Judicial Statistics of England and Wales. Reports for above years in *Parliamentary Papers* as follows:

1871 in 1872(LXV): c. 600 (England); c. 674 (Ireland)

1881 in 1882(LXXV): c. 3333 (England); c. 3355 (Ireland)

1891 in 1892(LXXXIX): c. 6734 (England); c. 6782 (Ireland)

1901 in 1903(LXXXIII), cd. 1441 (England); 1902(CXVII), cd. 1208 (Ireland); 1902(XLIII), cd. 1166 (DMP)

1911 in 1912–13(CX): cd. 6602 (England); cd. 6419 (Ireland)

1912–13(LXIX), cd. 6384 (DMP).

(10,000 or more per annum before 1899 and averaging 7,500 annually thereafter), the city still maintained an uncomfortable lead over all others. No mean contributor to this record was another Dublin "peculiarity"—an excessive flouting of the Highway Acts (e.g., obstructions, nuisances, and offenses by owners and drivers of carts). By 1909 over 10,000 persons were being charged annually for these offenses, numbers considerably in excess of those in other cities. The number so charged in the London metropolitan police district (population 7.4 million) in 1912, for example, was 13,286, or only about 2,000 more than in Dublin district (population 420,000), while the numbers in the other major centers ranged between 200 and 2,500. A similar pattern prevailed for the more serious offenses in the nonindictable category. Cruelty to children as measured by prosecutions had an unfortunate prominence in the Irish capital. There too both citizen and constable had a much greater chance of being the victim of common or aggravated assault. No offense, however, gave greater cause for scandal than drunkenness, a problem that in its public manifestation of disorderly conduct happily began to come under some control with the passing of the Victorian era.

Drunkenness had long been the great social problem of the age, its incidence suggesting the great amount of disorder that characterized street life in the nineteenth-century city. For all the purported devotional predilections of the Irish people, not much reverence was accorded in Dublin to the memory of the great Irish apostle of temperance, Father Theobald Mathew. From Barnaby Riche in 1610 (". . . the selling of Ale in Dublin . . . hath vent in every house in the Towne every day in the weeke, at every houre in the day and in every minute in the houre . . . the whole profit of the Towne stands upon Alehouses and selling of Ale") to the Lenten pastorals of Archbishop Walsh, there was no trait of the people more subject to denunciation than their propensity to tipple. The Catholic Church in particular was greatly opposed to the old Irish practice of "waking" the dead, whereby bodies were often kept in the room of a tenement house for as many days as it took to ensure a well-attended Sunday funeral, the intervening period providing the occasion for dissipation among the living. In 1870 over half of those arrested in Dublin for minor offenses were drunk and disorderly, a number (24,468 [!]) that exceeded even the figure for the London metropolis, an area with a population ten times greater. Such conditions lent credence to the brawling stereotype depicted in the novels of Charles Lever. Nor were the citizens of Dublin the chief offenders in this regard, for the cities of Waterford and Limerick in particular surpassed the capital in this form of iniquity and no comment on that social evil was more trenchant than Bishop O'Dwyer's: " . . . until the torrent of liquor flowing over Limerick was stopped the city would remain as it was—beggarly, wretched, filthy, and impoverished."[7] The assault on alcoholism and drunkenness was undertaken by the Irish Association for the Prevention of Intemperance, among whose sponsors were John Redmond, Michael Davitt, and other members of the Irish parliamentary party. The Association was formed in 1878 to secure the enforcement of Sunday closing and a reduction in the number of licenses. Fierce agitation accompanied the attempts in 1878 to curtail hours as organized groups of publicans in Dublin broke up meetings supporting the temperance legislation that was then being debated in parliament. In the event, Dublin and four other cities were exempted from the Sunday Closing (Ireland) Act.

Fortunately, the extremes of drunken behavior in Ireland were mitigated over the years (see Table 21) by the stricter penalties imposed by licensing acts; by the normal civilizing process of improved living standards; by the work of the churches, the Gaelic League, the various temperance associations; and outside the major cities, by Sunday closing. The improvement after 1870 was quite remarkable, an improvement that was, despite a few lapses in the late 1880s, well maintained in Dublin. By 1899 the number of arrests for drunkenness in the city had decreased to 9,000 (over a third of them of women) and continued to decline rapidly thereafter. Yet by the standards of English cities, Dublin in the early twentieth century deserved no laurels for sobriety. Indeed, as Table 21 suggests, the "way out of Dublin" was even shorter in 1901 than that familiar, well-trodden route out of Manchester. And the evils of drink could not be measured by statistics alone. All the social investigations of the period pointed to drunkenness as the predominant cause of misery and destitution among the working classes in the slums, including the cruelty to children by drunken fathers (far greater in Dublin, apparently, than elsewhere) and their neglect by drunken mothers. Few, however, made the opposite correlation between miserable surroundings and addiction to alcohol. Some "experts" preferred to see the causes of alcoholism in the "excitable, high-strung, nervous temperament of the Irish race, . . . in the essentially neurotic and mercurial Irishman . . . easily overjoyed and as easily depressed, and accustomed to treat both conditions by whisky"[8](!), a conclusion that hardly explains the tremendous improvements in the incidence of public drunkenness in Dublin since the besotted mid-Victorian years.

TABLE 21. **Dublin (Metropolitan Police District): Arrests for Drunkenness Compared to Similar Arrests in Belfast and the Largest English Boroughs, 1871–1911. Figures Shown Are Rates per 100,000 of the Population of the Police District in Each Case as Calculated from Census Data.**

	1871	1881	1891	1901	1911
Dublin	5,294	2,738	4,406	1,997	701
Belfast	4,594	3,489	2,963	1,113	1,142
Birmingham	636	585	652	640	913
Bradford	422	189	202	182	263
Bristol	633	662	528	358	222
Leeds	622	523	506	425	525
Liverpool	3,965	2,572	2,190	632	1,447
London	649	581	570	773	853
Manchester	3,008	2,722	1,393	1,489	995
Sheffield	467	275	493	337	330

SOURCES: Judicial Statistics of Ireland; Statistical Returns of the Dublin Metropolitan Police; Judicial Statistics of England and Wales (see references to *Parliamentary Papers* in Table 20).

Dublin had about 800 licensed public houses of all kinds (excluding over 300 "off license" spirit grocers and beer dealers) and an untold number of illegal "shebeens." In the poorer parts of the city, nearly every grocery store was licensed for the consumption of liquor on the premises (in separate adjoining quarters) and this widespread availability of liquor was doubtless responsible for the telling statistic in the police returns, which revealed that for a two-week period in June 1908 46,574 women and 27,999 children (including 5,807 babes in arms) were observed entering 22 selected public houses in the city.[9]

(One must suppose that an inordinate amount of police time was spent in supervising public houses.) Hence the vigorous campaign to curtail hours and extend the Sunday Closing Act to Dublin and the other exempted centers. Both the Dublin Total Abstinence Society (Catholic) and the Hibernian Band of Hope Union (Protestant) persisted mightily in beating the drum for temperance at open-air concerts and, with an eye to the future, strove to enroll the young in the crusade through school lectures. Perhaps these deserve some of the credit for the gains made in 1906, when the Intoxicating Liquors (Ireland) Act decreed an earlier Saturday (10 P.M.) closing and a two-hour reduction in the former 2 to 7 P.M. Sunday hours, not the least blessing of which must have been the greater possibility for many a household of a full family gathering at the Sunday evening meal.

It was the war that dealt the greatest blow to the drink trade, for the full implications of the vitiating force of alcoholism became all too apparent under the increased manpower and industrial needs from 1914 onward. Among the more noteworthy temperance crusades of this period was the Strength of Britain Movement. The names of some of the most influential people in public life—Thomas Hardy, Viscount Bryce, H. G. Wells, Patrick Geddes, and from Dublin, Professor Mahaffy and the ubiquitous Sir Charles Cameron—were lent to a movement that demanded prohibition during the war and the conversion of public houses into places of refreshment! If nothing else, the sponsors demonstrated that they had learned little about one aspect of human nature that had mocked even John Calvin himself. Mercifully, the controls introduced by the government were not so extreme and resulted in the continued decrease in arrests for drunkenness. In Dublin by 1916 the number was less than one-quarter of what it had been 16 years earlier, an improvement not matched in such centers of dissipation as Liverpool and Manchester.

The greatest "social evil," of course, was prostitution, not only for the outrage it gave to conventional morality but also because of its obvious association with the dreaded and insidious venereal diseases. Prostitution was, of course, a characteristic of urban life down through the ages. In his *View of Ancient and Modern Dublin* (1798), Ferrar mentions the establishment in 1792 of an association for discountenancing vice "to stem the torrent of vice and immorality which was deluging the nation." A half-century later Gustave Richelot's study of prostitution in British and Irish cities devoted barely 70 words out of 70,000 to Dublin and then only to record police statistics on some 1,200 ladies of the night.[10] Social conditions in the city of Dublin, as in other great urban centers with considerable poverty and deprivation, most certainly encouraged prostitution's growth among low-paid workers, many of them introduced to looser forms of morality through the general practice among the poor of mixed sleeping of related persons in one room or even in the same bed. One of the most forceful statements ever penned on the subject of prostitution was that of George Bernard Shaw on the occasion of the white slavery agitation in 1912:

> Until you change this condition of society (whereby women are more highly paid and better treated as prostitutes than as respectable women) and secure to every respectable woman a sufficient wage with reasonable hours of labor, you will never get rid of the White Slave Traffic. . . . There are always orphans and widows and girls from the country and abroad who have no family and no husband, and these must submit to the blackest misery that a slum garret and an income of from 8d. to 1s. a day can bring to a lonely, despised, shabby, dirty, underfed woman, or else add to their wages by prostitution.[11]

Our mid-Victorian forbearers acknowledged the oldest profession in the world by including it among the occupations of the people in the censuses of 1851 and 1861. According to this source the number of confessed or ascribed prostitutes numbered 740 (Dublin) and 590 (Leinster), respectively, but these figures were only a fraction of those actually arrested for soliciting. The census of 1861 listed 134 brothel keepers in Leinster (131 of them females and doubtless all operating in Dublin). The period before 1890 saw the heyday of prostitution in Ireland (see Table 22). Long before Mecklenburgh Street garnered its ill-fame through the activities of its "swell ladies . . . in pink wrappers," the upper class of prostitute played host to Dublin's officers and gentlemen in French Street (now Mercer Street, Upper) and Clarendon Street without interference from the law. In contrast to the continental practice of moral policing of prostitutes and brothels, the lack of any supervision in the United Kingdom was dictated by English prudery. For a brief period between 1866 and 1885, supervision was attempted in certain "protected areas" under the Contagious Diseases Acts (Dublin was not included), but public agitation based on fears of the abuse of virtuous women by arbitrary police rule resulted in the repeal of the Acts. The more modest aim pursued in England and Ireland, therefore, was the preservation of public order and propriety and, consequently, the arrest of "public women" who solicited their clients in a riotous or disorderly manner or the fining of publicans who allowed them to gather in public houses. In 1870 the number of women arrested in Dublin (DMP district) for prostitution totalled 3,255—more than in Liverpool, Manchester, or the London metropolis. It was often claimed that many of these were women who had come over with the troops—camp followers from England—or girls attracted from other parts of Ireland. Even more striking is the number of women, 8,271, adjudged to be prostitutes among those females tried summarily both for prostitution and various other indictable and nonindictable offenses, suggesting the obvious link between prostitution and ordinary crime. The corresponding figure for any of the aforementioned English cities did not exceed 6,000.

In the above context, the contemporary accounts of 1,500 well-known prostitutes choking Grafton Street or of young ladies being afraid to walk across town at night do not seem unduly exaggerated. Dr. Rawton Macnamara, senior surgeon at the Westmoreland Lock Hospital, explained how the brothels of French and Clarendon Streets were broken up following the Prevention of Crime Act of 1871. After the protests of local residents and priests (Clarendon Street contained a Roman Catholic church), policemen were placed at the doors of known brothels and took down the name of every visitor, thus effectively depriving the madams of their clientele. Apparently not even the clergy were secure from the advances of prostitutes, to judge from Dr. Macnamara's reference to a case of indecent assault on a priest who had braved entry into Bracken's Lane. The good doctor himself was surprised one evening on leaving Gresham's Hotel to find in his cab a prostitute who wished to force herself on him.[12] Naturally, the breaking up of one red-light district only pushed the girls into hotels and rooming houses elsewhere. Soon business was transferred across the Liffey to seedier Lower Mecklenburgh Street, where from around 1880 on the old elegance was maintained by the famous Mrs. Annie Mack in her "lodging house" at no. 20 (a former tenement), and to the lower-class "stews" of Purdon and Montgomery Streets. The increase in the number of brothels in this so-called "Monto" district in the early 1880s was the subject of comment in the evidence taken at the Royal Commission on Housing in 1885, attention being drawn to the new feature of the profession whereby a brothel was maintained on a single floor of a tenement house that also contained respectable families.[13]

The most serious blow struck organized prostitution in Dublin was the Criminal Law Amendment Act of 1885, which provided (part 2, section 13) for the outright suppression of brothels by summary conviction of brothel keepers and punishment leading to imprisonment with hard labor for repeated offenses. The act also raised the ages at which carnal knowledge of a female became either a felony (from 12 to 13 years) or misdemeanor (from 13 to 16 years). The moving force behind the more resolute intervention of the police was the newly established Dublin branch of the White Cross Association, an agency of the National Vigilance Association's crusade to repress criminal vice and public immorality. By all accounts some of the principal streets of the city seemed hardly less "choked" with prostitutes in 1884 than they had been during the infamous 1870s. By 1887, however, the Association was claiming the "greatest possible change now in Dublin compared to former times" through the strict application of section 13 (1885 Act) in closing unlicensed hotels of bad reputation as well as known brothels. In that same year the Association's volunteers took a house in Mecklenburgh Street from which they bravely emerged each night on lantern patrol to discourage would-be clients. But not even the clearing out of the worst kips nor the subsequent renaming of Mecklenburgh as Tyrone Street could entirely rid the district of its evil reputation nor certainly eliminate prostitution in a port and garrison town, especially one with a large proportion of young bachelors prone to marry, if at all, at a rather late age. Nevertheless, the Association did claim some success in running the brothel-keepers to ground and forcing them more and more to confine their business to those "few streets almost wholly given up to vicious inhabitants" to which even the arm of the law did not extend.[14] As for Mrs. Mack, she made the prudent decision to move her services from no. 20, which almost adjoined St. Patrick's School near Mabbot Street intersection, east along the street to no. 85, near Buckingham Street and only a few doors from St. Mary's Penitent Retreat, which offered both warning and (perhaps) opportunity.

The only figures issued by the authorities detailing the number of known brothels in Dublin cover the years 1891 to 1894. In this period between 75 and 82 houses (only about ten of which were of the "superior" type) were on record, a number exceeding, though hardly in elegance, that of the licensed *maisons closes* in "decadent" Paris but far below those of the worst English cities. They reportedly accommodated only about 270 prostitutes. Another 100 girls were known to be operating from their own private rooms in so-called "houses of assignation," and of course, hundreds more plied their trade directly on and off the streets. That the kips were flourishing a full decade after the 1885 Act suggests that the police for the most part had now turned a blind eye to the vice traffic, thankful at least that it was confined to only one small section of one police district, the C Division, in which "Monto" was located. No more than token suppression was executed during the four years referred to above, for the number of brothels reported to have been put out of business was only 14.[15] Yet if arrests for prostitution be any guide, Dublin at the turn of the century was a much purer and safer city than it had been ten and more years before, an improvement due not only to more concerted police efforts at suppression but also, even in Dublin, to the opening up of new and steadier avenues of employment (in factories and among the lower clerical occupations) for girls who formerly might have drifted into a life on the streets. But the visible evidence of prostitution continued to appall. The city, expectedly, still contained the largest number of streetwalkers in the country, though the ratio these bore to numbers in the rest of Ireland had been greatly reduced. And if a comparison be made with English cities, it is seen that her notoriety was surpassed only in Lancashire, though even there it was to become clear that by 1910 the Irish capital was again rising to meet the impure challenge of Liverpool (see Table 22).

TABLE 22. Dublin (Metropolitan Police District): Number of Arrests for Prostitution; Number of Alleged Prostitutes Tried Summarily for Various Offenses of All Kinds; and Comparison with Other Cities, 1870–1913 (rates per 100,000 of population[a] of each police district in parentheses).

	1870	1875	1880	1885	1890	1895	1900	1905	1910	1913
(a) *Arrests for prostitution:*										
Dublin	3,255	1,462	1,009	1,601	1,077	699	431	651	785	689
	(965)	(427)	(290)	(457)	(306)	(190)	(112)	(163)	(190)	(164)
Belfast	38	94	225	202	131	84	86	223	453	479
	(22)	(50)	(110)	(89)	(52)	(29)	(25)	(61)	(119)	(119)
Rest of Ireland	380	283	236	383	159	158	139	102	265	221
Liverpool	301[b]	3,865	2,783	2,390	2,423	2,806	2,267	1,876	1,472	1,208
	(62)	(748)	(509)	'(444)	(465)	(480)	(331)	(266)	(197)	(160)
Manchester	1,617	1,361	2,432	1,733	1,001	1,070	1,131	1,154	860	1,003
	(457)	(389)	(709)	(426)	(205)	(205)	(208)	(190)	(120)	(140)
London (Metropolitan police district)	2,163	1,373	2,334	2,861	2,206	633[c]	1,804	4,028	4,451	4,605
	(58)	(33)	(50)	(57)	(40)	(11)	(28)	(60)	(62)	(62)
(b) *Number of alleged prostitutes among certain offenders:*										
Dublin	8,271	4,288	3,419	2,867	4,132	1,692	1,907	1,218	.	.
Belfast	864	502	294	208	136	147	231	615	.	.
Rest of Ireland	2,729	2,274	1,660	1,292	995	621	832	451	.	.
Liverpool	4,585	6,233	5,255	5,368	2,744	3,885	.	.	.	.
Manchester	2,110	1,824	2,721	1,933	1,368	1,746	.	.	.	.
London (as above)	5,846	4,230	6,718	5,731	3,200	3,243	.	.	.	.

[a]Population figures used for calculating rates of arrest in (a) were as provided in official returns or estimated by reference to closest census.
[b]Actual figure reported. Arrests had been even lower in preceding years but jumped suddenly after 1870: e.g., 3,388 in 1871; 3,970 in 1872.
[c]Actual figure reported. Arrests had been decreasing since 1890 but increased again after 1897.
NOTE: Omissions signify that relevant data were not reported.
SOURCES: Judicial Statistics of Ireland; Statistical Returns of the Dublin Metropolitan Police; Judicial Statistics of England & Wales.

Prostitutes rarely saw the inside of prison, for virtually all were subject only to fines, a sharp contrast to the fate reserved for those convicted of begging; these were invariably sentenced to short terms of imprisonment. The total arrests of all females for prostitution offenses in the years 1899 to 1914 numbered 10,000, or an annual average of 625. The majority of offenders were in the 21 to 30 age group and few were minors. Excepting the years 1899 and 1912, when 20 and 13 percent, respectively, were aged between 16 and 21 years, minors accounted for less than 6 percent of all arrests, and only on two occasions between 1899 and 1914 was a child under 16 arrested for prostitution.[16] However, this kind of data can never give an entirely satisfactory picture of the number of prostitutes in the city.* In the early years of the century, the number of females treated at the Lock Hospital actually exceeded the number of prostitutes arrested on Dublin's "dark, slimy streets." Besides, the police showed little inclination to institute another dispersal by cleaning up "Monto," preferring instead to curb soliciting elsewhere by allowing relatively free traffic in vice in that sector. Furthermore, the twentieth century saw a growing tendency on the part of magistrates to adopt a greater leniency in the prosecution of first offenders and to forego altogether the less serious offenses, part of a general amelioration of the penal system, which saw such compassionate advances as the mitigation of prison discipline, the establishment of the Borstal system for youthful offenders, as well as the Probation of Offenders Act. Defenders of the moral credentials of Dublin's female population allowed that only .5 percent (a ridiculously low figure compared to other cities) were engaged in prostitution. With a female population in 1901 of almost 93,000 over the age of 20, this percentage yielded an estimated 465, or about the same number as those prostitutes arrested in that year—an unlikely circumstance indeed. Moreover, of the persons tried summarily for various offenses in 1901, the police concluded that 1,677 were operating as prostitutes, a figure equal to just under 2 percent of the adult female population. Doubtless the number that managed to steer clear of the law was much higher. Only ten years before, over 4,000 (about 5 percent of adult females) were listed as prostitutes in the arrest records of the DMP. And to complicate the picture further, experience in Germany, where prostitution was under strict controls, suggested that one could find an average of 64 "clandestine prostitutes" (women suspected of prostitution) for every one infected with venereal disease,[17] an estimate that would have yielded many thousands more if one could have arrived at the exact number of infected prostitutes throughout the year at the Lock Hospital, the Magdalen Homes, or elsewhere. Although it is impossible to arrive at a correct figure, it would not be unreasonable to suppose that at the very least (and allowing for attrition in the profession over the years) some 3 or 4 percent of adult females, say, between 3,000 and 4,000, were engaged in prostitution in Dublin in the early years of this century, quite enough to corroborate the charges of their contemporaries that the west side of O'Connell Street on any evening testified to the continuing shame of Dublin, albeit no more shameful surely than certain large cities in Britain. The charity sermons on behalf of the Magdalen Asylum at High Park, Drumcondra, gave annual reminder of this shame of Dublin. "The streets of this Christian and Catholic city of Dublin after nightfall," stated one such appeal in 1899, "preach a more powerful sermon in favor of High Park than the lips of the most eloquent advocate can frame."

Montgomery Street and adjacent areas continued to attract considerable notice as the "worst sink of iniquity in the British Isles." The former street in 1901, shortly before the Corporation undertook a slum clearance, had 35 inhabited houses containing 130 separate families. The "kips" appear to have been centered here in just 7 houses (nos. 56 to 62), for according to census schedules, the 33 "families" listed for those few tenements included 28 in which anywhere from one to five unattached females of young age cohabited, their occupations in most cases being given as "domestic servant." The pattern was repeated for the smaller Purdon Street, with, again, an unusual number of young single girls of menial or no occupation. By 1905 the former tenements of nos. 51 to 70 Montgomery Street had been demolished to make way for the new Corporation Buildings and

---

*In 1888, for example, the year in which Jack the Ripper was instilling panic among the streetwalkers of Whitechapel, *Lancet* reported an estimated 10,000 prostitutes in that London district alone!

the street itself renamed Foley Street. Only a few years later, as will be recalled, Lower Ty-rone Street and Mabbot Street had also sufficiently redeemed their evil reputations to merit similar renaming as Railway and Corporation Streets. Foley Street continued to re-main an undesirable area and, as indicated in an earlier chapter, never succeeded in at-tracting the type of tenant desired by the new landlord, the Dublin Corporation.[18] As for the dispossessed prostitutes, they either took up residence in the cheap one-room Corpo-ration flats or launched yet another hegira.

The moral outrage that had abated with the clearing out of the Montgomery Street tenements was soon stirred again when a local Jesuit priest, Fr. J. Gwynn, delivered a frontal attack on the immorality of Dublin in a Mansion House address to the Catholic Truth Society in October 1910. It caused a sufficient reaction for the Corporation to hold a special meeting of the councillors to consider the charge. The attack was also unusual since the Roman Catholic clergy had always been remarkably reticent on such matters, reserving their energies rather to condemn purveyors of "dirty" postcards (mostly pic-tures of nude statuary in European museums!), torrid film posters that "suggested ideas fatal to many minds," English Sunday newspapers, which served to "undermine the mo-rale and faith of our Catholic people," Dublin dailies (*Irish Independent* and *Daily Express*) reporting the details of divorce court proceedings, or even that notorious import from Latin America—the tango! "Dublin," Gwynn stated, was "rapidly earning for itself the reputation of being one of the most immoral of cities . . . the principal streets of London, Brussels and of the great cities of Germany and France had by no means that air, what-ever be the reality, of looseness and depravity which invaded our main thoroughfares at night." Twenty-five years before, Dublin would have been placed in the first rank of "im-moral" cities, so at least some improvement had been recognized. But the claim un-leashed a flood of charges and countercharges, though these lacked the intensity that had distinguished the crusade of distraught "heads of families" against the public nuisance before 1870 or so, when the streets of the city were reportedly "scandalous by day and dangerous by night." Defenders of the city on this occasion dubbed the reverend's charge a gross exaggeration. He was being misled, it was said, by the "army of young ser-vants and factory girls" who promenaded on one side of O'Connell Street and both sides of Dame Street each evening as the young men of Dublin and the British soldiery held their nocturnal levee. Others extended the sway of the demimondaines to the northern quays from the North Wall to Phoenix Park between 11 P.M. and 1 A.M. and to the banks of the Dodder between Ringsend and Dartry Road. According to yet another correspon-dent, Dublin's social evil held an international threat for "the worst possible news which can reach those interested in the moral welfare of the military in India is that a regiment has been ordered to Dublin. . . . Dublin holds absolutely the lowest reputation amongst the cities of the homeland as a contaminating center." The final comments were made in an *Irish Times* editorial in which Dublin was not accounted to be especially immoral, though it held that anyone familiar with the streets at night would have to admit that "there is a good deal" of prostitution.[19]

The last public flurry of concern about the evils of prostitution attended the agitation over the white slavery legislation of 1912. It was the "White Slave Traffic" Bill that had prompted Shaw's scathing attack on the hypocrisy that would permit the flogging of pro-curers when the only remedy for the abolition of the evil traffic was a minimum wage law. The White Cross Association, active in discountenancing vice in Dublin since the evil days of 1887, took the leading role in pressing for the application of the proposed legislation to Ireland. Newspapers were scanned for suspicious advertisements, and the public appetite for salacity was titillated with variations of the story of the two well-educated girls answering the advertisement for a typist who found themselves in a house of ill fame but who fortunately escaped in the nick of time. The citizens were reminded once more that "immorality in Dublin is more public, more aggressive, and more squalid than in any other city of the same size . . . footpaths thronged with women whose calling is distressingly obvious . . . the appalling youth of the girls most noticeable in the past five or six years."[20] The statistics of crime did indeed reveal a considerable increase in arrests for brothel-keeping between 1907 and 1912, an average of over 50 per annum in contrast to the 5 or 6 of the preceding years. The Bill was passed and the ensuing legislation, extended to Ireland, may have been responsible for the apparent decrease in brothel-keeping in Dublin, at least as measured by arrests. But no one could feel sanguine that public morality had been vindicated. Observers were forced to admit that the clearing out of the "plague spots" had contributed little to the reduction of prostitution and that further campaigns were needed to purify the streets. By 1913 Ashe Street was being spoken of as the final refuge of the former hostesses of the Monto bawdy houses, and the street walkers were reported to have invested the Grand Canal between Dolphin's Barn and Baggot Street Bridge as well as the roads of Donnybrook and Rathmines. Few could doubt it would remain thus as long as unemployment, boredom, or starvation wages continued to be the lot of the young girls of the city. Nor could those local women's groups who in January 1915 planned to organize themselves into "women's patrols" (the prototype of a future female police force, it was hoped) for the protection of those "excited girls who congregate in the neighborhood of barracks and recruiting stations" expect much cooperation from their quarry.

By far the most unfortunate aspect of crime and its treatment up through the early years of this century was the punishment meted out to youthful offenders. Their number happily was never very great: in 1901 children under 16 years represented less than one percent of the 14,000 individuals who were convicted in the Dublin courts of summary jurisdiction after being apprehended (i.e., not dealt with on summons) for crimes and other offenses. Where the penalty was not payment of a fine, it usually meant prison or the reformatory. That the law did not make adequate distinction between mere "naughtiness" and criminal activity is evident from the harsh sentences imposed for what were often trifling misdemeanors. Whether it was for petty larceny or the sometimes destructive consequences of stone-throwing, the punishment was equally severe. Typical of police reports is the case of the 14-year-old ("not of a whippable age") sent to Glencree Reformatory for 5 years for breaking a pane of glass in a grocery store with a stone. The "larceny of a piece of timber" earned an 11-year-old 14 days in jail *and* 5 years in a reformatory as did an 8-year-old's "larceny of two bottles." Begging could merit imprisonment with hard labor, and few culprits escaped the almost mandatory additional 5 years in a reform school, the minimum term considered essential for reformation of the character. The cold statistics of the General Prisons Board further illustrate the cruel face of official justice throughout the United Kingdom during the Victorian and Edwardian eras, examples of which, in the case of offenders in Ireland, are shown in Table 23.

TABLE 23. Representative Offenses and Corresponding Sentences in the Case of Juvenile Offenders in Ireland, 1899–1904.

AGE OF OFFENDER IN YEARS	OFFENSE	SENTENCE
7	Riotous and indecent (sic) behaviour and throwing stones	48 hrs. imprisonment or 3s. 6d. fine
8	Assault (sic)	14 days imprisonment plus 5 yrs. in Reformatory
9½	Throwing stones on street	7 days imprisonment or 6s. 6d. fine
10 (female)	Larceny of a prayer book	14 days imprisonment plus 6 yrs. in Reformatory
10	Stealing a pair of shoes	5 yrs. in Reformatory
10	Playing hurley in street	4 days imprisonment or 4s. fine
10	Trespassing on railway premises	14 days imprisonment or 22s. fine
10	Obstructing footpath by playing pitch and toss	7 days imprisonment or 11s. 6d. fine
11	Larceny of lemonade	5 yrs. in Reformatory
11	Larceny of £16	14 days with hard labour plus 5 yrs. in Reformatory
11½	Illegal possession of a blanket	14 days imprisonment plus 5 yrs. in Reformatory

SOURCE: *Parliamentary Papers,* 1900 (XLI), cd. 293; 1902 (XLVII), cd. 1241; 1904 (XXXV), cd. 2194; and *passim.*

The Inspectors of the Irish Prisons Board were outraged by these harsh sentences and added the following comment to the official report for 1905–1906:

> We cannot too strongly express our regret that children of from 9 to 11 years are still sent to Prison by some Magistrates. . . for such offences as throwing stones into a harbour or in the street, loitering at a harbour or near goods or trespassing in pursuit of game. Although the common objection to sending children to jail, viz., the allegation that they "herd with common criminals" is absolutely untrue, the practice is deplorable on other grounds. They become for life branded with the Prison taint, and being well and kindly treated, lose the salutary dread of Prison of which they acquire no experience in its severer disciplinary aspect.[21]

Fortunately, the extremes of punishment were reserved for the very few children. In 1905 there were nearly 200 juveniles under 16 years in Irish prisons, a number considerably less than the 1,000 and more one would have found languishing there a generation earlier. But youthful offenders were obliged to "herd with common criminals" when they appeared before the magistrates until that practice was abolished in Dublin in 1904 with the establishment of a special Children's Court. Children were not as a rule incarcerated with adult prisoners, separate facilities being set aside for their reception, as was the case at Mountjoy Prison for juveniles sentenced to terms of one month and upward. More usually, however, youthful offenders convicted for offenses that in the case of an adult would have brought imprisonment or penal servitude worked out their punishment in Reform and Industrial Schools.

Reformatories were credited with the great decrease in juvenile crime during the latter part of the nineteenth century. As one official report put it, they had been the means of "breaking up the societies of little pickpockets and burglar apprentices in cities and towns." Two of Ireland's six Reform Schools were situated in and around Dublin: the small High Park facility for Roman Catholic girls at Drumcondra and St. Kevin's for Roman Catholic boys at Glencree, County Wicklow. When first established at mid-century, St. Kevin's Reform School instituted special provisions for "removing" boys to other countries as a form of forced emigration. Gradually, however, these centers of detention concentrated on the industrial training of youthful offenders aged 18 years and under and their placement in employment upon release. As Appendix E indicates, no more than a few score of convicted juveniles in Dublin were sent for reformatory treatment in any year. Industrial Schools likewise were supposed to have rescued thousands of "street arabs and vagrants from the snares of temptation." Certainly they saved many from slow starvation, for these institutions primarily held children aged 14 and under who had been committed when found wandering, destitute, or abandoned. Only a very small proportion of children committed to Industrial Schools were sent there for offenses against the law, and some of these hardly merited the harsh penalty of separation from families that the residential Schools imposed. Proper discipline for truant or unruly children might have been achieved more humanely in Day (i.e., nonresidential) Industrial Schools of the type that had been operating in England for decades. Local voluntary child-welfare agencies pleaded in vain for their establishment in Ireland, especially in Dublin and Belfast, where numbers of wayward children roamed the streets at all hours. Yet as late as 1916, eight years after municipal authorities in Ireland had been empowered to provide for them from local funds, Dublin was still without such a much needed facility.

Welcome though minor reforms such as the establishment of children's Courts did not satisfy those who felt that there was still some way to go in humanizing the system of detention for young offenders. Gradually, however, the worst features of the system were eliminated by the introduction of the English Borstal system and the coming into operation of the so-called "children's charter"—the Children Act of 1908. Under the new Borstal system, introduced to Ireland in 1906, all male criminal prisoners between the ages of 16 and 21 years and serving prison terms of nine months or more were to be transferred to a specially organized wing of the old Clonmel Prison to receive instruction in useful trades, enjoy better diet and facilities, and be described officially as "inmates" instead of "prisoners." The new system was in full operation by late 1909, and within two years a modified version of the treatment was extended to Mountjoy and other prisons for young offenders sentenced to prison terms of one month or more. The Children Act was hailed by reformers as the most notable event in the history of penal legislation affecting youthful offenders. It provided that no child under 14 years would thenceforth be sent to prison under any circumstances and that prison terms could be meted out to convicted young persons (14 and under 16 years) only if they were unruly or depraved. In addition children under 12 could no longer be sent to Reform School. Also, instead of remanding young offenders to prison to await trial, local Places of Detention were set up (in Dublin at 54 Summerhill) for their temporary custody. The effects of the Act were felt immediately: in 1910 only four children under 16 years were held in Irish prisons.

The greater leniency in the treatment of young offenders neither precipitated a crime wave nor reduced the numbers involved in offenses of all kinds. Juvenile crime remained much as before in Dublin, with some 1,800 being charged annually in the courts, of whom about half were convicted. But punishment for children and virtually all young persons would henceforth be fines or sureties, probationary care, or for the few incorrigibles, Reform and Industrial Schools. No longer would children playing football or hurley in the streets, "bathing in the public view," or throwing stones into the harbor be branded with imprisonment. It is ironic that though much that constituted youthful offenses during those years has virtually disappeared from court calendars, youthful criminality has at last come home to roost in all the major cities of the modern world. Thus in one respect at least our forebears escaped one of the more distressing features of modern urban life—those savage enclaves that now threaten in varying degree the security and well-being of citizens in Dublin and most other metropolitan centers.

8

CHAPTER

Labor

Not to recognize Trade Unions in any shape; employ any person who presents himself; if a strike pending try and get the ringleader, dismiss him quietly, assigning no cause; this method has been successful with us.

Advice of Dublin employer to Royal Commission on Labour on how to avoid strikes, *Parliamentary Papers*, 1892

FOR OFFICIAL purposes the working population was classified in accordance with a scheme that recognized the fine distinctions of status, toil, and remuneration. In the professional and independent class were members of the professions (medical, legal, and such) as well as military officers, higher civil servants, the great merchants and manufacturers, along with individuals of rank and property. The middle class comprised the officials of government and banking, the traders and business managers, clerks and commercial assistants. Below them was the class of artisans and petty shopkeepers, the former including skilled workers in the various trades or comparable callings. Lowest of all was the general service class, which included, in addition to personnel of the armed forces, police, postal and prison service, the varied but low-paid class of laborers, porters, hawkers, vanmen, domestic servants, and the like. Since this chapter deals almost entirely with the so-called "working classes," it is desirable to define that much discussed social entity more accurately. Section 16 of the Housing of the Working Classes (Ireland) Act, 1908, offers a suitable definition: "The expression 'Working Classes' shall include mechanics, artizans, labourers, and others working for wages; hawkers, costermongers, persons not working for wages but working at some trade or handicraft without employing others except members of their own family; and persons, other than domestic servants, whose income in any case does not exceed an average of 60s. per week; and the families of any such persons who may be residing with them."

Table 25 offers a general impression of the occupations followed by the citizens of Dublin. For the years 1901 and 1911, the census surveys revealed almost identical figures for the numbers of people having specific or undefined occupations despite a population increase of 14,000 over the decade. But this was to be expected considering that there was a net increase in the same period of a mere 1,000 persons of both sexes (excluding married females) in the age group 15 to 64 years. The employment opportunities, naturally, were vastly greater for men. For approximately 100,000 males in the productive age groups (i.e., 15 to 64 years, excluding students and pensioners but including those outside these age limits having specific or undefined occupations), the 1911 census classified over 92,000 (92 percent) as following some occupation. The corresponding figures for females in the same categories were 63,000 (again excluding wives) and 40,000 (64 percent), revealing a gap signifying the massive unemployment and lack of opportunity facing females at all ages, one which would be widened only if the unknown number of working wives included in the figure of 40,000 could be ascertained. It should be noted, also, that some of the figures in Table 25 offer less than a true picture of total employment in the city owing to the proximity of a considerable "labor pool" in the four suburban districts of Kingstown, Blackrock, Pembroke, and Rathmines and Rathgar. For instance, it is probable that the majority of the more than 900 teachers shown as resident in these four districts (the combined population of which after 1900 remained at only 30 percent of the city's) were employed in city rather than suburban schools. The same would doubtless have been true of the 439 lawyers (an exclusively male profession), 1,960 clerks and, certainly, the 1,157 civil servants also shown as residing in these suburban areas, data which confirm the essentially middle-class character of the suburban population. This latter fact is clearly noted in the case of suburban-resident lawyers whose number exceeded by as much as one-third the total number residing in the more populous county borough. On the other hand, the approximately 9,000 domestic servants employed in these four townships would have included many who had formerly resided in the city proper.

A remarkable feature of labor in Dublin was the predominance of the class of general laborers. They numbered over 14,000 in 1901, between one-quarter and one-third of the male industrial work force, a proportion suggesting that this class of worker arose, not as in England or Scotland from the needs of the established trades, but out of the general lack of varied and widespread industrial employment. The proportion of such low-paid workers would be higher if the porters, messengers, watchmen, and others classified in the census under the "commercial" category were included. Ten years later the number of general laborers had increased to over 17,000 in the city, whereas in such large urban centers as Birmingham, Manchester, and Liverpool the corresponding numbers ranged from 3,000 to 7,000. The same pattern is revealed in the case of female employment with the decided prevalence of the class of indoor domestic servant, over 14,000 of them in 1901 representing about 40 percent of all female workers in domestic and industrial employment. Thus, a large section of the working class consisted of men and women compelled to earn their living in domestic service (women) or, in the case of males, in cyclical employment as general laborers in the building trades or as part of a floating population of casuals in search of work at docks and wharves. Therefore, Dublin, with a paucity of industry and skilled artisans, possessed a work force that was extremely vulnerable to victimization by employers and in addition suffered long hours and low wages in a city where the consequences of the loss of a job could often mean not alternative employment but either emigration or the workhouse. The capital, situated in a nonindustrial region, had no great manufacture of its own, nor was it the locus of commercial activity for any surrounding regional centers. The absence of any marked increase in population during the second half of the nineteenth century also testified to the city's arrested economic development. There was nothing to compare with the mighty shipbuilding yards and textile factories of the Belfast region. The numbers involved in heavy industry were quite small, only 2,000, for example, in engineering and ironworking occupations, whereas Glasgow (though exceeding Dublin's population by two-and-a-half times) boasted 90,000 such workers. Likewise, in the production of textiles Dublin, with its 1,000 or so operatives, did not rank alongside Belfast's 37,000. Dublin's most notable business enterprise was the Guinness firm, with reputedly the largest output of any brewery in the world and a little over 2,000 workers of all grades. Other main avenues of employment in Dublin in addition to building, brewing, and dockside labor were in distilling, printing, the clothing trades, and assorted occupations serving the railway system. The largest single skilled occupations for males in the industrial category were in carpentry, printing, tailoring, and bootmaking, only one of which (carpentry) was followed by more than 2,000 workers, according to the census of 1901. The opportunities for females were few and, more so than in most cities, in a decided disproportion to those available for men, owing to the virtual absence of textile factory labor. There were no great factories, apart from Jacob's biscuit factory, offering much escape from the drudgery and servitude of domestic service. Bookbinding and, naturally, the dressmaking trades were occupations attracting most females who could avoid domestic service. Also, the figures for female employment reveal a welcome trend after 1900, for the number of servants declined and young girls found alternative employment in the growing commercial sector as telephonists and general office workers. However, the dearth of opportunity ultimately meant that large numbers of females were forced to live in a state of involuntary indolence. Even in the nonmanual category, female commercial clerks numbered under one-sixth of the total, the profession of teacher alone being dominated by women.

TABLE 24. **Proportion of Persons Employed in Specific Occupations (rate per 10,000 males of ten years and above), 1891 and 1901.**

	IRELAND		ENGLAND AND WALES		SCOTLAND	
	1891	1901	1891	1901	1891	1901
General laborer	626	661	561	338	449	332
Building trades	262	311	602	749	660	785
Iron and steel	105	103	347	333	449	471
Commercial clerk	86	108	217	254	225	238

SOURCE: *Parliamentary Papers,* 1908 (XCVIII), cd. 4413 (Abstract of Labour Statistics, 1906–1907, pp. 208–11).

The quotation at the head of this chapter should leave one under no illusion regarding the nature of the unequal relationship between masters and men. Blacklisting was common in the building trade, as evidenced by the practice (outlined at the Royal Commission on Labour) of employers distributing to other employers lists of known "agitators" and men who refused to work with nonunion labor, the latter attitude being a most distinctive characteristic of the Dublin tradesman. Other information given to the Royal Commission suggested not only rigid discipline, including unbearable fines, but also a low level of wages, especially for those in the unskilled category. It will be recalled that the social investigations of working-class families in this period were suggesting that the barest necessities of life, enough for "merely physical efficiency," could not be maintained on less than about 22s. per week, whereas others concluded that the bare essentials of a decent standard of living demanded half as much again and more. In Dublin it was estimated that few tradesmen and no unskilled worker of any kind earned above £2 per week, the proportions being roughly as follows: (a) tradesman—average earnings 30s. to

40s. weekly—about 30 percent of the work force; (b) unskilled workers in regular employment—20s. to 25s.—30 percent; (c) casual laborers—12s. to 15s.—25 percent; (d) the "very poor" or those unable to obtain regular employment—15 percent of the work force. Thus a majority of working-class employed was forever on the fringes of poverty however defined. Wages, therefore, always took priority in labor relations. The general course of wages in the United Kingdom followed an upward trend in the decade preceding 1900, when, as in the late 1880s, wages once more remained stationary, not rising again until 1906, though only then for a short period before becoming stationary again in 1908. Wage rates in Ireland were generally lower than those prevailing in Britain. This was particularly true in the case of textile workers, the wages of men, women, and lads not reaching 70 percent of the average earnings of corresponding operatives in England. However, there were few such workers in Ireland outside the northeastern counties of Antrim and Down, but any differences also prevailed in Dublin, where, compared to London, the gap in wages was wider than the proportionate difference in the cost of living. London rates in the building trades were at least 2d. per hour greater than the corresponding Dublin rates, and this gap was not narrowed until the general advance in Dublin wages in 1913, the first in the building trades since 1896.

Specific examples of wages and working conditions are afforded by the evidence taken at the Royal Commission on Labour. The information on wages relates to 1892, of course, and would need to be adjusted upward *if* the employer followed the general trend of wage increases (12 percent) over the next eight years. The employer cited at the heading to this chapter, the engineering firm of Stephens and Company, Windmill Lane, paid skilled mechanics 32s., laborers 14s., and boys 5s. to 10s., depending on age, for a week of 54 hours. Weekly rates in the timber trade ranged from 24s. to 36s. for carpenters and machine hands, 16s. to 22s. for unskilled laborers, and 9s. to 30s. for female polishers. Wages of the unskilled employees of the coal merchants were from 20s. to 35s. weekly, but this was for 60 hours worked between 6 A.M. and 6 P.M. (weekdays) and 6 A.M. and 3 P.M. on Saturday. Wages at Boland and Company, the bread makers, were 34s. for work performed at night (8 P.M. to 8 A.M.), with no special rate for Sunday work. Notice was neither given nor required for termination of employment. Building tradesmen appeared to enjoy some leverage against the masters, to judge by the contracting firm of S.H. Bolton and Sons, where only union labor was generally employed because the men refused to work with nonunionists. But remuneration still averaged only 34s. for a 54-hour week with no allowance for "wet time." Some workers enjoyed unique privileges but only when they worked for unusual masters. The Guinness brewing firm was one such employer. In addition to trade-union rates of pay, there was a daily allowance of two pints of beer per man or exchangeable "scrip" for use at the company's cooperative store. Pensions up to two-thirds of working wages were payable to retirees at 60. All employees and their families were entitled to free medical service (including the services of a midwife) either at the company's dispensary or on visit by the medical officer. There were liberal sick allowances. And the company also gave annual grants-in-aid to the tradesmen's benefit societies and maintained a savings bank, library, and cafeteria. Nor did benefits end there. There were also excursion allowances in summer, Christmas "boxes" (though for foremen only), and free breakfasts for draymen and office cleaners. Work hours ranged from 48 to 58 per week. It need hardly be added that trade disputes were practically unknown at Arthur Guinness, Son and Company, Ltd.[1]

TABLE 25. City of Dublin: Total Employed and Residents Employed in Selected Occupations, 1881–1911 (figures include both sexes except where otherwise indicated).

CLASS OF OCCUPATION	1881	1891	1901	1911
I. *Professional* (note 1)	13,560	11,689	13,718	15,820
Lawyer (barrister, solicitor)	656	451	406	326
Medical doctor	403	349	329	342
Teacher	1,152	1,372	1,446	1,472
Civil servant	946	1,012	1,804	2,344
Clergyman: Roman Catholic	198	191	279	308
Other	117	111	114	107
Nun	242	425	749	829
II. *Domestic*	25,914	20,686	22,183	18,232
Domestic indoor servant	16,736	15,042	14,661	11,611
Charwoman	942	1,273	1,457	1,246
III. *Commercial*	13,695	16,063	20,390	22,945
Commercial clerk	2,862	3,714	5,331	6,299
Carter, drayman, etc.	1,855	1,546	2,862	3,083
Messenger, porter, etc. (not in government or railway employment)	2,948	4,202	4,244	4,641
IV. *Agricultural*	1,790	1,383	1,889	2,276
V. *Industrial* (note 2)	69,938	68,414	74,245	73,175
Printer	1,486	1,661	1,837	1,679
Engineering (fitter, boilermaker)	377	613	873	1,148
Building (carpenter, bricklayer, mason, slater, plasterer, plumber, painter)	7,138	6,619	7,487	6,561
Baker	890	987	1,031	1,340
Tailor, tailoress	2,604	3,082	3,060	2,989
Dressmaker, seamstress, etc. (female)	8,250	7,916	7,020	5,554
Coalheaver	837	697	898	975
Factory laborer	100	408	1,050	2,044
General laborer	13,400	13,223	14,728	17,269
Total employed (class I–V)	124,897	118,235	132,425 (note 3)	132,448
Total population	249,602	245,001	290,638	304,802

NOTE 1. Totals for this class adjusted to exclude various categories of student listed under occupations in census tables.
NOTE 2. Census did not make distinction between employer and employee under this classification.
NOTE 3. Increase over 1891 partly accounted for by extension of city boundaries in 1900.
SOURCE: Census of Ireland—City of Dublin, Occupations of the People.

Further information on the conditions of labor and the aspirations of the working classes is available in the replies of various trade unions to the queries of the Royal Commission. The Cabinet Makers' Association complained of long hours (56 per week) and that members could be dismissed at one hour's notice. As usual in the trades, there were no paid holidays except for foremen and certain other classes of employees. Long hours and low wages were mentioned by the Irish National Federal Union of Bakers as being responsible for most disputes. There was apparently no limit to the number of hours the men could be asked to work, the union citing up to 100 hours (overtime included) as standard. A weekly half-holiday was not granted, nor were there paid holidays of any kind. The union also claimed that shops were seldom inspected as provided under the Factory Acts, resulting in the employment of 12-year-old apprentices at night contrary to law. The Bookbinders and Machine Rulers' Consolidated Union had about 300 members, and their complaints centered on the "almost perpetual aggression" on the part of employers in general "through their anxiety to encroach upon our rights by introducing cheap and female labour." Again it was claimed that there was a total neglect of safety and inspection in unsanitary workshops, though the lavatory facilities, for example, must have been far ahead of those that prevailed (if they existed at all) in the provincial towns. The employers also had complaints, the head of a Dublin van-making concern with 70 people reporting that with only eight exceptions he was unable to get honest work out of the men.

Among the benefits deriving from union membership were the vital payments for loss of time due to disputes, accident, illness, as well as lump sum funeral benefits and legal aid. Contributions were levied weekly with additional levies required for special purposes as well as fines if a job were lost due to drink. Membership in a union required an entrance fee. For example, the Ancient Guild of the Incorporated Brick and Stonelayers demanded a 20s. fee for those who had served their time. Weekly contributions were 2d. and the following benefits applied: accident—15s. p.w. for 3 months, 7s. 6d. for second 3 months, 5s. thereafter; dispute—15s. p.w.; death—£5 for member or wife. The plasterers, carpenters, and others who paid higher weekly dues (up to 1s.) also enjoyed superannuation benefits of around 5s. per week at age 60 after 20 or 25 years of membership. Some union rules gave open expression to workers' solidarity, the Grain Weighers and Tally Clerks union vowing "no member to work with a nonmember as long as any member is wanting employment."[2]

The building trades were among the most important groups of industry affording employment to males. Of that work force 82 percent earned less than £2 per week on basic rates during pre-war years, the average weekly earnings for skilled labor being 33s. in Great Britain, compared with 27s. 9d. in Ireland. Apprenticeships in the trade were extremely long (seven years), and a second seven-year period followed in which cumulative pay increases brought the worker to full scale only in his fourteenth year of employment.

Between 1905 and 1912 the wages of building tradesmen advanced by only 2 percent, for laborers 6 percent, though as mentioned above a general increase in all trades soon followed.[3] In the same period there was a sharp rise in the retail price index resulting in higher prices in Dublin for all foodstuffs except meat and making coal considerably dearer. Combined rent and retail prices showed a 7 percent increase, much lower incidentally than in most other towns in the United Kingdom. But it was clear that the ordinary worker was suffering a reduction in real wages and doubtless also in his standard of living. The great disparity in the wages of tradesmen and laborers is especially noticeable in Dublin, and this was not corrected until the general advance of 1913. Among the lowest paid workers were employees of the railway companies. Men worked a full six days at an average 58.2 hours exclusive of mealtimes and overtime. Only engine drivers earned in excess of £2 weekly, while the wages of porters, laborers, gangers, carmen, ticket collectors, and firemen ranged from 15s. to 24s. 6d. despite the long hours. Wages of tramway employees were also low, and in contrast with other trades had hardly changed since the 1880s. The wages of the first-class motormen ranged from 26s. to 31s. per week, or 5s. to 10s. below the rates prevailing in Great Britain in 1913. Of all occupations, dock labor

TABLE 26. Building Trades: Hourly Wage Rates (summer) in Dublin and Selected Cities as of October 1, 1908, and October 1, 1914.

| | DUBLIN | | BELFAST | | GLASGOW | | MANCHESTER | | LONDON | |
	1908	1914	1908	1914	1908	1914	1908	1914	1908	1914
Bricklayers	8½d.	9½d.	8½d.	9d.	9½d.	10½d.	10d.	10½d.	10½d.	11½d.
Masons	8d.	9½d.	8½d.	8½d.	9d.	10d.	10d.	10½d.	10½d.	11½d.
Carpenters	8d.	9d.	8½d.	9d.	9¼d.	10½d.	9½d.	10½d.	10½d.	11½d.
Plumbers	8½d.	9d.	8½d.	9½d.	9d.	10½d.	9½d.	10d.	11d.	12d.
Plasterers	8d.	9½d.	8½d.	8½d.	9½d.	10d.	10d.	11d.	11d.	11½d.
Painters	8d.	8d.	8d.	8½d.	9d.	10d.	9d.	9½d.	9d.	10d.
Laborers (hodmen)	4½d.	7d.	4½d.	.	6d.	6½d.	7d.	7d.	7d.	8d.

NOTE: 1914 rates exclusive of war bonuses
SOURCE: *Parliamentary Papers:* 1908 (XCVIII), cd. 4413; 1914–1916 (LXI), cd. 7733.

was one to which in the general opinion something of a stigma was attached. Although many a bona-fide skilled dock worker in regular employment could earn higher wages than the general laborer, dock labor was of such a nature that a surplus labor pool needed to be on hand at all times and this attracted an army of unskilled "casuals" with a reputation for thriftlessness and intemperance who because of their precarious existence seemed destined sooner or later for the workhouse. Many of these so-called dockers were lucky to earn as little as 5s. a week.

Work in the clothing trades may have brought respectability but hardly better wages. In tailoring and dressmaking only fitters and cutters of each sex earned high pay, that is, between £2 10s. and £3 10s. per week, for their special skills, enough to qualify them for "middle-class" status. Tailors in regular employment were only a few shillings below tradesmen in wages, but journeymen's wages were quite low, only 26s. for a 55-hour week. Women and juveniles were the worst off. The average full-time earnings of female dressmakers before the Trade Boards Act of 1909 assured them a modest 4.25d. per hour were a mere 10s. per week, barely 70 percent of the sum paid their equals in London. Rates for boys and girls did not reach 6s. per week, but even so, such earnings were a welcome addition to the slender resources of most working-class families. The drapers' assistants had special problems besides low wages and "instant dismissal." The majority in this employment were recruited from country districts, some 90 percent being unmarried, a fortunate circumstance in view of their low wages of about £1 weekly. For many of them the "living-in" system (i.e., sleeping accommodation on employer's premises) was common down to 1910. The general secretary of the drapers' assistants union gave evidence before the departmental committee on the Truck Acts in 1908 that affirmed that in one large Dublin firm over 300 assistants, or about one-seventh of the total in the city, "lived in"—herded together, as the union complained, "like cattle, irrespective of personal taste as regards association." In smaller establishments, board and lodging was often provided and, as the union again commented, "in many cases one bed is shared by two persons and in some cases perhaps a healthy person has to share his bed with a consumptive" in a room containing perhaps a dozen others ranging in age from 15 to 40 years.[4]

No adult worker could have been more abused than the poor shop girls with their paltry 7s. to 10s. per week. Their condition was often offered as evidence for the prevalence of prostitution in large cities. James Larkin's *Irish Worker* was especially active in exposing the "slavery" imposed on these young girls in shops and laundries. Female clerical workers and bookkeepers were not paid much better, the average pre-war wage in these occupations being 8s. and 12s. 6d. per week, respectively. Little wonder that the idea of a minimum wage was continuously pressed by labor spokesmen in this period. But the shop girls and others enjoyed a measure of independence denied to their sisters in domestic service. On the other hand, the lower wages of the latter were compensated for somewhat by free board and lodging. And there was always the chance for advancement—from a 3s. per week juvenile to a 4s. general servant at age 16 and so onward and upward to a young and energetic housemaid (5s.), a prim parlormaid (6s.), a mature cook (7s.), and should fortune smile, a supercilious lady's maid at a handsome 9s. 3d. These were the rates prevailing in Ireland in 1899 and, naturally, were 20 to 25 percent under English rates.[5] There was little change in the following years as is evident from the classified advertisements in newspaper columns, where the usual £12 to £15 per annum was offered to parlormaids as late as 1916. The chances of demanding higher wages were slim, for the dissatisfied could easily be dismissed and replaced by the young and timid. And more than performance was often required in these servile occupations. Quite frequently such jobs were reserved for those with the necessary Catholic or Protestant religious affiliation, although occasionally some ambiguity intruded with such distinctions as "Christian lady preferred."* Other qualifications were harder to come by, as in the case of the dispatch department of a large concern that required a 16-year-old, "well-educated and respectable," to work from 8 A.M. to 7 P.M. for 6s. per week!

Hours of work were second only to wages among the concerns of working people. The trend was downward in most trades during the second half of the nineteenth century, though in most cases substantial reductions took place only after 1870. As with wages, hours were least favorable for those in unskilled occupations. Railway porters on passenger trains worked an average 78-hour week before gains reduced it to 72 hours around 1880 and to 60 hours a decade later. General railway servants were expected to work anywhere from 60 to 120 hours a week, though by century's end the upper limit had been reduced to 100 hours. These were exceptional cases, however, for the standard work week was generally around 60 hours for most of the period. Those workers whose skills or organization encouraged the solicitude of employers naturally gained most. Thus, the craft unions of the building trades took the lead in the campaigns for a shorter work week and succeeded by 1896 in obtaining a reduction to 54 hours. Workers could suffer by such changes if the consequent reduction in overall wages was not compensated for by increased rates of pay or overtime. But few workers could have regretted the change whatever the outcome. Even a 54-hour week meant the following grinding schedule for the "summer" months of February through November, which kept men away from home for at least 12 hours each day: weekdays—6:30 A.M. to 5:30 P.M., with breaks for breakfast (8:30 to 9:15 A.M.) and dinner (2 to 2:45 P.M.); Saturday—6:30 A.M. to 1:45 P.M., with one break. The "outdoor" men—masons, bricklayers, and slaters—enjoyed the shorter 46½-hour "winter" work week during December and January. As a rule, tradesmen in the great cities and towns worked the least number of hours, yet in the capital of Ireland the building trades craftsmen did not obtain the 50- or 51-hour week long enjoyed by their brethren in London and Glasgow until 1913, when a general reduction to 50 hours was effected in many trades. Others were not so lucky: carters worked in excess of 60 hours;

*Discrimination still persists in other forms, now based on different though equally insupportable grounds of age and sex.

tram conductors only won a 66-hour week in 1911, a gain from 73 hours; and as late as 1916 the bakers were still agitating for the 50-hour week of *day* work.[6]

The various Factories and Workshops acts also provided some regulation of the labor of females and juveniles. In fact, our knowledge of local abuses derives from the legal proceedings attending infractions against this legislation. Two cases among the many undetected instances of abuse were brought to light in which Dublin shopowners worked young persons for as many as 92 hours a week, fines of 20s. being imposed in each case. On another occasion a newsagent was fined 10s. for employing young girls for 74 hours, and so on. In some instances ridiculous ½d. token fines were imposed, Ireland generally being notorious for the paltry fines levied for infringement of the acts. The annual reports of the chief inspector of factories and workshops rarely omit references to the "absurdly low," "utterly inadequate," and "miserable" penalties exacted through prosecutions for illegal employment. Institutions such as the convent laundries attached to orphanages or Houses of Mercy often succumbed to exploitative impulses, as evidenced by the employment of young girls under 16 years in the hard labor of laundry work—turning heavy handles, carrying loads, and working mostly in a standing position (under the rule of silence and dressed in hideous clothes) for as many as 55 hours a week with little or no wages beyond their support. Such labor was quite profitable, of course, and some mothers superior refused grants from the Technical Education Board for the training of girls in domestic or industrial subjects because these had conditions attached requiring a shorter work week for girls.[7] The acts are also revealing of the conditions of employment deemed tolerable for women and young persons. Under the act of 1901 women and those aged 14 years and under 18 could be employed up to 60 hours per week (Sundays and meal times excluded) in nontextiles employment. Women working in laundries could extend their hours to 66 per week, via overtime, for over two months in each year. In 1911 another Shops Act was passed—the "shop assistants' charter"—that gave legal recognition for the first time to a weekly half-holiday whereby shops, with some exceptions (pubs, newsagents, and such), were obliged to dismiss employees at 1:30 P.M. on a fixed day of the week. Though the act did not specifically decree any reduction in hours, it proved something of a boon to drapers' assistants, who had hitherto worked as many as 72 hours a week and even 14 hours on the busy Saturday trading day. Some of the better drapery houses had already granted a Saturday half-holiday during the summer months, but now officially began the early closing on Saturdays of the large drapery establishments in Grafton and Henry Streets and of the butchers' shops on Mondays. Some employers, especially drapery houses (which with the aforementioned exceptions had chosen early Wednesday closing), attempted to circumvent the act by spreading the few hours off over the entire week, thus avoiding the loss of business supposedly resulting from an early closing. These efforts prompted a procession of some 700 assistants through the city streets in protest on June 8, 1912. But as late as 1914 the drapers' assistants union admitted considerable difficulty in compelling observance of the Shops Act and yet, despite the lack of a minimum wage and the desire for a 48-hour week, congratulated itself that its members had not been directly involved in the bitter labor strife of the previous year.[8]

The years during which these gains in the conditions of labor were won, albeit slowly, also coincided with the resurgence of militant unionism in the United Kingdom. Many of the craft or larger unions in Dublin, particularly in the building trades, were locals of English-based parent associations such as the Operative Stonemasons, the United Operative Plumbers, the Amalgamated Society of Carpenters and Joiners, along with the National Union of Dock Labourers, Amalgamated Society of Railway Servants, and others. The smaller and weaker unions were usually native growths, but some of these local unions had a long history in the city, extending back to the old days of the trade guilds—the House Painters and Stucco Plasterers (1670), the Operative Bakers (1752), Dublin Typographical Society (1809), Dublin Brass Founders (1817), Operative Butchers and Assistants (1828) (see Appendix G). "Trade unionism flourishes in Ireland," claimed one observer, "the desire for association being one of the strongest traits in the Irish character."[9] However, unions in Dublin did not apparently acquire a cohesive public identity until the amnesty agitation (for release of the Fenian prisoners, many of them of the artisan or urban laboring class) of the late 1860s. Their image was consolidated at the Daniel O'Connell centenary celebrations in 1875, a decade or so after John Keegan, a local cabinetmaker, had started a United Trades Association that lasted until 1883. Two years later, after political life and organization revived with the advent of Gladstone's proposal for Irish home rule, the labor element in the city formed a provisional committee to create a local Trades Council. This project was soon realized with the formal establishment in May 1886 of the United Trades Council and Labour League.[10] By 1892 the Council claimed an affiliated membership of 11,000 workers, including 4,000 of the unskilled. A trades council was essentially consultative in character and had no control over the actions of its affiliate unions. However, it could act to promote the cause of a particular union and allow the use of its name for the collection of support funds during a dispute. The Dublin Trades Council, for example, was active during 1909 in support of the drapers' assistants' campaign for early closing, advising trade unionists not to shop late on Saturdays. The Council began with 23 affiliated unions and by 1900 this figure had more than doubled. The annual conference delegates were a cross-section of all the established trades and also included representatives of such disparate groups as the coopers, corporation laborers, fire brigade men, hairdressers, and carpet planners. The annual labor day demonstration in May brought the members together in a public show of fellowship and fraternity. The objectives of the Council included the standard claims for improved working conditions and housing for the working classes but also extended to support of technical education, public libraries and, significantly, labor representation on public boards as well as (before 1898) the assimilation of the parliamentary franchise to local government (i.e., Dublin Corporation) elections.

TABLE 27. **Trades Councils. Number of Unionists Represented: Ireland, 1899–1913; Dublin and Belfast, 1899–1910.**

	IRELAND	DUBLIN	BELFAST		IRELAND	DUBLIN	BELFAST
1899	37,595	16,000	19,000	1907	38,059	13,000	14,919
1900	32,243	15,000	15,000	1908	39,556	14,000	15,234
1901	27,291	13,000	11,700	1909	29,525	13,000	11,545
1902	29,637	14,170	12,672	1910	31,704	13,000	12,177
1903	27,895	14,000	10,000	1911	39,496	.	.
1904	32,818	13,500	14,186	1912	40,914	.	.
1905	32,672	.	.	1913	38,181	.	.
1906	35,181	13,000	15,335				

SOURCE: Board of Trade (Labour Department) Reports (various) on Trade Unions.

The more radical objectives were pursued by socialist intellectuals who, in the early stages, attached themselves to labor demonstrations. Thus we find reports of a socialist demonstration in 1887 at a public meeting of the unemployed. There the Irish branch of the Socialist League distributed handbills in Beresford Place (site of the future Liberty Hall), which may have caused some uneasiness in Capel Street (headquarters of the Trades Council) but doubtless evoked little concern from those without jobs: "True freedom lies far ahead even of Home Rule. We must destroy all tyranny, native or foreign. Then, when the people own the people's goods . . . when there will be no excess wealth nor degrading poverty, all Ireland will be free."[11] These were sentiments that were to flare up briefly a decade later and suffer similar disregard by the organized working classes when James Connolly founded the Irish Socialist Republican Party. Neither did all unionists pay heed to Connolly's call to elect only members of their own class to Dublin Corporation. The very first elections to the Corporation after the broadening of the franchise by the Local Government Act of 1898 saw the following advice issued to its members by one local union in pursuance of a unanimous resolution: "That we, the members of the Mineral Water Operatives Trade Association, recommend the candidature of Alderman Sir Henry Cochrane to the workingmen of the Mansion House ward, he being a large employer, employing trade unionists, paying the standard rate of wages, and being in every respect worthy of their unanimous respect." The cause of labor was saved, however, by the defeat of Sir Henry, a Unionist, and the election of the labor candidate. Another strange emanation was the City and County of Dublin Conservative Workingmen's Association, whose spurious origins were suggested by the presence of Unionist councillors at their annual dinner and toasts to the success of the "Unionist cause" and the renewal of the "imperialist spirit."[12] A more naked opposition to working-class solidarity was expressed by the trade magazine *Irish Builder* as it purveyed the theme of union domination of the fortunes of the building trade, where "contractors are nonentities on their own jobs, . . . foremen [are] afraid to face their men," this being in strong contrast, it was alleged, to the "strong-hand methods of American managers who defy union leaders and bring in 'scabs' if unions refuse to bow to demands."[13] This assessment, at least in relation to Irish workers, was quite untrue and represented one example of the hysterical bleating of those who apparently would have preferred the tradesman and his laborer to be the willing tools of their capitalist master. Wages, hours, severe unemployment, a weak political voice, the static nature of trade union membership (see Table 27), the availability of as well as the will to use strike-breaking nonunion or foreign labor—all these gave evidence enough of the vulnerability rather than the strength of labor in Dublin in the early twentieth century.

Unemployment was a recurring nightmare for most of the period, worse for the army of the unskilled than for the artisans and mechanics. A grim example of the despairing quest for work in Dublin was an occurrence in August 1899 at the North Wall. It had been announced that quarry laborers and navvies were required for work on the Portland docks. Extraordinary scenes took place when 2,000 men assembled to find that only 100 were needed, whereupon all rushed the steamer standing by for the trip to England. Police had to be called to restore order.[14] Reliable figures of unemployment cannot be ascertained for this period, but an informal measure is furnished in the District Reports on Employment published by the Board of Trade in the monthly *Labour Gazette*. The designations "dull," "slack," and "bad" figure prominently as a general description of the level of employment in the building trades for the years 1903 through 1907, 1911 and 1913, some years—1904 and 1913 especially—being periods of unrelieved gloom. The years 1903 through 1909 were disastrous for employees in the engineering trades; the printers suffered in 1904 and from 1909 on; and almost every year was bad for the tailors and bootmakers. More accurate data on unemployment became available after the Labour Exchanges Act of 1909. A divisional office was established under the act in Copper Alley off Lord Edward Street in March 1910 and thereafter thousands registered each month for the few hundred vacancies that needed to be filled. It is revealing of conditions in Dublin that the number remaining on the live register was invariably considerably greater than the corresponding figure for the more populous Belfast, often exceeding it by two or three times. The data in Table 28 is not an untypical record for the Irish capital, reveal-ing the alarming proportion of the unemployed in the city (even by the lower official esti-mates) compared to the condition in British cities with over twice Dublin's population.

TABLE **28.** Labor Exchange—Dublin, 1912: Applications for Adult Employment, Number on Live Register, and Comparison with Other Cities for Selected Periods.

	DUBLIN			BELFAST	GLASGOW	MANCHESTER
	(i) NUMBER REGISTERED AT BEGINNING OF PERIOD	(ii) NUMBER OF APPLICATIONS RECEIVED DURING PERIOD	(iii) NUMBER ON REGISTER AT END OF PERIOD	(iii)	(iii)	(iii)
4 w.e. 23 Feb.	1,549	2,086	1,427	696	1,677	1,290
4 w.e. 24 May	1,208	2,119	1,250	625	1,382	991
4 w.e. 23 Aug.	1,978	3,099	2,010	614	1,612	1,382
4 w.e. 22 Nov.	2,259	2,932	2,432	827	1,503	1,692

SOURCE: *Labour Gazette,* 1912.

The labor exchanges were only partially successful in finding jobs for the unem-ployed. Records show that the number of vacancies notified numbered only 25 percent of the number of workers in search of them. Besides, not every unemployed person chose to register at the exchange, many doubtless foregoing what had in the past proven to be a fruitless quest. The numbers of unemployed applying for relief to the Dublin Distress Committee almost always exceeded those registered at the Labour Exchange. Unemploy-ment, of course, had become a national issue long before the Act of 1909. The onset of winter each year signaled local trade unions to canvass municipal intervention to relieve distress, and throughout the United Kingdom local authorities provided relief works for the worst cases. In Dublin the Corporation had always attempted to provide some assis-tance through the employment of casual laborers in the paving and cleansing depart-ments. However, as so often happened, when the funds ran out this pool of casual labor was thrown back on the streets, inevitably leading to recrimination from men and unions alike. The only groups expressing satisfaction at such setbacks were the Dublin Citizens (ratepayers) Association and the Chamber of Commerce, who all along strenuously resist-ed Corporation borrowing to provide money for public works to relieve unemployment. Witness, for example, the parading over several days in August 1904 of the "Corporation unemployed" bearing black flags in protest against their firing. These finally had to be dispersed by the police so that the great annual Dublin event, Horse Show Week, could take place without discomfort for visitors.[15] Those who administered the Poor Law often claimed that municipal relief works served only to swell the ranks of the unemployed by luring hopeful aspirants into the city from country districts. Notwithstanding, from about 1904 on the cry of winter distress was rarely absent in Dublin. Processions of the idle were noted in the artisan quarters of Francis, Bolton, and North King Streets; the local charitable organizations were inundated with requests for aid; and various deputations importuned the city fathers for measures to relieve the situation. The Corporation held a special meeting on December 3, 1904, and voted funds that enabled over 300 persons to work an average of two weeks each during the winter months. Soon official recognition of the crisis resulted in the Unemployed Workmen Act of 1905. This measure, which received the royal assent on August 11, arranged for distress committees to be set up in the more populous boroughs and urban districts to collect information with regard to labor conditions and distribute the relief funds made available by the Treasury. Amazingly, the Dublin Corporation declined to adopt the Act, thus depriving itself of much needed funds for relief of the unemployed. Perhaps it was loath to become officially associated with relief programs for a situation that seemed certain to become an annual liability with the cost of administration being borne by the rates. In the event, the Corporation was shamed into adoption of the Act when the Philanthropic Reform Association, an organization similar in purpose to the Charitable Organization Society in England, acted on its own to wheedle a £500 grant through the Local Government Board to set up a relief fund. In November 1906 the Corporation formally established a distress committee and set a two-year residency requirement for recipients of relief, an obvious device to answer the criticism that municipal largesse attracted casual laborers to the city from the rest of Ireland. In that winter only £500 of government money found its way to the Dublin distress committee, the bulk of the £5,000 in grants to Ireland going to relieve the needy congested districts in the West. This was only enough to employ some 600 laborers for *one* week at the "relief" rate of 4d. per hour. Inasmuch as 4,000 or so applications representing anywhere from 8,000 to 13,000 dependents were received by the Dublin committee between November and March, it remained to the Corporation to encroach upon the budgets of its works departments to make available opportunities for wage labor.

There was never enough employment for those who wanted it. In an editorial of April 6, 1909, the *Irish Times* estimated that unemployment had struck 7,000 heads of families of the unskilled class, leaving over 20,000 people in destitution. The hundreds of unemployed skilled workers (almost half of the city's printers were out of work in March) at least received some relief from the trade unions via special weekly levies of 2s. 6d. on each employed member. During seven months of 1911 when an average of 2,500 unemployed registered each month with the committee, work was available only for 200; for 1912 the corresponding monthly totals were 2,800 and 300. Mass attempts were made to solicit voluntary contributions from the general public, but the amounts realized were small, though sometimes even these exceeded the sums provided by the rates:[16]

Period	From rates	From subscriptions	From Treasury
1908/1909	£ 430	£469	£5,650
1909/1910	575	661	5,110
1910/1911	600	594	3,182
1911/1912	595	366	3,500
1912/1913	1,050	80	2,600
1913/1914	850	56	6,500
1914/1915	1,150	816	3,400

Disappointment was also felt at the amount contributed by the government. Out of £100,000 or more voted annually by parliament, Ireland as a whole was allocated an average £8,000 per year and, as indicated above, a little over half of this was the average amount set aside for Dublin distress. Some British cities, Glasgow for example, actually received more on occasion than the entire sum voted for Ireland. Therefore, only a few days of employment in any month could be expected by applicants if the funds were to be distributed evenly. In Dublin the majority of applicants were laborers, even though it was the intention of the act to provide mainly for exceptional and short-term unemployment (such as was occasioned by a strike or shut-down) among otherwise regularly employed workmen, *not* to relieve chronic unemployment of the type that prevailed among the unskilled men and women of Dublin. Of the £3,000 expended by the committee in wages during the year 1911-12, 85 percent went to pay able-bodied unskilled laborers, including a few score women workers. Even the Local Government Board itself was forced to admit that the Dublin Distress Committee could never alleviate the mass of chronic poverty the city faced with such limited resources. In fact, the situation was so urgent in the winter of 1910-11 that no grant was allocated for that year to Belfast, a relatively prosperous city, to reserve as much as possible for the capital.

Similar urgency arose in the early months of 1912, when the great coal miners' strike in Great Britain sent its shock waves of distress along the quays of Dublin, resulting in the laying off of about 500 coal workers. At a Mansion House meeting on April 5, the Lord Mayor told the assembled representatives of local government and trade unions that the amount available for Dublin from the Royal Relief Fund then opened in England was a mere £180. Furthermore, since the municipal estimates had then been adopted, no relief projects were possible, nor could a special rate be levied unless the Poor Law Guardians declared that *exceptional* distress existed (alas, the exceptional was normal in Dublin). This grim news prompted the immediate canvassing of local subscriptions to relieve the families of those thrown out of work. The response, though modest, was surprisingly good as far as such collections went in Dublin, ready admission indeed of the extent of privation in the city. In one week of unaccustomed generosity for the needs of the poor, about £1,000 was collected, including contributions from as far afield as Sydney, Australia, and a surprising £50 from the acknowledged "enemy" of organized labor, William Martin Murphy. The effect of this generosity was even more remarkable. On Saturday, April 6 the Trades Hall in Capel Street, distribution center for the relief, was besieged by 2,000 men scrambling for admission in a manner reminiscent of the rush for the boat at the North Wall thirteen years before. The relief committee was forced to adjourn to the newly opened Liberty Hall, headquarters of James Larkin's Transport Workers' Union. About 2,500 families eventually received the small sum of 5 shillings each. Interestingly enough, the sum of £2,000 was collected during the same month and in as many days through the agency of the *Irish Times* as Dublin's initial contribution for the relief of the survivors and dependents of the *Titanic* disaster.[17] Despite all this, repeated requests for additional government aid were met by arguments that the proper remedy for *continuing* distress was the Poor Law. The solution offered to the unemployed by the War Office was more to the point—join the Special Reserve for the six months of winter and get free food and lodging and 7s. per week! Grants therefore continued in the normal manner until the pressure of war expenditures caused the suspension of the Unemployed

Workmen Act in 1916. By then it was hoped that the ministry of munitions would step in to absorb the unemployed who had not already rallied to the colors.

One other private effort for the relief of the unemployed in Dublin during these years is worthy of mention. This was the City Labour Yard committee, organized also in 1905 by one of the most energetic and socially conscious women in Dublin—Miss Sarah Harrison, artist, crusader for the municipal gallery, and in 1912 the city's first woman town councillor. Unceasingly, she used the newspapers to canvass subscriptions to her committee (never more than a few hundred pounds) and expose the misery and degradation that daily faced men compelled to idleness. Located at 33 Harcourt Street, the Yard gave employment each season to those who failed to secure relief from the distress committee, from a handful to several hundred, depending on contributions. These men were put to work at 1s. or 1s. 6d. per day chopping timber (usually donated) for sale to the public as firewood at prices below those of the private traders, a circumstance that naturally excited their anger. These efforts, however laudable, were made perforce on too small a scale to make much difference in the overall situation, though at a personal level a few shillings was all that was needed to keep a family out of the workhouse at least.

The general crisis of unemployment, generated not only by trade depression in Great Britain but, in Dublin, by factors unique to that city continued intermittently between 1904 and 1912. The problem had become, in the words of a spokesman at the Irish Trade Union Congress in 1911, "the vastest and most appalling of the age." This was ultimately conceded by the government in the passage of Lloyd George's great measure of social legislation, the National Insurance Act of 1911. It came into effect in July 1912 and ensured that all those engaged in manual labor in the specified trades (building construction, iron founding, sawmilling, and so forth) would thenceforth be compulsorily insured against unemployment. Benefits, supported by equal contributions from worker and employer, were to become payable after January 15, 1913, and consist of 7s. per week for eligible insured workers over 18 years and 3s. 6d. for 17- and 18-year-olds. No benefits were payable to clerks or those under 17 years. It seemed therefore that by 1913 the shadow of the workhouse, which had receded already for the aged poor with the introduction of old age pensions, might now also vanish for some able-bodied victims of the more malign economic forces, at least for those in insured trades. Since the act required that the unemployed lodge their "books" at the local labor exchange or approved association to claim benefits, a further index of unemployment was provided. At the end of February 1914, for example, the ratio of unemployed to total insured in the building trades was 12.9 percent for Ireland as a whole compared to 3.6, 2.4, and 5.4 percent, respectively, for Scotland, Wales, and the worst-hit regional division of England. This pattern, reflecting the dire situation in Dublin (now improved after the intense labor struggles of the previous months), was maintained subsequently, though by December 1915 the ratio had been reduced to 9 percent for the Irish building trades and to 1.2, 0.9, and 3.1 percent for the other three centers.[18]

It is suggested by the foregoing and will become clearer throughout the rest of this chapter that the working class in the Irish capital, organized or not, possessed little bargaining power for any struggle with that truculent breed of Irishman—the Dublin capitalist. Yet the campaign for better working conditions and recognition of trade union rights was not shirked, and these early years of the century saw many occasions when the more militant elements of that working class went over to the offensive in sometimes long and bitter contests with employers who had long profited from the weakness of organization and cooperation among the Dublin trade unions (see Appendix H). The notion that trade unions in Dublin were the dominant factor in the relations between masters and men was one of long standing and dated from the early years of the nineteenth century when the capital was the scene of violent labor clashes in such established trades as building and printing, caused principally by the aggression of employers in paying low wages, overhiring apprentices, insisting on harsh rules, and discharging men belonging to trade combinations. "No portion of the United Kingdom has suffered so materially as Ireland from the evil effects of trade combinations," reported a correspondent of *The Times* in 1859, assigning to them the cause for the decline of shipbuilding and the foundry trade in Dublin.[19] The reality was otherwise for, despite the sporadic outbursts of the Billy Welters and other violent factions, trade unions in Ireland throughout the century were rarely a "terror" to employers. Not until the very end of the century, when union strength and determination revived, did Dublin become the venue for two of the largest trade disputes in the United Kingdom: the corn porters in 1891 and the building trades in 1896, each of which resulted in the loss of over 100,000 man-days of work. Trade disputes almost always involved wages, with workers striking for an increase or against a decrease in remuneration. When not involving such bread and butter issues, strikes were most often the consequence of union men refusing to work alongside nonunion labor. In about two-thirds of all strikes, the matter at issue was resolved in favor of the employer or by compromise, with the latter assuming increasing importance after the introduction of conciliation machinery in 1900. The years 1897 to 1901 and from 1907 onward were periods of great industrial unrest in the United Kingdom, and this pattern also prevailed in Dublin, where some of the fiercest trade disputes, culminating with the epic struggles of 1913, took place.

The first major contest between masters and men in the period under review concerned the grievances of the painters. In June 1899 they repeated an old tactic of refusing to work with nonunion men. Three years before, a similar resolve had been abandoned after wage and hour claims had been conceded, but that agreement had now expired. The response of the masters demonstrated which party had the upper hand: 300 men were locked out and strike-breakers imported from across the channel. The lockout lasted for over a month and was settled by "mutual concession," a phrase that invariably meant continued freedom of action for the employers in hiring and firing. The dockers' union met with even firmer resistance when they went against the City of Dublin Steampacket Company in September for an increase in wages. The standard rate along the quays was about 24s. for a 60-hour week. The City of Dublin paid 27s. but allowed no recompense for overtime worked. The dockers' demand was for a uniform 4s. 6d. per day and a separate 7d. per hour overtime rate. The two-week strike was broken by the importation of scabs from England and the men returned under existing conditions. Four other minor disputes in that year illustrate the nature of the grievances that upset relations with the employers: 50 coal laborers won their demand for payment while awaiting the unloading of vessels; over 60 bricklayers struck for two days while awaiting an apology for an employer's charge of dilatoriness against one of their fellows; a score of brass finishers fought for two months against a reduction in piece rates; and over 50 dockers walked off the job in a show of sympathy for their striking brothers in Liverpool—all were replaced.[20]

The year 1900 saw the virtual breakup of the National Union of Dock Labourers in Dublin. The trouble began in early July when the Coal Merchants Association rejected the coal laborers' claim for an increase in wages and ignored their demand that nonunion workers be let go. Within days, between 1,000 and 1,200 dock and coal laborers struck, being joined by a number of sympathetic carters. The employers immediately advertised for men at 24s. per week and in addition imported 90 "free laborers" from England. On July 14 a group of about 50 strike-breaking scabs was accosted by men of the dockers' union wielding shovels, iron bars, bricks, and bottles. Though the English free laborers were put to flight during the 15-minute melee, the ultimate victory lay with the masters, who insisted on their sole right to hire and fire without interference. The arrest of 24 dockers cooled matters considerably, and within days the men began to trickle back to work and suffer the humiliation of being forced to work with nonunion laborers.[21] Disputes of this nature invariably reduced employment for local men, for not every free laborer or hired nonunion worker vacated the job he had secured. The same year saw a lockout in the tailoring trade when the men demanded the abolition of out-work, which they regarded as conducive to "sweating" and the undermining of their own jobs. The subject of sweating had arisen only a few weeks earlier at the public health inquiry where examples of the system were given by a member of the Amalgamated Society of Tailors. Although it was there claimed that the system was worse in Dublin than in the rest of the United Kingdom, this was an exaggeration since Belfast was certainly the "sweating center" of Ireland. (In the 1910 Report of the Chief Inspector of factories and workshops, some 1,600 known outworkers were enumerated for the city of Dublin, in contrast to over 6,600 for Antrim, i.e., Belfast and environs.) At any rate, it was estimated that there were at least 700 outworkers maintained in tenement rooms by the clothiers but, of course, there was no way of arriving at any correct total. On this occasion, however, 600 tailors felt strongly enough about the evil to maintain a violent opposition for over four months while 34 businesses closed down and others imported "aliens" or sent work to England for completion. The masters refused arbitration, with the result that the tailors, or rather those who had not been forced to emigrate, finally withdrew their demands on September 20 under a promise that grievances would be referred to a joint committee of masters and men.[22]

The next few years brought a lull, although flareups were never absent—the plumbers suffering defeat after a two-month strike in 1901, the engineers after a four-month struggle in 1902. A small but interesting dispute was initiated by a handful of carpenters in June 1901 when they refused to fix foreign-made joinery, an act of seeming patriotism that rivalled the exertions of the drapers' assistants who once earned the plaudits of Arthur Griffith's *United Irishman* for their resolve never to put any substitute before their customers when an Irish article was asked for. Not until the spring of 1905 did the next dispute occur and, again, it was a lockout, this time of the bricklayers and stone masons, who had refused to accept the Master Builders Association plan that employers should be free to hire men from any recognized society of brick and stone layers in the United Kingdom, an obvious attempt to break the Dublin union. One thousand men were directly and indirectly involved and the lockout lasted for four months until referred to local arbitration. The dispute, as usual, saw the use of free laborers. Although the employers won their point, the union ultimately profited from the stipulation that any new employees would be required to join the Dublin Society of Bricklayers and Stone-layers within twelve months. A trouble-free 1906 was followed by a comparatively mild 1907 in which only one major dispute of note occurred, the year-end strike of over 200 gas workers evolving from the introduction of mechanical time-saving devices by the Alliance Gas Consumers Company. Here too the employers demonstrated that, like weavers in Glasgow or cotton workers at Wigan, unskilled gas workers in Dublin could easily be replaced from the ready pool of unemployed laborers.

With the year 1908 a new and vital phase in the history of labor in Ireland is reached. For James Larkin is to descend like a thunderbolt among the cowed and dispirited masses of unskilled laborers in the city of Dublin and be soon followed by his equal in courage, tenacity, and commitment, James Connolly. Two excellent biographies have described their role in the labor struggles in Dublin in this period; the reader who desires a wider perspective of the issues involved is advised to consult them.[23] It was Larkin who as an official of the National Union of Dock Labourers reorganized the battered remnants of its Dublin branch in 1907. Larkin in his evidence before the departmental committee on piece-work wages in dock labor in 1908 stated that the union claimed about 2,500 men in Dublin. These men principally handled coal, with about 60 percent assigned to work at tonnage rates, a device that allowed unscrupulous employers to pay men for less tonnage than they handled.[24] In his many forays to Dublin, Larkin left his union colleagues in the Dublin Trades Council under no illusion about what his tactics would be. On one of these occasions, a meeting of the Council and the T.U.C. parliamentary committee on the government's old age pension proposals (one poorly attended by union members), he gave a strongly socialist speech and, significantly, deplored the action of the workers of Dublin for their lack of assistance to the gas workers in their recent strike.[25]

The year 1908 was one of revival in other respects. For the first time in thirteen years, the traditional Labor Day celebration was again held under the auspices of the Dublin Trades Council. Over thirty of the city trades associations were represented in the procession, along with delegates from the newly constituted Socialist Party of Ireland. During the following weeks relations between the Dublin branch of the N.U.D.L. and the Coal Masters Association became strained as the employers revealed a decided preference for nonunion workers and refused to negotiate with union representatives. Early in July the men, over 4,000 according to one newspaper report, threatened to strike unless full recognition of the union was conceded by the coal merchants and general carriers. They would cease work on July 20 if the companies then retained men who did not bear on their lapels the badge of the union. The main companies involved were the City of Dublin Steampacket, Palgrave-Murphy, Tedcastle and McCormick, Laird Line, T. Heiton and Sons, B and I Steampacket, and Clyde Shipping. Their reply was to threaten the discharge of any man who refused to work with nonunion labor and also issue a notice on Thursday, July 9 that men belonging to the N.U.D.L. would not be allowed to resume work on the following Monday. Two employers declined even to wait that long, having fired over 400 men who refused to give up their union badges on the Friday. The union (Larkin's hand is evident) distributed its own notice: "Unemployed men, keep away from the harbour of Dublin. Don't scab on your fellow-countrymen who are locked out by the employers. Don't Carey.* Before accepting employment call at 10 Beresford Place." Events now moved swiftly, an indication at least that the union commanded more respect than in the dark days of 1899 and 1900. A public meeting brought unexpected support from local political bigwigs, all critical of the arbitrary action of the employers. These included Timothy Harrington, Nationalist MP and barrister, who had shown little regard for the working classes when he was Lord Mayor of Dublin; William Field, another Nationalist MP who, though retail butcher and president of the Victuallers' Association, had somehow become the party's "labor" representative; Alderman J. J. Farrell, soon to be branded with flunkeyism; and councillor Lorcan Sherlock, lawyer, retail tobacconist, and in time a fierce critic of the "clever Socialists prostituting the labor movement." And over the weekend an official of the Board of Trade arranged a meeting between the Under Secretary and the union, at which Sir Antony MacDonnell persuaded the latter to authorize the resumption of work by the men, as if no dispute had arisen, until the issues could be resolved by a conference between masters and men. It was only with difficulty that some employers could be induced to accept this interim agreement, for on Monday men returning to the City of Dublin Steampacket Company and Tedcastle and McCormick found themselves locked out and their places taken by others.[26] The dispute, which worked itself out without the violence accompanying a similar set of circumstances in Belfast in the previous year, finally ended on July 30 with an agreement yielding points to each side. The employers were again ceded the right to employ nonunion labor, whereas the men gained recognition of the union as final bargaining agent for their grievances, though they were not to display their badges. And it was hoped that in the future the extension of the system of conciliation boards to Ireland might avert the worst consequences of trade disputes.

A far more serious affair was the carters' strike at the end of the year. These workers in the carrying trade had become affiliated to the N.U.D.L. and had for some time sought recognition of their union as well as a wage increase and other concessions from the master carriers. Receiving no response, over 100 carters belonging to four firms of general carriers finally struck on November 16. With the approach of the Christmas season, few desired any disruption of trade. In fact, the extent of unemployment was severe enough in the winter of 1908 for the men to be branded by the *Irish Times* for their "criminal stupidity." Things became ugly when the 64 scabs hired immediately to take the place of strikers were attacked and a dray of goods (including an expensive dynamo, which was later recovered) was dumped into the Liffey. During that first week the carters were joined by the loaders, bulkers, and boatmen of the Grand Canal Company, which distributed goods from Dublin throughout the country. The number on strike soon mounted to some 600 carters and almost as many canal workers. The potential for further violence being so grave, police protection was ordered for the blacklegs, while in Dublin Castle and at the Board of Trade the wheels of conciliation were put in motion to induce the strikers to return to work pending arbitration proceedings. Although the strike appeared to have ended on November 23 with the interim agreement worked out at Dublin Castle, tempers could not be cooled so quickly on either side: by the end of November

*James Carey (a member of the Dublin municipal council in 1883) was the notorious informer who betrayed his fellow assassins after the murder of the Viceroy in Phoenix Park in 1881. He himself was later murdered for his treachery.

the carters and canal men had resumed the strike, and further incidents took their toll of company property. In one case a cart was overturned and the goods scattered all over Lower Abbey Street, the horse mercifully being unyoked beforehand. Since a providential fog had closed in at the time, no arrests could be made. Vanmen delivering goods in the city were accompanied by police to protect them from pickets. The streets were so denuded of police for ordinary duty that the Irish Life Boat Committee canceled its yearly fund-raising procession for fear of the danger to spectators in a city wracked daily by violent affrays.[27]

Apart altogether from the issue of union recognition, the men certainly had a grievance in the matter of wages. The plight of the carters may be inferred from the demands made on the employers: 24s. per week (single horse) minimum wage and weekday hours 6 A.M. to 6 P.M. (Saturdays 6 A.M. to 3 P.M.) and two hours for meals. According to Larkin the average wage of the Dublin carter was 15s. 4d. for a week of 82 hours. There was undoubtedly some exaggeration here, especially as regards hours, but the wage of a carter on daily or weekly earnings most assuredly did not exceed 20s. per week. Considering that wages had not changed during the decade and that retail prices of food and coal were on the increase from 1905 onward, reaching a combined total increase since that year of 9 percent by 1912 and an index number of 97, a mere 3 points below London as base, the standard of living of the ordinary worker was not improving. In December 1908, for example, the price of bread, a staple item in the working-class diet, was 6d. for the 4 lb. loaf, which was ½d. to 1d. higher than in London and Manchester, where wages were appreciably greater. For the low-paid worker with a family of three children and earnings of around 20s. per week, it was estimated that as much as 67 percent of income went towards food (the proportion must have been higher for those irregular employees working "on earnings").[28] This left a Dublin carter and his family with something less than 7s. for rent, clothes, tramfare, union dues, tobacco, alcohol, and amusements. But in December 1908 some 1,000 men (a figure soon doubled) and their dependents had to survive somehow on 10s. per week strike pay from the union or whatever could be culled from local charities. Little wonder that the two archbishops of Dublin should intervene in that holy season on behalf of charity and understanding.

The following days did not bring peace, however, but rather an extension of the strike when some 400 men from the malting houses (the Guinness Company excepted) whom Larkin claimed had joined the N.U.D.L. in sympathy with the striking carters also came out for higher wages. These men, who worked a full seven days (6 A.M. to 6 P.M.) and earned only 16s. to 19s. per week during the eight months or so per year they were in regular employment, now sought the Guinness weekly rate of 23s. and the abolition of the "back shilling," whereby the employer retained that sum each week until the end of the working season, being returned if conduct was satisfactory. Thus, by mid-December the business of 19 carrier firms and all but one of the malting houses was interrupted and about 3,000 workers (including those indirectly involved) were idle. Public sympathy appeared to lie with the strikers, Archbishop Walsh openly suggesting that the men had not been treated sympathetically by the employers and Lord Mayor O'Reilly (the slum landlord who came to grief in 1913) contributing to the strike fund. A proposal by Alderman M'Walter that the Lord Mayor's salary be reduced to enable the Corporation to divert funds to help alleviate local poverty lost by only one vote. The master carriers also had sympathizers—one of the most powerful corporations in the United Kingdom, the Shipping Federation. In an attempt to repeat what they had accomplished in Belfast in the previous year the Federation offered to send 700 men from Liverpool to break the strike as well as a passenger steamer to accommodate them while in the port. The Belfast experience had already demonstrated the serious results these tactics could have and that prompted the Lord Lieutenant to intervene. Only the personal representation of Lord Aberdeen through Sir James Dougherty, the new Under Secretary, induced the Federation to forego this scheme. It was these two officials who finally arranged the arbitration proceedings that brought an end to the strike only a few days before the Christmas holiday. But there was little of cheer for those men who found that their jobs were no longer available on December 21: one firm took back only 21 of the 100 who had gone on strike. And several of the more militant strikers who had been arrested found themselves in jail over the holidays. As to the final award of the arbitration, some important concessions were made on overtime rates, the maltmen saw an end to the hated "back shilling" practice, and all became entitled to two weeks' notice from employers. But pay scales for normal hours remained unchanged, no minimum wage was set, and it was decreed that early closing (3 P.M.) could not be enforced on Saturdays owing to the exigencies of the trade.[29]

These hectic months were followed by over two years of peace. It was but the calm before the stormy events of a summer of industrial unrest in 1911. The syndicalist militancy of those few years before the war was now firmly implanted in Dublin under the leadership of the organizer Larkin, who had divested himself of his N.U.D.L. shackles to found his own Irish Transport and General Workers Union, and the theorist Connolly, lately returned from the U.S.A. to lend the weight of his experience and authority to the advancement of socialist ideas among the Irish working class. The first dispute to rock the capital in 1911 had its origins in British ports, where seamen, firemen, and stewards employed by the shipping companies struck for higher wages. Their success encouraged the dock laborers, who now also struck, an action that again brought the seamen and firemen out in sympathy. In a similar move, seamen in the employ of Palgrave, Murphy, and Company walked off the job along Dublin's North Wall quays on June 30. During the whole of July the trade of the port of Dublin was interrupted as strike, sympathetic strike, and lockout affected in turn seamen, dockers, carters, and employees of the Port and Docks Board. There were no sailings as cattle, Guinness stout, and other export commodities piled up along the quays. Five hundred men were unemployed on June 30, double that number on July 1, and up to 2,000 by mid-month. There was the now customary intimidation and violence against the blacklegs, in many cases men whose own tenuous hold on subsistence presumably prevented their indulging the moral consideration in taking away the jobs of those of their own class. The masters discovered it was somewhat more difficult than usual to find replacements on this occasion, but scabs were nevertheless found to deliver coal despite the dangers. A partial settlement of the seamen's strike was arranged on July 22 at a Dublin Castle conference whereby the terms won by the Liverpool seamen were yielded by the Dublin shipping companies and other outstanding matters were referred to arbitration. Within a week the carters and the Port and Docks men had also returned to work in a major victory for the organized militancy of Larkin's new union. Though there were no arrests on this occasion to mar the results for the men, there was a certain amount of family disruption for those few strikers and locked-out carters who had been ejected from their tenement dwellings for nonpayment of rent during the struggle.[30]

These new sympathetic-strike tactics of the Transport Union lost it much of the public favor it had garnered during the events of December 1908. Moreover, Larkin's newly founded weekly, the *Irish Worker*, alienated the bourgeois Nationalist politicians of both the Irish Parliamentary Party and Dublin Corporation through its uncompromising and withering attacks on their alleged cynical disregard of the workers' interests.[31] The growing strength of the labor party in Britain coupled with Lloyd George's radical legislation induced the men of property to draw together against what were described as the accelerating forces of socialism in Ireland. Not unnaturally, the Dublin employers devised their own defenses by the creation of the Employers' Federation, designed to coordinate action against the syndicalist methods of the Transport Union. The general public also received solemn warnings from the press and pulpit. There was talk of the establishment of Leo Guilds to unite capital and labor under the aegis of the St. Vincent de Paul Society. The activist laity was congratulated at the Catholic Truth Society conference in June 1912 for its work in counteracting the "pernicious influence exercised by socialism and rationalism." The message was expressed in much clearer terms at the Dublin conference of the Catholic Truth Society held at the Mansion House in October: "The last thing in the world that socialists want to see is any redress of the workers' wrongs or any bettering of their social status." Cardinal Logue spoke to the same gathering and, while recognizing the severe lack of employment in Dublin as well as the low wages paid, hardly helped the solution of this social question by suggesting that there would be "less of this contrast of the luxury of the rich and the suffering of the poor" if the people kept the doctrines of the gospel before their eyes.[32]

The month of August 1911 saw more repercussions in Dublin of events in Britain. A short-lived railway strike in Britain was supported in Ireland and seemed to be the trigger that set off a mass of wage demands by such disparate groups as newsboys, timber carriers, bakers, mineral water operatives, and Grand Canal workers. Serious violence or intimidation attended all these outbursts, evidence of the pent-up rage and discontent that drew the least paid workers in the city under the protection of Larkin's union. On Saturday, August 19 the ragged army of newsboys, Larkin's younger disciples, staged a demonstration against the newspaper owners arising out of grievances relating to prices paid on returns. Riots developed in which the police were stoned and shops looted in O'Connell Street. The trouble continued into Sunday, when attempts were made to stop the distribution of papers. A number of arrests were made and scores of persons were treated for injuries at Jervis Street Hospital. According to one newspaper report, shots were fired at a constable. This strange affair ended as quickly as it began but without benefit to the newsboys, who resumed their trade under existing terms. The wounds of this fracas had hardly been treated when 500 men employed by the timber merchants, 70 percent of whom belonged to the Transport Union, were locked out as part of the employers' plan to cut losses resulting from the trade disruption caused by the railway strike. This developed into a strike when the men refused to return without an increase in wages and recognition of their union, leading in turn to the hiring of scabs and the use of clerical workers as carriers. The latter were branded by name in the *Irish Worker*, one of them being a ward-heeler for the Nationalist grass-roots organization, the United Irish League.[33] The building trade was seriously affected, and citizens once more saw police-protected drays rumble through the streets of the city.

This situation was further complicated on September 15 when two employees of the Great Southern and Western Railway Company at Kingsbridge refused to handle a consignment of timber from one of the firms involved in the strike. This action spread to other terminals and soon brought the railway system in certain areas to a standstill. When the railway companies refused to negotiate with the union, the latter retaliated on September 21 by calling a general strike on Irish railways. The timber dispute paled into insignificance before this massive escalation, which saw over 7,000 railway workers throughout the country directly and indirectly involved. Soldiers and police were placed on the ready. The Lord Lieutenant returned from England to bring both parties into the discussion of differences. There were rumors in Dublin that the carters might be brought out in sympathy. But what lent urgency to negotiations was the amount of food rotting at railway terminals as well as the desire of the government to avoid using the military to run the trains. The employers gained the sympathy on this occasion since those who had formerly been found to side with the workers now condemned the sympathetic strike, the latter also being damned by a meeting of the Roman Catholic bishops in October as "fatal to trade unionism as well as to industry and civilization." Those who had precipitated the crisis were described by the bishops as "mischief makers," and the Irish executive was blamed by the *Irish Times* for a lack of courage in not using the troops to man the trains, a tactic that according to the *Irish Worker* was also advocated by Arthur Griffith. The struggle ended in a complete triumph for the companies and bitter humiliation for the workers. The settlement of October 4 was dictated by the Great Southern, whose workers had comprised the overwhelming majority of those on strike. In a show of "generosity" the directors offered to take back at once all the locomotive and permanent way men (about 2,000 in number) and 90 percent of the 1,600 traffic men. But they refused either to dismiss the men taken on during the strike or cancel the promotions already granted to those who had remained loyal to the company. The union yielded and on the insistence of the directors expressed on behalf of the men regret for their leaving work without notice and undertook to handle all traffic from whatever source. The strike of the timber workers, which had initiated the month-long crisis, also ended disastrously for the men. They neither won an advance in wages nor recognition of the union, and those 70 or so who found their jobs given to nonunion workers were unable to return in their former capacity.[34]

While all these events were creating dislocation of trade and distress for workers and their families, an even more startling situation followed in the wake of disputes in the bakery trade. The Dublin Operative Bakers and Confectioners union had been faced with the implications of the introduction of new machinery for bread and confectionery processes since around 1904, when the companies began to introduce the "time system" (fixed wage for fixed hours, irrespective of output) in place of the traditional "results system" whereby men in regular employment only produced a stipulated number of loaves and no more. As more and more masters adopted the new system, the men began to press for wage increases to compensate for higher production: the issue here was not disemployment by machines, for there were about 20 percent more workers in the trade in 1911 compared to 1901 despite the technological advances. The latest agreement was made in November 1910, when new wage and hourly rates were set. On those few occasions when isolated strikes took place, they were usually broken by "free" labor or through employment of bakers from the rival (since 1907) though small Metropolitan Bakers Society, which declined to merge with the older organization. One such dispute involving 90 bakers took place in February 1911. Another one-day strike took place on August 22, when the biscuit and cake makers struck for higher wages and other concessions. On that occasion occurred one of the most remarkable instances of workers' solidarity in the history of the city when 2,000 girls in the employment of Messrs. Jacob came out in sympathy.[35]

The most serious dispute, however, began on September 26, when some 350 members of the Dublin Operative Bakers (about 40 percent of the total male operatives) went on strike for higher wages and the abolition of the time system. All the major firms were involved—Boland, Monks, Kennedy, D.B.C., and Downes. The last named was owned by Sir Joseph Downes, long-time Nationalist alderman of Dublin Corporation. Such widespread disruption in a vital trade had immediate consequences among the citizens. The poor were the first to feel the effects of the resulting scarcity. It was claimed that the more unscrupulous small retailers were charging double prices for the 2 lb. loaf and that large numbers of people were on the verge of starvation. While the drays of the timber merchants were being attacked by strikers, the vans of the bread companies were being rifled of their contents by marauding bands of women and children. Attacks of this nature took place on September 30 in several of the poorer quarters of the city. It required charges by mounted police to disperse a hostile crowd at Beresford Place and police escorts to guard consignments of bread to hotels from firms not affected by the strike. There were claims that patients were being refused admittance to hospitals because of the shortages. When in early October the employers indicated a willingness to discuss the question of wages, only some men began to trickle back to work. The employers' concessions did not extend however to the firing of the "free" laborers hired during the strike, with the result that a considerable number of men remained in enforced unemployment for some time.[36] As late as January 9 the plight of these men became a matter for discussion at a meeting of Dublin Corporation.

The year 1912 passed almost without incident after these hectic months, much as the unrest of 1909 was followed by the quiet of 1910. Perhaps the excitement of the Home Rule Bill banished for the moment more immediate concerns. For Larkin the year was one of organization in that the unskilled workers of Dublin were gathered in increasing numbers into the Transport Union. The National Insurance Act, which allowed for contributions to be made through trade unions, also gave an undoubted fillip to labor organization since 1911. By 1913, therefore, the masters of Dublin were confronted by workers organized as never before and led by a man who had become "the virtual dictator of the port of Dublin."[37] Twelve months later, when the opportunity arrived to review the many events of that year, some writers naturally reflected on the sinister significance attaching to the number 13. For 1913 was the *annus terribilis* of the Dublin working class. Before it ended, a bewildering variety of strikes, often with no obvious relation to one another, rocked the port and city of Dublin in a manner characterized by the Lord Mayor as tantamount to "civil war." Involved in strikes, lockouts, and sympathetic strikes were agricultural laborers, bill posters, biscuit makers, bottle makers, box makers, brass finishers, bricklayers, builders laborers, cabinet makers, canal loaders, carpenters, carriers, carters, coach makers, confectioners, dockers, electricians, engineers, farm workers, gas workers, glaziers, hairdressers, horse shoers, iron founders, linen workers, manure workers, market

gardeners, match workers, millers, newsboys, painters, paviors, plasterers, plumbers, pop-
lin workers, seamen and firemen, soap makers, stevedores, stonecutters, tobacco workers,
tramway employees, van drivers, wood machinists—even schoolboys at the national
schools in Rutland Street. A gloom had descended on the city that caused some observers to remark on the absence in Dublin of that open-air gaiety that was the abiding charm
of continental cities. They may have included the lady who wrote a despairing letter to
the *Irish Times* bemoaning the dearth of social functions in recent years and suggesting
that Dublin society had also gone on "strike."

Predictably, the gauntlet was first thrown down by the Transport Union. On Thursday, January 30 over 100 dockers in the employ of the City of Dublin Steampacket Company went on strike, ostensibly on the grounds that they would not any longer work
alongside nonunion men: the foremen had refused to join the men's union. It was market
day in Dublin and the cross-channel cattle trade was dislocated. It soon became apparent
that the action related to wage and hour claims when another 200 dockers joined the
strike. Violence, by now the usual accompaniment of Transport Union strikes, soon followed; lorries were overturned at the North Wall in the presence of police and any carters
who did not support the strikers were constantly intimidated. It was a repeat of earlier occurrences: goods were removed from ships and carried through the city under police protection. The union had the support of the Dublin Trades Council and appeared to be well
prepared to withstand a long struggle; strike pay was 17s. 6d. per week for married men
(about 75 percent of regular wages) and 12s. for the unmarried. The dispute was protract-
ed, lasting until a general agreement was concluded on April 19, an agreement that eventually conceded wage and overtime increases to both constant and casual laborers along
the quays.[38]

Between the dockers' strike and the momentous events of August, several unrelated
minor disputes took place that illustrate widespread grievance and militancy in the skilled
and unskilled trades during that fateful year. The bottle makers fought unavailingly for
three weeks against the introduction of machines; 350 biscuit workers struck for one day
for the reinstatement of a suspended worker; 500 coachbuilders were out for six weeks
before they won a minimum wage; over 100 sawyers won a 50-hour week, as did 50 bill-
posters of David Allen and Company; hairdressers struck to protest the abolition of the
tipping system and their strike was honored by the glaziers and carters of Brooks, Thomas, and Company, who refused to install a pane of glass in a hairdressing establishment in
sympathy with the strikers. In one case the strike of 90 factory girls in a recently opened
subsidiary of a northern linen firm led to the precipitous flight of the business, lock,
stock, and barrel, back to the more congenial atmosphere of Belfast. In all, about thirty
separate disputes involving over 2,200 workers, many resulting in arrests and violence,
took place between January 29 and August 15.[39]

The major Dublin employers—the steamship companies, building contractors, coal
merchants—had viewed with growing apprehension the events of the past six years. To
them, as to many members of the public, the idea of the sympathetic strike was anathema. It was to counter this trend that the Dublin master builders united together in July
1913 to form the Building Trades Employers' Association, embracing every trade connected with the building industry, a combination of one group of like employers that
paralleled the all-embracing Dublin Employers' Federation of 1911. The employers' plan
of campaign had already been mapped out for them by the *Irish Times* on January 31,

1913: ". . . the extravagant claims of this union [i.e., Larkin's] must be crushed once and for all." And the man who was responsible for it all made no bones about the fact that he was waging class warfare. "I am a Socialist myself," Larkin had said, "and I believe in State control of all industry"[40]—sentiments that in themselves provided allies enough for the capitalists of Dublin. He also believed in the "one big union" of *all* workers, from seamen to agricultural laborers. It was in line with this latter idea that he now entered into a contest with William Martin Murphy for the allegiance of the tramway workers, setting off one of the longest (22 weeks) and costliest industrial disputes in British trade union history.

Trouble between the Dublin United Tramways Company (DUTC) and the Irish Transport and General Workers' Union (ITGWU) had been brewing for several weeks before the work stoppage in late August. As usual, the grievance had to do with the low wages paid, rates of pay that had remained virtually unchanged over the previous three decades. Motormen earned a standard 25s. 6d. to 31s. per week according to grade, and the minimum for conductors was 22s. 6d. A tramworker was obliged to buy his own uniform, which cost £2, the amount being stopped weekly by the company and refunded either on dismissal or retirement. Two years earlier the men had petitioned for a shorter work week and more free days for older men. Now, against the company's offer of a 1s. per week wage increase, the men presented a demand for 2s. 6d. Angered that a number of employees should have joined Larkin's union, the DUTC on August 12 posted a notice stating that no demands would be acceptable from James Larkin on behalf of the men. In anticipation of a strike, the DUTC attempted to exact a written promise from each employee that he would remain loyal to the company. At the same time the DUTC parcels delivery department was closed down and the men there were discharged because they had joined the ITGWU, the distinctive union lapel badge (a red hand) proclaiming that fact. This resistance of the company to the organizing attempts of Larkin was personified by Murphy, the chairman of the board of the DUTC. Murphy also extended his anti-Larkin measures to his own employees at the plant of his own newspaper, the *Irish Independent*, by hiring scabs on August 21 to replace discharged dispatchers and vanmen. Naturally, this action was followed by the union's attempts to stop the distribution of Murphy's papers, a tactic that was resisted by the largest of the distributors, Eason and Son, Ltd. Meanwhile, mindful of the serious violence that had enveloped the streets of the city when the newsboys struck in 1911, the authorities decided to prepare for further trouble by swearing in 60 pensioners of the DMP to do duty as jailers and special constables to relieve policemen for street duty and the guarding of Murphy's and Eason's delivery vans.

All attention, of course, was focussed on the trams. There was as yet only rumor of a strike, and the lines were operating as usual. Certainly no one outside the union desired any interruption in the tram service, particularly at that time of year. At least one irate citizen made his feelings public when he assaulted Larkin in the street with a cane. Dublin was in readiness for the gala event of the social season, the Royal Dublin Society Horse Show at Ballsbridge, which was to open on Tuesday, August 26. The city had on its best face—clean streets, renovated statues and monuments, and busy crowds of visitors expecting pleasure and profit. The public was encouraged in these expectations: "We refuse to contemplate this [tramway strike] seriously," editorialized the *Irish Times* on August 23, "for it is almost incredible that any Irishman could plan such a blow at the welfare of our capital." By August 25, however, a "cloud on the horizon" was espied, and on the following day the incredible happened—the tramway strike began at 10 A.M., coinciding with the opening of the Horse Show.[41]

The strike took place without warning when about 200 motormen and conductors left their vehicles stranded in College Green and O'Connell Street at the appointed hour.* During the same day an estimated 150 DUTC laborers, fitters, and boilermen at the company's Ringsend power plant also left work in support of the union. The *Irish Times* reported that 70 vehicles out of 200 had been abandoned, probably a fair estimate: in 1910 the DUTC had 330 electric cars in stock, and according to the company's own advertisements operated about 230 cars daily in the city. At any rate the company was able to maintain a curtailed service with the aid of "loyal" employees and newly hired men from the DUTC list of casuals (a newspaper report stated that the DUTC offices were "besieged by an army of applicants" for the vacant positions).[42] Service was to be suspended each evening after 7 P.M. in accordance with Murphy's pre-strike promise to the men, a promise made to encourage them to be loyal in the event of trouble. This tactic was hailed by Larkin as a victory for the union, but it delighted nobody as much as the city's jarvies and taxicab drivers. Police began to patrol the streets in force almost immediately, and scuffles broke out as strikers paraded. The DMP was strengthened by imported contingents of the RIC, the latter appearing in the city for the first time in many years and reportedly being rendered conspicuous for their lack of height alongside the "giants" of the metropolitan force. Before the day had ended, the police courts were busy handling cases of intimidation and obstruction, while small retailers in some quarters were refusing to sell food to the wives of nonstriking tram workers. That same evening Larkin addressed the men who had gathered outside Liberty Hall and offered his own version of the events of the morning, when, in a reference to the action of Murphy a few days before in discharging the men of the parcels department, he claimed: "This is not a strike, it is a lockout of the men who have been tyrannically treated by a most unscrupulous scoundrel."

The remarkable thing about the strike of August 26 was not only the rapidity with which it spread to other trades but also the aggressive unity of the employers against Larkin and the ITGWU. In the following days the employees of a local flour milling firm struck when the owners announced their plan to dismiss members of Larkin's union. On August 30 over 600 men struck Jacob's biscuit factory because the company had taken a delivery of "tainted" flour. And demonstrating the same spirit they had shown in August 1911, over 1,700 of that company's female employees also left rather than remove their union badges. Jacob's thereupon closed down operations, intimating that they would reopen after sufficient applications from workers not connected with the ITGWU were received (the company reopened on September 15). On September 1 the coachbuilders locked out all unskilled men who wore the union badge as well as those skilled men who refused to repair Murphy's newspaper delivery vans. Next, about 1,000 carters were locked out by the Coal Merchants' Association for refusing to deliver coal to "black" firms. The steamship companies followed with a threat to dismiss any member of Larkin's union: dockers had refused to handle "tainted" goods despite the agreement

*Accounts vary of the number of men who struck on that day. The total number of men employed on the trams, according to company figures, was 368 motormen and 258 conductors, and Murphy later claimed that two-thirds of them remained "loyal."

worked out earlier in the year to submit all grievances in writing and terminate employment only after one month's notice. On the following day, September 3, the Master Carriers' Association also promised instant dismissal to those refusing to obey orders. Employer antagonism culminated with a "declaration of war" by about 400 members of the Employers' Federation who pledged themselves in future "not to employ any persons who continue to be members of the Irish Transport and General Workers' Union . . . a menace to all trade organisation." In addition the famous "document" was issued to all workers exacting a written declaration not to join or support the ITGWU as a condition of employment, a scheme that was later condemned by an official Court of Inquiry as "contrary to individual liberty and which no workman or body of workmen could reasonably be expected to accept." Obviously the masters had determined on a fight to the finish and were using the lockout as the weapon to crush the union. Retaliation proceeded from workers in a wide variety of trades and firms throughout the city. The builders' laborers refused to sign and brought a halt to building operations. Employees of timber importing and cement and brick-making firms also refused, and more firms were added during the next three months. By mid-September some 9,000 workers (including about 4,000 building trade employees) were out of work and the number was constantly growing.

The first few days of the strike saw little violence beyond the usual posturing before police-protected trams and drays. Of marches and meetings there were many as men vainly demanded wages due them at the time they struck, and Beresford Place and the Custom House steps resounded with the lurid declamations of union representatives. The events of Saturday and Sunday (August 30 and 31) saw scenes of violence that were long remembered and became a minor saga in the history of Dublin labor.[43] During the two-day period there were twelve separate riots throughout the city. The clashes between police and strikers began near the Dodder Bridge at Ringsend on Saturday afternoon, when a large crowd, numbering 500 to 600 according to police estimates, attacked a number of trams and assailed 16 constables and inspectors—from a safe distance—for several hours with stones, bricks, and bottles. This was only a foretaste of the riot in Great Brunswick (now Pearse) Street on the same day when another wild crowd of men and women were held at bay by a tiny force of police who succeeded in arresting six rioters. This particular uproar elicited a colorful account from a local priest, whose testimony was used at the official inquiry to support the police account of the event:

> At every street corner along Brunswick Street there were large groups of people, chiefly women and children, of a degraded class. . . . As the tram passed each group they lost all control of themselves and behaved like frenzied lunatics. They shouted coarse language and threats at the tramwaymen, and with violent gestures indicated the fate that awaited the 'scabs' if the 'scabs' fell among them. . . . Not only men, but women with hair all dishevelled, and even young girls of fifteen or sixteen, rushed and surged around the police. . . . One obsessed creature seized an empty coal-bag from a cart and belaboured the constable to the utmost of her power. . . . [The behavior of the police] was the only redeeming feature of what was for a Dublin citizen a really humiliating and disgusting spectacle.[44]

Violence turned to tragedy that same evening when the hard-pressed police used their batons to disperse missile-wielding crowds in the vicinity of Beresford Place, leaving two men, both married laborers, on the street with fractured skulls. Both died within a few days. A few blocks away the Foley Street Corporation dwellings became a haven for those fleeing police batons in Corporation Street. The balconies were later used to shower the police below with bricks, stones, crockery, saucepans, chamber pots, and bottles. Responding to the baiting though misdirected challenge "Come on, you whores," a number of police entered the buildings and losing all control dispensed severe beatings to a few tenants, arrested others, and did considerable damage to property. This episode was treated at great length in the subsequent inquiry because of the involvement of the Corporation and its tenants: over £60 was paid in compensation by the government, one-third of it to the municipal landlord for replacement of glass and broken locks. Tenant witnesses were rather unfairly treated at the hearing even by Corporation counsel, the reputation of the Foley Street residents preceding them. Their combative spirit and verbal resourcefulness, illustrative of a certain type of Dublin character, is worth demonstrating by the following examples in which two female witnesses are being cross-examined on the events of August 30 and 31:

Witness no. 1.
- Q. And your "da," does he always live with you?
- A. My "da" is a man, and he is not to be belittled anyway.
- Q. Not at all?
- A. Age is honourable.
- Q. When he is not in gaol he is with you?
- A. Certainly; he would have no home, and surely you don't think that I would throw him on the ways of the world. I am not one of the quality, they desert them.
- Q. Where were you enjoying yourself on Saturday night then?
- A. It is no matter where, but I enjoyed myself.
- Q. You did?
- A. Of course, when I came home I came home like you go rolling home in the morning.
- Q. You came home rolling drunk?
- A. As you say so.
- Q. Had you the baby with you all the time?
- A. The child is sticking there no matter what happens.

Witness no. 2.
- Q. Are you a peaceable woman yourself?
- A. I am.
- Q. Did you get 14 days' imprisonment last year for assault?
- A. I did, sir, for my sister.
- Q. You didn't think it any harm to assault your sister?
- A. Not in the least. When she deserved it, why not give it to her?
- Q. I believe the weapon you used on your sister . . . was a red-hot poker?
- A. It was not red-hot.
- Q. I apologise, but it was hot?
- A. I could not tell you.
- Q. You forget, I suppose.
- A. I don't forget my 14 days.
- Q. And on Saturday night your general frame of mind is that you don't care whether the poker is hot or cold when you want to assault anyone?
- A. Anyone who would try to insult me I would hit with a hot poker.[45]

The most famous incident of this two-day battle was the baton charge in O'Connell Street on the Sunday, a moment captured in one of the most striking photographs of the period. A meeting scheduled for that day, and at which Larkin was to speak even though a warrant had been issued for his arrest, was proclaimed by the government. In expectation of trouble, the authorities had posted 300 policemen along the thoroughfare. Nevertheless, the disguised leader managed to evade them until his fleeting appearance before the expectant crowds shortly after 1 P.M. on the balcony of the Imperial Hotel over Clery's department store. As Larkin was being led away, a section of the crowd surged forward only to be driven back by the line of 50 police in front of Clery's. The constables, never ones to brook any challenge to their control of city streets, inevitably employed considerable force, doubtless brutal in some cases, to repel what they saw as an attempt to release their prisoner. As *The Times* was later to explain in justification of their action, " . . . the flame of a street riot cannot be put out with a spray of rose water." Over a period of a few minutes several hundred persons, many of them innocent passers-by, were either batoned or trampled underfoot in the wild rush to escape the encircling squads of police. Many of these were among the more than 200 persons (including a score of policemen) who were treated at Jervis Street Hospital for scalp wounds between Saturday and Sunday evenings. Later on that afternoon and into Monday, mobs 200-and-more-strong wrecked trams, looted shops, and fought policemen in several areas of the city, the men being assisted by women bearing stones in their aprons. In Cornmarket two lone policemen were chased into a presbytery and besieged until rescued. At Inchicore the ferocity of the crowd was so great that a detachment of the West Kent regiment had to be called out to escort trams to their depot.[46] It was estimated that 500 people received injuries during that wild weekend, over 400 of them being treated in city hospitals. The victims might well have regretted the recent decision of the Corporation to postpone for another year the question of providing the Fire Brigade (which handled first-aid calls) with its first motorized ambulance. The police later claimed that about 200 of their own number had been injured, but this was probably an overestimate designed to draw sympathy: a dozen police were usually enough to strike terror into any crowd, as was proven by those several instances in which a handful of them was able to put hundreds to flight.

The rioters were by no means regarded everywhere as the downtrodden battalions of labor being starved into submission by unrelenting capitalists. These outbursts of late August were of such a character that the fear of anarchy overcame for many both sympathy and understanding. There was after all a considerable amount of property damage in the wake of the riots, resulting in 58 firms submitting claims for compensation. The most biting criticism came from the *Irish Catholic*, whose insensate hatred of socialism and Larkin's methods blinded it to the Christian charity it might have shown to the victims of the lockout:

> In the majority they are beings whose career is generally a prolonged debauch, seldom broken by the call of labour—their only thought is to work destruction and havoc in the existing order of society. It is this type who have made the streets during the past four or five nights hideous with bloodshed and disorder.[47]

Some more neutral observers could appreciate that it was not socialism or depravity that drove on the rioters—socialism in Dublin only existed in the obiter dicta of a Larkin or

The famous melee in O'Connell Street on Sunday, August 31, 1913. Police scatter and baton the surging crowd following the arrest of James Larkin on the balcony of the Imperial Hotel.

Connolly—but their frustrations and anger at the employers' implacable hostility to their brand of trade unionism. Nor was that great ally of business and order, the *Irish Times*, unaware of the real issue. "Our large employers of labour have still much to do for their workers. That fact has been brought home to them very disagreeably by recent events," it wrote on September 17. More direct sympathy for the workers came from English railwaymen at Liverpool, Birmingham, and elsewhere when several thousand of them refused to handle "tainted" goods from Dublin consignors; usually this type of sympathetic action between Irish and English workers was the other way round. The gesture did not last long, for the executive of the National Union of Railwaymen, disinclined to condone anything that might lead to a general strike, especially under these circumstances, ordered the men back to work. But other help was forthcoming in the form of money from British unions to support the ITGWU, now hard-pressed in doling out strike pay. Indeed, money had already been contributed to support workers in Dublin—funds solicited by a committee that included councillor J. Crozier (soon to be revealed as the owner of considerable tenement property) "to reward the loyal tramwaymen," a project that also had the support of the sectarian A.O.H. (Board of Erin), the political ally of the Irish party. By the end of September the amount subscribed to this fund exceeded £1,000.

During September there was no letup in the violence directed against the trams, carts, vans, and coal lorries; and there was one further serious riot in Townsend Street, on September 21, during one of the frequent monster processions of the workers—"the most determined and disgraceful riot that took place in Dublin during the disturbances," ac-

The Dublin lockout, 1913. Tramway passengers travel under the protection of a formidable member of the Dublin Metropolitan Police.

cording to the Commission set up to investigate all those events. Constant battles continued to be waged between striking and nonstriking workmen. Police continued to be drafted into the city until eventually some 1,000 RIC were placed on special duty in Dublin alongside the 1,000-man metropolitan force. Soldiers stood guard over carts carrying fuel to military barracks or cartloads of coal for consignment to Curragh Camp. Between August 19 and September 30, almost 700 offenses directly related to the labor unrest (assault, intimidation, breaking of street lamps, destruction of property, and the like) were reported to the police, of which 350 were prosecuted. Of these, 178 cases resulted in imprisonment, ninety persons were fined, and a small number of juvenile offenders was sent to reformatories.[48] At the licensing renewal sessions in the police courts, objections were lodged against those publicans who had refused to serve drink to persons alighting from trams, employees of DUTC, and policemen in plain clothes. Any worker who used a tram was now regarded as a scab, a prohibition that according to Larkin should be extended even to those riding trams to the football matches in Shelbourne Road. One wonders how Larkin regarded the Primate of Ireland, Cardinal Logue, who made special arrangements with the DUTC to run late cars for delegates to the October conference of the Catholic Truth Society.[49] Many employers had their employees licensed to carry revolvers for protection while police continued to ride trams and escort carters. By mid-month more and more firms had been affected by either sympathetic strikes or decisions to lock out those who refused to sign the "document." Many were advertising for blackleg labor. Hardly any work was being done along the docks, where food was rotting on the quayside. The streets were constantly full of people anxious to observe developments, participate in processions, or attend meetings to hear the encouraging words of an English sympathizer (Ben Tillett), cheer the delivered hunger-striker (James Connolly), or savor the vituperative oratory of James Larkin.

The condition of the families of the locked-out men was becoming daily more precarious. Young girls roamed the streets with collection boxes on behalf of the union or followed the banner-waving processions of the unemployed to solicit contributions from spectators along the route. Observers contrasted the "ridiculously large" police with the pale and hollow-eyed pickets, ill clad in miserable weather. Misery hung about the pawn shops, some of which had become so congested that they ceased to accept further pledges. Food and coal prices increased, potatoes almost doubling in price and a bag of coal (the poor could only buy in small quantities) jumping from 1s. 6d. to 3s. 4d. Some men had received ejectment notices as tenants of employer-owned dwellings, a move that prompted Larkin to promise to house families under canvas tents in Croydon Park, the ITGWU recreation grounds. Hospitals were running out of supplies of cotton wool because no ships were arriving in Dublin from England; even their coal supplies had to be furnished under police escort. Business in the city was virtually at a standstill since many firms were unable to make deliveries owing to lack of police protection. W.M. Murphy made representations to the Chief Secretary requesting the use of the military, and for the first time since a detachment of the West Kents were employed at Inchicore on August 31, troops began on September 25 to replace the police at the DUTC depots and power station and thereby relieve them for patrol duty. It seemed impossible that such a state of affairs should continue, for by this time it was estimated that at least 20,000 workers were directly involved in the dispute through strike or lockout or, as in the case of the building tradesmen laid off when the laborers refused to disavow Larkin, were indirectly involved. This large number included about 500 farm laborers from the county for whom Larkin had won a wage increase before the trouble began in the city. These now went on strike rather than agree to the demand by the Farmers' Association (conveniently presented after the harvest had been brought in) that they give up their membership in the ITGWU. But the strangest addition of all to the ranks of the strikers were the schoolboys of St. Thomas' National School in Lower Rutland Street, not far from the tenements of Summerhill. There, according to one report, the "chislurs" demanded free books and a weekly half-holiday and insisted that they not be compelled to purchase books ("tainted" goods?) published by Easons![50]

Attempts to settle the dispute were made through the agency of the Trades Union Congress, but they foundered on the employers' resolve not to treat with Larkin or his union. The Board of Trade next took a hand by appointing a court of inquiry presided over by the veteran industrial conciliator Sir George Askwith, but this only produced a draft conciliation scheme as a basis of discussion between employers and men which the employers completely ignored. The Protestant Archbishop of Dublin offended no one when he called for prayers in his parish churches for the return of peace. More material peace efforts were made by a group of local intellectuals (Thomas Kettle, Oliver St. John Gogarty, Padraic Colum, Thomas McDonagh, Joseph Plunkett, and others) who formed an Industrial Peace Committee to negotiate between the opposing sides. This got as far

Cloth caps and 'boaters' mingle in a demonstration at Liberty Hall, headquarters of Larkin's Irish Transport and General Workers' Union, during the labor troubles in 1913.

as inducing the directors of the DUTC to accept proposals for a conference, but this too failed to break their resolve not to treat with Larkin. Neither were the efforts of the Lord Mayor any more successful with the Employers' Federation. This adamantine resolve of the masters placed them in a very unfavorable position, and they were now increasingly accused of attempting a "settlement by starvation" that could not fail to inaugurate an era of class warfare in Dublin. Dublin had become the stage on which was reenacted with grim reality the theatrical confrontation of an unyielding labor against "that white-faced monster with the bloody lips" of the Galsworthy play, *Strife*, which had been presented to audiences at the Gaiety Theatre a few weeks earlier. The most striking response to these developments was George Russell's Open Letter to the Masters of Dublin—those "blind Samsons pulling down the pillars of the social order."[51]

Most remarkable was the silence of the Irish MPs (including Dublin City representatives Field, Brady, Abraham, and Nannetti) during all these attempts at negotiation. In their 30-year domination of politics in three provinces of Ireland, the Nationalists had never failed to champion the victims of distress—evicted tenants, rack-rented farmers, land-hungry peasants, victims of coercion—but their inaction in this crisis only gave Larkin the opportunity to accuse their leader, John Redmond, of letting Dublin rot. One of the few to speak out was David Sheehy, MP, but only to make the obtuse claim in a speech at Navan that "it was the most absurd thing that ever emanated from the brain of man to think that there was antagonism" between capital and labor and suggest subtly

Another aspect of the Dublin lockout. Homeless children guard treasured possessions after eviction of the family for nonpayment of rent.

that it only needed Larkin's removal to effect an agreement.[52] This was the position maintained by the Employers' Federation. The general attitude among the parliamentarians appeared to be that they must steer clear until home rule granted them the authority to intervene, an eventuality whose likelihood of realization would recede with each passing month. It seemed more credible that their basic hostility to Larkin and his ideas, an attitude shared by priest and bishop, urged the policy of neutrality. Moreover, any success of his militant labor movement could only work to weaken the local Irish party machine in Dublin and in time threaten the Nationalist parliamentary movement itself. Meanwhile, the attacks on the evils of "syndicalism" could be left to the clerical press while the *Freeman's Journal* drove home the charge that the activities of Larkin were aiding the enemies of Ireland in Great Britain by disrupting the united front needed to win Home Rule.

The positive influence of the Catholic Church in Ireland was also notably absent. Archbishop Walsh was away from Dublin during August and September, but on his return both he and the Protestant Archbishop refused to intervene when invited to do so in a resolution of Dublin Corporation. Incredibly, the activities of clergymen were mainly confined to sermons on socialism as the antithesis of sound Christian principles, a theme that had figured prominently in the statements of clerical spokesmen on matters of social reform for some years. Only when the humane plan was mooted in late October to send half-starved children to temporary homes in Great Britain did the most basic instincts of the clergy rise up in fear against what was perceived as an opportunity for proselytizing by English Protestants in an atmosphere that despite all assurances priests and lay Catholics alike refused to believe could be other than non-Catholic and Socialistic.

The "deportation of the children" affair was yet another curious episode among the many strange and startling events of 1913 in Dublin and arose out of the cruel suffering that a "settlement by starvation" had imposed on the Dublin working classes. With anywhere between 20,000 and 25,000 citizens out of work, representing along with dependents at least one-quarter of the city's population, the amount of suffering among those least able to withstand prolonged privation had approached crisis proportions. For two months tens of thousands had been living on charity and strike pay (5s. per week). The annual operations of the Distress Committee were usually in abeyance during the summer months, with the result that nothing was expended in wages during September and October. When taken up again in November, the fund provided only about £10 to 47 persons employed on piece work during that month and an average of 6s. per week to fewer than 200 persons subsequently. The situation would have been rendered absolutely intolerable had not the benevolence of Englishmen and the sympathy of the British trade union movement been forthcoming. A local relief fund to provide free meals for school-children received a cold reception by the main organs of the daily press. The *Irish Times* had taken a definite stand against Larkin, and the neutrality of the nationalist daily, the *Freeman's Journal*, was soon to turn to hostility also. When the Lord Mayor was urged to raise such a fund, he admitted that such was the economic dislocation of the city that it was "next to impossible to raise funds for any object, even for the dependents of Nolan and Byrne."[53] (Nolan and Byrne were the laborers who were bludgeoned to death during the riots in late August.) Only about £400 was raised by the Lady Mayoress and her committee of ladies, a sum that was dwarfed fortunately by corresponding funds raised in England and Scotland: from newspaper subscription lists (especially the *Daily Citizen*, organ of the Labour Party), trade union associations (the Miners' and Transport Federations), the Trade Union Congress—even the London taxi drivers. Hitherto the only support received by the ITGWU was the dues of members not affected by the dispute (i.e., the dockers) and voluntary contributions from other trade unionists not directly involved. From October onward large amounts of money began to flow to the coffers of the union from its British supporters, eventually reaching the stupendous sum of £150,000, or about three-quarters of a million dollars.[54] What captured the imagination, however, was the arrival of the first food ship, S.S. *Hare*, alongside the south wall of the Liffey shortly after noon on Saturday, September 27. This was the first of a dozen or so such TUC-sponsored operations over the next four months. It was not the first food gathered for the relief of the citizens; only a few hours earlier the cooperative bakeries of Dublin and Belfast had donated 12,000 loaves of bread for distribution by the union. But the cargo of the *Hare* provided the necessities of life, 60,000 packages containing butter, sugar, tea, bread, jam, potatoes, fish, and biscuits for the "kiddies." The drapers' assistants on their weekly half-holiday nobly offered their services at Liberty Hall to help with the distribution. From now on the union was able to issue tickets to men and their families for the daily dinners at the union headquarters in Beresford Place. Yet these ventures could not feed everybody; hence the scheme to rescue the "starving children of Dublin" suggested by a group of English suffragists and arranged with Larkin by Mrs. Dora Montefiore, an English social worker.

Six children had already been sent to homes in Surrey when Archbishop Walsh publicly made known his opposition, despite the assurances that had been received that the children would as far as possible be received into Catholic homes and schools and in every case be placed under the spiritual care of the local parish priest. This was the cue for the unleashing of a disgraceful campaign of vilification against the promoters of the scheme by the more fanatical members of the priesthood, especially when it became known that offers to take 350 more children were still awaiting fulfillment. But the attacks were not confined to "scoundrels in clerical garb" (Connolly's phrase). Maud Gonne, supporter of the Transport Union, whose public activities were latterly confined to canvassing for the Ladies School Dinner committee, incurred the wrath of Larkin for her support of Walsh's position. Extraordinary scenes followed when priests from Westland Row Church played on the apprehensions of mothers as a group of 50 children, ranging in age from 5 to 13 years, were being washed at the Tara Street baths on October 22 in preparation for the journey. Only 19 children got as far as the steamer at Kingstown, but there too victory lay with the priests, no child leaving on that occasion. But despite the vigilance of the clergy and the picketing of steamers, another 18 children were gotten off safely at the North Wall. On October 24 Larkin's sister, Delia, was foiled in her attempt when the clergy, with fanatics of the Nationalist, sectarian and anti-Larkin Ancient Order of Hibernians in tow, intimidated parents with cries of "socialism," this at a time when the newspapers were reporting an increase in street begging by children. The last attempt of the union to carry out its humanitarian endeavors also ended in failure when several children were stopped at Kingsbridge Station and Francis Sheehy-Skeffington, the well-known Dublin pacifist and socialist who was detested by Nationalist politicians for his eccentric radicalism, was manhandled by 100 vigilantes and clergy in an action that did little credit to the spirit of lay Catholicism in Dublin in 1913.

Though the union might seem to be winning the hearts and minds of many at home and abroad, it now appeared to be losing the struggle itself. It had agreed to every proposal to sit down and negotiate with the employers, but the latter refused the offer on each occasion. It could not induce the parliamentary representatives to intervene on their behalf, for the latter declined to take sides. And the influence of the most respected man in Dublin, Archbishop Walsh, was also denied them since he had publicly owned that the employers had been to some extent justified in hesitating to enter into an agreement until they obtained guarantees of good faith from the ITGWU, which in the view of employers could only come after the removal of Larkin." Some comfort could be taken however in the new-found concern of the clergy for the material welfare of the children, a distress fund having been organized by the Archbishop that by mid-November had collected over £3,000. But on the labor front, employers had begun to import "free" laborers to move the enormous amount of goods that had been accumulating along the quays—timber for T. & C. Martin, barley for Guinness's. These latter companies were among the first to use the scabs arriving in late October from England and the rural parts of Leinster. Within a month some 500 were employed in the city, and by the end of the year estimates of the number ranged as high as 900. This strike-breaking action (of a type that had often characterized English disputes when employers hired Irish scabs) naturally heightened tempers in the city and led to renewed acts of violence and intimidation. On December 25 an attempt was made to drown a sergeant of the DMP who had interfered with picketers. He was pushed into the Liffey and his rescuers were obstructed. Although the ring-leader was arrested, he in turn was rescued by force from the arms of the police. Many of the "free" laborers carried arms (the repeal of the Arms Act in 1906 having rendered the control of firearms for personal use a dead letter in Ireland), and on one tragic occasion a shot fired by one of them wounded young Alice Brady as she was returning home from Liberty Hall with her allowance of food. She died shortly after and the funeral on January 4 provided the occasion for a great labor demonstration in which 500 members of the Larkinite Irish Women Workers' Union marched in the cortege. Equally tragic were the murders of two scabs, one found drowned in Alexandra Basin on January 15, the other beaten to death on a Dublin street two days later. Much of the "free" labor had been pro-vided through the British Shipping Federation, and consequently the ITGWU felt no compunction in breaking the earlier agreement with the Steampacket Company when it called out the dock laborers on November 12. For the next four weeks the cross-channel trade of the port of Dublin was completely paralyzed, and a general resumption was not effected until the dispute began to draw to a close in late January 1914. Meanwhile, work-ers who had managed to avoid becoming involved in the great struggle chose this mo-ment to demonstrate their support for the strikers by striking in sympathy with them. Such was the action of 200 manure workers of Morgan, Mooney, and Company and 100 tobacco workers throughout the city.

In December the general feeling began to develop that the struggle was winding down. Negotiation was again in the air, and though a conference between the two sides arranged, finally, by Archbishop Walsh broke down on the employers' refusal to reinstate *all* employees, the union was now prepared to abandon the sympathetic strike as its part of a bargain. The port was opening up again as some men resumed work on the quays and "free" laborers continued to arrive. The manure workers who had left work in No-vember returned at the end of December on the employers' terms. Larkin's call to the British Trade Union Congress for a general strike in support of the Dublin struggle was rejected in favor of further negotiation, which when held on December 18 only saw the confirmation of the employers' refusal to guarantee rehiring by promising to discharge the "free" laborers. Financial support from England was also dwindling, though the food ships continued to arrive until the end of January thus enabling the union to maintain its free-meal service. But both food supplies and union funds now ran out, the *Irish Times* reporting on February 2 that no strike pay had been doled out at Liberty Hall—two loaves of bread for each applicant was all that remained and this on the day when the children who had been "deported" in the previous October began to return to their fam-ilies and the special duty RIC men were returning to their barracks throughout the country.

Few men gave up the fight in December, but as January progressed there were signs of surrender. The seamen and firemen returned to work under threat of their British union officials that no further strike payments would be made if they continued the dis-pute. The ITGWU as much as admitted defeat on January 18 when it advised the men to apply for reinstatement provided they were not obliged to give up their union member-ship.[56] The union also suffered the political defeat of almost all its candidates at the mu-nicipal elections in the same month, a reversal that appeared to endorse the violent platform condemnations by Lord Mayor Sherlock and his UIL colleagues of those "clev-er socialists prostituting the labor movement" who had insulted priests, attacked nuns, deported children, and were indifferent to religion. Most of the men who had left the

DUTC works at Inchicore in sympathy with the coachbuilders' refusal to repair wrecked tramcars now submitted, as did increasing numbers of tramway employees, farm workers, and practically all the men in the employ of the shipping companies. The Master Builders, intransigent to the last, continued to insist throughout January on the "document" even though their vendetta with the laborers idled thousands of tradesmen who had no connection with Larkin's union. The Masters were in a favorable position, given the usual slackness in building operations at the height of winter, though their action roused Alderman Kelly to threaten them with direct labor by Corporation workmen on municipal construction sites. Finally, on January 27, in his presidential address to the Dublin Chamber of Commerce, W. M. Murphy triumphantly announced the "defeat of syndicalism." The men returned on the employers' terms, though not all were obliged to sign the "document." This latter humiliation was reserved for the 2,000 builders' laborers who surrendered to the Master Builders' Association on February 1, pledging not to remain in or become a member of the ITGWU, to disavow the sympathetic strike and obey all instructions of the employer. With that settlement an additional 3,000 men of some 160 firms—1,200 carpenters, 700 bricklayers, 600 painters, 500 plasterers and plumbers, electricians, stonecutters, and sawyers—returned the building trade to normal. The longest to hold out were the ever-faithful carters, who as late as January 29 were still refusing to load material bound for Jacob's biscuit factory, which company implacably waited till mid-March to take on hundreds of discharged women employees. The carters were also the ones to suffer most in the long run, for the vacancies were far fewer in that line of work, the employers having decided to retain large numbers of "free" laborers. Moreover, some cartage firms now went over to motorized lorries for conveying goods in an ominous development that put the carter in much the same position of restricted opportunity as the advent of the motor taxi and private automobile had placed the jarvey.

It is pointless to ask who won the battle. There could be no real victory for anyone after such an exhausting and bitter 22-week struggle, with nearly 2 million man-days of work lost, five persons killed* and hundreds injured, the social and economic life of the city entirely dislocated, the trade of the port crippled under staggering blows, over £1 million lost to businessmen, and untold expenses incurred by the government for police and military duty—all this in addition to losses by ratepayers owing to destruction of property and to landlords for nonpayment of rents. It is strange to read that someone actually profited from the struggle—the Poor Law Guardians of the South Dublin Union, who were glad to be able to report at their December meeting that the workhouse then contained 355 fewer pauper children than at the same time in the preceding year, the result allegedly of food and money distributed to the poor by Larkin's union. The working class, or rather the 12,000 or so men and women of the Transport Union allied to several thousand more in other organizations, had also suffered cruelly. They and their families had endured loss of wages, lack of food, the abuse of their pastors, the batons of the police, and, for the unfortunate few, the toils of imprisonment. Some others faced the choice of seeking work in England or continued poverty at home due to unemployment: as late as the end of March 1914 it was estimated that 4,000 workers still awaited reinstatement in their former jobs.

*These deaths (of Nolan and Byrne, two "free" laborers, and Alice Brady) do not include another casualty, James Byrne, a Transport Union official in Kingstown who was arrested in October, went on hunger strike, and died of pneumonia after his release.

The lockout had also revealed the paralysis that was undermining the social conscience of the city. Even William Martin Murphy himself, by no means the worst of employers, had conceded at the opening of these tragic events that the plight of the unorganized workers in the city left much to be desired: "I consider that some employers in Dublin have bred 'Larkinism' by the neglect of their men," he reminded his fellow employers in the Dublin Chamber of Commerce. The *Irish Times*, also no friend of the ITGWU, drew the same moral on several occasions: "The classes have been too uncurious about one another's welfare and ways of life. . . . The employers and the comfortable public of Dublin have not done their whole duty by the working classes." And in a final comment as the men returned to work, the paper brought attention once more to facts that the "comfortable public of Dublin" had ignored:

> . . . The unrest which made the employment of such conditions [the sympathetic strike] possible had real and urgent causes. The brooding discontents which exploded in the mad attempt to "hold up" Dublin gathered force and volume in the pestilential atmosphere of the Dublin slums . . . it is a cynical commentary on our social sense that we needed the stimulus of the strike to realise the squalor and misery which, in the last analysis, produced it.[57]

Just how great the cynicism and how widespread the squalor was in this period was revealed a few days later when the forbidding details of the Dublin Housing Inquiry were made public. Perhaps the greatest failure of conscience was to be found among the Irish parliamentary representatives, who to a man (Redmond, Dillon, and the members for the Dublin constituencies included) voted with their Liberal allies to defeat (233 to 45) a Labour party amendment deploring the fact that the Royal Address had contained no reference to the recent labor disturbances in the Irish capital. Their ineffective neutrality policy during the great lockout was finally revealed as latent hostility when P. J. Brady, the member for St. Stephen's Green Division, chose the same occasion to damn the activities of the Dublin "syndicalists" as the worst enemy of "responsible" Trade Unionism. But disinterest finally won the day: "My colleagues and I want to forget these five sad months in Dublin," concluded Brady,[58] a condition most likely to be realized now that the prospect of home rule was capturing the headlines in the spring of 1914. The bishops also pronounced on the epic conflict, but their plea in a joint pastoral letter for those "who have not received a fair share of the wealth they do so much to produce" came much too late in the day. But at least the pastoral did not descend to the fatuity of the ubiquitous Fr. Bernard Vaughan, who lectured the Lord Mayor and citizens on his favorite topic, the "socialist nonsense," only weeks after the men returned to work, reporting that he had discovered "a wonderful spirit growing in Dublin—a brotherly feeling between employer and employee"[59]—a statement that carried as much conviction as the claim by P. J. Brady, MP, that the Irish party had always been a labor party.

As for the Irish Transport and General Workers' Union, its members had stood up to the Dublin capitalists with unparalleled discipline and courage and with something of the ferocity that had distinguished the elemental outbursts of their rural compatriots against the exactions of Irish landlords a generation earlier. Yet the union had also paid a bitter price in demonstrating the purpose and resolve Larkin had brought to Irish trade unionism. Nevertheless, with its new strength it was able to survive a capitulation that many felt should have been blamed on British trade union executives for their opting for discipline over revolution. But any criticism of the latter must be tempered by recognition of the generous support in money and food that flowed unstintingly to relieve the distress of thousands of Irish families during their dark winter of discontent. The departure of Larkin for the United States at the end of 1914 brought the union under the control of his chief lieutenant, James Connolly, in whose hands it became the instrument of a higher purpose than the pursuit of better wages and conditions of labor. Connolly's fusion of the nationality and labor questions was foreshadowed in the creation of a paramilitary contingent of workers—the Irish Citizen Army—to defend the interests of Dublin labor against rapacious capitalists and baton-wielding police. Organized in late November 1913, when the labor troubles were drawing to a close, the "army" took little part in the events of that year. But the Citizen Army, raised in 1913 to advance the cause of labor, fought in 1916 to further the cause of Ireland. For Connolly the two aims were indistinguishable. His death in the Rebellion added a luster to the ITGWU that played no small part in enabling it to become in a few more years the largest association of organized workers in a new Ireland.

The remainder of the story is briefly told. Dublin, having emerged from a war of the classes, soon had to adjust to the war of nations. That great war brought no quickening of the motor of industry, for the city had little to offer besides recruits for the infantry. In fact, the outbreak led to considerable unemployment in the building trade for men and the clothing industry for women. The employment opportunities were in Britain while in much of Ireland distress committees continued to operate, and when these ceased in 1916 assistance from the National Relief Fund was necessary, particularly for those women unlucky enough not to get the few jobs available in Dublin: making shirts under War Office contracts. The controls on alcohol production also greatly affected the staple industry of Dublin—brewing and distilling—while the shipping trade suffered when vessels were commandeered for war purposes. And despite the continued requests of local politicians, Dublin received only a very small share in munitions work.

The war also resulted in a sharp increase in the cost of living, which prompted tradesmen and other workers to seek increased wages or war bonuses. The second half of 1915 saw this new round of wage demands involving dockers, carters, seamen and firemen of the shipping companies, bookbinders, bakers, printers, and building tradesmen. Some of their claims resulted in strikes, but in general the demands of the men prevailed owing to the increased cost of foodstuffs. The most serious dispute and one that gave an echo of "1913" was another strike of the dockers in October 1915. The rapid increase in the cost of living had prompted the ITGWU to demand an advance in wages to 7s. per day (from 5s. 8d.) for the several hundred quay laborers in the employ of the shipping companies. When negotiations fell through, Connolly called out his men on October 11 in a strike that immediately received the support of several hundred carters who refused to handle goods at the company sheds and added a wage demand of their own for good measure. The Employers' Federation, now faced with the materialization of a ghost that was thought to have been laid to rest in February 1914, recommended to the Master Carriers that they lock out the carters. Fortunately, the Masters declined the advice and compromised with the men, while the personal attention of Sir George Askwith also induced all but one of the shipping companies to conclude an agreement on October 23 that won a 37s. week of 60 hours for the dockers. But the City of Dublin Steam Packet covering the Dublin-Liverpool run remained as obdurate as ever and refused to comply. Their laborers endured a lone six-month struggle before Askwith finally arbitrated the issue on June 27 and secured for the men (from May 18, 1916) the wages won by their fellow workers in the previous October.[60]

More widespread in effect was the dispute in the building trade in April 1916 when about 1,800 tradesmen (plasterers, bricklayers, and carpenters) struck for wage and hour concessions. This of course threw another 1,000 laborers out of work through indirect involvement. After a five-week strike the men accepted arbitration that gave them a penny an hour extra (double the employers' offer) and a reduction to the 50-hour week. At 10d. per hour the building tradesmen for the first time got beyond the long-maintained weekly wage barrier of £2. This settlement was certainly opportune, for by the time the strike was settled in mid-May the dust was beginning to settle on the pile of rubble that was O'Connell Street after the fires and shells of Easter Week. The Dublin workers, a few of whom had given their lives to restructure Irish government, were to be assigned the more modest task of reconstructing the Irish capital. The smouldering fire of Irish nationalism and the gathering clouds of revolt that catapulted the city of Dublin to the center of the political stage in Ireland are the central matter of the next and last chapter.

9

War and Rebellion

I have been some five years in this House; and the conclusion with which I leave it is that no cause, however just, will find support, no wrong however pressing or apparent, will find redress here unless backed up by force.

> Resignation speech of MICHAEL DAVITT in House of Commons,
> October 25, 1899

The spirit of what today is called Sinn Feinism is mainly composed of the old hatred and distrust of the British connection, always noticeable in all classes and in all places, varying in degree and finding different ways of expression, but always *there*, as the background of Irish politics and character.

> Evidence of AUGUSTINE BIRRELL, Chief Secretary for Ireland, at the
> Royal Commission on the Rebellion in Ireland, May 19, 1916

IN THE early years of this century, the forces of Irish political disaffection began to gather in and radiate from Dublin to an extent that the Irish capital became sharply distinguished from the rest of Ireland for the sustained vigor with which the idea of British rule in Ireland came under attack. Hitherto the countryside had been the locus of discontent as agrarian agitation, often accompanied by crime and violence, ranged tenant farmer (almost always Irish and Catholic) against landlord (usually Anglo-Irish and Protestant) in a struggle to achieve purely economic gains, viz., lower rents or transfer of ownership. The progressive settlement of these questions by land acts and land purchase acts between 1881 and 1903 greatly improved the social condition of the Irish tenantry and enrolled the farmers as firm supporters of those who were working for the peaceful and constitutional settlement of outstanding Irish problems. Chief among the latter was home rule, which by its very nature implied that Irish self-government should arrive via the legislative sanction of the British parliament. This was the position maintained by the Irish parliamentary party and promoted with little difficulty throughout the country (excluding, naturally, the Unionist strongholds in the northeastern sector). There was, of course, an alternative political attitude that envisaged something other than a political connection under the Crown or the indissoluble union demanded by Orangemen. This was the republican tradition handed down by Wolfe Tone a century before and later nurtured by the abortive Fenian episode.

The decade of the 1890s in Ireland was one of revival among literary, cultural, and new nationalist groups. The Gaelic League, despite its avowedly nonpolitical aims, could hardly fail to attract the forward elements of a more uncompromising nationalism than could be comprehended by the moderate constitutional objectives of the official Nationalists whose nominees dominated the Dublin Corporation. Furthermore, the futile squabbles among parliamentarians and their supporters, originating in the deposition of Parnell as leader of the Irish party in 1890, had operated somewhat to alienate the younger generation from the parliamentary tradition that since O'Connell's day looked to Westminster for the working out of Ireland's political destiny. This trend was most noticeable in Dublin, where the more concrete goal of the Irish parliamentary party—the resolution of the land question—offered little to attract the interest of the urban masses.

It was natural that the capital should play the leading part in the more demonstrative aspects of Irish nationalism. It had historic traditions as the seat of the independent (even if Ascendancy) Irish parliament in the late eighteenth century. All the great state trials of rebel Irishmen took place in Dublin, and the headquarters of every nationalist body since O'Connell's Catholic Association were located there. The annual rituals of nationalist sentiment, the annual conventions of the National League, were held there. Dublin, besides, was a hotbed of sedition and the forum for every manifestation of political extremism. The city now began to recapture the limelight of nationalist revivalism when the centenary of the Rebellion of 1798 stirred the becalmed sea of Irish politics. For the heroism recalled was the attempt to sever the British connection in bloody revolt. Though that event was sufficiently remote in 1898 to be celebrated even by the constitutional spirits of the Irish parliamentary party, there were some who became infused with more than the usual rhetorical flourishes on that occasion. Though small in number and having neither organization nor support, the separatists cells attracted notoriety by their appeal to the most atavistic national aspirations of Irish men and women. Their strength lay in an unbending resolve to claim custody of the separatist and republican tradition bequeathed by the United Irishmen and measure political action by that standard. It lay in an unfailing desire to regard England's difficulty as Ireland's opportunity. As self-appointed guardians of the national honor, they would make of "flunkeyism" a major element in the national demonology. As rebels without guns, they would strike at England's power by demoralizing her would-be Irish soldiers. As revolutionaries in the making, they would conspire to make the bid that the tradition demanded—the blood sacrifice of revolt.

These aggressive spirits were considered dangerous only by the super-sensitive secret society experts in Dublin Castle. Their milieu was the city, their instruments the public meeting, the conspirator's cellar, the antienlistment handbill, the seditious press. It was they who initiated the scheme of erecting a memorial to Wolfe Tone in the centenary year at the southern end of Grafton Street. Only the foundation stone was laid, the project succumbing to the greater interest surrounding the Parnellites' proposal for a monument to commemorate the dead Chief—a symbolic victory for the forces of moderation. But of far greater advantage to their purposes than the transient effusions of the centenary celebrations was the approaching crisis in South Africa following years of imperialist pressure against the Boer republic of the Transvaal. Here again republicans and their sympathizers were able to capitalize on the endemic anti-British feeling now fanned to fever pitch by the imminent imperial assault on the nationality of the Boers. An Irish Transvaal Committee was formed and attracted a broad support from moderates and militants alike, all united only in their anti-imperialism. Its more extreme supporters were the republican followers of Major John McBride, one of the few Irishmen to fight on the side of the Boers, and James Connolly, then busily canvassing support for his Irish Socialist Republican party. These two were joined on public platforms by the doyen of Fenianism, John O'Leary, by the aged bard of Young Ireland, T. D. Sullivan, by the Gaelic sports enthusiast, Michael Cusack, as well as the poet Yeats, Maud Gonne, Michael Davitt (soon to resign his parliamentary seat in protest against the attack on the Boers), William Redmond, MP, and several members of Dublin Corporation. Their mouthpiece (assuming the opinions of such disparate elements could be expressed as one voice) was Arthur Griffith's *United Irishman*. The authorities were not unaware of the potential for trouble from these disloyal elements. Reviewing the situation a year later, Commissioner J.J. Jones of the DMP informed Dublin Castle that "The Irish Republican Socialists [*sic*] are a bad lot. . . . The Irish Transvaal Committee embraces all that is dangerous in Dublin."[1] To muster support for the Boer cause, the Transvaal Committee organized one of the largest public meetings held in Dublin for many years, on Sunday, October 1, 1899, at Beresford Place, a favorite open-air venue adjoining the Custom House.

During the opening weeks of the war, when British armies were on the defensive following early Boer victories, the citizens were treated to a novel outdoor display by the *Nation*. This newspaper had erected an outdoor projection screen in College Green on which was flashed nightly the news of Boer successes, giving the assembled crowd the opportunity to cheer Boer generals and groan at British politicians when their likenesses appeared on the screen, all greatly to the discomfiture of the residents of nearby Trinity College. A few days later the students themselves were goaded into retaliation against the nationalist maligners of Joseph Chamberlain when he arrived in the city to accept an honorary degree from the college. Doubtless Chamberlain was confirmed in the view ascribed to him of regarding Ireland much as he did his gout—"both very detestable and . . . absolutely incurable."

This outpouring of anti-British sentiment ("hostilities" were perforce out of the question) coalesced into a single-minded campaign against recruiting for the army, which effort was conducted both in the pages of *United Irishman* and through the widespread dissemination of antirecruitment handbills that posed the question: "Irishmen, will you keep your country enslaved and under the heels of England by joining the English army, navy or police forces?" The constabulary was singled out for special attention as "traitors" to their country. Another stratagem employed during 1900 at least gave some merriment—a green handbill stating on the authority of a priest that any Irish Catholic who died taking part in "England's Robber War" must "suffer the loss of his soul." When the Irish members were questioned in the Commons on this elusive theology, William Redmond (who was later to die in British uniform in another war) suggested facetiously that it could only have been the work of the "Orange" party. Yet the army reports for the Dublin Area show that the years of the Boer war (1899–1902) furnished the highest number of Irish recruits to the regular army. Even the national celebration of the rebellious deeds of Wolfe Tone during the centenary year did nothing to reduce enlistments, the figures for Dublin exceeding by about 50 percent and 25 percent, respectively, those for 1896 and 1897. And more embarrassing still to patriots, Dublin not only provided on the average over one-quarter of total Irish regular army enlistments in each year but also gave Britain far more soldiers than did "loyal" Belfast. Idle hands and empty stomachs are a powerful antidote to patriotic idealism, however, and there were more of these in Dublin than in any other part of the country.

General harassment by the police soon quieted the more disruptive aspects of nationalist activity, and the end of the war in South Africa removed an effective means of concentrating Irish opinion against Imperial rule. The seditious elements returned to their "cellars" and politics adapted once more to the plodding pace set by the parliamentarians. Yet the rebellious activism of these years only lay below the surface during the ensuing years of industrial unrest and political hopes. The forces that had emerged soon became identified (and not always accurately) with the Irish-Ireland, anti-English movement championed by Arthur Griffith and after 1905 known as Sinn Fein. Thus, individuals as different in temper and purpose as the revolutionaries of the Irish Republican Brotherhood (IRB), the language revivalists of the Gaelic League, and the sports enthusiasts of the Gaelic Athletic Association, along with the followers of Griffith, were dubbed Sinn Feiners by the Irish government at Dublin Castle whether or not all of them actually subscribed to the Sinn Fein principles of Griffith. What united them was the general de-Anglicizing crusade begun in *United Irishman* and its practical results in opposing royal visits, refusing toasts to the health of the King, and, most of all, maintaining vigorously the movement to reduce the enlistments of Irishmen in the British army. Hence it became necessary for nationalists at all times to heighten the distinction between things English and things Irish: from the politicians who insisted that no Irish nationalist take office under the Crown to the cranks who would have the organ grinders convert the "Galloping Major" to "A Nation Once Again." Thus, the freedom of the city was assured for political prisoners (P. A. McHugh, MP) and former rebels (E. O'Meagher Condon); streets acquired bilingual nameplates; Irish bricks had to be used on Corporation contracts and Gaelic letterhead on municipal correspondence. This could be taken too far, of course, as Sinn Fein alderman Walter Cole discovered when he had his name printed in Gaelic on one of his business vans; refusing to pay the 10s. fine for this offense, he suffered distraint of that value of his goods.

The anti-recruiting campaign outlasted the Boer War and was regarded with some concern by the Irish administration at Dublin Castle. In his report for 1905, the Director of Recruiting also felt constrained to make special mention of Ireland, where press articles and seditious posters broadcast continual hostility to the British army. The campaign was cited as responsible for the marked reduction in the numbers of recruits after 1904. There was in fact for the decade before the First World War a decline in the number of soldiers (NCOs and men) whose country of birth was Ireland—from 30,654 in 1904 to 20,780 in 1913. The decline was general for all four home countries, but the rate of reduction of Irish-born in the ranks (32 percent) greatly exceeded the rate for Scottish-born (21 percent) and English- and Welsh-born (11 percent) during the period. Thus, there was a corresponding decrease in the proportion of Irish-born soldiers to total regular army strength—from 11.5 percent in 1904 to 9.4 percent in 1913. Nevertheless, Ireland, in keeping with her martial tradition, was contributing more than her share of men to the service, for the number of Irish-born soldiers in all years exceeded the combined total for Scotland and Wales (areas of greater combined population), and to that number might be added a fair proportion of those several thousand Roman Catholics in the army who were of English birth though doubtless of Irish origin.[2]

It would be unwise to assume that the activities of Sinn Feiners and others were

TABLE 29. Numbers of Recruits Raised for the Regular Army, 1899–1913.[a]

	DUBLIN RECRUITING AREA	BELFAST RECRUITING AREA	IRELAND (total)	SCOTLAND[b]	WALES	ENGLAND
1899	1,016	795	3,987	4,387	985	30,149
1900	1,054	1,188	4,040	5,323	1,063	36,553
1901	1,209	748	3,778	5,164	1,251	33,906
1902	1,232	798	4,691	5,363	2,257	38,440
1903	—data not given in usable form—					
1904	869	620	3,604	4,159	1,277	31,391
1905	1,125	411	3,166	3,842	1,321	25,993
1906	764	362	2,739	3,781	1,125	27,622
1907	791	620	2,949	3,873	841	25,853
1908	882	801	3,265	4,207	744	27,662
1909	657	505	2,727	3,241	603	25,878
1910	505	293	2,069	2,723	444	20,275
1911	726	260	2,549	2,686	600	22,956
1912	899	286	2,756	2,835	683	23,451
1913	832	380	2,655	2,376	653	21,860

[a]These figures omit a small number of men who were not included in the area enumeration compiled by the army. On the average, this amounts to an additional 1,300 recruits per year for the period shown (country of origin not given) or slightly over 3 percent of the total.
[b]The year 1899 was the first in at least two decades in which the number of Scottish recruits exceeded the Irish.
SOURCE: *Parliamentary Papers*—General Annual Reports on the British Army (annual reports of recruiting).

alone, if at all, responsible for the decrease in Irish recruitment. It should be noted that the population of Ireland was still in decline owing to continued emigration, while elsewhere numbers were growing. Besides, the increased prosperity of Irish farming families as well as improved conditions for agricultural laborers probably worked to deny to the military some of the young men who once would have had little other option at age 19 than to emigrate or don a uniform for seven years.[3] Also, from 1910 onward the new Labour Exchanges may have had a similar effect in some urban areas. But such qualifying factors had only slight impact on the splendid record of the Dublin recruiting district. In 1905, the year in which Sinn Fein as a movement was formally established in the capital, the area gave an exceptionally high number of recruits to the army and by 1912 had managed to exceed for the third time the number recruited in 1904. Indeed, regular army recruitment from the Dublin area for the years 1899 to 1913 inclusive (a total of 12,561 men) approached 87 percent of the number for Glasgow district, with its huge catchment area, and exceeded the number recruited in Edinburgh by over 1,700 men for the same period. The contrast with Belfast* (see Table 29) is especially noteworthy and must have rankled the Irish Irelanders as much as the embarrassing statistic that some 30,000 of their fellow-countrymen had helped to defeat the Boers. But success in the antirecruiting campaign was less important at this early stage than the propaganda effect and nuisance value of openly seditious behavior by those who had enrolled in a movement that was fast becom-

*The breakdown of recruitment by provinces also shows Ulster trailing Leinster and Munster in military zeal, though this, naturally, is indicative more of the greater opportunities for employment in that loyalist province than any disinclination to meet the needs of the empire. The numbers of men reporting to local recruiting and regimental districts for service in the regular army (i.e., excluding the militia) are given below. These dising a school for rebels. It was these more extreme elements of Irish opinion that Augustine Birrell, the Chief Secretary, had in mind in 1916 when he told the Royal Commission on the Rebellion: "I always thought that I was very ignorant of what was actually going on in the minds, and in the cellars if you like, of the Dublin population. I was always exceedingly nervous about that. Therefore, I distinguish very much in my own mind between the state of things going on in Dublin and the state of things going on in the rest of the country."[4]

A large military force was always maintained in Ireland, and for obvious reasons. There were throughout between 20,000 and 25,000 troops of the Irish Command, about four to five times the numbers garrisoned in Scotland. These were distributed throughout the four provinces and commanded from eight regimental districts from which were recruited the replacements for some of the most famous territorial regiments of the British army: the Connaught Rangers (Galway), the Royal Irish Regiment (Clonmel), the Munster Fusiliers (Tralee). Naas was the headquarters of another famous unit, the Royal Dublin Fusiliers, whose origins could be traced back to 1645 and whose battle honors were won in India under Clive and at Lucknow and, lately, in exploits against the Boers.* But Irish-born soldiers usually served overseas, and one was far more likely to see a South Wales Borderer, a Royal West Kenter, or a Scots Fusilier in the streets of Dublin or elsewhere in Ireland than one of the "Pals" or "Faugh-a-Ballaghs." About 4,000 troops were quartered in barracks throughout metropolitan Dublin—including infantry at the Royal, Richmond, and Beggar's Bush barracks; cavalry at Marlboro' and Portobello; artillery at Islandbridge—while another 4,000 or so were stationed comfortably close at the Curragh of Kildare. Though used to enforce eviction decrees in country districts during the 1880s, the military were only rarely employed in the capital, but their very presence on the streets—a visible manifestation of English power—was anathema to all shades of nationalist opinion. Foreign visitors may have been attracted by the novelty and picturesqueness of street scenes as groups of soldiers carrying canes or whips swaggered by in scarlet jackets, tight-fitting trousers and top boots, a tiny skull-cap held in place by a strap under the chin. To Irish nationalists, however, the nocturnal levee of British soldiery along O'Connell and Westmoreland Streets represented an immoral incubus on the city and a lasting source of fear and resentment. "When tourists came to Dublin and saw these streets," complained one angry councillor, "they were apt to go away under the impression that they had been in a market in Cairo." The Corporation, of course, was powerless to restrict the perambulations of the soldiery. Yet thousands of natives no less than tourists must have enjoyed those occasions when all the trappings of imperial power and privilege were on show: streets lined with soldiers as the monarch made the ritual passage

---

tricts are here grouped by province, and in the case of Ulster at least, the figures should furnish a reasonably accurate guide to the provincial origin of Irish recruits.

Province	Population in 1901 (in millions)	Total recruits to regular army, 1899 to 1913 inclusive
Ulster	1.582	13,739
Leinster	1.153	19,000
Munster	1.076	12,567
Connaught	0.647	2,321
Ireland	4.458	47,627

*The arch at the northwest corner of St. Stephen's Green was erected to commemorate their valor in the South African War.

from Kingstown harbor to the Viceregal Lodge in the Phoenix Park in 1900, 1903, 1904, and 1911; the visit of the channel squadron (eight battleships and four cruisers under Vice Admiral Lord Charles Beresford) in connection with Horse Show Week in 1904, with 2,000 marines and sailors enveloping the city to make way for citizens touring the anchored vessels; the arrival of the Home Fleet with its impressive dreadnoughts in 1911 and 1913.

The years following the Boer war saw little political unrest in Ireland. The capital too was undisturbed by nationalist agitators, the police being well able to handle any disorderly scenes such as those that usually occurred at City Hall or elsewhere when loyal addresses hung in the balance or "flunkeys" needed to be run to ground. There was never any reason to call out the military, and when this finally did happen it arose not from the threat of rebellious nationalists but rather to protect supplies of food and fuel from rioting workers during the labor troubles of 1913. But there were many frustrated nationalists smarting under an alien rule that had endured for a century and seemed unlikely to end in a manner consonant with the aspirations of a younger and more radical generation of Irishmen. Hence the mounting show of support for Sinn Fein, manifested not least by its appearance as a political party in Dublin Corporation after 1905. And the Irish parliamentary party could do little in the circumstances to arrest an apparent decline in its own support. Their Liberal allies, returned to Westminster with an overwhelming majority in 1906, felt little compulsion to cede them no more than a derisory down-payment on Gladstonian home rule. The abortive measure, the Irish Council Bill of 1907, reserved so much to Imperial authority as to be regarded by nationalists as an insult. Though there was no serious attempt to contest the mandate now wielded for almost a generation by the aging Nationalist party, there were ominous stirrings that boded ill for that party's continued political control in Ireland. For the cream of the younger generation was being attracted to all those movements asserting pride in race, language, culture, and nationality—Gaelic League, Gaelic Athletic Association, Dungannon and Oliver Bond clubs, Daughters of Erin, Sinn Fein, and their like. And in the background stood the violent men of the IRB silently waiting on England's difficulty.

The political fortunes of the Irish party took a turn for the better in 1910 when the elections of that year rendered the Liberal government dependent on Irish votes. Popular opinion was still on the side of the parliamentarians, and even their Irish opponents were now constrained to give them a fair hearing. On Sunday, March 31, 1912, one of the greatest of nationalist gatherings took place in Dublin in anticipation of the home rule bill to be introduced in the Commons some days later. An estimated 100,000 persons from all over Ireland assembled in O'Connell Street to be assured by their representatives that Irish self-government was to become a reality. John Redmond appropriately took the platform at the Parnell memorial while his chief lieutenant, John Dillon, addressed the crowd at Fr. Mathew's statue. At the Abbey Street platform, separatist (Patrick Pearse) and constitutionalist (Joe Devlin, MP) both spoke. At the "students" platform near the O'Connell Monument, the crowd was addressed in Gaelic by Professor Eoin MacNeill and heard Michael Davitt's son declaim, "We want home rule" and, to the dismay of some listeners, "We trust the Irish party."

Not everyone indulged in this show of allegiance to the party. The suffragists of the Irish Women's Franchise League were up in arms at the lack of a woman suffrage clause in the Bill: they had showered the crowd with Votes for Women leaflets from their offices in O'Connell Street after having been roughly handled by Nationalist stewards in the streets below. It bears recalling that these progressive women of the capital were yet another element in the increasing militancy that was now bestirring Ireland once more. In earlier years their activities had been confined to hiring "sandwich-men" to carry their placards throughout the city. They seemed respectable enough in 1910 to win a Dublin Corporation resolution in support of the Conciliation Bill. In the same year Mrs. Pankhurst spoke in middle-class Rathmines in the company of Tom Kettle and with Alderman M'Walter deputizing for the Lord Mayor. A year later, on April 4, another resolution passed the municipal council requesting the Lord Mayor to journey to London and, as was his right, present a petition to parliament in favor of women's suffrage. The occasion did not endear the Sinn Fein members to the vocal feminists in the gallery when Alderman Kelly, supported by Councillor Cosgrave, dismissed the move as a "class movement" (for no woman living in a tenement would get a vote) and a waste of money. Scorn, derision, and abuse were added to these strictures as the ladies, led in Dublin by Mrs. Hannah Sheehy-Skeffington, began to emulate their suffragist sisters in England. At the height of the agitation in 1912, Bishop O'Dwyer of Limerick came out against votes for women in his Lenten pastoral. Cardinal Logue, speaking at Maynooth on June 25, condemned those "masculine females who wanted not alone to be equal to men in everything but to supplant them if possible" and even found a few words of praise for Trinity College, which had avoided, in contrast to the new National University in Dublin (UCD), the "unseemly mixture of sexes." Much more unseemly were the feminist outrages in 1912 and 1913: a hatchet-throwing incident involving Prime Minister Asquith, as he rode with John Redmond through the city to address a Nationalist meeting at the Theatre Royal; the attempt by two women (allegedly "English militants") to set fire to the theater on the same day; the window-smashing at government buildings and at offices of the United Irish League; the attack on the Dublin home of John Dillon. This latter incident resulted in a trial at which Dillon, so far forgetting his own fearless and rambunctious days as an agrarian agitator in the 1880s, declared that "militancy is disgraceful."[5]

Militancy, however, became the order of the day, and in the course of the next few years all the hopes of moderate nationalists were to be shattered as the political initiative passed from constitutional elements into the hands of extremists. The Irish party fatally undermined its position in the country at large in the spring of 1914 by submitting under extreme government pressure to special treatment for Ulster and agreeing to the temporary exclusion of six northeastern counties from the operation of home rule. It had also lost much of its credibility in Dublin labor circles through its aloofness to the bitter industrial struggles of the previous year. And to add to the party's troubles, it seemed certain that the establishment of paramilitary formations in the country precluded any peaceful settlement of the national question. In the north the Ulster Volunteers pledged themselves to protect the special interests of Ulster Unionism, and in the south the Sinn Fein-IRB-sponsored Irish Volunteers resolved to defend the larger interests of Ireland. Dublin labor, as we have seen, made its own special contribution to these portentous events when James Connolly and his comrades established the Citizen Army late in 1913. Thereafter the citizens were treated to the unusual sight of workingmen gathering at Liberty hall with staves and hurleys for the drilling exercises conducted at Croydon Park, the ITGWU grounds in the Marino district of Clontarf. Soon the hurleys were exchanged for rifles, and W.M. Murphy for one was glad that this show of force had not been present during the tension-filled days of September 1913.

By July 1914 the nationalist "troops" in Dublin numbered about 5,000 Volunteers (out of some 180,000 in the country at large) and a few hundred men of the Citizen Army, the latter now pledged also to protect greater interests than merely the cause of labor. What gave these developments notoriety in the eyes of the authorities was the appearance of rifles and revolvers in the hands of ordinary citizens in a city that had an unarmed police force. W.M. Murphy, labor's antagonist in 1913, later complained before the Royal Commission on the Rebellion that this development was "one of the most amazing things that could happen in any civilized country outside of Mexico." The consequences were tragically demonstrated on Sunday, July 26, after the successful landing of arms at Howth harbor shortly after noon on that day. This ostentatious daylight version of the earlier secret gun-running episode of the Ulster Volunteers at Larne brought rifles and ammunition to over 1,000 waiting Irish Volunteers. After taking possession, at least 800 men accompanied by a tiny force of helpless RIC proceeded in orderly fashion to march the 8½ miles to the city in a show of their new-found military strength.

Having been advised of the landing by the Howth police, the assistant commissioner of the metropolitan police, W.V. Harrel, acting on his own authority as magistrate, called out a military detachment of 100 King's Own Scottish Borderers from the Royal (now Collins) Barracks to intercept and disarm the Volunteers.[6] Police and soldiers arrived at Clontarf by trams and confronted the Volunteers on the Malahide Road at Clontarf—170 vs. 800. The latter refused to give up their arms and, amazingly, there was only a minor scuffle in which the police seized 19 rifles before the Volunteers jettisoned their plans and disappeared across neighboring fields and yards. A disaster was avoided through the judicious reckoning of the military officer in command, Captain Cobden, who did not feel justified in shedding blood to recover what could only have proved to be a few rifles. Unfortunately, this was not the end of the affair, for tension heightened as the company of soldiers, now joined by another 60 men of the same regiment, arrived at Fairview: false rumors had spread that several Volunteers had been killed in the fracas at Clontarf. It would have been wiser for them had they returned to barracks the way they had come (by tram) or at least been accompanied by police, for stones and abuse followed their march back to town, the crowd being undeterred by the feigning attacks with bayonets all along the way. At 6:30 P.M. the soldiers had turned onto Bachelor's Walk along the northern quays and had reached the corner of Liffey Street opposite the Metal Bridge when the officer in charge gave the order to halt. By this time the men, young and inexperienced soldiers, had become highly excited—2 had been wounded by revolver shots at Clontarf and several had been injured in the stone-throwing. It was apparently the intention of the commanding officer to warn the crowd that unless the stone-throwing ceased his men would be ordered to shoot. The subsequent inquiry produced the usual conflicting evidence from each side: the soldiers maintaining missiles were freely used; Alderman Byrne, who was accompanying the crowd, denying that he saw any stones thrown; and Thomas Johnson of the Irish Trades Union Congress remarking that he had seen more stones thrown at a football match in Belfast without interruption of the game. At any rate the raised-hand warning gesture of Major Haig was misinterpreted by the 30 or so men already told off and ready to fire. Several volleys rang out, leaving 3 dead and at least 35 injured, including 6 women and 4 children under 16 years. It was also established that one of the dead and some of the injured had suffered bayonet wounds. The victims were eventually paid about £800 compensation by the government, but another "massacre" had been added to the national litany of remembrances.

Other casualties of the affair were W. V. Harrel, discharged after nearly 30 years of faithful service to the Crown for having acted *ultra vires* in employing police and military for the prevention of smuggling, and Sir John Ross, the chief commissioner, who resigned to protest his colleague's removal. A quite remarkable turn of events was the refusal of eighteen policemen to obey the order to seize rifles, thus demonstrating a sharper understanding of the legal technicalities involved than did Commissioner Harrel, although their reason for not doing so—that no disarming had been enforced in similar circumstances at Belfast—perhaps revealed a latent sympathy for the Volunteers. For this two constables were dismissed from the force, though they were later restored to duty when the Royal Commission set up to investigate the incident concluded that Harrel's order was illegal. General Cuthbert, commander of troops in Dublin, was strongly criticized for collaborating in the attempt "to put soldiers to a duty which the law did not impose, and would not warrant." The soldiers themselves, now demoted by the mob to "King's Own Sons o'Bitches," did not long have to endure their scorn. Within one month they were to leave the city (to cheering crowds, according to reports) for a far more chilling baptism of fire in France and Belgium alongside the Munster Fusiliers. A curious aftermath of the affair, as reported in the Minutes of the municipal council for 1915, was an attempt by citizens to erect a memorial tablet at Bachelor's Walk, intended, obviously, as a reminder of the heinous crime of British soldiers. Although the Paving Committee gave its approval to the idea, it was scotched by Major General Friend, commander of H.M. Forces in Ireland, who in a letter to the Lord Mayor explained that the proposed inscription was likely to cause disaffection and prejudice recruiting. The erection of a tablet either at the site of the massacre or anywhere else in the city was expressly forbidden.

Harrel received no support from Dublin Castle for his actions, and in the ensuing debate in the House of Commons the Chief Secretary laid the entire blame on the "wholly unnecessary intervention of the military," admitting that the Irish government could not very well discriminate against the southern Volunteers when those in the north were behaving in open defiance of the government,[7] a rationale that Royal Commissioners in 1916 may have had in mind when they declared that that government was "almost unworkable in times of crisis." The Under Secretary, Sir James Dougherty, who handled the day-to-day affairs of the Irish administration, had made frantic but futile efforts on July 26 to contact Harrel (who, incidentally, did not much appear to wish to be contacted) and prevent deployment of the military, believing that armed Volunteers in the streets of Dublin could not be expected by any reasonable man to constitute, in the circumstances of the times, an incitement to riot or disorder. It was a peculiar state of affairs indeed that the Irish government should find itself in the position of virtually condoning armed parading by self-styled military formations. But the Volunteers were not then considered much of a threat, being regarded only as the natural answer to the earlier organization of the Ulster Volunteers. It became apparent only after the outbreak of war that the ostensibly loyal and respectable Irish Volunteers contained a revolutionary core dedicated to using their easily obtained arms to strike a blow for Ireland. The government would come to regret the decision of 1906, urged on it by John Redmond, to allow the Peace Preservation (Ireland) Act to lapse. After 1881 the so-called Arms Act had proven an effective check on the possession and sale of arms because each applicant for a license had to be certified as loyal by the local police inspector. In 1906, however, all restrictions disappeared, rendering it an easy matter to import arms from England or abroad, provided the normal regulations of the civil law were complied with. But in Ireland not even the ordinary excise duty on carrying a gun (which would have enabled the compilation of a firearms register) was levied on the grounds that, as the chief commissioner of police later explained, the people concerned would have refused to take out the license and pay the duty.[8] Thus, unknown quantities of weapons and ammunition entered the country between 1906 and December 1913, at which time a royal proclamation again placed an embargo on the importation of arms. It was in defiance of this decree that the illegal gun-running at Larne and Howth occurred. Yet the government took no action in either case and, more remarkable still, withdrew the December proclamation to produce the rather bizarre situation on August 5, 1914, one day after war had been declared, that allowed the importation of arms once more into Ireland. Most of these arms were destined to be used for seditious purposes—by the Ulster Volunteers, the IRB wing of the Irish Volunteers, and the Citizen Army.

As tensions in Europe heightened in the summer of 1914, the needs of the military became paramount in Ireland as in Great Britain. The antirecruiting campaign, never entirely absent over the years and certainly not materially damaging to army strength as long as only small numbers were needed, took on serious dimensions once the call went out for vastly greater enlistments. Sinn Fein had been especially active during 1913, issuing postcards illustrated with antienlistment cartoons from its headquarters at 6 Harcourt Street. Pamphlets turned up in letter boxes, portraying the imminent destruction of the British Empire in a war with Germany. On one occasion a British army propaganda film being shown in an O'Connell Street theater was treated to the boos, groans, and pro-German cheers of an organized body of nationalists.[9] The extremist elements were still only a small minority of the city's nationalists, and this was demonstrated in September 1914 when the Irish Volunteers split into two factions, the result of Redmond's famous recruiting speech at Woodenbridge, county Wicklow. On that occasion, only two days after home rule received the royal assent on September 18 (though prevented from coming into operation by an accompanying Suspensory Act and the promise of eventual special treatment for six of Ulster's counties), the grateful leader of the Irish parliamentary party urged Irishmen to join in common defense of the Empire. What to Redmond and his colleagues was a debt of honor became in the eyes of separatists tantamount to a national humiliation. About 12,000 Volunteers, barely 6 percent of the total number, refused accordingly to acknowledge Redmond's authority and, retaining their name, set themselves up in opposition to the majority faction that remained loyal to the Irish party and was now styled the National Volunteers. At the outbreak of war the police estimate of the actively disloyal persons in Dublin was given as 2,325, which included 100 of the Citizen Army, but it was conceded that this was probably an underestimate, though not in any case exceeding 3,000.[10] In normal circumstances hardly a threat at all, under the extraordinary conditions introduced by the war the disruptive potential of these elements could prove a hindrance to the war effort.

The war brought some changes to the city. Within hours a number of suspects were arrested—not, as might be thought, members of secret societies but the bewildered foreign-born hotel waiters and shopkeepers (eighty of them) who had to be registered and certified under the Aliens Act. Within days troops were embarking at the North Wall, and before a month had passed the roll of honor brought news of the casualties at Mons. There appeared to be an effusion of pro-war fervor on the part of many citizens as departing soldiers in Dublin and elsewhere left with cheers for England ringing in their ears. Many of those on their way to the front were the city's builders' laborers, men already in the army reserve. Trinity College advanced its examination schedule to give senior students the opportunity to place themselves at the disposal of the War Office. Surgeons and nurses left their hospitals and medical students their classes to volunteer their professional services. These skills were soon needed in Dublin when the first groups of wounded soldiers began to arrive. The shortage of hospital beds necessitated the conversion of the state apartments in Dublin Castle via public subscription into a reception center for the wounded under the administration of the local branch of the Red Cross Society. From now on the horrors of war were to be brought home vividly to the citizens by the continuous arrival of sick and mutilated bodies for hospital care, the lengthening lists of war dead and missing, and the sight of despairing Belgian refugees, some 300 of whom received temporary accommodation in the city.[11] Among the lesser effects of the war was the cancellation of the Dublin Horse Show, the showgrounds being commandeered by the military for mobilization. The annual pilgrimages to Lourdes, a growing Irish "industry," were also interrupted. But the restrictions that were sought to be imposed on drink unleashed a furor in Ireland. As early as November 1914 the Dublin police had applied to the courts for permission to close the pubs between 8 P.M. and 7 A.M. owing to the drunkenness of soldiers in the city. The Recorder instead decided to impose a 10 P.M. closing (9:30 P.M. Friday and Saturday)—a victory for the publicans. The proposals of the government, however, were a more serious threat. Lloyd George expressed the moral outrage of many British citizens early in 1915 when he termed drink a more deadly enemy than either Germany or Austria. He therefore proposed to double the taxes on spirits, impose taxes on beer and wine, and dilute spirits up to 35 percent in an attempt to curb the alleged effects of drunkenness among recruits and munitions workers. In Dublin these proposals rallied "the swollen tyranny of 'the trade'" against what was regarded as an attack on the economic life of the nation. The outcry found priest and politician together in unlikely common cause and led to public meetings in the Mansion House and Phoenix Park and elsewhere in May 1915. Perhaps the most unusual protest of all was that of Dr. Fogarty, bishop of Killaloe, delivered at Ennis before a group of children waiting to be confirmed![12] The protests brought favorable treatment for Ireland, but they did not prevent the military from ordering the Dublin pubs off limits to soldiers after December.

Public energy was almost wholly consumed by the recruiting campaign. In a letter to Dublin Corporation in July 1915, John Redmond reminded the citizens that "it is the highest duty and most vital interest of Ireland to do everything in her power to support the cause of the Allies." The campaign got under way in earnest as soon as Kitchener issued his initial call for 100,000 men in August. A Dublin Recruiting Committee was set up immediately under the chairmanship of Sir Maurice Dockrell and received the unstinted support of the people's representatives. The earliest demonstration of recruiting fervor was a Mansion House meeting on September 5. There Redmond along with his colleagues Devlin and Field and his supporters, Lord Mayor Sherlock and Sir Joseph Downes, together with W. M. Murphy, promised to add to the 60,000 or so soldiers and

WAR!!

ENGLAND, GERMANY AND IRELAND.

The mighty British Empire is on the verge of destruction. "The hand of the Lord hath touched her." The English live in daily terror of Germany. War between England and Germany is at hand. England's cowardly and degenerate population won't make soldiers: not so the Germans. They are trained and ready.

WHAT WILL ENGLAND DO?

She'll get Irish Fools to join her Army and Navy, send them to fight and die for her Empire. England has never fought her own battles. Irish traitors have ever been the backbone of her Army and Navy. How has she rewarded them? When they are no longer able to fight she flings them back to Ireland, reeking with foul filthy diseases to die in the workhouses.

WHY SHOULD YOU FIGHT FOR ENGLAND?

Is it in gratitude for the Priest-hunters and the rack of the Penal days! The Gibbet! The Pitch Cap! The Half-hangings and all the Horrors of '98?

Is it in gratitude for the Famine when One Million of our people were slowly starved to death, and Christian England thanking God that the Celts were going, going with a vengeance?

Is it in gratitude for the blazing homesteads and the people half-naked and starved to death by the roadside?

STAND ASIDE

and have your revenge. Without Ireland's help England will go down before Germany as she would have gone down before the Boers had not the Irish fought her battle in South Africa. The English know this and they have offered us a bribe and call it

HOME RULE.

It is not yet law, but believing us to be a nation of fools she wants payment in advance, and has sent her warships to our coasts to entrap young Irishmen.

THE VIGILANCE COMMITTEE

feels bound to issue this solemn warning to young Irishmen against joining the English Army or Navy—for your own sake, as well as for your country's sake. You denounce as traitors the men who sold their votes to pass the Union. You denounce Judas who sold Christ, but generations yet unborn will curse YOU who now join England's Army or Navy. Aye, will curse not alone the dupes who join, but also those who neglect to aid the VIGILANCE COMMITTEE in their crusade against the most Immoral Army and Navy in the world.

Antirecruiting handbill circulated during 1913.

sailors who were serving with or called up by the military at the outbreak of war.[13] Elsewhere in the city, antirecruiting meetings suggested the difficulties in this undertaking. One observer, revealing perhaps something of his own Unionist bias, regarded the results of the Mansion House demonstration with considerable skepticism: "A special recruiting office was set up in Grafton Street for the National Volunteers to save them the 'ignominy' of entering the recognized Army Recruiting office in Great Brunswick Street . . . six recruits presented themselves, apparently at some risk to their lives from the indignant populace. From the first the Grafton Street office has been a fiasco . . . it is quite possible that an actual majority of the Dublin recruits have been Unionists."[14] Things did not remain quite this bad, however, for by October about 200 enlistees were presenting themselves each week, over ten times the pre-war rate. By the end of 1915 some 86,000 recruits had been raised in Ireland, of which nearly 17,000 hailed from the recruiting area of the city and county of Dublin (only 60 percent of the number from Belfast district).[15] Yet these figures were far from satisfactory and necessitated renewed measures to entice apathetic or unwilling Irishmen into uniform, varying from the employment of sandwichmen conveying the needs of the Dublin Fusiliers to an inculcation of a martial spirit by the marching bands of the Irish Guards. Perhaps not too many donned the khaki because it entitled their wives and children to free entrance to the Dublin Zoo, but the separation allowances to wives (12s. 6d. weekly), mothers, and sisters dependent on the soldier's earnings in civilian life was a powerful inducement indeed.

The higher clergy and some priests also gave strong support initially to the recruiting campaign. Their statements condemning secret societies (Archbishop of Dublin), urging Irishmen to forget the penal laws (Bishop of Kildare and Leighlin), or calling Irish farmers to their duty to the flag of the Empire (Archbishop of Tuam), perhaps were responsible for the truculent antirecruiting poster "Away with the priests." The Dublin Chamber of Commerce undertook the responsibility for convincing employers to assist recruiting efforts by promising to rehire men who enlisted. Another tactic attempted with employers was a circular letter from the recruiting committee requesting particulars on employees of military age: it was claimed by opponents of this invasion of privacy that men in that category had been dismissed from employment in public bodies in order to compel them to join up.[16] The city was also host to continuous platform oratory through which Irish politicians and other worthies attempted to convince the people that the proper way to fight for dear Ireland was to don a British army uniform. A hero from the trenches was usually on hand on these occasions to belabor the "shirkers." One of the more famous of these was Sgt. Mike O'Leary from Inchigeela, county Cork, one of two early Irish VCs. Having already received a hero's welcome in Cork, O'Leary earned a civic reception from the Lord Mayor of Dublin at which he imposed the impossible demand on his countrymen that they should emulate his own splendid bravery: he had killed eight Germans single-handedly! His valor was not appreciated everywhere, most especially at Labor's stomping grounds at Beresford Place, where his presence in the city provoked a counter-demonstration from James Connolly and his comrades. It was Connolly who shortly after the outbreak of war hoisted the Irish flag (a harp, minus the crown, on a green background) over Liberty Hall and emblazoned that building's façade with the taunting sign "We Serve neither King nor Kaiser but Ireland." The Mansion House, official residence of the Lord Mayor, was an open house for recruiters, imparting an official sanction to the work of the recruiting committee. The "loyalty" of the Corporation was acknowledged by the action of the majority Nationalists in the case of Professor Kuno Meyer, the well-known German authority on Celtic studies. Meyer, co-founder of the summer school of Irish learning in Dublin, had been honored with the freedom of the capital city in 1911. He had lately justified Germany's position on the war, was avowedly anti-British, and had contacts with the revolutionary Clan-na-Gael in New York. For this his name had already been expunged from the roll of freemen by Cork Corporation. Similar action was now taken by the municipal administration in Dublin in March 1915.[17] All these actions encouraged the loyalty of others. The president of University College in Dublin made a formal application to the G.O.C. in Ireland for approval to establish a contingent of the officers' training corps among the students. A negative reply prompted him to plead with John Redmond for assistance.[18] The Royal Dublin Fusiliers were an obvious instrument for recruiting in the capital. Not only were the workaday citizens to be provided for in the first nine battalions of the regiment but the tenth, the "scholars" battalion, was reserved for professional men and clerks. Sentiment also operated to widen involvement as local theaters (the Abbey and Theatre Royal) arranged benefit concerts to raise funds for "comforts" for the troops.

The *Freeman's Journal* played a leading and controversial role in the campaign. For long the premier Nationalist daily, the paper now seemed to vie with the *Irish Times* in an effusion of imperial fervor. With the *Freeman*'s circulation of 50,000, few Dublin homes escaped exposure to its fawning adulation of Lord Wimborne ("our Sporting Viceroy"), its exaltation of the exploits of Irish regiments, or the grisly details of alleged German atrocities in Belgium. By 1916, at a time when the enthusiasm of the clergy for the war was beginning to wane, the *Freeman* was pleading editorially for the honoring of "obligations" along the lines framed from the outset by Redmond, Dillon, and others. Like other pro-war papers, it was a willing vehicle for the propaganda of the recruiters, some of which spared no feelings:

TO THE YOUNG WOMEN OF IRELAND

. . . If your young man neglects his duty to Ireland, the time
may come when he will neglect you.
. . . If he does not think that you and your country are worth
fighting for—do you think he is *worthy* of you.

YOUNG MAN

. . . Is anyone proud of you?
Is your mother proud of you?
Is your . . . [sister, sweetheart, employer, Ireland] proud of you?

And there were the oft-repeated "5 Questions" and "5 Reasons" why Irishmen not already engaged in munitions work in Ireland (few were) should join an Irish regiment to defend "the sacred rights and liberties of Belgium." Even the leaders of the Irish parliamentary party came to regard their erstwhile ally as an encumbrance for its obvious alienation of a considerable segment of nationalist opinion that failed to understand why England's war should be Ireland's battle too. The bishop of Killaloe expressed privately what had become clear to many: "The *Freeman* is but a government organ and the National Party but an Imperial instrument."[19]

The recruiting drive met with difficulties in Dublin from the beginning. As early as

November 1914 the committee advised the government that its efforts on behalf of Lord Kitchener were being undermined by seditious literature and antirecruiting demonstrations. Large, well-designed placards told of "England's Growing Hypocrisy," "England's Last Ditch," and the "Pretence of the Realm Act," while thousands of leaflets published at Liberty Hall offered "5 Reasons" why Dubliners should join the Citizen Army. Pro-German, anti-British newspapers flourished and invited suppression by the authorities. Their small circulation gave little assurance that the opinions they expressed were shared only by the few: as was demonstrated in Ireland in 1918 and in many other contexts before and since, dissenting opinion can be transformed into majority votes. A round of seizures brought the *Irish Freedom, Irish Worker, Sinn Fein*, and other weeklies into the government's net, but soon these reappeared in another guise to taunt the authorities as *The Worker, Nationality, Scissors and Paste*, and so on. But the suppression of seditious literature was not consistently pursued, partly because the advice of the Irish party that suppression would only bring public sympathy for the revolutionary movement prevailed. Arrests under the Defence of the Realm Act (D.O.R.A.) only made martyrs and provided further embarrassment for Irish party representatives. The arrest and imprisonment in May 1915 of that man of sterling character, the Dublin pacifist editor Francis Sheehy-Skeffington, led to a public outcry that brought the caustic comment from George Bernard Shaw that if Britain could not win the war without putting him into prison for depleting the army by a few men, she deserved to be beaten by Germany (he was released due to ill health after a few days). The effectiveness of D.O.R.A. was considerably reduced in Ireland and more especially in Dublin in March 1915 when amending legislation provided for trial by jury, a departure that in the opinion of both the Under Secretary and the Director of Military Intelligence rendered it extremely difficult to obtain convictions, evidence of the sympathy (or perhaps fear) engendered by the revolutionary elements.[20]

The clash of pro- and anti-war sympathies was demonstrated on the first anniversary of the outbreak. Dublin War Week was proclaimed by the authorities to usher in yet another recruiting drive by the Lord Mayor, uniformed Irish MPs, and others to the accompaniment of street-corner performances by the band of the Dublin Fusiliers. Also on Sunday of that first week in August 1915, the body of the old Fenian dynamitard O'Donovan Rossa lay in state at City Hall, a prelude to one of the most memorable public funerals ever held in the city. Two unbroken lines of marchers extended from College Green to the gates of Glasnevin cemetery, including Irish Volunteers (armed), National Volunteers (unarmed), and contingents of local labor and nationalist groups. At the graveside, Pearse, in the uniform of an Irish Volunteer, invoked the tradition of Tone, Mitchel, and Rossa in a call for Irish freedom.

It was the threat of conscription that finally demonstrated the lack of enthusiasm for enlistment in Ireland. Rumors about it had surfaced soon after the war had begun and, according to newspaper reports, set off an exodus to the United States of farmers' sons. Conscription became the main topic of conversation throughout the country in the second half of 1915, and the efforts of Irish MPs, now following rather than leading public opinion, were concentrated on persuading the government that conscription could not be enforced in Ireland without bloodshed or at any rate not until a settlement had been reached on the home rule question, which sentiment corresponded fully with nationalist aspirations. The antirecruiting meetings hitherto held only by "seditious" elements were now replaced by anticonscription demonstrations that joined both the loyal and disloyal

TABLE 30.   Recruiting in Ireland, August 1914 to October 1916.

AREA	NO. RECRUITED	ESTIMATED NUMBER AVAILABLE FOR MILITARY SERVICE (October 1916)
Dublin Police District	21,412	21,970
Belfast County Borough	38,543	7,806
Leinster (incl. Dublin)	37,048	52,788
Ulster (incl. Belfast)	66,674	45,205
Munster	21,079	42,742
Connaught	5,440	20,504
Ireland (total)	130,241	161,239

SOURCE: *Parliamentary Papers,* 1916 (XVII), cd. 8390 (Men of Military Age in Ireland).

elements among Irish nationalists. The use of the municipal council chamber, for example, was granted in July to groups protesting conscription, a move promoted by Sinn Fein
Alderman Thomas Kelly though, strangely enough, opposed by a score of Nationalist
members, including Lord Mayor Gallagher, Patrick Shortall (who was knighted in 1916),
and Alderman M'Walter, M.D. (who was soon to don the uniform of a captain in the
R.A.M.C.). The disgraceful harassment and abuse meted out to emigrating Irishmen at
the Liverpool docks further inflamed opinion in Ireland and was directly responsible for a
stinging anti-British outburst by Dr. O'Dwyer, bishop of Limerick, in a letter that received wide distribution as a pamphlet in November and December; it was later dubbed
by Chief Secretary Birrell as "one of the most formidable anti-recruiting pamphlets ever
written." The agitation of these months served to bring over more and more adherents to
the cause of Sinn Fein and reduce the authority of the Irish party. In the country at large
the strength of the National Volunteers decreased while the Irish Volunteers grew in
numbers. In Dublin the 4,000 or so National Volunteers ceased activity altogether as the
streets were given over to the drilling and parading of some 2,500 extremists owing allegiance to either the IRB or the Citizen Army. The effect of all this on recruiting was dramatic. By October 1916, at which time recruiting had dwindled to small proportions,
only half the estimated number that was expected should have joined from the Dublin
district had enlisted, although many of the so-called "shirkers" could have been presumed to have taken up munitions work in England. This trend was in sharp contrast
with Belfast, where only about 15 percent of all effectives still awaited enlistment. According to one official estimate, the army lost 50,000 potential recruits as a result of the
antirecruiting movement alone.[21]

As the year 1916 opened, few sensed that there was any other purpose behind the
arming and drilling of the Irish Volunteers than the vague assertion by their nominal
leader, Professor MacNeill, of furthering the interests of Ireland by securing its peace and
prosperity and protecting her against aggressors. There was, of course, some apprehension on the part of the authorities because, as Birrell later explained, ". . . the impression
that one gained in walking about the streets [of Dublin] almost was as if the Sinn Feiners
were in a certain sense in possession."[22] But the policy of nonintervention that had benefited the gun-runners in the North now also worked to the advantage of the anti-British
forces in the South. These were the circumstances in which the review of 1,600 men of
the Irish Volunteers, mostly armed with rifles and revolvers, took place under the aegis of
Sinn Fein on St. Patrick's Day. The physical difficulty of disarming these Volunteers—

Lord Wimborne estimated 100,000 troops would be needed—precluded any drastic action being taken in Dublin or elsewhere. The dangers appeared to have escaped the leader of the Irish parliamentary party, whose opinion on the state of the country contemplated the withdrawal of a few thousand men from the RIC to keep depleted Irish battalions up to strength. A more realistic appraisal, however, had been conveyed to Redmond in a confidential letter from the Chief Secretary late in 1915:

> During the last few <u>weeks</u> I have been reading nothing but uncomfortable figures about the Irish Volunteers, who are steadily month by month <u>increasing</u>. . . . Whenever there is a plucky priest and two or three men with a little courage, the <u>movement</u> is <u>stamped out</u>—but unluckily such priests and laymen are not always to be found . . . the <u>Revolutionary</u> propaganda grows in strength and I think, in sincerity of purpose. . . . The newspapers are poor enough both in circulation and ability, but reading them as I have to do, I think I notice an increasing <u>exaltation of spirit</u> and a growth of confidence, in some of the better written articles which indicates more <u>belief</u> in the possibilities of the future than was the case 6 months ago . . . and having regard to the uncertainty of our military operations, gloomy possibilities in the East and elsewhere, parliamentary upsets and so on, I feel the <u>Irish</u> Situation one of actual menace.
>
> I don't think therefore this is the time to underrate the services of the <u>Police</u> or to draw a rosy, <u>however truthful</u>, picture of the <u>crimelessness</u> of Ireland. We may want the police and if so shall have to arm them.[23]

The political and military details of the Easter Rising, that enduring monument to the valor of fewer than two thousand citizens of Dublin in the spring of 1916, hardly needs another retelling here; the event has been the subject of numerous descriptive and analytical books and articles.[24] Only the bare outlines of the major occurrences are included to support the lesser account of the effects of the insurrection on the city and the populace after fewer than one thousand Irish Volunteers and about two hundred men and women of the Citizen Army marched out on Easter Monday to obey, as their simultaneous declaration of an Irish republic explained, the call of the dead generations to strike for the freedom of their country. That the insurrection would be almost solely confined to Dublin was assured by the cancellation by MacNeill of the planned Sunday maneuvers throughout the country of the Irish Volunteers.

The city was in festive mood on April 24, the last day of a holiday weekend. Those citizens planning to holiday "on the cheap" could contemplate enjoying a pleasant afternoon of varied pleasures at Phoenix Park, strolling in Stephen's Green, or taking in the invigorating air along the foreshore of the bay. Trains would take other holiday-makers to the more distant resort of Bray in county Wicklow, while the more irrepressible spirits could find outlet at the great race meeting at Fairyhouse. It was from the latter venue that all the junior officers of the Dublin military headquarters would be recalled on that fateful day: many had left on early trains to catch the first race. Citizens could also expect to end their day of leisure with an enjoyable reprise of *The Gondoliers*, due to usher in the annual D'Oyly Carte season at the Gaiety, or savor the melodrama and musical mélanges of Dublin's other palaces of entertainment now to be reopened again after the ritual silence of Holy Week. The more discriminating might ponder the political implications of Yeats's *Cathleen Ni Houlihan*, due to be given another airing at the Abbey, and visitors from the country would look forward to extending their holiday so as to take in the Royal Dublin Society's Spring Show at Ballsbridge. Indeed, the first to experience the effects

of the Easter Rising were the casual strollers in Stephen's Green who were unceremoniously driven out of the park a few minutes before midday by the occupying Volunteers.
Holiday-makers at Westland Row railway station were also surprised to find their plans
interrupted by a similar occupation by the rebels. Within an hour or so the insurgents,
fewer than a thousand in number, had also taken as strongpoints the General Post Office,
the Four Courts, the buildings of the South Dublin Union, City Hall, Jacob's biscuit factory, the College of Surgeons, Boland's flour mills, as well as key approaches from the
north and south of the city. The holiday atmosphere evaporated quickly. Everyone, including the Irish Administration and the forces of law and order, had been taken by surprise as Birrell's worst fears were realized.

One of the more striking alterations in the appearance of the city following the events
of Monday afternoon was the disappearance of the Dublin Metropolitan Police, now reduced to a cipher in a confrontation they were not equipped to handle—their large
frames and imperial mien presenting both target and excuse for the bullets of the rebels.
The tramway system that during the worst days of the labor troubles of 1913 managed to
carry its passengers now ground to a halt for the duration of what was euphemistically
described in Hansard as the "disturbances in Ireland." Holiday-makers who had gotten
off to an early start on that morning found that the return journey was possible only on
foot or in somewhat undignified fashion on passing carts and wagons. Soon there would
be no postal and telegraph service (the telephone exchange, however, was secured by the
military) nor gas supply. Street lighting, which had already been curtailed by the Corporation due to budgetary constraints, was also withdrawn. Banks, stores, and public houses
in the center of the city were closed as well as museums, cinemas, and theaters. And as a
military cordon began to be drawn around Dublin, the citizens would be denied the use
of the Phoenix Park, with its popular zoological gardens and horserace meetings. Bewildered pedestrians became spectators of gun battles or in some cases victims to wayward
bullets.

The outbreak, as stated, caught both the authorities and military command by surprise. There had, of course, been fears of what was brewing, but they had been lulled not
only by MacNeill's cancellation of the maneuvers on the previous day but by the earlier
capture of Roger Casement and the German arms ship he had chartered to support the
insurrection. The Lord Lieutenant was hardly speaking for his colleagues when in ad-
dressing the Royal Commission one month later he recalled that "at that time of day it
did not look very much like a rebellion. The idea is that these things generally begin earlier than half-past twelve"! There were 120 officers and 2,265 men in military barracks in
the city, 400 of them detailed to be able to turn out at a moment's notice to handle such
emergencies as might be anticipated from Volunteer maneuvers. But the authorities were
faced with something more than a military exercise, and little use could be made of the
troops on that first day. Also, by a strange turn of events, three of the four detachments
of military in the city had been drawn from Irish regiments, one of them consisting of 467
officers and men of the 10th ("scholars") battalion of the Royal Dublin Fusiliers. "The
Dublins behaved magnificently in the rebellion," stated Lord Wimborne. "They were
called upon to fire on their own fellow-citizens, and, possibly, their own relatives."[25] It
would take more than the 2,000 or so additional troops arriving that afternoon and evening from the Curragh and Belfast to weight the odds in favor of the military: the rebels
had declined to use barricades—"the ordinary tactics of revolutionists," according to

Wimborne—from which they could have been easily dislodged by superior forces of armed police and soldiers.

Martial law was proclaimed throughout the city and county on Tuesday. The only newspaper published on this and the two following days was the *Irish Times*, its useless theater listings marking a strange contrast with the grim conditions of the city. Information on the outbreak was forbidden by the censor. Because of the proclamation no parades, political meetings, or organized sports events could take place without the permission of the authorities. Only those with military passes and doctors and nurses in uniform were exempt from the 7:30 P.M. to 5:30 A.M. curfew imposed by Major General Friend, G.O.C. in Ireland. When General Maxwell arrived on Friday to assume supreme command and exercise plenary powers, the curfew was extended from 6 P.M. to 9 A.M. Under these circumstances of enforced idleness, the *Irish Times* on Thursday felt obliged to offer its readers suggestions on how to pass the time during the long evening hours —cultivate a habit of easy conversation . . . tend the garden . . . mend and paint the house . . . acquire the art of reading, Shakespeare being especially appropriate in the poet's tercentenary year. The daylight hours were passed by some in a frenzy of looting. With the withdrawal of the police on Monday, the poor descended on O'Connell Street, Camden Street, and other shopping centers and at great risk to their lives (for they were fired on both by the rebels in the G.P.O. and the O.T.C. detachment defending Trinity College) reaped the windfall of material comforts in undefended clothing and footwear establishments. All contemporary accounts testify to this desperate emanation of Dublin's "underworld," each relating a particular example of serious or amusing character— Sean MacDiarmada leaving his post at the G.P.O. to remonstrate with looters for disgracing the fight for Ireland's freedom, an army of children laying siege to Lawrence's toy bazaar, Noblett's candy store pillaged of its contents, drunken citizens fighting each other for the bottles of stout and whiskey lifted from a public house, the Lord Mayor and civilians keeping a mob at bay in fashionable Grafton Street until the arrival of a military guard. Further lurid details were provided by the police courts, where over 130 persons were charged with looting during May, the police having entered homes in search of the culprits. Those arrested included ten-year-old boys who stole footballs and running shoes from Elvery's sports shop and scores of adults in possession of equally selective plunder—boots and shoes, topcoats and jackets, teapots and delph, toilet soap and cocoa. The grand looting prize must go to Winnie O'Byrne and her daughter Agnes, who were caught with two hair mattresses, one pillow, eight window curtains, one pair of corsets, one piece of flannelette, one quilt, one topcoat, two ladies' coats, a half-dozen ladies' hats, and four chairs! The greatest loss was suffered by the B & I Steam Packet Company, whose warehouse was stripped of goods to the value of £5,000. Those convicted received sentences of one or two months' imprisonment, and cases did not cease to be heard until mid-July. According to police statistics for 1916, 425 persons were proceeded against for looting during the Rebellion and 398 of these were either fined or imprisoned.[26]

The fighting, which no one had expected would last more than a day or two, dragged on throughout the week, increasing in severity and isolating citizens trapped between rebel-held areas and the tightening cordon of the military. The movement of troops was facilitated by improvised "armored cars" constructed by mounting loopholed boiler plate on lorries supplied by Guinness's. In the battle zones Englishmen and Irishmen in the army of the Empire faced Irish soldiers in the army of the new Republic—12,000 against

The Easter Rising: the burned-out hulk of the General Post Office. The site remained a ruin for years and the building was not finally reopened to the public until 1929.

fewer than 2,000. Rifle and machine-gun fire raked the city, killing and wounding combatants and civilians alike. Residents in the vicinity of the strongly held rebel redoubt about the Four Courts suffered vindictive reprisals at the hands of the attacking soldiery. Snipers' bullets found innocent targets in a raised hand or misunderstood gesture. Terror mounted for ordinary citizens when the first artillery shells began to pound the abandoned Liberty Hall in a vengeful assault on the "citadel of anarchy." Incendiary shells wreaked destruction on O'Connell Street and started fires that were quite beyond the capacity of the municipal fire brigade to handle even if Captain Purcell's men had been foolhardy enough to operate amidst a hail of bullets and machine-gun fire. The military by securing Dublin Castle and Trinity College had effectively divided the rebel forces in two and consequently concentrated their fire on the city's main thoroughfare in the expectation (correct, as it turned out) that the destruction of the rebel headquarters in the G.P.O. would bring about the surrender of the outlying positions in the southern half of the city. By Thursday evening the flames had enveloped such city landmarks as the pagoda-topped D.B.C. cafe, the Imperial Hotel and Clery's department store, the Royal Hibernian Academy, Elvery's sports shop, and the offices of the *Freeman's Journal*. The night sky bore witness to the rumors of death and destruction that reached the suburbs. It was

The Easter Rising: a view of Lower O'Connell Street looking northward to Nelson's Pillar. The ruined D.B.C. restaurant is on the right and farther down the street can be seen the canopied entrance to what was the Imperial Hotel.

fire that hastened the tragic end of the insurrection when flames gutted the G.P.O. on Friday afternoon, driving the defenders, including Pearse and the wounded Connolly, into the surrounding streets and houses. Within 24 hours an unconditional surrender was forced on the leaders of the rebellion, and one by one the remaining rebel positions submitted, though the men at Jacob's factory held out until 3 P.M. on Sunday afternoon and isolated rebels continued to snipe at soldiers throughout that night until finally cleared out in house-to-house searches by the military with, once more, the aid of the DMP and some five hundred "special constables."

The Easter Rising, which with the exception of minor skirmishes in Galway, Wexford, Meath, Louth, and county Dublin was largely confined to the capital, resulted in an estimated 3,000 casualties. The following official figures were later disclosed:[27]

		Killed		
	Military	*Police*	*Civilians*	*Total*
Dublin	116	3	310	429
(DMP district)				
Rest of Ireland	—	13	8	21
Total	116	16	318	450

		Wounded		
	Military	*Police*	*Civilians*	*Total*
Dublin	367	7	2208	2582
(DMP district)				
Rest of Ireland	1	22	9	32
Total	368	29	2217	2614

Of the civilian casualties it has been estimated that some 180 (60 killed, 120 wounded) belonged among the insurgents. These do not include the grisly executions of 14 rebel leaders in a backyard at the disused Kilmainham jail under the martial-law regime of General Maxwell nor the brutal murder of Francis Sheehy-Skeffington by a demented British officer during the week of hostilities. Thus the greatest number of casualties was suffered by ordinary citizens, especially in the northern side of the city, where due to the lack of food deliveries many had to choose between bullets and starvation. Much credit is due the Red Cross Society, St. John's Ambulance brigade, and the doctors, nurses, medical students, clergymen, and volunteer stretcher-bearers who at great risk (a nurse and an ambulance worker were killed) tended the wounded in the streets. Many bodies had to be retrieved from ruined buildings only to be buried under the most distressing circumstances—only one mourner allowed—with the coffin liable to be halted for search allegedly for identification purposes, in reality to ensure against the smuggling or disposal of arms. When the fighting ceased, it became the duty of the sanitary officers of the public health department to safeguard the city from the danger of epidemic disease owing to the decomposition of horse carcasses and unburied corpses or those lying in shallow graves. In this manner the hastily interred bodies of several soldiers were discovered and handed over to the military authorities. The city morgue became the repository for the large number of bodies that had to remain unburied owing to the temporary shortage of coffins. Over 60 unidentified bodies picked up off the streets or collected from city hospitals were buried in pits at the rear of Dublin Castle, though some of these were later exhumed for proper interment by relatives.[28]

No citizen was unaffected by the Rising, for all were subject to curfew and few indeed escaped some privation arising from the interruption of milk and food deliveries, the closing of shops, and the cessation of the gas supply. Those individuals and businesses connected to the electric supply service fared better, for only a small section of the city served by a damaged sub-station was affected. Observers commented on the unexpected conjunction of society dames and "shawlies" at the baker's cart and the sight of staid professional men homebound with loaves of bread and joints of meat under their arms or dragging bags of coal behind them. There were reports of gangs of poor people invading the vegetable patches of market gardeners in outlying suburbs owing to the scarcity of food. And, of course, the shortages were compounded by the fact that the military had first call on available food stocks. The attempt by the rebels at Boland's bakery to distribute loaves of bread did little to relieve the situation because of the dangers involved for civilians. When the factory was recovered by the owners after the surrender, thousands of loaves still unused were distributed to the poor of the district. The urgency of the food shortage prompted the Local Government Board to set up a Food Supply Committee to administer the direct free distribution of food at 31 depots in the city, work that was soon transferred to the charitable Society of St. Vincent de Paul. Relief vouchers were also distributed at the Salvation Army hostel at Peter Street, but the worst was soon over when goods trains loaded with food supplies began to arrive from May 4. But there could be no speedy return to normal after such total dislocation of the industrial and commercial life of the city. For there were the added consequences of increased unemployment and the necessity of securing relief for families in distress, especially those of clerks, shop assistants, and small shopkeepers. The National Relief Fund made over £5,000 available for emergency relief operations during the crucial first two weeks of May, and for two months thereafter the Board of Guardians were ordered to dispense outdoor relief to the most urgent cases, without disability to the recipients (i.e., loss of the franchise) from funds placed at their disposal: 8s. per week for husband and wife, 5s. for widow or widower, and supplementary payments of 1s. and more for children and adult dependents.[29] Subscriptions to the Lord Mayor's Fund for similar relief of unemployment brought in over £5,000 within a month, including about £1,000 raised by a concert given by John McCormack for Irish relief in New York. Most of the money was expended to give employment over the ensuing months to between 300 and 400 persons on various relief projects: market gardening in Fairview, clearing derelict sites, training for munitions making in the technical schools, knitting gloves and socks for the troops, and making dolls in local convents. Similar funds were started for the dependents of police and soldiers who fell during the fighting.

Many businesses were able to resume operation on May 5 after the appearance of public notices advising employees to return to work. The gas service was restored by May 10, and four days later the trams were in full operation. Free movement in and out of the city was again possible with the removal of the military cordon. Cinemas reopened on Saturday, May 6, followed by the Theatre Royal and the Abbey on May 8, not even a silent protest being made against the judicial slaughter of 14 Irish nationalists between May 3 and 12. Even before the last executions had taken place, citizens were able to mix entertainment with the latest cinematographic pictures of *The Dublin Rising and the Ruins of the City* at the Bohemian Theatre. Because of the curfew, performances were at first confined to matinees but gradually evening performances were added, and with the delaying of the curfew until midnight on May 14 the remaining theaters reopened. The city's public houses, which had been ordered closed during the executions, also resumed business but were subject to even further curtailment of hours (8 P.M. weekday closing). The city was slowly returning to normal.

"When we are all wiped out, people will blame us for everything," said Pearse to his comrade Desmond Ryan while they were both under fire in the G.P.O. "So far it [the Rising] has met with no evidence of popular sympathy and we owe it as much to the loyal population as to ourselves to exhibit determination," wrote Lord Wimborne to Asquith.[30] And it must be said that the overwhelming public opinion shared Redmond's feelings of "detestation and horror" at what a resolution of Irish parliamentary representatives later described as "futile revolution and anarchy." Contemporary observers and participants alike bear witness to the hostile feelings of the general public toward the rebels. James Stephens, mixing among the crowds during the days of fighting, heard middle- and lower-class women exclaim: "I hope every man of them will be shot!" De Valera, the Volunteer leader at Boland's Bakery, was appalled at seeing British soldiers being fed by the residents of Northumberland Road while Irishmen were under fire in nearby houses. Frank Robbins, a soldier in the Citizen Army contingent at the College of Surgeons, recalled with amazement the cries of encouragement offered by his fellow citizens to the English battalion escorting Commandant Mallin (executed on May 8), Countess Markievicz, himself, and other combatants to the Richmond Barracks—"Good old Staffords," "Shoot the traitors," "Bayonet the bastards." One can well believe the story related of another rebel prisoner surrounded by a similar hostile mob who when asked by a companion whether he and his comrades might after all be released by their military guardians replied, with an eye to the mob: "Bejasus, I hope not." John Dillon, MP, another observer of some of the events of Easter Week, also corroborated the friendliness of the general population toward the soldiers, among whom were their very own Dublin Fusiliers.[31] The degree of revulsion varied, of course, it being strongest among those middle-class elements who well knew that their vision of a new Ireland under an anticipated Home Rule regime accorded ill with the kind of society envisaged by Connolly's socialism or Pearse's Gaelic idealism. Their judgment of the insurrection was given its most extreme expression in the *Irish Catholic* and *Irish Independent*. The former editorialized on the "German conspiracy" on May 13, condemning Sinn Fein as being in thrall to anticlericals, socialists, and non-Catholics. Pearse was ridiculed as "a crazy and insolvent schoolmaster" while General Maxwell, whom Bishop O'Dwyer of Limerick later virtually denounced as a cold-blooded murderer, was given high praise as the "gallant officer" who with his admirably disciplined troops had saved Dublin from anarchy and socialism. And, finally, in a complete misreading of the changed mood of the people in the wake of the executions, the paper found "no reason to lament that the rebel leaders have met the fate which from the very dawn of humanity has been universally reserved for traitors." William M. Murphy's *Irish Independent* recommended leniency for the rank and file who had believed on Easter Monday that they were "only going out for a march"! These and other Irishmen could atone for the crime of the insurrection by presenting themselves at army recruiting stations. For the leaders and organizers of the revolt, however, there could be no show of mercy. The fate of two of them, Connolly and MacDiarmada, still hung in the balance, but in a brutal gesture on May 10 the paper ignored the cries for clemency and advised that "the worst of the ringleaders be singled out and dealt with as they deserve." Both men were shot two days later. Among those executed were two officials of Dublin Corporation: Edward T. Kent, a clerk in the City Treasurer's department, and John MacBride, of Boer War fame, who had been employed as water bailiff. John Connolly, slain in the attack on Dublin Castle on April 24, was employed as a clerk in the Paving Committee. The municipal council itself also figured in the Roll of Honor: Councillor Richard O'Carroll and ex-Alderman Peter Macken, both members of the Labour Party, fell in the fighting.

The municipal council was tamely silent on the events that had brought such destruction to the city. It was perforce prevented from meeting according to its regular schedule early in May and only convened on May 10 in answer to the request of the Board of

Guardians of the South Dublin Union to formally request the Local Government Board to authorize the distribution of outdoor relief under the Poor Law. But at the regular meeting on June 5, though the occasion was used to express regret at the death of Councillor O'Carroll and pass a resolution of sympathy with the relatives of citizens who had lost their lives during the Rebellion, there was no outburst of nationalist fervor such as had often disrupted proceedings when merely formal verbal affronts to patriotism had to be endured. No cue was taken from the passionate outburst of Dillon in the House of Commons a few weeks earlier. Instead the council, bereft of its Sinn Fein and Labour stalwarts, returned, as might have been expected by the ratepayers at least, to its normal routine of business—approving committee reports, passing on candidates for jobs, scrutinizing salary recommendations, and accepting tenders for contracts while finding time also to plead with the Royal Dublin Society to reconsider its decision not to hold that gayest event of the social season, the Horse Show. Later in the year, Dublin's first citizen had no qualms about proposing a toast to the King at the first mayoral banquet in 35 years to be graced by the Lord Lieutenant, who, incidentally, chose the occasion to give yet another recruiting speech.[32]

As things began to return to normal by mid-May the Chamber of Commerce, the Port and Docks Board, the *Irish Times*, and several business associations in the city called for the continued application of martial law. The *Irish Times* in particular was accused by the *Freeman's Journal* of inciting an "Alva's campaign" in Ireland. Indeed, it appears that some Dublin employers actually dismissed workers whose relatives had participated in the rebellion. Outside opinion on the events in Dublin was equally condemnatory, as judged by the resolutions of rural and urban district councils and boards of guardians. The South Tipperary county council distinguished itself by failing to provide a seconder for a resolution expressing pride in the "clean, honourable fight made by Irish Volunteers," a concession that even the *Irish Times* made on July 22. In Galway, the most troubled area outside Dublin (530 arrests in connection with the Rising), the academic council of University College branded the insurrection a "disgrace and dishonour inflicted upon Ireland." In the welter of denunciations, the early protest in the House of Commons on May 3 of the maverick nationalist MP, Laurence Ginnell, against the "shooting of innocent men by this Hunnish Government" stood alone until the passionate defense uttered by John Dillon eight days later on behalf of those who had fought "a clean fight, a brave fight, however misguided. . . ."[33] Gradually, however, the executions and deportation of prisoners created the climate for a reversal of sentiment in favor of the rebels. The earliest manifestation of this tendency was the nationalist demonstrations accompanying the masses for the souls of those executed, gatherings in defiance of the martial law regulations. Moreover, there was increasing bitterness against the repressive regime of General Maxwell. This attitude was best expressed by Bishop O'Dwyer of Limerick in his rejection of Maxwell's request that certain nationalist priests in the Limerick diocese be disciplined. The bishop's refusal betrayed no mincing of words:

> You took great care that no plea for mercy should interpose on behalf of the poor young fellows who surrendered to you in Dublin. . . . Personally, I regard your action with horror and I believe that it has outraged the conscience of the country. Then the deporting of hundreds and even thousands of poor fellows without a trial of any kind, seems to me an abuse of power as fatuous as it is arbitrary; and altogether your regime has been one of the worst and blackest chapters in the history of the misgovernment of the country.[34]

Whereas the events of Easter week had involved fewer than 2,000 rebels in Dublin and a handful in other areas, the roundup of suspected Sinn Feiners brought home the repressive methods of the government to 27 of Ireland's 32 counties, only Carlow, King's county, Armagh, Antrim, and Fermanagh escaping the military dragnet.[35] Consequently, over 1,700 persons were added to the approximately equal number of men and women rounded up in the metropolitan area. The first batch of prisoners, about 500, were sent to England on Sunday, April 30, just hours after the surrender. These were distributed among the internment camps at Frongoch and elsewhere.

TABLE 31. Number of Persons Arrested in Dublin Metropolitan Area in Connection with the Rebellion of 1916.

NUMBER TRIED BY COURTS MARTIAL		ARRESTED BUT NOT TRIED BY COURTS MARTIAL		TOTAL ARRESTED
EXECUTED	IMPRISONED	INTERNED	RELEASED WITHOUT INTERNMENT	
14	73	947	749	1,783
	(note 1)	(note 2)	(note 3)	(note 4)

NOTE 1. Includes 1 female.
NOTE 2. Includes 3 females.
NOTE 3. Includes 72 females.
NOTE 4. Excludes one additional male tried by courts martial but discharged as not guilty.
SOURCE: Statistical Returns of the DMP, *Parliamentary Papers,* 1919 (XLII), cmd. 30.

During May and June, deportations continued and newspapers added to the ironies of the situation by printing the names of deportees along with those of the men of the Royal Dublin Fusiliers and other Irish regiments who had become casualties of the war in France. A study of some 700 names and occupations of deportees listed in the *Irish Times* on May 11, 13, and 14 reveals the following general categories and indicates the largely working-class background of the Irish Volunteer rank and file arrested immediately after the Rising:

General unskilled labor	273
Tradesmen and allied occupations	201
Clerks	102
Shop assistants	54
Apprentices	9
Seamen/Dockers	4
Students	6
Farmers	11
Other (grocers, insurance agents, etc.)	58
Total:	718

Dublin Corporation, which had already yielded 5 victims to the cause, also contributed names to the growing number of those arrested: Sinn Fein Alderman Thomas Kelly; his colleagues John T. Kelly and W. T. Cosgrave, both Rising participants and the latter reprieved from a sentence of death; councillor P. V. Mahon, printer of the IRB-influenced *Irish Volunteer*; Labour councillors P. T. Daly and William Partridge; and ex-councillor T. Farren. About 3,500 prisoners in all were arrested during the Rebellion, only 1,000 being released immediately and some 2,000 deported. The piecemeal return of the internees provided recurring opportunities for the expression of nationalist sympathies in the streets of Dublin. Men who months before had been hooted as "toy soldiers" drilling with mock rifles were now hailed as returning heroes. Postcard photos of the executed rebel leaders and Irish republican songbooks were added to antienlistment handbills as material to be seized by the police. A resurgence of patriotism and national pride infected those who had for long supported the bland nationalism of the Irish parliamentary party. Even the schoolboys of Summerhill, who had distinguished themselves as "strikers" in 1913, became "patriots" in 1916, when they started a riot to protest the order of the school commissioners against the wearing of nationalist badges in school. The military authorities were also conscious of the changed mood, although the apprehensive report made by General Maxwell to the cabinet in late June may have been framed to steel the nerves of civilians in the event further tough measures should be necessary:

> It is impossible to conceive a more inflammable or dangerous condition than Ireland has been allowed to drift into . . . the social conditions of the cities in the South are deplorable, especially Dublin City; whether this is due to the incompetence of the municipality or to economic reasons, I am not in a position to say; but as long as the labour questions, the incidence of wages, the housing of the poor, remain as they are, rioting and disorder can be expected on the least provocation.[36]

The withdrawal of loyalist sentiment was perhaps most evident in the fortunes of the recruiting campaign. Unsatisfactory before the Rebellion, recruiting declined catastrophically soon after, the yellowing recruiting posters on barrack walls symbolic of dwindling enlistments. English and Scottish soldiers now had to be added to "Irish" divisions to fill the vacancies not taken up by Irish recruits. Redmond, blissfully unaware that the Irish party no longer spoke for Ireland, erred in choosing to speak for the citizens of Dublin when, in correspondence with General Macready on how best to find more recruits for the army, he suggested the formation of a Dublin Brigade: "I am sure that this creation would arouse a great deal of interest and satisfaction in Dublin City." The feelings of the citizens were more accurately appraised by Sir Matthew Nathan, the Under Secretary, in his own analysis of events at the Royal Commission:

> Apart from its general ultimate futility, the planning and conduct of the insurrection showed greater organising power and more military skill than had been attributed to the Volunteers, and they also appear from all reports to have acted with greater courage. These things and the high character of some of the idealists who took part in the insurrection no doubt account for some of the sympathy which the beaten Volunteers have undoubtedly excited among a large—probably the larger part of the people of Dublin—and in many places in the country. There are also the deeper grounds of a passionate national feeling for Ireland and of a long hatred of England.[37]

There remained one final victim of the Rising—the city itself. Damage to buildings was extensive in the wake of fire and artillery, but it was almost entirely confined to Lower O'Connell Street, from O'Connell Bridge northwards. The fires had begun on Tuesday evening during the looting of Lawrence's photographic and toy store, exploding fireworks, rockets, and Roman candles adumbrating in macabre fashion the destructive shellfire that was soon to rain down on Liberty Hall, the G.P.O., and other buildings in the area. Between the imposing monuments of Nelson and O'Connell—smoke-enshrouded and bullet-ridden—lay a scene of utter devastation. A heap of broken bricks marked

The Easter Rising: the destruction by bombardment of Liberty Hall.

the site of Messrs. Hopkins, the familiar jeweller's shop at the corner of Eden Quay. A stone's throw along the quay stood the gutted Liberty Hall—"no more than a sinister and hateful memory," gloated one newspaper. Of the shops and houses that ran the length of the block to the corner of Lower Abbey Street, only the skeleton of the D.B.C. premises remained. Two other familiar landmarks, Mooney's pub on Eden Quay and Wynn's Hotel in Abbey Street, disappeared in the wreckage. On this block also perished the valuable collection of paintings and sculpture worth an estimated £40,000 in the home of the Royal Hibernian Academy. Between Abbey Street and North Earl Street only ruined hulks of buildings and tottering walls stood on the sites of Clery's and other establishments. Alderman Downes's new bakery in North Earl Street was totally destroyed, and similar destruction was visited on the block extending to the next corner at Cathedral Street on which Lawrence's had provided a pyrotechnic display to accompany the looting. On the western side of the thoroughfare, Bachelor's Walk, the scene two years earlier of the famous shooting affray in connection with the Howth gun-running, suffered only superficial damage. Around the corner, the large chiming clock at Chancellor's next door to the bullet-ridden Gunpowder Office of Messrs. Kelly reportedly still kept going despite being shot through. Most of the houses on the block extending northward to Middle Abbey Streeet escaped serious damage, though Elvery's at the northern end was destroyed by fire. The destruction in Middle Abbey Street and down as far as Prince's Street was almost total, the Hotel Metropole vanishing without a trace and important business establishments such as Eason's, Freeman's Journal Company, and other printing and publishing houses being levelled to the ground. On the next block stood what remained

The Easter Rising: a view of the destruction of the Imperial Hotel and Clery's department store from atop Nelson's Pillar. The blocks south from Sackville Place to Lower Abbey Street and from there to the bridge are also totally destroyed.

of the G.P.O., the rebel headquarters. The famous creation of Francis Johnston (whose portrait, incidentally, was destroyed in the fire at the Royal Hibernian Academy) had only just undergone extensive internal reconstruction and on August 16 would have celebrated the 100th anniversary of the laying of the foundation stone. Now the interior lay in ruins surrounded by gaping walls and the bullet-chipped columns of the portico. Along the adjoining Henry and Moore Streets destruction was equally great. Elsewhere damage was only slight, with the exception of those houses destroyed in the fierce battle waged near the Mount Street Bridge over the Grand Canal. Remarkably, the Custom House, the old Parliament House (Bank of Ireland), Trinity College, and Kingsbridge Railway Station escaped damage.[38]

These scenes of desolation, which had attracted only the "hooligan" element during the fighting, now became the venue of sightseeing citizens, souvenir hunters, and the desperate few for whom pieces of wood and other combustible material meant added comfort. Soldiers, police, and special constables were out in force to prevent further looting and enforce the repressive paraphernalia of martial law. Damaged shops had to be boarded up, tottering structures pulled down, and mountains of brick, stone, and twisted steel removed. More important, reconstruction had to be undertaken as soon as possible to heal the ugly gashes in the historic city. In this regard building experts and town planners added their voices in the hope that a restored O'Connell Street would be notable for something other than being merely the widest thoroughfare in Europe. Many of the old patchwork collection of buildings that had been destroyed possessed little of architectural merit and were quite devoid of aesthetic interest. Thus, town planners felt that the ill wind of rebellion had presented a great opportunity to an Irish Nash or Haussman. Coincidentally, the future of Dublin had shortly before been under consideration by those architects who had entered Lord Aberdeen's town planning competition in 1914. There was no shortage of ideas therefore on what that future might be. Some civic-minded observers expressed regret for the insurgents' failure to remove that formidable obstruction to traffic, Nelson's Pillar (a matter since righted!). Others bemoaned the continued presence of the equally obstructive Parnell Monument and an "eyesore" Metal Bridge. The prospect of reconstruction also resurrected the idea of a Catholic cathedral for the city, Archbishop Walsh proposing that at least a site might be acquired and held in trust until money for building should become available (a matter not yet righted). The most comprehensive plan was the winning design in the Aberdeen competition submitted by Professor Abercrombie and his associates.[39] The outstanding feature of that plan was the displacement westward of the city's existing main artery (O'Connell Street) through the creation of a new city center along a line extending from Christ Church on the south bank to the Four Courts area on the north. A series of radial roads from all four quadrants would concentrate on this new center, about which would run concentric circumferential routes, on one of which O'Connell Street—freed of the "tram incubus"—would represent a chord. On the north bank of the Liffey would develop a prosperous business and commercial life, while the south bank would boast the new legislative buildings of the home rule parliament as well as the seats of learning. Other important features of the Abercrombie plan included a massive power citadel in the harbor, a national theater and music auditorium to replace the Rotunda, the removal of Butt Bridge and the building of a new road bridge to connect the splendid Custom House with the southern quays, and a Catholic cathedral in Capel Street in whose courtyard would rise a round tower, 500 feet high and topped with a figure of St. Patrick, whose "colossal shaft . . . would serve as the spiritual emblem of the city, as the power citadel chimney is the sign of its material sanity"!

The spoils of war. Children gather firewood from destroyed buildings in the wake of the Easter Rising.

These, however, were grandiose plans for a city as penurious as Dublin, where budgetary deficiencies had already curtailed street lighting and public interest in town planning was confined to a tiny few. Such planning had been rejected in 1914, when immediate concerns ran to housing for the working classes. Now once more town planning was subordinated to the immediate needs of businessmen and small traders. In O'Connell Street alone some 90 establishments had either been destroyed or heavily damaged. There were problems in providing capital as well as difficulties arising from the effects of the war in procuring supplies of timber, steel, and other building materials. Insurance companies were not liable under the circumstances, and special legislation (6 & 7 Geo. 5, cap. 46) had been introduced to waive the liability of local authorities for criminal or malicious injuries arising out of the recent "disturbances," a welcome decision to ratepayers. Property owners, therefore, looked to the government for redress. Indeed,

The Easter Rising: citizens inspect the destruction in Henry Street. The Post Office is on the right.

there was every encouragement to do so considering that the report of the royal commission inquiring into the events leading up to the rebellion lent credence to the general notion of government culpability for the outbreak by its strong criticism of both the negligence and indulgent policies of the Irish administration. An early announcement of the Lord Lieutenant assured owners that the State would assume liability up to the amount that would have been payable by insurance companies had damages been recoverable, as in the case of fire and the like. For this purpose looting was to be treated as if the losses occasioned thereby had also been due to fire. Accordingly, in anticipation of the *ex gratia* grants promised by the government, an association was formed to process the claims of over 1,200 individuals. Estimates of losses incurred were as high as £2.5 million and included such individual claims as £47,000 (Messrs. Arnott) and £157,000 (the Gas Company). Many individuals would also suffer irreparable losses in goodwill and irrecoverable debts, for the resulting government grants for rebuilding and property damage did not exceed £1.75 million.[40] The Corporation was also a sufferer inasmuch as rates could no longer be recovered on the former valuation of ruined property, a circumstance that could only introduce further stringencies in municipal services.

The final consideration was the actual rebuilding of the destroyed areas. As early as July 5 a deputation from Dublin Corporation headed by the Lord Mayor met with the prime minister to impress on the government the necessity of financial help in enabling the Corporation to make street improvements and lend money to those owners whose premises had been destroyed. Eventually a bill was introduced in Parliament during the summer—the Dublin Reconstruction (Emergency Provisions) Bill. Its intent, as the new Chief Secretary explained during the second reading, was to provide for the reconstruction of the main parts of Dublin "in a manner consistent with the traditions which attach to the almost historic main thoroughfare in Dublin . . . to prevent a shanty being erected where there was formerly a noble structure."[41] From the outset, however, property owners indicated their opposition to architectural constraints that would delay building operations or create added expense. Under the Dublin Reconstruction Act, which was passed into law in December 1916 (6 & 7 Geo. 5, cap. 66), the city architect was given the authority to approve all rebuilding plans and reject those of a character that would be injurious to the amenity of the street fronting thereon. The Act also provided for temporary rates exemption and protected the interests of license holders of destroyed public houses. Alas, there was to be no planning on the grand scale, for the Corporation was given little power to impose designs on owners. The tentative plans offered so few concessions to art that one observer quipped that the destructive effects of the rebellion might not prove half so bad as the projected rebuilding: apparently there was some danger at one point that red brick might triumph over cut stone for O'Connell Street frontages. The disillusion of the town planners was expressed by the *Irish Builder*: ". . . the property owners and those who control such matters had so little enthusiasm, were so concerned in narrow interests . . . [that they] failed completely to rise to the great and noble traditions of eighteenth-century Dublin."[42]

But the city that emerged from the ashes of 1916 could no longer be measured only by stone and brick. Dublin, which had known its share of poverty, shame, and tragedy, now tasted glory as it sanctified the national cause with the blood of martyrs. In the months and years that followed, the "terrible beauty" that was born in Dublin continued to radiate its claim on the allegiance of Irishmen and Irishwomen and mock the parting words of Augustine Birrell as Chief Secretary for Ireland: "I hope . . . that this insurrection in Ireland will never, even in the minds and memories of that people, be associated with their past rebellions, or become an historical landmark in their history."[43]

Epilogue

The bitter struggle for Irish independence that culminated in 1921 saw the establishment of an Irish Free State and the conferring on Dublin a status she had not hitherto enjoyed as seat both of a national government and an independent, freely elected legislature. The city had become a capital in fact as well as in name. It was not, however, the capital of a united Ireland. The new state represented only 26 of the country's 32 counties, leaving Dublin to vie with Belfast as one of two Irish capital cities. And the year of civil war in 1922, which once more brought bloodshed and killing to the streets of Dublin, could not alter the reality of that political compromise. The cherished dream of nationhood was placed in abeyance while a new political identity was being created for three million Irishmen. The practical results of this national endeavor would have their most immediate effect in Dublin with the establishment of Dail Eireann and the sweeping away of all the agencies of British rule that had formerly operated from Dublin Castle. Ironically, among the casualties of administrative restructuring was the Dublin Corporation, dismissed unceremoniously in 1924 by W. T. Cosgrave, a former councillor and then prime minister—a bold stroke that not even Dublin Castle had attempted against that "voice of Ireland" in its most provocative moments.[1] For the next six years the city was administered by three commissioners appointed by the government. To them is due the credit for the civic improvements that transformed the streets of the city from the old and inadequate cobblestone surfaces to concrete and asphalt. Among their achievements also was the financing of house purchase schemes for a growing population. When a local government act extended the boundaries of the city in 1930, thus realizing the 50-year-old dream of incorporating the southern urban districts of Pembroke and Rathmines along with the townlands of Cabra, Killester, Clonskeagh, Terenure and others, the population stood at 416,000, an increase of over one-third since the census of 1911. The city continued to exert its pull on the rural parts of Leinster while growing numbers of educated country youth took up official employment in the highly centralized bureaucracy. By 1946 the population of the city had passed the half-million mark, although the rest of the country continued to experience the population decline characteristic of economically stagnant and underdeveloped areas.

The city retained for a considerable period of time some of the worst features of its former distressful circumstances—poverty, unemployment, and inadequate housing. Even the walls of the General Post Office, a victim of the Easter Rising, lay in ruins for almost a decade, and O'Connell Street and the Four Courts area bore for several years the marks of the destruction they had suffered during the civil war. True, gains were readily won in advancing public health, reducing death rates, and eradicating the worst forms of poverty; and, as always, the unemployed were "exported" to Britain and elsewhere. But the clearing out of the slums and the building of new homes defied quick solution. After 1930 the reconstituted 35-member Dublin Corporation took up this task begun by its predecessor over 40 years before. Under the Housing Act of 1932 the new body undertook the slum clearances that led to the creation of vast, working-class housing estates in the southern suburban district of Crumlin. Yet at the end of that decade it was estimated that over 20,000 dwellings were still needed to provide for those families still living in tenement houses regarded unfit for human habitation. In the course of time the housing problem too was solved, though at the cost of ringing the city with dreary and characterless public housing.

Dublin can no longer be accused of possessing, as Patrick Abercrombie once claimed, "the most architectural slums in Europe." Happily, only minor pockets of blight remain in a city that now enjoys the flourishing affluence of Western European capitals. The city is now the center of a growing conurbation whose numbers will soon approach one million residents, or about one-third of the country's entire population. But, strangely, the terms used by architects and planners to describe this present-day metropolis are redolent of the anguished cries of yesteryear—city in crisis, city in decline, city rotting at the heart! Not the social dilemmas of the past but rather the depredations of the developer have generated this new concern for the future of Dublin. Dublin, like many cities, has fallen victim to the regressive effects of the automobile. The desire for suburban living, facilitated over the past quarter-century by mass use of the private motor car, has had disturbing consequences for the form and vitality of the old central core of historic Dublin. The resulting depopulation of inner urban areas has placed the city at the mercy of speculators and developers. Car parks have silenced the mingled chorus of urban voices. The sealed monoliths of public and corporate enterprise have replaced the living social tissue of family dwelling and local store. Waste sites, derelict spaces, deteriorating housing abound. Nothing remains to evoke the nostalgic associations of old Moore Street. Boarded-up hulks disfigure deserted streets where rehabilitation might have restored a living presence. The inner city has been abandoned to the less well-off citizens, the helpless sufferers of the traffic congestion and environmental pollution that are the hallmarks of the commuter civilization. Elsewhere, the suburban sprawl, especially to the favored southeast, still promises security, relaxation, child-rearing advantages, and social status. But at such high cost—the deprivation, deterioration, and segregation of the central city, a city upon which descends at the end of each working day "an interminable deathly hush."[2]

The future of Dublin is far from clear. There is hope in the city's avoidance of the worst excesses of criminality and vandalism. There is no hint of the civil disorder that has made a battlefield of her sister city in the north. Nor does the racial prejudice that has produced unbearable tensions in other metropolitan centers exist in Dublin. The city of Yeats and Joyce—Dublin within the canals—still possesses noble qualities in its natural beauty, fine architecture, and picturesque quays. It lacks, however, the wide-ranging cultural amenities and cosmopolitan atmosphere that have enabled world cities like Paris, London, and New York to retain an enduring attraction for those in the grip of the metropolitan spirit. Dublin will not become a world city, but its politicians, planners, and people can do nothing less than attempt to realize that hope Patrick Geddes expressed in 1913—that the city become what it was in the eighteenth century, one of the most important secondary cities in the world. It will not be an easy task to persuade those who have forsaken the civic ideal to remake the urban environment. Their mission for the Dublin of the future must be, to borrow the words of Lewis Mumford, "to put the highest concerns of man at the center of all his activities: to unite the scattered fragments of the human personality, turning artificially dismembered men—bureaucrats, specialists, 'experts,' depersonalized agents—into complete human beings, repairing the damage that has been done by vocational separation, by social segregation, by the over-cultivation of a favored function, by tribalisms and nationalisms, by the absence of organic partnerships and ideal purposes."[3]

Appendices

APPENDIX A. Dublin City and County: Religious affiliations of the people expressed as percentages of the population in each city ward and in suburban areas, 1871–1926.

	1871					1881					1891				
	RC	E	P	M	O	RC	E	P	M	O	RC	E	P	M	O
A. DUBLIN CITY															
North city wards:															
Arran Quay	82.9	13.2	1.6	0.9	1.4	82.2	13.6	2.5	0.9	0.8	85.0	12.5	1.2	0.8	0.5
Inns Quay	86.0	10.8	1.7	0.4	1.1	84.0	12.2	2.3	0.4	1.1	86.5	10.6	1.9	0.4	0.6
Mountjoy	72.0	21.4	3.3	1.3	2.0	75.9	18.9	2.7	1.2	1.3	83.5	13.4	1.4	0.8	0.9
North City	80.2	14.2	3.1	1.1	1.4	83.5	12.0	2.3	1.0	1.2	87.2	10.3	1.2	0.6	0.7
North Dock	77.7	14.1	3.8	1.3	3.1	80.3	14.0	2.4	1.0	2.3	81.9	12.8	2.4	0.9	2.0
Rotunda	73.5	22.2	2.4	0.3	1.6	78.3	18.3	2.2	0.5	0.7	83.6	13.6	1.5	0.4	0.9
South city wards:															
Fitzwilliam	57.9	34.1	1.7	1.5	4.8	62.3	32.2	1.4	2.1	2.0	64.7	27.8	1.7	1.3	4.5
Mansion House	74.8	20.8	0.7	0.8	2.9	75.3	21.5	0.8	0.6	1.8	78.7	18.9	0.6	0.6	1.2
Merchants' Quay	88.5	9.6	0.8	0.6	0.5	87.4	10.9	0.7	0.5	0.5	84.4	12.4	1.7	0.6	0.9
Royal Exchange	75.8	18.4	1.8	0.7	3.3	75.0	19.3	3.0	1.0	1.7	74.4	21.8	1.2	1.5	1.1
South City	77.1	17.4	2.2	1.0	2.3	80.7	15.5	1.7	0.9	1.2	77.5	17.3	1.7	0.8	2.7
South Dock	73.1	20.4	2.2	0.2	4.1	76.8	19.8	1.5	0.4	1.5	79.6	17.5	1.0	0.5	1.4
Trinity	78.9	16.4	1.2	0.5	3.0	81.2	16.6	1.1	0.1	1.0	83.0	14.2	1.4	0.5	0.9
Usher's Quay	86.9	11.4	1.0	0.2	0.5	87.2	11.0	1.1	0.4	0.3	87.6	11.2	0.7	0.3	0.2
Wood Quay	81.0	16.2	0.9	0.7	1.2	80.8	16.2	1.0	1.0	1.0	79.5	14.9	1.3	1.0	3.3
Added areas:															
Clontarf East															
Clontarf West															
Drumcondra					(see note 1)										
Glasnevin															
New Kilmainham															
Total for City	79.2	16.2	1.8	0.8	2.0	80.4	15.9	1.8	0.8	1.1	82.2	14.4	1.4	0.7	1.3
B. SUBURBS															
Blackrock	61.4	32.2	1.6	1.2	3.6	63.2	30.2	1.6	1.0	4.0	64.1	28.9	1.4	1.5	4.1
Kingstown[a]	63.4	31.5	1.5	1.1	2.5	66.3	28.9	1.4	1.1	2.3	67.7	28.5	1.6	0.8	1.4
Pembroke	56.2	36.3	3.6	1.7	2.2	60.4	33.2	2.4	1.7	2.3	59.8	30.8	5.1	2.0	2.3
Rathmines & Rathgar	47.8	42.3	3.6	1.9	4.4	49.1	40.3	4.0	2.5	4.1	49.9	38.7	3.9	2.9	4.6
Total for suburbs	56.0	36.5	2.8	1.5	3.2	58.5	34.1	2.6	1.7	3.1	58.5	32.9	3.5	2.0	3.1
C. REST OF COUNTY	80.7	16.4	1.2	0.4	1.3	80.5	16.6	1.5	0.5	0.9	78.7	17.8	1.6	0.9	1.0

[a]under revived official name of Dun Laoghaire in 1926 census.

Note 1: population included in C, 1871–1891; areas became part of city after annexation in 1900.

Abbreviations: RC = Roman Catholic; E = Episcopalian (Church of Ireland); P = Presbyterian; M = Methodist; O = Other (including no information)

Sources: Census of Ireland: Dublin City and County, 1871–1926 (% calculated by author).

	1901					1911					1926			
RC	E	P	M	O	RC	E	P	M	O	RC	E	P	M	O
83.2	13.9	1.3	0.7	0.9	84.7	12.9	0.9	0.6	0.9	92.7	5.9	0.5	0.3	0.6
87.8	9.7	1.4	0.4	0.7	90.8	7.8	0.7	0.2	0.5	94.8	4.4	0.4	0.1	0.3
85.0	12.6	1.1	0.6	0.7	88.7	9.6	0.9	0.3	0.5	94.3	5.0	0.3	0.2	0.2
89.6	8.6	0.6	0.4	0.8	92.0	5.9	1.0	0.3	0.8	95.1	3.4	0.4	0.1	1.0
84.6	11.3	1.7	0.6	1.8	85.6	10.5	1.8	0.5	1.6	91.9	6.3	1.1	0.2	0.5
85.3	12.0	1.4	0.4	0.9	88.8	9.4	1.1	0.2	0.5	94.5	4.5	0.4	0.2	0.4
67.3	23.7	1.9	1.7	5.4	71.0	20.4	1.8	1.7	5.1	79.4	14.7	1.1	1.2	3.6
84.0	13.6	0.8	0.5	1.1	85.5	12.2	0.9	0.2	1.2	91.0	7.5	0.6	0.1	0.8
82.8	13.5	1.0	0.7	2.0	83.2	12.1	0.9	0.6	3.2	89.8	6.8	0.4	0.4	2.6
78.5	17.9	1.5	0.1	2.0	80.0	16.5	1.4	0.8	1.3	87.7	10.4	0.7	0.2	1.0
79.4	17.1	0.1	0.7	2.7	81.6	14.4	1.1	0.5	2.4	90.0	7.3	0.8	0.3	1.6
80.8	16.3	1.0	0.5	1.4	84.8	12.7	1.0	0.4	1.1	91.1	7.4	0.5	0.2	0.8
85.2	13.0	0.7	0.2	0.9	87.5	10.8	0.7	0.3	0.7	91.5	6.8	0.9	0.2	0.6
88.3	10.3	0.6	0.4	0.4	87.5	10.7	0.7	0.6	0.5	91.1	7.1	0.6	0.7	0.5
77.7	14.8	1.1	0.8	5.6	79.5	12.2	0.9	0.5	6.9	85.5	7.3	0.5	0.5	6.2
60.5	27.6	5.3	4.2	2.4	63.0	24.9	5.8	3.8	2.5	73.9	18.2	3.7	2.4	1.8
56.3	29.7	7.1	3.7	3.2	55.9	26.3	8.4	5.4	4.0	79.1	13.5	3.5	1.7	2.2
73.6	19.1	3.3	1.8	2.2	75.7	17.7	2.7	1.7	2.2	84.6	12.0	2.2	0.6	0.6
61.9	28.6	4.1	2.9	2.5	64.7	26.6	4.7	1.7	2.3	83.1	12.6	2.7	0.8	0.8
76.5	20.1	1.2	1.5	0.7	75.9	20.5	0.9	1.8	0.9	91.9	6.6	0.3	0.7	0.5
81.8	14.3	1.4	0.8	1.7	83.1	12.9	1.4	0.8	1.8	90.0	7.4	0.8	0.5	1.3
66.7	25.6	2.1	1.5	4.1	67.4	26.1	2.1	1.9	2.5	77.7	17.2	1.8	1.4	1.9
68.9	26.9	1.7	1.1	1.4	69.5	25.5	2.1	1.1	1.8	75.2	19.9	1.9	1.2	1.8
64.3	28.9	2.8	1.9	2.1	67.2	25.4	3.1	2.2	2.1	77.0	17.6	2.1	1.5	1.8
52.8	35.3	4.2	3.5	4.2	54.0	34.1	4.4	3.1	4.4	66.8	23.4	3.4	2.5	3.9
61.1	30.6	3.0	2.3	3.0	62.3	29.1	3.3	2.3	3.0	72.7	20.3	2.6	1.8	2.6
81.2	16.1	1.4	0.5	0.8	81.2	15.5	1.6	0.7	1.0	86.1	11.1	1.2	0.6	1.0

APPENDIX B. Dublin City and County: Population of wards and suburban areas, 1851–1926.

	1851	1861	1871	1881	1891	1901	1911	1926
A. DUBLIN CITY								
North city wards:								
Arran Quay	30,148	27,726	26,720	27,405	26,546	31,109	35,019	33,461
Inns Quay	21,533	21,188	21,009	22,707	22,496	24,940	23,305	22,600
Mountjoy	14,305	15,421	19,427	19,407	22,469	24,840	25,998	27,381
North City	15,307	14,150	11,327	10,885	9,774	8,784	7,886	6,719
North Dock	17,211	18,573	20,248	22,707	23,075	23,634	24,506	27,317
Rotunda	11,019	12,059	9,945	12,210	12,549	14,580	15,617	18,038
South city wards:								
Fitzwilliam	8,825	10,187	9,984	10,786	11,949	12,455	12,404	13,762
Mansion House	12,475	13,526	13,734	11,767	11,096	11,892	11,189	10,587
Merchants' Quay	24,907	22,417	20,576	20,281	23,034	25,434	25,705	26,772
Royal Exchange	14,137	13,990	11,764	9,778	8,766	7,648	6,532	5,355
South City	10,101	9,370	7,885	6,176	4,599	4,385	3,857	3,298
South Dock	14,156	13,515	14,426	15,051	14,895	14,766	15,074	16,084
Trinity	15,955	17,267	14,992	13,662	12,176	12,331	11,081	10,027
Usher's Quay	24,931	22,864	22,607	22,779	21,129	23,655	25,793	25,573
Wood Quay	23,351	22,260	21,682	24,001	20,448	20,654	21,986	21,869
Added areas: (note 1)								
Clontarf East	.	.	.	.	.	3,081	3,303	4,275
Clontarf West	.	.	.	.	.	3,849	5,662	9,232
Drumcondra	.	.	.	.	.	7,545	9,774	11,712
Glasnevin	.	.	.	.	.	6,273	10,481	11,461
New Kilmainham	.	.	.	.	.	8,783	9,630	11,170
Total A	258,361	254,513	246,326	249,602	245,001	290,638	304,802	316,693
B. SUBURBS (note 2)								
Blackrock	.	.	8,089	8,902	8,401	8,719	9,080	9,934
Kingstown	.	.	16,378	18,586	17,352	17,377	17,219	18,987
Pembroke	.	.	20,982	23,222	24,269	25,799	29,294	33,383
Rathmines & Rathgar	.	.	20,562	24,370	27,796	32,602	37,840	39,984
Total B			66,011	75,080	77,818	84,497	93,433	102,288
C. REST OF COUNTY	146,778	155,444	92,885	94,228	96,397	72,856 (note 3)	78,961	86,673

Note 1. Population of "added areas" included in C, 1851–1891. These areas annexed to municipality in 1900, adding five new wards as shown.

Note 2. Population of southern suburbs included in C, 1851–61: Blackrock and Pembroke townships not incorporated until 1863.

Note 3. Decrease over preceding decade brought about by annexation of county areas to the city in 1900 (see note 1).

SOURCE: Census of Ireland: Dublin City and County, 1851–1926.

APPENDIX C. Dublin Corporation: Members of the council and political affiliations, 1899–1915.

Abbreviations: I = Independent; IN = Independent Nationalist; L = Labour; SF = Sinn Fein; U = Unionist. Where no identifying letter is given, member is Nationalist.

The Lord Mayor for each year is indicated by an asterisk. Names of aldermen are in block capitals. Blank space(s) under names signify incumbent continued in office for year as indicated.

†denotes member elected during previous year on death or resignation of incumbent.

‡denotes same member served in different ward at another time during the period.

(sources: Dublin Corporation, Minutes of the Council, 1899–1915; *Irish Times*; *Freeman's Journal*).

YEAR	ARRAN QUAY WARD			
1899	‡J. CUMMINS	R. Jones	W. Coffey	J. Keogh
1900			P. Monks	
1901				
1902	W. GAYNOR			
1903	W. COFFEY			T. Dunne
1904		J. Carolan		
1905				
1906			T. Rooney	
1907				
1908				
1909	*			
1910				
1911				
1912				
1913		J. Nugent		
1914	J. KEOGH			M. J. Kelly
1915				

YEAR	CLONTARF EAST WARD (begins 1901)			
1899				
1900				
1901	H. GIBSON (U)	G. Booker (U)	G. Tickell (U)	M. J. Judge
1902				
1903			‡J. Brady	
1904	(vacant)	‡J. Crozier VS(U)		
1905	‡G. HEALY (U)			E. Higginbotham (U)
1906				
1907				
1908			G. Birney (U)	
1909				
1910				
1911				
1912			‡J. Clancy	
1913				
1914	J. Ryan		J. CLANCY	‡W. Reigh
1915		†P. Meehan	and ‡J. MORAN	

YEAR	CLONTARF WEST WARD (begins 1901)			
1899				
1900				
1901	W. GRAHAM (U)	A. Lyon	A. Noble (U)	W. Woodhams (U)
1902				
1903			‡F. Vance (U)	
1904	W. McCarthy (U)			W. WOODHAMS (U)
1905		A. LYON		J. Doyle
1906			M. Cahill	
1907				
1908		‡W. Ireland (U)		W. WOODHAMS (U)
1909			T. R. Scott (U)	
1910				
1911				
1912			S. Crawford (U)	
1913	T. P. Bradshaw (I)			†J. MAGUIRE
1914		W. Coulter (U)	(vacant)	W. McCARTHY (U)
1915	†M. J. Moran		‡J. Moran and J. Foley	

YEAR	DRUMCONDRA WARD (begins 1901)			
1899				
1900				
1901	J. DERWIN	P. Murray (I)	‡F. Vance (U)	T. Lawler
1902				
1903			‡D. Daly	
1904		A. Dawson (U)		
1905				
1906			F. Vance (U)	
1907		D. Doyle (SF)		
1908	C. J. Murray		F. VANCE (U)	D. Quaid
1909				
1910		J. Derwin		
1911				
1912				
1913				
1914			J. Dillon	D. QUAID
1915	J. P. McAvin	and D. Daly		

YEAR	FITZWILLIAM WARD			
1899	‡W. IRELAND (U)	P. Corrigan	T. Pile	T. Joynt (U)
1900			*(knighted)	
1901				
1902				J. Keys MD (U)
1903				
1904			T. Kennedy	
1905	J. Hatch	P. CORRIGAN		P. Lennon
1906				
1907				
1908	J. Gallagher			
1909				
1910				
1911				
1912				
1913				
1914				
1915	*(see note below)			

NOTE: Councillor Gallagher assumed the mayoralty on the death of Alderman Clancy (Clontarf East) shortly after the latter's election to the mayoralty in January 1915.

YEAR	GLASNEVIN WARD (begins 1901)			
1899				
1900				
1901	J. F. McCARTHY	‡J. Crozier VS (U)	Garrett Begg	W. Dinnage (U)
1902				
1903		M. Crowe		
1904				
1905				
1906	†F. KEEGAN			
1907				C. Monks
1908		‡J. Cummins	†‡D. Daly	
1909			M. Maher	
1910				
1911				
1912			J. Thornton (I)	
1913				
1914	W. DINNAGE (U)			
1915				

YEAR	INNS QUAY WARD			
1899	T. LENEHAN	J. Downes	T. O'Neill	E. Richardson (L)
1900		(knighted)		
1901				M. Fitzpatrick
1902				
1903			T. O'Loughlin	
1904	W. L. COLE			A. Madden
1905				
1906	(joined SF)		J. T. Kelly (SF)	
1907				
1908	Gerald Begg	J. DOWNES		
1909				‡T. O'Reilly
1910				
1911				
1912				
1913				W. Delany
1914	W. O'Hara			
1915				

YEAR	MANSION HOUSE WARD			
1899	P. DOWD (L)	*D. Tallon	T. Kelly	P. Little
1900				
1901				
1902				
1903				
1904		W. Rippingale (U)		
1905	T. Clear		T. KELLY	
1906	(joined SF)	†J. Reynolds (SF)	(joined SF)	†J. J. Ryan (SF)
1907		M. Cole		
1908				R. O'Carroll (L)
1909				
1910				
1911	T. O'Brien			
1912				
1913				
1914				
1915				

YEAR	MERCHANTS' QUAY WARD			
1899	J. HENDRICK	J. Hutchinson	J. P. Cox	M. McGovern
1900				
1901				J. Vaughan
1902				
1903				
1904		*		
1905	C. DOWLING	*		
1906				
1907				
1908			D. McCarthy (SF)	
1909				
1910				
1911	W. O'CONNOR		‡J. Scully	
1912		J. Bohan (L)		
1913				
1914				
1915		E. Brooks (L)		

YEAR	MOUNTJOY WARD			
1899	J. J. FARRELL	W. Leahy (L)	J. Kennedy	J. Clarke (L)
1900			J. C. Briscoe	
1901				
1902				
1903				
1904		J. Parkinson		
1905				
1906				L. Sherlock
1907				
1908				
1909				
1910		P. V. Mahon		
1911	*			
1912				*
1913				*
1914				*
1915				

YEAR	NEW KILMAINHAM WARD (begins 1901)			
1899				
1900				
1901	J. McCANN	J. Cooney	C. Kelly	J. Cronin
1902				‡ W. Reigh
1903			M. J. Lord (L)	
1904				
1905	† W. Partridge (L)	P. O'Carroll		W. REIGH
1906		(joined SF)		
1907	M. J. O'Lehane (L)		P. J. Rooney	
1908	J. Gleeson			
1909				
1910				
1911				J. MURRAY
1912			J. S. Kelly (L)	
1913	W. Partridge (L)	† T. O'Hanlon (L)		
1914		H. Donnelly (L)		
1915		† J. Gleeson		

YEAR	NORTH CITY WARD			
1899	J. HENNESSY	M. Canty (L)	J. Long	P. White
1900		J. Irwin		
1901			P. J. McCabe	(elected MP)
1902				
1903				
1904			C. Grimes	
1905			J. O'Reilly	J. C. M'Walter MD
1906	C. A. James	J. IRWIN		
1907				
1908		J. Maloney (L)	R. J. Union	J. C. M'WALTER MD
1909				
1910		J. J. Fox		
1911				
1912				
1913			J. Gately	
1914				
1915	J. O'Doherty			

YEAR	NORTH DOCK WARD			
1899	E. FLEMING (L)	D. Bergin	T. C. Harrington MP	E. Holohan
1900				
1901			*	T. Byrne
1902	M. Mullally (L)	D. BERGIN	*	
1903	P. Ryan		*	
1904				
1905				
1906	P. O'Reilly			
1907	†J. Kavanagh			
1908			P. Gregan (SF)	
1909	C. L. Ryan			
1910				J. P. Farrelly
1911			A. Byrne	
1912	J. Larkin (L)			
1913	†P. MACKEN (L)	†W. Richardson		M. Brohoon (L)
1914	J. Higgins		A. BYRNE	
1915		‡P. T. Daly (L)		

YEAR	ROTUNDA WARD			
1899	W. DOYLE	H. B. Kennedy MD	P. O'Hara	J. P. Nannetti
1900				
1901		T. McAuley		(elected MP)
1902				
1903				
1904			†‡P. T. Daly (L)	
1905				
1906		†J. Lawlor		*
1907				*
1908				
1909			P. McCarten (SF)	
1910		P. Shortall	L. O'Neill (IN)	
1911				
1912				P. J. Duffy
1913				
1914	C. McGuinness		L. O'NEILL (IN)	
1915				

YEAR	ROYAL EXCHANGE WARD			
1899	W. RUSSELL	‡A. Beattie (U)	‡J. Brady	‡M. Murray
1900				
1901				
1902	E. W. Smyth (U)			J. DELAHUNT
1903			J. Cahill (L)	
1904		J. Cogan		
1905	J. Doyle			
1906				
1907				
1908				
1909			J. J. McKee	
1910				
1911				
1912				
1913				
1914	J. Devlin			
1915			and M. O'Connor	

YEAR	SOUTH CITY WARD			
1899	Sir R. SEXTON (U)	G. Macnie (U)	H. Brown (U)	‡G. Healy (U)
1900				
1901				
1902	†R. O'REILLY			
1903			E. P. Monk	
1904		‡M. Murray		
1905				T. Cahill
1906				
1907		E. Bewley (U)		
1908				
1909				
1910				
1911	J. J. O'Neill	E. BEWLEY (U)		‡A. Beattie (I)
1912			S. Harrison (IN)	
1913				
1914				
1915		†J. J. CORRY	J. Isaacs	

YEAR	SOUTH DOCK WARD			
1899	W. F. COTTON	D. Burke	J. J. O'Meara	‡J. Clancy
1900				
1901				T. J. Fitzgerald
1902				J. Clancy
1903				
1904				J. Camac
1905				
1906				
1907				J. Clancy
1908		A. Dickson		
1909				
1910				T. O'Beirne
1911	(elected MP)			
1912				
1913				
1914		M. Keogh MD		
1915				

YEAR	TRINITY WARD			
1899	J. MEADE	L. Doyle	P. Meagher	G. O'Reilly
1900			J. Lyons	
1901	G. Moore			G. O'REILLY
1902				
1903	†‡T. O'Reilly			
1904		M. Doyle		
1905				
1906			E. Meade	
1907	P. Comerford (SF)			
1908			†R. Bradley	*
1909				
1910	L. O'Toole (SF)	*		
1911				
1912			W. Hopkins (L)	
1913		W. Tierney (SF)		
1914		W. Chase (L)		
1915			P. Power	

YEAR	USHER'S QUAY WARD			
1899	M. FLANAGAN	W. Redmond MP	J. Gibbons (L)	B. Gorevan
1900			W. Crimmins	
1901		†G. Lawless		
1902			†A. Altman	
1903				
1904			W. Johnston (L)	
1905		‡J. Scully		
1906				†W. Kavanagh
1907			M. Altman	
1908		D. Healy (SF)		
1909				W. T. Cosgrave (SF)
1910				
1911		D. Cogan		
1912			and T. Farren (L)	
1913			H. Doyle	
1914		C. Donaghy		
1915			†J. Groome	

YEAR	WOOD QUAY WARD			
1899	J. DAVIN	M. Kernan	P. J. McCall	R. J. Dodd
1900		†F. McKenna		
1901				
1902				
1903				W. Fanagan
1904				
1905				
1906				J. Byrne (SF)
1907		T. J. Sheehan (SF)		
1908				
1909				O. Brady
1910		M. J. Swaine		P. J. Dwyer
1911	J. J. KELLY		P. O'Reilly	
1912				T. Lawlor (L)
1913				
1914				
1915				M. T. Byrne

APPENDIX **D.** Dwellings completed by Dublin Corporation under Housing of the Working Classes Acts from 1887 to 1921.

COMPLETION	SCHEME	NUMBER AND TYPE	1 RM	2 RM	3 RM	4 RM
1887	Benburb Street	144 flats	63	67	10	4
1889	Bow Lane	86 flats		76	10	
1895, 1911	Bride's Alley	173 flats		94	79	
1896, 1913	Blackhall Place	86 flats		81	5	
		23 cottages				23
1896	St. Joseph's Place	80 cottages			80	
1904	Elizabeth Street	14 cottages			14	
1905	Clontarf	57 cottages		24	24	9
1905	Foley Street	458 flats	378	64	16	
1907	Townsend Street	20 flats		15	5	
1912	Inchicore	333 cottages			279	54
1914	Cook Street	45 cottages			45	
1914	Lurgan Street	48 cottages			48	
1917	Trinity Ward	28 cottages			28	
		48 flats		48		
1917	Church Street	146 cottages		28	94	24
1917, 1921	Ormond Market	61 cottages			61	
		56 flats		56		
1917	M'Caffrey Estate	262 cottages		20	40	202
1918	Spitalfields	75 cottages			75	
	Totals:	1,071 flats				
		1,172 cottages				

SOURCE. Report of Inquiry into the Housing of the Working Classes in the City of Dublin, 1939/43 (App. 1, Table A, p. 231).

APPENDIX E. Dublin Metropolitan Police District: Total offenses, persons proceeded against for selected offenses, and disposition of cases in selected years, 1899–1913.

	1899	1901	1906	1911	1913
1. Total Offenses					
A. Indictable (crimes):					
Against the person	86	113	111	130	202
Against property *with* violence (robbery, burglary, etc.)	86	153	249	353	237
Against property *without* violence (simple larceny, etc.)	2,074	2,251	2,657	2,607	2,328
Other (malicious damage, suicide attempts, etc.)	200	179	134	339	223
Totals	2,446	2,696	3,151	3,429	2,990
B. Nonindictable (persons proceeded against)	36,195	29,736	27,659	27,050	26,542
2. Selected Offenses					
A. Indictable (number of crimes):					
Murder (persons over 1 year)	2	2	2	3	—
Rape	2	6	5	1	—
Assault	23	38	44	38	35
Suicide attempts	65	36	47	33	33
Simple and minor larcenies	1,599	1,804	2,257	2,288	1,980
B. Nonindictable (persons proceeded against):					
Assault	2,714	2,061	1,752	1,839	2,076
Cruelty to children	153	225	325	349	443
Drunkenness	9,023	7,791	4,713	2,915	2,759
Prostitution	494	472	601	605	689
Vagrancy	912	981	1,099	915	783
3. Disposition of cases					
Number of persons made amenable:					
for indictable offenses	1,256	1,204	1,300	1,696	1,792
(conviction rate—%)	(65.1)	(67)	(63.8)	(57.8)	(53.2)
for nonindictable offenses	36,195	29,736	27,659	27,050	26,542
(conviction rate—%)	(84)	(83.6)	(83)	(74.1)	(74.1)
Total net convictions:	31,226	25,671	23,785	21,015	20,608
sent to prison	3,309	3,014	2,691	2,262	2,361
sent to reformatory	36	33	69	60	70
sent to industrial school	20	21	13	27	9
fined	27,784	22,260	20,861	18,397	17,862
4. Population of police district (i.e., city and suburbs) at each census	—	392,797	—	415,866	—
Police strength	1,137	1,172	1,184	1,202	1,173

SOURCE: Statistical Returns of the Dublin Metropolitan Police in *Parliamentary Papers* as follows: 1899 in 1900 (XL), cd. 176; 1901 in 1902 (XLII), cd. 1166; 1906 in 1907 (XXXI), cd. 3551; 1911 in 1912–13 (LXIX), cd. 6384; 1913 in 1914 (LXVII), cd. 7587.

APPENDIX F. Comparative statistics of crimes and offenses for Dublin and selected major English cities, including those with highest incidence in each category, 1900–13. (Based on annual statistical returns of the D.M.P. and judicial statistics—England & Wales).

(1) Crimes: Total Crimes Reported and Number of Criminal Offenses in Selected Sub-Categories
(Rates per 100,000 of the Population)

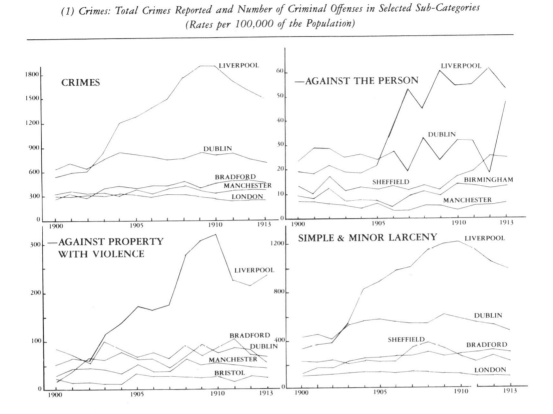

APPENDIX **F.** (con't.)

(2) Non-Indictable Offenses: Total Persons Proceeded Against and Numbers Involved in Selected Offenses
(Rates Per 100,000 of the Population)

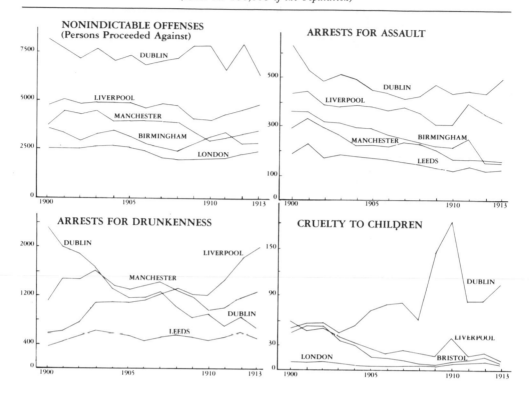

APPENDIX **G.** Registered trade unions in the City of Dublin, 1899–1916 (note 1).

NAME	YEAR ESTABLISHED OR REGISTERED	HIGHEST RECORDED MEMBERSHIP DURING PERIOD	REMARKS
A. BUILDING, CONSTRUCTION, ETC.			
1. Ancient Guild of Incorporated Brick and Stonelayers	1670	1,385	Irish-based union with branch in Dublin
2. City of Dublin Marble Polishers	1881	72	
3. City of Dublin Stonecutters	1900	134	Dissolved in 1907 to amalgamate with #10
4. Dublin Builders' Laborers	1896	450	Dissolved in 1906
5. Dublin Operative Plasterers	1893	390	See #12
6. Dublin Regular Paviors	1860	34	Dissolved in 1903 and reorganized in following year
7. Dublin Tile Mosaic and Faience Fixers Association	1909	15	
8. Dublin Whiteners	1891	80	
9. Metropolitan House Painters	1670	600	Membership reduced to 307 by 1913
10. Operative Stone Cutters of Ireland	1891	660	Irish-based union with branch in Dublin
11. Regular Glass Cutters, Glaziers and Lead Sash Makers	1890	33	Branch of UK union before 1902
12. Regular Stucco Plasterers	1670	280	Name changed as in #5 after 1903
13. Stonecarvers' Society of Ireland	1909		No data
14. United Builders' Laborers and General Workers of Dublin	1889	1,600	No data
15. United Operative Brick and Stone Layers	1904	46	No data after 1905

Note 1: Does not include amalgamated UK unions with local affiliation in Dublin (e.g., carpenters and other building trade employees, etc.)

SOURCE: *Parliamentary Papers*: Reports by the Chief Labour Correspondent of the Board of Trade on Trade Unions (various); Reports by the Chief Registrar of Friendly Societies: Trade Unions, 1899–1916 (annual).

NAME	YEAR ESTABLISHED OR REGISTERED	HIGHEST RECORDED MEMBERSHIP DURING PERIOD	REMARKS
B. CONVEYANCE, DOCK WORK, ETC.			
16. Belfast and Dublin Locomotive Engine Drivers and Firemen	1872	438	Irish-based union with branch in Dublin
17. Coal and Grain Laborers	1894		No data
18. Dublin Amalgamated Grain Laborers	1895	900	Dissolved in 1901
19. Dublin and District Tramwaymen	1890	497	Dissolved in 1904
20. Dublin United Grain and Coal Laborers	1905	67	Dissolved in 1906
21. Irish Automobile Drivers Society	1910	162	No data
22. Irish Railway Workers	1910	152	
23. Irish Transport and General Workers	1909	24,135	
24. Mail Cart Drivers	1905	1,300	Includes Dublin branch
25. National Union of Coal Laborers	1898	456	Dissolved in 1902
26. Port of Dublin Grain Weighers and Tally Clerks	1888	40	Dissolved in 1903
27. United Job Carriage Drivers	1899	106	Dissolved in 1902
C. SHIPPING, ENGINEERING, METALWORKING, ETC.			
28. Amalgamated Coach Body Makers	1899	88	Branch of U.K. union before 1899. Dissolved in 1902
29. Dublin United Brass Founders, Finishers and Gasfitters	1817	152	
30. Dublin Silver Plate Workers	1898	23	Dissolved in 1900
31. Dublin Tinsmiths and Sheet Metal Workers	1899	85	
32. Hammermen's Society of Dublin	1901	100	Dissolved in 1903

NAME	YEAR ESTABLISHED OR REGISTERED	HIGHEST RECORDED MEMBERSHIP DURING PERIOD	REMARKS
33. Independent Stationary Steam and Gas Engine Drivers, Steam and Hydraulic Crane and Motor Drivers, Greasers, Firemen and Trimmers	1902	158	Name changed in 1909 to substitute "Electric" for "Hydraulic." Dissolved in 1913
34. Operative Society of Mechanical Engineers, Whitesmiths, Iron Workers and Pipe Fitters, Locksmiths, Bellhangers, etc.	1893	40	
35. Regular Cart, Van and Wagon Builders	1876	22	
36. United Smiths of Ireland	1886	114	
37. United Stationary Engine Drivers, Cranemen and Firemen	1876	253	

D. FOOD, DRINK, ETC.

NAME	YEAR ESTABLISHED OR REGISTERED	HIGHEST RECORDED MEMBERSHIP DURING PERIOD	REMARKS
38. City of Dublin Pork Butchers and Bacon Curers	1875	90	Dissolved in 1907
39. Dublin Biscuit Operatives			No data
40. Dublin Butchers, Porters and Vanmen	1894		No data
41. Dublin Mineral Water Operatives	1906	117	Branch of U.K. union before 1906
42. Dublin Operative Bakers	1752	600	Dissolved in 1911
43. Dublin Operative Confectioners and Sugar Boilers	1892	24	Dissolved in 1902
44. Dublin Operative Poulterers and Fishmongers	1903	40	
45. Irish National Bakers and Confectioners	1890		Irish-based union with branch in Dublin

NAME	YEAR ESTABLISHED OR REGISTERED	HIGHEST RECORDED MEMBERSHIP DURING PERIOD	REMARKS
46. W. & R. Jacob & Co., Ltd. Employees	1911		No data
47. Journeymen Fishmongers	1898	12	Amalgamated with #44
48. Metropolitan Bakers Society	1907	144	Dissolved in 1911
49. Operative Butchers and Assistants	1828	136	
50. Progressive Bakers of Dublin	1905	60	Dissolved in 1909
51. Purveyors' Assistants	1885	180	
52. Regular Hotel Workers International	1912	50	
E. TEXTILES, ETC.			
53. Carpet Planners of the City of Dublin	1898	42	
54. Dublin International Tailors' Machiners and Pressers	1908	182	
55. Dublin Silk and Poplin Weavers		320	
56. Dublin Upholsterers	1872	70	No data after 1900
57. Irish Drapers' Assistants	1901		Irish-based union with 1600 members in Dublin branch
F. GOVERNMENT, MUNICIPAL			
58. Asylum Attendants of Ireland	1896	67	
59. Dublin Corporation Lamplighters	1909	22	Dissolved in 1910
60. Dublin Corporation Waterworks Employees Association	1907	59	
61. United Corporation Workmen of Dublin	1894	1,384	
62. Dublin Fire Brigade Union	1892	47	

NAME	YEAR ESTABLISHED OR REGISTERED	HIGHEST RECORDED MEMBERSHIP DURING PERIOD	REMARKS
63. Dublin Municipal Engine Drivers, Firemen, Cranemen and Motormen	1914		No data
64. Irish Post Office Clerks	1900		Irish-based union with branch in Dublin
G. COMMERCIAL			
65. Prudential Assurance Agents Association	1912		No data
66. Refuge Assurance Company Employees	1910	47	
67. United Collectors and Salesmen	1894		No data
H. WOODWORKING			
68. Coffin Makers Society	1903	13	Dissolved in 1909
69. Dublin Basket Makers	1854	30	Joined UK union in 1902
70. Dublin Coopers		350	
71. Dublin Operative Lath Makers		20	
72. Dublin Woodworking	1898		No data
I. MISCELLANEOUS			
73. Dublin Journeymen Hairdressers	1876	120	
74. Dublin Newspaper Machinists	1891	31	Dissolved in 1901
75. Dublin Newspaper Packers	1899	50	Dissolved in 1904
76. Dublin Regular Operative Farriers		120	
77. Dublin Rope Makers	1884	35	Dissolved in 1899
78. Dublin Theatrical and Music Hall Employees	1891	62	
79. Dublin Typographical Provident Society	1809	1,270	

NAME	YEAR ESTABLISHED OR REGISTERED	HIGHEST RECORDED MEMBERSHIP DURING PERIOD	REMARKS
80. General Warehousemen, Drivers, Shopworkers and Kindred Trades	1907	85	Dissolved in 1909
81. Irish Glass Bottle Makers	1867	276	Irish-based union with branch in Dublin
82. Irish National Labor Union	1892	129	Dissolved in 1907
83. St. James' Gate Brewery Labor Union	1891		No data

APPENDIX **H.** Major labor disputes (strikes and lockouts) in Dublin, 1899–1916.

YEAR	TRADE AFFECTED	NUMBER OF WORKERS INVOLVED (DIRECTLY OR INDIRECTLY)	STRIKE COMMENCEMENT AND DURATION	REMARKS
1899	Glass Bottle Makers	250	Dec. 31, 1898 (25 days)	Wage demand conceded
	Bricklayers and Laborers	180	May 9 (2 days)	Rules dispute
	Painters	500	June 1 (35 days)	Refusal to work with nonunionists followed by lockout. Settled amicably by mutual concessions
	Coal Laborers	50	June 22 (2 days)	Wage demand conceded
	Dock Laborers	52	Sept. 7 (1 day)	Sympathetic strike with Liverpool dockers. Men replaced
1900	Dock Laborers	47	Feb. 17 (3 days)	Sympathy strike. Resolved in favor of men
	Tailors	600	April 26 (124 days)	Grievance over outworking system. Lockout. Referred to arbitration
	Dock, Coal Laborers and Carters	1,000	July 20 (7 days)	Wage demand. Work resumed on employers' terms
	Plumbers	260	Nov. 23 (59 days)	Wage demand. Work resumed at old rates. Agreement on new rules
1901	Carpenters	40	Mar. 23 (11 days)	Sympathetic strike. Referred to conference
	Carpenters	22	June 13	Refusal to work on foreign-made joinery. Men replaced
	Upholsterers	70	Aug. 29 (7 days)	Rules dispute. Hours reduced
1902	Engineers	226	May 23 (126 days)	Wage demand. Work resumed on old conditions
1905	Bricklayers and other Building Operatives	1,000	Mar. 1 (102 days)	Rules dispute followed by lockout. Referred to arbitration
1907	Gasworkers	295	Dec. 20 (12 days)	Wage demand. Men replaced or reinstated at discretion of employer

YEAR	TRADE AFFECTED	NUMBER OF WORKERS INVOLVED (DIRECTLY OR INDIRECTLY)	STRIKE COMMENCEMENT AND DURATION	REMARKS
1908	Dock Laborers	500	July 11 (2 days)	Men locked out after refusal to work with nonunion men. Referred to conference
	Carters, Dock Laborers, Canal Workers and Maltsters	3,000	Nov. 16 (33 days)	Wage demands and union recognition. Referred to arbitration
1911	Firemen and Seamen, Dockers and Coal Porters	2,000	June 30 (31 days)	Wage demands, sympathetic strikes and lockout. Referred to arbitration
	Timber workers (carters, laborers)	500	Aug. 21 (46 days)	Recognition of union and wage demand. Demands refused. Some men replaced
	Biscuit and Cake Makers	876	Aug. 22 (1 day)	Wage demand. Return on employers' terms. Many men replaced
	Railwaymen (mechanics and servants of G. S. & W. Railway)	7,300 (total in Ireland)	Sept. 15 (19 days)	Sympathetic strike. Return on employer's terms
	Bakers	480	Sept. 26 (12 days)	Rules dispute and wage demand. Return on employers' terms. Many men replaced
	Canal Boatmen	350	Sept. 29 (25 days)	Sympathetic strike. Return on employers' terms
1913	Dock Workers	325	Jan. 30 (78 days)	Wages and hours demand. Agreement arrived at
	Bottle Makers	179	Mar. 31 (23 days)	Dispute over work rules. Settled on agreement
	Biscuit Workers	350	April 12 (1 day)	For reinstatement of suspended worker
	Cabinetmakers	100	May 31 (70 days)	—
	Sawyers and Machinists	176	June 17 (11 days)	Wages and hours demand. Reduction in hours conceded
	Coach and Van Builders	500	June 28 (68 days)	Wage demands conceded

YEAR	TRADE AFFECTED	NUMBER OF WORKERS INVOLVED (DIRECTLY OR INDIRECTLY)	STRIKE COMMENCEMENT AND DURATION	REMARKS
	Transport Workers, Building Trade Operatives and workers in other industries	20,000 (est.)*	August 26, 1913 to February 1914	Lockout, strikes and sympathetic strikes in various trades arising out of refusal of Dublin employers to recognize the Irish Transport and General Workers Union
1915	Bakers	500	November	Dispute over hours of work. Referred to arbitration
	Dock Laborers	300	Oct. 15 (8 days)	Wage concessions after conference. Settlement with all companies except City of Dublin Steampacket Co., which also settled by arbitration in May 1916
	Printers	300	Dec. 3 (28 days)	Wage concessions made
1916	Building Trades	2,650	April 1 (33 days)	Wage dispute. Modified advance granted
	Bakers	500	November	Work rules dispute. Arbitrator appointed
	Gasworkers	250	Oct. 16 (5 days)	Wage concessions after arbitration

*In the period January 1 to August 25, 1913 (i.e., before the great lockout of that year), a series of strikes involving small firms (about 24 in all) and resulting in the loss of almost 20,000 man-days took place in addition to those referred to above.

SOURCES: *Labour Gazette* (Board of Trade); Labour Statistics of the United Kingdom (various reports in *Parliamentary Papers*)

Notes

1. Dear, Dirty Dublin

1. Rev. G. N. Wright, *Historical Guide to Ancient and Modern Dublin* (London, 1821), p. 9. Italics are mine. For another contemporary account of post-Union Dublin, see S.M.T., "Dublin in 1822" in *The New Monthly Magazine and Literary Journal* (London), IV (1822), pp. 503-11.

2. *Parliamentary Papers*, 1833 (XXXV), no. 5 (Summary of documents relating to the new valuation of the City of Dublin, 1830). This item is a full listing by street of the houses in the city together with the annual value of each as of October 1828. For a brief treatment of some of the more favorable aspects of the city after the Union, see R. B. McDowell (ed.), *Social Life in Ireland, 1800-45* (Dublin, 1957), pp. 13-20.

3. *Parliamentary Papers*, 1822 (VII), no. 394 (Select Committee on the Local Taxation of the City of Dublin), pp. 3-4.

4. *Ibid.*, 1820 (VIII), no. 84 (Commission on the House of Industry), p. 15. For the reference to George IV's progress through Dublin, see *ibid.*, 1846 (XII), no. 519 (Committee on the Dublin Wide Streets Bill), p. 20.

5. *Ibid.*, 1831-32 (XIX), no. 678 (Select Committee on the Silk Trade), pp. 836-38, 930.

6. *Ibid.*, 1871 (LXII), no. 440 (Factories and Workshops). The returns were incomplete, but fuller data would not have materially changed the picture in the case of Dublin. See, also, *ibid.*, 1884-85 (IX), no. 288 (Select Committee on Industries), *passim*.

7. *Ibid.*, 1854 (XII), no. 338 (Select Committee on Dublin Hospitals), pp. 245-46. An earlier example of this familiar complaint dates from 1823 and was made by a witness before the Select Committee on the Local Taxation of the City of Dublin at a time when the population of the county was increasing more rapidly than the city's: "The population are quitting Dublin, owing, as I believe, to the pressure of local taxes, and are taking houses in the county out of their reach" [*Ibid.*, 1823 (VI), no. 549, p. 6]. The "population" in this statement would have meant the better-off elements, of course, for as is indicated earlier in this chapter, Dublin was gaining citizens in the first half of the century.

8. Municipal Boundaries Commission (Ireland), Part I (Minutes of Evidence) in *ibid.*, 1880 (XXX), c. 2725, pp. 22, 52. See, also, *ibid.*, 1876 (X), no. 352, p. 289.

9. *Ibid.*, 1881 (L), c. 2827, p. 19.

10. *Ibid.*, 1809 (VII), no. 148.

11. *First Report of the General Board of Health* (Dublin, 1822). Though information was collected from all over Ireland, this first report was confined to the province of Munster. It was the Board's intention to publish the results of its investigations in the other three provinces, but that does not appear to have been realized.

12. For a brief outline of sanitary progress in Dublin, see Sir Charles Cameron, *Municipal Public Health Administration* (Dublin, 1914). A concise review of sanitary legislation in Great Britain is given in *Sanitary Record* (London), January 17, 1896.

13. This paragraph is based on the proceedings of the Royal Commission on Sewerage and Drainage in Dublin in *Parliamentary Papers*, 1880 (XXX), c. 2605, mainly pp. 2, 169, 218.

14. A report of the Commission of Investigation held in 1860 is given in National Library of Ireland (pamphlet collection), I6281 D7.

15. Quoted in Royal Commission on Sewerage and Drainage, *op. cit.*, p. xviii.

16. Wilde's supplementary data showed that in the 10 years preceding the taking of the census, there were 1,151,254 deaths in Ireland of persons of specified ages. Of these, 435,117 were of children up to 5 years [*Parliamentary Papers*, 1843 (XXIV), no. 504 (IV), pp. xlv-xlvii]. See, also, T. Antisell, *Suggestions Towards the Improvement of the Sanatory Condition of the Metropolis* (Dublin, 1847); T. Willis, *Social and Sanitary Condition of the Working Classes in the City of Dublin* (Dublin, 1845).

17. See Royal Commission on Sewerage and Drainage, *op. cit.*, p. 191.

18. The death rates in this and in the two preceding paragraphs were obtained from the annual reports of the Registrars General for Ireland and for England and Wales.

19. Royal Commission on Sewerage and Drainage, *op. cit.*, pp. xxi-xxii.

20. *The Times*, September 15 and November 24, 1853; *The Dublin University Magazine*, vol. 52 (September 1858), p. 296.

21. *Parliamentary Papers*, 1878 (XXIII), c. 2060 (Board of Works Inquiry), p. 51 and Appendix F. for a summary of the Board's loan operations covering the years 1866 to 1910, see *ibid.*, 1910 (LVI), cd. 5301 (Appendix C to the 78th annual report of the Commissioners of Public Works in Ireland). During that period £1.2 million was advanced to public authorities and private builders throughout Ireland (including about £240,000 borrowed by Dublin Corporation) in connection with schemes to accommodate over 12,000 families in cities and towns under the various housing acts.

22. *Ibid.*, 1906 (XCVII), no. 337. As an indication of the inflated costs involved in the Coombe and Plunkett Street schemes, the cost of clearance, improvements *and* erection of buildings for the 80-family St. Joseph's Place scheme undertaken entirely by the Corporation only came to £26,000.

23. Cameron, *Municipal Public Health*, p. 57.

24. See Dublin Corporation: Reports and Documents, 1903-III no. 176, which provides the following details of working-class housing completed in Dublin and vicinity up to 1903:

Builder	Families accommodated	
Dublin Corporation	518	
Private companies:		
Dublin Artisans' Dwellings Company	2660	(see note)
Dublin & Suburban Artisans' Dwellings Company	288	
Industrial Tenements Company	52	
Association for the Housing of the Very Poor	36	
Iveagh Trust (New Bride Street)	336	
Guinness's Brewery (for employees)	87	
Watkin's Brewery (for employees)	87	
Great Southern & Western Railway (for employees)	148	
Midland Great Western Railway (for employees)	42	
Private individuals	835	
Total	5089	

Note: Figure in report in error; above figure more nearly accurate. By 1906 or thereabouts the Dublin Artisans' Dwellings Company had built 3,300 houses in the city and sububs, but only 134 of them (i.e., 4 percent) were let at weekly rents of 2s. 6d. and below while almost 50 percent demanded 5s. and above [see *Parliamentary Papers*, 1914 (XIX), cd. 7317 (Dublin Housing Inquiry), Appendix XXVIII].

25. First Report from the Select Committee on the State of Disease and the Condition of the Labouring Poor in Ireland, in *Parliamentary Papers*, 1819 (VIII), no. 314 (Report of Dr. J. Cheyne).

26. Select Committee on the Health of Towns, 1840: Report and Minutes of Evidence in *ibid.*, 1840 (XI), c. 384 (data on Dublin is contained in replies to Questions 3168/3396).

27. *Ibid.*, 1847 (XXVI), no. 124: Report and Minutes of Evidence on the preliminary inquiries respecting the Dublin Improvement Bill.

28. *The Times*, September 15, 1853.

29. Sir Charles Cameron, *Reminiscences* (Dublin, 1913), p. 106. The incident occurred during the royal visit in 1885.

30. Dublin Corporation: Reports and Documents, 1884-I no. 29.

31. Dublin Sanitary Association: Report for 1874. For details of the activities of the Public Health Committee, see *Parliamentary Papers*, 1876 (X), no. 352 (Select Committee on Local Government and Taxation), Appendix 8.

32. *Sanitary Record*, October 14 to December 23, 1876.

33. Censuses prior to 1901 did not provide data on room occupancy. The figures quoted here are those of Dr. Cameron, who conducted a sanitary survey of Dublin in 1882 for the Public Health Committee (Cameron, *Municipal Public Health*, p. 82).

34. *Annual Register*: 1873-Part II, p. 54; 1875-Part II, pp. 53-55.

35. *Parliamentary Papers*, 1884-85 (IX), no. 288, Appendix 22 (evidence of P. McDonald and C. Dennehy, members of the Dublin municipal council).

36. *The Times*, October 30, 1841. For examples of the exclusive nature of the Protestant-dominated council in the period before the 1840 reform, see *Parliamentary Papers*, 1830 (XXVI), no. 521 (Names of common councilmen of the City of Dublin, 1824-30).

37. L. M. Cullen, *An Economic History of Ireland since 1660* (New York, 1972), p. 166.

38. Joseph Lee, *The Modernization of Irish Society, 1848-1918* (Dublin, 1973), pp. 14-20. Sentiments expressing a similar unfavorable comparison of the late-eighteenth century Protestant middle classes in Ireland with their English and Dutch counterparts were offered by Samuel Crumpe in his prize essay for the Royal Irish Academy, *On the Best Means of Providing Employment for the People* (2nd ed.: London, 1795): "To stand behind a counter, superintend a farm, or calculate in a compting-house, would be beneath the dignity of such exalted beings [the sons of the gentry]. . . . To the same general aversion to industry, and tendency to dissipation, and to a considerable share of family vanity, are we to ascribe the silly . . . propensity of *gentlemen*, to educate their children in *gentlemanly* professions. Hence arise the daily increasing numbers of curates with scanty salaries, or none, attorneys preying on the public, ensigns without the means of rising higher, physicians without patients, and lawyers without briefs" (pp. 169-70). For an assessment of the retardation of economic growth in pre-Famine Ireland, see G. L. Barrow, *The Emergence of the Irish Banking System, 1820-1845* (Dublin, 1975), pp. 58, 191, 195-96.

39. *Parliamentary Papers*, 1884-85 (IX), no 288 (Q. 14: evidence of W. K. Sullivan).

2. The Faded Capital

1. See the provocative and illuminating article by L. Wright et al., "A Future for Dublin," in *Architectural Review*, CLVI (November 1974). This article has been reprinted and published by The Architectural Press Ltd. as *A Future for Dublin* (London, 1975).

2. The relevant figures for Justices of the Peace as of August 1911 were:

	Catholics	Protestants	Jews	Other	Total
Dublin City	84	145	4	–	233
Dublin County (excluding the city)	68	163	1	1	233
Belfast City	43	129	2	2	176
Total for Ireland	2,275	3,663	8	13	5,959

Source: *Parliamentary Papers*, 1911 (LXV), no. 306, pp. 29-30.

3. For an excellent historical study of Dublin's architectural greatness, see Maurice Craig, *Dublin, 1660-1860* (London, 1952). There is an appendix dealing with "Some Characteristics of the Dublin House."

4. *Parliamentary Papers*, 1892 (XVIII), no. 240 (Select Committee on Theatres and Places of Entertainment), Q. 3677-78.

5. "My Dublin Year" in *Studies* (December 1912), pp. 694-708. This article has been reproduced with commentary in the autumn and winter 1971 issues of the same periodical.

6. Select Committee on Theatres and Places of Entertainment, *op. cit.*, Appendix 4, p. 439. Some of the nostalgia associated with Dan Lowrey's music hall is evoked in Eugene Watters, *Infinite Variety* (Dublin, 1979).

7. *Irish Times*, April 2, 1912. See, also, *Freeman's Journal*, December 30, 1915.

8. *Irish Times*, November 3, 1905.

9. For various comments on the state of musical life in Dublin, see *ibid.*, March 2 and April 21, 1899; June 13/14, 1900; January 18, 1901; March 19, 1903; February 6/9, 1906.

10. *Ibid.*, June 30, 1913.

11. A. Birrell, *Things Past Redress* (London, 1937), p. 214.

12. *Irish Times*, August 5, 1904. There is an account of the patent hearings in the *New Irish Jurist*, August 12, 1904, p. 270.

13. For accounts of the *Playboy* fracas, see *Irish Times*, January 29-31 and February 1, 1907. A detailed commentary of contemporary reactions to the play is given in R. Hogan et al., *The Modern Irish Drama*, vol. 3 (Atlantic Highlands, N.J., 1978), pp. 123-62.

14. *Leader*, July 30, 1910.

15. For a contemporary account, with illustrations, of the works in the gallery, see *The Connoisseur* (April 1908), pp. 219 ff.

16. *Parliamentary Debates*, 4th series, XCVII (July 22, 1901), col. 1245.

17. *Irish Times*, April 12, 1901.

18. *Ibid.*, November 30, 1912. Incidentally, lest Shaw's ruminations be taken too literally, it may be noted that newspaper reports of weekly gallery attendance in 1870 (about the time the young Shaw might have made his artistic perambulations) ranged as high as 3,000 persons and had averaged 2,500 a week since the gallery had been opened in 1864. Attendance appeared to have decreased thereafter, for the director's reports covering the years 1886 to 1899 (general attendance figures were not published subsequently) claimed an average annual attendance of 75,000.

19. *Ibid.*, June 24, 1913. See, also, *ibid.*, March 17 and April 23, 1913.

20. Extract from the poem "To a shade." See, also, his poem "To a wealthy man who promised a second subscription to the Dublin Municipal Gallery if it were proved the people wanted pictures." In a private letter to Lady Gregory, Yeats concluded that only a "fear of culture" as the "enemy of faith and morals" (the latter phrase, as Yeats remarked, having been uttered allegedly by someone on the staff of the new National University in Dublin) could have produced such hostility to Lane's gallery [Lady Gregory, *Hugh Lane's Life and Achievement* (London, 1921), p. 127]. The story of the municipal gallery is recounted in Thomas Bodkin's *Hugh Lane and his Pictures* (Dublin, 1956), which includes illustrations of all 39 paintings along with sketches of Lutyens' design for the Bridge site. The famous controversy hinged on Lane's unwitnessed codicil to his will written shortly before his departure on the ill-fated voyage. Mollified perhaps by his recent appointment as a director of Dublin's National Gallery, Lane had relented and was prepared to give the city a second chance at the collection. According to the amended will, the pictures were to be returned to Dublin if a suitable building to house them were provided within 5 years of his death. But as Lane failed to observe the legal formalities, the pictures remained in London despite the best efforts of a united Irish opinion (from Lady Gregory to Lord Carson) to get them back. They had to wait a decade before finding a permanent home at the Tate, where they formed the nucleus of that institution's foreign collection of modern art. Not until 1933 (18 years after Lane's death) did the paintings and sculptures at Harcourt Street find their permanent home in a fine old Georgian mansion (Charlemont House) in Parnell (formerly Rutland) Square, which building has since been appropriately renamed the Hugh Lane Municipal Gallery. Lane would not have approved of the hours of opening at the new location—evening hours on Wednesdays only and Sunday closing between May and September. Eventually, Dublin's "moral claim" to the disputed pictures was partially satisfied in 1959 with the conclusion of an arrangement between the two parties providing for the exhibition in Dublin of half the collection, each half to be loaned alternately for a 5-year term. This agreement expired in 1979 and further negotiations between the Irish authorities and the Trustees of the National Gallery in London are expected to produce further arrangements for the continued exhibition of the pictures in both countries.

21. *Irish Times*, January 10 and 11, 1951.

22. For details of the development of the public library system in Dublin, see Dublin Corporation: Reports and Documents, 1883-II no. 160; 1885-I no. 69; 1886-III no. 131; 1909 no. 19. See, also, *Freeman's Journal*, September 29 and October 2, 1884; *Library Association Record*, December 15, 1883/December 15, 1906/June 1920; *Library Chronicle*, 1884-I, p. 161/ 1888-V, p. 56; *Irish Times*, May 25, 1904/ January 27, February 11, May 7 and

15, 1908/ March 7, 1916; W.G.S. Adams, *A Report on Library Provision and Policy* (Edinburgh, 1915), pp. 62-64. For comparative data on U.K. libraries, see *The Libraries, Museums and Art Galleries Year Book*.

23. *Parliamentary Debates*, LIV (March 14, 1898), col. 1511.

24. For data and comments on the city's open spaces, see *Parliamentary Papers*: 1866 (LX), no. 460; 1878-79 (XIX), c. 2276; 1901 (LX), no. 341. See, also, *Dublin Civic Survey* (London, 1925), pp. 16-20; *Lancet*, August 26, 1899; *Irish Times*, July 28, 1880/ July 17, 1899. The case for opening Mountjoy Square dragged on for a very long time, being brought before the Free State parliament on several occasions from 1924 onward. The park was finally opened to the public, via enabling legislation, in 1938.

25. Figures are from the annual reports of the Commissioner of Public Works (Ireland) in *Parliamentary Papers*: 1913 (XXXVIII), cd. 6971; 1914 (XLVII), cd. 7563; 1914-16 (XXXIV), cd. 8119. Although the reduction in the figures for soccer in 1914-15 is certainly due to the war, one can only surmise that the proportionately great reduction in Gaelic games played in 1913-1914 was the result of the labor disturbances of the period. For the remark of the Chief Secretary on the use of the Phoenix Park, see *Parliamentary Debates*, CXXXVII (June 30, 1904), col. 171. See, also, *ibid.*, CLII (February 28, 1906), col. 1146.

26. See, for example, *Parliamentary Papers*, 1910 (LXXIV), no. 209.

27. Only the daily newspaper can give one a sense of the nature of traffic problems in these years. Other sources found useful here include the following *Parliamentary Papers*: 1904 (LXXIX), no. 292, p. 5; 1906 (XLVIII), cd. 3081, pp. 622-23; 1913 (IX), no. 278 (Select Committee on Motor Traffic), pp. 1030-38.

28. See in particular Dublin Corporation Reports, 1909-II no. 101; *Irish Builder*, December 3, 1903; *Irish Times*, February 28, 1901/December 6, 1912; *Medical Press*, December 4, 1907/ October 21, 1908; *Sanitary Record*, August 24, 1905.

29. *Irish Times*, January 8, 1901/September 21, 1903. See, also, *Irish Builder*, February 13, 1902 and January 2, 1909; Dublin Corporation, Reports and Documents: 1906-I no. 29.

30. P. Mairet, *Pioneer of Sociology* (London, 1957), p. 150.

31. H.T. O'Rourke, *The Dublin Civic Survey* (London, 1925), pp. xviii-xix. The successful entry in the competition was the plan submitted by Professor Abercrombie in association with a Liverpool team of architects. It was published by the Civics Institute of Ireland as *Dublin of the Future* (London, 1922).

3. Politics and the Dublin Corporation

1. See, for example, the election campaign notice of A.M. Sullivan, proprietor of the *Nation*, in *Freeman's Journal*, November 5, 1870.

2. The eligibility of women for municipal office holding meant little in practice. In 1913 the various county boroughs of Ireland numbered only 3 female councillors among a total of 316 members. The proportion was even worse in the case of the district councils, where the concession had earlier been won by the Local Government Act of 1898: 5 women among 1,361 urban district councillors; 1 among 313 town commissioners; 47 out of 7,480 members of rural district councils. The largest female representation was on Boards of Guardians, where women held but 109 of 8,164 places. The 1911 Act also rendered women eligible for membership of *county* councils, but the opportunity to serve did not arise there until the county elections in 1914 [*Parliamentary Papers*, 1913 (XXXII), cd. 6978, p. ii].

3. This number of voters, though a five-fold increase over the pre-1899 register, was far from representing the "one man, one vote" electorate later decreed by the reforming legislation of 1918. According to the 1901 census, for example, over 160,000 persons of both sexes aged 20 and over resided in the borough's 15 "old city" wards, and it may be inferred that most of these would have automatically been burgesses under a truly democratic franchise. The number of municipal electors changed little over the years. At the elections of 1914 the registered voters numbered 49,284, which included 8,469 burgesses from the five new wards carved out of the added areas in 1900, thus leaving the electoral roll for the "old city" about where it was in 1899 regarding numbers. The virtual disfranchisement of "lodgers" owing to the residency requirements is suggested by the list of parliamentary electors for all four city divisions (including the two University seats), which, according to the 1913 register, barely exceeded 40,000 persons and included only 1,126 lodgers [*Parliamentary Papers*, 1912-13 (LXVII), no. 53].

4. *Parliamentary Debates*, LVI (April 26, 1898), col. 1244.

5. *Freeman's Journal*, January 16, 1899; *The Times* (London), January 19, 1899.

6. For the discussion, see *Parliamentary Debates*, LXXII (June 13, 1899), cols. 1008 ff. See, also, *Irish Times*, April 19, 21, 22, 26, 1899.

7. The former northern townships of Clontarf, Glasnevin, and Drumcondra had a greater proportion of non-Catholic (i.e., Protestant) inhabitants than all but one of the existing city wards. The percentages were 42, 38 and 26, respectively, compared to less than 17 percent in the northern wards and 11 percent to 23 percent in the southern wards, the one exception being Fitzwilliam ward with a non-Catholic population of one-third. Incidentally, Lord Ardilaun, who had been a town commissioner in Clontarf township before it became annexed to the city, declined to join his colleagues in contesting the ward seats at the municipal elections in 1901.

8. *Irish Times*, March 7, 1899. When one such resolution subsequently passed the council chamber in May 1908, the plan foundered on the refusal of officials of the Corporation Departments to undertake the onerous work schedules and personal inconveniences that evening sittings would have entailed: the council and its various committees were then convening over 700 times a year.

9. *Ibid.*, January 27, 1903.

10. *Parliamentary Debates*, LXXX (March 8, 1900), col. 66.

11. State Paper Office (Dublin), D.M.P. Criminal Department-Special Branch, #23504/S, Chief Commissioner to Under Secretary, November 21, 1900.

12. *Irish Times*, October 2, 1901. For Dillon's speech, see *ibid.*, January 14, 1901.

13. *Ibid.*, April 2, 1901.

14. *Ibid.*, January 15, 1903.

15. Dublin Corporation: Minutes of the Council, 1907 no. 704; *Irish Times*, September 3, 1907.

16. For an analysis of the general fortunes of Sinn Fein in the country at large during these years, see F.S.L. Lyons, *Ireland Since the Famine* (London, 1973), pp. 256-58.

17. *Freeman's Journal*, January 20, 1910.

18. For the background to these events, see A. Mitchell, *Labour in Irish Politics* (New York, 1974), pp. 22-28

19. A motion in the council expressing regret at the means taken to unseat Larkin received the support of Sinn Fein councillors, one Unionist and even UIL-sponsored Nationalists (Dublin Corporation: Minutes of the Council, September 16, 1912).

20. *Irish Times*, October 8, 1912 (speech to the Irish Trades Union Congress).

21. *Ibid.*, May 1, 1911.

22. *Parliamentary Debates*, LXXII (June 13, 1899), col. 1036.

23. Dublin Corporation: Minutes of the Council, 1908 no. 335. See, also, *ibid.*: 1906 no. 635; 1908 no. 689; 1911 no. 129. The General Account of Salaries for each year is contained in the annual Accounts of the Dublin Corporation.

24. *Freeman's Journal*, February 7, 1903; *Evening Telegraph*, February 7, 1903.

25. Dublin Corporation: Minutes of the Council, 1909 no. 34; *Irish Times*, January 22, 1909.

26. *Irish Times*, October 8, 1912. Clerkships had been open to competitive examination since 1899.

27. *Freeman's Journal*, October 3, 1899. Incidentally, the bribery charges (made at a public meeting) were supported by then councillor Thomas Kelly, who at this stage was less than friendly to the Labour interest, an attitude that soon enough changed to active support.

28. *Irish Times*, December 14, 1907.

29. *Ibid.*, October 3, 1910.

30. *Ibid.*, October 2, 1916. George Russell had earlier expressed the same sentiments in his famous letter to the Masters of Dublin (see Chapter 8): "You are bad citizens, for we rarely, if ever, hear of the wealthy among you endowing your city with the munificent gifts which it is the pride of merchant princes in other cities to offer."

4. Public Health

1. Dublin Corporation, Reports and Documents: 1901-III no. 212.

2. *Lancet*, November 25 and December 2, 16, 23, 30, 1899; January 20, 27, 1900.

3. *Parliamentary Papers*, 1900 (XXXIX): cd. 243 (Report of Committee); cd. 244 (Minutes of Evidence and Appendices).

4. A glance at the general mortality tables in any recent issue of the United Nations *Demographic Yearbook*

will demonstrate the virtual elimination of infectious disease as a major cause of death in the developed countries.

5. See George Rosen's article, "Disease, Debility, and Death," in H. Dyos and M. Wolff, *The Victorian City*, II, pp. 625-67, for an informative account of the incidence and impact of disease in nineteenth-century Britain.

6. Board of Superintendence of Dublin Hospitals: Report for 1910, in *Parliamentary Papers*, 1910 (XXII), cd. 5335.

7. For a detailed analysis of the infant mortality problem, see the various supplements to the Local Government Board (England and Wales) Reports for 1909-1910 to 1912-1913 inclusive, especially the study conducted in 1913 by the Board's medical officer and appearing as cd. 6909 in *ibid.*, 1913 (XXXII).

8. *Parliamentary Papers*, 1913 (XXXII), cd. 6909.

9. See the annual reports of the Public Health Committee in Dublin Corporation, Reports and Documents, and the reports of the Local Government Board (Ireland).

10. Dublin Public Health Inquiry, *op. cit.*, cd. 244 (Q. 722-57 and Appendix 44).

11. For comparative TB rates of international cities, see U.S. Department of Commerce, Bureau of the Census, *Mortality Statistics, 1910*.

12. *Irish Times*, July 23, 1912. For details of the many activities of the W.N.H.A., see *British Journal of Tuberculosis* (London), V, no. 2 (April 1911), pp. 69-82.

13. Dublin Corporation, Reports and Documents (September 11, 1908); *Irish Times*, July 3, 13 and August 10, 1909.

14. For interesting surveys of the incidence of TB in post-1921 Ireland, see the statistical studies by R.C. Geary and J.E. Counihan et al. in *Journal of the Statistical and Social Inquiry Society of Ireland*, 83rd session (October 1930), pp. 67-103 and 97th session (1943-1944), pp. 169-88.

15. Report for the year ending March 31, 1900 in *Parliamentary Papers*, 1900 (XXVI), cd. 215. For data on individual hospitals in Dublin and in the rest of the United Kingdom, see Burdett's *Hospitals and Charities* (annual yearbook of philanthropy).

16. *Lancet*, April 4, 1903; *British Medical Journal*, April 25, 1903 and January 6, 1912.

17. Figures compiled from annual reports of the Registrar General for Ireland. The highest mortality was in the years 1905-1909 and 1914.

18. *Lancet*, March 19, 1864.

19. For the evidence and statistics cited, see the annual reports of the Army Medical Department. See, also, *Parliamentary Papers*, 1868-1869 (VII), no. 306 (p. 77 and Appendix 4); 1871 (XIX), c. 408 (Q. 4312); 1880 (VIII), no. 114 (Appendices 1 and 3); 1881 (VIII), no. 351 (Q. 6431 ff. and Appendix 16); 1898 (LIV), c. 9019.

20. Witness at the Dublin Hospitals Commission, *Parliamentary Papers*, 1887 (XXXV), c. 5042 (p. 94). For the number of cases treated and other information on the early years of operation of the Lock hospital, see evidence of Dr. T. Byrne before the select committee on Dublin hospitals in *ibid.*, 1854 (XII), no. 338.

21. *Parliamentary Papers* (Dublin Hospitals Reports): 1878 (XL), c. 1936; 1880 (XXIII), c. 2565; 1883 (XXVII), c. 3739. See, also, *ibid.*, 1854 (XII), no. 338, p. 19.

22. *Ibid.*, 1916 (XVI), cd. 8189, p. 23.

23. For the evidence relating to Dublin given before the Royal Commission, see *ibid.*: 1914 (XLIX), cd. 7475 (p. 87-93/265-75); 1916 (XVI), cd. 8190 (pp. 203-11). See, also, *ibid.*, 1913 (XXXII), cd. 7029 for the special report to the Local Government Board on venereal diseases.

24. Dublin Public Health Inquiry, *op. cit.*, cd. 244 (Q. 2168A and 2446).

25. *Irish Worker*, September 2, 1911. Payments for dead flies were not uncommon in public health-conscious cities. In the United States they were bought at 5 cents per bag in those days. Even as recently as 1974 the ploy was used in Turkey.

26. *Lancet*, October 11, 1913; *Medical Press*, October 1, 1913.

27. *Lancet*, May 19, 1906/March 30, 1918; *British Medical Journal*, February 15, 1908; *Parliamentary Papers*, 1913 (XXIX), cd. 6684 (Irish Milk Commission), Q. 73-74, 776-80, 905; Dublin Public Health Inquiry, *op. cit.*, Q. 4545, 4669; Dublin Corporation, Reports and Documents: 1917 no. 121 (June 1917).

28. *Lancet*, September 14 and 28, 1907; *Irish Times*, March 6, 1899 and May 31, 1916; Dublin Public Health Inquiry, *op. cit.*, cd. 244, Q. 3218-89, 4735, 4894.

29. Dublin Public Health Inquiry, *op. cit.*, cd. 244, Q. 194. For data concerning the main drainage system, see *Parliamentary Papers*, 1903 (XXXI), cd. 1487 (Royal Commission on Sewage Disposal), Q. 13029-221; Dublin Corporation *Souvenir Handbook* (1906); *Irish Times*, September 25, 1906/October 2, 1909/January 20, 1975.

5. Housing

1. The figures for housing construction to 1900 are based on the Report of the Departmental Committee (the Dublin Housing Inquiry) in *Parliamentary Papers*, 1914 (XIX): cd. 7273, pp. 17-19; cd. 7317, pp. 18-19. Further information is contained in Dublin Corporation, Reports and Documents: 1903-III no. 176 and in the annual reports of the Dublin Sanitary Association. For press reports of annual meetings of the various building societies, see, for example, *Irish Times*: January 17, 1900 and February 8, 1907 (Artisans' Dwellings Co.); May 23, 1904 (Alexandra Guild); March 12, 1908 (Iveagh Trust); April 15, 1909 and April 19, 1913 (Housing of the Very Poor Association). See, also, *Irish Builder*, September 27, 1913 and *Dublin Civic Survey* (London, 1925), pp. 77-78.

2. *Parliamentary Papers*, 1908 (XXXI), cd. 4128 (Belfast Health Commission), p. 78; *ibid.*, 1913 (LXXVII), cd. 6910 (Tenements in Administrative Areas), Table XIX.

3. *Ibid.*, 1914 (XIX), cd. 7317, p. 102.

4. *British Medical Journal*, May 9, 1903.

5. Reported in *Sanitary Record*, October 20, 1904.

6. For general remarks on all these matters, see Dublin Public Health Inquiry in *Parliamentary Papers*, 1900 (XXXIX), cd. 244, p. 21; Dublin Housing Inquiry, *op. cit.*, cd. 7317, pp. 43, 49, 57, 118, 166-67 and Appendix XXV.

7. See Table "Offences against the Sanitary Laws" in the annual reports (statistical returns) of the Dublin Metropolitan Police. See *Irish Times*, October 6, 1908, for the allegations against councillor Sherlock.

8. Information in this and in the preceding paragraph based on Philanthropic Reform Association Report for year ending April 30, 1899; *Irish Builder*, February 1, 1899; *Irish Times*, December 19, 1900/October 18, 1913; Dublin Corporation: Public Health Reports (various); *British Medical Journal*, September 27, 1913; Dublin Housing Inquiry, *op. cit.*, cd. 7317, pp. 102, 237 and *passim*.

9. Public Record Office (Dublin). Manuscript schedules of 1901 Census for streets named in text.

10. *Irish Builder*, August 27, 1903. See, also, *ibid.*, May 7 and December 3, 1903; *Parliamentary Papers*, 1908 (CVII), cd. 3864, p. xxi; *ibid.*, 1913 (LVI), cd. 6955; Dublin Housing Inquiry, *op. cit.*, cd. 7317, pp. 6, 18-20, 30, 37-38, 56, 62, 83 and Appendixes XXII-XXIV.

11. *Irish Times*, August 14 and 22, 1899.

12. *Parliamentary Papers*, 1900 (XXXIX), cd. 243 (Public Health Inquiry), p. 12.

13. Public Record Office (Dublin). Manuscript schedules of 1901 Census, 39/86-87.

14. *Irish Times*, December 16, 1902/October 15, 1904/ March 9, 1908; Dublin Corporation, Reports and Documents: 1902-III no. 183; 1904-II no. 108; 1905-III no. 253. See, also, Dublin Housing Inquiry, *op. cit.*, cd. 7317, pp. 22, 29, 208.

15. *Parliamentary Debates*, CI (January 17, 1902), cols. 218-21, 233-36; *Irish Times*, September 14 and December 19, 1903; Dublin Housing Inquiry, *op. cit.*, cd. 7317, pp. 262-64; Dublin Corporation, Reports and Documents: 1903-III no. 176.

16. *Irish Times*, February 26/March 5, 6, 10, 16/April 9, 1908; Dublin Housing Inquiry, *op. cit.*, cd. 7317, pp. 152, 265.

17. *Parliamentary Debates*, CLXXXVI (March 20, 1908), cols. 929-37.

18. *Irish Times*, July 15, 1904 and July 23/November 12, 1910; Dublin Corporation, Reports and Documents: 1909-III; 1909-II no. 178; Dublin Housing Inquiry, *op. cit.*, cd. 7317, p. 22 and Appendix III.

19. *Irish Builder*, April 29, 1911; *Irish Times*, October 14, 1912.

20. *Irish Times*, November 3, 1903.

21. *Irish Times*, July 4, 1914; Dublin Corporation, Reports and Documents: 1912-I no. 5; 1914-I no. 15; Dublin Housing Inquiry, *op. cit.*, cd. 7317, p. 13.

22. For a list of Corporation housing schemes up to 1921, see Appendix D.

23. *Irish Times*: October 10, 1902; November 24, 1909; April 12-13, 1911; September 4, 1913. *Medical Press*, December 1, 1909; *British Medical Journal*, September 13, 1913; Dublin Housing Inquiry, *op. cit.*, cd. 7317, pp. 189-91.

24. *The Leader*, January 25, 1913; *Irish Times*, September 17, 1913; *British Medical Journal*, September 27, 1913; *Irish Builder*, October 25, 1913.

25. *Parliamentary Papers*, 1914 (XIX): cd. 7273 (Report of Committee); cd. 7317 (Minutes of Evidence and Appendices). Appended to the volume is a brief summary of housing construction undertaken by several urban authorities elsewhere in Ireland along with an interesting series of photographs of the Dublin slums.

26. *Ibid.*, cd. 7273, p. 5.

27. *Ibid.*, cd. 7317, p. 16.

28. *Ibid.*, p. 212. The three labor spokesmen were W. O'Brien, Larkinite vice-president of the Dublin Trades Council, Walter Carpenter, sometime socialist candidate in municipal elections and chairman of the Independent Labour Party of Ireland, and M.J. O'Lehane of the Drapers Assistants' Association.

29. *Ibid.*, p. 7.

30. *Ibid.*, see Appendix XV-XVI. Another politically prominent owner of tenements (3 houses in Beresford Street which were willed to him) was John Dillon, chief lieutenant of John Redmond in the Irish parliamentary party (see *Irish Times*, October 10, 1913).

31. *Ibid.*, p. 210.

32. The various Labourers (Ireland) Acts were first instituted in 1883 and were a valiant attempt to rid the country (principally in Munster and Leinster) of the sooty, insanitary cabins with little or no land that had been the shame of rural Ireland. The scheme at Midleton, Co. Cork was reputedly a model of its kind. The local sanitary authorities were given compulsory powers to buy land and borrow on the security of the rates to build cottages with half-an-acre (later increased to one acre) attached. Rents did not exceed 1s. 6d. per week and averaged 11d. per week, the result of the contributions (after 1906) of the Imperial Exchequer (1/3rd) and the ratepayers (1/5th) toward the building costs. The schemes were notable for the involvement of the Catholic clergy in the work of canvassing support and action from both ratepayers and agricultural laborers, either of whom could make representations to the local authority for a building scheme under the Acts.

33. Dublin became a greater Mecca with the birth of the Irish Free State. For the next few decades the number of city residents with a birthplace in Ireland (32 counties) outside of County Dublin hovered around 25 percent in a rising population, a trend reversed only since the 1960s.

34. E. Gauldie, *Cruel Habitations*, p. 299.

35. See *Irish Times*, July 4, 1914 for evidence of a workman at Local Government Board hearing into Ormond Market scheme. The Law Agent's remarks were made at the Housing Inquiry, *op. cit.*, cd. 7317, p. 266.

36. *Parliamentary Debates*, LXI (16 April 1914), cols. 392-93.

37. *Irish Times*, May 5 and 27, 1914.

38. *Ibid.*, March 4, 1916.

39. *Ibid.*, September 15 and November 4, 1916; *Parliamentary Debates*, LXXXII (June 1, 1916), cols. 3071-72.

40. Report of the Local Government Tribunal, 1938 (P. 3163), p. 18. See, also, *Dublin Civic Survey* (London, 1925), p. 58; F. McGrath, "Homes for the People" in *Studies* (1932), pp. 269-82; T. Dillon, "Slum Clearance, Past and Future" in *Studies* (1945), pp. 13-20.

6. Poverty

1. The spokesman was the Bishop of Ross in evidence given before the Inter-Departmental Committee on Physical Deterioration, *Parliamentary Papers*, 1904 (XXXII), cd. 2210 (Minutes of Evidence), Q. 11279-80.

2. *Irish Times*, August 29, 1899 (speech to Catholic Truth Society at Stockport).

3. *Parliamentary Papers*, 1904 (XXXII), cd. 2210 (Physical Deterioration Committee), Q. 5335, 12568-71.

4. *Ibid.*, 1900 (XXXIX), cd. 244, p. 86.

5. S. Meacham, *A Life Apart* (Cambridge, Mass., 1977), p. 215. For data on prices and incomes, see *Parliamentary Papers* (Labour Statistics of the U.K.): 1908 (XCVIII), cd. 4413; 1914 (LXXX), cd. 7130.

6. The results of this interesting survey conducted over periods of four to ten weeks in 1904 is contained in *Parliamentary Papers*, 1910 (L), cd. 5070 (Royal Commission on the Poor Laws), pp. 143-91.

7. *Ibid.*, pp. 38-45 (evidence of J.P. Nannetti).

8. *Irish Times*, November 25, 1912.

9. The story of the Foundling Hospital is without parallel in the annals of institutional care in Ireland for young children. The worst phase, between 1790 and 1797, saw 9,200 infants out of 14,700 admitted perish in the nursery. This record of abuse, inhumanity, and mismanagement became the subject of an inquiry by a committee of the Irish parliament in 1797, and even though new standards and regulations were instituted thereafter, infant mortality in the Hospital always remained at an extremely high level. The basic source material on this appalling record is to be found in the following official reports: *Journal of the* (Irish) *House of Commons*, XVII (1797), Appendix pages cclvii-cclxxiii; *Parliamentary Papers*: 1810 (X), no. 193 (Report of the Board of Education); 1826-27 (XIII), no. 13 (Irish Education Inquiry).

10. *Parliamentary Papers*, 1887 (XXXV), c. 5042 (Dublin Hospitals Commission), p. 24; *ibid.*, 1902 (XXXVII), cd. 1259.

11. *Irish Times*, January 8, 1914. For a review of workhouse practice, see W. Mackenzie, *The Poor Law Guardian*, 4th ed. (London, 1895).

12. *Irish Times*, October 6, 1904; *Parliamentary Debates*, CLII (February 22, 1906), col. 517.

13. See, for example, the evidence of Dr. J.C. M'Walter (councillor, North City ward) in *Parliamentary Papers*, 1906 (LII), cd. 3204 (Commission on Poor Law Reform), vol. III, p. 565.

14. *Ibid.*, 1900 (XXXV), cd. 338 (Report of Local Government Board), p. 362. See *Irish Times*, July 18, 1912 for the "smuggling" offenses at the workhouse of the South Dublin Union.

15. *Parliamentary Papers*, 1900 (X), cd. 67 (Aged Deserving Poor), Appendix V, pp. 66-72.

16. *Ibid.*, 1902 (XLIX), cd. 1144 (Street Trading Children Committee), p. 179.

17. *Ibid.*, Appendix no. 3, pp. 145, 147, 150.

18. *Irish Times*, April 4, 1908. See, also, *Parliamentary Papers*, 1910 (XXVIII), cd. 5229 (Committee on Employment of Children), p. 8.

19. *Irish Times*, November 30, 1910 and July 1, 1913; *Irish Catholic*, February 1, 1913.

20. Dublin Corporation, Reports and Documents: 1915-I no. 39. For Bishop Kelly's comment, see *Parliamentary Papers*, 1904 (XXXII), cd. 2210 (reply to Q. 11386).

7. Police and Crime

1. *Parliamentary Papers*: 1900 (XL), no. 181; 1907 (XXXI), no. 128. See, also, *Parliamentary Debates*, CLXXIII (May 2, 1907), col. 1097.

2. Sir Francis Head, *A Fortnight in Ireland* (New York, 1852), p. 49. Incidentally, the DMP recruited few ex-soldiers, perhaps because of the lower physical standards set for members of H.M. Forces. The annual reports of the British Army disclose that of the 969 vacancies arising in the DMP between 1899 and 1913, only 23 were filled by former soldiers, a proportion similar to that for the RIC but only about one-fifth of the rate of employment of ex-soldiers by the London Metropolitan Police.

3. Chief Commissioner (DMP) to the Under Secretary, July 22, 1916 in Public Record Office (London), C.O. 904-174-4: "I think the Government will be faced with a serious situation unless an increase of pay is considered. The DMP rates of pay are lower than the rates obtaining in police forces of similar importance in England, while the work, during the last three years, of the Dublin Police has been of an unpleasant and onerous character. . . . There is a general feeling throughout the force that they are underpaid and although the RIC are not recruiting we find it almost impossible to secure suitable candidates for the DMP." Legislation was soon passed to soften the inequity (6 & 7 Geo. 5, cap. 59), giving the men only their second increase in pay in over 30 years.

4. *Parliamentary Papers*, 1902 (XLII), cd. 1095, pp. 4, 5, 11.

5. *Irish Times*, November 7, 1916.

6. *Parliamentary Papers*, 1901 (XXXII), cd. 707 (Report of the General Prisons Board).

7. *Irish Times*, February 23, 1902. The greatest offenders were the cities of Waterford, Londonderry, and Limerick—with drunkenness arrest rates (per 100,000 of the population) of 5758, 4333 and 4063, respectively, in 1901.

8. Address by Dr. T. J. O'Meara to the Irish Temperance Association (*British Medical Journal*, June 18, 1904).

9. *Parliamentary Papers*, 1909 (LXXIII), cd. 4575. The corresponding figures for 22 public houses in Belfast were 5,963 women and 6,449 children.

10. Gustave Richelot, *The Greatest of Our Social Evils* (London, 1857), p. 290.

11. Quoted in R. Weintraub (ed.), *Fabian Feminist* (University Park, Penn., 1977), p. 255.

12. Evidence before the Select Committee on the Contagious Diseases Acts in *Parliamentary Papers*, 1881 (VIII), no. 351 (Q. 6431 ff.).

13. *Ibid.*, 1884-85 (XXXI), c. 4547-I, pp. 55-56.

14. For accounts of the activities of the Dublin branch of the White Cross Association, see *The Vigilance Record* (London), especially issues of April 15, 1887 and April 15, 1892.

15. *Parliamentary Papers*, 1895 (LV), c. 7734 (DMP Statistical Returns for 1894), Table XXXV.

16. See the annual statistical returns of the Dublin Metropolitan Police.

17. *Parliamentary Papers*, 1913 (XXXII), cd. 7029 (Report of Dr. R. W. Johnstone to the Local Government Board), p. 14.

18. For the subsequent fortunes of this infamous quarter of Dublin, see John Finegan, *The Story of Monto* (Dublin, 1978).

19. The controversial episode can be followed in the *Irish Times*, October 10-28, 1910. For an earlier example of this type of concern about prostitution in the city, see *Freeman's Journal*, September/October 1866.

20. *Irish Times*, December 7, 1912 and February 18, 1913.

21. *Parliamentary Papers*, 1906 (LI), cd. 3103, p. viii.

8. Labor

1. *Parliamentary Papers*, 1892 (XXXVI), c. 6795 (Royal Commission on Labour), VI-pt. 3, IX-pts. 4, 5.

2. *Ibid.*, IX-pt. 4, XII-pt. 5. For evidence of Dublin Trades Council representatives see *ibid.*, vol. II, Group C (Q. 16235-519/16682-709).

3. Data on wage rates in the U.K. is given in the annual abstracts of labor statistics issued by the Board of Trade. Reports found useful in this instance include *Parliamentary Papers* as follows: 1908 (XCVIII), cd. 3690/4413; 1909 (LXXX), cd. 4545; 1910 (LXXXIV), cd. 5086; 1912-13 (CVIII), cd. 6053; 1913 (LXVI), cd. 6955. See also *Irish Times*, October 3, 1913 and Dublin Housing Inquiry, *Parliamentary Papers*, 1914 (XIX), cd. 7317, p. 2; *Parliamentary Debates*, CLIII (14 March 1906), col. 1223.

4. *Parliamentary Papers*, 1908 (LIX), cd. 4444; Q. 14033-186; 1909 (LXXX), cd. 4844, p. 39.

5. *Ibid.*, 1899 (XCII), c. 9346, pp. 9-13 (Report on the money wages of indoor domestic servants).

6. *Ibid.*, 1910 (LXXXIV), cd. 5086/5196/5460; 1914 (LXXX), cd. 7131; 1914-16 (LXI), cd. 7635.

7. *Ibid.*, 1906 (XV), cd. 3036 (Factories and Workshops Report for 1905). See, also, *Irish Times*, June 10, 1899 and November 18, 1905.

8. *Irish Times*, April 27, 1912 and April 14, 1914.

9. Cyril Jackson in report to the Royal Commission on the Poor Laws and Relief of Distress in *Parliamentary Papers*, 1909 (XLIV), cd. 4890, p. 6.

10. *Trade and Labour Journal* (Dublin), Vol. 1, no. 1, May 1909.

11. *The Times* (London), February 22, 1887.

12. *Workers' Republic*, May 16, 1900; *Irish Times*, January 14, 1899 and March 2, 1908.

13. *Irish Builder*, January 30, 1901 and December 4, 1902.

14. *Irish Times*, August 17, 1899.

15. *Ibid.*, August 19, 1904.

16. See annual reports of the Local Government Board for Ireland for data on the operation of the Act. See, also, *Labour Gazette*, 1906-1916 (Distress Committee Reports).

17. *Irish Times*, April 4, 8 and November 12, 1912. See, also, *Parliamentary Papers*, 1911 (XXXIII), cd. 5847 (Reports of Distress Committees).

18. *Labour Gazette*, February 1914 et seq.

19. *The Times* (London), August 22, 1859. The canard about the unions' responsibility for the decline of shipbuilding in Dublin was an old one. It figured prominently, naturally enough, in the unconvincing evidence of shipbuilders before the Select Committee on Combinations of Workmen in 1838 [see *Parliamentary Papers*, 1837-38 (VIII), no. 646 (Second Report), Questions 5900-6000].

20. *Labour Gazette*, May-July and October 1899; *Irish Times*, September 7 and 9, 1899.

21. *Labour Gazette*, August 1900; *Irish Times*, June 5 and July 5-17, 1900.

22. *Labour Gazette*, May 1900; *Irish Times*, May 8, June 5, July 26, September 20, 1900; *Parliamentary Papers*: 1900 (XXXIX), cd. 244, pp. 223-4; 1910 (XXIX), cd. 5110.

23. E. Larkin, *James Larkin* (Cambridge, Mass., 1965); C. Desmond Greaves, *The Life and Times of James Connolly* (London, 1961).

24. *Parliamentary Papers*, 1908 (XXXIV), cd. 4381 (Q. 494-563).

25. *Irish Times*, January 4, 1908.

26. *Ibid.*, July 9-11, 14, 1908. For Sherlock's attacks on Larkinism, see *ibid.*, January 14 and April 2, 1914.

27. *Ibid.*, November 18 and December 1 and 4, 1908; *Labour Gazette*, January 1909.

28. Cost of living data from Bureau of Labour Statistics tables in *Parliamentary Papers*: 1908 (XCVIII), cd. 4413; 1913 (LXVI), cd. 6955; 1914 (LXXX), cd. 7131.

29. *Labour Gazette*, March 1909; *Irish Times*, December 5, 14, 16, 22, 23, 1908 and February 17, 1909.

30. *Irish Times*, July 1, 17, 24, 28, 1911.

31. A. Mitchell, *Labour in Irish Politics* (New York, 1974), p. 29; E. Larkin, *James Larkin*, p. 76.

32. *Irish Times*, October 11, 1911.

33. *Ibid.*, August 21, 1911 and January 5, 1912; *Irish Worker*, September 27, 1911.

34. *Labour Gazette*, October 1911; *Irish Times*, October 5, 7, 11, 1911; *Irish Worker*, October 7, 1911.

35. *Weekly Irish Times*, August 26, 1911; *Irish Times*, October 10, 1911.

36. *Irish Times*, September 28 and October 2, 16, 1911.

37. Larkin, *James Larkin*, pp. 111, 114.

38. *Irish Times*, January 31/February 25/April 21, 1913.

39. *Ibid.*, July 9, 1913. For a listing of strikes occurring between January and August 1913 in Dublin, see *Parliamentary Papers*, 1914 (XVIII), cd. 7272 (Dublin Disturbances Commission), pp. 429-30.

40. *Parliamentary Papers*, 1913 (XXVIII), cd. 6953 (Inquiry into Industrial Agreements), Q. 7715-7874.

41. The details of the strike and accompanying lockout as outlined in the following paragraphs are based mainly on the day-to-day reports in the *Irish Times*. A convenient calendar of the events from August 12 onward is given in the issue dated December 22, 1913. Additional information on the course of the dispute is contained in *Parliamentary Papers*, 1914-16 (XXXVI), cd. 7658, pp. xxv-xxxi. For Larkin's involvement, see Larkin, *James Larkin*, Ch. 6-7. For contemporary comments, see the compilation by D. Nevin, *1913—Jim Larkin and the Dublin Lock-Out* published by the Workers' Union of Ireland (Dublin, 1964), which also contains an interesting series of photographs.

42. *Irish Times*, August 28, 1913. For information on company rolling stock, see *Parliamentary Papers*, 1911 (LXXI), cd. 5839 (Board of Trade Report on Tramway Orders).

43. These events became the subject of an official inquiry because of the allegations of police brutality and the bludgeoning to death of two citizens. The investigation was published as the Dublin Disturbances Commission in *Parliamentary Papers*, 1914 (XVIII): cd. 7269 (Report); cd. 7272 (Minutes of Evidence).

44. *Ibid.*, cd. 7272, p. 432.

45. *Ibid.*, pp. 331 2, 354.

46. *Ibid.*, cd. 7269, p. 9.

47. *Irish Catholic*, September 6, 1913. For an enlightening discussion of the "absurdly hysterical denunciation" of the "phantom" of socialism by the Catholic clergy and press, see E. Larkin, "Socialism and Catholicism in Ireland" in *Church History*, XXXIII (December 1964), 462ff.

48. Dublin Disturbances Commission, *op. cit.*, cd. 7272, p. 452.

49. *Irish Times*, October 16, 1913.

50. *Ibid.*, September 19, 1913.

51. The letter appeared in *Irish Times*, October 7, 1913. The full text is quoted in D. Nevin (comp.), *1913—Jim Larkin and the Dublin Lock-Out* (Dublin, 1964), pp. 55-57.

52. *Irish Times*, September 23, 1913.

53. *Ibid.*

54. Larkin, *James Larkin*, p. 128.

55. *Irish Times*, October 21, 1913.

56. Larkin, *James Larkin*, p. 156.

57. *Irish Times*, February 3, 1914. See, also, *ibid.*, September 20, 23, 1913. For Murphy's comments, see Nevin, *1913—Jim Larkin and the Dublin Lock-Out*, p. 65.

58. *Parliamentary Debates*, 5th series, LVIII (18 February 1914), cols. 989-95.

59. *Irish Times*, April 2, 1914. For the bishops' pastoral, see *ibid.*, February 23, 1914.

60. *Labour Gazette*, July 1916, p. 265.

9. War and Rebellion

1. State Paper Office (Dublin): DMP Criminal Department-Special Branch, #23504/S, Jones to Under Secretary, November 21, 1900.

2. *Parliamentary Papers*, 1912-1913 (LI), cd. 6656. More than Irish antienlistment activities engaged the army's attention, though the Director of Recruiting appeared to be grasping at straws in his efforts to explain his

problem to his superiors. In his report for 1904 he noted: "In some districts prejudice still exists against service in the Regular Army. . . . Influence is sometimes even from the pulpit against the work of the recruiter. In other cases exhibitions [i.e., public entertainments] purporting to represent incidents in the life of a soldier are calculated to cast ridicule on His Majesty's Service" [*Ibid.*, 1905 (IX), cd. 2265, p. 30].

3. Army recruits, in the main, had an urban background, only about 15 percent overall hailing from agricultural districts. In Ireland, however, the rural component was closer to one-third of recruits. The following gives the occupational background of a number of individuals (mainly from Dublin but with country districts added) offering themselves for enlistment during 1904. The rejection rate (327 per 1,000) is fairly typical for the period.

Occupational data	*No. inspected*	*No. rejected*	*No. finally approved*
Rural unskilled (farm servants and country casuals)	113	48	65
Urban unskilled (general laborers, porters, carters, casuals, etc.)	328	121	207
Skilled workers (tradesmen, etc.)	149	45	104
Tradesmens' assistants	40	14	26
Clerks	80	24	56
Students	4	2	2
Boys under 17	62	–	62
Total	776	254	522

Source: *Parliamentary Papers*, 1905 (IX), cd. 2265 (Appendix F).

4. *Parliamentary Papers*, 1916 (XI), cd. 8311, p. 22.

5. *Irish Times*, May 17, 1913. See, also, *ibid.*, June 14 and 19, 1912.

6. These events along with the subsequent shootings at Bachelor's Walk are fully outlined in the Report of the Royal Commissioners on the Landing of Arms at Howth in *Parliamentary Papers*, 1914-16 (XXIV), cd. 7631/7649.

7. *Parliamentary Debates*, LXV (July 27, 1914), cols. 1031-36.

8. Royal Commission on the Rebellion in Ireland, *Parliamentary Papers*, 1916 (XI), cd. 8279, p. 4; cd. 8311, p. 56.

9. *Parliamentary Debates*, LIX (March 19, 1914), col. 2219. For examples of Sinn Fein postcards, see Colonial Office Records in P.R.O. (London), C.O. 904 162(2).

10. Royal Commission on the Rebellion, *op. cit.*, cd. 8311, p. 3.

11. During the four years of the war, over 2,300 refugees were received in Ireland for whom the Belgian Refugees Committee collected over £46,000 (including the proceeds of collections at the doors of Dublin churches). Some were placed in workhouses for lack of accommodation; in one case (Dunshaughlin, county Meath) the paupers were cleared out by the military to make way for 125 refugees. According to a Local Government Board report, "public interest in the business chilled when Belgians showed little inclination to accept Irish hospitality, preferring to remain in England." Perhaps there they were not reduced to displacing unfortunate paupers. At any rate, the number of refugees in Ireland gradually declined from 1,500 in June 1915 to 900 the following year and to 500 by the end of the war [*Parliamentary Papers*, 1914-16 (XXV), cd. 8016].

12. *Freeman's Journal*, May 4, 1915.

13. *Ibid.*, September 6, 1915. For Redmond's letter, see Dublin Corporation: Minutes of the Council, 1915 no. 683.

14. Extract from typescript diary of Arthur Steel Maitland, MP (former chairman of the Unionist party organization in Britain) in Bonar Law Papers (49/D/6) at House of Lords Record Office, London.

15. *Parliamentary Papers*, 1914-16 (XXXIX), cd. 8168 (Report on recruiting in Ireland). The proportion of enlistments was considerably less for Ireland than for the other three home countries.

16. *Freeman's Journal*, December 17, 1915. For the attitude of the Catholic hierarchy to the war effort as the conflict progressed, see David W. Miller, *Church, State and Nation in Ireland, 1898-1921* (Pittsburgh, 1973), pp. 310 ff.

17. The reason for this action against Meyer was his speech of December 6, 1914 to a meeting of Clan-na-Gael in New York. Councillor Cosgrave's attempt to prevent the removal of his name (which lost by 22 votes to 30) had the support of Sinn Fein and Labour members and a dozen or so Nationalists. Naturally, the anglophobe Herr Doktor's name was restored to the roll of honorary burgesses after the "takeover" of the municipal council by Sinn Fein in 1920.

18. Redmond Papers (National Library of Ireland), MS. 15177/3.

19. *Ibid.*, MS. 15188/5 (Dr. Fogarty to Redmond, June 3, 1915).

20. Royal Commission on the Rebellion, *op. cit.*, cd. 8311, pp. 15, 57. See, also, memorandum of H.E. Duke to Lloyd George, January 30, 1917 in Lloyd George Papers (House of Lords Record Office), F/37/4/10.

21. Royal Commission on the Rebellion, *op. cit.*, cd. 8311, p. 57.

22. *Ibid.*, p. 22.

23. Redmond Papers (National Library of Ireland), MS. 15169/4, Birrell to Redmond, December 19 (1915). See, also, Redmond's memorandum enclosed with letter to General Sclater, August 9, 1915 in *ibid.*, MS. 15225.

24. A favorite contemporary account is James Stephens, *The Insurrection* (Dublin, 1916). A later study, by one who participated in the rebellion, is Desmond Ryan, *The Rising* (Dublin, 1949). For a readable popular account, see Max Caulfield, *The Easter Rebellion* (New York, 1963).

25. Royal Commission on the Rebellion, *op. cit.*, cd. 8311, pp. 38, 69.

26. *Parliamentary Papers*, 1919 (XLII), cmd. 30 (DMP Statistical Returns), p. iv.

27. *Ibid.*, 1918 (XXV), cd. 9066 (Judicial Statistics of Ireland), Table 31. For additional information relating to participants in the Rising, see B. Mac Giolla Choille, *Intelligence Notes, 1913-16* (Dublin, 1966). For the military aspects of the Rising, see the article by G.A. Hayes-McCoy in Kevin B. Nowlan (ed.), *The Making of 1916* (Dublin, 1969), 255-304.

28. For public health aspects of the Rising, see Dublin Corporation, Reports and Documents: 1917-III no. 183. See, also, *Lancet*, May 13, 1916 and *Irish Times*, May 20, 1916.

29. *Parliamentary Papers*, 1917-1918 (XVI), cd. 8765 (Local Government Board Report for year ended March 31, 1917).

30. D. Ryan, *The Man Called Pearse* (Dublin, 1919), p. 58; Asquith Papers (Bodleian Library), Wimborne to Prime Minister, April 25, 1916.

31. For Redmond's speech in the Commons on April 27, see *Parliamentary Debates*, LXXXI, col. 2512. See, also, *ibid.*, LXXII, col. 948 (speech of John Dillon); Robbins, *Under the Starry Plough*, p. 128; T.M. Coffey, *Agony at Easter* (London, 1970), p. 260; T.P. O'Neill et al., *Eamon De Valera* (Boston, 1971), p. 47.

32. *Irish Times*, November 30, 1916.

33. Dublin Corporation: Minutes of the Council, August 7, 1916 (no. 574); *Irish Times*, May 10 and 11, 1916; *Parliamentary Debates*, LXXXII, col. 31; F.S.L. Lyons, *John Dillon* (London, 1968), p. 382. Dillon had been "marooned" in the city during the fighting, with the result that his intervention in the Commons debate was delayed.

34. *Irish Times*, May 31, 1916.

35. For details of the number arrested in each county, see *Parliamentary Papers*, 1918 (XXV), cd. 9066 (Judicial Statistics of Ireland, Table 31).

36. Quoted in G. Dangerfield, *The Damnable Question* (Boston, 1976), pp. 246-47.

37. Royal Commission on the Rebellion, *op. cit.*, cd. 8311, p. 10. For Redmond's remarks see Lloyd George Papers (House of Lords Record Office), E/3/2/3, Redmond to Macready, October 31, 1916 (copy).

38. This account of the destruction is based on the report in *Irish Builder*, May 13, 1916.

39. Details of the plan became known during the summer of 1916, though it was not formally published until 1922, when it appeared as volume one of the publications of the Civics Institute of Ireland under the title *Dublin of the Future*. The other competitive designs were appended to volume two of the Institute's publications under the title *The Dublin Civic Survey* (London, 1925).

40. *Parliamentary Papers*, 1918 (XXV), cd. 9066 (Judicial Statistics of Ireland, Table 31). See also *Parliamentary Debates*, LXXXVI (October 12, 1916), col. 174; *Irish Builder*, May 27, 1916; *Irish Times*, May 18, 1916.

41. *Parliamentary Debates*, LXXXV (August 17, 1916), col. 2099.

42. *Irish Builder*, January 6, 1917.

43. *Parliamentary Debates*, LXXXII (May 3, 1916), col. 35. Birrell, as if to delude himself (or his readers)

about an event that had blighted his own political career and had indeed become a "political landmark," referred to the Rising in his memoirs as "really nothing more than a Dublin row"! (*Things Past Redress*, p. 219).

Epilogue

1. See *The Irish Statesman* (Dublin), May 31, 1924. The Corporation may be said to have hastened its own demise. Before the dissolution, the municipal council was dominated by the type of republican whose sympathies had lain with the anti-Treaty faction in the civil war. Consequently, the council often behaved in its last two years of life in a manner calculated to provoke the Free State government in much the same way that in the past the former members had acted to antagonize the British authorities. For example: the council attempted to compensate ex-Corporation employees who had been on the wrong (i.e., anti-Treaty) side in the civil war; it refused to strike the police rate; and it rejected government relief funds that would have been used to give employment to demobilised Free State soldiers.

2. L. Wright et al., "A Future for Dublin," in *Architectural Review* (November 1974), p. 292. See, also, U. Mac-Eoin, "Dublin: City in Decline" in *Hibernia* (Dublin), January 21, 1977.

3. *The City in History* (New York, 1961), p. 573.

Bibliography

1. TRAVEL, DESCRIPTION, etc.

(a) Nineteenth century and before (as the titles in some cases suggest, references to Dublin form only part of the traveler's account of his or her itinerary).

Brewer, J. N. *The Beauties of Ireland*. 2 vols. London, 1825.

Campbell, Thomas. *Philosophical Survey of the South of Ireland*. London, 1777.

Carr, John. *The Stranger in Ireland*. London, 1806.

Carrick, J. & J. *The Picture of Dublin for 1812—A Correct Guide*. Dublin.

Craig, Maurice. *Dublin, 1660-1860*. London, 1952.

Cromwell, Thomas. *Excursions through Ireland*. London, 1820.

De Bovet, M. *A Three Month Tour in Ireland*. London, 1891.

Dubois, Edward. *The Stranger in Ireland in 1805*. New York, 1807.

Ferrar, J. *A View of Ancient and Modern Dublin*. Dublin, 1796.

Fisk, Wilbur. *Travels in Europe*. New York, 1838.

French Emigrant, A (M. De Latocnaye). *Rambles through Ireland*. 2 vols. Cork, 1798.

Gamble, John. *Sketches of History, Politics and Manners in Dublin and the North of Ireland in 1810*. London, 1826.

Gregory, William. *The Picture of Dublin*. Dublin, 1817.

Griscom, John. *A Year in Europe . . . in 1818 and 1819*. 2 vols. New York, 1824.

Harris, W. *History and Antiquities of the City of Dublin*. London, 1766.

Head, Sir Francis. *A Fortnight in Ireland*. London, 1852.

Inglis, Henry D. *A Journey throughout Ireland during the Spring, Summer and Autumn of 1834*. 4th ed. London, 1836.

Irish Times. "The Last 50 Years in Dublin." Jubilee issue, June 8, 1909.

Johnson, James. *A Tour in Ireland*. London, 1844.

Kohl, J. G. *Ireland*. London, 1844.

Luckombe, Philip. *A Tour through Ireland*. London, 1780.

Maxwell, Constantia. *Dublin under the Georges, 1714-1830*. London, 1936.

———. *The Stranger in Ireland*. London, 1954.

Nicolson, A. *Ireland's Welcome to the Stranger*. New York, 1847.

O Muirithe, Diarmaid. *A Seat behind the Coachman*. Dublin, 1972 (compilation of comments on Dublin and other parts of Ireland by 19th-century travelers).

Parliamentary Gazeteer of Ireland. Dublin, 1844 (entry for Dublin).

Twiss, Richard. *A Tour in Ireland in 1775*. London, 1776.

Whitelaw, Rev. James. *An Essay on the Population of Dublin*. Dublin, 1805 (the "essay" is reprinted in Gregg International Publishers Ltd., *Slum Conditions in London and Dublin*. Farnborough, Hants., 1974).

Wright, G. N. *Historical Guide to Ancient and Modern Dublin*. London, 1821.

(b) Twentieth century

Carmichael, F. *Dublin*. Dublin, 1907.

Cole, G. A., and Praeger, R. L. *Handbook of the City of Dublin and the Surrounding District*. Dublin, 1908.

Cooke, John (ed.). *Handbook for Travellers in Ireland*. London, 1902.

Cosgrave, E. MacDowel, and Strangways, Leonard R. *The Dictionary of Dublin*. Dublin, 1908.

Englishman, An (Douglas Goldring). *Dublin Explorations and Reflections*. Dublin, 1917.

Fitzpatrick, Samuel. *Dublin*. London, 1907.

Gillespie, Elgy. *The Liberties of Dublin*. 3rd ed. Dublin, 1977 (has some interesting photographs).

Gwynn, Stephen. *The Famous Cities of Ireland*. Dublin, 1915.

Harvey, John. *Dublin*. London, 1949.

Kain, Richard M. *Dublin in the Age of William Butler Yeats and James Joyce*. Norman, Okla., 1962.

Longford, C. *A Biography of Dublin*. London, 1936.

Pearl, Cyril. *Dublin in Bloomtime*. New York, 1969 (a guide for Joyceans—contains interesting photographs of Dublin at the turn of the century).

Stewig, Reinhard. *Dublin: Funktionen und Entwicklung*. Kiel, 1959.

2. OFFICIAL RECORDS.

(a) Dublin Corporation: Accounts
   Minutes of the Municipal Council
   Reports and Documents

(b) Dail Eireann. *Report of Inquiry into the Housing of the Working Classes of the City of Dublin*. Dublin, 1943.

(c) Public Record Office (Dublin): Manuscript Census Schedules, 1901.

(d) British *Parliamentary Papers*. The following is not a complete listing of the Papers found useful for this study. Only the more important items are included. The method of citation is: Year or Session (Number of Bound Volume), Paper or Command Number.

   (i) Public Health: 1819 (VIII), no. 314. First Report from the Select Committee on the State of Disease and the Condition of the Labouring Poor in Ireland.

      1840 (XI), c. 384. Select Committee on the Health of Towns (evidence relating to Dublin).

      1854 (XII), no. 338. Select Committee on Dublin Hospitals.

      1880 (XXX), c. 2605. Royal Commission on Sewerage and Drainage of the City of Dublin.

      1887 (XXXV), c. 5042. Dublin Hospitals Commission.

      1900 (XXXIX), cd. 243/cd. 244. Dublin Public Health Inquiry.

      1904 (XXXII), cd. 2210. Inter-Departmental Committee on Physical Deterioration (evidence relating to Dublin).

      1914 (XLIX), cd. 7475; 1916 (XVI), cd. 8169. Royal Commission on Venereal Diseases (evidence relating to Dublin).

(ii)   Housing: 1833 (XXXV), no. 5. Summary of Documents relating to the New Valuation of the City of Dublin, 1830.

1884-85 (XXXI), c. 4547/c. 4547-I. Royal Commission on the Housing of the Working Classes (evidence relating to Dublin).

1914 (XIX), cd. 7273/cd. 7317. Housing Conditions of the Working Classes in Dublin.

(iii) Labor:1837-38 (VIII), no. 646. Select Committee on Combinations of Workmen (2nd Report).

1884-85 (IX), no. 288. Report of the Select Committee on Industries (Ireland).

1892 (XXXVI), c. 6795: vol. II-Group C; vol. VII-pt. 3; vol. IX-pts. 4, 5; vol. XII-pt. 5. Royal Commission on Labour (evidence relating to Dublin).

1913 (XXVIII), cd. 6953. Report of Inquiry into Industrial Agreements (evidence relating to Dublin).

1914 (XVIII), cd. 7269/cd. 7272. Dublin Disturbances Commission.

(iv)   Local Government: 1822 (VII), no. 394. Select Committee on the Local Taxation of the City of Dublin.

1823 (VI), no. 549. Select Committee on the Local Taxation of the City of Dublin (Second Report).

1835 (XXVII), no. 23. Municipal Corporations (Ireland). Report on the City of Dublin, Part I.

1836 (XXIV), no. 26. Municipal Corporations (Ireland). Report on the City of Dublin, Part II.

1847 (XXVI), no. 124. Report of the Surveying Officers on the Dublin Improvement Bill.

1850 (XXV), no. 559. Report made by the Commissioners appointed for Dividing the City of Dublin into New Wards.

1876 (X), no. 352. Select Committee on Local Government and Taxation of Towns (Ireland).

1878 (XXIII), c. 2062. Inquiry into the Collection of Rates in the City of Dublin.

1880 (XXX), c. 2725; 1881 (L), c. 2827. Municipal Boundaries Commission (Ireland).

1900 (XXXVI), cd. 383. Royal Commission on Local Taxation in Ireland.

(v)   Census of Population (Ireland):
City of Dublin, 1851: 1852-53 (XCI)
         "   1861: 1863 (LIV)
         "   1871: 1872 (LXVII)
         "   1881: 1881 (XCVII)
         "   1891: 1890-91 (XCV)
         "   1901: 1902 (CXXII)
         "   1911: 1912-13 (CXIV)

(vi)   Miscellaneous: 1883 (XXXII), c. 3576. Report of Committee of Inquiry into the Dublin Metropolitan Police.

1902 (XLII), cd. 1088/cd. 1095. Committee of Inquiry into the Dublin Metropolitan Police.

1902 (XLIX), cd. 1144. Street Trading Children (Ireland).

1906 (LI), cd. 3202/cd. 3203; 1906 (LII), cd. 3204. Vice-Regal Commission on Poor Law Reform in Ireland.

1909 (XXXVIII), cd. 4630; 1910 (L), cd. 5070. Royal Commission on the Poor Laws and Relief of Distress (evidence relating to Dublin).

1910 (XXVIII), cd. 5229/cd. 5230. Employment of Children Act, 1903 Committee (evidence relating to Dublin).

1914-16 (XXIV), cd. 7631/cd. 7649. Royal Commission on the Landing of Arms at
Howth on July 26, 1914.

1916 (XI), cd. 8279/cd. 8311. Royal Commission on the Rebellion in Ireland.

(vii) Annual Reports:

Board of Superintendence of the Dublin Hospitals
Chief Inspector, Factories and Workshops
Chief Registrar of Friendly Societies: Trade Unions
Commissioners of Public Works in Ireland
Dublin Metropolitan Police, Statistical Returns (from 1894)
General Prisons Board (Ireland)
Inspector of Reformatories and Industrial Schools (Ireland)
Judicial Statistics of Ireland
Labour Statistics of the U.K. (Trade disputes, Unions, etc.)
Local Government Board (Ireland)
Registrar General of Births, Marriages and Deaths (Ireland)
Reports of the British Army (Recruiting, Medical Dep't, etc.)
Returns of Local Taxation in Ireland

(e) *Parliamentary Debates*, 4th and 5th series

3. SPECIAL SUBJECTS

(a) Public Health:

Antisell, Thomas. *Suggestions towards the Improvement of the Sanatory Condition of the Metropolis.* Dublin, 1847 (pamphlet).

Birmingham, Charles L. *Handbook of Irish Sanitary Law.* Dublin, 1905.

Cameron, Sir Charles. *Municipal Public Health Administration.* Dublin, 1914.

Dublin Corporation. Public Health Committee, Annual Reports (reference no. Ir 614094183 D3 in pamphlet collection of National Library of Ireland).

Dublin Corporation. *Souvenir Handbook* (issued on the inauguration of the Main Drainage). Dublin, 1906.

Dublin Sanitary Association. Annual Reports, 1873-1910 (reference no. Ir 6140941 D5 in pamphlet collection of National Library of Ireland).

Philanthropic Reform Association. Annual Reports (reference no. Ir 361 P1 in pamphlet collection of National Library of Ireland).

Rice, Ignatius J. *Notes on the Law of Public Health in Dublin.* Dublin, 1900.

Willis, T. *Social and Sanitary Condition of the Working Classes in the City of Dublin.* Dublin, 1845 (pamphlet).

(b) Housing:

Aldridge, Henry R. *The National Housing Manual.* London, 1923.

Brady, J. Vincent. *The Future of Dublin—Practical Slum Reform.* Dublin, 1917.

Bolton, A.D. *Housing of the Working Classes (Ireland) Acts, 1890-1908.* Dublin, 1914.

Dawson, Charles. "The Housing of the People with special reference to Dublin" in *Journal of the Statistical and Social Inquiry Society of Ireland*, XI (1901).

Dillon, T. "Slum Clearance, Past and Future" in *Studies*, XXXIV (March 1945).

Kaim-Caudle, P.R. *Housing in Ireland: Some Economic Aspects.* Dublin, 1965.

McGrath, F., S.J. "Homes for the People" in *Studies*, XXI (June 1932).

McKenna, Lambert, S.J. "The Housing Problem in Dublin" in *Studies*, VIII (June 1919).

O'Connell, John R. *The Problem of the Dublin Slums.* Dublin, 1913 (pamphlet).

Robinson, Nugent. *The Condition of the Dwellings of the Poor in Dublin*. London, 1862 (pamphlet).

Synnott, Nicholas J. *The Housing Question in Irish Towns*. Dublin, 1908 (pamphlet).

Thompson, W. *The Housing Handbook*. London, 1903.

————. *Housing Up-To-Date*. London, 1907.

(c) Town Planning and Development:

Civics Institute of Ireland. *Dublin of the Future*. London, 1922 (the prize design of Patrick Abercrombie and associates for the Marquis of Aberdeen town-planning competition of 1914).

Craft, Maurice. "The Development of Dublin" in *Studies*, Autumn 1970 and Spring 1971.

Delaney, Patrick (ed.). *Dublin: A City in Crisis*. Dublin, 1975 (a "plan of action" for the modern metropolis).

Haughton, Joseph P. "The Social Geography of Dublin" in *Geographical Review*, XXXIX (1949).

O'Rourke, Horace T., et al. *Dublin Civic Survey*. London, 1925 (has excellent set of plans and photographs).

Wright, Lance, et al. "A Future for Dublin" in *Architectural Review*, CLVI (November 1974).

(d) Miscellaneous:

Blythe, E. P. "The D.M.P." in *Dublin Historical Record*, XX (June 1965).

Chart, D. A. *Unskilled Labour in Dublin*. Dublin, 1914 (pamphlet).

Church of Ireland Social Service Union. *Social Service Handbook*. Dublin, 1901.

Dawson, Charles. "The Valuation of the City of Dublin" in *Journal of the Statistical and Social Inquiry Society of Ireland*, X (1897), pp. 320-25.

Dublin Metropolitan Police. *Standing Orders and Regulations*. Dublin, 1889.

Dublin Municipal Council. *Miscellaneous By-Laws* (pamphlet in National Library of Ireland collection: Ir 352 D8).

Mackenzie, W. *The Poor Law Guardian*. 4th ed. London, 1895.

Meehan, P. "Early Dublin Public Lighting" in *Dublin Historical Record*, V (June 1943).

Reed, Sir Andrew. *The Policeman's Manual*. Dublin, 1898.

Smith Gordon, Lionel, and O'Brien, Cruise. *Starvation in Dublin*. Dublin, 1917 (pamphlet).

Thompson, W. H., M.D. *War and the Food of the Dublin Labourer*. Dublin, 1915 (pamphlet).

A Vindication of the Municipal Council of the City of Dublin. Dublin, 1924.

4. **GENERAL AND RELATED WORKS**

Bodkin, Thomas. *Hugh Lane and his Pictures*. Dublin, 1956.

Cameron, Sir Charles A. *Reminiscences*. Dublin, 1913.

Caulfield, Max. *The Easter Rebellion*. New York, 1963.

Chart, D. A. *The Story of Dublin*. London, 1932.

Coffey, T. M. *Agony at Easter*. London, 1970.

Collins, James. *Life in Old Dublin*. Dublin, 1913.

Cullen, L. M. *An Economic History of Ireland Since 1660*. London, 1972.

Curriculum Development Unit. *Divided City*. Dublin, 1978 (a "portrait of Dublin in 1913" for school use but has interesting series of photographs of life and labor in early 20th-century Dublin).

Dangerfield, George. *The Damnable Question*. Boston, 1976.

Fallis, Richard. *The Irish Renaissance*. Syracuse, New York, 1977.

Finegan, John. *The Story of Monto*. Dublin, 1978. pb.

Greaves, C. Desmond. *The Life and Times of James Connolly*. London, 1961.

Hogan, Robert, and Kilroy, James. *The Modern Irish Drama*. 3 vols. Dublin, 1975-78.

Larkin, Emmet. *James Larkin*. Cambridge, Mass., 1965.

————."Socialism and Catholicism in Ireland" in *Church History*, XXXIII (December 1964).

Lee, Joseph. *The Modernization of Irish Society, 1848-1918*. Dublin, 1973.

Lyons, F. S. L. *Ireland Since the Famine*. London, 1971.

MacGiolla Choille, B. *Intelligence Notes, 1913-16*. Dublin, 1966.

McHugh, Roger (ed.). *Dublin 1916*. New York, 1966.

Miller, David W. *Church, State and Nation in Ireland, 1898-1921*. Pittsburgh, 1973.

Mitchell, Arthur. *Labour in Irish Politics*. New York, 1974.

Nevin, Donal. *1913—Jim Larkin and the Dublin Lock-Out*. Dublin, 1964 (contains photographs associated with the labor troubles of that year).

Norway, Mrs. Hamilton. *The Sinn Fein Rebellion as I Saw It*. Dublin, 1916.

Nowlan, Kevin B. (ed.). *The Making of 1916*. Dublin, 1969.

O'Brien, William. *Forth the Banners Go*. Dublin, 1969.

O Broin, Leon. *Dublin Castle and the 1916 Rising*. Dublin, 1966.

Osborough, Nial. *Borstal in Ireland*. Dublin, 1975.

Quaney, Joseph. *A Penny to Nelson's Pillar*. Waterford, 1971 (the development of the Dublin tramways).

Redmond-Howard, L. G. *Six Days of the Irish Republic*. Dublin, 1916.

Robinson, Lennox. *Ireland's Abbey Theatre*. London, 1951.

Ryan, Desmond. *The Rising*. Dublin, 1949.

————. *A Man Called Pearse*. Dublin, 1919.

Robbins, Frank. *Under the Starry Plough*. Dublin, 1977.

Stephens, James. *The Insurrection*. Dublin, 1916.

Swift, John. *History of the Dublin Bakers*. Dublin, n.d.

Watters, Eugene. *Infinite Variety*. Dublin, 1979.

Webb, J.J. *Municipal Government in Ireland*. Dublin, 1918.

Wright, Arnold. *Disturbed Dublin*. London, 1914 (to be used with caution: it is not the "impartial" study of the events of the 1913 labor disputes the author tells us he set out to write).

5. YEARBOOKS, DIRECTORIES, etc.

Burdett's *Hospitals and Charities* (The Year Book of Philanthropy and Hospitals). London.

Municipal Year Book. London.

Museums, Libraries and Art Galleries Year Book. London.

Pettigrew and Oulton's *Dublin Almanac*. Dublin (has street directory).

Thom's Directory. Dublin, 1844- (has street directory and map of city and environs).

Wilson's *Dublin Directory*. Dublin, 1765-1837 (has street directory).

6. NEWSPAPERS AND PERIODICALS (published at Dublin except where stated).

(a) Newspapers

Church of Ireland Gazette

Evening Telegraph

Freeman's Journal

Irish Catholic

Irish Times

Irish Worker

Leader
Sinn Fein
The Times (London)
United Irishman
Weekly Irish Times
Worker's Republic

(b) Periodicals:
British Medical Journal (London)
Dublin Historical Record
Dublin Quarterly Journal of Medical Science
Irish Builder
Journal of the Statistical and Social Inquiry Society of Ireland
Labour Gazette (London)
Lancet (London)
Medical Press (London)
Sanitary Record (London)
Studies

7. PHOTOGRAPHS

(a) The main source for photographs of early twentieth-century Ireland is the Lawrence microfilm collection at the National Library of Ireland. For photographs of Dublin, see Royal microfilm series:

Roll 9: frames 5927-29, 5933-34
 "   10:   "   5936-38, 5941-42
 "   13:   "   7880-82, 7884, 7887-90
 "   14:   "   8608, 8905

(b) Pictures of Dublin, 1916 (photographs in the National Library of Ireland showing the destruction in Dublin as a result of the Easter Rising: reference no. Ir 9410912 i5).

(c) The "Emerald Isle" Album Series. *The City and County of Dublin*. Dublin, n.d. (77 "platina-tone views" with descriptive guide of Dublin at the turn of the century—from photographs by William Lawrence).

(d) Gorham, Maurice (ed.). *Dublin from Old Photographs*. New York, 1975.

8. MAPS

Readers may have difficulty in locating suitable street maps of nineteenth- and early twentieth-century Dublin. Some excellent maps of the city and environs are to be found appended to various Parliamentary Papers. Examples are:

1837 (**XXIX**), no. 301
    ward boundaries existing before establishment of new wards in 1850
1880 (**XXX**), c. 2605
    6" (to the mile) street map and several 1" maps in connection with plans for a main drainage scheme
1881 (L), c. 3089-I
    4" map of city and townships
1883 (**XXXII**), c. 3576
    6" street map showing boundaries of the Dublin Metropolitan Police divisions and location of station houses

1900 (**XXXIX**), cd. 244
   6″ street map showing principal areas of poverty
1914 (**XIX**), cd. 7317
   6″ street map (including added areas) showing ward boundaries and particulars as to housing

Index

Abbey Theatre. *See* Entertainment, theaters
Abercrombie, Sir Patrick, 69, 271, 276
Aberdeen, Countess of, 69, 113
Aberdeen, Lord, 68, 69, 219, 271
Abraham, William, MP, 232
Act of Union, Effects of, 5-7, 10-11, 70
Alexandra College Guild, 128
Ancient Order of Hibernians (AOH), 182, 229, 235
Antisell, Dr. Thomas, 20
Ardilaun, Lord (Arthur E. Guinness), 55, 62, 79, 100
Army, British, in Ireland, 117-118, 194, 228, 230-231, 247, 249-250, 252, 258; barracks, 40, 246, 249; conscription, 256; and Easter Rising, 258-263 *passim,* 271; recruiting, 85, 162, 212, 243-245, 251-257 *passim,* 268; strength, 246
Arnold, Matthew, 57
Arnott, Sir John, 25, 72, 80
Askwith, Sir George, 231, 239
Asquith, H. H., 248

Bachelor's Walk massacre, 249-250
Bailey, W. F., 51
Belfast, 9, 82, 116, 212, 234, 275; compared with Dublin, 11, 40, 59, 65, 72, 74, 75, 76, 77, 80, 96, 104, 107, 110, 112, 123, 142, 162, 201; crime in, 185-186, 188; housing in, 24, 27, 130; industry in, 10, 200; labor, 205, 208, 210, 215, 217, 219; police, 180; population, 9, 35; recruiting, 243, 245, 254, 257
Belgian refugees, 252
Bernard, Dr. J. H., Protestant Archbishop of Dublin, 231, 233
Bewley, Ernest, TC, 83
Birmingham, 77, 104, 106, 107, 130, 180, 186, 188
Birrell, Augustine, Chief Secretary for Ireland, 50, 150, 155-156, 246, 250, 257-258, 274

Board of Works, 25-26
Bodkin, Thomas, 57
Boer War, 85, 87-88, 242-244
Bohan, J., TC, 92
Boyd, Ernest, 52
Bradford, 11, 77, 104, 106, 107, 186, 188
Brady, Alice, 236
Brady, P. J., MP, 232, 238
Bristol, 59, 77, 104, 106, 107, 186, 188
Brooks, Maurice, 72
Brothels, 117, 143, 171, 190-191, 195
Building Trades Employers' Association, 223
Burdett, Henry, 32
Byrne, A. ("Alfie"), TC, 147, 157, 249

Calcutta, 102
Cameron, Sir Charles, 31, 112, 121-122, 124, 128, 130, 135, 146, 147, 154, 158, 189
Campbell, John, 72
Carpenter, Walter, 92, 138
Carson, Edward, 83
Casement, Sir Roger, 259
Chamber of Commerce, Dublin, 144, 210, 254, 266
Chamberlain, Joseph, 243
Charitable societies, 168-170, 177, 211; Mendicity Institution, 8, 102, 168; St. Vincent de Paul, 33, 169, 220, 264; Salvation Army, 169, 264
Cheyne, Dr. J., 28
Children Act (1908), 174, 197
Church of Ireland Gazette, 170
Church Street disaster, 68, 135, 149
Churches, 4, 6, 271
Citizens Housing League, 148
Civic Exhibition, Dublin, 69
Clancy, J. J., MP, 145, 156
Clancy, John, TC, 85, 87, 148

Coal Merchants Association, 215-216, 225

Cobden, Capt. H., 249

Cochrane, Sir Henry, 209

Cole, Walter, TC, 244

Colum, Padraic, 231

Connolly, James, 85-87, 88-89, 92, 95, 209, 215, 216, 219, 229, 231, 235, 239, 243, 248, 254, 262, 265

Connolly, John, 265

Cork, 112, 117, 118, 185

Corrigan, P., TC, 98

Cosgrave, Dr. E. MacDowel, 162

Cosgrave, Wm. T., TC, 56, 90, 156-157, 248, 267, 275

Cost of living, 166-167, 201, 204, 218, 231, 239

Cowpock Institution, 16

Crime, 33, 182-187, 190; juvenile offenders, 193, 195-198

Crozier, J., TC, 229

Cusack, Michael, 243

Custom House, 10, 43, 64, 121, 271

Cuthbert, Brigadier-Gen. G., 250

Daly, P. T., TC, 89, 90, 267

Dargan, William, 55

Davitt, Michael, 65, 187, 243

Davitt, M., Jr., 247

Dawson, William, 45, 46

Death rates. See Public health

Defence of the Realm Act (D.O.R.A.), 256

De Valera, Eamon, 265

Devlin, Joe, MP, 247, 252

Dillon, John, MP, 87, 238, 247, 248, 255, 265, 266

Disease, 17, 19-20, 28, 101, 104 ff., 115-116, 121-123; cholera, 20, 101-102, 105; smallpox, 17, 101-102, 105, 115; TB, 101, 105, 107, 109, 110-114, 166, 333; typhus, 20, 101, 105, 109; VD, 105, 116-120, 193-194

Dockrell, Sir Maurice, 80, 252

Dockrell, Thomas, 72

Dodd, R. J., TC, 88

Domestic servants, 206

Donnelly, H., TC, 92

Dougherty, Sir James, 219, 250

Doyle, W., TC, 91

Dowd, P., TC, 84

Downes, Sir Joseph, TC, 80, 86, 98, 222, 252

Drama. See Entertainment

Drogheda, 21

Drunkenness, 34, 163, 183, 184, 187-189, 252

Dublin: description, 3-14 passim, 27-28, 34, 36, 39 ff., 56, 61-63, 68-69, 242, 276-277; monuments, 41-43, 57, 63, 65, 87, 91, 120, 242, 268, 271; Phoenix Park, 62, 88, 155, 247, 259; St. Stephen's Green, 4, 55, 61-62, 136, 259; Zoological Gardens, 43, 62

Dublin and Suburban Workmen Dwellings Company, 128

Dublin Artisans Dwellings Company, 25, 26, 127, 130, 139

Dublin Castle, 4, 5, 150, 252

Dublin Citizens Association, 96, 145, 146, 210

Dublin Corporation, 17, 18, 30, 35, 48, 62-67 passim, 74, 85, 97-99, 169, 176, 180, 194, 227-228, 233, 242, 244, 248, 254-255, 259, 275; and Bachelor's Walk massacre, 250; and Dublin Housing Inquiry, 150-156 passim; and Easter Rising, 265-267, 274; and extension of boundaries, 14-15, 76, 82-83, 275; and home rule, 84, 86, 95, 152; and housing, 26-27, 98, 127, 129-130, 134-136, 141-149, passim, 153, 155-157, 169-170, 276; and main drainage, 20, 124; and Municipal Art Gallery, 53-56; municipal franchise, 5, 35, 72, 73, 77; and public health, 17, 20, 22, 30-32, 67, 102, 109-116 passim, 120-124, 136, 170; and public libraries, 58-59; rates, 15, 17, 35-36, 74, 96; revenue and expenditure, 17, 74-77, 99; and royal visits, 86, 88, 91; and unemployment, 168, 210-212, 234, 264
    elections, 72, 80, 88, 90-93, 98; (1899), 77-79; (1900), 85; (1901), 83-84, 87; (1905), 83; (1906), 89; (1910), 90; (1912), 91-92; (1913), 92; (1914), 92, 236
    municipal council, 35-36, 71-74, 76-100 passim, 136, 242, 247; Labour faction, 56, 78-79, 84, 89-95 passim, 136, 148; Nationalist faction, 56, 78-79, 83, 85, 88, 90, 92, 93-95; Sinn Fein faction, 56, 89-90, 93-96, 144; Unionist faction, 56, 78-79, 83, 93, 95-96

Dublin Improvement Act (1849), 17

Dublin Sanitary Association, 22, 25, 30, 32, 112, 128

Dublin United Tramways Company (DUTC), 144, 151, 224-225, 231

Dublin Vigilance Committee, 23, 47

Dudley, Earl of, 133

Duke, H. E., 157

Dundalk, 57, 58

Easter Rising, 157, 258-274 passim; arrests, 267; casualties, 262-263; destruction, 268-273, 276; looting, 260

Edinburgh, 77, 104, 106, 107

Edward VII, 88, 91, 129

Elections. See Dublin Corporation, elections

Employers' Federation, Dublin, 220, 226, 232-233, 239

Employment of Children Act (1903), 176

Entertainment, 44-53 passim, 258, 264; cinema, 47, 264; music, 46, 47-50; music hall, 46-47
    theaters: Abbey Theatre, 50-52; Gaiety, 45, 46, 53, 232; Queen's, 46; Theatre Royal, 45-46

Esposito, Michele, 48-49

Fairview Park, 121
Falkiner, Sir Frederick, 184
Farrell, J. J., TC, 91, 217
Farren, T., TC, 267
Ferguson, Sir Samuel, 58
Field, William, MP, 123, 144, 217, 232, 252
Flanagan, M., TC, 93
Flinn, Dr. D. Edgar, 177
Fogarty, Michael, Bishop of Killaloe, 252, 255
Foundling Hospital, 170
Friend, Major-Gen. L. B., 250, 260

Gaelic Athletic Association, 62, 244, 247
Gaelic League, 50, 60, 95, 113, 188, 242, 244, 247
Gallagher, J., TC, 100, 257
Galway, 21, 266
Geddes, Patrick, 68, 143, 154, 277
George IV, 8
George V, 53, 91, 114
Gilbert, Sir John, 59
Ginnell, Laurence, MP, 266
Glasgow, 21, 64, 65, 77, 104, 106, 107, 110, 131, 134-
    135, 180, 201, 205, 210
Gogarty, Oliver St. John, 40, 231
Gonne, Maud, 85, 177, 235, 243
Goodbody, Marcus, 79
Goulding, W. J., 80
Gray, Edmund D., 71
Gray, Sir John, 18, 72
Gregory, Lady, 50-53
Griffith, Arthur, 51, 89-91, 118, 144-145, 221, 243-244
Grimshaw, Dr. Thomas, 22
Guinness, Arthur E. See Lord Ardilaun
Guinness, Sir Benjamin L., 72, 128
Guinness, Edward C. See Lord Iveagh
Guinness's Brewery, 149, 180, 201-202, 218, 235, 260
Gunn, Michael, 47
Gwynn, Fr. J., 194

Haig, Major A.E., 249
Harrel, W. V., 179, 249-250
Harrington, T. C., MP, TC, 58, 79, 84, 87, 88, 217
Harrison, Sarah, TC, 55, 92, 213
Harvey, John Martin, 52
Healy, T. M., MP, 54, 77, 86
Hicks, Rev. Savell, 163
Holloway, Joseph, 52
Home Rule, 36, 84, 86, 90, 95, 152, 156, 222, 238,
    241, 247-248, 251
Hospitals, 20, 112-116, 118-120, 122-123, 129, 170-
    171, 220, 228, 231; Westmoreland Lock, 118-120,
    193
House of Industry, 8, 170
Houseowners and Ratepayers Association, 147

Houses, number of, 6, 18, 23-24
Housing, 6, 12, 36, 42, 69, 156-157, 158; accommo-
    dation, 23-28 passim, 33, 133, 143, 146, 148, 152-
    154; and Dublin Corporation, 26-27, 98, 127, 129,
    134-149 passim, 153, 156-157, 276; Dublin Hous-
    ing Inquiry, 98, 133, 135, 138, 150-157, 166, 238;
    legislation, 25-27, 34, 142, 145-146; lodging
    houses, 29, 33, 169; rents, 25-27, 33, 127, 139,
    141-142, 143, 146, 148; schemes, 26, 127-130, 143-
    144, 146-149, 157, 276
    tenements: conditions in, 7-8, 18, 29-30, 32-
    33, 112, 134-139, 164; description of, 23, 28-
    29, 31, 103, 127, 131-135, 139, 147, 151;
    development of, 7, 14, 23, 40, 142; number
    of, 133-135, 152-153
Housing of the Very Poor Association, 128
Howth arms landing, 249-250
Hutchinson, Joseph, TC, 92

Industrial Tenements Company, 25
Infant mortality. See Public health
Irish Builder, 33, 142, 149, 209, 274
Irish Citizen Army, 239, 248-249, 251-252, 257-258
Irish parliamentary party, 71, 86, 144, 156, 238, 241-
    242, 247, 248, 256, 257, 268
Irish Republican Brotherhood, 244, 247, 251, 257
Irish Socialist Republican party, 78, 209, 243
Irish Transvaal Committee, 85, 242-243
Irish Volunteers, 248-251, 256-259, 267, 268
Irish Women Workers Union, 236
Irish Women's Franchise League, 96, 247
Iveagh, Lord, 62, 79, 100, 114, 129
Iveagh Hostel, 128-129, 169

Jacob, George, 79
Jameson, John, 80
Jameson, John, Jr., 72
Jews, 102, 162
Johnson, Thomas, 249
Jones, J. J., Commissioner (DMP), 243
Joyce, James, 40, 47, 50, 60

Keegan, John, 208
Kelly, Denis, Bishop of Ross, 173, 177
Kelly, J. S., TC, 91
Kelly, John T. (Sean T. O Ceallaigh), TC, 89, 90, 267
Kelly, Thomas, TC, 89-90, 144, 157, 237, 248, 257,
    267
Kenny, Dr. Joseph, 111-112
Kent, Edward T., 265
Kettle, Tom, 182, 231, 248
Knox, Capt. L., 72

Labor: hours, 202-204, 206-207, 218; Labour Exchanges, 176, 210, 213, 245; legislation, 205, 207, 210, 211, 213; riots, 217, 220, 222, 226-230; rules and discipline, 201, 203-205

 strikes and lockouts: (1899), 214; (1900), 215; (1901), 215; (1902), 215; (1905-07), 215-216; (1908), 216-219; (1911), 219-222; (1913), 222-238; (1915), 239-240; (1916), 240

 unemployment, 121, 168, 209-213, 264; wages, 166-167, 201-202, 204-206, 214, 218, 224. *See also* Trade unions

Labour Gazette, 209

Labourers' Acts, 34, 154, 156

Lancet, 102-103, 115, 117, 118

Lane, Hugh, 53-56, 60, 100

Larkin, Delia, 235

Larkin, James, 49, 89-90, 91-92, 121, 156, 216, 219, 220, 222, 224-225, 228-239 *passim*

LaTouche, C. D., 167

Lavery, John, 56

Leahy, W., TC, 84

Lecky, W. E. H., 83

Leeds, 21, 77, 104, 106, 107, 180, 186, 188

Lewis-Hill, Ada H., 168

Liberties, The, 7, 9-10, 40, 127, 158

Liberty Hall, 212, 225, 234, 236, 248, 254, 256, 261, 269

Libraries, 57-59

Liffey, River, 4, 18-20, 82, 99, 103, 124-125, 168

Limerick, 187

Liverpool, 20, 21, 59, 65, 77, 104, 107, 109, 130, 180, 186, 188, 192, 215, 219

Local Government Act (1898), 72, 73, 77

Local Government Board, 17, 26, 49, 65, 76, 96, 97, 99, 103, 110, 114, 146-150 *passim*, 155, 157, 170, 172, 206, 211-212, 264

Logue, Michael, Cardinal, 87, 91, 220, 230, 248

London, 21, 64, 65, 103, 104, 106, 107, 112, 120, 122, 131, 142, 166, 181, 186, 187, 188, 192, 202, 205, 218

Lutyens, Sir Edwin, 55

McBride, Major John, 85, 243, 265

McCabe, Sir Francis, 125

McCormack, John, 264

MacDiarmada, Sean, 260, 265

McDonagh, Thomas, 231

MacDonnell, Sir (later Lord) Antony, Under Secretary for Ireland, 76, 176, 217

McGough, Rev. E., 88

Mack, Mrs. Annie, 190-191

Macken, Peter, TC, 265

Mackey, Sir J. W., 72

Macnamara, Dr. Rawton, 190

MacNeill, Eoin, 247, 257, 258

M'Swiney, Peter, 72

M'Walter, J. C., M.D., TC, 47, 58, 96, 97-98, 115, 120, 147, 152, 218, 248, 257

Maguire, W. R., 79

Mahaffy, Dr. J. P., 49, 189

Mahon, P. V., TC, 267

Main drainage. *See* Public health

Manchester, 21, 59, 64, 65, 77, 104, 107, 130, 180, 186, 188, 192, 205, 210

Manufacturers, 5, 9-11, 36, 200-201, 239

Martyn, Edward, 52-53

Master Builders Association, 215, 237

Master Carriers Association, 226, 239

Maxwell, Lieutenant-Gen. Sir John, 260, 263, 266, 268

Meyer, Kuno, 255

Money, Chiozza, 166

Montefiore, Dora, 234

Moore, George, 55

Moran, D.P., 51, 52, 129

Moriarty, J.P., KC, 51

Moyers, George, 71

Mumford, Lewis, 277

Municipal Art Gallery, 53-56, 60

Municipal Corporations Act (1840), 71

Murphy, William Martin, 54-55, 63, 96, 144, 152, 212, 224, 225, 231, 237, 238, 249, 252

Music. *See* Entertainment

Nannetti, Joseph P., MP, TC, 79, 90, 144, 232

Nathan, Sir Matthew, 268

National Gallery of Art, 53-55, 57, 60

National Insurance Act (1911), 213, 222

National Volunteers, 251, 254, 256-257

Newspapers, 31, 60, 71-72, 85, 118, 194, 256; *Freeman's Journal*, 18, 52, 60, 72, 79, 87, 233, 234, 255, 266; *Irish Catholic*, 60, 163, 228, 265; *Irish Independent*, 194, 224, 265; *Irish Times*, 46, 48, 52, 53, 55, 60, 65, 68, 72, 83, 95, 99, 125, 145-149 *passim*, 163, 168, 177, 194, 211, 212, 217, 221-229 *passim*, 234, 236, 238, 255, 260, 266, 267; *Irish Worker*, 60, 90, 205, 220, 221; *Leader*, 60, 149, 169; *Nation*, 243; *Sinn Fein*, 60, 118; *United Irishman*, 60, 215, 243, 244

Nottingham, 120

O'Carroll, Richard, TC, 89, 91, 265-266

O'Connell, Daniel, 35, 208

O'Connell, Maurice, MP, 10

O'Dea, Thomas, Bishop of Galway, 95

O'Donovan Rossa, Jeremiah, 256

O'Dwyer, Edward T., Bishop of Limerick, 47, 91, 187, 248, 257, 266

O'Leary, John, 243
O'Leary, Sgt. Mike, 254
Old Age Pensions Act (1908), 172-173
O'Neill, Laurence, TC, 152
O'Reilly, George, TC, 98, 149, 218

Pankhurst, Mrs. E., 248
Park, Robert, 68
Parkinson, J., TC, 98
Parliamentary Gazeteer of Ireland, 11, 12
Parnell, Charles Stewart, 41
Partridge, William, TC, 267
Peace Preservation (Arms) Act (1881), 236, 250-251
Peacocke, Joseph F., Archbishop of Dublin, 218, 231, 233
Pearse, Patrick, 50, 247, 256, 262, 264, 265
Philanthropy, 163, 168-169
Phoenix Park. *see* Dublin
Pile, Sir Thomas, TC, 80, 86, 87-88, 108
Plunkett, Joseph, 231
Police, 65, 68, 73, 218, 230-231; DMP, 162, 179-182, 188, 191, 193, 224-229, 243-244, 250; and Easter Rising, 259, 263, 271; and labor unrest, 210, 218, 220, 222, 224-231 *passim*, 235-236
Poor relief, 74, 162, 170, 210, 212, 264, 266; workhouses, 74, 112, 115, 162, 170-173, 237
Population, 4, 5, 7, 9, 14, 22, 35, 39, 78, 155, 203, 275
Prisons, 184, 196
Prostitution, 10, 118-119, 171, 189-195
Public health, 16-18, 31-32, 102-103, 110, 120-121, 123, 135; dairy yards, 16, 122-123; death rate, 20-23, 102, 104-105; infant mortality, 21, 107-109, 116, 171; legislation, 16-17, 20, 66, 76, 82, 101, 105, 109-110, 114, 117-118, 170, 190; main drainage, 20, 76, 124-125; Public Health Inquiry (1900), 103-104, 112-113, 122, 142; Royal Commission on Sewerage and Drainage (1879), 19, 23, 103, 126; scavenging, 16, 31-32, 120-121; sewers, 6, 18-19; slaughter houses, 16, 102, 110, 122, 123-124; water supply, 16, 18-19, 30, 102
Publishing, 59-60
Purcell, Capt. Thomas, 65, 261

Redmond, John, MP, 85, 86, 88, 90, 95, 187, 232, 238, 247, 248, 250, 251, 252, 255, 258, 264, 268
Redmond, Wm., MP, 86, 243
Reformatories, 196-197
Robbins, Frank, 265
Roe, George, 72
Ross of Bladensburg, Sir John, 179, 250
Rowntree, Seebohm, 162-167 *passim*
Royal Commission on Venereal Diseases, 120
Royal Dublin Society, 266
Royal visits, 25, 31, 85-86, 88, 91, 129, 247

Russell, George (AE), 232
Russell, T.W., MP, 156

St. Patrick's Cathedral, 8, 128
St. Stephen's Green. *See* Dublin
Sanitary Record, 32, 102, 103
Saunderson, Colonel E. J., MP, 82, 95, 98
Schools, 103, 110, 169, 177-178, 231; Industrial Schools, 173-174, 197
Sexton, Sir Robert, TC, 72, 93
Shaw, G. Bernard, 45, 52, 54, 189, 194, 256
Sheehy, David, MP, 232
Sheehy-Skeffington, Francis, 235, 256, 263
Sheehy-Skeffington, Hannah, 248
Sheffield, 77, 104, 106, 107, 120, 155, 180, 186, 188
Sherlock, Lorcan, TC, 58, 92, 152, 157, 217, 236, 252
Shipping Federation, 219, 236
Shortall, Sir Patrick, TC, 80, 257
Sinn Fein, 89, 95, 244-245, 247, 251, 257
Sisson, Jonathan, 10
Sligo, 57
Sports, 62-63
Stafford, Dr. T. J., 166
Standard of living, 164-168, 175-176
Stephens, James, 265
Stewart, Sir Robert, 48, 58
Strauss, Nathan, 113
Streets and squares: condition of, 21, 28, 29, 31 32, 66-67; lighting, 4, 16, 67-68, 259; paving, 4, 6, 16-17, 66-67, 275
    names mentioned, 3-12 *passim*, 28, 40, 66, 110, 123, 127-133 *passim*, 139-141, 147, 154, 158, 269; Bride Street, 33, 110, 131, 139, 169; Bride's Alley, 26, 127, 130, 131, 142; Bull Alley, 124, 128, 130, 131, 158; Church Street, 28, 68, 112, 127, 131, 135, 137, 148-149; The Coombe, 9, 26, 31, 127, 133, 137, 139, 148; Fitzwilliam Square, 6, 61; Grafton Street, 43, 66, 67, 86, 190, 207, 242, 254, 260; Mecklenburgh Street, 40, 118, 143, 190, 191; Merrion Square, 4, 6, 55, 61; Montgomery Street, 40, 131, 139, 140-141, 143-144, 175, 190, 193; Mountjoy Square, 4, 6, 14, 40, 61; O'Connell Street, 40, 66, 67, 193, 194, 220, 228, 240, 247, 260-261, 268, 271, 276; Plunkett Street, 7, 18, 26, 127, 130; Rutland Square, 4, 14, 61; Sackville Street (*see* O'Connell Steet); Summerhill, 12, 40, 110, 127, 179, 197; Townsend Street, 103, 110, 118, 123, 127, 133, 149, 152, 229; Tyrone Street, 40, 143, 175, 191, 194 (*see also* Mecklenburgh Street)
Street trading, juvenile, 174-176
Strikes and lockouts. *See* Labor

Suburbs, 12, 14, 15, 39, 63, 82, 83, 105, 124, 179, 275; Clontarf, 14, 39, 83, 99; Drumcondra, 14, 39, 83; Glasnevin, 39, 83; New Kilmainham, 14, 39, 83; Pembroke, 14, 275; Rathmines, 14, 15, 275
Sullivan, A. M., 72
Sullivan, T. D., 243
Swift, Jonathan, 8, 29, 131
Synge, John M., 51-52

Tallon, Daniel, TC, 79, 85, 88
Tara Street Baths, 29, 102, 235
Tenements. *See* Housing
Theaters. *See* Entertainment
Thom's Directory, 131, 158
Tillett, Ben, 231
Times, The, 79, 228
Town planning, 68-69, 156-157, 271-272, 274
Trades Union Congress, Irish, 91, 144
Trade unions, 203-204, 207-217 *passim,* 220-223, 226, 231, 236, 239; bakers, 203, 221-222, 225; bookbinders, 204; building trades, 204, 215-216, 226, 237, 240; carters, 217-218, 225, 237, 239; dockers, 214-216, 223, 239; drapers' assistants, 205, 207, 215, 234; gas workers, 204; Irish Transport and General Workers' Union, 212, 219-239 *passim;* mineral water operatives, 209; painters, 214; railway workers, 221; tailors, 215. *See also* Labor
Trades Council, Dublin, 74, 84, 89, 91, 144, 208-209, 216, 223
Traffic, 64-66, 181

Tramways, 63-64
Travers, Charles, 151
Trevelyan, G.O., 57
Trinity College, 43, 83, 86, 128, 182, 243, 248, 252, 271

United Irish Leag .e (UIL), 78, 84-85, 88-90, 95, 147
Ulster Volunteers, 248-251

Valuation, 12, 17, 76-78, 82-83
Vance, F., TC, 90
Vaughan, Bernard, S. J., 238
Vaughan, Cardinal, 163
Victoria, Queen, 31, 85-86

Walsh, William J., Archbishop of Dublin, 68, 88, 91, 164, 169, 218, 233-236 *passim,* 271
Water supply. *See* Public health
White Cross Association, 191, 195
Whitelaw, Rev. James, 4, 7, 11, 28
Wide Streets Commissioners, 4, 6, 10, 16, 29
Wilde, Dr. William, 20
Willis, Dr. Thomas, 20, 30
Wimborne, Lord, 258-260, 264
Women's National Health Association, 109, 113-114, 150
Workhouses. *See* Poor relief

Yeats, Elizabeth, 60
Yeats, W. B., 50-52, 56, 243
York, 162, 164